Addison-Wesley

Pre-Algebra

Phares G. O'Daffer

Stanley R. Clemens

Randall I. Charles

Addison-Wesley Publishing Company

Menlo Park, California   Reading, Massachusetts   Don Mills, Ontario

Wokingham, England   Amsterdam   Sydney   Singapore

Tokyo   Madrid   Bogotá   Santiago   San Juan

Photograph Acknowledgments

Cover Craig Aurness/West Light

CR Studio: 1. Tom Stack/Tom Stack & Associates: 2. Ben Rose/The Image Bank West: 15. Wayland Lee*/ Addison-Wesley Publishing Company: 18. Bill Ross/West Light: 24. George B. Fry III*: 28. Mitchell Funk: 33. David Madison/Bruce Coleman Inc.: 40. Doug Lee/ Tom Stack & Associates: 49. Mark Perlstein/Black Star: 57. Brett Froomer/The Image Bank West: 59. NASA: 62. Arthur Meyerson/The Image Bank West: 67. W. H. Hodge/Peter Arnold Inc.: 68L. Phelps/West Light: 68R. Wayland Lee*/Addison-Wesley Publishing Company: 79. Wayland Lee*/Addison-Wesley Publishing Company: 89. Keith Murakami/Tom Stack & Associates: 96. Jay Freis/The Image Bank West: 101. Wayland Lee*/Addison-Wesley Publishing Company: 105. Horst Schafer/Peter Arnold Inc.: 108. P. Kelly/The Image Bank West: 113. Jeanne Carley*: 117. Erika Stone/Peter Arnold Inc.: 118. Peter Menzel/Stock, Boston: 129. J. Carmichael/The Image Bank West: 133. Wayland Lee*/ Addison-Wesley Publishing Company: 134. Stephen Frisch*: 142. Rick McIntyre/Tom Stack & Associates: 147. Jeanne Carley*: 160. Flip Chalfant/The Image Bank West: 165. David Madison/Bruce Coleman Inc.: 170. David Madison/Bruce Coleman Inc.: 183. Stacy Pick/Stock, Boston: 186. Andy Levin/Black Star: 191. David Madison/Bruce Coleman Inc.: 198. Lou Jones/The Image Bank West: 203. Michael Salas/The Image Bank West: 215. Bill Gallery/Stock, Boston: 217. Tom Stack & Associates: 224. Ken Cooper/The Image Bank West: 233. Wayland Lee*/Addison-Wesley Publishing Company: 234. Al Saiterwhite/The Image Bank West: 239. Joan Saxe/Bruce Coleman Inc.: 247. Richard Choy/Peter Arnold Inc.: 251. NASA: 253. Brian Parker/Tom Stack & Associates: 260. Michael Melford/The Image Bank West: 265. Cecile Brunswick/ Peter Arnold Inc.: 266. John Coletti/Stock, Boston: 272. Charles Gupton/Stock, Boston: 282. Jay Freis/The Image Bank West: 287. National Baseball Hall of Fame: 293. Wayland Lee*/Addison-Wesley Publishing Company: 296. Craig Aurness/West Light: 301. Cary Wolinsky/Stock, Boston: 302. Wayland Lee*/Addison-Wesley Publishing Company: 308. Mike Mazzaso/Stock, Boston: 312. D. Brewster/Bruce Coleman Inc.: 313. Gary Milburn/Tom Stack & Associates: 319. Suzi Barnes/ Tom Stack & Associates: 330. Ted Speigel/Black Star: 335. Steve Dunwell/The Image Bank West: 342T. Wayland Lee*/Addison-Wesley Publishing Company: 342B. NASA: 360. Wayland Lee*/Addison-Wesley Publishing Company: 368. Marc Solomon/The Image Bank West: 375. Eric Simmons/Stock, Boston: 384. Alvis Upitis/The Image Bank West: 395. T. Schneps/The Image Bank West: 399. Nicholar Foster/The Image Bank West: 409. Focus On Sports: 418. Marc Romanelli/The Image Bank West: 425. © Elliot Varner Smith 1975: 428. Focus On Sports: 431. Rich McIntyre/Tom Stack & Associate: 439. Ron Sherman/Bruce Coleman Inc.: 442. David Hiser/The Image Bank West: 447. Stephen Frisch*: 451. Focus On Sports: 461. Gus Schonefeld/Berg & Associates: 465. Wayland Lee*/Addison-Wesley Publishing Company: 468. Stephen Frisch*: 474. George B. Fry III*: 475. © Greg Pease 1986: 479. Gary Withey/Bruce Coleman Inc.: 490. Miguel/ The Image Bank West: 494.

*Photographs provided expressly for the publisher

ISBN 0-201-20480-0

HIJKL-KR-82109

Contents

Chapter 1
Expressions and Equations: Addition and Subtraction

Chapter 2
Expressions and Equations: Multiplication and Division

Chapter 3
Integers

Chapter 4
Decimals

Chapter 5
Number Theory

Chapter 6
Rational Numbers: Addition and Subtraction

Chapter 7
Rational Numbers: Multiplication and Division

Chapter 8
Equations and Inequalities

Chapter 9
Ratio, Proportion, and Percent

Chapter 10
Using Percent

Chapter 11
Equations in Geometry

Chapter 12
Area and Volume Formulas

Chapter 13
Probability, Statistics, and Graphs

Chapter 14
Square Roots and Special Triangles

Chapter 15
Graphs of Equations and Inequalities

Chapter One

Expressions and Equations: Addition and Subtraction

1-1 Variables and Expressions

The burner in a hot-air balloon heats air inside the balloon. The hot air makes it rise. When the burner is turned off, the air in the balloon cools and the balloon drops.

With its burner on, a balloon rose to an altitude of 300 meters above sea level. Then the pilot turned the burner off and the balloon dropped 50 meters. If the pilot turned the burner on again and the balloon rose 100 meters, what altitude would the balloon reach?

The solution to this problem can be found by using the **numerical expression** (300 − 50) + 100. A numerical expression is a name for a number. To **evaluate** a numerical expression you find the number it represents. When an expression includes parentheses ( ), do the operation inside the parentheses first.

Example 1

Evaluate. (300 − 50) + 100

Solution (300 − 50) + 100

= 250 + 100 Do the operation inside the parentheses first. 300 − 50 = 250.

= 350 Complete the calculation. 250 + 100 = 350.

Practice Evaluate.

a. 16 − 7 **b.** 8 + (17 − 9) **c.** (27 + 6) − 19

A **variable** is a letter, such as n, that reserves a place for a number. An expression such as $\boldsymbol{n + 7}$ that contains at least one variable is called an **algebraic expression**. To evaluate an algebraic expression, you replace each variable with a number, or value, and evaluate the numerical expression that results.

Example 2

Evaluate $n + 7$ for $n = 9$.

Solution $n + 7$

$9 + 7$ Replace the variable n with the number 9.

$= 16$

Practice Evaluate.

a. $32 - x$ for $x = 8$ **b.** $a + (13 - 8)$ for $a = 6$

An algebraic expression may contain more than one variable.

Example 3

Evaluate $(a + b) - 10$ for $a = 8$ and $b = 9$.

Solution $(a + b) - 10$

$(8 + 9) - 10$ Replace a with 8 and b with 9.

$= 17 - 10$

$= 7$

Practice Evaluate.

a. $(x - 6) + z$ for $x = 11$ and $z = 9$ **b.** $c - (c - d)$ for $c = 17$ and $d = 4$.

Oral Exercises

What letter is used as a variable? What number replaces it?

1. $x + 5$ $3 + 5$	**2.** $5 + a$ $5 + 7$	**3.** $12 - b$ $12 - 8$	**4.** $r - 7$ $9 - 7$
5. $9 + s$ $9 + 2$	**6.** $13 - c$ $13 - 4$	**7.** $y - 8$ $10 - 8$	**8.** $t + 8$ $6 + 8$

Exercises

A Evaluate each numerical expression.

1. $8 + 7$	**2.** $17 - 9$	**3.** $13 - 13$
4. $49 + 9$	**5.** $45 - 10$	**6.** $(36 - 8) + 5$
7. $43 - (6 + 7)$	**8.** $(19 + 9) - 10$	**9.** $(35 + 4) + 7$

Evaluate each numerical expression.

10. $26 + (12 - 4)$ **11.** $(16 - 5) + 4$ **12.** $(20 - 15) + 6$

13. $49 - (8 + 2)$ **14.** $23 + (8 + 10)$ **15.** $(19 - 8) - 6$

16. $(11 + 12) - 13$ **17.** $33 - (22 + 10)$ **18.** $28 + (19 - 4)$

Evaluate each algebraic expression.

19. $x + 4$ for $x = 6$ **20.** $n - 6$ for $n = 9$ **21.** $n + 5$ for $n = 7$

22. $b - 13$ for $b = 17$ **23.** $4 + c$ for $c = 29$ **24.** $16 - a$ for $a = 7$

25. $(x - 9) + 8$ for $x = 75$ **26.** $8 + (6 + c)$ for $c = 53$ **27.** $(e - 5) - 9$ for $e = 64$

28. $n + 7$ for $n = 5$, for $n = 7$, and for $n = 15$

29. $x - 8$ for $x = 12$, for $x = 14$, and for $x = 76$

Evaluate each expression for $a = 5$, $b = 8$, and $c = 9$.

30. $a + b$ **31.** $c - a$ **32.** $c - (13 - b)$

33. $(c - b) + 26$ **34.** $(b + b) - 8$ **35.** $(29 + 57) + (c - a)$

36. $(c + a) - (12 - 4)$ **37.** $(a + b) - (17 - 8)$ **38.** $(13 - c) + (14 - b)$

Evaluate.

39. $(x + 8) + (x - 7)$ for $x = 15$ **40.** $(p + 4) + (p - 7)$ for $p = 12$

41. $(9 - b) - (2 + b)$ for $b = 3$ **42.** $(12 - q) + (8 - q)$ for $q = 5$

43. $(z + 7) - (z + 5)$ for $z = 8$ **44.** $(8 + d) + (c - d)$ for $d = 5, c = 12$

B Evaluate each expression for $w = 47$, $x = 56$, $y = 94$, and $z = 123$.

45. $(w + x) + (z - y)$ **46.** $(z - x) - (y - w)$ **47.** $(z - y) + (x - w)$

Copy and complete each table, evaluating the algebraic expression for the numbers given.

	n	$n + n - 1$
	5	$5 + 5 - 1 = 9$
48.	10	
49.	9	
50.	20	

	x	y	$x + x - y$
	8	7	$8 + 8 - 7 = 9$
51.	7	6	
52.	9	8	
53.	6	9	

	a	b	$a + b + b$
	1	7	$1 + 7 + 7 = 15$
54.	3	10	
55.	6	8	
56.	15	20	

C Extending Thinking Skills

57. Choose numbers for a, b, and c so that $c - b = a$. Do this three times with different numbers. Does $a + b = c$ each time?

58. What is the value of the next expression in this pattern if $n = 9$?
$n + 1, n + 3, n + 6, n + 10, n + 15, ?$

59. Find number replacements for x and y so that $x + y = 16$ and $x - y = 2$.

Mixed Review

Add or subtract.

Examples:

1 11	5 99 13
3,346	6,003
+ 894	− 978
4,240	5,025

60. 104 + 86 **61.** 171 + 74 **62.** 16 + 191
63. 54 + 47 **64.** 936 + 243 **65.** 511 + 106
66. 518 + 166 **67.** 110 + 749 **68.** 219 + 371
69. 183 + 128 **70.** 308 − 225 **71.** 436 − 88
72. 221 − 96 **73.** 178 − 65 **74.** 2,104 − 196
75. 3,096 − 854 **76.** 2,004 − 857 **77.** 40,000 − 32,651
78. 7,841 − 538 **79.** 1,240 − 141 **80.** 14,326 − 2,134
81. 30,001 − 5,642 **82.** 50,129 + 11,297 **83.** 3,590 + 7,246
84. 65,667 − 25,340 **85.** 42,208 − 3,175 **86.** 90,128 + 3,808
87. 12,645 − 3,810 **88.** 7,775 + 3,816 **89.** 20,251 − 18,532
90. 31,190 + 4,325 **91.** 4,261 − 1,705 **92.** 30,672 + 3,488
93. 50,119 + 5,679 **94.** 24,307 − 2,867 **95.** 10,146 − 5,982
96. 10,085 + 4,709 **97.** 3,290 − 1,701 **98.** 128,104 + 9,685

CALCULATOR ACTIVITY

You can use the memory keys on a calculator to evaluate expressions.

Use the [M+] key to add the displayed number to the total in the memory.

Use the [M−] key to subtract the displayed number from the total in the memory.

Use the [MR] key to display the total in the memory.

Evaluate 956 − $(a - b)$ for $a = 342$ and $b = 178$.

342 [−] 178  [=]  [M+] Find the difference in parentheses first and store it in memory.

936  [−] 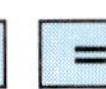 [MR]  [=] 772 Then subtract the difference in the memory from 936.

Use the calculator memory keys to evaluate each expression.

1. 5,392 − $(x + y)$ for $x = 849$, $y = 768$

2. 4,238 + $(c - d)$ for $c = 6{,}982$, $d = 748$

3. 3,479 − $(a - b)$ for $a = 1{,}603$, $b = 479$

4. 965 + $(p - q + 467)$ for $p = 640$, $q = 398$

1-2 Translating Phrases to Algebraic Expressions

Verbal phrases that suggest addition or subtraction can be translated into numerical or algebraic expressions.

Example 1

Write as a numerical expression. "5 increased by 3"

Solution $5 + 3$ The phrase "increased by 3" suggests adding 3.

Practice Write as a numerical expression.

a. 6 less than 10

b. 9 decreased by 4

c. the sum of 8 and 7

d. 7 more than 8

The phrase "5 increased by 3" is translated to the numerical expression $5 + 3$. The phrase "a number increased by 3" becomes the algebraic expression $n + 3$.

number	number increased by 3	
5	$5 + 3$	"5 increased by 3"
10	$10 + 3$	"10 increased by 3"
n	$n + 3$	"a **number** increased by 3"

Example 2

Write as an algebraic expression. "a number decreased by 4"

Solution $n - 4$ Think of a specific number, say 6. "6 decreased by 4" is $6 - 4$, so "a *number* decreased by 4" is $n - 4$.

Practice Write as an algebraic expression.

a. a number plus 5

b. a number decreased by 8

c. 7 more than a number

d. 5 less than a number

e. the difference of a number and 3

Example 3

Write as an expression. Jeff has \$68. How much will he have if:

a. he earns 43 dollars? **b.** he earns x dollars?

c. he spends 29 dollars? **d.** he spends y dollars?

Solutions

a. he earns 43 dollars? $68 + 43$

b. he earns x dollars? $68 + x$ Think about a number, write a variable.

c. he spends 29 dollars? $68 - 29$

d. he spends y dollars? $68 - y$ Think about a number, write a variable.

Practice Write as an expression. Tina's house is 23 years old. How old:

a. will it be in 9 years? **b.** will it be in y years?

c. was it 14 years ago? **d.** was it t years ago?

Oral Exercises

Tell whether the phrase suggests addition or subtraction.

1. the sum of **2.** decreased by **3.** minus

4. increased by **5.** make it greater **6.** added to

7. the difference of **8.** make it less **9.** plus

10. subtracted from **11.** make it more **12.** a total of

Exercises

A Write as a numerical expression.

1. the sum of 8 and 6 **2.** the difference of 12 and 4

3. 7 more than 9 **4.** 3 less than 10

5. 6 increased by 7 **6.** 14 decreased by 5

7. 8 added to 12 **8.** 12 subtracted from 15

Write as an algebraic expression.

9. the sum of x and 6 **10.** 4 taken away from t

11. 7 more than n **12.** 3 less than s

13. 8 added to r **14.** 12 subtracted from z

15. y decreased by 5 **16.** x more than 16

17. the difference of a number and 9 **18.** the sum of a number and 8

19. 6 more than a number **20.** a number increased by 11

21. 16 added to a number **22.** a number decreased by 56

23. 126 less than a number **24.** 9 increased by a number

Write an expression for each question.
Mr. Henderson is 64 years old. How old:

25. will he be in 9 years?
26. will he be in y years?
27. was he 16 years ago?
28. was he x years ago?

Beth weighs 45 kg. How much will she weigh:

29. after she gains 7 kg?
30. after she gains n kg?
31. after she loses 4 kg?
32. after she loses y kg?

Todd earned $75 by washing cars. How much money will he have:

33. after he earns 45 dollars more?
34. after he earns x dollars more?
35. after he buys some $37 shoes?
36. after he buys an item costing d dollars?

B The letter n represents an even number 0, 2, 4, 6, 8, ...
Write an algebraic expression for:

37. the whole number just after n.
38. the whole number just before n.
39. the even number just after n.
40. the even number just before n.

C Extending Thinking Skills

41. Choose two variables and write an algebraic expression for their sum. Write an expression for the difference of the same two variables. Find values for the variables that have a sum of 31 and difference of 3.

42. Look for a pattern in this sequence: 1, 1, 2, 3, 5, 8, 13, 21, 34, 55, . . . Let a represent a number in the sequence and b represent the next number after a. Write an algebraic expression for the next number in the sequence after b.

Mixed Review

Evaluate. **43.** 850 + 143 **44.** 248 − (20 + 28) **45.** 466 − (96 − 66)

Evaluate for $s = 136$, $s = 238$, and $s = 312$. **46.** $70 + (s - 86)$ **47.** $1000 - (s + s)$

MENTAL MATH

You can use **compensation** to find certain sums and differences mentally.

- To find 752 − **398**, think "752 − **400** is 352. I subtracted **2** too much, so I'll add it back. The difference is 352 + **2**, or 354."
- To find 645 + **296**, think "645 + **300** is 945. I added **4** too much, so I'll subtract it. The sum is 945 − **4**, or 941."

Use compensation to find each sum or difference mentally.

1. 642 − 299
2. 8,546 − 3,998
3. 874 − 549
4. 387 + 497
5. 4,638 + 2,995
6. 529 + 348

1-3 Properties of Addition

The **whole numbers** are the numbers 0, 1, 2, 3, 4, 5, . . . The basic properties for addition of whole numbers can make computation with numerical expressions easier. You can also use the properties to write **equivalent** expressions. Two algebraic expressions are equivalent if (and only if) they have the same value for any number that replaces the variable.

You can change the order in which two numbers are added and the sum will stay the same. For example, $578 + 964 = 964 + 578$.

$$\begin{array}{r} 578 \\ +\ 964 \\ \hline 1{,}542 \end{array} \qquad \begin{array}{r} 964 \\ +\ 578 \\ \hline 1{,}542 \end{array}$$

Variables can be used to state this property for all whole numbers.

Commutative Property of Addition

A change in the order in which two whole numbers are added does not change their sum.

For all whole numbers ***a*** and ***b***, $a + b = b + a$

Example 1

Use the commutative property to write an equivalent expression. $n + 5$

Solution $5 + n$ $5 + n$ has the same value as $n + 5$ for any number that replaces n.

Practice Use the commutative property to write an equivalent expression.

a. $45 + x$ **b.** $a + 5{,}138$ **c.** $479 + t$

You can change the way whole numbers are grouped for addition and the sum will stay the same.
For example, $(87 + 649) + 151 = 87 + (649 + 151)$.

$$\begin{array}{r} 87 \\ +\ 649 \\ \hline 736 \end{array} \qquad \begin{array}{r} 736 \\ +\ 151 \\ \hline 887 \end{array} \qquad \text{and} \qquad \begin{array}{r} 649 \\ +\ 151 \\ \hline 800 \end{array} \qquad \begin{array}{r} 87 \\ +\ 800 \\ \hline 887 \end{array}$$

Variables can be used to state this property for all whole numbers.

Associative Property of Addition

A change in the grouping of whole numbers for addition does not change the sum.

For all whole numbers **a, b, and c**, $\mathbf{a + (b + c) = (a + b) + c}$

Example 2

Use the associative property to write an equivalent expression.
$(x + 57) + 43$

Solution $x + (57 + 43)$ — $x + (57 + 43)$ has the same value as $(x + 57) + 43$ for any number that replaces x.

Practice Use the associative property to write an equivalent expression.

a. $(n + 145) + 68$

b. $125 + (75 + a)$

c. $m + (123 + 77)$

d. $(118 + 12) + c$

Zero is called the **additive identity** because when it is added to a number, the result is that same number. For example, $689 + 0 = 689$.

Identity Property of Addition

The sum of an addend and zero is the addend.

For every whole number **a**, $\mathbf{a + 0 = a}$ $\mathbf{0 + a = a}$

When zero is subtracted from a number, the result is that same number: $\mathbf{a - 0 = a}$. When a number is subtracted from itself, the result is zero: $\mathbf{a - a = 0}$.

Example 3

Use the identity property to write an equivalent expression. $x + 0$

Solution x — x has the same value as $x + 0$ for any number that replaces x.

Practice Use the identity property to write an equivalent expression.

a. $0 + t$ **b.** $a + 0$ **c.** $z + 0$ **d.** $0 + n$

Oral Exercises

Name the property shown by each equation.

1. $9 + 0 = 9$
2. $7 + 8 = 8 + 7$
3. $0 + 6 = 6$
4. $6 + (3 + 5) = (6 + 3) + 5$
5. $8 + 23 = 23 + 8$
6. $18 + (2 + 9) = (18 + 2) + 9$
7. $47 = 0 + 47$
8. $(14 + 6) + 15 = 14 + (6 + 15)$

Exercises

A Use the commutative property to write an equivalent expression.

1. $y + 4$
2. $9 + x$
3. $12 + n$
4. $x + 28$
5. $137 + b$
6. $c + 236$
7. $507 + y$
8. $p + 1578$

Use the associative property to write an equivalent expression.

9. $(n + 2) + 8$
10. $(y + 8) + 12$
11. $(t + 9) + 7$
12. $(a + 4) + 16$
13. $(z + 16) + 34$
14. $(n + 78) + 22$
15. $17 + (8 + b)$
16. $26 + (4 + c)$
17. $38 + (12 + r)$

Use the identity property to write an equivalent expression.

18. $x + 0$
19. $0 + y$
20. $a - a$

Write an equivalent expression and name the property you used.

21. $n + 7$
22. $y + 0$
23. $(n + 7) + 3$
24. $57 + x$
25. $p + 23$
26. $83 + (17 + x)$
27. $8 + s$
28. $0 + n$
29. $0 + (x + y)$

B Use the basic properties to find the value for each variable.

30. $7 + n = 9 + 7$
31. $6 + x = 6$
32. $b + 0 = 12$
33. $34 - z = 0$
34. $(c + 9) + 12 = 7 + (9 + 12)$

35. Evaluate $a - b$ for $a = 15$, $b = 8$. If the answer must be a whole number, can $b - a$ be evaluated for the same numbers? Is the commutative property true for subtraction of whole numbers?

36. Evaluate $(p - q) - r$ for $p = 12$, $q = 8$, $r = 4$. Evaluate $p - (q - r)$ for the same values. Is the associative property true for subtraction of whole numbers?

Use the commutative and associative properties to change the pairings of the numbers. Compute mentally. Look for **compatible numbers** such as 75 + 25 that make easy sums.

37. $(98 + 75) + 25$
38. $55 + (45 + 87)$
39. $(975 + 492) + 25$
40. $750 + (958 + 250)$
41. $64 + 9 + 36 + 11 + 3 + 79 + 97$
42. $125 + 555 + 375 + 445 + 237$

C Extending Thinking Skills

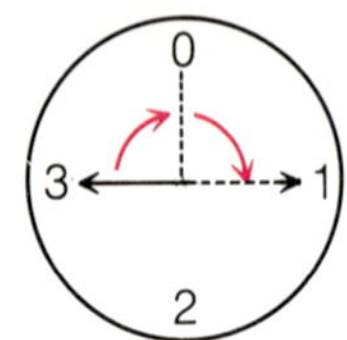

This "clock" can be used to find "clock sums." For example, $3 \oplus 2 = 1$, because two hours after pointing to 3 o'clock, the hand would point to 1 o'clock.

Find each clock sum. Do you think the operation $\oplus$ is commutative?

43. $2 \oplus 1$ **3** **44.** $2 \oplus 2$ **0** **45.** $2 \oplus 3$ **46.** $3 \oplus 2$

Mixed Review

Add or subtract. **47.** 954 − 765 **48.** 340 + 565 **49.** 2,506 − 987

Evaluate. **50.** (45 − 18) − 16 **51.** 23 + 49 + 85 **52.** 65 + 25

Evaluate for $a = 10$. **53.** $a + 16$ **54.** $a + 8$ **55.** $25 - a$

Evaluate for $b = 12$, $c = 13$. **56.** $b + c$ **57.** $c - b$

Write the word name. **58.** 2,017 **59.** 452 **60.** 6,906

NUMBERS TO ALGEBRA

A generalization that can be made about numbers can be expressed with variables. Check to see if the number examples are true. Then see how the variables are used to express the generalization.

Numbers	Algebra
(35 + 49) + 15 = (35 + 15) + 49	For whole numbers ***a*, *b*,** and ***c*,**
(75 + 89) + 25 = (75 + 25) + 89	
(88 + 76) + 12 = (88 + 12) + 76	$(a + b) + c = (a + c) + b$
(148 + 97) + 52 = (148 + 52) + 97	

Give two more number examples, then copy and complete the generalization.

Number Examples	Generalization
(50 + 6) + (30 + 7) = (50 + 30) + (6 + 7)	**For whole numbers**
(40 + 9) + (60 + 8) = (40 + 60) + (9 + 8)	***a*, *b*, *c*, and *d*,**
(200 + 52) + (600 + 48) = (200 + 600) + (52 + 48)	$(a + b) + (c + d) =$ __ ? __

1-4 Equations

An **equation** is a mathematical sentence that uses an equal sign to state that two expressions represent the same number or are equivalent.

The expression on the left side	names the same number as	the expression on the right side
24 + 6	=	30

An equation that contains only numbers can be either true or false. For example, $24 + 6 = 30$ is true, but $24 + 6 = 31$ is false. An equation that contains at least one variable is an **open sentence** and is neither true nor false. For example, $x + 6 = 30$ is neither true nor false because x has not been replaced with a number.

The set of numbers from which you can select replacements for the variable is called the **replacement set**. A replacement for a variable that makes an equation true is called a **solution** of the equation. You can **solve** an equation by finding all of its solutions. The collection of all the solutions is called the **solution set** of the equation.

When the replacement set contains only a few numbers, one way to solve the equation is to try all the numbers.

Example 1

Solve $x + 38 = 42$ for the replacement set $\{1, 2, 3, 4, 5\}$.

Solution

$\mathbf{x} + 38 = 42$

$\mathbf{1} + 38 = 42$ (false) — Replace the variable x with each number in the replacement set.

$\mathbf{2} + 38 = 42$ (false)

$\mathbf{3} + 38 = 42$ (false)

$\mathbf{4} + 38 = 42$ (true) $\surd$ — The number that makes the equation true is the solution. $x = 4$.

$\mathbf{5} + 38 = 42$ (false)

Practice Solve the equation for the replacement set $\{0, 2, 4, 6\}$.

a. $51 - n = 45$ **b.** $b + 79 = 81$ **c.** $31 = 27 + y$

Example 2

Solve the equation $x - 8 = 16$ for the replacement set $\{23, 25, 27\}$.

Solution

$x - 8 = 16$

$23 - 8 = 16$ (false) Replace the variable x with each number in the replacement set.

$25 - 8 = 16$ (false)

$27 - 8 = 16$ (false) Since no number makes the equation true, it has no solution for the replacement set given.

There is no solution.

Practice Solve the equation for the replacement set given.

a. $n + 15 = 45$ $\{31, 32, 33\}$ **b.** $x + 5 = 2$ $\{0, 1, 2, 3\}$

Oral Exercises

Is the value given for the variable a solution to the equation?

1. $n + 5 = 12, n = 8$? **2.** $9 + p = 13, p = 4$? **3.** $e - 5 = 9, e = 15$?

4. $9 = a - 6, a = 15$? **5.** $15 - y = 7, y = 8$? **6.** $13 = 6 + c, c = 8$?

Exercises

A Solve the equation for the replacement set given.

1. $n + 3 = 12$ $\{8, 9\}$
2. $q - 7 = 9$ $\{14, 15, 16, 17\}$
3. $9 + n = 13$ $\{0, 2, 4, 6\}$
4. $12 - r = 7$ $\{1, 3, 5, 7, 9\}$
5. $z + 8 = 17$ $\{7, 8, 9, 10\}$
6. $11 - s = 7$ $\{1, 2, 3, 4, 5\}$
7. $31 = 28 + x$ $\{0, 2, 4\}$
8. $12 + n = 20$ $\{2, 4, 6, 8, 10\}$
9. $17 = n - 3$ $\{20, 21, 22\}$
10. $24 = 5 + y$ $\{15, 16, 17, 18\}$
11. $p + 0 = 8$ $\{0, 4, 8, 12, 14\}$
12. $28 = t - 10$ $\{17, 18, 19, 20\}$
13. $z + 34 = 187$ $\{150, 151, 152\}$
14. $y - 37 = 241$ $\{277, 278\}$

B Describe the solution set. The replacement set is the set of all whole numbers.

15. $n + 4 = 0$ **16.** $x + 5 = 5 + x$ **17.** $y - y = 0$ **18.** $a + a = a$

C Extending Thinking Skills

19. Write an equation with no solution. Replacement set: all odd whole numbers.

Mixed Review

Write a numerical expression for each. **20.** 12 added to 7 **21.** 7 decreased by 6

Use the associative property to write an equivalent expression. **22.** $25 + (75 + 42)$

Evaluate for $a = 20$, $a = 30$, and $a = 40$. **23.** $(165 + a) + 35$ **24.** $a + 80$

1-5 Solving Equations: Using Mental Math

When the replacement set for an equation is the set of all whole numbers, it is impossible to try every number to find the solution. If an equation involves small numbers and a single operation, it often can be solved mentally.

To find the number of pins knocked down when 6 are left standing, you can solve the equation $p + 6 = 10$ mentally.

Example 1

Solve and check mentally. $p + 6 = 10$

Solution $p + 6 = 10$ Think: what number added to 6 gives 10?

Check $4 + 6 \stackrel{?}{=} 10$ Mentally substitute 4 for p in $p + 6 = 10$.

$10 = 10 \checkmark$ The equation is true, so 4 is the solution.

Practice Solve and check mentally.

a. $8 - a = 5$ **b.** $7 + n = 15$ **c.** $y - 6 = 2$

These equations illustrate the relationship between addition and subtraction.

addend		addend		sum		sum		addend		addend
65	+	35	=	**100**	→	**100**	−	35	=	65

Since addition can undo subtraction and subtraction can undo addition, addition and subtraction are called **inverse operations**. You can use this idea to solve equations mentally.

Example 2

Use the inverse operation to solve mentally. $x + 7 = 29$

Solution $x + 7 = 29$ Think "7 has been added to a number to produce 29,

$x = 29 - 7$ so 29 minus 7 should equal the number."

$x = 22$

Check $22 + 7 \stackrel{?}{=} 29$ Mentally substitute 22 for x in the equation.

$29 = 29 \checkmark$ The equation is true, so 22 is the solution.

Practice Use the inverse operation to solve mentally.

a. $n - 5 = 31$ **b.** $24 = y + 8$ **c.** $d + 7 = 21$

Oral Exercises

The solution of the equation $6 + x = 10$ is "the number that adds to 6 to give 10." Describe the solution of each equation.

1. $n + 5 = 13$ **2.** $4 + c = 20$ **3.** $x - 5 = 12$

4. $x - 9 = 7$ **5.** $24 = a + 12$ **6.** $13 = c - 7$

To solve the equation $x + 7 = 15$, you can use the inverse operation and find $15 - 7$. Tell how you can solve each equation.

7. $a + 4 = 15$ **8.** $y - 7 = 8$ **9.** $23 = x + 19$

10. $8 = n - 9$ **11.** $6 + r = 19$ **12.** $p - 16 = 2$

Exercises

A Solve and check mentally. The replacement set is the set of all whole numbers.

1. $n + 2 = 8$ **2.** $a + 4 = 9$ **3.** $7 + x = 9$

4. $8 + b = 9$ **5.** $c + 3 = 12$ **6.** $7 + z = 15$

7. $6 + p = 11$ **8.** $a + 7 = 12$ **9.** $t - 4 = 9$

10. $x - 8 = 9$ **11.** $c - 5 = 6$ **12.** $b - 10 = 8$

13. $13 - n = 5$ **14.** $17 - d = 8$ **15.** $a - 6 = 0$

16. $x - 7 = 9$ **17.** $50 = n + 20$ **18.** $40 + x = 90$

19. $b - 60 = 10$ **20.** $20 = 80 - n$ **21.** $31 = 28 + x$

22. $17 = n - 3$ **23.** $24 = 5 + y$ **24.** $28 = 10 + x$

25. $a - 19 = 2$ **26.** $120 = p + 70$ **27.** $0 = n - 13$

28. $125 + z = 200$ **29.** $n + 25 = 100$ **30.** $t - 300 = 700$

B Use a calculator and inverse operations to solve the equations in Exercises 31–41. For example, to solve $x + 346 = 923$, think: In the equation, 346 has been *added* to a number to produce the sum 923. Start with 923 on your calculator and *subtract* 346 to find the number.

				Display	
923	−	346	=	577	$x = 577$

31. $n + 479 = 1{,}235$ **32.** $b - 567 = 494$ **33.** $c + 5{,}926 = 13{,}415$

34. $y - 8{,}219 = 6{,}437$ **35.** $r + 3{,}643 = 9{,}008$ **36.** $t - 54{,}876 = 67{,}954$

37. After giving away 2,575 campaign buttons, a politician had 4,925 left. Solve the equation $b - 2{,}575 = 4{,}925$ to find how many she had at the beginning of her campaign.

38. The population of a city increased by 5,689 during a certain year, making a total of 157,743. Solve the equation $p + 5{,}689 = 157{,}743$ to find the population before the increase.

39. At a time when few people watch, a television commercial cost \$235,650. This was \$195,750 less than its cost during prime time. Solve the equation $p - 195{,}750 = 235{,}650$ to find the cost of the commercial during prime time.

40. After a salesman had flown enough miles to receive two free tickets, he flew an extra 5,478 miles. His total mileage was 81,453. Solve the equation $m + 5{,}478 = 81{,}453$ to find the number of miles he had to fly to win two free tickets.

41. The attendance at a major league baseball game on Tuesday was 5,679 less than the attendance on Sunday. Tuesday's attendance was 31,685. Solve the equation $s - 5{,}679 = 31{,}685$ to find Sunday's attendance.

For all whole numbers, a, b, and c, if $a - b = c$, then $a = c + b$. Use this relationship between addition and subtraction to rewrite each equation with the variable by itself on one side. Then solve for the variable.

42. $x - 38 = 72$ **43.** $y - 35 = 96$ **44.** $60 = z - 23$

C Extending Thinking Skills

45. Find numbers for x and y that make both equations true.

$x + y = 24 \qquad x - y = 2$

46. These 3 equations have the same solution. Find the solution. Look for a pattern and write two more equations that have the same solution.

$x + 2 = 5$
$x + 5 = 8$
$x + 8 = 11$

Mixed Review

Evaluate. **47.** $b + 45$ for $b = 55$ **48.** $35 - (7 + x)$ for $x = 8$

Use the commutative property to write an equivalent expression. **49.** $28 + y$

Solve the equation for the replacement set {10, 15, 20}. **50.** $y - 5 = 15$

MENTAL MATH

Breaking apart numbers is a mental math technique based on the associative and commutative properties. Study the examples.

- To find 76 + 9, think "70 plus 6 + 9 is 70 plus 15, or 85."
- To find 57 + 38, think "50 + 30 is 80. 7 + 8 is 15. 80 + 15 is 95."
- To find 347 + 526, think "300 + 500 plus 40 + 20 plus 7 + 6 is 800 + 60 + 13, or 873."

Find each sum mentally by breaking apart the numbers.

1. 67 + 6 **2.** 96 + 9 **3.** 37 + 65

4. 78 + 94 **5.** 437 + 328 **6.** 256 + 493

1-6 Solving Equations: Using Addition and Subtraction

Although some simple equations can be solved mentally, other methods are useful with equations that have larger numbers or more operations. Two ideas are used in solving equations involving addition or subtraction. The first is that addition and subtraction are inverse operations and each can undo the other.

Subtraction can undo addition.	Addition can undo subtraction.
$10 + 9 - 9 = 10$	$10 - 9 + 9 = 10$
$n + 9 - 9 = n$	$n - 9 + 9 = n$

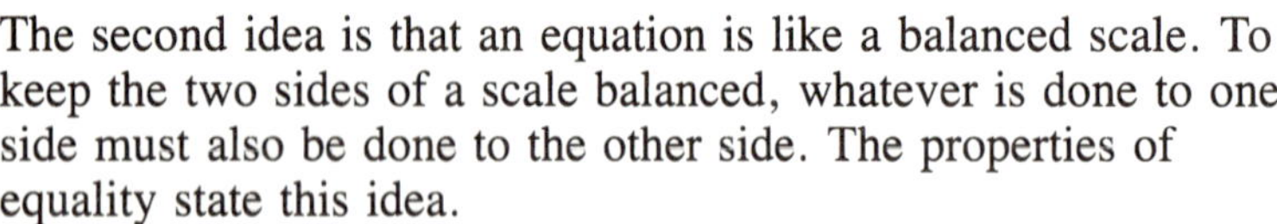

The second idea is that an equation is like a balanced scale. To keep the two sides of a scale balanced, whatever is done to one side must also be done to the other side. The properties of equality state this idea.

Addition and Subtraction Properties of Equality

You can add or subtract the same number on both sides of an equation and the two sides will remain equal.

For all numbers **a, b,** and **c,** if $a = b$, then $a + c = b + c$
and if $a = b$, then $a - c = b - c$

The following steps for solving equations show how to use the idea of inverse operations and the properties of equality to get the variable by itself on one side of the equation.

Solving Equations Using Addition and Subtraction

1. Decide which operation has been applied to the variable.
2. Use the inverse of this operation, adding or subtracting the same number on both sides of the equation.

The following examples show how to use these steps to solve equations.

Example 1

Solve and check. $n + 89 = 134$

Solution $n + 89 = 134$ — You need to get the variable by itself.

$n + 89 - 89 = 134 - 89$ — To undo adding 89, subtract 89 from both sides.

$n = 45$

Check $45 + 89 \stackrel{?}{=} 134$ — Replace n with 45.

$134 = 134 \checkmark$ — The solution is 45.

Practice Solve and check. **a.** $x + 77 = 394$ **b.** $123 = x + 87$

Example 2

Solve and check. $x - 89 = 176$

Solution $x - 89 = 176$ — You need to get the variable by itself.

$x - 89 + 89 = 176 + 89$ — To undo subtracting 89, add 89 to both sides.

$x = 265$

Check $265 - 89 \stackrel{?}{=} 176$ — Replace x with 265.

$176 = 176 \checkmark$ — The solution is 265.

Practice Solve. **a.** $m - 76 = 158$ **b.** $146 = y - 89$

Oral Exercises

Give the inverse of each operation.

1. Adding 58 **2.** Subtracting 97 **3.** Subtracting 123
4. Subtracting 29 **5.** Adding 456 **6.** Subtracting 43

Name the operation that would be used to solve the equation.

7. $x + 19 = 56$ **8.** $n - 28 = 56$ **9.** $467 = x + 85$
10. $98 = b - 35$ **11.** $c - 56 = 178$ **12.** $b + 278 = 562$

Exercises

A Solve and check.

1. $n + 38 = 84$ **2.** $x + 56 = 92$ **3.** $a + 47 = 85$
4. $y + 29 = 92$ **5.** $c + 76 = 154$ **6.** $n + 67 = 282$
7. $x + 79 = 194$ **8.** $b + 68 = 290$ **9.** $x - 87 = 63$
10. $y - 69 = 145$ **11.** $x - 58 = 139$ **12.** $y - 77 = 229$
13. $c - 167 = 85$ **14.** $n - 258 = 197$ **15.** $c - 376 = 488$

16. $b - 96 = 685$

17. $178 = n + 89$

18. $164 = n - 85$

19. $254 = a + 67$

20. $182 = y - 347$

21. $x + 87 = 264$

22. $183 = y - 259$

23. $n - 575 = 391$

24. $743 = c + 88$

25. $a + 86 = 842$

26. $b - 248 = 560$

27. $5{,}684 = n - 975$

28. $x + 437 = 1{,}065$

29. $a + 455 = 738$

30. $2{,}256 - x = 394$

B Solve and check.

31. $x + (157 + 29) = 342$

32. $a - (104 - 78) = 28$

33. $(358 + 76) + y = 500$

34. $(56 + 87) - b = 17$

35. Write and solve an equation in which the sum is 2,475 and the addend 1,697 is added to a number represented by the variable n.

36. Write and solve an equation in which 3,478 is subtracted from a number represented by the variable y to produce the difference 5,607.

C Extending Thinking Skills

In a magic square, the sum of the numbers in each row, column, and diagonal is the same.

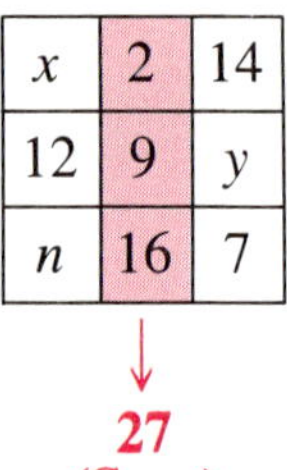

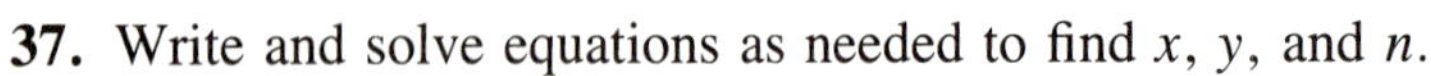

37. Write and solve equations as needed to find x, y, and n.

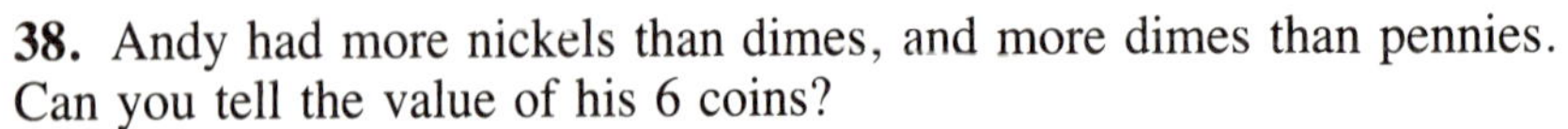

38. Andy had more nickels than dimes, and more dimes than pennies. Can you tell the value of his 6 coins?

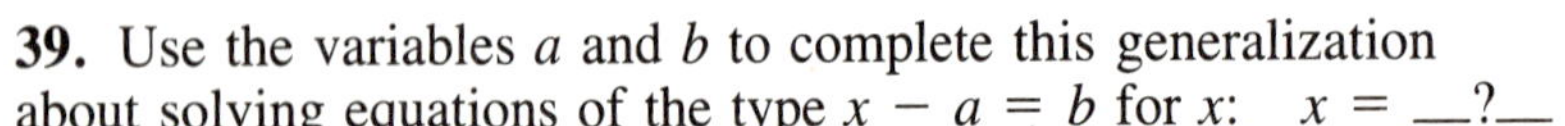

39. Use the variables a and b to complete this generalization about solving equations of the type $x - a = b$ for x: $x =$ __?__

Mixed Review

Write as an algebraic expression. **40.** 125 added to a number

Evaluate. **41.** $927 + 386$ **42.** $400 - 157$ **43.** $98 + 837 + 369$

Solve mentally and check. **44.** $n + 5 = 11$ **45.** $y - 6 = 10$

COMPUTER ACTIVITY

This computer program can be used to solve equations of the form $x + A = B$.

```
10 REM: SOLVE AN EQUATION X + A = B
20 PRINT "CHOOSE WHOLE NUMBERS A AND B WITH A < B"
30 INPUT A,B
40 PRINT "EQUATION: X + ";A;" = ";B
50 PRINT "SOLUTION: X = ";B-A
60 END
```

1. Run the program or show what the run would look like.
2. Change the program to solve equations of the form $x - A = B$.

More Practice

Solve and check.

1. $x - 31 = 19$
2. $b + 83 = 109$
3. $39 = y - 75$
4. $m - 104 = 127$
5. $z - 64 = 241$
6. $r + 27 = 46$
7. $b + 60 = 82$
8. $c + 535 = 1{,}024$
9. $m - 54 = 147$
10. $111 = w + 37$
11. $r - 97 = 406$
12. $t + 42 = 150$
13. $r - 104 = 90$
14. $a - 276 = 519$
15. $92 = k + 67$
16. $a + 94 = 163$
17. $h + 139 = 297$
18. $x - 192 = 12$
19. $w + 484 = 620$
20. $5{,}104 = r - 628$
21. $n - 4 = 97$
22. $516 = b + 377$
23. $267 = m - 734$
24. $c + 139 = 297$
25. $y + 84 = 110$
26. $p - 181 = 190$
27. $k - 4 = 97$
28. $c - 26 = 87$
29. $x + 19 = 27$
30. $62 = z - 18$
31. $t + 140 = 816$
32. $r - 152 = 28$
33. $a + 493 = 602$
34. $n - 218 = 672$
35. $120 = b + 49$
36. $f - 19 = 91$
37. $657 = k + 298$
38. $h - 46 = 47$
39. $w - 26 = 590$
40. $z + 97 = 406$
41. $n - 27 = 261$
42. $t + 184 = 901$
43. $r + 77 = 311$
44. $p - 19 = 74$
45. $z - 116 = 493$
46. $204 = m - 79$
47. $k + 183 = 291$
48. $n + 882 = 960$
49. $h + 68 = 390$
50. $406 = r + 297$
51. $b - 332 = 49$
52. $a + 76 = 375$
53. $54 = x - 127$
54. $117 = m - 83$
55. $86 = n + 53$
56. $m + 30 = 214$
57. $a + 599 = 604$
58. $w + 38 = 52$
59. $162 = t + 38$
60. $c - 745 = 267$
61. $z - 56 = 39$
62. $k + 137 = 514$
63. $r - 11 = 86$
64. $b - 129 = 92$
65. $y - 356 = 25$
66. $33 = p + 25$
67. $k + 16 = 108$
68. $r + 177 = 219$
69. $a - 36 = 25$
70. $93 = m - 15$
71. $x + 692 = 781$
72. $z + 63 = 87$
73. $r - 273 = 26$
74. $211 = x + 16$
75. $m - 47 = 44$
76. $c + 67 = 207$
77. $a - 669 = 241$
78. $k + 48 = 60$
79. $129 = t - 65$
80. $r + 114 = 177$
81. $b - 56 = 12$
82. $60 = r + 48$
83. $b + 18 = 29$
84. $w + 18 = 92$

1-7 Buying a Car

When solving a word problem, you can use the five guidelines on this Problem-Solving Checklist.

Problem The dealer adds $59 to the base list price of a Cyclone 500 for preparation and handling. If the car cost the dealer $7,189, what is the dealer's profit?

Problem-Solving Checklist

- Understand the **QUESTION**
- Find the Needed **DATA**
- **PLAN** What to Do
- Find the **ANSWER**
- **CHECK** Back

Price List Cyclone 500	
Base List Price:	$8,012
Extra Options, List Price:	
Air Conditioner	$575
Cruise Control	$139
Rear Defrost	$126
Tinted Glass	$ 98
PinStripe	$ 70
AM/FM Stereo Radio	$184
Power Steering	$209
Automatic Transmission	$439
Selling Price:	$9,852

Note that the price list shows the customer's cost. The customer's "base list price" equals the dealer's cost plus the dealer's profit.

Understand the QUESTION.
Read the problem carefully and decide what question is asked.

You are asked to find the amount of profit the dealer has included in the base list price.

Find the Needed DATA.
Decide what information is needed to solve the problem.

You can look at the data chart to find that the base list price is $8,012.

PLAN What to Do.
Choose a strategy that will help you solve the problem.

To *compare* the base price with the dealer's cost, first choose the operation *subtraction*.
To *include* the extra profit from the handling charge, choose the operation *addition*.

Find the ANSWER.

Complete the reasoning or computation needed to find the answer.

(8,012 + 59) − 7,189 = 882.

Add the preparation cost of 59 to the base list price of 8,012, then subtract the dealer's cost, 7,189.

The total dealer's profit is $882.

CHECK Back.

Reread the problem. Does your answer seem reasonable?

The dealer's cost was about $7,200. If a profit of about $800 was added, the base list price would be about $8,000. The answer is reasonable.

Problems

Solve. Use the data on p. 22.

1. What is the total cost of the extra options for the Cyclone 500?

2. The extra options actually cost the dealer $1,146. How much profit would the dealer make on the extra options?

3. The dealer's profit is the difference between the total dealer's cost and the total listed selling price. What is the dealer's profit for the Cyclone 500 with all the extra options?

4. Suppose a customer convinces the dealer to reduce the selling price by $500. How much profit would the dealer make?

5. What would the listed selling price be if a customer chose all the extra options except air conditioning?

6. How much lower would the selling price be without air conditioning, cruise control, power steering, and automatic transmission?

7. What would the total cost be if a customer chose all the options and paid the full selling price plus a sales tax of $493?

8. Suppose the dealer reduced the selling price by $375 and then the buyer decided to have the car rustproofed at a cost of $195. What would the total cost be before the addition of sales tax?

9. Which two extra options could a customer omit to save about $400?

10. The dealer wants to sell the car and is willing to take only $275 profit. What will the selling price be for a Cyclone 500 with all the extra options?

11. **Data Search** Find the listed selling prices of two of your favorite cars. By how much do the prices of these cars differ?

What's Your Decision?

You need a new car and have chosen the Cyclone 500. You can afford to spend only $8,700 plus tax. The dealer will not reduce the listed selling price. If you buy the car, which extra options will you choose?

1-8 Estimating

Three years ago, the Garcias bought a camper with an odometer reading of 16,329. Now the odometer reads 38,647. You could estimate to figure out about how many miles they had driven the camper.

It is often useful to **estimate** to find an approximate answer to a problem or to see if an answer found with a calculator makes sense. There are several ways to estimate sums and differences of whole numbers. One way is called **estimating using rounding**.

Estimating Using Rounding

- Round the numbers to the desired place.
- Compute with the rounded numbers to find the estimate.

Example 1

Round to the nearest thousand and estimate the value of the variable.
$n = 38{,}647 - 16{,}329$

Solution

$$\begin{array}{r} 39{,}000 \\ -\ 16{,}000 \\ \hline 23{,}000 \end{array}$$

Round 38,647 to 39,000.
Round 16,329 to 16,000.

The estimated value for n is 23,000.

Practice Round to the nearest thousand and estimate the value of the variable.
a. $a = 9{,}586 + 4{,}299$ **b.** $76{,}953 - 5{,}466 = y$

Front-end estimation is another useful technique for estimating sums and differences. It is most often used when the numbers have the same number of digits.

Front-end Estimation

- Add (or subtract) the first digits to get a rough estimate.
- Adjust your estimate by using the remaining digits and looking for numbers that are compatible.

Example 2

Use front-end estimation to estimate the value of the variable.
$3{,}527 + 7{,}969 + 5{,}493 = n$

Solution Rough Estimate: 15,000 — Add the "front-end" digits. **3**,527 + **7**,969 + **5**,493 is about **15** thousand.

Adjusted Estimate: 17,000 — Look at the other digits, 3,**527** + 7,**969** + 5,**493**, for compatible numbers. **527** + **493** is about 1,000. **969** is about 1,000. Increase the estimate by 2,000.

Practice Use front-end estimation to estimate.

a. 347 + 598 + 754 **b.** 8,802 − 2,319

Oral Exercises

Round to the place indicated.

1. 658 to nearest ten
2. 864 to nearest hundred
3. 6,523 to nearest thousand
4. 74,214 to nearest ten thousand
5. 91,096 to nearest hundred
6. 6,325 to nearest ten
7. 4,352 to nearest thousand
8. 54,986 to nearest hundred
9. 65,847 to nearest thousand
10. 724,063 to nearest ten thousand

Exercises

A Round to the nearest ten and estimate the value of the variable.

1. $59 + 87 = x$ **2.** $92 - 58 = b$ **3.** $94 + 78 = y$
4. $z = 149 - 62$ **5.** $s = 263 + 695$ **6.** $e = 865 - 243$

Round to the nearest hundred and estimate the value of the variable.

7. $n = 725 + 487$ **8.** $1{,}248 - 519 = x$ **9.** $z = 938 + 694$

Round to the nearest thousand and estimate the value of the variable.

10. $y = 8{,}399 + 6{,}508$ **11.** $12{,}778 - 7{,}499 = c$ **12.** $56{,}468 + 79{,}122 = x$

Use front-end estimation to estimate the value of the variable.

13. $346 + 657 + 498 = n$

14. $873 + 449 + 628 + 858 = y$

15. $2,543 + 7,986 + 4,478 = x$

16. $9,245 + 6,508 + 7,796 = n$

17. $36,247 + 43,572 = a$

18. $875,652 + 925,468 = y$

19. $9,704 - 6,218 = x$

20. $8,703 - 4,687 = a$

21. $74,907 - 35,186 = c$

22. $973,477 + 23,885 = c$

B Solve.

23. The first owner of a car drove it for 56,478 miles. The second owner put 37,517 miles on it. Estimate the total mileage, to the nearest thousand miles.

24. The total cost of a sports car was $17,485. An economy car cost $4,965. Estimate the difference in cost, to the nearest thousand dollars.

25. A bike trip around the mainland of the United States covered 12,092 miles. A trip directly from the west coast to the east coast covered 2,964 miles. About how much longer was the trip around the mainland?

26. Write two numbers, each of which is 24,000 when rounded to the nearest thousand.

27. A number, rounded to the nearest thousand, is 6,000. What letters on the number line below could show the position of this number?

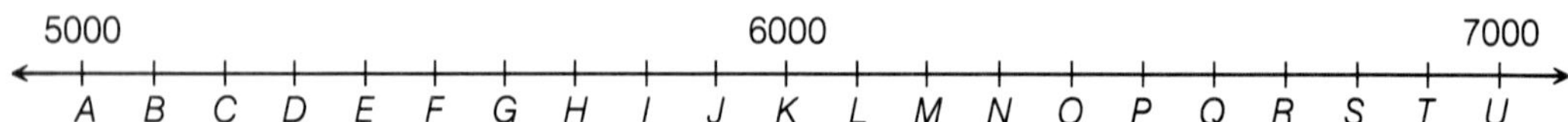

28. A used-car salesperson says that a car has been driven about 70,000 miles. If this number has been rounded to the nearest ten thousand, what is the greatest number of miles the car could have been driven? What is the smallest?

C Extending Thinking Skills

29. Estimate the sum of the whole numbers from one to 25. Use a calculator to check your estimate.

30. Whole numbers in order, such as 8, 9, and 10, are called **consecutive** whole numbers. Find 3 consecutive whole numbers whose sum is 111.

Mixed Review

Use the associative property to write an equivalent expression. **31.** $(78 + 65) + 135$

Write as an algebraic expression. **32.** a number decreased by 650

Solve and check. **33.** $65 - x = 38$ **34.** $48 + y = 93$ **35.** $n + 37 = 129$

Add or subtract. **36.** $1,295 + 1,128$ **37.** $5,007 - 3,985$

38. $22,423 + 10,525$ **39.** $13,254 + 8,098$ **40.** $500,821 - 39,827$

1-9 Guess, Check, Revise

In Section 1-7 you had to decide which operations to use to solve a problem. This strategy is called **Choose the Operations**. Think about what operations are needed to solve the following problem.

Problem A television set costs \$469. You could pay that amount in cash, or you could choose an installment plan and first pay a \$95 down payment and then pay 24 installment payments totaling \$456. How much more would you pay if you chose the installment plan?

To solve the problem, you might plan to use the operation of addition first, then subtraction.

$95 + 456 = 551$ The television costs \$551 on the installment plan.

$551 - 469 = 82$ You would pay \$82 more on the installment plan.

You need to use other strategies for word problems that cannot be solved by simply choosing the operations. You can solve some by guessing a solution, checking the guess, and using what you learned from the check to revise the guess. This strategy is called **Guess, Check, Revise.** You can use it to solve the following problem.

Problem A newspaper ad offered a soccer ball and soccer shoes for a total price of \$59. If the shoes cost \$15 more than the ball, what did each cost?

The chart below shows how you might use the Guess, Check, Revise strategy to find the solution to this problem.

Guess	Check	Revise
First Guess **Ball: \$20**	Shoes: \$20 + \$15 = \$35 Total Cost: \$20 + \$35 = \$55	55 is less than 59. Revise guess up. **Revised guess, \$25**
Second Guess **Ball: \$25**	Shoes: \$25 + \$15 = \$40 Total Cost: \$25 + \$40 = \$65	65 is more than 59. Revise guess down. **Revised guess, \$22**
Third Guess **Ball: \$22**	Shoes: \$22 + \$15 = \$37 Total Cost: \$22 + \$37 = \$59	This is correct!

The ball cost \$22 and the shoes cost \$37.

Problem-Solving Strategies

Choose the Operations

Guess, Check, Revise

Additional strategies will be introduced in later chapters.

Problems

Solve.

1. Denise scored 6 more points in this week's basketball game than she scored in last week's game. She scored a total of 30 points in the two games. How many points did she score in each game?

2. Mrs. Gentry sold 36 more computers in August than she did in July. She sold one more computer in September than she sold in August. In September, she sold 55 computers. How many did she sell in the three months?

3. Eric is 9 years old. In 4 years his father will be 13 years older than twice what Eric's age will be then. How old is Eric's father now?

4. While playing darts, Raul noticed that if he reversed the two digits of his score, it would produce Linda's score. Linda's score was a multiple of 9 and only 9 more than Raul's score. What were their scores? (Note: multiples of nine are 0, 9, 18, 27, 36 . . .)

5. The difference between Richard's and Harriet's weekly earnings is \$80. The sum of their earnings is \$560. Harriet earns the greater amount. How much does each earn?

6. Will is one year older than Phil and Phil is one year older than Gil. The sum of their ages is 75. How old is each?

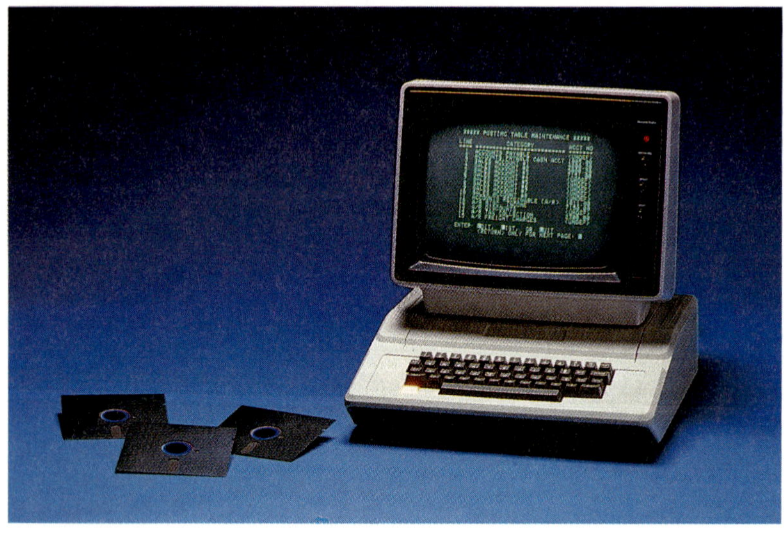

Enrichment

Logical Reasoning and Venn Diagrams

The words ***and, or, not,*** and ***if-then*** are used to express ideas in **logical reasoning**. A **Venn Diagram** is a drawing used to show logical relationships among members of sets. The set members can be numbers, people, cards, or any other elements. The Venn Diagrams below show some relationships.

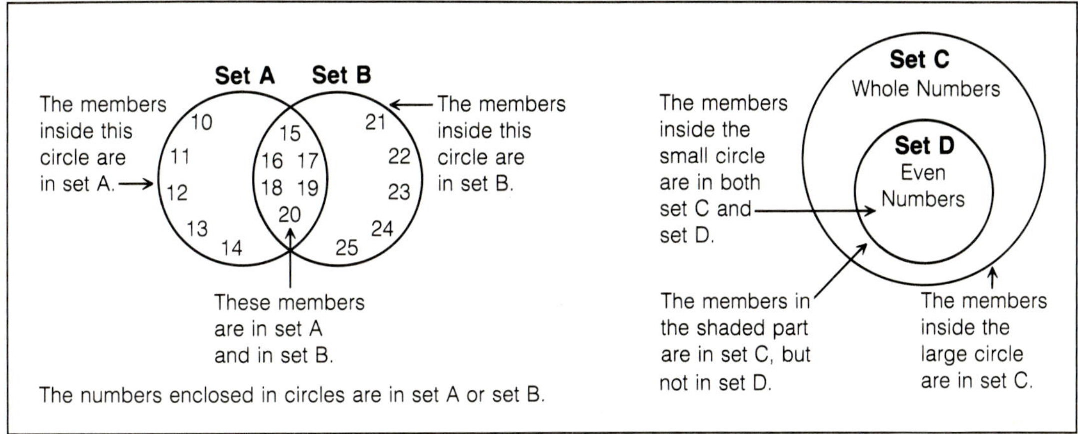

Refer to the Venn Diagrams above for Exercises 1–7. List the numbers in:

1. both set A ***and*** set B

2. set B, but ***not*** in set A.

3. set A, but ***not*** in set B.

4. set A ***or*** set B.

5. List the smallest five numbers that are in set C, but ***not*** in set D.

6. Are there any numbers that are in set D, but ***not*** in set C?

7. ***If*** a number is in set D, ***then*** what can you conclude?

Make a Venn Diagram to show: Set A = brown-haired people. Set B = green-eyed people. Describe the people in:

8. both set A ***and*** set B.

9. set A, but ***not*** set B.

10. set B, but ***not*** set A.

11. ***neither*** set A ***nor*** set B.

Make a Venn Diagram to show: Set C = people from the United States. Set D = people from Texas.

12. A person is in set C, but ***not*** in set D. What can you conclude?

13. A person is ***not*** in set D. What can you conclude?

14. A person is ***not*** in set C. What can you conclude?

Chapter 1 Review

1-1 Evaluate each numerical expression.

1. $24 + (15 - 6)$
2. $(16 + 4) - 8$
3. $44 - (12 + 6)$
4. $38 - (8 - 5)$
5. $27 + (6 - 4)$
6. $(13 + 3) - 6$

Evaluate each algebraic expression.

7. $r + 4$ for $r = 4$
8. $12 - s$ for $s = 8$
9. $(5 + a) + 1$ for $a = 3$
10. $18 - (3 + b)$ for $b = 4$
11. $x - y$ for $x = 7, y = 2$
12. $(a + 10) - 9$ for $a = 7$

1-2 Write as an algebraic expression.

13. 1 more than z
14. 9 added to p
15. v decreased by 2

Write an expression for each question.
Mark walks 9 miles a day. How far will he walk if

16. he walks m miles farther?
17. he walks 2 miles less?

1-3 Use the basic properties. Write an equivalent expression.

18. $(c + 1) + 3$
19. $k + 5$
20. $0 + w$

1-4 Solve the equation for the replacement set given.

21. $f - 4 = 6$ {9, 10, 11, 12}
22. $b + 3 = 11$ {8, 9, 10, 11}

1-5 Solve.

23. $15 - m = 6$
24. $4 + x = 17$
25. $b + 8 = 17$

1-6 Solve and check.

26. $t + 28 = 39$
27. $q - 45 = 22$
28. $691 + p = 777$
29. $121 = 193 - z$
30. $238 + a = 238$
31. $144 - m = 32$

1-7 Solve.

32. Teresa rode her bicycle 5 kilometers farther today than she did yesterday. She rode 17 kilometers yesterday. How far did she ride today?

33. Josh had 22 tapes. He gave all but 5 away. How many did he give away?

1-8 Round to the nearest thousand and estimate the value of the variable.

34. $9{,}862 + 6{,}490 = p$
35. $n = 2{,}714 - 1{,}152$
36. $3{,}561 + 5{,}126 = k$

Round to the nearest hundred and estimate the value of the variable.

37. $r = 927 + 610$
38. $683 - 274 = y$
39. $3{,}596 - 834 = c$

Use front-end estimation to estimate the value of the variable.

40. $m = 798 + 413 + 112$
41. $(3{,}418 + 1{,}113) + 2{,}976 = f$

Chapter 1 Test

Evaluate each numerical expression.

1. $17 - (3 + 6)$
2. $(25 - 5) + 4$
3. $12 + (8 + 6)$
4. $(7 - 4) + 8$
5. $18 - (7 - 5)$
6. $(16 - 7) + 5$

Evaluate each algebraic expression.

7. $y + 7$ for $y = 6$
8. $z - 3$ for $z = 9$
9. $(3 + 5) - m$ for $m = 4$
10. $13 - (x + 7)$ for $x = 2$
11. $r - k$ for $r = 7, k = 2$
12. $(a + b) - 3$ for $a = 8, b = 6$

Write as an algebraic expression.

13. 5 more than p
14. v decreased by 4
15. 7 added to a number

Write an expression to answer each question.
Hitoshi has $45. How much will she have if:

16. she earns $18 more?
17. she buys earrings for $36?

Use the basic properties. Write an equivalent expression.

18. $t + 0$
19. $(n + 5) + 4$
20. $6 + y$

Solve the equation for the replacement set given.

21. $x + 9 = 12$ $\{1, 2, 3, 4\}$
22. $n - 7 = 7$ $\{13, 14, 15, 16\}$

Solve and check.

23. $16 - n = 8$
24. $1 + y = 8$
25. $z + 7 = 16$
26. $g + 14 = 67$
27. $s - 74 = 12$
28. $255 + w = 500$
29. $166 = 212 - h$
30. $413 = 62 + r$
31. $113 - f = 113$

Solve.

32. Wayne practiced the piano 7 hours more this week than he did last week. He practiced 9 hours last week. How long did he practice in the two weeks?

33. Margaret gave 19 of her magazines to a friend. She has 24 magazines left. How many magazines did she have to start with?

Round to the nearest thousand and estimate the value of the variable.

34. $4{,}679 + 3{,}125 = a$
35. $s = 11{,}591 - 2{,}139$
36. $7{,}825 + 3{,}368 = p$

Round to the nearest hundred and estimate the value of the variable.

37. $j = 853 + 234$
38. $891 - 255 = w$
39. $1{,}316 - 402 = b$

Use front-end estimation to estimate the value of the variable.

40. $n = 143 + 978 + 245$
41. $1{,}708 + 1{,}125 + 6{,}855 = a$

Cumulative Review

Evaluate each numerical expression.

1. $13 - (7 + 4)$ **2.** $(12 - 9) + 8$ **3.** $23 + (5 + 6)$

Use front-end estimation to estimate the value of the variable.

4. $b = 212 + 583 + 785$ **5.** $5{,}258 + 9{,}295 + 4{,}502 = p$

Write as an algebraic expression.

6. 2 less than n **7.** k increased by 3 **8.** 7 added to a

Write an expression to answer each question.
Susan has \$15. How much will she have if:

9. she earns \$22 more? **10.** she buys a record for \$9?

Use the commutative, associative, or zero properties. Write an equivalent expression.

11. $r + 5$ **12.** $(y + 4) + 6$ **13.** $6 + 0$

Solve the equation for the replacement set given.

14. $z + 4 = 12 \{7, 8, 9, 10\}$ **15.** $a - 5 = 7 \{12, 13, 14, 15\}$

16. $20 - m = 14 \{6, 7, 8, 9\}$ **17.** $4 + g = 14 \{7, 8, 9, 10\}$

Solve.

18. $7 + x = 14$ **19.** $a - 8 = 15$ **20.** $13 - b = 6$

Solve and check.

21. $x + 16 = 35$ **22.** $k - 45 = 17$ **23.** $743 + n = 850$

24. $102 = 314 - f$ **25.** $555 = 770 - r$ **26.** $225 - p = 115$

Solve each problem.

27. Mickey played baseball 10 hours more this week than he did last week. He played baseball 12 hours last week. How long did he play this week?

28. Barbara gave 11 of her books to a friend. She had 31 left. How many did she have to start with?

Round to the nearest ten and estimate the value of the variable.

29. $55 + 23 = v$ **30.** $z = 693 - 58$ **31.** $47 + 21 = d$

Round to the nearest hundred and estimate the value of the variable.

32. $c = 697 + 162$ **33.** $836 - 642 = h$ **34.** $147 + 121 = d$

Evaluate each algebraic expression.

35. $t + 9$ for $t = 6$ **36.** $(4 + 7) - c$ for $c = 5$

37. $s + y - 2$ for $y = 6$, $s = 3$

Chapter 2

Expressions and Equations: Multiplication and Division

2-1 Evaluating Expressions: Order of Operations

Numerical expressions involving multiplication and division can be written in several ways.

9×8 can be written $9 \cdot 8$ or $9(8)$

$72 \div 8$ can be written $\frac{72}{8}$

Parentheses ( ) and brackets [ ] indicate the order in which operations should be done, and are called **grouping symbols**. The fraction bar, which serves as a division symbol, is also a grouping symbol.

Expression	Meaning of grouping symbols	Results
$(9 + 6) \div 3$	*Parentheses* indicate that addition is to be done first.	$15 \div 3 = 5$
$9 + (6 \div 3)$	*Parentheses* indicate that division is to be done first.	$9 + 2 = 11$
$7 - [(6 + 9) \div 5]$	*Inner parentheses* indicate that addition is to be done first. The division inside the *brackets* is to be done next.	$7 - [15 \div 5]$ $7 - 3 = 4$
$\frac{9 + 3}{3 \cdot 2}$	The *fraction bar* indicates that the addition above and the multiplication below are to be done before dividing.	$\frac{12}{6} = 12 \div 6 = 2$

When no grouping symbols are given, as in the expression $5 + 4 \cdot 7$, we need a rule for the order of operations. If addition is done first, $5 + 4 \cdot 7$ is 63. If multiplication is done first, $5 + 4 \cdot 7$ is 33. The following rule ensures that everyone gets the same answer.

Order of Operations

First do all multiplying and dividing in order from left to right.
Then do all adding and subtracting in order from left to right.

Example 1

Evaluate. $[18 + (4 \cdot 6)] \div 7$

Solution

$[18 + (4 \cdot 6)] \div 7$ Look for the inside grouping symbols. Compute $4 \cdot 6$ first.

$= [18 + 24] \div 7$ Next do the operation in the outer pair of grouping symbols. Compute $18 + 24$.

$= 42 \div 7$

$= 6$

Practice Evaluate.

a. $27 \div (5 + 4)$

b. $23 - [(56 + 7) \div 9]$

Example 2

Evaluate. $8 \cdot 2 + 45 \div 9$

Solution

$8 \cdot 2 + 45 \div 9$ Do multiplication and division from left to right. First compute 8×2.

$= 16 + 45 \div 9$ Then compute $45 \div 9$.

$= 16 + 5$ Next do addition and subtraction from left to right. Compute $16 + 5$.

$= 21$

Practice Evaluate.

a. $5 + 4 \cdot 7$ **b.** $24 + 40 \div 8 - 3$ **c.** $16 + 30 \div 3 \cdot 2$

Like numerical expressions, algebraic expressions involving multiplication and division can be written in several ways. For example, $\mathbf{9 \times s}$ can be written $\mathbf{9 \cdot s}$, $\mathbf{9(s)}$, or $\mathbf{9s}$. An expression such as $\mathbf{7 \times a \times b}$ is most often written $\mathbf{7ab}$.

The expression $\mathbf{y \div 3}$ can be written $\mathbf{\frac{y}{3}}$.

Example 3

Evaluate $x(7 + y)$ for $x = 9$ and $y = 3$

Solution $x(7 + y)$

$9(7 + 3)$ Replace x with 9 and y with 3. Add within the parentheses first.

$= 9(10)$ Remember that 9(10) means 9×10.

$= 90$

Practice Evaluate.

a. $3(a + 5)b$ for $a = 7$ and $b = 9$

b. $8 + \left(\frac{yz}{40}\right)$ for $y = 10$ and $z = 4$

Example 4

Evaluate. $\frac{x + 7}{6}$ for $x = 47$

Solution $\frac{x + 7}{6}$

$\frac{47 + 7}{6}$ Replace x with 47. Do the operations above the fraction bar first. Find 47 + 7.

$= \frac{54}{6}$

$= 9$

Practice Evaluate.

a. $\frac{9 + 6}{a}$ for $a = 3$ **b.** $\frac{7 + 9}{z + 6}$ for $z = 10$ **c.** $\frac{3y + 9}{2z}$ for $y = 9$ and $z = 9$

Oral Exercises

Which operation would you do first?

1. $5 + 3 \cdot 2$
2. $(7 + 4) \cdot 6$
3. $(36 - 32) \div 4$
4. $48 - 24 \div 6 \cdot 2$
5. $15 - 8 \div 2$
6. $7 + 6 \cdot 3 - 3$

Exercises

A Evaluate each numerical expression.

1. $13 + (54 \div 9)$
2. $63 \div (21 \div 3)$
3. $(7 \cdot 8) - 50$
4. $[9 + (9 \cdot 7)] \div 8$
5. $[15 - (4 \cdot 2)] + 9$
6. $[48 \div (32 - 26)] \cdot 12$
7. $16 - 7 \cdot 2$
8. $9 \cdot 4 \div 2$
9. $543 - 196 \div 28$
10. $12 + 9 \cdot 3 - 28$
11. $45 - 20 \div 4 + 9$
12. $96 \div 4 - 3 \cdot 5$
13. $54 + 24 \div 3 - 30$
14. $36 \div 3 + 4 \cdot 5 - 3$
15. $5 \cdot 6 - 56 \div 7 + 7 \cdot 4$

Evaluate each algebraic expression.

16. $5x$ for $x = 9$
17. $4bc$ for $b = 16$, $c = 17$
18. $(18 + 7)ab$ for $a = 2$, $b = 5$
19. $\frac{x}{8}$ for $x = 32$
20. $\frac{a}{b}$ for $a = 945$, $b = 9$
21. $\frac{3cd}{6}$ for $c = 18$, $d = 25$
22. $\frac{54}{b}$ for $b = 6$
23. $12(52 - p)$ for $p = 47$
24. $24 + bc$ for $b = 39$, $c = 16$
25. $\frac{s + 8}{16}$ for $s = 24$
26. $\frac{5x}{13}$ for $x = 26$
27. $\frac{43 - t}{9}$ for $t = 7$
28. $6y - 2y$ for $y = 24$
29. $\frac{5a}{b + 4}$ for $a = 9$, $b = 1$
30. $\frac{y + 7}{x - 5}$ for $x = 14$, $y = 20$
31. $n(n) + 2$ for $n = 8$
32. $\frac{56}{n} + 24$ for $n = 8$
33. $\frac{2a + 4}{b - 7}$ for $a = 20$, $b = 18$

B Copy and complete each table.

	a	b	$6a - b$
	3	3	$6(3) - 4 = 14$
34.	5	30	
35.	9	4	
36.	7	5	

	x	y	$x \div 3 + y \div 3$
	6	9	$6 \div 3 + 9 \div 3 = 5$
37.	12	18	
38.	24	45	
39.	63	99	

Find the final answer without writing down intermediate answers.

40. Evaluate. $959 \div 7 - 16 \cdot 8$ **41.** Simplify. $24 \cdot 57 + 1{,}424 \div 89$

C Extending Thinking skills

42. Use each of the numbers 2, 4, 6, 8, and 12 exactly once, with any operation signs and grouping symbols you wish, to write an expression for the smallest possible whole number.

43. Use the digits for this year with any grouping symbols and operations to write expressions for as many of the whole numbers from 0 to 10 as you can.

Mixed Review

Solve mentally. **44.** $120 + n = 135$ **45.** $80 = 105 - m$ **46.** $m - 45 = 55$

Write as an expression. **47.** x less than 27 **48.** x more than 12

Round to the nearest hundred and estimate the sum. **49.** 3,647 + 2,891

CALCULATOR ACTIVITY

Some calculators are programmed to follow the order of operation rules. With others, you must think about the rules and enter the computations into the calculator in the order in which they should be performed. Test your calculator by entering $4 \cdot 3 + 8 \div 2$ as follows:

4 [×] 3 [+] 8 [÷] 2 [=]

What answer will the calculator display if it uses the order of operation rules? What answer will it display if it simply performs the operations from left to right? Which answer is correct?

Use a calculator to evaluate each expression.

1. $56 + 9 \cdot 57$

2. $84 - 240 \div 16$

3. $832 \div 8 + 4 \cdot 26$

4. $254 - 19 \cdot 13 + 68$

5. $16 + 4 \cdot 7 - 36 \div 9$

6. $536 + 18 \cdot 53 - 9$

2-2 Translating Phrases to Algebraic Expressions

Verbal phrases that suggest multiplication or division can be translated to numerical or algebraic expressions.

Example 1

Write as a numerical expression. "the product of 9 and 8"

Solution 9×8 The phrase "the product of" suggests multiplying the two numbers.

Practice Write as a numerical expression.

a. the quotient of 24 and 6

b. twice 8

c. 12 multiplied by 7

The phrase "9 times 8" translates to the numerical expression 9×8. The phrase "9 times a number" translates to the algebraic expression $9n$.

number	9 times the number	
8	9×8	"9 times 8"
10	9×10	"9 times 10"
n	$9n$	"9 times a **number**"

Example 2

Write an algebraic expression for "a number divided by 6."

Solution $\frac{n}{6}$ Think of a specific number, say 24. "24 divided by 6" is $\frac{24}{6}$, so "a *number* divided by 6" is $\frac{n}{6}$.

Practice Write as an algebraic expression.

a. the product of 6 and a number

b. double a number

c. the quotient of a number and 5

A phrase may suggest a combination of operations, as in the following example.

Example 3

Write an algebraic expression for "6 less than twice a number."

Solution $2n - 6$ "6 less than" suggests subtracting 6.

Practice Write as an algebraic expression.

a. 5 increased by twice a number **b.** 7 times the sum of a number and 4

Example 4

Write as an expression.
Rita earned $24. How much will she have if:

a. she earns 7 times as much? **b.** she earns n times as much?

c. she divides it among 3 people? **d.** she divides it among n people?

Solutions

a. she earns 7 times as much? 24×7

b. she earns n times as much? $24n$ Think about a number, write a variable.

c. she divides it among 3 people? $24 \div 3$

d. she divides it among n people? $24 \div n$ Think about a number, write a variable.

Practice Write as an expression.

A machine produces 645 items in an hour. How many does it produce in: **a.** 8 hours? **b.** h hours?

How many items are in each box if 645 items are divided equally among: **c.** 5 boxes? **d.** b boxes?

Oral Exercises

Tell whether the phrase suggests multiplication or division.

1. the product of **2.** divided by **3.** the quotient of

4. doubled **5.** multiplied by **6.** times

7. one-third of **8.** halved **9.** tripled

Exercises

A Write as a numerical expression.

1. the product of 8 and 7 **2.** 7 times 9 **3.** twice 46

4. 6 multiplied by 7 **5.** 48 shared among 4 **6.** 45 divided by 15

Write as an algebraic expression.

7. the product of a number and 9 **8.** the quotient of a number and 8

9. a number times 15 **10.** a number multiplied by 11

11. 6 times a number

12. half of a number

13. a number divided by 5

14. double a number

15. 35 increased by twice a number

16. 6 less than the sum of a number and 3

17. 12 less than twice a number

18. 100 less than a number divided by 1,000

19. 24 less than 3 times a number

20. 8 times the sum of 18 and a number

21. 5 times a number, plus 4

22. 5 more than the quotient of a number and 6

Write an expression for each question.

There are 36 cars in the parking lot. How many will there be when there are:

23. 9 times as many?

24. y times as many?

25. the number there now divided by 4?

26. the number there now divided by n?

Kristy sold 48 calculators in one week. How many will she sell in a week when:

27. her sales are multiplied by 4?

28. her sales are multiplied by x?

29. her sales are divided by 12?

30. her sales are divided by z?

B The expression $2n + 1$ represents an odd number such as 1, 3, 5, 7, 9, . . .
Write an algebraic expression for:

31. the even number that comes just after $2n + 1$

32. the even number that comes just before $2n + 1$

33. the odd number that comes just after $2n + 1$

34. the odd number that comes just before $2n + 1$

C Extending Thinking Skills

35. In a championship football game, the Rams scored 25 points more than the Dolphins. If the Dolphins had scored 3 times as many points, they would have scored 1 point more than the Rams. How many points did each team score?

36. Look for a pattern in the equations below.

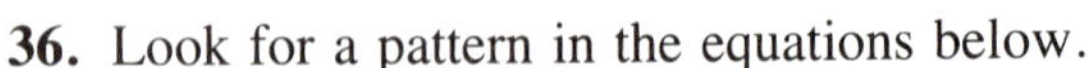

Sum of the first **1** odd number	$1 = \mathbf{1}$
Sum of the first **2** odd numbers	$1 + 3 = \mathbf{4}$
Sum of the first **3** odd numbers	$1 + 3 + 5 = \mathbf{9}$
Sum of the first **4** odd numbers	$1 + 3 + 5 + 7 = \mathbf{16}$

Write an algebraic expression for the sum of the first n odd numbers. Use it to find the sum of the first 100 odd numbers.

Mixed Review

Solve and check. **37.** $n - 163 = 291$ **38.** $x + 62 = 157$ **39.** $26 = r - 45$

Solve for the replacement set given. **40.** $c + 16 = 42$ {24, 25, 26, 27}

Use the associative property to write an equivalent expression. **41.** $(x + 7) + 3$

2-3 Basic Properties of Multiplication

The basic properties of multiplication and division can be used to write equivalent expressions.

You can change the order in which two numbers are multiplied and their product will stay the same.

For example, $32 \times 15 = 15 \times 32$.

$$\begin{array}{r} 32 \\ \times 15 \\ \hline 160 \\ 32 \\ \hline 480 \end{array} \qquad \begin{array}{r} 15 \\ \times 32 \\ \hline 30 \\ 45 \\ \hline 480 \end{array}$$

With variables, this property can be stated for all whole numbers.

Commutative Property of Multiplication

A change in the order in which two numbers are multiplied does not change their product.

For all whole numbers ***a*** and ***b***, $ab = ba$

Example 1

Use the commutative property to write an expression equivalent to $5y$

Solution $y(5)$ $y(5)$ has the same value as $5y$ for any number that replaces y.

Practice Use the commutative property to write an equivalent expression. **a.** xy **b.** $z(6)$ **c.** $24p$

You can change the way three numbers are grouped for multiplication and the product stays the same.

For example, $(17 \times 25) \times 4 = 17 \times (25 \times 4)$.

$$(17 \times 25) \times 4 = 425 \times 4 = 1700$$

$$17 \times (25 \times 4) = 17 \times 100 = 1700$$

With variables, this property can be stated for all whole numbers.

Associative Property of Multiplication

A change in the grouping of three whole numbers for multiplication does not change the product.

For all whole numbers **a, b,** and **c,** $a(bc) = (ab)c$

Example 2

Use the associative property to write an expression equivalent to $6(4n)$.

Solution $(6 \cdot 4)n$ $(6 \cdot 4)n$ has the same value as $6(4n)$ for any number that replaces n.

Practice Use the associative property to write an equivalent expression.

a. $(n \cdot 12)7$ **b.** $25(4a)$ **c.** $(6a)b$

The number **1** is called the **multiplicative identity** because when it is multiplied by a number, the result is that same number.
For example, $\mathbf{49 \times 1 = 49}$.

Identity Property of Multiplication

The product of a factor and one is the factor.

For all whole numbers **a,** $a(1) = a$ $1(a) = a$

Any number divided by 1 equals that same number: $a \div 1 = a$.
Any number divided by itself equals one: $a \div a = 1$.

The number 0 also has special properties. When any number is multiplied by 0, the product is always 0: $\mathbf{6 \times 0 = 0}$.

Zero Property of Multiplication

The product of any number and zero is zero.

For all whole numbers **a,** $a(0) = 0$ $0(a) = 0$

When 0 is divided by another number, the quotient is always 0. When you consider dividing by 0, you will see that every number could be a solution to the equation $0 \div 0 = n$. An equation such as $24 \div 0 = n$ would have no solution. Division by 0 is undefined for these reasons.

Example 3

Use the zero or identity property to write an equivalent expression.

a. $0 \cdot x$ **b.** $1 \cdot x$

Solutions **a.** 0 $0 \cdot x = 0$ for any number that replaces x.

b. x $1 \cdot x = x$ for any number replacing x.

Practice Use the zero or identity property to write an equivalent expression.

a. $0 \cdot t$ **b.** $1n$ **c.** $p(0)$

The numbers below show that $9 \cdot (10 + 6) = 9 \cdot 10 + 9 \cdot 6$. The result is the same whether the two numbers are added first and their sum is multiplied by 9, or the products are found first and then added.

$9 \cdot (10 + 6)$	$9 \cdot 10 + 9 \cdot 6$
$9 \cdot (16)$	$90 + 54$
144	**144**

This important property ties multiplication and addition together.

Distributive Property of Multiplication Over Addition

When two numbers have been added and then multiplied by a factor, the result will be the same when each number is multiplied by the factor and the products are then added.

For whole numbers **a, b, and c,** $a(b + c) = ab + ac$

$(b + c)a = ba + ca$

Example 4

Use the distributive property to write an expression equivalent to $5(x + y)$

Solution $5x + 5y$ $5(x + y)$ has the same value as $5x + 5y$ for any numbers that replace the variables.

Practice Use the distributive property to write an equivalent expression.

a. $6(r + 4)$ **b.** $(5 + 3)n$

Oral Exercises

Name the property shown by each equation. Do not compute.

1. $12 \times 0 = 0$
2. $17 \times 8 = 8 \times 17$
3. $16 \times (3 \times 5) = (16 \times 3) \times 5$
4. $1 \times 26 = 26$
5. $83 \times 14 = 14 \times 83$
6. $6 \times (12 + 7) = 6 \times 12 + 6 \times 7$
7. $8 + 23 = 23 + 8$
8. $9(14) + 9(6) = 9(14 + 6)$

Exercises

A Use the commutative property to write an equivalent expression.

1. $y(4)$
2. $9x$
3. cd
4. $x(28)$
5. $68b$
6. $c(36)$
7. $15r$
8. $9(43)$

Use the associative property to write an equivalent expression.

9. $(n \cdot 3)8$
10. $(y \cdot 7)13$
11. $8(5 \cdot a)$
12. $50(4n)$

Use the zero or identity property to write an equivalent expression.

13. $1y$
14. $0 \cdot s$
15. $y \div y$
16. $0 \div m$

Use the distributive property to write an equivalent expression.

17. $4(x + 3)$
18. $8(s + 7)$
19. $y(6 + 9)$
20. $(n + 4)3$
21. $(6 + s)5$
22. $(8 + 7)y$
23. $5(z + 3)$
24. $y(2 + 8)$

B

25. Evaluate $(12a)b$ and $12(ab)$ for $a = 7$ and $b = 13$. Are the values equal?
26. Evaluate $a(7 + b)$ and $7a + ab$ for $a = 9$ and $b = 6$. Are the values equal?

Use basic properties to solve the equations.

27. $8n = 13(8)$
28. $8(16 + 24) = 8(16) + 8m$
29. $(54 \cdot 36)23 = 54(b \cdot 23)$
30. $8(4x) = (8 \cdot 4)100$
31. Evaluate $a \div b$ for $a = 10$ and $b = 5$.
If only whole number answers are allowed, why can't you evaluate $b \div a$ using these same numbers? Is the commutative property true for division of whole numbers?

32. Evaluate $a(b - c)$ for $a = 7$, $b = 14$, and $c = 8$.
Evaluate $ab - ac$ for the same numbers.
Try some other numbers for a, b, and c. When would a distributive property involving multiplication with subtraction be true?

33. Choose values for a, b, and c to show that a distributive property for addition over multiplication, $a + (b \cdot c) = (a + b) \cdot (a + c)$, does not hold true for all whole numbers.

C Extending Thinking Skills

34. Suppose the symbol @ represents the operation "doubleadd" so that $3 @ 4 = 2(3) + 4 = 10$. That is, double the first number and add the second. Give examples to show that neither the commutative nor the associative properties hold true for this operation.

35. How could you calculate answers to these problems quickly?

a. $26(6) + 26(4)$ **b.** $38(57) + 38(43)$ **c.** $56(64) + 56(36)$

Mixed Review

Find the product or quotient.

Examples:

$$\begin{array}{r} 376 \\ \times\ 23 \\ \hline 1128 \\ 752 \\ \hline 8648 \end{array} \qquad \begin{array}{r} 306 \\ 45\overline{)13,770} \\ \underline{13\ 5} \\ 270 \\ \underline{270} \\ 0 \end{array}$$

36. $236 \cdot 43$ **37.** $95 \cdot 307$ **38.** $119 \cdot 45$

39. $472 \cdot 11$ **40.** $8586 \div 53$ **41.** $513 \div 27$

42. $1848 \div 56$ **43.** $1292 \div 76$ **44.** $67 \cdot 29$

45. $1311 \div 57$ **46.** $94 \cdot 280$ **47.** $8100 \div 36$

48. $732 \cdot 58$ **49.** $35322 \div 42$ **50.** $3000 \div 25$

NUMBERS TO ALGEBRA

When an expression has the same number as a factor in each addend, a reversed form of the distributive property, $\boldsymbol{ab + ac = a(b + c)}$ may be used to write an equivalent expression that is a product.

Check the number examples to see that they are true.

This property is used to **factor** algebraic expressions

Numbers	Algebra (factored form)
$\mathbf{4} \cdot 3 + \mathbf{4} \cdot 5 = \mathbf{4}(3 + 5)$	$4b + 4c = 4(b + c)$
$\mathbf{6} \cdot 5 + \mathbf{6} \cdot 7 = \mathbf{6}(5 + 7)$	$6x + 6y = 6(x + y)$
$\mathbf{5} \cdot 8 + \mathbf{5} \cdot 4 = \mathbf{5}(8 + 4)$	$5m + 5n = 5(m + n)$

Use the distributive property to factor each expression.

1. $2a + 2b$ **2.** $5y + 5z$ **3.** $6n + 6(7)$

4. $8s + 16$ **5.** $3p + np$ **6.** $ax + az$

2-4 Simplifying Algebraic Expressions

To **simplify an algebraic expression**, you replace it with a simpler equivalent expression. An expression in its simplest form does not contain parentheses. The table below suggests that $6n$ has the same value as $3(2n)$ for every number that replaces the variable n. $3(2n)$ can be simplified to $6n$ because $6n$ is a simpler expression that is equivalent to $3(2n)$.

n	$3(2n)$	$6n$
1	6	6
2	12	12
3	18	18
⋮	⋮	⋮

You can use the basic properties to simplify algebraic expressions.

Example 1

Use the associative property of multiplication to simplify. $3(2n)$

Solution $3(2n) = (3 \cdot 2)n$ $(3 \cdot 2)n$ has the same value as $3(2n)$ for any value of n.

$= 6n$

Practice Simplify. **a.** $5(6x)$ **b.** $9(7b)$ **c.** $12(8y)$

Example 2

Use the associative property of addition to simplify. $(x + 7) + 6$

Solution $(x + 7) + 6 = x + (7 + 6)$ $x + (7 + 6)$ has the same value as $(x + 7) + 6$ for any value of n.

$= x + 13$

Practice Simplify. **a.** $(n + 24) + 8$ **b.** $(z + 13) + 7$ **c.** $(r + 25) + 7$

The parts of an algebraic expression that are separated by an addition or subtraction sign are called **terms**. The expression $4x + 2y - 3$ has three terms.

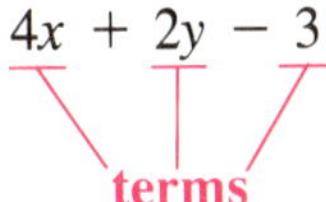

Terms with the same variable factors are called **like terms**. $2n$ and $3n$ are like terms, but $4x$ and $2y$ are unlike terms because their variable factors, x and y, are different.

To simplify expressions with addends that are like terms, you can **combine like terms** by using the distributive property: $\boldsymbol{ba + ca = (b + c)a}$. The number replacements for n in the table below suggest that $2n + 3n$ can be simplified to $5n$.

n	$2n + 3n$	$5n$
1	5	5
2	10	10
3	15	15
⋮	⋮	⋮

Example 3

Use the distributive property to simplify by combining like terms. $5x + 8x$

Solution $5x + 8x = (5 + 8)x$ $(5 + 8)x = 5x + 8x$ for any number replacing x.
$= 13x$

Practice Combine like terms. **a.** $6n + 5n$ **b.** $25b + 15b$ **c.** $37z + 4z$ **d.** $x + 5x$

Oral Exercises

Name the property that could be used to simplify the expression.

1. $5(4x)$ **2.** $(n + 9) + 6$ **3.** $7(5 \cdot b)$
4. $6y + 9y$ **5.** $(c \cdot 5)7$ **6.** $12c + 17c$
7. $8 + (9 + r)$ **8.** $23t + 1t$ **9.** $6(2n)$

Exercises

A Use the associative property of multiplication to simplify.

1. $13(16c)$ **2.** $5(3 \cdot s)$ **3.** $8(6p)$ **4.** $6(10 \cdot n)$
5. $7(8x)$ **6.** $7(4 \cdot y)$ **7.** $27(3y)$ **8.** $10(100n)$
9. $46(3b)$ **10.** $4(9 \cdot z)$ **11.** $34(46z)$ **12.** $56(89x)$

Use the associative property of addition to simplify.

13. $(x + 7) + 9$ 14. $(p + 13) + 8$ 15. $(b + 27) + 5$

16. $(z + 45) + 25$ 17. $(n + 18) + 5$ 18. $(c + 24) + 9$

19. $(b + 36) + 47$ 20. $(q + 67) + 8925$ 21. $(y + 135) + 68$

Use the distributive property to simplify by combining like terms.

22. $4x + 6x$ 23. $7a + 5a$ 24. $9p + 7p$ 25. $4z + 12z$

26. $8s + 9s$ 27. $15y + 8y$ 28. $5a + 36a$ 29. $86c + 37c$

B The distributive property can be extended. For whole numbers $a, b, c, d, \ldots, a(b + c + d + \ldots) = ab + ac + ad + \ldots$

Use the **extended distributive property** to simplify.

30. $5x + 4x + 3x$ 31. $6a + 8a + 9a + 7a$

32. $23y + 6y + 5y$ 33. $27c + 23c + 6c$

Use the basic properties as needed to simplify each expression.

34. $(5 + y) + 9$ 35. $5(3x + 4x)$ 36. $7(x + 8)$ 37. $\frac{6a + 4a}{7a + 3a}$

C Extending Thinking Skills

38. Nancy sold tickets to the school play. Compared to the number she sold on Monday, Tuesday's number was double, Wednesday's was triple, and Thursday's was quadruple. If Nancy sold a total of 80 tickets, how many did she sell each day?

39. Try this "number trick": choose a number; add 7; subtract 2; multiply by 2; subtract 10; divide by 2. What is the result? Choose a variable to express the number and write an algebraic expression to help explain why this works.

Mixed Review

Write as an algebraic expression. 40. 9 less than 6 times a number

Solve and check. 41. $x - 19 = 6$ 42. $304 = x - 24$ 43. $167 + x = 540$

MENTAL MATH

Because of the distributive property, you can find products such as 3(24) by "breaking apart" 24 and thinking "3(20) plus 3(4), or 60 + 12. The product is 72." Break apart numbers to find each product mentally.

1. 2(34) 2. 3(26) 3. 4(23)

4. 5(33) 5. 6(43) 6. 7(24)

2-5 Solving Equations: Using Mental Math

To find the average speed of a raft on a 5-hour trip with a distance of 35 km you can solve the equation $5n = 35$.

An equation that involves small numbers and a single operation, either multiplication or division, can often be solved mentally.

Example 1

Solve and check mentally. $5n = 35$

Solution $5n = 35$ Think: what number multiplied by 5 gives 35?

$n = 7$

Check $5(7) \stackrel{?}{=} 35$ Mentally substitute 7 for n in the equation.

$35 = 35 \checkmark$ The equation is true, so 7 is a solution.

Practice Solve and check mentally.

a. $\frac{x}{4} = 9$ **b.** $56 = 7r$ **c.** $9 = \frac{c}{3}$

The equations below show the relationship between multiplication and division.

Product		Factor		Factor		Factor		Factor		Product
240	÷	**40**	=	**6**	⟷	**6**	·	**40**	=	**240**

Since multiplication can undo division and division can undo multiplication, multiplication and division are inverse operations. You can use this idea to solve simple equations mentally.

Example 2

Use the inverse operation to solve mentally. $\frac{x}{6} = 5$

Solution $\frac{x}{6} = 5$ Think "A number has been divided by 6 to produce 5, so 5 times 6 should equal the number."

$x = 5 \cdot 6$

$x = 30$

Check $\frac{30}{6} \stackrel{?}{=} 5$ Mentally substitute 30 for the x in the equation.

$5 = 5 \checkmark$ The equation is true, so 30 is the solution.

Practice Use the inverse operation to solve mentally.

a. $r \cdot 8 = 40$ **b.** $\frac{a}{6} = 9$ **c.** $6y = 48$

Oral Exercises

The solution of the equation $6x = 42$ is "the number that multiplied by 6 gives 42." Describe the solution of each of these equations.

1. $\frac{n}{5} = 9$ **2.** $4c = 20$ **3.** $\frac{x}{7} = 4$

4. $x \cdot 9 = 7$ **5.** $4 = \frac{a}{8}$ **6.** $63 = 7c$

To solve the equation $\frac{x}{21} = 7$, you can use the inverse operation and find $21 \cdot 7$. How can you solve each of these equations?

7. $\frac{a}{4} = 9$ **8.** $7y = 28$ **9.** $7 = \frac{x}{9}$

10. $72 = 9n$ **11.** $6r = 42$ **12.** $\frac{p}{6} = 6$

Exercises

A Solve and check mentally.

1. $3n = 27$ **2.** $4a = 28$ **3.** $7x = 49$ **4.** $8b = 72$

5. $\frac{t}{4} = 9$ **6.** $\frac{x}{8} = 9$ **7.** $\frac{c}{5} = 6$ **8.** $\frac{b}{10} = 8$

9. $30p = 150$ **10.** $40x = 80$ **11.** $\frac{b}{60} = 4$ **12.** $20 = \frac{n}{4}$

13. $240 = 8x$ **14.** $10 = \frac{n}{3}$ **15.** $100 = 5y$ **16.** $250 = 10x$

17. $\frac{a}{50} = 250$ **18.** $3 = \frac{p}{70}$ **19.** $100 = \frac{n}{5}$ **20.** $80 = \frac{t}{4}$

21. $25n = 100$ **22.** $350t = 700$ **23.** $125z = 250$ **24.** $\frac{r}{1000} = 3$

B Use a calculator and inverse operations to solve the equations in Exercises 25–32. For example, to solve $\frac{x}{38} = 26$, think: a number has been *divided* by 38 to produce the factor 26. Start with 26 and *multiply* by 38.

Display

26 [×] 38 [=] 988 $x = 988$

25. $\frac{n}{49} = 135$ **26.** $57c = 684$ **27.** $\frac{c}{78} = 41$ **28.** $\frac{y}{82} = 137$

29. An amusement park director divided the total attendance for a two-week period by 14 to find that the average daily attendance was 8,654. Solve the equation $\frac{t}{14} = 8{,}654$ to find the total two-week attendance.

30. A detective divided her earnings for an 8-week case by 8 to find that her average weekly salary had been $4,535. Solve the equation $\frac{a}{8} = 4{,}535$ to find the total amount she earned.

31. If the monthly sales dollars made by a salesman were multiplied by 9, he would reach his yearly sales goal of $508,275. Solve the equation $9s = 508{,}275$ to find the amount of his monthly sales.

32. A scientist knew that the time a satellite had traveled, 3,699 seconds, times its speed in miles per second would equal the 25,893 miles it had traveled. Solve the equation $3{,}699s = 25{,}893$ to find the speed of the satellite.

33. For all whole numbers a, b, and c, if $\frac{a}{b} = c$, then $a = c \cdot b$. Use this relationship to rewrite each equation with the variable by itself on one side. Then solve for the variable. **a.** $\frac{x}{28} = 42$ **b.** $\frac{n}{24} = 53$ **c.** $\frac{z}{125} = 17$

C Extending Thinking Skills

34. Find numbers for x and y that make both $x \cdot y = 144$ and $x \div y = 4$ true.

35. The product of the ages of a teenager and her grandmother was 1024. The sum of their ages was 80. What was the quotient of their ages?

Mixed Review

Evaluate each expression. **36.** $(9 - 6) \cdot 3$ **37.** $21 \div 7 - 6 \div 3$ **38.** $(6 \cdot 2) - 9$

Solve and check. **39.** $x + 71 = 90$ **40.** $27 = x - 14$ **41.** $x + 26 = 53$

ESTIMATION

Since the addends in the sum 598 + 613 + 587 cluster around 600 you can use **clustering** to estimate this sum as 3 × 600, or 1800. Use clustering to estimate the following sums.

1. 275 + 314 + 326 **2.** 923 + 879 + 894

3. 1232 + 1187 + 1199 **4.** 708 + 674 + 719 + 697

5. 196 + 226 + 175 + 213 **6.** 2417 + 2373 + 2386 + 2394

2-6 Solving Equations: Using Multiplication and Division

Although some simple equations can be solved mentally, other methods are useful with equations that have larger numbers or more operations. Two ideas are used to solve equations involving multiplication and division. The first is that multiplication and division are inverse operations, and each can be used to undo the other.

Division can undo multiplication.	Multiplication can undo division.
$\frac{4 \cdot 8}{4} = 8$	$\frac{8}{4} \cdot 4 = 8$
$\frac{4 \cdot n}{4} = n$	$\frac{n}{4} \cdot 4 = n$

The second idea is that an equation is like a balanced scale. Whatever is done to one side must also be done to the other side. The properties of equality state this idea.

Multiplication and Division Properties of Equality

You can multiply or divide by the same number on both sides of the equation and the two sides will remain equal.
For all numbers **a, b, and c,** if **$a = b$, then $ac = bc$**

and, when **$c \neq 0$,** if **$a = b$,** then $\frac{a}{c} = \frac{b}{c}$

To solve an equation, you need to change it into an equation with the variable by itself on one side. The following steps use the idea of inverse operations and the properties of equality to help you do this.

Solving Equations Using Multiplication and Division

1. Decide which operation has been applied to the variable.
2. Use the inverse of this operation, multiplying or dividing by the same number on both sides of the equation.

Example 1

Solve and check. $4n = 72$

Solution $4n = 72$

$\frac{4n}{4} = \frac{72}{4}$ To undo multiplying by 4, divide by 4.

$n = 18$ Divide both sides by 4 so they remain equal.

Check $4 \cdot 18 \stackrel{?}{=} 72$ Replace n with 18 in $4n = 72$.

$72 = 72\ \checkmark$ The solution is 18.

Practice Solve and check. **a.** $6x = 78$ **b.** $192 = 8n$

Example 2

Solve and check. $\frac{n}{4} = 26$

Solution $\frac{n}{4} = 26$

$\frac{n}{4} \cdot 4 = 26 \cdot 4$ To undo dividing by 4, multiply by 4.

$n = 104$ Multiply both sides by 4 so they remain equal.

Check $\frac{104}{4} \stackrel{?}{=} 26$ Replace n with 104 in $\frac{n}{4} = 26$.

$26 = 26\ \checkmark$ The solution is 104.

Practice Solve and check. **a.** $\frac{n}{6} = 12$ **b.** $4 = \frac{x}{8}$

Oral Exercises

Name the operation that would be used to solve the equation.

1. $27c = 513$ **2.** $17r = 765$ **3.** $504 = 56x$

4. $\frac{b}{36} = 24$ **5.** $125 = z \div 94$ **6.** $35 = \frac{y}{16}$

Exercises

A Solve and check.

1. $6y = 48$ **2.** $2c = 98$ **3.** $9n = 99$ **4.** $4c = 68$

5. $5x = 115$ **6.** $9c = 234$ **7.** $12a = 144$ **8.** $21x = 168$

9. $32b = 192$ **10.** $43n = 172$ **11.** $54y = 162$ **12.** $72n = 432$

13. $\frac{n}{24} = 8$ **14.** $\frac{x}{32} = 9$ **15.** $\frac{c}{41} = 5$ **16.** $\frac{b}{26} = 5$

17. $\frac{y}{16} = 12$ **18.** $\frac{a}{23} = 11$ **19.** $\frac{x}{32} = 16$ **20.** $\frac{n}{44} = 15$

21. $\frac{a}{36} = 54$ 22. $\frac{b}{75} = 28$ 23. $\frac{c}{38} = 69$ 24. $\frac{y}{54} = 183$

25. $432 = 36b$ 26. $38 = \frac{y}{78}$ 27. $527 = 31n$ 28. $23 = \frac{c}{35}$

29. $16n = 5216$ 30. $1924 = 52y$ 31. $\frac{y}{361} = 27$ 32. $94 = \frac{x}{57}$

B Solve and check.

33. $(32 + 45)n = 231$ 34. $(54 - 9) = 15y$ 35. $\frac{a}{27(3)} = 24 + 36$

36. $\frac{x}{3 \cdot 18} = 4$ 37. $(126 \div 9) = \frac{z}{5}$ 38. $266 = (46 - 8)p$

39. Write and solve an equation in which the product is 612, one factor is 3, and the other factor is represented by the variable n.

40. Write and solve an equation in which m is divided by 9 and the quotient is 5.

C Extending Thinking Skills

41. Use inverse operations to find the missing number n in this flow chart.

Start with n	→	subtract 1492	→	multiply by 6	→	add 282	→	end with 1986

42. If a number is multiplied by 3 and added to 9, the result is 54. What is the number?

Mixed Review

Write as an expression. 43. 13 added to the product of 6 and 9

Solve and check. 44. $n - 36 = 17$ 45. $41 + x = 63$ 46. $9 = x - 334$

COMPUTER ACTIVITY

This computer program can be used to solve equations of the form $\frac{x}{A} = B$.

```
10 REM: SOLVE AN EQUATION X/A=B
20 PRINT "CHOOSE WHOLE NUMBERS A AND B, A<>0"
30 INPUT A,B
40 PRINT "THE EQUATION IS X/"A;"=";B
50 PRINT "THE SOLUTION IS X=";A*B
60 END
```

1. Run the program or show what the run would look like.
2. Change the program to solve equations of the form $Ax = B$.

More Practice

Solve.

1. $x - 37 = 110$
2. $r - 83 = 26$
3. $m + 74 = 231$
4. $t - 462 = 19$
5. $w - 396 = 47$
6. $215 = r + 86$
7. $k - 59 = 317$
8. $x + 34 = 416$
9. $t + 21 = 387$
10. $a + 68 = 156$
11. $z - 87 = 216$
12. $y + 87 = 206$
13. $a + 67 = 914$
14. $m - 53 = 422$
15. $c + 23 = 111$
16. $n - 45 = 74$
17. $\frac{a}{7} = 56$
18. $16w = 288$
19. $9c = 207$
20. $12h = 312$
21. $\frac{m}{8} = 24$
22. $276 = 23k$
23. $\frac{r}{12} = 406$
24. $\frac{z}{7} = 116$
25. $n \cdot 11 = 561$
26. $\frac{y}{27} = 13$
27. $242 = \frac{t}{8}$
28. $19w = 475$
29. $\frac{x}{27} = 15$
30. $\frac{t}{9} = 63$
31. $27m = 216$
32. $104 = \frac{a}{12}$
33. $16 = \frac{n}{21}$
34. $t + 38 = 415$
35. $a - 35 = 180$
36. $12 \cdot c = 384$
37. $z + 19 = 111$
38. $26x = 910$
39. $\frac{r}{64} = 11$
40. $y - 908 = 21$
41. $w + 87 = 126$
42. $13 = \frac{h}{19}$
43. $43k = 731$
44. $m - 88 = 316$
45. $\frac{t}{30} = 26$
46. $c - 86 = 104$
47. $n + 77 = 254$
48. $36a = 936$
49. $191 = x - 29$
50. $z + 92 = 647$
51. $930 = 15 \cdot y$
52. $\frac{w}{42} = 15$
53. $21 \cdot t = 693$
54. $387 = a - 26$
55. $r + 49 = 513$
56. $\frac{k}{8} = 404$
57. $760 = 8m$
58. $\frac{n}{5} = 160$
59. $t - 57 = 487$
60. $x + 81 = 360$
61. $z - 109 = 26$
62. $1395 = 31 \cdot h$
63. $\frac{w}{9} = 18$
64. $r + 75 = 463$
65. $\frac{y}{16} = 25$
66. $v + 67 = 104$
67. $486 = 18n$
68. $476 = c - 738$

PROBLEM SOLVING: APPLICATIONS

2-7 Keeping Physically Fit

A calorie is a heat unit that can measure the food energy taken in and used by the body. Average calorie amounts used by activities are shown in the table at right. Calorie needs are shown below.

To keep your weight the same take in 15 calories per pound of your weight, per day.

To gain a pound take in 3500 extra calories.

To lose a pound use 3500 extra calories.

Calorie Use	
Activity	**Calories per minute**
Running	14
Bicycling	11
Swimming	9
Tennis	7
Bowling	5

Problems

Use the information given above to solve. Decide whether to use **pencil and paper, mental math, estimation,** or a **calculator** to find the answer. Use each of these techniques at least once.

1. How many calories would you use by swimming for 30 minutes?

2. Would you use more than or less than than 460 calories by bicycling for 45 minutes?

3. How many calories would you use by running for 1 hour and 5 minutes?

4. How many minutes would you have to run to use 350 calories?

5. How many more calories would you use by running than by playing tennis for 55 minutes?

6. How many calories are needed daily to keep the weight of a 137-pound adult the same?

7. An athlete weighs 129 pounds. Will she gain or lose weight if she eats 15 calories per pound of weight and uses a total of 2000 calories each day?

8. During one month, Enrique took in 31,576 fewer calories than he needed to keep his weight the same. How many pounds (to the nearest pound) did he lose?

9. ***Data Search*** How many calories do you need each day to maintain your weight?

What's Your Decision?

Suppose you want to lose 10 pounds by either running or swimming. How will you do it and how long will it take?

2-8 Evaluating Formulas

A **formula** is an equation that shows a relationship between two or more variables. The formula $\boldsymbol{W = 5H - 190}$ expresses the relationship between a person's height in inches ($\boldsymbol{H}$) and a predicted weight in pounds ($\boldsymbol{W}$).

Example 1

Evaluate the formula $W = 5H - 190$ for $H = 60$.

Solution $W = 5H - 190$

$W = 5(60) - 190$ Replace the variable H with 60.

$W = 110$ Evaluate the resulting numerical expression.

Practice Evaluate the formula above for the heights given.

a. $H = 65$ **b.** $H = 68$

Example 2

Evaluate the following formula to find Dave's arm strength rating. He weighs 110 lbs., is 63 inches tall, and did 12 dips and 10 pullups. Formula: $A = S\left(\frac{W}{10} + H - 60\right)$. A is arm strength, S is sum of dips and pullups a person can do, W is weight in pounds, and H is height in inches.

Solution

$$A = S\left(\frac{W}{10} + H - 60\right)$$

$$A = 22\left(\frac{110}{10} + 63 - 60\right)$$ Replace the variable S with 22, W with 110, and H with 63. Evaluate.

$$A = 22(11 + 3)$$

$$A = 22(14) = 308$$

Jeff's arm strength rating is 308.

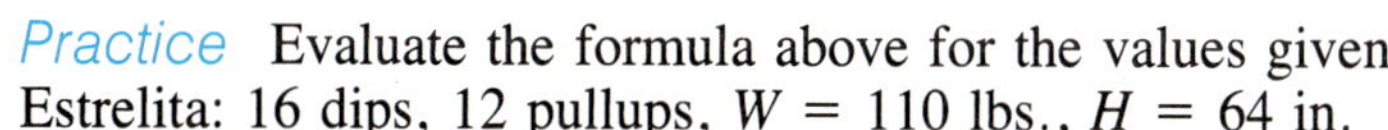

Practice Evaluate the formula above for the values given.
Estrelita: 16 dips, 12 pullups, $W = 110$ lbs., $H = 64$ in.

Oral Exercises

Evaluate mentally. **1.** $95 - ab$ for $a = 9$, $b = 7$ **2.** $r + 23$ for $r = 45$

3. $A + B$ for $A = 199$, $B = 78$

4. $\frac{q}{7}$ for $q = 154$

5. $x - y$ for $x = 200$, $y = 99$

6. $5x$ for $x = 15$

Exercises

A Evaluate the formula for the values given.

1. $W = 5H - 190$ for $H = 66$
2. $S = 16t + 64$, for $t = 12$
3. $P = S - 38$ for $S = 124$
4. $D = 16r - 57$ for $r = 6$
5. $P = 2L + 76$ for $L = 98$
6. $A = 3rr$ for $r = 9$

7. Formula: $D = r \cdot t$ where D is distance in miles, r is rate in mi/hour, and t is time of ride in hours. Find how far Jenny rode her bicycle in 3 hours at 17 mi/hour.

8. Formula: $W = r \cdot t + e$ where W is total wages, r is hourly rate of pay, t is time worked in hours, and e is overtime pay. Find how much Brian earned working 37 hours at \$6 an hour, and earning \$58 in overtime pay.

9. Formula: $S = p - d$. Find the sale price of a television when the regular price (p) is \$325 and the discount (d) is \$48.

B Copy and complete the table for each formula.

Formula: $T = t - \frac{a}{300}$

Temperature in degrees Celsius (T) at an altitude in meters (a) when the ground temperature in degrees Celsius is (t).

	10.	11.	12.	13.	14.
a	900	1200	2,400	4,800	6,000
t	20	20	20	20	20
T					

15. Formula: $W = 5000d(d + 1)$ where W is weight in thousands of pounds that a rope with diameter (d) in inches will hold without breaking. Make a table showing values of W for $d = 1, 2, 3, 4$, and 5.

C Extending Thinking Skills

16. Test the formula $S = 3F - 24$ where S = shoe size and F = length of foot in inches. Make a table to show your data. Is the formula accurate?

17. The formula for finding the total points scored in a basketball game is $P = 2g + f$, in which P is the total points scored, f is the number of free throws and g is the number of field goals. Write a formula for finding the number of field goals when the total points scored and the number of free throws are known.

Mixed Review

Solve and check. **18.** $m \div 19 = 11$ **19.** $23t = 437$

Write as an algebraic expression. **20.** The sum of 37 and a number

2-9 Estimating

An airline pilot or navigator might estimate the time for a trip, the speed of the plane, or the total number of miles flown.

You have used rounding to estimate sums and differences. You can also use rounding to estimate products and quotients.

Example 1

Estimate the value of the variable by rounding. $807 \cdot 19 = y$

Solution $807 \cdot 19$ Round 807 to 800. Round 19 to 20.

$800 \cdot 20 = 16{,}000$

The estimated value for y is 16,000.

Practice Estimate the value of the variable by rounding.

a. $876 \cdot 79 = n$ **b.** $x = 2{,}449 \div 79$

When rounding to estimate a quotient does not result in an easy division, you can **choose a compatible number** that makes the division easier.

Example 2

Estimate the value of the variable by choosing a compatible number.
$1{,}419 \div 28 = c$

Solution $1{,}400 \div 30$ Round the numbers.

$1{,}500 \div 30 = 50$ Choose a number compatible with 30.

The estimated value for c is 50.

Practice Estimate. **a.** $738 \div 9 = t$ **b.** $m = 1{,}694 \div 37$

Oral Exercises

Choose a number compatible with the divisor and estimate the quotient.

1. $1{,}100 \div 60$ **2.** $2{,}300 \div 40$ **3.** $1{,}300 \div 60$ **4.** $4{,}600 \div 90$

5. $5{,}700 \div 80$ **6.** $6{,}400 \div 70$ **7.** $19{,}000 \div 40$ **8.** $170{,}000 \div 60$

Exercises

A Estimate the value of the variable by rounding.

1. $28 \cdot 82 = x$ **2.** $93 \cdot 57 = y$ **3.** $n = 78 \cdot 19$

4. $p = 45 \cdot 39$ **5.** $786 \cdot 43 = a$ **6.** $318 \cdot 18 = t$

7. $b = 54 \cdot 995$ **8.** $n = 513 \cdot 289$ **9.** $89 \div 29 = c$

10. $243 \div 57 = z$ **11.** $r = 348 \div 73$ **12.** $s = 724 \div 89$

13. $1{,}599 \div 43 = p$ **14.** $a = 2{,}779 \div 68$ **15.** $5{,}589 \div 69 = t$

16. $z = 8{,}068 \div 85$ **17.** $792 \cdot 564 = n$ **18.** $3{,}984 \div 832 = n$

Estimate the value of the variable by choosing a compatible number.

19. $342 \div 7 = s$ **20.** $532 \div 6 = t$ **21.** $n = 653 \div 8$

22. $c = 437 \div 5$ **23.** $294 \div 58 = y$ **24.** $d = 372 \div 55$

25. $553 \div 79 = b$ **26.** $2{,}438 \div 53 = c$ **27.** $2{,}652 \div 68 = d$

B Estimate, then compute the value of the variable in Exercises 28–30.

28. $p = 58 \cdot 94 \cdot 75$ **29.** $z = (1848 \div 56) \cdot 98$ **30.** $x = (684 \cdot 423) \div 12$

31. A store sold 96 regular tires at an average price of \$56 a tire and 28 snow tires at an average price of \$79 per tire. Estimate the total sales.

32. The total weekly salary for 12 supervisors was \$6,696. Their total weekly overtime pay was \$492. Estimate a supervisor's average weekly earnings.

33. Estimate, then find, the number of flight hours logged by a pilot who made six 895-mile trips at an average speed of 618 mi/hour.

C Extending Thinking Skills

34. Copy the division problem at right and fill in the missing digits.

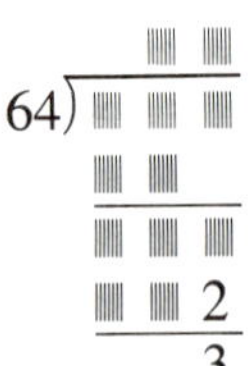

35. Mrs. Ward rounded her monthly salary to the nearest hundred and arrived at an estimate of \$40,800 for her yearly salary. Describe her actual monthly salary as accurately as possible.

Mixed Review

Solve and check. **36.** $169 = \frac{b}{13}$ **37.** $61 = x - 24$ **38.** $19a = 304$

Evaluate the formula $M = 6w + 12$ for: **39.** $w = 9$ **40.** $w = 3$

2-10 Draw a Picture

The problem-solving strategy called **Draw a Picture** can often help you better understand a problem situation and give you a start toward a solution.

Problem The head of a tropical fish is $\frac{1}{3}$ as long as its midsection. Its tail is as long as its head and midsection combined. The total length of the fish is 48 cm. How long is each part of the fish?

It is helpful to draw and label a picture to show the conditions of the problem.

The picture shows that 8 equal segments make up the 48 cm. Each segment must be 6 cm long, so the head is 6 cm long, the midsection is 18 cm long, and the tail is 24 cm long.

Problem-Solving Strategies

Choose the Operations

Guess, Check, Revise

Draw a Picture

This chart shows the strategies introduced so far.

Problems

Solve.

1. The tail of a salamander is three times as long as its midsection. Its head is $\frac{1}{2}$ as long as its midsection. If the total length of the salamander is 27 cm, how long is its tail?

2. Joliet is 564 km from Canton. A bus started at Canton and drove 248 km towards Joliet. A jeep started at Joliet and drive 216 km towards Canton. How far apart were the two vehicles at the end of these trips?

3. Alfredo correctly answered 22 questions on a test for a score of 84. There were 15 questions worth 3 points and 11 questions worth 5 points. How many questions of each type did he answer correctly?

4. A special rubber ball is dropped from the top of a wall 16 feet high. Each time it hits the ground it bounces half as high as its previous high point. If the ball is caught just as it bounces 1 foot high, how far has it traveled?

5. Kiyoko scored her test by multiplying the number of problems correct by 3 and subtracting 1 for each of the 16 problems she missed. She answered twice as many problems correctly as the number she missed. What was the total number of problems on the test? What was her score?

6. Sam's class took twice as long as Mark's class to build a homecoming float. Mark's class took 8 hours longer than Randy's class. The total number of hours spent by all classes was 60. How long did it take each class to build its float?

7. Mr. Ashby sold 37 small carved wooden whistles for $5 each, and his last 5 large whistles for $25 each. How many more small whistles will he have to sell to reach a sales total of $500?

8. An explorer astronaut completed a 152-km trip around a crater on the moon in 4 hours of traveling time in a moon buggy. She plans to make a 114-km trip at the same speed around another crater and stop for 1 hour along the way to explore on foot. How long will this take?

9. A construction engineer wants to make a tunnel through a rock that is 10 meters thick. Each hour the drilling tool goes in 5m, but as the engineer rests the rock caves in and the drilling tool slides back 4m. At this rate, how many hours will it take the engineer to break through the rock?

Enrichment

Functions

A **function** can be thought of as a rule that pairs each member of one set, called the **domain**, with one and only one member of another set, called the **range**.

The "Function Machine" below illustrates the idea, using numbers as elements. The set of "input" numbers is the domain. The set of "output" numbers is the range.

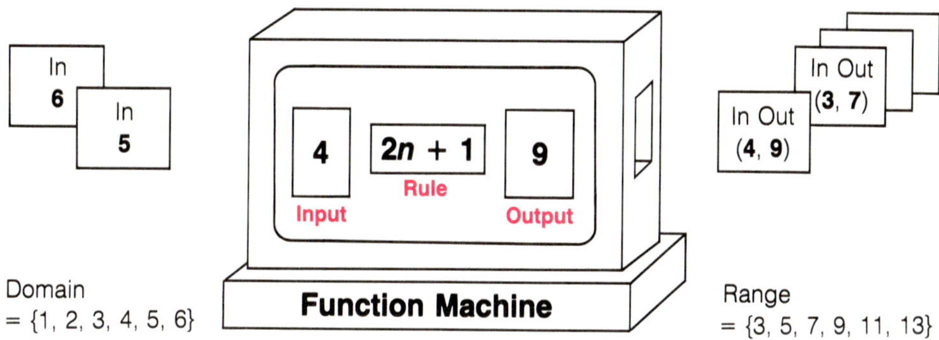

In the rule $f(n) = 2n + 1$, the function is named by the letter f and the input number is represented by the variable n. The output number is represented by either $f(n)$ or $2n + 1$. Using this rule for the input number 4, the output number, $f(n)$, would be found as follows: $f(4) = 2(4) + 1$.

You may use a table to describe the function:

Rule $f(n) = 2n + 1$

Input	1	2	3	4	5	6
Output	3	5	7	9	11	13

Or you may list the pairs as
$f = \{(1, 3), (2, 5), (3, 7), (4, 9), (5, 11), (6, 13)\}$.

1. Domain: {1, 2, 3, 4, 5}, Function rule: $f(n) = 3n + 4$. List the set of pairs for the function f.

2. Function Rule: $g(x) = \frac{x}{2} + 1$. Find $g(24)$, $g(100)$, $g(498)$, and $g(2)$.

3. Function Rule: $h(t) = t \cdot t \cdot t$. Find $h(2)$, $h(4)$, $h(5)$, and $h(10)$.

4. Function Rule: $f(n) = 5n - 3$. Find the value for n if $f(n) = 17$.

5. Domain: {1, 2, 3, 4, 5, 6, 7, 8}, Rule: $f(b) = (b + 3)(b + 3)$. Use a table to show the function.

6. Function: {(2, 2), (4, 3), (6, 4), (8, 5), (10, 6)}. Give the domain, range, and function rule.

Chapter 2 Review

2-1 Simplify.

1. $64 \div (4 + 4)$
2. $6 + [(2 + 1) \div 3]$
3. $2 \cdot 6 + 2 \cdot 5$

Evaluate.

4. $\frac{3x}{y}$ for $x = 8$
5. $z(c + 4)$ for $z = 6$
6. $6(x - y)$ for $x = 7, y = 5$

2-2 Write as an algebraic expression.

7. twice x
8. m divided by 4
9. b multiplied by 5

2-3 Use the commutative property to write an equivalent expression.

10. $f(4)$
11. ab
12. $14x$

Use the associative property to write an equivalent expression.

13. $12(3p)$
14. $(7t)k$
15. $(v \cdot 3)6$

Use the distributive property to write an equivalent expression.

16. $4(h + 6)$
17. $w(7 + 1)$
18. $(9 + n)5$

2-4 Use the basic properties to simplify.

19. $3 + (17 + r)$
20. $9(3m)$
21. $12(2x)$
22. $y + 8y$
23. $4a + 7a$
24. $18p + 12p$

2-5 Solve.

25. $6n = 36$
26. $\frac{40}{x} = 8$
27. $\frac{y}{7} = 5$

2-6 Solve and check.

28. $5x = 75$
29. $255 = 5v$
30. $\frac{c}{8} = 15$
31. $\frac{d}{8} = 23$

2-7 Solve.

32. If Andy uses 9 calories per minute while swimming, how many calories will he use if he swims for 30 minutes?

2-8 Solve.

33. Formula: $D = rt$. D is distance in miles, r is rate in miles per hour, and t is time in hours. How far did Brad drive in 6 hours at an average speed of 50 miles per hour?

2-9 Use rounding to estimate the value of the variable. Choose compatible numbers as needed.

34. $415 \cdot 42 = t$
35. $6129 \div 28 = p$
36. $1466 \div 32 = r$

Chapter 2 Test

Simplify.

1. $72 \div (6 + 2)$
2. $9 + [(3 + 7) \div 2]$
3. $3 \cdot 8 + 7 \cdot 4$

Evaluate.

4. $9y$ for $y = 5$
5. $\frac{2c}{d}$ for $c = 8$
6. $v(6 + m)$ for $v = 6$
7. $\frac{6m}{4}$ for $m = 8$
8. $5(16 - x)$ for $x = 8$
9. $3(a - b)$ for $a = 8, b = 6$

Write as an algebraic expression.

10. twice f
11. 6 divided by r
12. 13 less than twice a number

Use the commutative property to write an equivalent expression.

13. $7w$
14. $c(8)$
15. np

Use the associative property to write an equivalent expression.

16. $(2x)y$
17. $15(2v)$
18. $(b \cdot 4)9$

Use the distributive property to write an equivalent expression.

19. $r(2 + 5)$
20. $7(e + 7)$
21. $(4 + a)8$

Use the basic properties to simplify.

22. $7(8p)$
23. $5(6k)$
24. $21(11s)$
25. $w + 6w$
26. $2z + 3z$
27. $15n + 20n$

Solve.

28. $8n = 32$
29. $\frac{56}{y} = 8$
30. $\frac{a}{3} = 9$

Solve and check.

31. $6z = 78$
32. $220 = 11n$
33. $\frac{r}{7} = 12$
34. $\frac{b}{6} = 19$

Solve.

35. If you use 11 calories per minute bicycling, how many calories would you use on a 30-minute bicycle ride?

36. Formula: $A = lw$; A is the area of a rectangle in square centimeters, l is the length of the rectangle, and w is the width of the rectangle. What is the area of a rectangle with width 17 centimeters and length 19 centimeters?

Use rounding to estimate the value of the variable. Choose compatible numbers as needed.

37. $394 \cdot 28 = m$
38. $5776 \div 19 = c$
39. $8122 \div 23 = h$

Cumulative Review

Solve.

1. $35 - x = 18$ **2.** $b + 28 = 42$ **3.** $45 + c = 82$

4. $v - 21 = 50$ **5.** $48 = z - 27$ **6.** $39 = 13 + t$

Round to the nearest thousand and estimate the value for each variable.

7. $7{,}154 + 1{,}738 = a$ **8.** $n = 3{,}606 - 908$ **9.** $3{,}847 + 2{,}929 = b$

Round to the nearest hundred and estimate the value for each variable.

10. $f = 576 + 114$ **11.** $703 - 515 = x$ **12.** $2639 - 482 = g$

Use rounding to estimate the value of each variable.

13. $216 \cdot 82 = s$ **14.** $3844 \cdot 17 = c$ **15.** $8639 \div 27 = m$

Use front-end estimation to estimate the value of the variable.

16. $v = 221 + 592 + 485$ **17.** $4348 + 4369 + 2947 = p$

Simplify.

18. $49 \div (5 + 2)$ **19.** $7 + [(4 + 4) \div 4]$ **20.** $(2 \cdot 9) + (3 \cdot 4)$

Use the commutative property to write an equivalent expression.

21. $f + 4$ **22.** $17 + h$ **23.** $c + 981$

24. $6t$ **25.** $z(4)$ **26.** uk

Use the associative property to write an equivalent expression.

27. $(a + 44) + 235$ **28.** $101 + (555 + w)$ **29.** $m + (16b + 580)$

30. $(4e)g$ **31.** $22(2s)$ **32.** $(y \cdot 8)3$

Use the distributive property to write an equivalent expression.

33. $k(1 + 7)$ **34.** $2(e + 9)$ **35.** $(3 + p)6$

Use the associative property for multiplication to simplify.

36. $2 \cdot (7 \cdot n)$ **37.** $9(6y)$ **38.** $50(10j)$

Use the distributive property to simplify by combining like terms.

39. $v + 5v$ **40.** $8k + 2k$ **41.** $12h + 33h$

Chapter 3
Integers

3-1 Integers

Positive and negative numbers can be used to describe situations that are opposites of each other, such as profit and loss, temperatures above and below zero, or yards gained and lost.

The complete set of **integers** consists of the positive integers, the negative integers, and 0. On the number line, the **positive integers** are to the right of 0, and the **negative integers** are to the left of 0.

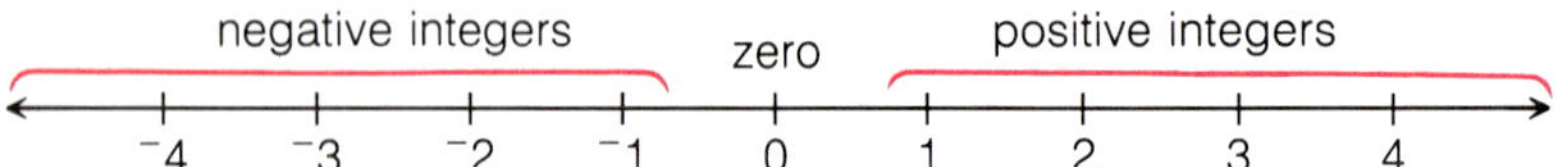

The integer **4** is read as "positive four," or "four." The integer **⁻4** is read as "negative four." Numbers such as 4 and ⁻4 that are the same distance from 0 on the number line but on opposite sides of it, are called **opposites**. The opposite of 0 is 0. We use a minus sign that is *not* raised to indicate "the opposite of."

The *opposite of 4* is written as -4

The *opposite of* ⁻*4* is written as $-(^{-}4)$.

Example 1

Give the integers for points *A* and *B* on this number line.

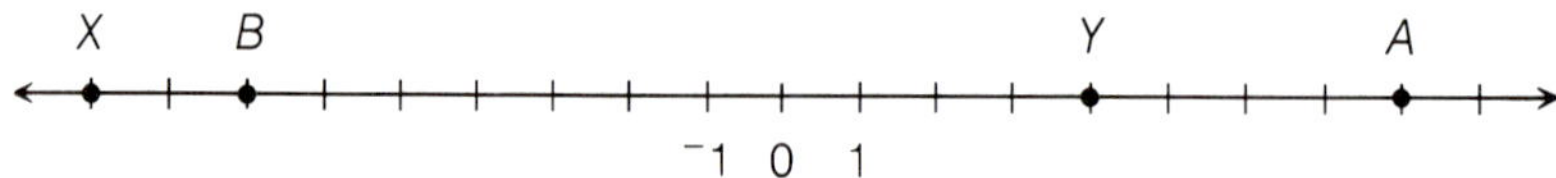

Solution *A*: 8 Point *A* is 8 units *to the right* of 0 on the number line.

B: ⁻7 Point *B* is 7 units *to the left* of 0 on the number line.

Practice Give the integers for points *X* and *Y* on the number line above.

The **absolute value** of an integer is the number of units the integer is from 0 on the number line.

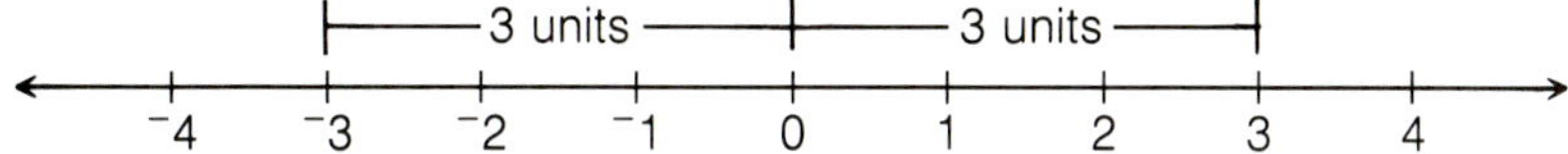

The absolute value of 3 is written $|3|$.
Since 3 is 3 units from 0, $|3| = 3$.
Since $^-3$ is 3 units from 0, $|^-3| = 3$.

Whether a number is positive or negative, its absolute value is always a positive number.

Example 2

Find the absolute value. $|^-7|$

Solution $|^-7| = 7$ $^-7$ is 7 units from 0 on the number line.

Practice

Find the absolute value. **a.** $|9|$ **b.** $|^-85|$

As with whole numbers, the integer farther to the right on the number line is the greater number. The symbols $>$ (greater than) and $<$ (less than) express inequalities.

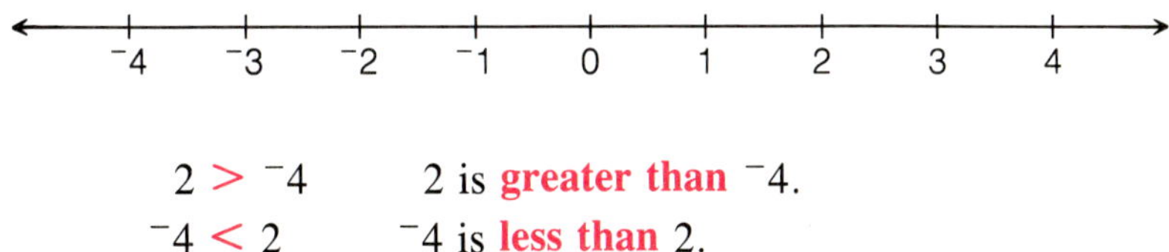

$2 > {}^-4$ 2 is **greater than** $^-4$.
$^-4 < 2$ $^-4$ is **less than** 2.

To order a set of integers, you need to compare each integer to the others in turn.

Example 3

Use the symbols $<$ or $>$ to order from least to greatest. $^-8$, 5, $^-2$

Solution $^-8 < {}^-2 < 5$ $^-8$ is farthest to the left on the number line, $^-2$ is next, and 5 is farthest to the right, so $^-8 < {}^-2$ and $^-2 < 5$.

Practice Use the symbols $<$ or $>$ to order from least to greatest.

a. 6, $^-8$, $^-16$

b. $|^-6|$, 9, 0, $^-3$

Oral Exercises

Give the integer suggested by the situation. Give the opposite of that integer.

1. A gain of \$9 **2.** 900 ft below sea level **3.** 4° below zero

4. Decrease by 7 kg **5.** 6 sec before blastoff **6.** Lose 4 points

7. Gain 7 yards **8.** 5 strokes under par **9.** Spent \$50

10. 6 flights up **11.** Put in 8 liters **12.** 4 floors down

Exercises

A

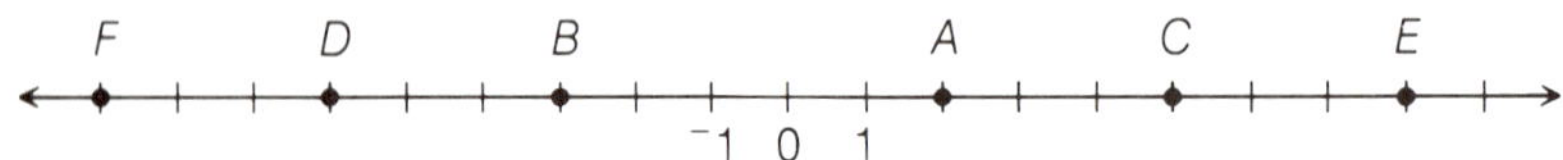

Give the integer for each point on the number line.

1. *A* **2.** *B* **3.** *C* **4.** *D* **5.** *E* **6.** *F*

Give the absolute value.

7. $|5|$ **8.** $|^{-}9|$ **9.** $|123|$ **10.** $|^{-}15|$ **11.** $|-36|$

12. $|0|$ **13.** $|199|$ **14.** $|^{-}152|$ **15.** $|^{-}1|$ **16.** $|1000|$

Use the symbols < or > to order from least to greatest.

17. 2, $^{-}21$ **18.** $^{-}7$, 0, 7 **19.** $^{-}1$, $^{-}6$, 4

20. $^{-}5$, $^{-}3$, 6 **21.** $^{-}1$, $^{-}6$, $^{-}9$, $^{-}2$ **22.** 6, $^{-}4$, $^{-}8$

23. $^{-}23$, 8, $^{-}24$ **24.** $^{-}2$, $|^{-}3|$, $^{-}1$, $|4|$ **25.** $^{-}13$, 12, $|^{-}18|$, 6, $^{-}4$

B For Exercises 26–29, give the integer for the point on the number line.

26. A point 27 units to the right of 0 **27.** A point 124 units to the left of 0

28. A point 20 units to the right of $^{-}2$ **29.** A point 16 units to the left of 4

30. What integer is the opposite of $|^{-}8|$? **31.** Give the integer represented by $-(^{-}8)$.

32. Find 2 values for x that make the equation $|x| = 5$ true.

Complete the following.

33. The opposite of a positive integer is a ______ integer.

34. The opposite of a negative integer is a ______ integer.

35. The integer __ is neither positive nor negative.

36. The absolute value of a nonzero integer is always a ______ integer.

37. The opposite of the opposite of a negative integer is a ______ integer.

C Extending Thinking Skills

Find the next 3 numbers in each pattern by thinking about the number line.

38. 16, 9, 2, __, __, __ **39.** $^-13$, 2, 17, __, __, __ **40.** $^-8$, $^-4$, 0, __, __, __

41. If you were to fold a piece of notebook paper in half twice and make a straight cut across the corner with only folded edges, what would the cut-off piece look like when unfolded?

Mixed Review

Solve and check. **42.** $\frac{x}{221} = 16$ **43.** $56 = m - 133$ **44.** $24w = 3144$

Estimate the value of the variable. **45.** $t = \frac{(83 \cdot 28)}{17}$

Simplify. **46.** $3n - n$ **47.** $11(9x)$ **48.** $26a + 7a$ **49.** $\frac{t}{t}$

Evaluate. **50.** $5 \cdot 4 - \frac{36}{9}$ **51.** $\frac{12 + 6}{10 - 7}$ **52.** $5 \cdot 1 \cdot 1$

Basic Property Update

The basic properties for whole number operations are also true for integer operations.

Identity Properties

For every integer **a**,

$a \cdot 1 = 1 \cdot a = a$ $a + 0 = 0 + a = a$

Commutative Properties

For all integers **a** and **b**,

$a + b = b + a$ $a \cdot b = b \cdot a$

Associative Properties

For all integers **a** and **b**,

$(a + b) + c = a + (b + c)$ $(a \cdot b) \cdot c = a \cdot (b \cdot c)$

Distributive Property

For all integers **a**, **b**, and **c**,

$a(b + c) = ab + ac$

Other properties of integers that follow from the basic properties are:

$a - 0 = a$ $a - a = 0$ $a \cdot 0 = a$

$0 \div a = 0$ $a \div 1 = a$ $a \div a = 1$

3-2 Adding Integers

You can use arrows on the number line to find integer sums. Adding a *positive integer* is shown by an arrow to the *right*. Adding a *negative integer* is shown by an arrow to the *left*. The number line below shows how to find the sum $^{-}4 + 6$.

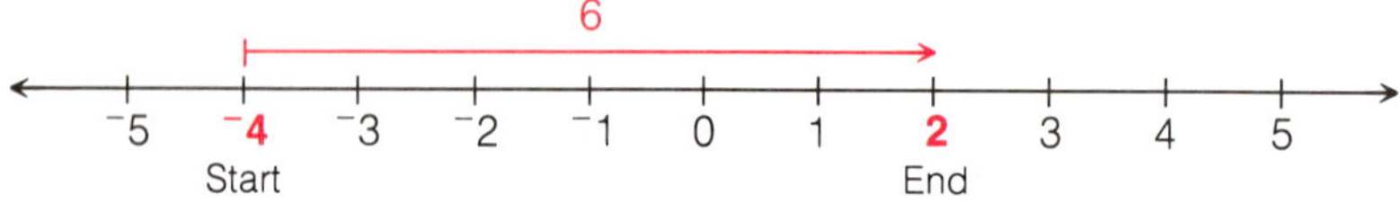

Start at the first number, $^{-}4$. To add positive 6, move to the right 6 units. The ending point, 2, is the sum. $^{-}4 + 6 = 2$.

On the number line, you can see that $4 + {}^{-}4 = 0$.

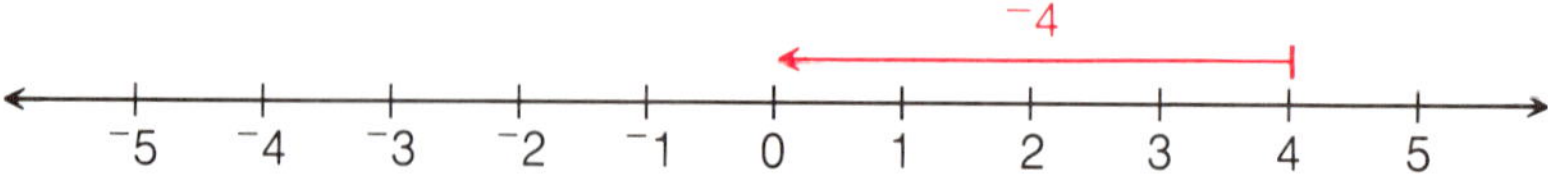

This suggests the following property for adding integers.

Inverse Property of Addition (Opposites Property)

The sum of any integer and its opposite is zero.

For every integer $\mathbf{a}$, $\mathbf{a + (-a) = 0}$ and $\mathbf{-a + a = 0}$

This property and addition on the number line lead to the following rule for finding the sum of any two integers.

Adding Integers

To add integers with like signs,

- Add their absolute values
- Give the sum the sign of the integer addends.

To add integers with unlike signs,

- Find the difference of their absolute values.
- Give the difference the sign of the integer addend with the greater absolute value. If the difference is zero, omit the sign.

Example 1

Find the sum. $^-2 + ^-3$

Solution $^-2 + ^-3 = ^-5$ $|^-2| + |^-3| = 5$. Since both original addends are negative, the sum is negative, $^-5$.

Practice Find the sum.

a. $^-14 + ^-16$ **b.** $35 + 29$ **c.** $^-34 + ^-26$

Example 2

Find the sum. $^-6 + 4$

Solution $^-6 + 4 = ^-2$ $|^-6| - |4| = 2$. Since $|^-6|$ is larger than $|4|$, the sum is negative, $^-2$.

Practice Find the sum.

a. $^-4 + 6$ **b.** $25 + ^-9$ **c.** $18 + ^-43$

Example 3

Evaluate. $n + 8$ for $n = ^-24$

Solution $n + 8$

$^-24 + 8$ Replace n with $^-24$.

$= ^-16$

Practice Evaluate.

a. $^-9 + x$ for $x = ^-11$ **b.** $a + b$ for $a = ^-24$ and $b = 36$

Oral Exercises

Tell whether the sum will be positive, negative, or zero.

1. $9 + 5$ **2.** $^-6 + ^-7$ **3.** $^-8 + ^-5$ **4.** $8 + 7$
5. $^-9 + ^-7$ **6.** $^-7 + 3$ **7.** $^-6 + 5$ **8.** $^-7 + 12$
9. $5 + ^-14$ **10.** $9 + ^-19$ **11.** $^-8 + 8$ **12.** $^-4 + 6$

Exercises

A Find each sum.

1. $^-5 + (^-7)$ **2.** $9 + 4$ **3.** $^-8 + (^-7)$ **4.** $^-7 + (^-6)$
5. $12 + (^-8)$ **6.** $16 + (^-9)$ **7.** $23 + (^-4)$ **8.** $13 + (^-6)$
9. $^-3 + 11$ **10.** $^-8 + 14$ **11.** $^-5 + 13$ **12.** $^-9 + 25$
13. $^-10 + 4$ **14.** $^-3 + (^-9)$ **15.** $^-6 + 7$ **16.** $26 + 8$
17. $3 + (^-12)$ **18.** $17 + (^-8)$ **19.** $^-24 + 0$ **20.** $^-26 + (^-23)$

Evaluate each expression.

21. $n + (^{-}5)$ for $n = {}^{-}7$

22. $^{-}13 + x$ for $x = 35$

23. $r + (^{-}45)$ for $r = 71$

24. $x + (^{-}24)$ for $x = 16$

B Find each sum.

25. $25 + |^{-}12 + {}^{-}15|$

26. $(43 + {}^{-}29) + (^{-}43 + 29)$

27. On the first down, Jerry's football team gained 6 yards. On the second down it lost 14 yards. On the third down it gained 16 yards. If it lost 13 yards on the fourth down, what was its total gain or loss?

28. The temperature was recorded at 15° Celsius. It then rose 8°, fell 6°, rose 12°, and fell 23°. What was the temperature after these changes?

C Extending Thinking Skills

29. Add mentally. $^{-}57 + 46 + 178 + (^{-}45) + 199 + 58 + (^{-}178)$

30. This proof uses basic properties to show that $^{-}5 + 8 = 3$.

$^{-}5 + 8$

$= {}^{-}5 + (5 + 3)$ Substitute 5 + 3 for 8.

$= (^{-}5 + 5) + 3$ Associative Property.

$= 0 + 3$ Additive Inverse Property.

$= 3$ Zero Property.

Write a proof for $9 + {}^{-}4 = 5$.

Mixed Review

Solve mentally and check. 31. $4m = 24$ 32. $\frac{c}{5} = 7$ 33. $n - 2 = 18$

Order from least to greatest. Use inequality symbols. 34. $^{-}6, 4, 0, 1, {}^{-}1$

NUMBERS TO ALGEBRA

In algebra, $-n$, which means "the opposite of n," is negative when n is replaced with a positive integer, but it is positive when n is replaced with a negative integer.

$-n$	Replace n with 5	$-n$	Replace n with $^{-}5$
-5		$-{}^{-}5$	
$^{-}5$	The result is a negative integer.	5	The result is a positive integer.

Complete each statement.

1. If $n = 8$, then $-n =$ __.

2. If $n = {}^{-}9$, then $-n =$ __.

3. If $n = {}^{-}24$, then $-n =$ __.

4. If $n = 45$, then $-n =$ __.

3-3 Subtracting Integers

These number lines show that subtracting an integer and adding the opposite of the integer produce the same result.

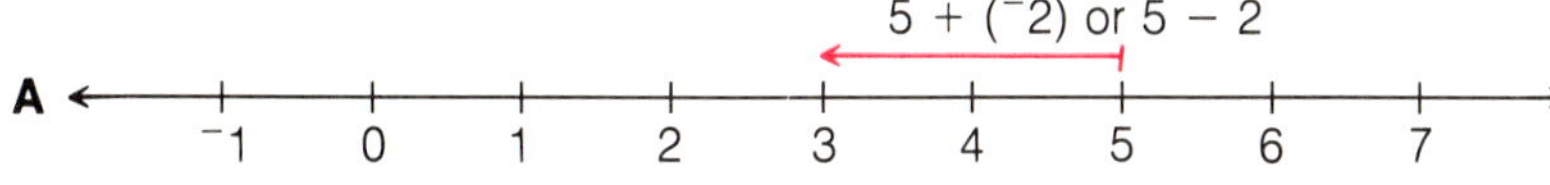

Adding ⁻2 is the same as subtracting 2.

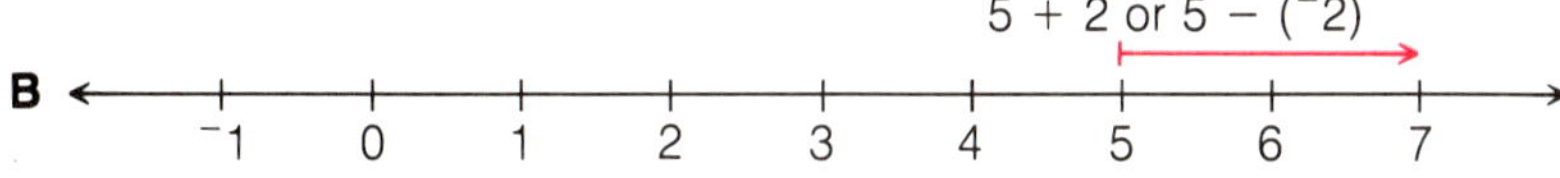

Adding 2 is the same as subtracting ⁻2.

This suggests the following rule.

Subtracting Integers

To subtract an integer, add its opposite.

For all integers **a** and ***b***, $a - b = a + (-b)$

You learned earlier in this chapter that -5 represents "the opposite of five" and that ⁻5 (with raised sign) represents the integer "negative five." Since -5 and ⁻5 name the same number, either can be used to represent that integer. Beginning with the following examples, a minus sign that is not raised will always be used to represent a negative integer.

Example 1

Subtract. $-5 - 8$

Solution $-5 - 8$

$= -5 + (-8)$ Subtracting 8 is the same as adding -8.

$= -13$

Practice Subtract. **a.** $2 - 7$ **b.** $-4 - 6$ **c.** $-8 - 3$ **d.** $15 - 9$

Example 2

Subtract. $7 - (-4)$

Solution $7 - (-4)$
$= 7 + 4$ Subtracting -4 is the same as adding 4.
$= 11$

Practice Subtract. **a.** $9 - (-3)$ **b.** $4 - (-10)$ **c.** $-9 - (-2)$

Example 3

Evaluate. $-8 - n$ for $n = -5$

Solution $-8 - (-5)$ Replace n with -5.
$= -8 + 5$
$= -3$

Practice Evaluate. **a.** $x - (-7)$ for $x = -13$ **b.** $-9 - b$ for $b = -15$

Oral Exercises

Give an addition expression that has the same answer as the subtraction expression.

1. $8 - 4$ **2.** $3 - 9$ **3.** $-2 - 7$ **4.** $-11 - 6$
5. $-8 - 8$ **6.** $-5 - 6$ **7.** $3 - 6$ **8.** $-4 - 7$

Exercises

A Subtract.

1. $9 - 3$ **2.** $8 - 12$ **3.** $4 - 10$ **4.** $9 - 13$
5. $1 - 7$ **6.** $-3 - 11$ **7.** $-6 - 8$ **8.** $-12 - 5$
9. $-8 - 14$ **10.** $-20 - 6$ **11.** $4 - (-9)$ **12.** $6 - (-15)$
13. $17 - (-8)$ **14.** $24 - (-10)$ **15.** $7 - (-7)$ **16.** $-3 - (-12)$
17. $-8 - (-16)$ **18.** $-14 - (-7)$ **19.** $-18 - (-12)$ **20.** $-50 - (-30)$
21. $7 - 15$ **22.** $-8 - 11$ **23.** $6 - (-8)$ **24.** $-9 - (-13)$
25. $45 - 94$ **26.** $-34 - (-58)$ **27.** $57 - (-24)$ **28.** $-75 - 48$

Evaluate.

29. $n - 9$ for $n = -6$ **30.** $-7 - n$ for $n = 14$ **31.** $12 + n$ for $n = -18$
32. $n + (-6)$ for $n = 11$ **33.** $n - (-11)$ for $n = 5$ **34.** $n - (-13)$ for $n = 9$
35. $-7 + n$ for n -6 **36.** $-16 - n$ for $n = -10$ **37.** $-10 + n$ for $n = 12$
38. $n - (-4)$ for $n = -12$, for $n = 16$, and for $n = -53$
39. $6 - r$ for $r = 23$, $r = -9$, and $r = -87$.

B Simplify.

40. $5 - (-6) - 20$

41. $-8 - (-2) - (-7)$

42. $-13 - (-7) + (-5)$

43. $(-5 - 3) + (-9) - (-15)$

44. $-6 + (-9 - 12)$

45. $7 - (-8 - 13) + (-5)$

46. Evaluate the formula P = I − E to find the Profit (P) when Income (I) = \$85,654 and Expenses (E) = \$92,472.

47. Replace a and b with integers to show that $a - b = b - a$ is not true for all integers.

48. Replace a, b, and c with integers to show that $(a - b) - c = a - (b - c)$ is not true for all integers.

49. Death Valley is 282 ft below sea level. Mt. Whitney is 14,494 ft above sea level. How much higher is the elevation of Mt. Whitney than the elevation of Death Valley?

50. One day the nation's high temperature was 75°F. The low temperature was −8°F. What is the difference between these temperatures?

C Extending Thinking Skills

51. In a magic square, the sum of the numbers in each row, column, and diagonal is the same. Find the missing numbers in this magic square, assuming the magic sum is −2.

4	−6		
−7		2	
	−3	−8	
		5	−5

52. An elevator went up 6 floors, down 9 floors, down 12 more floors, up 8 floors, and down 4 floors. It stopped on the 43rd floor. On what floor did it start?

Mixed Review

Solve and check. **53.** $8y = 216$ **54.** $t + 163 = 204$

Find the sum. **55.** $-5 + 3$ **56.** $5 + 3$ **57.** $5 + (-3)$

58. $-5 + (-3)$

CALCULATOR ACTIVITY

The change-sign key [+/−] allows you to show a negative integer by changing the displayed number to its opposite.

To add 86 + (−123): 86 [+] 123  [+/−] [=]

To subtract −67 − (−239): 67 [+/−] [−] 239 [+/−] [=]

Add or subtract, using the change-sign key.

1. $258 + (-689)$

2. $-9674 + 6739$

3. $-783 - (-975)$

4. $-7386 + 2978$

5. $4547 - (-8964)$

6. $-435 + 848$

More Practice

Find the sum.

1. 13 + 9 **2.** 28 + (−9) **3.** −76 + (−84) **4.** −37 + 19

5. 64 + (−9) **6.** 21 + 107 **7.** −6 + (−37) **8.** −26 + 13

9. 0 + (−11) **10.** 64 + 136 **11.** −57 + 84 **12.** 111 + 99

13. −6 + (−6) **14.** 6 + (−6) **15.** −36 + 271 **16.** −28 + (−57)

17. −14 + 7 **18.** −21 + (−108) **19.** 147 + 239 **20.** 65 + (−19)

Find the difference.

21. −5 − 3 **22.** 15 − 3 **23.** 21 − 38 **24.** −6 − (−31)

25. 19 − (−21) **26.** −49 − 51 **27.** −5 − (−3) **28.** 26 − 57

29. −12 − 4 **30.** 43 − 62 **31.** −9 − (−6) **32.** 25 − (−14)

33. 180 − 97 **34.** −34 − (−37) **35.** 74 − 105 **36.** −34 − 62

37. 62 − 87 **38.** 91 − (−45) **39.** −81 − 14 **40.** 504 − 367

Find the sum or difference.

41. 67 − 71 **42.** 46 + (−13) **43.** −19 + 27 **44.** −41 − 16

45. −41 + 16 **46.** 219 − 167 **47.** 50 + (−61) **48.** 29 − 40

49. −35 − (−17) **50.** −64 + 12 **51.** −24 − 12 **52.** −240 − (−13)

53. 42 − 384 **54.** −27 − (−16) **55.** −30 − (−42) **56.** 120 + (−49)

57. 27 + (−62) **58.** 51 − 17 **59.** 6 − 31 **60.** −32 + 19

61. 106 − 112 **62.** 102 + (−31) **63.** 19 − (−32) **64.** 19 + (−40)

65. −6 + 30 **66.** 28 − 35 **67.** −9 + (−11) **68.** 64 − (−16)

69. 37 − (−42) **70.** −54 + 17 **71.** −116 + 24 **72.** 46 − 59

73. −23 + (−66) **74.** 15 − 102 **75.** 83 − 117 **76.** −30 + (−47)

77. 27 − 16 **78.** −47 − 14 **79.** 92 + (−18) **80.** 143 + (−51)

81. −27 − 6 **82.** −16 + 39 **83.** 64 + (−128) **84.** 138 − (−12)

85. −30 + 19 **86.** 240 − 192 **87.** 457 + 393 **88.** 19 − 30

89. −26 − 17 **90.** −6 + 40 **91.** −319 − (−67) **92.** −126 + (−12)

93. 104 + (−35) **94.** 48 − (−52) **95.** −16 − 12 **96.** −41 + 93

3-4 Solving Integer Equations: Addition and Subtraction

To solve integer equations such as $t + 34 = 28$ or $x - 18 = -35$, you need to get the variable by itself on one side of the equation. The following steps show you how to use the ideas of inverse operations or the additive inverse property and the properties of equality to do this.

If the temperature increased 34°C to reach a high of 28°C, you could solve the equation $t + 34 = 28$ to find the original temperature.

Solving Equations Using Addition and Subtraction

1. Decide which operation (addition or subtraction) has been applied to the variable.

2. Use the inverse operation or use the additive inverse property, adding or subtracting the same number on both sides of the equation.

Examples 1 and 2 show how to use inverse operations and the same steps you used with whole number equations to solve integer equations. Example 3 shows how to use the additive inverse property to solve integer equations.

Example 1

Solve and check. $t + 34 = 28$

Solution $t + 34 = 28$ — You need to get the variable by itself on one side.

$t + 34 - 34 = 28 - 34$ — To undo adding 34, subtract 34 from both sides of the equation so they remain equal. (Subtraction property of equality.)

$t = -6$

Check $-6 + 34 \stackrel{?}{=} 28$ — Replace t with -6 in $t + 34 = 28$.

$28 = 28 \checkmark$ — The solution is -6.

Practice Solve and check.

a. $x + 19 = -47$ **b.** $-42 = y + 76$ **c.** $z + (-35) = (-164)$

Example 2

Solve and check. $x - 18 = -35$

Solution $x - 18 = -35$

$x - 18 + 18 = -35 + 18$

$x = -17$

To undo subtracting 18, add 18 to both sides so they remain equal. (Addition property of equality.)

Check $-17 - 18 \stackrel{?}{=} -35$

$-35 = -35$ √

Replace x with -17 in $x - 18 = -35$.

The solution is -17.

Practice Solve and check.

a. $b - (-15) = 43$ **b.** $n - 29 = -45$ **c.** $y - (-37) = -64$

Since subtracting an integer is the same as adding the opposite integer, an equation that can be solved by subtracting can also be solved by using the additive inverse property.

Example 3

Solve and check. $n + (-25) = 46$

Solution $n + (-25) = 46$

$n + (-25) + 25 = 46 + 25$

$n = 71$

To undo adding -25, use the additive inverse property and add the opposite of -25, or 25. $-25 + 25 = 0$.

Check $71 + (-25) \stackrel{?}{=} 46$

$46 = 46$ √

Replace n with 71 in $n + (-25) = 46$.

The solution is 71.

Practice Solve and check. **a.** $a + (-17) = -75$ **b.** $43 = p + (-26)$

Oral Exercises

To solve, what integer would you add to or subtract from each side?

1. $x + 19 = -48$ **2.** $n - 28 = -56$ **3.** $-379 = x + 85$ **4.** $78 = b - (-45)$

5. $c - 56 = -198$ **6.** $b + (-37) = 84$ **7.** $z + 53 = -53$ **8.** $0 = n - 67$

Exercises

A Solve and check.

1. $n + 27 = -84$ **2.** $x + 97 = 42$ **3.** $a + 157 = -96$

4. $y + 79 = -32$ **5.** $c + 76 = 154$ **6.** $n + 67 = -282$

7. $x + 279 = 194$ **8.** $b + 68 = -253$ **9.** $y + (-36) = 273$

10. $a + (-285) = -643$ **11.** $c + 947 = -765$ **12.** $x + (-258) = 1752$

13. $x - 47 = -63$
14. $y - 86 = 175$
15. $x - 86 = 59$
16. $y - 86 = -254$
17. $c - 47 = -195$
18. $n - 58 = -127$
19. $c - (-56) = 498$
20. $b - (-76) = 485$
21. $n - 226 = -46$
22. $y - (-75) = 60$
23. $x - 158 = 42$
24. $c - 63 = -441$
25. $-278 = n + (-69)$
26. $-263 = n - 45$
27. $-274 = a + 37$
28. $142 = y - (-349)$
29. $x + 367 = 294$
30. $-217 = y - 87$

B Solve and check.

31. $x + (-74 + 39) = 546$
32. $a - (-72 + 78) = 17$
33. $(-49 + 86) + y = -84$

34. Write and solve an equation with sum -75, one addend -16, and the other addend represented by the variable n.

35. Write and solve an equation in which 78 is subtracted from a number represented by the variable y to produce the difference -29.

C Extending Thinking Skills

36. When $n + n + n + n$ is evaluated, the result is 9 less than n. Find n.

37. If 5 cards are moved from stack A to stack B, both stacks will contain 12 cards. How many cards were in each stack to begin with?

Mixed Review

Add or subtract. 38. $7 - (-2)$ 39. $-9 - (-2)$ 40. $-4 + (-1)$

Write as an algebraic expression. 41. twice the sum of 7 and a number

MENTAL MATH

You can find the sum of any number of positive integers in order, starting with 1, by multiplying the last number by the number that follows it and dividing by 2. Check the equations below to see whether they are true. Fill in the blank to complete the generalization.

$$1 + 2 = 2(3) \div 2$$
$$1 + 2 + 3 = 3(4) \div 2$$
$$1 + 2 + 3 + 4 = 4(5) \div 2$$
$$1 + 2 + 3 + 4 + 5 = 5(6) \div 2$$
$$1 + 2 + 3 + 4 + 5 + \ldots + n = \underline{\quad ? \quad}$$

Find each sum mentally.

1. $1 + 2 + 3 + 4 + 5 + 6 + 7$
2. $1 + 2 + 3 + 4 + 5 + 6 + 7 + 8 + 9$
3. The positive integers from 1 through 20.
4. The positive integers from 1 through 99.

3-5 Keeping Checkbook Records

A **checking account** at a bank or savings and loan company allows a customer to write checks to pay bills or get needed cash. To keep money in the account, the customer makes deposits.

A deposit of money to an account is called a **credit** (+). A payment (check) or withdrawal is called a **debit** (−). The **balance** is the amount of money in the account at a given point. The balance changes after each withdrawal, payment, or deposit. If an account's debits are greater than its credits, the balance that remains is less than zero and the account has been **overdrawn**. The customer must keep an accurate record of all account **transactions**, or activities.

NUMBER	DATE	DESCRIPTION OF TRANSACTION	PAYMENT/ DEBIT (−)		√ T	(−)FEE (IF ANY)	DEPOSIT/ CREDIT (+)		BALANCE $125	00
126	2/9	Terry's Service Station	$ 79	00						
	2/9	Deposit from Salary					215	00		
127	2/11	Record Land	48	00						
128	2/14	Cancer Research Donation	125	00						
	2/15	Transfer from Savings					575	00		
129	2/15	Food Mart	56	00						
130	2/17	Snapit Camera Shop	279	00						

Problems

Solve problems 1–4, using the transaction record above. For problems 5–8, decide whether to use **pencil and paper, mental math, estimation,** or a **calculator** to find the answer. Use each of these techniques at least once.

1. The amount of money in the account before check number 126 is shown in the balance column. What is the balance after check number 126 is written?

2. What is the new balance following the deposit on 2/9?

3. What is the new balance following: check number 128? the deposit on 2/15?

4. What is the new balance following: check number 129? check number 130? Check your answers by writing credits as positive integers and debits as negative integers and finding their sum.

5. A customer wrote a check for $79, wrote a check for $156, made a deposit of $275, and wrote a check for $398. If the balance before these transactions was $517, what was the balance after the transactions?

6. Decide whether or not this checking account has been overdrawn: beginning balance: $1353; check for $798; check for $206; deposit of $449; check for $747.

7. A checking account with a beginning balance of $150 had debits of $1250 and credits of $900. By how much was it overdrawn?

8. A checking account had a beginning balance of $435. Deposits were made in the amount of $1196. Checks were written in the amount of $1952. Three of these checks were written when the account was overdrawn. The bank fee for overdrawn checks is $12 per check. How much must be deposited to pay the fee and bring the balance up to $400?

9. ***Data Search*** Find a record form for a checking account. Make up a beginning balance, then 3 checks and 2 deposits. Fill out the record form for the transactions and find the ending balance.

What's Your Decision?

At the National Bank you can choose between the two types of non-interest checking accounts shown below.

Regular Account		Zero Balance Account
Account Balance	**Fee for Writing Checks**	
Below $100	$6/month	Annual fee of $24, plus $0.20 for each check.
$100–$200	$5/month	
$200–$300	$4/month	
$300–$400	$3/month	
Over $400	No charge	

You want to open a checking account, and expect to write no more than 10 checks per month. You usually keep a little over $100 in your account. Would you choose a Regular Account or a Zero Balance Account? Why?

3-6 Multiplying Integers

You can use repeated addition to show that the product of a positive integer and a negative integer is a negative integer.

$$3(-4) = (-4) + (-4) + (-4) = -12$$

The following statement uses the fact that 3 is the opposite of -3 to suggest that the product of two negative integers is a positive integer:

Since $3(-4) = \mathbf{-12}$, then $-3(-4) = \mathbf{12}$

The equation pattern below, in which the product increases by 4 each time, also suggests that $-3(-4) = 12$.

$$\begin{aligned} 3(-4) &= -12 \\ 2(-4) &= -8 \\ 1(-4) &= -4 \\ 0(-4) &= 0 \\ -1(-4) &= 4 \\ -2(-4) &= 8 \\ -3(-4) &= 12 \end{aligned}$$

These ideas support a procedure for multiplying integers.

Multiplying Integers

Find the product of the absolute values. Then use the following rules for determining the sign.

- The product of two positive integers is positive.
- The product of two negative integers is positive.
- The product of a positive integer and a negative integer is negative.

Example 1

Find the product. $-6(-4)$

Solution $-6(-4) = 24$ The product of two negative integers is a positive integer.

Practice Find the product. **a.** $9(6)$ **b.** $-7(-8)$ **c.** $-9(-5)$

Example 2

Find the product. $-8(5)$

Solution $-8(5) = -40$ A positive times a negative integer is a negative integer.

Practice Find the product. **a.** $-5(4)$ **b.** $6(-8)$ **c.** $9(-4)$ **d.** $-7(3)$

Oral Exercises

Tell whether the product is positive or negative.

1. $6(3)$	**2.** $-7(4)$	**3.** $-6(-9)$	**4.** $5(-9)$
5. $-8(-3)$	**6.** $-2(-17)$	**7.** $-12(15)$	**8.** $24(-45)$
9. $-19(-78)$	**10.** $28(-14)$	**11.** $10(-6)$	**12.** $8(8)$

Exercises

A Find the product.

1. $9(7)$	**2.** $-5(-3)$	**3.** $-4(-8)$	**4.** $8(6)$
5. $-9(-4)$	**6.** $-6(-8)$	**7.** $-7(-2)$	**8.** $-3(-8)$
9. $7(8)$	**10.** $-6(-7)$	**11.** $9(-5)$	**12.** $-8(7)$
13. $-7(0)$	**14.** $-1(8)$	**15.** $-9(9)$	**16.** $6(-5)$
17. $-3(-6)$	**18.** $-7(7)$	**19.** $8(-6)$	**20.** $-8(-9)$
21. $-10(-46)$	**22.** $-12(35)$	**23.** $-24(-52)$	**24.** $54(-23)$
25. $-76(-98)$	**26.** $86(-45)$	**27.** $124(-36)$	**28.** $-246(-35)$

B

29. Find the product: $2(-3)(-4)(-5)$. Is the number of negative factors odd or even? Is the product positive or negative?

30. Find the product: $(-5)(-6)(-2)(-1)$. Is the number of negative factors odd or even? Is the product positive or negative?

31. Consider your answers to exercises 29 and 30, try other examples as needed, and complete the following:

a. The product of an odd number of negative factors is __?__ (positive, negative).

b. The product of an even number of negative factors is __?__ (positive, negative).

Find the product.

32. $-5(-4)(6)$	**33.** $7(-4)(6)$
34. $-36(-25)(-4)(-2)$	**35.** $-36(-25)(-4)(3)$
36. $4(-6)(-5)(-23)(-1)$	**37.** $7(-6)(-5)(-3)(-1)(-8)$

Evaluate each expression.

38. $-3n$ for $n = 47$

39. $15(z + 6)$ for $z = -23$

40. $-12pq$ for $p = 32$ and $q = -9$

41. $4a - 3b$ for $a = -5$, $b = 7$

42. Show that $2b + 3b$ has the same value as $5b$ when $b = 4$, $b = -8$, and $b = -34$. What property does this show?

43. Show that $-9(a + 25)$ has the same value as $-9a + (-9)(25)$ when $a = -9$, $a = 12$, and $a = -24$.

44. The formula $s = -0.4y + 1020$ has been used to predict the record time (s, in seconds) for the mile run in a chosen year (y). Evaluate the formula for $y = 1990$.

45. The air temperature decreases 7°C for each kilometer of increase in altitude. If the temperature was 0°C at a certain altitude, what would the temperature be outside an airplane flying 4 km above this altitude?

Use the change-sign key to find each product. Check your answer with an estimate.

Example: $-578(-637)$ 578  637  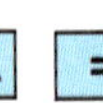

46. $-956(498)$

47. $-853(-32)(-46)$

48. $535(-726)(-43)$

C Extending Thinking Skills

49. Find the pattern for each sequence. Give the next 3 integers in the sequence.

a. 3, −6, 6, −12, 9, −18, __, __, __.

b. 6, 2, −2, −6, __, __, __.

50. Mindy tripled the temperature reading on a cold day and the result was 6 less than the original temperature. How could this be possible? What was the original temperature?

Mixed Review

Solve and check. 51. $r + 23 = -36$ 52. $m + 19 = 12$ 53. $25t = 1075$

Estimate the value of the variable. 54. $503 \div 9 = a$

MENTAL MATH

Because of the commutative and associative properties, you can choose any pair from among 3 factors $\boldsymbol{a}$, $\boldsymbol{b}$, and $\boldsymbol{c}$ to multiply first. That is, $(\boldsymbol{ab})\boldsymbol{c} = (\boldsymbol{bc})\boldsymbol{a} = (\boldsymbol{ac})\boldsymbol{b}$. Choosing **compatible numbers** makes it easier to find products mentally.

Choose compatible numbers to find each product mentally.

1. 4(687)(250)
2. 68(50)(20)
3. 20(579)(−5)
4. −674(385)(0)
5. 96(4)(25)
6. 250(127)(40)

3-7 Dividing Integers

The relationship between multiplication and division can be used to find the quotient of two integers.

factor	factor	product		product	factor	factor
$4 \cdot$	$6 =$	24	$\longrightarrow$	$24 \div$	$6 =$	4
$4 \cdot$	$(-6) =$	-24	$\longrightarrow$	$-24 \div$	$-6 =$	4
$-4 \cdot$	$6 =$	-24	$\longrightarrow$	$-24 \div$	$6 =$	-4
$-4 \cdot$	$(-6) =$	24	$\longrightarrow$	$24 \div$	$-6 =$	-4

The equations above suggest the following procedure.

Dividing Integers

To divide integers, find the quotient of their absolute values. Then use the following rule for determining the sign:

- The quotient of two positive integers is positive.
- The quotient of two negative integers is positive.
- The quotient of a positive and a negative integer is negative.

Example 1

Find the quotient. $-35 \div (-7)$

Solution $-35 \div (-7) = 5$ The quotient of two negative integers is positive. This checks, since $5(-7) = -35$.

Practice Find the quotient. **a.** $30 \div 6$ **b.** $-45 \div (-9)$ **c.** $\frac{-72}{-8}$

Example 2

Find the quotient. $-32 \div 4$

Solution $-32 \div 4 = -8$ The quotient of two integers with unlike signs is negative. This checks, since $-8(4) = -32$.

Practice Find the quotient. **a.** $-48 \div 8$ **b.** $\frac{20}{-4}$ **c.** $40 \div (-5)$

Oral Exercises

Check each quotient by multiplying. Is it correct?

1. $35 \div (-5) = -7$ **2.** $-18 \div 6 = 3$ **3.** $24 \div 8 = 3$

4. $-42 \div (-7) = 6$ **5.** $48 \div (-6) = -8$ **6.** $0 \div (-12) = 0$

Exercises

A Find the quotient.

1. $56 \div 8$ **2.** $-24 \div (-8)$ **3.** $-20 \div (-4)$ **4.** $81 \div 9$

5. $-36 \div 4$ **6.** $42 \div (-7)$ **7.** $-64 \div 8$ **8.** $72 \div (-9)$

9. $45 \div (-5)$ **10.** $36 \div 6$ **11.** $-48 \div (-8)$ **12.** $-90 \div 10$

13. $9 \div (-1)$ **14.** $0 \div (-12)$ **15.** $-66 \div (-11)$ **16.** $30 \div (-5)$

17. $-54 \div 3$ **18.** $-60 \div (-5)$ **19.** $52 \div (-4)$ **20.** $-51 \div (-3)$

21. $\frac{125}{-5}$ **22.** $\frac{-168}{7}$ **23.** $\frac{-96}{12}$ **24.** $\frac{-75}{-15}$

B Simplify.

25. $(-6)(4) \div (-8)$ **26.** $-40 \div (-8) - 9$ **27.** $-56 \div (2 - 10)$

28. $-18 \div (-3 + 9)$ **29.** $\frac{(-4)(-4)}{2}$ **30.** $\frac{-8 - 19}{-6 - 3}$

Evaluate.

31. $n \div (-8)$ for $n = 48$ **32.** $(-9 + a) \div (-6)$ for $a = 63$

33. Does $a \div (b + c)$ have the same value as $a \div b + a \div c$ when $a = -48$, $b = 12$, and $c = -4$?

34. When an integer is divided by 9, the quotient is -6. What is the integer?

35. The net change in the price of a stock over a three-month period was -27. What was the average change per month?

Find the quotient. Check by estimating.

36. $5,239,374 \div (-6958)$ **37.** $\frac{-1024(-75)}{-32}$ **38.** $\frac{-94 + 1886}{-108 + 164}$

C Extending Thinking Skills

39. Find integers a and b for which $a + b = 6$ and $a \div b = -4$.

40. Half an integer is five more than the integer. What is the integer?

41. The temperature rose at the rate of 3°F per hour to reach 0°F at noon. At what earlier time had the temperature been -21°F?

Mixed Review

Solve and check. **42.** $y - 63 = 14$ **43.** $w - (-4) = 61$ **44.** $24r = 384$

Simplify. **45.** $12(9c)$ **46.** $112w + 13w$ **47.** $(9 + t) + 4$

3-8 Solving Integer Equations: Multiplication and Division

To solve equations such as $7d = -91$ or $\frac{n}{-9} = 78$, you can use the same steps you used with whole number equations.

- Decide what operation (multiplication or division) has been applied to the variable.
- Use the inverse operation, multiplying or dividing both sides of the equation by the same number.

If quick-freezing for 7 minutes lowers the temperature 91°C, you can solve the equation $7d = -91$ to find the temperature change per minute.

Example 1

Solve and check. $-6n = 78$

Solution

$$-6n = 78$$

$$\frac{-6n}{-6} = \frac{78}{-6}$$ To undo multiplying by 6, divide by 6 on both sides.

$$n = -13$$

Check $-6(-13) \stackrel{?}{=} 78$ Replace n with -13 in $-6n = 78$.

$78 = 78 \checkmark$ The solution is -13.

Practice Solve and check. **a.** $-4x = 68$ **b.** $-182 = 7n$

Example 2

Solve and check. $\frac{n}{-4} = 17$

Solution $\frac{n}{-4} = 17$ To undo dividing by -4, multiply by -4 on both sides.

$$\frac{n}{-4}(-4) = 17(-4)$$

$$n = -68$$

Check $\frac{-68}{-4} \stackrel{?}{=} 17$ Replace n with -68 in $\frac{n}{-4} = 17$.

$17 = 17 \checkmark$ The solution is -68.

Practice Solve and check. **a.** $\frac{a}{6} = -72$ **b.** $25 = \frac{x}{-8}$

The following property of -1 is useful when solving equations such as $-n = 24$.

Property of −1

The product of −1 and a number is the opposite of the number.

For each number $\boldsymbol{n}$, $\quad \mathbf{-1n = -n} \quad$ and $\quad \mathbf{-n = -1n}$

Example 3

Solve and check. $\quad -n = 24$

Solution

$-n = 24$

$-1n = 24 \qquad -n = -1n$

$\frac{-1n}{-1} = \frac{24}{-1} \qquad$ Divide (or multiply) each side by −1.

$n = -24$

Check $\quad -(-24) \stackrel{?}{=} 24 \qquad$ Replace n with 24 in $-n = 24$.

$24 = 24 \ \checkmark \qquad$ The solution is −24.

Practice Solve and check. **a.** $-x = -15$ **b.** $36 = -b$

Oral Exercises

Check. Is the given number a solution to the equation?

1. $-3c = 18, c = 6$? **2.** $5n = -40, n = -8$? **3.** $-63 = -9x, x = -7$?

4. $\frac{y}{-4} = 7, y = -28$? **5.** $8 = \frac{b}{-3} = b = -24$? **6.** $\frac{x}{-9} = -9, x = 81$?

Tell what operation you would use to solve the equation.

7. $36c = -324$ **8.** $-b = 29$ **9.** $-272 = -34x$

10. $24r = -144$ **11.** $-169 = \frac{z}{-13}$ **12.** $\frac{y}{-57} = 29$

Exercises

A Solve and check.

1. $-8y = 96$ **2.** $2b = -86$ **3.** $-7n = -105$ **4.** $-b = 72$

5. $-4z = 92$ **6.** $8c = -272$ **7.** $-14a = -168$ **8.** $-23y = 161$

9. $\frac{n}{17} = -9$ **10.** $\frac{b}{-26} = 7$ **11.** $\frac{r}{-31} = -6$ **12.** $\frac{t}{36} = -8$

13. $\frac{a}{18} = -15$ **14.** $\frac{a}{-29} = 13$ **15.** $\frac{x}{46} = -11$ **16.** $\frac{y}{-54} = -13$

17. $-282 = 47b$ **18.** $47 = \frac{y}{-16}$ **19.** $-882 = 14n$ **20.** $31 = \frac{b}{-35}$

21. $-28n = -1288$ **22.** $-2226 = 42t$ **23.** $\frac{c}{-66} = 77$ **24.** $-49 = \frac{x}{-34}$

25. $-16c = 256$ **26.** $\frac{b}{-9} = -347$ **27.** $-576 = 16p$ **28.** $127 = \frac{r}{-85}$

B Solve and check.

29. $(-16 + 25)b = 162$ **30.** $\frac{x}{(-12)(-16)} = -8$ **31.** $(235 - 421) = -31d$

32. Write and solve an equation in which the product is −518, one factor is −7, and the other factor is represented by the variable *n*.

33. A football team lost an average of 12 yards (−12) a play for a total loss of 72 yards (−72). How many plays were run?

34. When cooked vegetables were put in a freezer, the temperature dropped an average of 19°C (−19) each hour for 6 hours. If the cooking temperature was 108°C, what was the temperature after the 6-hour drop?

C *Extending Thinking Skills*

35. Find the solutions to these equations and look for a pattern. Write the next 3 equations in the pattern. $2a = -2$, $3a = -6$, $4a = -16$, $5a = -40$, $6a = -96$

Use estimation and a calculator to find two solutions to each.

36. $n \cdot n = 1369$ **37.** $n \cdot n = 4624$ **38.** $n \cdot n = 18{,}769$

Mixed Review

Solve and check. **39.** $30x = 210$ **40.** $t - 26 = 14$ **41.** $m \div 12 = 18$

Multiply. **42.** $9(-2)$ **43.** $-9(-12)$ **44.** $11(-1)$ **45.** $-1(-11)$

COMPUTER ACTIVITY

The following program can help you use a "guess, check, revise" procedure to solve the equation $(n \cdot n) - 3n - 18 = 0$.

```
10 PRINT "GUESS A SOLUTION TO THIS EQUATION"
20 PRINT "NXN-3XN-18=0":INPUT N
30 IF N*N-3*N-18=0 THEN 80
40 PRINT "NO, NXN-3XN-18="N*N-3*N-18
50 PRINT "TRY AGAIN? TYPE YES OR NO.":INPUT T$
60 IF T$="YES" THEN 20
70 PRINT "BYE!":GOTO 90
80 PRINT "YOU'VE FOUND A SOLUTION! GREAT JOB!"
90 END
```

1. Use the program to find two solutions to the equation.
2. Change the program to help find solutions to the equation $n \cdot n + n - 12 = 0$.

More Practice

Solve and check.

1. $-2m = 144$
2. $26 + c = 11$
3. $t - 16 = 4$
4. $\frac{r}{4} = -28$
5. $\frac{x}{-5} = -19$
6. $m - 28 = 42$
7. $41 = a + (-19)$
8. $15n = -540$
9. $k - (-6) = 11$
10. $\frac{t}{9} = -16$
11. $-12a = 636$
12. $r + 6 = 0$
13. $97 + m = -6$
14. $350 = -14c$
15. $\frac{h}{-3} = -27$
16. $x - 6 = -8$
17. $12t = 144$
18. $16 = n - 3$
19. $w + 30 = 4$
20. $\frac{a}{16} = -23$
21. $\frac{m}{-7} = 46$
22. $t + 16 = 100$
23. $r - 5 = 0$
24. $-6k = -594$
25. $c - 6 = -4$
26. $\frac{z}{9} = -42$
27. $19y = -304$
28. $17 = n + 12$
29. $x + 31 = 16$
30. $11c = -297$
31. $\frac{w}{32} = 9$
32. $t - (-2) = 0$
33. $\frac{m}{-6} = -29$
34. $z + 26 = 18$
35. $h - 0 = -4$
36. $-5n = 1035$
37. $24a = -792$
38. $99 + h = 67$
39. $m - 6 = 21$
40. $\frac{t}{11} = -20$
41. $992 = -31n$
42. $14 = z - 10$
43. $-36 = \frac{r}{6}$
44. $46 = 7 + k$
45. $14 = \frac{k}{-9}$
46. $21n = 882$
47. $(-2) + r = -3$
48. $m - 6 = 103$
49. $36 + n = -9$
50. $k - 12 = -9$
51. $\frac{k}{-3} = 67$
52. $14t = -1260$
53. $-26r = -910$
54. $-19 = \frac{m}{-21}$
55. $t - 12 = 36$
56. $n + 3 = 0$
57. $a + 67 = 24$
58. $-9w = 1116$
59. $47 = m - 14$
60. $\frac{z}{21} = -37$
61. $r - 14 = -37$
62. $\frac{a}{9} = -54$
63. $r + 19 = 101$
64. $8k = 520$
65. $z - 39 = -6$
66. $t + 91 = 17$
67. $6a = -432$
68. $\frac{z}{-13} = 25$
69. $\frac{c}{27} = -11$
70. $w - (-6) = 12$
71. $40 = x + 100$
72. $-5m = 575$
73. $984 = 8r$
74. $-34 = \frac{t}{-12}$
75. $c - 19 = 40$
76. $n + 12 = -31$

PROBLEM SOLVING: WRITING EQUATIONS

3-9 Translating Sentences into Equations

To translate a verbal statement into an equation, read the verbal statement carefully, thinking about the meaning of each phrase. Then decide what the variable will represent. Notice how the following statement about numbers translates directly to an equation.

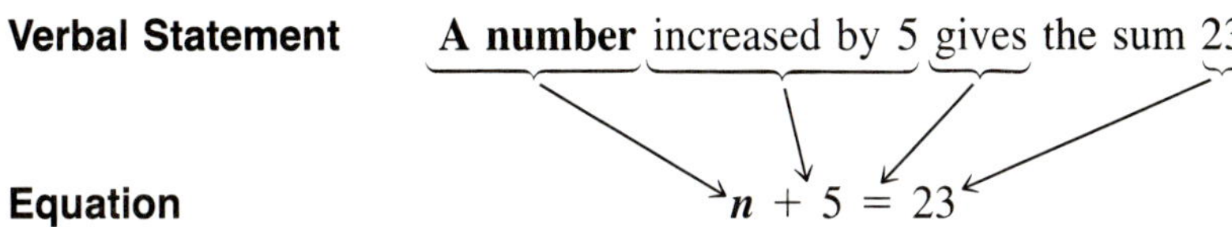

Sometimes the translation is less direct.

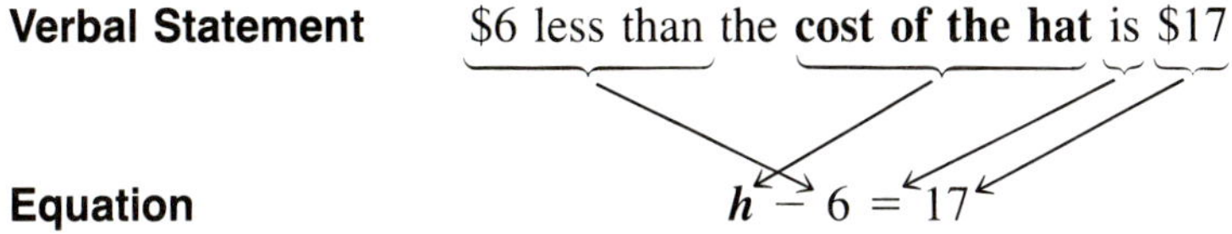

Example 1

Write an equation. A number increased by 8 is 23.

Solution Let n = a number — First decide what the variable represents.

$n + 8 = 23$ — "a number increased by 8" translates to $n + 8$. "is" translates to "=."

Practice Write an equation. **a.** A number decreased by 9 gives 54.
b. The sum of a number and 47 is −112.

Example 2

Write an equation. The $45 baseball glove costs 5 times as much as a ball.

Solution Let b = cost of the ball

$45 = 5b$ — "5 times as much" translates to $5b$.

Practice Write an equation. **a.** 55 times the number of hours is 220.
b. The number of people divided by 9 gives 12 teams.

Oral Exercises

Give an algebraic expression for the phrase.

1. Three times a number

2. 6 more than a number

3. A number divided by -17

4. The product of 9 and a number

5. A number decreased by 5

6. The quotient of a number and 8

Exercises

A Write an equation.

1. 17 less than a number is 101.

2. The quotient of a number and -8 is 216.

3. 35 more than a number is 372.

4. A number decreased by 13 gives 87.

5. 56 more than a number is 104.

6. The difference of a number and 9 is 47.

7. A number n divided by 25 is -12.

8. 57 added to a number gives a total of 123.

9. 9 times a number is -171.

10. The sum of a number and -73 is 145.

11. 17 less than a number is 15.

12. A number increased by 45 gives 77.

13. Six times the number of days is 91.

14. The price decreased by \$29 is \$258.

15. \$9 more than the total restaurant bill is \$72.

16. A number increased by 56 produces a total of 124.

17. 34 multiplied by a number produces the product 272.

18. 28 is the result of multiplying -4 by a number.

19. The difference between the cost of the car and \$6,000 is \$59,820.

20. 369 items divided into boxes of 3 gives the number of boxes.

21. The present temperature increased by 19 degrees gives a reading of 56 degrees.

B Write a verbal statement that describes each equation.

22. $x + 9 = 23$ **23.** $\frac{p}{-4} = 9$ **24.** $-8c = 72$ **25.** $16 - n = 7$

C Extending Thinking Skills

26. The sum of 5 times x and 7 times y is 110. Translate into an equation. Find integers x and y that make the equation true.

27. Write and solve an equation for "the sum of 3 page numbers in a row in a book is 828."

Mixed Review

Solve and check. **28.** $m + 19 = -31$ **29.** $14c = 434$ **30.** $\frac{z}{6} = -6$

Divide. **31.** $\frac{56}{-8}$ **32.** $\frac{-18}{-6}$ **33.** $\frac{-169}{13}$ **34.** $\frac{-324}{-9}$

3-10 Make a Table, Look for a Pattern

Problem-solving strategies called **Make a Table** and **Look for a Pattern** are helpful when solving problems involving numerical relationships. Consider the following problem.

Problem A secret agent was hired for a special assignment that would take exactly 14 days. He could choose to be paid one of the following two ways. Under payment plan A, he would receive $6000 for the job. Under payment plan B, his employer would put $1 into a safe for the first day and increase the amount in the safe to $2 the second day, $4 the third day, $8 the fourth day, and so on, doubling the amount in the safe each day. At the end of the assignment, the agent could claim the contents of the safe. Which payment plan should the agent choose?

To find the amount for payment plan B, you can use the data in the problem to begin a **table**. The red numbers show the data given in the problem. Look for a **pattern** to help extend the table and provide new information.

Notice that the numbers in the second column are found by multiplying 1 less factor of two than the number for the day. On day **4** there were **3** factors of 2, or 2(2)(2), dollars in the safe. So on day **14** there would be **13** factors of 2, or 8192 dollars in the safe.

Day	Number of dollars in the safe
1	**1**
2	**2** ← 2
3	**4** ← 2(2)
4	**8** ← 2(2)(2)
5	16
6	32
⋮	⋮
14	?

Payment plan A: $6000. Payment plan B: $8192. The agent should choose plan B.

Problem-Solving Strategies	
Choose the Operations	**Make a Table**
Guess, Check, Revise	**Look for a Pattern**
Draw a Picture	

This chart shows the problem-solving strategies introduced so far.

Problems

Solve.

1. Nina started a computer users club. On the first day, she was the only member. Each day after that, one more member joined than on the previous day. What was the membership of the club after 30 days?

2. A generous millionaire had an unusual plan for giving away her money. Beginning on her birthday, she would give away $1 the first day, $3 the second day, $5 the third day, and so on. How much money would she have given away after 100 days?

3. Scientists use a radio telescope to send the following sequence of "beeps" into outer space: 1, 1, 2, 3, 5, 8, 13, 21, 34. They hope that intelligent life will receive these signals and send return signals that continue the sequence. What are the next 5 numbers of "beeps" that intelligent life would send back?

4. A sandwich shop has 3-legged stools and 4-legged chairs at its tables. Altogether there are 31 seats and 104 legs. How many of the seats are stools and how many are chairs?

5. Emilio said, "A 1-year-old dog is 7 'dog years' old. My dog is 6 years old in regular years. If you change my age into dog years, I am 49 dog years older than my dog's age in dog years. How old am I?"

6. Suppose it takes newborn rabbits two months to mature and produce a new pair of rabbits. After that, they produce a new pair of rabbits on the first day of each month. The new pairs of rabbits grow and reproduce at the same rate. If you started on January 1 with a pair of newborn rabbits and no rabbits died, how many pairs of rabbits would you have on July 1?

7. George had 12 cherry trees. On January 1, 1780, he cut down 2 of the trees. On December 31, 1780, he planted 1 tree. Each year on the same dates he did the same things. On what date did he first have no cherry trees in his yard?

Enrichment

Sequences

A **sequence** is a set of numbers in a particular order. The numbers in a sequence are called **terms** of the sequence. The table below shows the sequence **1, 3, 5, 7, 9,** . . . The numbers in the top row show the *order* of the terms. The *first* term is 1, the *second* term is 3, the *third* term is 5, and so on. The general rule for finding a particular term of the sequence is called the **rule for the *n*th term**.

Number of the term	1st	2nd	3rd	4th	5th	6th	7th	8th	. . .	*n*th
Terms of the Sequence	1	3	5	7	9	11	13	15	. . .	$2n - 1$

Rule for the *n*th term.

To find the 9th, 10th, and 11th terms of the sequence above, you would replace the variable in the rule for the *n*th term by the number of the term you want to find.

Rule $\mathbf{2n - 1}$: $\mathbf{2(9)} - 1 = 17$, $2(\mathbf{10}) - 1 = 19$, $2(\mathbf{11}) - 1 = 21$

The **9**th, **10**th, and **11**th terms of the sequence are **17, 19, 21.**

1. The rule for the *n*th term of a sequence is $\frac{n(n + 1)}{-2}$. Write the first five terms.

2. The rule for the *n*th term of a sequence is $n(n) - 1$. Give the 8th term of the sequence. Give the 25th term of the sequence.

3. Find the rule for the *n*th term of this sequence: 1, 4, 9, 16, 25, 36, 49 . . .

4. Find the rule for the *n*th term of this sequence: −3, −7, −11, −15, −19, −23, −27, . . .

5. The *n*th term of a sequence is 0 when *n* is even and 1 when *n* is odd. Write the first eight terms of this sequence.

6. Write the next five terms in the **Fibonacci sequence**: 1, 1, 2, 3, 5, 8, 13, 21, 34, . . .

7. Square any term of the sequence in exercise 6. Then find the product of the term preceding and the term following that term. What do you discover?

8. Estimate how many of the first 25 Fibonacci numbers are even. Extend the sequence to check your guess.

Chapter 3 Review

3-1 Find the absolute value.

1. $|6|$ **2.** $|-3|$ **3.** $|-17|$

Use the inequality symbols. Order from least to greatest.

4. $-8, 2, -2$ **5.** $-7, -1, 0$ **6.** $0, -8, -5$

3-2 Find the sum.

7. $-3 + (-3)$ **8.** $-7 + 4$ **9.** $5 + (-2)$

10. $-20 + (-4)$ **11.** $-15 + 7$ **12.** $12 + (-6)$

Evaluate.

13. $s + (-4)$ for $s = -12$ **14.** $-17 + k$ for $k = 9$

3-3 Subtract.

15. $-7 - 6$ **16.** $5 - 8$ **17.** $-14 - 3$ **18.** $8 - (-3)$ **19.** $6 - 13$

Evaluate.

20. $v - 5$ for $v = 2$ **21.** $-3 - n$ for $n = 9$

3-4 Solve and check.

22. $r + 42 = -7$ **23.** $s - 17 = -34$ **24.** $t - 66 = 15$

25. $-37 = z + 56$ **26.** $v - (-28) = -77$ **27.** $w + (-15) = 56$

Solve.

28. A checking account with a beginning balance of \$120 has credits of \$600 and debits of \$944. By how much is it overdrawn?

3-6 Find the product.

29. $-1(-9)$ **30.** $7(8)$ **31.** $-5(-5)$ **32.** $6(-8)$ **33.** $-4(2)$

3-7 Find the quotient.

34. $-54 \div 6$ **35.** $-81 \div (-9)$ **36.** $28 \div (-4)$

37. $16 \div (-4)$ **38.** $-6 \div (-2)$ **39.** $72 \div (-3)$

3-8 Solve and check.

40. $-81 = 3n$ **41.** $-9y = 27$ **42.** $7 = \frac{r}{-7}$ **43.** $\frac{a}{4} = -6$ **44.** $91 = -r$

3-9 Write an equation.

45. 10 multiplied by a number n produces the product 110.

46. The sum of a number and -15 is 60.

Chapter 3 Test

Find the absolute value.

1. $|23|$ **2.** $|-8|$ **3.** $|0|$

Use inequality symbols. Order from least to greatest.

4. 7, −5, 8 **5.** −3, −9, 1 **6.** −2, 0, −3

Find the sum.

7. $-3 + 8$ **8.** $7 + (-1)$ **9.** $-2 + (-3)$

10. $-1 + (-1)$ **11.** $-8 + 3$ **12.** $13 + (-5)$

Evaluate.

13. $m + (-11)$ for $m = 5$ **14.** $20 + r$ for $r = -7$

Subtract.

15. $1 - 6$ **16.** $-13 - 2$ **17.** $12 - 14$ **18.** $16 - (-5)$ **19.** $-8 - 7$

Evaluate.

20. $-6 - n$ for $n = 7$ **21.** $-4 - n$ for $n = -7$

Solve and check.

22. $k + 35 = -50$ **23.** $m - 90 = -10$ **24.** $73 = p - 2$

25. $-48 = n + 35$ **26.** $p - (-15) = 43$ **27.** $s + (-18) = -35$

Solve.

28. By how much is Fred's checking account overdrawn? He started with a balance of $176, wrote a check for $140, then wrote a check for $90.

Find the product.

29. $-5(-4)$ **30.** $6(8)$ **31.** $-3(-1)$ **32.** $9(-2)$ **33.** $-7(4)$

Find the quotient.

34. $-18 \div 9$ **35.** $-48 \div (-6)$ **36.** $24 \div (-3)$

37. $25 \div (-5)$ **38.** $-9 \div (-3)$ **39.** $64 \div (-4)$

Solve and check.

40. $-84 = 4s$ **41.** $-6x = 36$ **42.** $\frac{t}{5} = -40$ **43.** $7 = \frac{m}{-8}$ **44.** $-c = -22$

Write an equation.

45. 24 less than a number x is 12.

46. 49 is the result of multiplying −7 by a number m.

Cumulative Review

Write an algebraic expression for each phrase.

1. g added to 9 **2.** k decreased by 3 **3.** the sum of v and 10

4. half of m **5.** y times 7 **6.** 9 divided by w

Write an expression for each question.

Wendy has 16 records. How many will she have if

7. she gives away r records? **8.** she buys b more records?

Simplify.

9. $28 \div (3 + 4)$ **10.** $2 + [(7 + 2) \div 3]$ **11.** $4 \cdot 5 + 3 \cdot 9$

Evaluate each algebraic expression.

12. $s + 2$ for $s = 9$ **13.** $(4 + 8) - c$ for $c = 10$

14. $f - g$ for $f = 5$, $g = 1$ **15.** $8k$ for $k = 8$

16. $\frac{2x}{z}$ for $x = 8$, $z = 4$ **17.** $n(m + 6)$ for $n = 2$, $m = 3$

18. $\frac{7w}{2}$ for $w = 4$ **19.** $3(10 - c)$ for $c = 5$

20. $y + (-10)$ for $y = 2$ **21.** $35 + b$ for $b = -10$

22. $-4 - t$ for $t = 5$ **23.** $-7 - x$ for $x = 3$

Use the commutative property to write an equivalent expression.

24. $y(6)$ **25.** pq **26.** $12 + z$

Use the associative property to write an equivalent expression.

27. $20(8p)$ **28.** $(5f)n$ **29.** $(y + 2) + 9$

Use the distributive property to write an equivalent expression.

30. $3(c + 4)$ **31.** $a(8 + 9)$ **32.** $(7 + b)8$

Use the associative property for multiplication to simplify.

33. $2(5 \cdot t)$ **34.** $6(4k)$ **35.** $15(2d)$

Use the distributive property to simplify by combining like terms.

36. $g + 7g$ **37.** $3v + 3v$ **38.** $25p + 50p$

Compute.

39. $3 - 7$ **40.** $-12 \cdot 8$ **41.** $18 \div (-9)$

Chapter 4
Decimals

4-1 Decimals and Place Value

Numbers are represented in the decimal system by using the digits 0 through 9 and grouping by tens. The value of each digit in a decimal depends on its place. The chart below shows the **place value** names for the decimals 24.5 and 6.263.

thousands	hundreds	tens	ones	decimal point	tenths	hundredths	thousandths	
1000	100	10	1		$\frac{1}{10}$	$\frac{1}{100}$	$\frac{1}{1000}$	
		2	4	.	5			twenty-four and five tenths
			6	.	2	6	3	six and two hundred sixty-three thousandths

Example 1

Write $\mathbf{3}(100) + \mathbf{1}(10) + \mathbf{3}(1) + \mathbf{4}\left(\frac{1}{10}\right) + \mathbf{7}\left(\frac{1}{100}\right)$ as a decimal.

Solution 313.47

Practice Write as a decimal.

a. $4(100) + 7(10) + 8(1) + 3\left(\frac{1}{10}\right) + 6\left(\frac{1}{100}\right)$

b. $9\left(\frac{1}{100}\right) + 3\left(\frac{1}{1000}\right)$

Decimals can be used to name points on a number line. The number line shown below is divided into ten equal spaces between 0 and 1. Point *A*, which is at the end of the seventh space, represents the number seven tenths and can be named by the decimal 0.7.

$\frac{7}{10} = 0.7$

Positive numbers represented by decimals are shown to the right of zero on the number line, and negative numbers represented by decimals are shown to the left of zero.

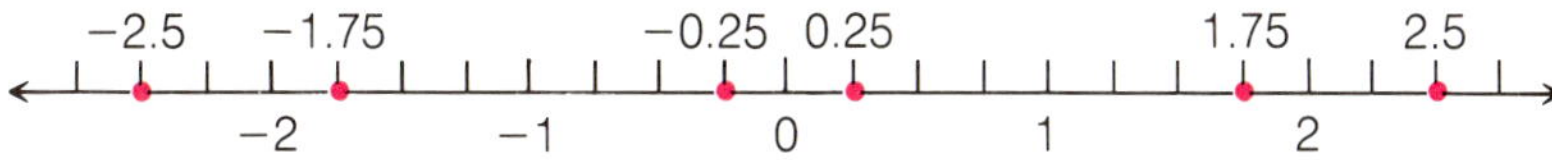

Example 2

Give the decimal names for points A and B.

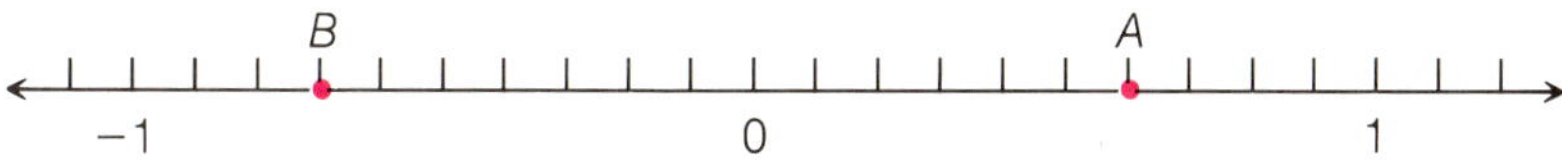

Solution point $A = 0.6$ Point A is at the end of the sixth of 10 equal spaces between 0 and 1.

point $B = -0.7$ Point B is at the end of the seventh of 10 equal spaces between 0 and −1.

Practice

Give the decimal name for point A.

a. A; −2.8 to −2.7

b. A; 2.7 to 2.8

The number farther to the right on the number line is the greater number. To compare decimals without a number line, start on the left, find the first place in which the digits are not equal, and compare the digits.

Example 3

Write $>$, $<$, or $=$ for □. 19.31 □ 19.23

Solution $19.31 > 19.23$ Start on the left. The tenths place is the first place in which the digits are not equal. Since $3 > 2$, $19.31 > 19.23$.

Practice

Write $>$, $<$, or $=$ for each □.

a. 47.14 □ 47.13 **b.** −7.003 □ −7.03 **c.** 18.06 □ 18.060

Oral Exercises

Read each decimal.

1. 8.3 **2.** 45.8 **3.** 390.1 **4.** 7.64 **5.** 35.18

6. 123.15 **7.** 3014.39 **8.** 0.034 **9.** 0.803 **10.** 493.319

Exercises

A Write as a decimal.

1. $5(100) + 4(10) + 7\left(\frac{1}{10}\right) + 6\left(\frac{1}{100}\right)$ **2.** $3(100) + 4(1000) + 3(10) + 7(1) + 5\left(\frac{1}{10}\right)$

3. $7(100) + 8(1) + 7\left(\frac{1}{100}\right) + 4(10)$ **4.** $4(100) + 5\left(\frac{1}{10}\right) + 8(10) + 6\left(\frac{1}{100}\right) + 7(1000)$

5. $8(1) + 7(10) + 5(100) + 3\left(\frac{1}{10}\right)$ **6.** $4\left(\frac{1}{100}\right) + 0(10) + 0(1) + 4(100)$

Give the decimal name for point A.

7. A, 0, 1

8. 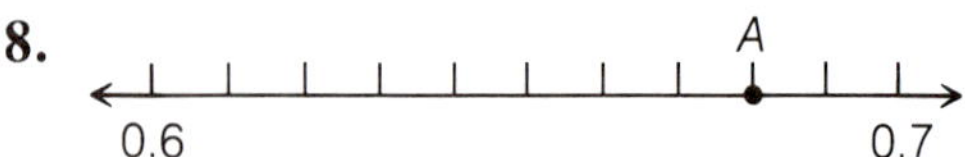

9. A, 1.3, 1.4

10. 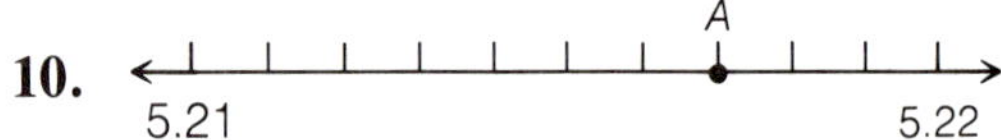

11. A, −0.4, −0.3

12. 

Write >, <, or = for each □.

13. 6.93 □ 6.930 **14.** 1.01 □ 1.101 **15.** −4.658 □ −4.685

16. 4.1 □ 4.100 **17.** 7.001 □ 7.010 **18.** −14.3 □ −14.29

B Write the numbers in order from least to greatest.

19. 3.7, 3.07, 3.069 **20.** 0.004, 0.039, 0.0041

21. 6.101, 6.010, 6.0101 **22.** 4.01, 4, 4.001

23. −5.404, −5.044, −5.040 **24.** −0.001, −0.101, −0.011, −0.01

Write two decimal replacements for x that make the sentence true.

25. $0.4 < x < 0.5$ **26.** $8.12 < x < 8.13$ **27.** $4.06 > x > 4.05$

28. $12.3 > x > 12.03$ **29.** $9.1 < x < 9.11$ **30.** $-7.6 > x > -7.601$

C Extending Thinking Skills

31. Use only the digits 0 and 1 to write four decimals that are > 0 and < 1.

32. Use only the digits 5 and 6 to write four decimals that are > 5 and < 6.

Mixed Review

Solve and check. **33.** $\frac{x}{13} = -17$ **34.** $-24n = -360$ **35.** $16t = -400$

Evaluate for $x = 6$. **36.** $9x - 2$ **37.** $\frac{-36}{x}$ **38.** $-6x - 2$

4-2 Estimating Using Rounding

This computerized gasoline pump records gallon amounts to the third decimal place. The attendant rounds the number of gallons before writing it on a receipt. The procedure for rounding decimals is given below.

Rounding Decimals

Look at the digit to the right of the place to which you are rounding.

- If it is less than 5, do not change the digit in the place to which you are rounding.
- If it is 5 or more, add 1 to the digit in the place to which you are rounding.

Replace the digits to the right with zeros, or drop them if they are to the right of the decimal point.

Example 1

Round 4.679 to the nearest hundredth.

Solution 4.68 4.679 Since 9 > 5, round 7 up to 8. Drop the digits to the right of the 8.

Practice Round.

a. 7.087 to the nearest hundredth.

b. 9.783 to the nearest whole number.

c. 0.925 to the nearest tenth.

Example 2

Round 593.827 to the nearest tenth.

Solution 593.8 593.827 Since 2 < 5, leave the 8 unchanged and drop the digits to the right of the tenths place.

Practice Round.

a. 73.484 to the nearest tenth. **b.** 0.253 to the nearest hundredth.

c. 4.82 to the nearest tenth.

You can use rounding with decimals to make estimates.

Estimating Using Rounding

- Round each decimal.
- Compute with the rounded decimals.

Example 3

Estimate the value of n by rounding. $n = 505.3 + 294.8$

Solution $500 + 300 = 800$ Round 505.3 to 500. Round 294.8 to 300.

The estimated value of n is 800.

Practice Estimate the value of x by rounding.

a. $x = 21.71 + 11.29$

b. $x = 352.92 - 147.19$

Oral Exercises

To round to the indicated place, would you increase the digit in that place or leave it unchanged?

1. 3.578, tenths
2. 5.294, hundredths
3. 32.925, tenths
4. 59.139, hundreds
5. 23.598, whole number
6. 258.37, tenths

Exercises

A Round to the nearest whole number.

1. 146.73
2. 93.48
3. 126.55
4. 14.73
5. 34.61
6. 8.499
7. 19.501
8. 999.99

Round to the nearest tenth.

9. 23.78
10. 1.725
11. 42.73
12. 76.39
13. 8.294
14. 39.149
15. 17.0051
16. 4.286

Round to the nearest hundredth.

17. 4.5869
18. 5.497
19. 0.2848
20. 3.0089
21. 9.896
22. 0.999
23. 8.8944
24. 2.09839

Estimate the value of the variable by rounding.

25. $n = 218.6 + 101.2$
26. $x = 24.5 - 10.3$
27. $y = 18.603 + 21.2218$
28. $z = 125.3 + 34.8$

29. $s = 724.91 + 575.36$

30. $x = 84.78 - 42.32$

B

31. Find four numbers that, when rounded to the nearest tenth, result in 23.5.

32. Find four numbers that, when rounded to the nearest hundredth, result in 4.23.

33. Use front-end estimation to estimate the sum.
5.53 + 9.48 + 7.24 + 8.77

34. Use estimation to decide which is the better buy: 5 bars of soap for $1.98 or 3 bars of the same soap for $1.10.

35. Keiko and Sara need to buy 80 hot dogs for a class picnic. They can buy packages of 8 hot dogs for $1.05 or packages of 10 hot dogs for $1.53. Use estimation to decide which is the better buy.

C Extending Thinking Skills

Look for a pattern. Give the next three numbers.

36. 1, 1, 2, 3, 5, 8, 13, 21, . . .

37. 0.001, 0.1, 0.101, 0.201, 0.302, 0.503, 0.805, 1.308, . . .

38. −0.03, 0.1, −0.13, 0.26, −0.49, 0.88, −1.63, 3.00, . . .

39. 0.001, 0.11, 0.111, 0.221, 0.332, 0.553, 0.885, . . .

Mixed Review

Find the value of the variable. **40.** $m = 2\,\frac{17 \cdot 62}{9 - 77}$

Solve and check. **41.** $-36m = 648$ **42.** $t - 26 = -8$ **43.** $\frac{w}{-9} = 14$

Simplify. **44.** $6t - 8t$ **45.** $6(-12)m$ **46.** $-9 + x + 3$

COMPUTER ACTIVITY

This program rounds a decimal to the nearest hundredth.

```
10 REM: ROUNDING DECIMALS
20 PRINT "TYPE A DECIMAL THAT HAS THREE OR MORE DECIMAL
   PLACES"
30 INPUT N
40 PRINT N; " ROUNDED TO HUNDREDTHS IS ";
50 PRINT INT(N*100+.5)/100
60 END
```

1. Type and run this program.
2. Change the program so it will round decimals to the nearest tenth.
3. Change the program so it will round decimals to the nearest thousandth.

4-3 Adding and Subtracting with Decimals

An 800-meter relay team had individual times of 21.38 seconds, 22.81 seconds, 22.93 seconds, and 21.12 seconds. The time for the team is the sum of the four decimals.

To add or subtract with decimals, align the decimal points and add or subtract as with whole numbers. Place the decimal point in the sum or difference, in line with the other decimal points.

Example 1

Add. 21.83 + 22.81 + 22.93 + 21.12

Solution

$$\begin{array}{r} 21.83 \\ 22.81 \\ 22.93 \\ +\ 21.12 \\ \hline 88.69 \end{array}$$

Write the numbers vertically, aligning the decimal points, and add.

Place the decimal point in the answer.

Practice Add. **a.** 34.28 + 259.3 **b.** 46.08 − 2.485

Example 2

Add. −5.3 + 2.7

Solution −5.3 + 2.7 = −2.6 Find the difference in absolute values. Since −5.3 has the larger absolute value, the sum is negative.

Practice Add. **a.** −17.4 + 75.3 **b.** −3.8 + (7.9 − 3.7)

Example 3

Evaluate. $v - 7.62$ for $v = 6.1$.

Solution

$$\begin{aligned} & v - 7.62 \\ & 6.1 - 7.62 \\ &= 6.1 + (-7.62) \\ &= -1.52 \end{aligned}$$

Practice Evaluate.

a. $w - 7.65 + 4.8$ for $w = -2.1$

b. $z - 3.9 + 9.31$ for $z = 8.63$

Oral Exercises

Place the decimal point and read the answer.

1. $3.2 + 6.7 = 99$

2. $9.51 + 1.3 = 1081$

3. $63.7 - 1.2 = 625$

4. $123.4 + 6.3 = 1297$

5. $13.56 - 6.4 = 716$

6. $406.5 - 25.6 = 3809$

Exercises

A Add or subtract.

1. $35.82 + 12.3$

2. $9.6 + 49.2$

3. $92.3 - 21.5$

4. $7.9 + (-3.8)$

5. $9.73 + (-3.7)$

6. $2.81 + (9.73 - 3.7)$

7. $254.87 - 73.62$

8. $-48.52 + 73.36$

9. $-38.15 + 8.24 + 17.28$

10. $35.9 - 24.8$

11. $71.05 - 39.23$

12. $4.98 + (2.89 + 0.82)$

13. $973.2 - 48.38$

14. $21.03 - (-19.128)$

15. $398.237 - 59.83$

16. $129.36 - 3.295$

17. $79.24 - (-42.48)$

18. $8.083 - 3.591$

Evaluate.

19. $75.92 - y$ for $y = 35.1926$

20. $(u - 45.2) + 21.04$ for $u = -97.2$

21. $(45.23 + v) + 38.3$ for $v = -17.5$

22. $x - 93.2 + 17.3$ for $x = -0.36$

B

23. Evaluate $a - (b - c)$ and $(a - b) - c$ for $a = 12.5$, $b = 5.3$, and $c = 1.4$. Are the two expressions equivalent?

24. A cross-country course has an uphill section of 0.82 km, a flat section of 1.3 km, a downhill section of 1.1 km, and a wooded section of 1.05 km. How long is the course?

25. A company that makes stereo components had profits for the year, in millions, of \$5.62 on speakers and \$4.38 on turntables. It had losses of \$0.21 on headphones and \$1.03 on amplifiers. What was its net profit?

Use a calculator with a memory key to evaluate each expression.

26. $x - 2.73$ for $x = 7.9$, $x = 9.32$, and $x = 17.21$

27. $19.8 - x$ for $x = 3.91$, $x = 11.82$, and $x = 6.5$

28. $(x + 5.2) - 3.1$ for $x = 19.6$, $x = 5.3$, and $x = 4.7$

29. $(12.5 - x) + 3.8$ for $x = 5.1$, $x = 7.92$, and $x = 3.3$

30. Use clustering to estimate the sum.
$45.68 + 56.79 + 49.53 + 52.75$

31. Explain how you can use compensation to find this difference mentally.
$68.73 - 25.99$

C Extending Thinking Skills

Copy each problem and find the missing digits.

32. $\begin{array}{r} 6\blacksquare.7 \\ -\ 46.\blacksquare \\ \hline 14.8 \end{array}$

33. $\begin{array}{r} 6\blacksquare\blacksquare.92 \\ -\ 231.\blacksquare 5 \\ \hline 384.77 \end{array}$

34. A business executive can fly from one city to another and then return by train for a total travel time of 7.5 hours. To fly both ways would take a total of 2.5 hours. How long would it take to go both ways by train?

Mixed Review

Solve and check. **35.** $m - 36 = -15$ **36.** $33r = -594$ **37.** $\frac{x}{-26} = 18$

Evaluate for $n = 3$. **38.** $6n \div 9$ **39.** $-3n + 11$ **40.** $12n \div (-6)$

NUMBERS TO ALGEBRA

The Numbers to Algebra section in Chapter 1 gave the generalization that if a, b, c, and d represent whole numbers, then $(a + b) + (c + d) = (a + c) + (b + d)$. You can use this idea to simplify both numerical and algebraic expressions.

Numbers	Algebra
$(17 + 14) + (3 + 16)$	$(2a + 3b) + (5a + 6b)$
$= (17 + 3) + (14 + 16)$	$= (2a + 5a) + (3b + 6b)$
$= 20 + 30$	$= 7a + 9b$
$= 50$	

Use the idea above to simplify each expression.

1. $(3x + 4y) + (4x + 2y)$

2. $(4a + 3b) + (7a + 6b)$

3. $(7u + 3n) + (4u + 2n)$

4. $(3e + 5f) + (9e + 2f)$

4-4 Solving Decimal Equations: Using Addition and Subtraction

To solve decimal equations involving addition and subtraction, you can use the same steps you used to solve integer equations.

Example 1

Solve and check. $x + 0.21 = 7.32$

Solution $x + 0.21 = 7.32$ — You need to get the variable by itself on one side.

$x + 0.21 - 0.21 = 7.32 - 0.21$ — To undo adding 0.21, subtract 0.21 from both sides.

$x = 7.11$

Check $7.11 + 0.21 \stackrel{?}{=} 7.32$ — Replace x with 7.11 in $x + 0.21 = 7.32$.

$7.32 = 7.32$ ✓ — The solution is 7.11.

Practice Solve and check.

a. $x + 2.39 = -14.85$

b. $s + 4.287 = 6.24$

Example 2

Solve and check. $x - 0.01 = 4.35$

Solution $x - 0.01 = 4.35$ — You need to get the variable by itself on one side.

$x - 0.01 + 0.01 = 4.35 + 0.01$ — To undo subtracting 0.01, add 0.01 to both sides.

$x = 4.36$

Check $4.36 - 0.01 \stackrel{?}{=} 4.35$ — Replace x with 4.36 in $x - 0.01 = 4.35$.

$4.35 = 4.35$ ✓ — The solution is 4.36.

Practice Solve and check.

a. $x - 2.39 = 14.85$

b. $x - 5.92 = -2.813$

Oral Exercises

Tell what operation you would use to solve the equation.

1. $x - 0.78 = 3.7$

2. $x + 8.92 = 13.5$

3. $y + 19.3 = 31$

4. $x + 25.7 = 14.3$

5. $x + 9.6 = 31.7$

6. $z - 2.84 = 51.82$

7. $s - 0.05 = 0.12$

8. $u - 1.24 = 4.82$

9. $w + 0.342 = -6.82$

Exercises

A Solve and check.

1. $y + 0.05 = 7.95$ **2.** $z + 17.5 = 46.82$ **3.** $u + 0.99 = 5.72$

4. $x - 12.3 = -6.28$ **5.** $x + 29.6 = 142.8$ **6.** $x - 29.6 = -14.3$

7. $s + 19.4 = 46.7$ **8.** $s - 79.4 = -46.7$ **9.** $y - 17.9 = 583.6$

10. $u + 1.53 = -26.91$ **11.** $v - 23.7 = -7.41$ **12.** $z + 0.5 = -5.03$

13. $x - 23.4 = 345.61$ **14.** $x - 5.05 = -4.38$ **15.** $x - 4.32 = 145.8$

16. $38.06 + x = 91.5$ **17.** $z - 2.04 = 48.13$ **18.** $-14.95 + t = 25.87$

B Solve and check.

19. $-84.02 + z = 46.3$ **20.** $12.3 + x = -6.28$ **21.** $-46.3 = z + 84.02$

22. $(x - 5.2) + 0.47 = 25.84$ **23.** $32.7 + x + 25.2 = 124.8$

24. Write and solve an equation with sum of 35.82, one addend of 13.08, and the other addend represented by the variable y.

25. Write and solve an equation with sum of 17.36, one addend of 8.24, and the other addend represented by the variable x.

C Extending Thinking Skills

26. Find values for x and y that solve both equations: $x + y = 1.5$ and $x - y = 0.5$.

27. The numbers in each row, column, and diagonal of this magic square have the same sum. Write equations for finding the values of w, x, y, and z.

1.6	0.2	x	1.3
w	1.1	1.0	0.8
0.9	0.7	0.6	y
0.4	z	1.5	0.1

Mixed Review

Compute. **28.** $120 - (65 \cdot 12) \div 15$ **29.** $15 + 8 \cdot 6 - 12$

Solve and check. **30.** $16m = -384$ **31.** $r - 16 = -4$

MENTAL MATH

You can "break apart" numbers to add or subtract decimals mentally. For example, to find 9.45 + 11.55, think "9 + 11 is 20 and 0.45 + 0.55 is 1. The sum is 21."

Find each sum or difference by breaking apart the numbers.

1. 7.35 + 9.65 **2.** 23.95 + 9.05 **3.** 45.85 − 5.40 **4.** 96.89 − 46.80

4-5 Multiplying with Decimals

Casey is a mountain climber. While planning an expedition and buying supplies, she chose a type of rope priced at \$1.89 per meter. She wanted to buy 19.5 meters of rope, but wasn't sure she had enough money to pay for it. You can estimate the total price by rounding each decimal to the nearest whole number.

Example 1

Estimate the product by rounding. $19.5 \times \$1.89$

Solution

$19.5 \times \$1.89$

$\approx 20 \times 2$ — Round 19.5 to 20 and round 1.89 to 2. Multiply.

$= 40.00$

$19.5 \times \$1.89$ is about \$40.00.

Practice Estimate the product by rounding.

a. 9.8×12.1

b. 19.2×43.9

c. 186.2×5.3

d. 493.6×39.4

Sometimes you need an exact answer rather than an estimate. The steps for multiplying decimals are given below. The *sign* of the product of two decimals is determined in the same way as is the sign for an integer product. The product of two decimals with like signs is positive. The product of two decimals with unlike signs is negative.

Multiplying with Decimals

- Multiply as with whole numbers.
- Place the decimal point in the product so that it has the same number of decimal places as the total number of decimal places in the factors.
- Determine the sign of the product, as with integers.

Example 2

Multiply. $1.02 \times (-0.36)$

Solution

$$\begin{array}{r} 1.02 \\ \times\ 0.36 \\ \hline 612 \\ 306\ \ \\ \hline 0.3672 \end{array}$$

Since the sum of the decimal places in the factors is 4, the product has 4 decimal places.

-0.3672 The product of a positive and a negative number is negative.

Practice Multiply. **a.** 4.12×2.1 **b.** $-7.3 \times (-0.02)$

Sometimes you need to write zeros to the left of the calculated number in order to place the decimal point.

Example 3

Multiply. 4.3×0.02

Solution

$$\begin{array}{r} 4.3 \\ \times\ 0.02 \\ \hline 0.086 \end{array}$$

Write a zero to the left of the calculated number to give the product 3 decimal places.

Practice Multiply. **a.** -3.7×0.003 **b.** $23.1 \times (-0.002)$

Oral Exercises

Place the decimal point mentally and read the answer.

1. $3.46 \times 57.9 = 200334$

2. $146.2 \times 0.013 = 19006$

3. $12 \times 17.32 = 20784$

4. $29.83 \times 0.0035 = 0104405$

5. $9.18 \times 1.018 = 934524$

6. $93.12 \times 33.4 = 3110208$

Exercises

A Estimate the product by rounding.

1. 19.8×5.25

2. 8.1×4.5

3. 3.9×0.75

4. 25.2×9.8

5. 399.6×20.03

6. 996.8×37.5

Multiply.

7. 18.9×0.01

8. $4.01 \times (-0.32)$

9. $-34.6 \times (-0.1)$

10. 16.32×1.03

11. -4.38×0.08

12. 196.3×0.01

13. -84.6×-3.05

14. 0.193×100

15. 21.3×0.481

16. 471.32×0.001

17. 5280×-0.01

18. -75.2×100

B Estimate the product, then compute.

19. 23.2×1.08
20. 0.515×0.02
21. 7.3×0.003
22. $2.3 + (3.2 \times 5.3)$
23. $4.2(1.3 + 6.7)$
24. $5.9(2.1 + 8.3)$

Evaluate for $u = 2.3$.

25. $5.2u - 3.1$
26. $9.4u + 32.1$
27. $3.1u + 8.3$

The relationship between temperature in degrees Fahrenheit (°F) and temperature in degrees Celsius (°C) is given by the formula $F = 1.8C + 32$. Evaluate the formula to find F for each value of C.

28. $C = 0°$
29. $C = 17°$
30. $C = 37°$

31. The hottest temperature ever recorded in North America was 56.7°C, in Death Valley. Use the formula above to find the temperature in degrees Fahrenheit.

32. A record was set by a driver in a three-wheeled car that averaged 157.19 miles per gallon while using 2.871 gallons of fuel. How many miles (to the nearest tenth) did the car travel?

C *Extending Thinking Skills*

33. Leslie, Beth, Rafael, and Jason are joining Casey on a mountain climb. In how many different orders can the five climbers tie themselves to the safety rope if Casey is always the lead member of the party?

34. A mountain climb has four routes from the base camp to the first campsite, two routes from there to the second campsite, and one route from there to the peak. How many different routes are there to the peak?

Mixed Review

Simplify. **35.** $46c - 3c$ **36.** $35 + (m + 6)$ **37.** $7(-9k)$

Evaluate for $a = 6$, $b = 4$, $c = 2$. **38.** $a + b - c$ **39.** $2(a - c) + b$

Round to the nearest tenth and estimate the value of n. **40.** $n + 0.196 = 0.662$

Order from least to greatest. Use inequality symbols. **41.** 1.04, 1.4, 0.14

MENTAL MATH

When multiplying mentally with decimals, it is often helpful to use the distributive property to "break apart" numbers. To find 3×2.3, think "3×2 is 6 and 3×0.3 is 0.9, a total of 6.9."

Use the distributive property to find each product mentally.

1. 3×9.25
2. 4×5.25
3. 5×3.02
4. 2×7.05
5. 4×3.6
6. 3×4.2

4-6 The Metric System

The metric system of measurement uses the meter (m) as the basic unit of length, the liter (L) as the basic unit of capacity, and the gram (g) as the basic unit of mass.

A series of prefixes is used with the basic units. The table below shows how each prefix corresponds to a decimal place value.

kilo-	hecto-	deka-	--	deci-	centi-	milli-
1000 thousands	100 hundreds	10 tens	1 ones	0.1 tenths	0.01 hundredths	0.001 thousandths

When a prefix is attached to one of the basic units, a new unit is created. Look at the table below. Multiply a unit by 0.1 to obtain the unit on its right. Multiply a unit by 10 to obtain the unit on its left.

← larger **Metric Units of Length** smaller →						
kilometer (km)	**hecto**meter (hm)	**deka**meter (dkm)	meter (m)	**deci**meter (dm)	**centi**meter (cm)	**milli**meter (mm)
1000 m	100 m	10 m	1 m	0.1 m	0.01 m	0.001 m

The basic units of length, capacity, and mass are related to one another.

A cube with edges the *length* of one **decimeter** has the *capacity* of one **liter**. The *mass* of one liter of water is 1 **kilogram**.

Problems

Solve.

1. How many kilometers long is a 1500-meter race?
2. A man's waist size might be 90 cm. How many meters is that?
3. If the width of the palm of your hand is 0.8 dm, how wide is it in centimeters?
4. A football field is about 90 m long. How long is it in decimeters? In dekameters?

5. A penny is about 18 mm in diameter. How many centimeters is that?

6. A building is 12.34 meters long. How long is it in centimeters?

7. A stack of five pennies is about 1 cm high. Approximately how many millimeters thick is one penny?

8. If a person's stride is 50 cm long, how many strides equal one kilometer?

9. How many millimeters are there in one kilometer?

10. A thimble has a capacity of about 2 ml. What is the approximate mass of the water contained by a full thimble? (1 liter = 1 kilogram)

11. ***Data Search*** Weigh a milk carton full of water to find the mass of the water in grams. Approximately how many liters does the milk carton hold?

What's Your Decision?

To find the mass of the water in a swimming pool, would you prefer to know the number of liters or the number of gallons it holds?

One dm^3 has a capacity of 1 liter.

4-7 Dividing with Decimals

A university charges $5789.40 for tuition, fees, room, and board for the school year. A student is permitted 12 monthly payments. What is the amount of the payment each month? You can estimate an answer to this question. When estimating, use the symbol ≈, which means "is approximately equal to."

Example 1

Round and choose compatible numbers to estimate.
5789.40 ÷ 12

Solution

$5789.40 \div 12$	
$\approx 5800 \div 12$	Round 5789.40 to 5800.
$\approx 5500 \div 11$	Change 5800 to 5500 and 12 to 11 to get compatible numbers for division.
≈ 500	5789.40 ÷ 12 ≈ 500.

Practice Round and choose compatible numbers to estimate.

a. 25.20 ÷ 8.10 **b.** 46.30 ÷ 5.91

You will often need an exact answer rather than an estimate. When the divisor is a whole number, place the decimal point in the quotient directly above the decimal point in the dividend.

Example 2

Divide. 13.5 ÷ 12

Solution

```
     1.125
12)13.500
   12
    15
    12
     30
     24
      60
      60
       0
```

Since the divisor is a whole number, place the decimal point in the quotient directly above the decimal point of the dividend.

Annex zeros to the dividend as needed in the division process.

Practice Divide. **a.** 382.5 ÷ 18 **b.** 223.2 ÷ 24

When the decimal point is moved one place to the right in both dividend and divisor, the same quotient results.

$$2.0\overline{)6.0}\;=\;3. \qquad 20.\overline{)60.}\;=\;3.$$

This supports the following procedure for dividing with decimals.

Dividing with a Decimal Divisor

- Move the decimal point the same number of places to the right in both divisor and dividend until the divisor is a whole number.
- Divide.
- Determine the sign as you would for division with integers.

Example 3

Divide. $17.25 \div 1.5$

Solution

$$\begin{array}{r} 11.5 \\ 1.5\overline{)17.25} \\ \underline{15} \\ 22 \\ \underline{15} \\ 75 \end{array}$$

Since the divisor is a decimal, move the decimal point until the divisor is a whole number. Move the decimal point one place to the right in both divisor and dividend. Place the decimal point in the quotient.

Practice Divide.

a. $262.2 \div 2.3$ **b.** $1.353 \div 4.1$ **c.** $33.37 \div 4.7$ **d.** $187.59 \div 3.9$

Sometimes you need to annex zeros in the quotient when placing the decimal point.

Example 4

Divide. $-0.0483 \div 2.1$

Solution

$$\begin{array}{r} 0.023 \\ 2.1\overline{)0.0483} \\ \underline{42} \\ 63 \\ \underline{63} \end{array}$$

Move the decimal point in both the divisor and the dividend and place the decimal point one place to the right. In the quotient, annex a zero.

-0.023 The quotient is negative because the divisor and the dividend have unlike signs.

Practice Divide.

a. $0.0045 \div 1.8$ **b.** $0.00496 \div 0.0031$ **c.** $0.0315 \div 0.7$ **d.** $0.00338 \div 2.6$

Oral Exercises

Place the decimal point in the quotient mentally and read it.

1. 29.61 ÷ 9 = 329 **2.** 16.3 ÷ −5 = −326 **3.** 104.4 ÷ 6 = 174

4. 4.816 ÷ 43 = 112 **5.** 129.93 ÷ 61 = 213 **6.** 135.47 ÷ 7.13 = 19

Exercises

A Round to the nearest whole number and choose compatible numbers to estimate.

1. 23.72 ÷ 4.9 **2.** 37.2 ÷ 5.78 **3.** 121.4 ÷ 40.3

4. 65.7 ÷ 8.48 **5.** 76.8 ÷ 26.1 **6.** 82.1 ÷ 9.8

Divide.

7. 33.58 ÷ 73 **8.** −0.4611 ÷ 53 **9.** 6.201 ÷ 53

10. 1.6758 ÷ 21 **11.** 129.89 ÷ 31 **12.** 87.99 ÷ (−21)

13. 4.42 ÷ 1.3 **14.** −51.3 ÷ (−1.9) **15.** 2.88 ÷ 0.18

16. 10.4 ÷ (−0.02) **17.** 109.5 ÷ 0.05 **18.** −131.58 ÷ (−8.6)

19. 3.24 ÷ 2.7 **20.** 46.08 ÷ 12.8 **21.** 27.12 ÷ 2.4

B Estimate an answer, then divide.

22. (4.63 + 25.5) ÷ 2.3 **23.** (24.7 ÷ 6.5) + 4.53 **24.** (1.3 + 1.82) ÷ 2

Evaluate.

25. $x \div 7.5$ for $x = 12$ **26.** $x \div 2.25$ for $x = 72$ **27.** $x \div 3.5$ for $x = 17.5$

Solve.

28. An insurance policy has an annual premium of $317.96 and there is an annual service charge of $2.50 if it is billed quarterly. Estimate the quarterly payments.

C Extending Thinking Skills

Find the pattern in the quotients and write one more equation.

29.
1.21 ÷ .11 = _?_
12.321 ÷ 1.11 = _?_
123.4321 ÷ 11.11 = _?_

30.
0.05 ÷ .99 = _?_
0.08 ÷ .99 = _?_
0.123 ÷ .999 = _?_

Mixed Review

Solve and check. **31.** $n + 0.65 = 1.7$ **32.** $r - 0.83 = -1.26$

Evaluate for $m = 1.63$. **33.** $m - 19.09$ **34.** $1.27 - m$ **35.** $3.2 + m$

Round to the nearest tenth and estimate the value of x. **36.** $9.02 + x = 1.49$

Write as an algebraic expression. **37.** 0.95 added to a number

4-8 Writing Equations to Solve Problems

You can use the Problem-Solving Checklist as a guide for solving problems when your plan involves the strategy **Write an Equation**.

Problem-Solving Checklist: Writing Equations

Understand the Question/Find the Needed Data
What do you need to find? Can you show the data in the problem?

Plan What to Do
Can you use a variable to represent an unknown number?
Can you represent other conditions in terms of the variable?
What is equal in the problem? Can you write and solve an equation?

Find the Answer/Check Back
Does the solution of the equation check?
What is the answer to the question in the problem?
Does the answer seem reasonable?

Example

Find the solution by writing and solving an equation. Check your answer.

Karla was running in a 26 km marathon. A friend held up a sign saying, "Only 8 km more to run." How far has Karla run?

Solution

You need to find how many kilometers Karla has run so far.

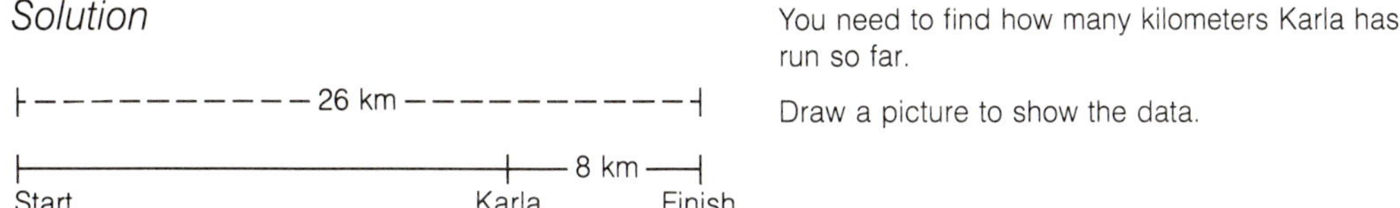

Draw a picture to show the data.

Let d = the distance Karla has run. — Choose a variable to represent what you want to find.

$$d + 8 = 26$$
$$d + 8 - 8 = 26 - 8$$
$$d = 18$$

The distance Karla has run plus 8 km is equal to the total distance of the race. Write and solve an equation.

Check $18 + 8 \stackrel{?}{=} 26$ — Check the equation solution.

$26 = 26 \checkmark$ — The equation solution checks

Karla has run 18 km. — 18 km and 8 km is 26 km. The answer is reasonable.

Practice Find the solution by writing and solving an equation. Students who sell 25 yearbooks win a radio. Karen needs to sell 6 more yearbooks to win a radio. How many has she sold so far?

Oral Exercises

Answer **a** through **e** for each problem.

a. What are you trying to find?

b. What are the important data?

c. What will the variable represent?

d. What is equal in the problem?

e. What is the equation?

1. A salesman sold $3440 worth of merchandise. This was half his goal for the month. What was his goal?

2. After Mr. and Mrs. Wong gave their children 45 rare coins, they had 129 left in their collection. How many coins were in their original collection?

3. Lupe can start driving in 3 years. If the driving age is 16, how old is Lupe now?

4. Phil saves $2 from his allowance each week. How many weeks will he have to save to buy a $36 camera?

5. Robin scored twice as many points in tonight's game as she did in last night's game. Tonight she scored 22 points. How many did she score last night?

Exercises

A Find the solution by writing and solving an equation.

1. A movie was set in a year 16 years before the year 2005. In what year was it set?

2. A theater sold $789 worth of tickets. Each ticket cost $3. How many tickets did the theater sell?

3. Mr. Bolt sold 17 fewer cars than Ms. Johnson sold. Mr. Bolt sold 53 cars. How many cars did Ms. Johnson sell?

4. A sweater costs $24.75. Dana needs $8.50 more to buy the sweater. How much money does Dana have now?

5. A runner's time was 4.52 seconds more than the school's record. The runner's time was 29.32 seconds. What was the school's record?

6. Barry spent $3.75 of his allowance. He had $4.25 left. How much was his allowance?

B

7. Jan made two dresses, using 6 m of fabric altogether. Each dress took 0.15 of a bolt of fabric. How many meters of fabric were on one bolt?

8. Elaine earns $4.25 an hour as a part-time clerk at a grocery store. Last week, she earned $85.75, which included a $5 bonus. How many hours did she work last week?

9. A number of people signed up for a recreation program. When 17 more enrolled the next day, 15 groups of 8 people could be formed. How many people signed up the first day?

C Extending Thinking Skills

Write a word problem that could be solved using the equation.

10. $x + 15 = 43$ **11.** $5x = 115$

Mixed Review

Solve and check. **12.** $t - 1.863 = -2.1$ **13.** $m + 3.6 = 8$

Evaluate for $a = 1.5$, $b = 2.0$. **14.** $2a - b$ **15.** ab **16.** $a + b - 8$

Round to the nearest whole number and estimate the product. **17.** 9.2(0.89)

CALCULATOR ACTIVITY

Some calculators have a [K] key that can be used for repeated multiplication by the same factor. The key sequence 3 [×] [K] makes 3 the repeating factor, as shown in the example below.

This key sequence completes the problems $3 \cdot 4$, $3 \cdot 6$, and $3 \cdot 9$, with the answers displayed after each press of the [=] key.

A store owner is raising all prices by the factor 1.05. Use the constant multiplier key to complete this table of new prices. Round prices to the nearest cent, if necessary.

Current price	New price
$ 53.95	$56.65
1. 72.85	
2. 92.60	
3. 126.98	
4. 361.89	
5. 455.99	

More Practice

Evaluate.

1. 12.35×0.13	**2.** $2.73 + 9.08$	**3.** $\frac{0.232}{0.02}$	**4.** $12.62 - 1.57$
5. $0.67 + 1.93$	**6.** 6.24×3.45	**7.** $8.03 - 9.99$	**8.** $\frac{-4.29}{1.65}$
9. $\frac{14.3}{-0.55}$	**10.** $15.62 - 13.77$	**11.** $4.8 + 0.673$	**12.** 9.05×4.4
13. $1.66 - 0.84$	**14.** $\frac{8.25}{3.75}$	**15.** -12.05×4.2	**16.** $-11.4 + 0.391$
17. $10.6 + 1.04$	**18.** -2.6×1.03	**19.** $11.62 - 7.92$	**20.** $\frac{15.21}{0.65}$
21. 6.05×3.2	**22.** $\frac{5.2}{-1.25}$	**23.** $8.11 + 6.84$	**24.** $44.1 - 37.6$
25. $27.04 - 1.62$	**26.** $26.1 + 13.9$	**27.** $\frac{23.1}{-6.6}$	**28.** 1.75×0.35
29. $\frac{9.45}{4.5}$	**30.** $16.74 - 3.62$	**31.** 16.2×11.5	**32.** $49.02 + 0.199$
33. 11.6×-5.2	**34.** $12.62 - 18.04$	**35.** $6.25 + 7.75$	**36.** $\frac{4.08}{2.4}$
37. $11.6 + 4.3$	**38.** $\frac{-45}{(-0.09)}$	**39.** $29.41 - 27.6$	**40.** 0.75×9.4
41. $\frac{-61.56}{8.1}$	**42.** $13.11 + 17.49$	**43.** 6.1×0.75	**44.** $3.62 - 1.99$
45. $41.35 - 9.16$	**46.** -19.25×16.4	**47.** $\frac{1.69}{1.3}$	**48.** $8.62 + 1.38$
49. $12.62 + 8.17$	**50.** $\frac{-2.07}{-0.23}$	**51.** $7.92 - 1.09$	**52.** -9.2×6.45
53. $6.34 - 4.76$	**54.** $14.02 + 6.973$	**55.** 84×7.14	**56.** $\frac{67.32}{1.02}$
57. $\frac{47.3}{-5.5}$	**58.** $8.52 - 6.66$	**59.** 10.25×2.4	**60.** $47.9 + 61.43$
61. $1.904 + 0.685$	**62.** 1.335×2.5	**63.** $\frac{33.063}{103}$	**64.** $14.11 - 16.8$
65. -4.28×1.6	**66.** $21.6 - 14.03$	**67.** $1.673 + 0.499$	**68.** $\frac{2.25}{-4.5}$
69. $3.49 - 6.004$	**70.** $16.37 + 9.642$	**71.** $\frac{-0.196}{98}$	**72.** 19.5×30.8

4-9 Solving Decimal Equations: Using Multiplication and Division

To solve an equation in which the variable has been multiplied by a decimal, divide both sides of the equation by that decimal.

Example 1

Solve and check. $0.12x = 60$

Solution

$$0.12x = 60$$

To undo multiplying by 0.12, divide by 0.12 on both sides.

$$\frac{0.12x}{\mathbf{0.12}} = \frac{60}{\mathbf{0.12}}$$

$$x = 60 \div 0.12$$

$$x = 500$$

Check

$$0.12(500) \stackrel{?}{=} 60$$

Replace x with 500 in $0.12x = 60$.

$$60 = 60 \checkmark$$

The solution is 500.

Practice Solve and check.

a. $1.5x = 225$ **b.** $0.05x = -46$

To solve an equation in which the variable has been divided by a decimal, multiply both sides of the equation by that decimal.

Example 2

Solve and check. $\frac{x}{2.15} = -1.4$

Solution

$$\frac{x}{2.15} = -1.4$$

$$\frac{x}{2.15}(\mathbf{2.15}) = -1.4(\mathbf{2.15})$$

To undo dividing by 2.15, multiply by 2.15 on both sides.

$$x = -3.01$$

Unlike signs result in a negative product.

Check

$$\frac{-3.01}{2.15} \stackrel{?}{=} -1.4$$

Replace x with -3.01 in $\frac{x}{2.15} = -1.4$.

$$-1.4 = -1.4 \checkmark$$

The solution is -3.01.

Practice Solve and check.

a. $\frac{x}{0.14} = 5.2$ **b.** $\frac{z}{-3.2} = 5.8$

Oral Exercises

To solve, would you multiply or divide in the first step?

1. $\frac{x}{2.1} = 5.98$ **2.** $-8.21y = 5.7$ **3.** $23.5z = 8.3$

4. $19.6 = 3.5w$ **5.** $\frac{u}{7.1} = -83.5$ **6.** $-19.7 = \frac{z}{-3.9}$

Exercises

A Solve and check.

1. $2.1x = 11.13$ **2.** $0.15z = 0.24$ **3.** $1.41y = -9.87$

4. $\frac{w}{6.5} = 7.2$ **5.** $\frac{z}{8.3} = -2.3$ **6.** $\frac{w}{3.2} = 48$

7. $-4.5x = 67.5$ **8.** $\frac{y}{1.7} = -3$ **9.** $3.6z = -43.2$

10. $-0.002u = -576.4$ **11.** $1.005x = 20.1$ **12.** $\frac{x}{-0.09} = 81$

13. $\frac{u}{4.98} = -1.2$ **14.** $\frac{-x}{0.55} = 0.2$ **15.** $\frac{y}{-5.4} = 3.2$

B Solve and check.

16. $-321.3 = 5.1x$ **17.** $-306.9 = 17.05x$ **18.** $21 = 67.2z$

19. $\frac{-u}{12.5} = -1.4$ **20.** $-0.91 = \frac{u}{1.2}$ **21.** $4.3 = \frac{x}{3.7}$

22. $(1\ 4 + 3.6)x = 15.5$ **23.** $\frac{x}{4.2} = 5.8 + 21.3$ **24.** $\frac{z}{8.5 - 2.3} = 25.4$

Write and solve an equation.

25. A number is multiplied by 1.2 and results in the product 264.

26. A number is divided by 3.4 and results in the quotient 25.3.

C Extending Thinking Skills

Use inverse operations to find the missing number in each flow chart.

27. Start with ? → multiply by 1.2 → Add 4.3 → end with 7.9

28. Start with 2.3 → Add 4.6 → Multiply by ? → end with 36.57

Mixed Review

Evaluate for $x = 1.5$, $y = 3.6$. **29.** $2x - 2y$ **30.** xy **31.** $2x + y$

Solve and check. **32.** $m + 1.04 = 3.1$ **33.** $-12k = 144$

PROBLEM SOLVING: STRATEGIES

4-10 Simplify the Problem

Solving some problems can be quite difficult if you try to find the solution using the numbers given in the problem. The strategy **Simplify the Problem** can help. To simplify, substitute smaller numbers. Then solve the simplified problem, and use your solution to it to help you solve the original problem.

Problem Ms. Corelli needs to install phone lines for a political convention. She has to install lines connecting each committee chairperson's desk with each of the others' desks. Ten desks are to be connected in all. A separate phone line is needed for each connection so people won't listen in on conversations. How many phone lines should Ms. Corelli install?

To solve, try **simplifying** the problem. Suppose there were only 2 desks, rather than 10, that needed phone lines. You could draw a **picture**.

If there were 2 desks, 1 line would be needed.

With 3 desks, 3 lines would be needed.

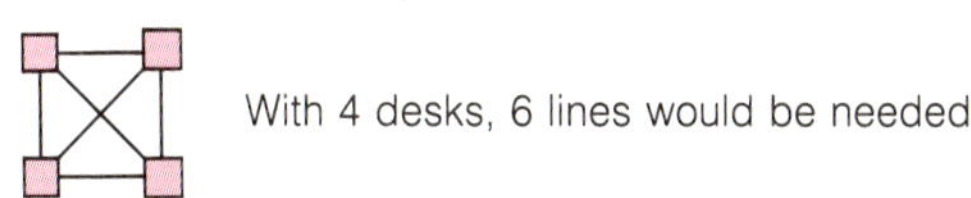

With 4 desks, 6 lines would be needed.

Recording the results from these simpler problems in a **table** helps you see a **pattern**. The difference in the number of lines needed increases by 1 each time.

Number of desks	2	3	4	5	6	7	8	9	10
Lines needed	1	3	6	10	15	21	28	36	45

Differences: 2 3 4 5 6 7 8 9

A total of 45 lines is needed to connect the 10 desks.

Problem-Solving Strategies	
Choose the Operations	Look for a Pattern
Guess, Check, Revise	Write an Equation
Draw a Picture	Simplify the Problem
Make a Table	

This chart shows the strategies presented so far. The strategy "Write an Equation" was introduced on page 121.

Problems

Solve.

1. A major company gave a large financial gift to a university. The plan was that $1 million would be given to the university the first year. In each of the following years, the university would receive an amount that was double the amount it received the previous year. What was the total amount of the gift through 12 years?

2. A grocer made a display with boxes arranged as in the illustration below. Each row had one less box than the row below it and the top row had one box. If 12 boxes were placed on the bottom row, how many were used all together?

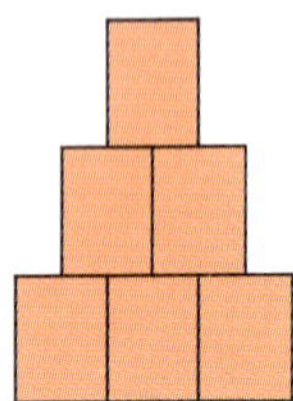

3. A 100 km bicycle race was held on roads near a large city. Markers were placed at the starting line of the race, at the finish line, and at every 10 km in between. How many markers were used for this race?

4. In a recent basketball game, the Giants beat the Lions by 25 points. The coach of the Lions said, "If we had scored twice as many points, we would have beaten the Giants by 14 points." What was the final score of the game?

5. A boat was having engine trouble. Each day, it could go forward 20 miles. At night, it had to rest its engines and would drift back 5 miles. At this rate, how many days would it take the boat to get 100 miles from its starting point?

6. A light bulb inspector found an alarmingly high number of defective bulbs in a recent shipment. Of the 25 bulbs she selected to test, she found 7 bulbs to be defective. How many might she expect to be defective out of the shipment of 275 bulbs?

Enrichment

The Binary System and the Computer

A microcomputer that has an 8-bit microprocessor processes information that is coded in strings of 8 digits of zeros and ones.

A digital computer uses only two digits, 0 and 1, to code information. Numbers are represented by a place value system called the **binary system**.

As in the decimal system, each digit in the binary system has a place value. The first seven place values are shown in red below.

Binary Place Value	64	32	16	8	4	2	1
Binary Number	1	1	0	1	1	0	1

The base 10 number represented by the binary number 1101101 is found by multiplying the digit in each place by its place value and adding together all the values.

$$\begin{aligned}(1101101)_2 &= 1(64) + 1(32) + 0(16) + 1(8) + 1(4) + 0(2) + 1(1)\\ &= 109\end{aligned}$$

Find the base 10 number represented by each binary number.

1. 1011 **2.** 1101 **3.** 110111 **4.** 100011

Chapter 4 Review

4-1 Write as a decimal.

1. $6(10) + 3(1) + 8\left(\frac{1}{10}\right)$

2. $2\left(\frac{1}{1000}\right) + 5(1) + 7\left(\frac{1}{100}\right)$

Write >, <, or = for each □.

3. -4.23 □ -4.28

4. 1.01 □ 1.010

5. 0.51 □ 0.514

4-2 Estimate the value of x by rounding.

6. $x = 94.27 - 13.66$

7. $x = 801.7 + 200.1$

8. $x = 47.27 + 15.25$

9. $x = 62.85 - 10.13$

4-3 Add or subtract.

10. $7.13 + 1.3$

11. $67.19 + 7.17 + 11.11$

12. $-3.87 + 9.75$

13. $61.3 + (-17.4) + 2.93$

Evaluate.

14. $u - 16.45$ for $u = -12.3$

15. $93.5 - t$ for $t = 6.8$

4-4 Solve and check.

16. $c - 6.29 = -4.83$

17. $e + 16.14 = -12.05$

18. $m - 8.35 = 21.06$

19. $-13.67 + n = 32$

4-5 Estimate the product by rounding.

20. 25.1×7.6

21. 3.12×96.78

22. 299.6×0.8

Find the product.

23. 7.17×3.2

24. 19.8×-0.07

25. -3.8×-9.2

26. -1462×-0.001

4-6 Solve.

27. A fence is 17.5 meters long. How many centimeters long is the fence?

28. Hector's cat weighs 4 kilograms. How many grams does the cat weigh?

4-7 Solve and check.

29. $4.4m = 92.4$

30. $-0.03x = 5.4$

31. $1.4s = 12.32$

32. $\frac{c}{0.14} = 7.1$

33. $\frac{f}{-3.3} = 1.1$

34. $\frac{h}{6.1} = -2.3$

4-8 Solve by writing an equation.

35. Ann got a $10.75 discount on a sweater with an original price of $37.90. How much did she pay for the sweater?

36. A scout troop collected 88.6 kilograms of newspaper on Saturday and 97.4 kilograms on Sunday. How many kilograms did they collect in the two days?

Chapter 4 Test

Write as a decimal.

1. $1(10) + 5(1) + 3\left(\frac{1}{10}\right)$

2. $4(100) + 6\left(\frac{1}{100}\right) + 8\left(\frac{1}{10}\right)$

Write $>$, $<$, or $=$ for each □.

3. 290 □ 7.29

4. 6.01 □ 6.1

5. −3.25 □ −3.45

Estimate the value of x by rounding.

6. $33.89 - 19.25 = x$

7. $x = 415.2 + 75.5$

8. $x = 391.37 - 106.93$

9. $59.82 + 16.05 = x$

Add or subtract.

10. $32.83 + 12.93$

11. $3.14 + 23.36$

12. $45.2 + (-2.2)$

13. $-0.33 + 24.81 + 2.66$

14. $88.2 - 35.5$

15. $-2.76 - 67.21$

Solve and check.

16. $f + 17.6 = -12.9$

17. $g - 6.43 = 29.62$

18. $38.7 + z = 25.86$

19. $18.06 + w = -7$

Estimate the product by rounding.

20. 4.38×6.1

21. 19.6×9.8

22. 1.02×0.98

Find the product.

23. 16.4×0.02

24. -71.43×-0.01

25. -9.4×8.5

26. 144.7×-0.1

Solve.

27. A container with a volume of 1 cubic centimeter has a capacity of 1 milliliter. What is the capacity of a container with a volume of 75 cubic centimeters?

28. Lisa ran a 500 meter race. How many kilometers is the race?

Solve and check.

29. $-0.5z = 3.15$

30. $1.2p = -5.76$

31. $0.18v = 3.24$

32. $\frac{a}{0.8} = -4.4$

33. $\frac{s}{-1.9} = -2.7$

34. $\frac{w}{3.8} = 4.2$

Solve by writing an equation.

35. Jorge made a deposit of \$16.50 on a \$46.50 jacket. How much does he still owe?

36. Sophie had 24.7 meters of fencing. She bought a 50-meter roll of fencing. How much fencing does she have now?

Cumulative Review

Write as a numerical expression.

1. 7 less than 18

2. 15 more than 32

3. 12 increased by 8

Write as an algebraic expression.

4. m less than 7

5. c decreased by 9

6. a number added to t

Solve the equation for the replacement set given.

7. $c + 4 = 12$ {6, 7, 8, 9}

8. $z - 8 = 8$ {13, 14, 15, 16}

9. $10 - n = 3$ {6, 7, 8, 9}

10. $4 + g = 14$ {7, 8, 9, 10}

Evaluate each algebraic expression.

11. $d + 1$ for $d = 6$

12. $h - i$ for $h = 7, i = 0$

13. $g + (-10)$ for $g = 3$

14. $35 + t$ for $t = -10$

15. $-4 - c$ for $c = 3$

16. $-5 - z$ for $z = 2$

Find the sum or difference.

17. $-2 + 6$

18. $-6 + 9$

19. $-3 + (-8)$

20. $-2 + (-3)$

21. $-6 + 19$

22. $12 + (-6)$

23. $5 - 3$

24. $-11 - 1$

25. $19 - 10$

Solve and check.

26. $x + 22 = 88$

27. $g - 31 = 17$

28. $300 + k = 414$

29. $506 = 472 - v$

30. $383 = 209 - j$

31. $365 = h + 100$

32. $p + 45 = -25$

33. $c - 77 = -30$

34. $88 = k - 1$

Solve.

35. Clyde read 4 more books this month than he read last month. If he read 10 books this month, how many books did he read last month?

36. Marquita gave some of her t-shirts away. If she had 14 t-shirts to begin with and has 8 now, how many did she give away?

37. A checking account has a beginning balance of \$405. How much money is in the account after a check is written for \$175 and a deposit is made for \$613?

38. By how much is this checking account overdrawn? Beginning balance: \$206; check for \$310; check for \$22.

Chapter 5
Number Theory

5-1 Multiples and Factors

The product of two whole numbers is a **multiple** of each of the whole numbers. The multiples of a number can be found by multiplying the number by 0, 1, 2, 3, 4, and so on.

$$0 \times 2 = \boldsymbol{0}, \quad 1 \times 2 = \boldsymbol{2}, \quad 2 \times 2 = \boldsymbol{4}, \quad 3 \times 2 = \boldsymbol{6}, \ldots$$

0, 2, 4, 6, . . . are multiples of **2**. All whole numbers that are multiples of 2 are called **even numbers**. All whole numbers that are not multiples of 2 are called **odd numbers**.

On some calculators, you can enter a number and press [+] [=] [=] [=] . . . *to display its multiples.*

Example 1

Write the first five nonzero multiples of 6.

Solution 6, 12, 18, 24, 30 Multiply 6 by 1, 2, 3, 4, and 5.

Practice

a. Write the first three nonzero multiples of 7.

b. Write the first five nonzero multiples of 9.

When two or more whole numbers are multiplied to form a product, each is called a **factor** of the product.

factors of 20 → 4 × 5 = 20 ← The product of 4 times 5

$$4 \times 5 = 20$$

When a whole number is divided by one of its nonzero factors, the quotient is a whole number and the remainder is zero. Thus, you can find out if one number is a factor of another by dividing. If the quotient is a whole number with a remainder of 0, then the divisor and the quotient are each factors of the dividend.

Example 2

Is 9 a factor of 153?

Solution $153 \div 9 = 17$ Since $153 \div 9 = 17$, with a remainder of 0,

9 is a factor of 153. then $17 \times 9 = 153$, and 9 and 17 are factors of 153.

Practice

a. Is 13 a factor of 106?

b. Is 7 a factor of 84?

To find all the factors of a whole number, divide the number by each whole number, beginning with 1. Stop dividing when the factors begin to repeat.

Example 3

Find all the factors of 12.

Solution The factors of 12 are 1, 2, 3, 4, 6, and 12.

12 ÷ 1 = 12, so **1** and **12** are factors of 12.
12 ÷ 2 = 6, so **2** and **6** are factors of 12.
12 ÷ 3 = 4, so **3** and **4** are factors of 12.
12 ÷ 4 = 3 produces no new factors. The factors 3 and 4 repeat. Stop.

Practice

a. Find all the factors of 18.

b. Find all the factors of 32.

Oral Exercises

Is the statement true or false?

1. 25 is a multiple of 5.

2. 24 is a factor of 7.

3. 4 is a multiple of 16.

4. 28 is a multiple of 4.

5. 5 is a factor of 25.

6. 32 is a multiple of 9.

7. 7 is a multiple of 35.

8. 21 is a multiple of 3.

9. 8 is a multiple of 64

10. 40 is a multiple of 5.

Exercises

A Give the first four nonzero multiples of each number.

1. 3 **2.** 5 **3.** 7 **4.** 2 **5.** 6 **6.** 8

7. 9 **8.** 10 **9.** 4 **10.** 11 **11.** 20 **12.** 100

Is the first number a factor of the second?

13. 4, 20 **14.** 5, 32 **15.** 3, 37 **16.** 8, 40 **17.** 9, 63

18. 6, 54 **19.** 8, 70 **20.** 7, 42 **21.** 4, 96 **22.** 5, 75

23. 3, 48 **24.** 2, 124 **25.** 3, 252 **26.** 4, 256 **27.** 9, 576

Find all the factors of the given number.

28. 16 **29.** 20 **30.** 28 **31.** 84

32. 40 **33.** 60 **34.** 34 **35.** 105

B

36. Solve the equations. Use the results to list all the factors of 72.

a. $1m = 72$ b. $2n = 72$ c. $3p = 72$
d. $4q = 72$ e. $6r = 72$ f. $8s = 72$

37. Solve the equation $18b = 1638$. Then give two 2-digit factors of 1638.

38. Find a number that has only two factors.

39. Find four numbers that have only three factors. Describe these numbers.

40. If n is any whole number, which expressions represent even numbers?

a. $2n$ b. $3n$ c. $4n$ d. $2n + 1$ e. $2n - 1$ f. $2n + 2$ g. $n + 2$

41. Describe five ways in which twenty-four cars can be parked in rows in a parking lot, with the same number in each row.

C Extending Thinking Skills

42. Complete these generalizations about even (E) and odd (O) numbers.

a. E + E = __ b. O + O = __ c. E + O = __
d. E × E = __ e. O × O = __ f. E × O = __

43. The number 6 is called a **perfect** number because the sum of its factors other than itself is 6. Show that 28 is a perfect number.

Mixed Review

Solve and check. **44.** $-9x = 59.4$ **45.** $m \div 3.7 = 3.92$

Evaluate for $h = -9.45$, $p = 4.5$. **46.** $(h \div p) + 2$ **47.** $2p - h + 1.75$

CALCULATOR ACTIVITY

You can use a calculator with a memory to find the factors of a given whole number quickly. First enter the number and push [M] or [M+] to record it in the calculator's memory. Then try each divisor 2, 3, 4, 5, . . . in order, as shown below.

trial divisor

This key causes the number in memory to be displayed. → [MR] [÷] 2 [=]

When the answer is a whole number, the trial divisor and the whole number are factors of the number in the memory.

Find the factors of each number.

1. 78 2. 90 3. 105 4. 210

5-2 Divisibility

A whole number is **divisible** by another whole number if, when it is divided by that number, the result is a whole number quotient with a remainder of zero. For example, **21** is divisible by ***3*** because **21** ÷ ***3*** gives the quotient 7 with the remainder 0. A whole number is divisible by each of its factors.

Every number has 1 as a factor. The divisibility rules below are shortcuts for determining whether a whole number has 2, 3, or 5 as a factor.

Divisibility by 2, 3, and 5

- A number is **divisible by 2** if its ones digit is even (0, 2, 4, 6, or 8).
- A number is **divisible by 3** if the sum of its digits is divisible by 3.
- A number is **divisible by 5** if its ones digit is 0 or 5.

The examples below show how these rules are applied.

Example 1

Is 3,764 divisible by 2?

Solution 3,764 is divisible by 2. Since the ones digit (4) is even, the number is divisible by 2.

Practice Which numbers are divisible by 2?

a. 58 **b.** 27 **c.** 36 **d.** 80 **e.** 653 **f.** 7254

Example 2

Is 560 divisible by 5?

Solution 560 is divisible by 5. Since 560 ends in **0**, it is divisible by 5.

Practice Which numbers are divisible by 5?

a. 204 **b.** 375 **c.** 800 **d.** 5,509

Example 3

Is 837 divisible by 3?

Solution 837 is divisible by 3. $8 + 3 + 7 = 18$. Since the sum of the digits is divisible by 3, 837 is divisible by 3.

Practice Which numbers are divisible by 3?

a. 81 **b.** 243 **c.** 953 **d.** 9,613

Oral Exercises

Is the digit odd or even?

1. 6 **2.** 0 **3.** 5 **4.** 8 **5.** 3

Find the sum of the digits of the number.

6. 49 **7.** 357 **8.** 986 **9.** 5,768 **10.** 57,643

Exercises

A State whether the number is divisible by 2.

1. 45 **2.** 36 **3.** 74 **4.** 67
5. 48 **6.** 170 **7.** 299 **8.** 594

State whether the number is divisible by 5.

9. 58 **10.** 75 **11.** 60 **12.** 125
13. 702 **14.** 66,345 **15.** 100,000 **16.** 400,551

State whether the number is divisible by 3.

17. 48 **18.** 63 **19.** 98 **20.** 173
21. 147 **22.** 273 **23.** 2,706 **24.** 3,195
25. 2,897 **26.** 54,623 **27.** 81,659 **28.** 97,497
29. 43,248 **30.** 386,322 **31.** 872,724 **32.** 497,333

B A whole number is **divisible by 6** if it is divisible by 2 *and* by 3. State whether each number is divisible by 6.

33. 468 **34.** 2,678 **35.** 42,672 **36.** 54,987

A whole number is **divisible by 9** if the sum of its digits is divisible by 9. State whether each number is divisible by 9.

37. 81 **38.** 342 **39.** 5,670 **40.** 8,769

A whole number is **divisible by 4** if its last 2 digits are divisible by 4. State whether each number is divisible by 4.

41. 532 **42.** 9,366 **43.** 24,847 **44.** 57,936

45. Write a rule for divisibility by 10.

46. Fill in the missing hundreds and ones digits in 3,▮4▮ so that the number will be:

a. divisible by 2 **b.** divisible by 3 **c.** divisible by 5

C Extending Thinking Skills

47. Find the smallest number that is divisible by each of the numbers 1 through 9.

48. Give an example to show that a number that is divisible by both 2 and 4 is not necessarily divisible by 8.

49. A number is divisible by 1, 5, and 7. It is not an odd number, and it is less than 100. Find the number. Find three other divisors of the number.

Mixed Review

Write $<$, $>$, or $=$ for each □. **50.** 1.01 □ 10.1 **51.** −6.25 □ −7.19

52. −0.01 □ 0.001 **53.** 0.14 □ 0.14 **54.** 4.031 □ 4.013

Evaluate. **55.** $k - 61.73$, for $k = 16.937$ **56.** $m - 10.62$, for $m = 10.637$

57. $(17 - r) + 26.1$, for $r = 16.937$ **58.** $\frac{11.776}{x}$, for $x = 5.12$

Solve and check. **59.** $r - 9.05 = 6.21$ **60.** $-1.3y = 1.69$

Use the variable n to write an equation for each statement.

61. 11 more than twice a number gives 27.

62. Half of a number equals the product of 3 and 4

MENTAL MATH

A way of deciding mentally whether a number is divisible by 3 is to "cast out multiples of 3" before adding the digits. Study the following mental steps for deciding whether the number 356,937 is divisible by 3.

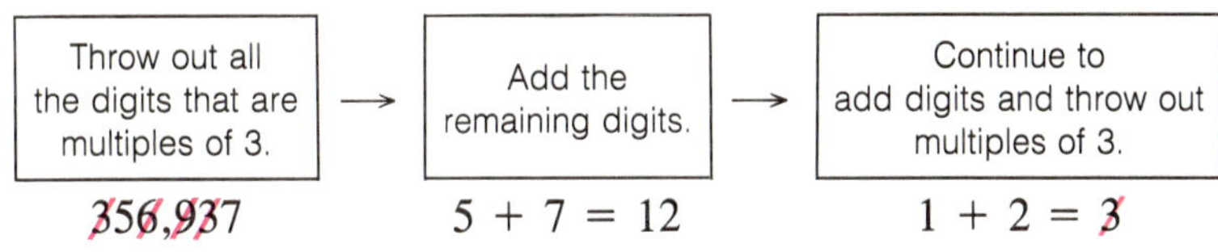

If all the digits in the original number are thrown out, or if the final digit is thrown out, the number is divisible by 3.

Cast out multiples of 3 to decide mentally whether each number is divisible by 3.

1. 919,536 **2.** 837,654 **3.** 273,649

4. 943,761 **5.** 6,589,335 **6.** 74,239,436

5-3 Writing Equations to Solve Problems

As shown in Chapter 4, the Problem-Solving Checklist can be a guide for solving problems when your plan is to write and solve an equation.

Problem-Solving Checklist: Writing Equations

Understand the Question/Find the Needed Data
What do you need to find? Can you show the data in the problem?

Plan What to Do
Can you use a variable to represent missing data?
Can you represent other conditions in terms of the variable?
What is equal in the problem? Can you write and solve an equation?

Find the Answer/Check Back
Does the equation solution check?
What is the answer to the question in the problem?
Does the answer seem reasonable?

Example

Find the solution by writing and solving an equation. Gloria had $51, which was just enough to pay for school yearbooks for herself and 2 friends. How much did a yearbook cost?

Solution Let c = cost of a yearbook — You want to find the cost of a single yearbook. Choose a variable to represent this.

$$3c = 51$$

Look for what is equal. $51 equals 3 times the cost of a yearbook.

$$\frac{3c}{3} = \frac{51}{3}$$

Write and solve an equation.

$$c = 17$$

Check $3(17) \stackrel{?}{=} 51$

$$51 = 51 \checkmark$$

The equation solution checks.

Each yearbook costs $17.

Estimate: three $20 yearbooks would cost $60. The answer is reasonable.

Practice Find the solution by writing and solving an equation. Todd divided the price of a stereo system by six to find the amount of one of six equal payments. The payment was \$84. What was the total price?

Exercises

A Solve by writing an equation. Check your answer.

1. Tim picked up a pizza for himself and three friends. Later, when they divided the cost of the pizza equally, each of them paid \$2.41. What was the total cost of the pizza?

2. A bandleader earns \$48 more per performance than the saxophonist. If the bandleader earns \$125 for a performance, how much does the saxophonist earn?

3. The even number 146 is twice an odd number. What is that odd number?

4. Sixteen years ago, Sylvia was 26 years old. How old is Sylvia now?

5. A class sold a total of 453 tickets to a play. This was three times the number they had sold on a certain day. How many did they sell on that day?

B

6. To make a 20-percent profit on an item, a store manager must sell the item for 1.2 times the amount he paid. On a compact-disc player that sells for \$354, the manager makes a 20-percent profit. Did the manager pay more or less than \$300 for it?

7. Mrs. Luzinski bought 12 video cassettes in packages of 4. She multiplied the cost of 1 cassette to find a total cost of \$84. How much did each cassette cost?

8. An egg farm shipped out 8064 eggs on Friday. The eggs were packed in boxes of 1 dozen. How many boxes were used? The boxes were packed in crates that held a dozen boxes each. How many crates were used?

C Extending Thinking Skills

9. Write a word problem that could be solved using the equation $3x = 78$.

10. Write a word problem that could be solved using the equation $x - 26 = 19$.

Mixed Review

Evaluate for $n = 9$. **11.** $n - 11$ **12.** $-n - 11$ **13.** $n + 11$

14. $-n + 11$ **15.** $n - n$ **16.** $2n$ **17.** $\frac{n}{-3}$ **18.** $6 - 2n$

Solve and check. **19.** $-3r = 8.22$ **20.** $\frac{t}{1.6} = 32.2$

21. $m - 19.26 = 0.004$ **22.** $\frac{a}{-9.2} = -6.15$ **23.** $-6.1 = \frac{x}{7.5}$

5-4 Prime and Composite Numbers

The number 5 has exactly two factors, 1 and 5. Any whole number that has exactly two factors, 1 and itself, is called a **prime number**.

Any whole number greater than 1 that has more than two factors is called a **composite number**. The number 1 has only one factor, so it is neither prime nor composite. The table below shows whether each number from 1 to 12 is prime, composite, or neither. The first five prime numbers are 2, 3, 5, 7, and 11.

Scientists have sent signals of prime number sequences into space in hopes of communicating with life on other planets.

Number	Factors	Type
1	1	neither
2	1, 2	prime
3	1, 3	prime
4	1, 2, 4	composite
5	1, 5	prime
6	1, 2, 3, 6	composite
7	1, 7	prime
8	1, 2, 4, 8	composite
9	1, 3, 9	composite
10	1, 2, 5, 10	composite
11	1, 11	prime
12	1, 2, 3, 4, 6, 12	composite

To decide whether a number is prime or composite, find and count its factors.

Example

State whether the number 14 is prime or composite.

Solution Factors of 14: 1, 2, 7, 14. Since 14 has more than 2 factors,
14 is a composite number. it is composite.

Practice State whether the number is prime or composite. **a.** 21 **b.** 17 **c.** 39

Oral Exercises

Give all the factors. Is the number prime or composite?

1. 16	**2.** 13	**3.** 15	**4.** 24
$16 = 1 \times 16$ $16 = 2 \times 8$ $16 = 4 \times 4$	$13 = 1 \times 13$	$15 = 1 \times 15$ $15 = 3 \times 5$	$24 = 1 \times 24$ $24 = 2 \times 12$ $24 = 3 \times 8$ $24 = 4 \times 6$

Exercises

A State whether the given number is prime or composite. If it is composite, give a factor of the number other than itself and 1.

1. 6 **2.** 7 **3.** 9 **4.** 14
5. 18 **6.** 22 **7.** 26 **8.** 32
9. 40 **10.** 33 **11.** 34 **12.** 45
13. 2 **14.** 49 **15.** 29 **16.** 41
17. 47 **18.** 57 **19.** 77 **20.** 51

B

21. List all prime numbers less than 25.

22. Find the smallest number for n that gives a composite value for $6n + 1$.

23. Find the smallest number for n that gives a composite value for $6n - 1$.

24. Evaluate the formula $P = (n \cdot n) - n + 11$ for $n =$ each of the whole numbers 1 through 11. For which value of n is P not prime?

C Extending Thinking Skills

25. Consecutive primes, such as 3 and 5, that have a difference of 2 are called twin primes. Find three more pairs of twin primes.

26. Continue this pattern until you arrive at a number that is not a prime.
11, 13, 17, 23, . . .

27. A mathematician named Goldbach claimed that every even number greater than 2 is the sum of two prime numbers. No one has proven this true, but no one has proven it false! Show that it is true for the even numbers 4 through 30.

Mixed Review

Solve and check. **28.** $12.3 = r + 6.72$ **29.** $n \div 0.35 = 1.75$ **30.** $2.4c = 4.08$
31. $t + 0.8 = 1.1$ **32.** $-0.09y = -45$ **33.** $m \div 3.2 = -6.05$

5-5 Powers and Exponents

A product in which the factors are identical is called a **power** of that factor. $32 = 2 \cdot 2 \cdot 2 \cdot 2 \cdot 2$, so 32 is the fifth power of 2. **Exponents** are used to write powers in short form. The exponent indicates the number of times the **base** is used as a factor.

$$2 \cdot 2 \cdot 2 \cdot 2 \cdot 2 = 2^5$$ ← **Exponent** (5); **Base** (2)

We read this as "two to the fifth power."

Other examples in which exponents are used to show powers are given below.

4^2 is 4 to the **second power** (or 4 squared) and means $4 \cdot 4$, or 16.

10^3 is 10 to the **third power** (or 10 cubed) and means $10 \cdot 10 \cdot 10$, or 1000.

3^4 is 3 to the **fourth power** and means $3 \cdot 3 \cdot 3 \cdot 3$, or 81.

a^6 is a to the **sixth power** and means $a \cdot a \cdot a \cdot a \cdot a \cdot a$.

A number raised to the first power is that number. For example, $10^1 = 10$.

To show the factors of a number expressed using exponents, you write the number in **expanded form**, also called factored form.

Example 1

Write in expanded form. Simplify if possible. 10^6

Solution $10^6 = 10 \cdot 10 \cdot 10 \cdot 10 \cdot 10 \cdot 10$ The exponent, 6, indicates that 10 is a factor 6 times.

$= 1{,}000{,}000$

Practice Write in expanded form and simplify.

a. 3^4 **b.** $(-2)^4$ **c.** a^3

Example 2

Write using exponents. $7 \cdot 7 \cdot 7 \cdot 7$

Solution 7^4 The base, 7, is a factor 4 times.

Practice Write using exponents.

a. $10 \cdot 10 \cdot 10$ **b.** $-2(-2)$ **c.** $bbbb$

To find the product of numbers expressed using exponents, you can simply add exponents to find the total number of factors in the product.

$$2^4 \cdot 2^3 = \underbrace{(2 \cdot 2 \cdot 2 \cdot 2)}_{4 \text{ factors}} \cdot \underbrace{(2 \cdot 2 \cdot 2)}_{3 \text{ factors}} = 2^{7}$$

4 factors + 3 factors = 7 factors

This leads to a rule for *multiplying* numbers with like bases.

Multiplying Powers with Like Bases

To multiply two or more powers with like bases, first add the exponents. Use this sum as the exponent together with the original base to express the product.

For any number ***a***, and whole numbers ***m*** and ***n***, $a^m \cdot a^n = a^{m+n}$

Example 3

Multiply. Give the answer in exponent form. $3^2 \cdot 3^4$

Solution $3^2 \cdot 3^4 = 3^6$ To multiply powers with like bases, add the exponents. $2 + 4 = 6$.

Practice Multiply. Give the answer in exponent form.

a. $(-5)^2 \cdot (-5)^4$ **b.** $10^2 \cdot 10^5$ **c.** $x^2 \cdot x^3$

The rule above works only when two powers with the *same bases* are *multiplied*. It does not apply when multiplying powers with unlike bases or when *adding* powers with like bases.

Example 4

Simplify. $3^2 + 3^4$

Solution $3^2 + 3^4 = 9 + 81$ Find $3^2 = 3(3) = 9$, and find $3^4 = 3(3)(3)(3) = 81$.

$= 90$ Add.

Practice Simplify. **a.** $10^2 + 10^3$ **b.** $(-5)^2 + (-5)^4$

Oral Exercises

Name the base and exponent, then read the expression.

1. 10^4 **2.** 9^5 **3.** 3^{17} **4.** 5^7

5. 11^4 **6.** 7^6 **7.** 2^8 **8.** $(-4)^{19}$

9. 12^3 **10.** $(-8)^6$ **11.** 8^{12} **12.** $(-3)^2$

Exercises

A Write in expanded form. Simplify if possible.

1. 10^5 **2.** 5^4 **3.** 7^3 **4.** 12^5 **5.** 9^3
6. $(-10)^6$ **7.** 8^2 **8.** $(-6)^3$ **9.** n^4 **10.** b^5

Write using exponents.

11. $5 \cdot 5 \cdot 5 \cdot 5$ **12.** $(-3)(-3)(-3)(-3)(-3)$ **13.** $10 \cdot 10 \cdot 10 \cdot 10$
14. $2 \cdot 2 \cdot 2 \cdot 2 \cdot 2$ **15.** $(9)(9)(9)(9)$ **16.** $yyyyyy$

Multiply. Give answers in exponent form.

17. $3^2 \cdot 3^4$ **18.** $2^4 \cdot 2^6$ **19.** $10^7 \cdot 10^3$ **20.** $(-5)^1 \cdot (-5)^3$
21. $10^5 \cdot 10^9$ **22.** $(-3)^8 \cdot (-3)^9$ **23.** $7^{23} \cdot 7^4$ **24.** $4^5 \cdot 4^8$
25. $2^3 \cdot 2^8$ **26.** $5^5 \cdot 5^2$ **27.** $3^8 \cdot 3^6$ **28.** $10^5 \cdot 10^8 \cdot 10^3$
29. $p^3 \cdot p^1$ **30.** $r^4 \cdot r^3$ **31.** $c^3 \cdot c^5 \cdot c^7$ **32.** $a^2 \cdot a^4$

Add.

33. $2^4 + 2^5$ **34.** $5^2 + 5^3$ **35.** $10^2 + 10^1$ **36.** $(-3)^4 + (-3)^2$

Simplify.

37. $2^3 + 2^2$ **38.** $(-3)^2 \cdot (-3)^3$ **39.** $5^1 \cdot 5^2$ **40.** $4^2 + 4^3$

B Write using exponents.

41. 100 **42.** 1,000 **43.** 10,000 **44.** 100,000

Evaluate the expression.

45. $y^5 \cdot y^3$ for $y = 4$ **46.** $10^a \cdot 10^b$ for $a = 2, b = 3$
47. $5^x \cdot 5^y$ for $x = 4, y = 3$ **48.** $10^a + 10^b$ for $a = 2, b = 3$
49. $10^a + b$ for $a = 2, b = 23$ **50.** $4^p \cdot 4^q \cdot 4^r$ for $p = 3, q = 5, r = 2$

Complete the equations in 51. Then answer the questions in 52–53.

51. $(-2)^1 = ?$ $(-2)^2 = ?$ $(-2)^3 = ?$ $(-2)^4 = ?$ $(-2)^5 = ?$ $(-2)^6 = ?$

52. When a negative integer is raised to an odd power, is the result a positive or a negative integer?

53. When a negative integer is raised to an even power, is the result a positive or a negative integer?

C Extending Thinking Skills

54. Jesse suggested to his parents the following plan for his monthly allowance. He would get 1 penny on the first day, 2 pennies on the second day, 4 pennies on the third day, 8 pennies on the fourth day, and so on. If Jesse's parents agree to the plan, how much should he get on the 30th day?

55. A *googol* and a *googolplex* are very large numbers that are defined as follows.

10^{100} = one googol $\qquad$ 10^{googol} = one googolplex

a. One googol is one followed by how many zeros?

b. One googolplex is 1 followed by how many zeros?

Mixed Review

Evaluate for $a = 2.5$, $b = 3$, $c = 3.25$. **56.** abc **57.** $a - c$

58. $3a - 2b + c$ **59.** $bc - a$ **60.** $bc \div (-a)$ **61.** $2a - b$

Solve. **62.** $10.4 + x = 8.7$ **63.** $9.8(x) = 22.54$

64. $396.49 - x = 177.5$ **65.** $18.4x = 86.48$ **66.** $\frac{x}{24.64} = 250.3$

ESTIMATION

To gain a feeling for certain large number amounts, it helps to compare them to powers of ten. Choose the power of ten, 10^4, 10^5, 10^6, 10^7, 10^8, or 10^9, that you would estimate is closest to each of the following amounts. Use an atlas or other reference book to check your estimates.

1. the population of the city in which you live, or the nearest large city.

2. the population of the United States.

3. the population of the world.

4. the population of the largest city in the world.

5-6 Prime Factorization

A factor tree shows a number as a product of prime factors. This factor tree shows that $24 = 2 \cdot 2 \cdot 2 \cdot 3$, or $2^3 \cdot 3$.

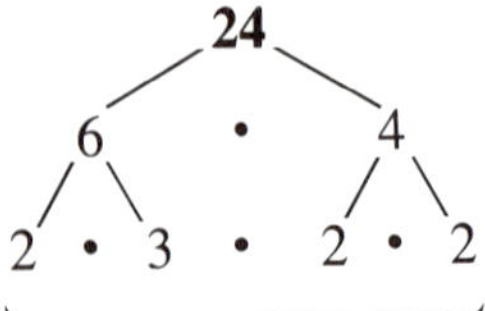

Prime factorization of 24

This expression of 24 as a product of prime factors is called the **prime factorization** of 24. We say that 24 has been **factored completely**. A factor tree for 24 that begins with $8 \cdot 3$ will have the same prime factors appearing in the bottom row, but perhaps in a different order. This suggests the following theorem.

Unique Factorization Theorem

Every composite number can be expressed as the product of prime numbers in only one way, except for the order of the factors.

Example 1

Make a factor tree to find the prime factorization of 60.

Solution

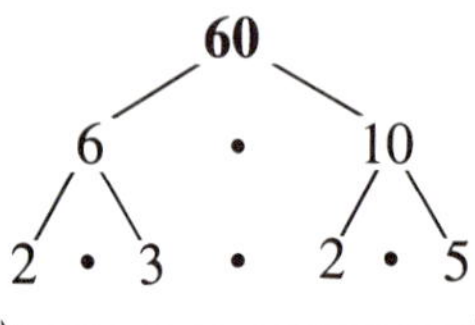

For the first row, look for any two numbers with product 60.

The prime factorization of 60 is $2 \cdot 2 \cdot 3 \cdot 5$.

Practice Make a factor tree to find the prime factorization of each number.

a. 40 **b.** 54

Example 2

Write the prime factorization of 84, using exponents.

Solution $84 = 2 \cdot 42 = 2 \cdot 6 \cdot 7 = 2 \cdot 2 \cdot 3 \cdot 7 = 2^2 \cdot 3 \cdot 7$

First find any 2 factors. Then continue to find factors until all are prime.

Practice Write the prime factorization of each, using exponents.

a. 28 **b.** 72

Another way of finding the prime factorization of a number is to use repeated division.

Example 3

Use repeated division to find the prime factorization of 60.

Solution

2|60
2|30
3|15
5|5
1

Beginning with 2, check whether each prime is a factor of the number. If it is, divide the number by the prime. Continue until you arrive at a quotient of 1.

$60 = 2 \cdot 2 \cdot 3 \cdot 5$

The product of the divisors is the prime factorization of the number.

Practice Use repeated division to find the prime factorization of each.

a. 42 **b.** 315

Oral Exercises

Give each number as the product of two factors.

1. 6 **2.** 8 **3.** 4 **4.** 9 **5.** 12

6. 15 **7.** 14 **8.** 16 **9.** 21 **10.** 26

Exercises

A Copy and complete each factor tree to find the prime factorization of each number.

1.

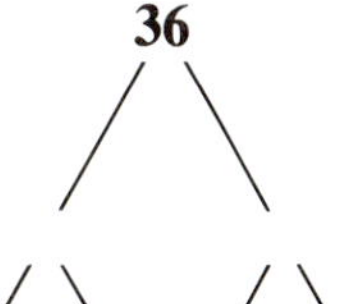

2.

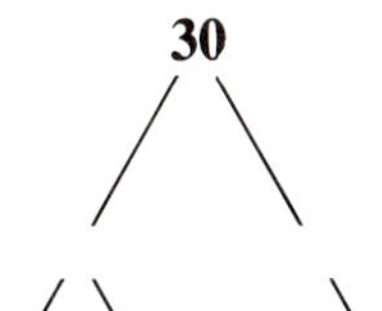

3.

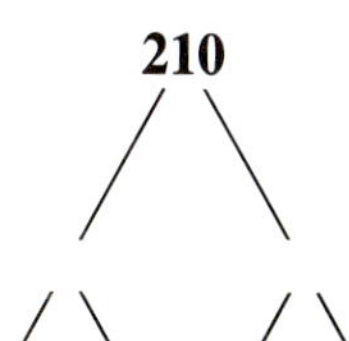

Make a factor tree to find the prime factorization of each number.

4. 32 **5.** 48 **6.** 63 **7.** 140 **8.** 150

Use exponents to show the prime factorization of each number.

9. 12	**10.** 18	**11.** 36	**12.** 45
13. 507	**14.** 75	**15.** 90	**16.** 84
17. 240	**18.** 126	**19.** 330	**20.** 288
21. 225	**22.** 236	**23.** 462	**24.** 585

Use repeated division to find the prime factorization of each number.

25. 297 **26.** 108 **27.** 216 **28.** 625 **29.** 9,282

B Solve the equation to complete the prime factorization.

30. $546 = 2 \cdot 3 \cdot 7 \cdot n$

31. $385 = n \cdot 7 \cdot 11$

32. $285 = 3 \cdot 5 \cdot n$

33. $2093 = 7 \cdot 13 \cdot n$

Solve the equation to find the number whose prime factorization is given.

34. $3^2 \cdot 5^3 = n$

35. $2^2 \cdot 3^4 \cdot 7 = x$

36. $z = 5^3 \cdot 7^2 \cdot 13$

37. $t = 2^4 \cdot 5^2 \cdot 7^3$

Use a calculator for exercises 38 and 39.

38. Evaluate the expression $n \cdot 7 \cdot 11 \cdot 13$ for the following values of n: $n = 263$, $n = 389$, $n = 59$. Do you see a shortcut for evaluating such an expression? Use the shortcut to evaluate the expression for $n = 974$.

39. Rima's teacher asked her to replace a with her age in the expression $a \cdot 3 \cdot 37 \cdot 91$, and then evaluate the expression. If Rima is 14 years old, what is the value of the expression? Evaluate the expression for $a = 23$, $a = 47$, $a = 75$, $a =$ your age. What do you discover?

C Extending Thinking Skills

40. Jeffrey's teacher told him that her age was a 2-digit number that was equal to twice the product of its digits. How old was Jeffrey's teacher?

41. Find the smallest number that has six different primes in its prime factorization.

42. Look for a pattern in the prime factorization of each of the four numbers in the sequence. Give the next two numbers. 2, 6, 30, 210, __, __.

Mixed Review

Use the variable n to write an equation for each statement.

43. 9 times the sum of 12 and a number gives 135.

44. 266 is 56 more than the product of a number and 15.

45. A number added to 36 gives the product of 5 and 4.

Solve and check. **46.** $36n = -558$ **47.** $c - 19.65 = -17.3$

5-7 Greatest Common Factor

The **Greatest Common Factor (GCF)** of two whole numbers is the greatest whole number that is a factor of *both* the numbers.

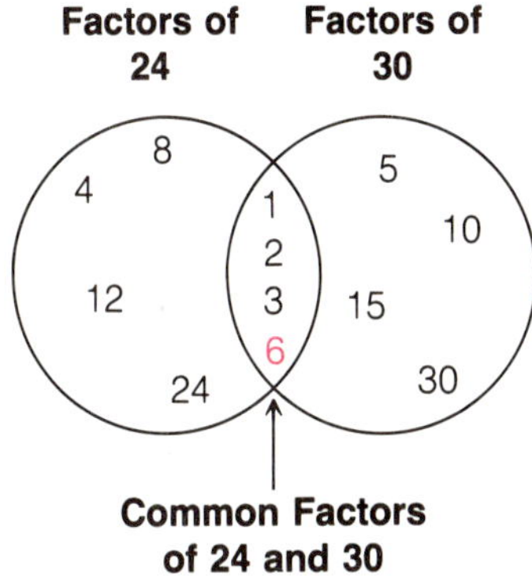

Factors of 24	**Factors of 30**
1, 2, 3, 4, 6, 8, 12, 24	1, 2, 3, 5, 6, 10, 15, 30

Common Factors of 24 and 30 1, 2, 3, 6

Greatest Common Factor of 24 and 30 6

In the example above, the factors of both numbers were listed to find the GCF. A method often used for finding the GCF of two whole numbers is to list the factors of the smaller number only, then look for the largest of these factors that is also a factor of the larger number.

Example 1

List factors of the smaller number to find the GCF of 18 and 24.

Solution Factors of 18: 18, 9, 6, 3, 2, 1 — Neither 18 nor 9 is a factor of 24.
6 is the GCF of 18 and 24. — 6 is the largest factor of 18 that is also a factor of 24.

Practice List factors of the smaller number to find the GCF of each pair.

a. 18, 27 **b.** 20, 12

Another way of finding the GCF is to use the prime factorization of the numbers. This method is useful in work with algebraic expressions. Factors that occur in the prime factorizations of both numbers are included as factors in the GCF.

Example 2

Use prime factorization to find the GCF of 36 and 60.

Solution $36 = \mathbf{2} \times \mathbf{2} \times \mathbf{3} \times 3$ Write the prime factorizations of 36 and 60.

$60 = \mathbf{2} \times \mathbf{2} \times \mathbf{3} \times 5$

GCF of 36 and 60 $= 2 \times 2 \times 3 = 12$ The GCF is the product of all the common prime factors.

Practice Use prime factorization to find the GCF. **a.** 12, 16 **b.** 24, 30

Oral Exercises

Give the GCF of the two numbers. The set of factors of each number is given.

1. 12: {1, 2, 3, 4, 6, 12}
20: {1, 2, 4, 5, 10, 20}

2. 18: {1, 2, 3, 6, 9, 18}
24: {1, 2, 3, 4, 6, 8, 12, 24}

3. 12: {1, 2, 3, 4, 6, 12}
16: {1, 2, 4, 8, 16}

4. 20: {1, 2, 4, 5, 10, 20}
28: {1, 2, 4, 7, 14, 28}

5. 21: {1, 2, 3, 7, 21}
56: {1, 2, 4, 7, 28, 56}

6. 70: {1, 2, 5, 7, 10, 14, 35, 70}
42: {1, 2, 3, 6, 7, 14, 21, 42}

Exercises

A List factors of the smaller number to find the GCF of each pair.

1. 8, 27 **2.** 18, 30 **3.** 16, 24 **4.** 21, 28
5. 12, 36 **6.** 18, 27 **7.** 48, 64 **8.** 36, 54
9. 24, 40 **10.** 30, 45 **11.** 10, 21 **12.** 16, 40
13. 27, 36 **14.** 18, 45 **15.** 32, 40 **16.** 18, 24

Use prime factorization to find the GCF of each pair.

17. 30, 105 **18.** 42, 44 **19.** 36, 54 **20.** 60, 126
21. 45, 60 **22.** 28, 42 **23.** 48, 72 **24.** 26, 51
25. 63, 84 **26.** 90, 189 **27.** 56, 90 **28.** 84, 108
29. 144, 216 **30.** 136, 162 **31.** 130, 182 **32.** 154, 192

B Use prime factorization to find the GCF of each set of numbers.

33. 12, 18, 24 **34.** 28, 42, 90 **35.** 30, 36, 48
36. 16, 28, 40 **37.** 32, 56, 72 **38.** 30, 45, 60

39. Two numbers whose GCF is 1 are said to be **relatively prime**. Are these number pairs relatively prime?

a. 9, 10 **b.** 20, 27 **c.** 165, 182

40. Carver Junior High School has 210 students in 8th grade and 180 students in 9th grade. The principal wants to divide the students into classes that are all the same size but keep the grades separate. What is the largest possible class size that could be used?

C Extending Thinking Skills

41. The number n is between 60 and 70. The GCF of n and 27 is 9. Find n.

42. A rectangular meeting room in a hotel is 66 feet by 78 feet. The room is to be covered with square pieces of carpet that are all the same size. If the square carpet pieces cannot be cut, what is the largest square piece that can be used?

Mixed Review

Simplify. **43.** $t(6 - 4)$ **44.** $6m + 9m$ **45.** $n \div (-n)$
46. $6(2c)$ **47.** $2(3x) - 4$ **48.** $9(y + 2y)$ **49.** $n - n$

Evaluate for $n = 6$. **50.** $2(4n)$ **51.** $3n + 2n$ **52.** $n(0)$

Solve and check. **53.** $2x + 3x = 45$ **54.** $-1.5c = 30$

NUMBERS TO ALGEBRA

Prime factorization is used to find the GCF of two algebraic expressions in the same way it is used to find the GCF of two whole numbers.

Numbers	Algebra
▪ Find the GCF of 108 and 120. $108 = 2 \cdot 2 \cdot 3 \cdot 3 \cdot 3$ $120 = 2 \cdot 2 \cdot 2 \cdot 3 \cdot 5$ Since 2 is a common factor twice and 3 is a common factor once, the CGF is $2^2 \cdot 3$, or 12.	▪ Find the GCF of x^2y^3 and x^3yz. $x^2y^3 = x \cdot x \cdot y \cdot y \cdot y$ $x^3yz = x \cdot x \cdot x \cdot y \cdot z$ Since x is a common factor twice and y is a common factor once, the GCF is x^2y.

Find the GCF of each pair of expressions.

1. xy^3 and x^3y **2.** $x^2y^5z^2$ and x^3y^4 **3.** $12x^3y^2$ and $18xy^3$

4. xy^2z^3 and x^2y^3z **5.** $16x^2z^3$ and $24x^3z^2$ **6.** $27ab^3$ and $45a^2b$

5-8 Driving a Car

Most states require that anyone applying for a driver's license take a written examination. Questions about reaction, braking, and stopping distances are often included in such an exam. The information in the graph below, taken from a driving manual, is important in road safety.

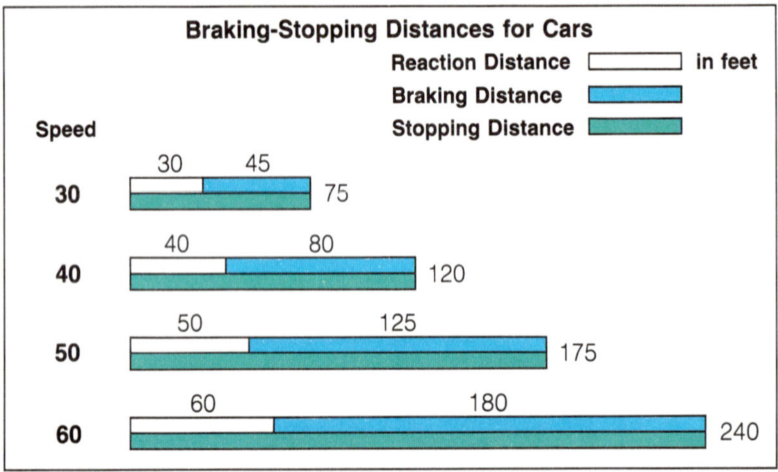

In the graph, the Stopping Distance is the sum of the Reaction Distance and the Braking Distance. The *Reaction Distance* is the number of feet the car travels *after* the driver decides to stop and *before* he or she applies the brakes.

Problems

Use the graph above to solve problems 1–4.

1. If a car is traveling at a speed of 40 mi/h and the driver sees an animal in the road, the reaction distance before the brakes are applied is the same number of feet as the speed. After the driver applies the brakes, how far will the car go before it stops?

2. What is the reaction distance when a car is traveling 60 mi/h? What are the braking and stopping distances?

3. How much farther is the stopping distance at 60 mi/h than at 50 mi/h?

4. Estimate the amount by which the stopping distance increases when a car's speed doubles from 30 to 60 mi/h. Is the increase about two, three, four, or five times the original speed?

Use the following formulas as needed to solve problems 5–12.

The ***Reaction Distance,*** **R**, in feet has been determined to be about the same as the speed the car is traveling in miles per hour.

The ***Braking Distance,*** **B**, is the distance in feet traveled after the brakes are applied:

$$\mathbf{B = 0.05R^2}$$

The ***Stopping Distance,*** **S**, is the Reaction Distance plus the Braking Distance:

$$\mathbf{S = R + 0.05R^2}$$

5. What is the braking distance when a car is traveling 70 mi/h?

6. What is the stopping distance when a car is traveling 70 mi/h?

7. Find the braking and stopping distances for the speed of 55 mi/h.

8. Some states have suggested that the speed limit be raised to 65 mi/h. How does the stopping distance at this speed compare with that at 55 mi/h?

9. If the driver of a car traveling 45 mi/h sees a truck stopped in the road ahead and immediately applies the brakes, how far will the car travel before coming to a stop?

10. A driver education instructor wanted to place 72 sophomores and 120 juniors in driver education classes so that each class would be the same size and would be as large as possible, but the grades would be kept separate. How many students will be in each class, and how many classes will be needed?

11. A highway planner wants to place rest stops at equal distances along an interstate highway connecting three cities. The distance from the first to the second city is 475 miles. The distance from the second to the third city is 285 miles. There is to be a rest stop in each of the cities, and the distance between the rest stops is to be as great as possible. How far apart will the rest stops be?

12. Data Search Find three different speed limits posted on streets in your community and calculate the stopping distance for each speed.

What's Your Decision?

How many feet of space should you keep between your car and the car in front of you for every 10 mi/h of speed? Use the data from the graph on page 154 to help you decide. Give reasons for your decision.

5-9 Least Common Multiple

The **Least Common Multiple (LCM)** of two whole numbers is the smallest *nonzero* whole number that is a multiple of *both* of the whole numbers.

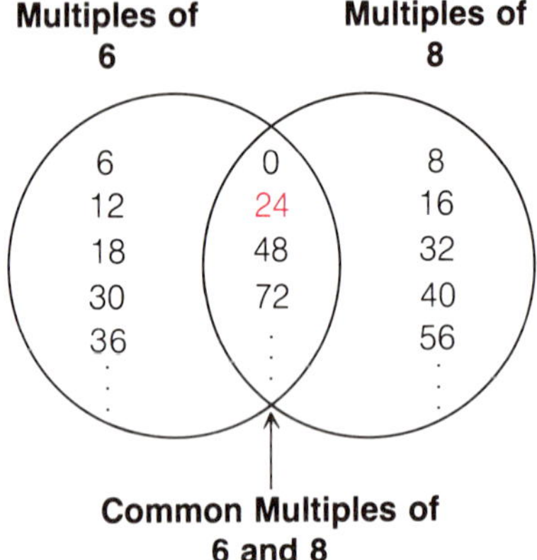

Multiples of 6
0, 6, 12, 18, 24, 30, 36, . . .

Multiples of 8
0, 8, 16, 24, 32, 40, 48, . . .

Common Multiples of 6 and 8 0, 24, 48, 72, . . .

Least Common Multiple of 6 and 8 24

In the example above, multiples of both numbers were listed to find the LCM. A method often used to find the LCM of two numbers is to list multiples of the larger number, then look for the smallest of these that is also a multiple of the smaller number.

Example 1

List multiples of the larger number to find the LCM of 9 and 12.

Solution 12, 24, 36 — Start a list of the nonzero multiples of the greater number, 12.

The LCM of 9 and 12 is 36 — Find the lowest number in the list that is also a multiple of the lesser number, 9.

Practice List multiples of the greater number to find the LCM of each pair.

a. 6, 9 **b.** 8, 12

You can use the prime factorizations of two numbers to find the LCM of the numbers. This method is useful in work with algebraic expressions. The factors in the LCM are only those factors needed so that the prime factorization of each number occurs in the LCM.

Example 2

Use prime factorizations to find the LCM of 42 and 60.

Solution

$$42 = \mathbf{2 \times 3 \times 7}$$
$$60 = 2 \times 2 \times 3 \times 5$$
$$\text{LCM}(42, 60) = \mathbf{2 \times 3 \times 7} \times 2 \times 5$$
$$= 420$$

Write the prime factorization of the lesser number. Then include factors from the greater number as needed to include the prime factorization of the greater number in the LCM.

Practice Use prime factorization to find the LCM of each pair. **a.** 12, 15 **b.** 24, 30

Oral Exercises

Give five nonzero multiples of each number.

1. 4	**2.** 5	**3.** 8	**4.** 6	**5.** 7
6. 10	**7.** 12	**8.** 9	**9.** 15	**10.** 11

Exercises

A List multiples of the larger number to find the LCM of each pair.

1. 8, 10	**2.** 4, 6	**3.** 6, 10	**4.** 6, 8
5. 8, 12	**6.** 6, 15	**7.** 9, 15	**8.** 12, 16
9. 6, 21	**10.** 9, 5	**11.** 10, 15	**12.** 8, 20
13. 6, 14	**14.** 3, 4	**15.** 4, 10	**16.** 8, 18

Use prime factorization to find the LCM of each pair.

17. 20, 25	**18.** 8, 18	**19.** 30, 70	**20.** 18, 60
21. 28, 40	**22.** 27, 36	**23.** 42, 70	**24.** 20, 24
25. 63, 90	**26.** 50, 75	**27.** 60, 80	**28.** 72, 84

B Find the LCM of the three numbers given.

29. 4, 6, 15	**30.** 8, 10, 12	**31.** 9, 12, 15	**32.** 8, 15, 18
33. 6, 12, 18	**34.** 30, 42, 48	**35.** 45, 63, 75	**36.** 30, 40, 60
37. 28, 40, 56	**38.** 27, 36, 45	**39.** 27, 45, 60	**40.** 28, 35, 56

41. What is the shortest length of ribbon that can be cut either into a whole number of 24-cm pieces or into a whole number of 30-cm pieces?

42. Suppose two race cars pass the flag at the same time and each continues to travel at a constant rate of speed. If the first car travels around the track in 24 seconds and the second car goes around in 27 seconds, how long will it be before they are at the flag at the same time again?

Using a calculator, list multiples and find the LCM of the numbers given.

43. 108, 135 **44.** 84, 126 **45.** 60, 126, 210

C Extending Thinking Skills

46. Mr. Lint goes to the laundromat every 10th day. Mr. Tidy goes every 6th day and Ms. Suds goes every 9th day. If they all go on January 1, on what date will they all go there on the same day again? (Assume that it is a leap year.)

47. Carlos said, "You can always find the LCM of two numbers by dividing the product of the numbers by their GCF. You can also find the GCF of two numbers by dividing the product of the numbers by their LCM." Test his idea with these pairs of numbers:

a. 6, 8 **b.** 10, 15 **c.** 12, 18 Is Carlos' generalization true for these three cases?

Mixed Review

Write in exponent form.

48. $x \cdot x \cdot x \cdot x$ **49.** $(-2)(-2)(-2)$

Solve and check.

50. $-12.5n = 50$ **51.** $t - 16.45 = 2.37$

COMPUTER ACTIVITY

This program finds the LCM of two numbers.

```
10 PRINT"TO FIND THE LCM"
20 PRINT "OF A AND B WHERE A>B"
30 PRINT "TYPE IN NUMBERS FOR A AND B"
40 INPUT A,B
50 FOR X=1 TO B
60 LET N = A*X
70 IF N/B=INT(N/B) THEN 90
80 NEXT X
90 PRINT "LCM(";A;",";B;")=";N
100 END
```

1. Run the program to find the LCM of 84 and 126.

2. Use the generalization suggested in exercise 47 to make additions to the program so that it will also find the GCF of the two numbers.

PROBLEM SOLVING: STRATEGIES

5-10 Make an Organized List

A strategy called **Make an Organized List** is helpful for solving problems that involve finding all possible ways to accomplish something. Making an organized list helps determine when all possible ways have been found. Consider the problem below.

Problem A computer club's members use two letters followed by three numbers to form identification codes. They use the letters C and I and the numbers 2, 3, and 4. They allow repetition of the letters, but not of the numbers. How many members can there be before they must change their method of making identification codes?

To solve this problem, you might make an organized list to show all the different identification codes that could be formed. There are four possible letter combinations, CI, IC, II, and CC. You can use these to list all possibilities systematically.

CI-234	IC-234	II-234	CC-234	Notice that the numbers starting with 2 are listed first.
CI-243	IC-243	II-243	CC-243	
CI-324	IC-324	II-324	CC-324	then the numbers starting with 3,
CI-342	IC-342	II-342	CC-342	
CI-423	IC-423	II-423	CC-423	and finally, the numbers starting with 4.
CI-432	IC-432	II-432	CC-432	

Twenty-four different identification numbers can be made from the letters C and I and the numbers 2, 3, and 4. After 24 members join the club, the system for forming ID numbers will have to be expanded.

Problem-Solving Strategies

Choose the Operations	**Look for a Pattern**
Guess, Check, and Revise	**Write an Equation**
Draw a Picture	**Simplify the Problem**
Make a Table	**Make an Organized List**

This chart shows the strategies presented so far.

Problems

Solve.

1. How many different arrangements of 3 letters can be made from the letters in the word MATH if no repetition of letters is allowed? How many of these are actual words?

2. A baseball coach listed the possible batting orders for his first four batters, Allen, Burge, Cotton, and Denby. His only requirement was that Cotton could not bat immediately after Denby. How many different batting order choices did the coach have?

3. The oil well on Mr. Greeley's property produces 19.7 barrels of oil each day. If a barrel contains 42 gallons and oil is worth $33 a barrel, how much money does the oil well yield per year?

4. When Tim puts his coins in groups of 2, 3, or 4, he always has one coin left over. He can put the coins in groups of 5 with none left over. What is the lowest number of coins Tim can have?

5. Jeral's chess club has 9 members. They are planning to have a holiday tournament in which every member plays every other member just once. How many games would be played?

6. A school with 900 students has exactly 900 lockers. The principal, who used to be a math teacher, met the students outside the building on the first day of school, and described the following weird plan. The first student is to enter the school and open all the lockers. The second student will then follow the first and close every even-numbered locker. The third student will follow and reverse every third locker by closing open lockers and opening closed lockers. The fourth student will reverse every fourth locker, and so on until all 900 students have walked past and reversed lockers. The students who can predict which lockers will remain open will get first choice of lockers. Which lockers will remain open?

Enrichment

More About Prime Numbers

Euclid, who lived about 300 B.C., proved that there is an infinite number of prime numbers. Today, mathematicians still study the properties of prime numbers, and continue to find larger and larger primes. By studying a list of prime numbers, you can find some interesting patterns and relationships. The table below shows the first 99 primes.

To use the table, notice that the 56th prime, for example, is found in the row labeled "5" and in the column labeled "6." It is 263.

The First 99 Prime Numbers

	0	1	2	3	4	5	6	7	8	9
0		2	3	5	7	11	13	17	19	23
1	29	31	37	41	43	47	53	59	61	67
2	71	73	79	83	89	97	101	103	107	109
3	113	127	131	137	139	149	151	157	163	167
4	173	179	181	191	193	197	199	211	223	227
5	229	233	239	241	251	257	263	269	271	277
6	281	283	293	307	311	313	317	331	337	347
7	349	353	359	367	373	379	383	389	397	401
8	409	419	421	431	433	439	443	449	457	461
9	463	467	479	487	491	499	503	509	521	523

1. What is the 23rd prime? the 50th prime? the 89th prime? the 99th prime?

2. Where are these in the sequence of primes? 59, 113, 227, 379, 521

3. Count the primes between 0 and 100, 100 and 200, 200 and 300, 300 and 400, and 400 and 500. Do you think the primes get fewer and fewer as the whole numbers get larger?

4. Consecutive primes with a difference of 2, such as 3 and 5, are called twin primes. How many pairs of twin primes are there in the first 99 primes?

5. How many groups of three consecutive odd numbers are there in the first 99 primes?

6. Look at the ones digit of the 2- and 3-digit primes. What do you discover?

7. If you square a whole number and add 1, will you get a prime over half the time?

8. Prime numbers 17 and 71 are "reversal primes." What other reversal primes can you find in the table?

Chapter 5 Review

5-1 Give the first five nonzero multiples of each number.

1. 5 **2.** 10 **3.** 70

Find all the factors of the given number.

4. 16 **5.** 32 **6.** 85

5-2 Tell whether the number is divisible by 2, by 3, and by 5.

7. 286 **8.** 207 **9.** 732

10. 1,345 **11.** 9,940 **12.** 6,532

5-3 Find the solution by writing and solving an equation.

13. The even number 218 is twice an odd number. What is the odd number?

14. Roberto needs 144 bottles of juice for a party. If juice comes 12 bottles to a case, how many cases does he need?

5-4 State whether the number is prime or composite.

15. 39 **16.** 24 **17.** 55

5-5 Write in expanded form. Simplify if possible.

18. 8^3 **19.** $(-6)^4$ **20.** s^6

Write using exponents.

21. $6 \cdot 6 \cdot 6 \cdot 6 \cdot 6$ **22.** $a \cdot a \cdot a$ **23.** $-2(-2)(-2)(-2)$

Multiply. Give the answers in exponent form.

24. $8^2 \cdot 8^1$ **25.** $(-3)^4 \cdot (-3)^2$ **26.** $x^3 \cdot x^2$

Simplify.

27. $3^3 + 3^2$ **28.** $(-10)^4 + (-10)^1$

5-6 Use exponents to show the prime factorization of each number.

29. 36 **30.** 75 **31.** 150 **32.** 378

5-7 Find the Greatest Common Factor (GCF) of each pair.

33. 15, 21 **34.** 39, 52 **35.** 60, 144

5-8

36. Use the formula $D = r \cdot t$ to find the rate (r) at which Greg traveled when he went the distance (D) of 100 miles in the time (t) of $2\frac{1}{2}$ hours.

5-9 Find the Least Common Multiple (LCM) of each pair.

37. 8, 12 **38.** 16, 24 **39.** 18, 32

Chapter 5 Test

Give the first five nonzero multiples of each number.

1. 3 **2.** 8 **3.** 40

Find all the factors of the given number.

4. 12 **5.** 28 **6.** 48

Tell whether the number is divisible by 2, by 3, and by 5.

7. 6,372 **8.** 4,715 **9.** 2,596

10. 9,360 **11.** 6,580 **12.** 3,505

Find the solution by writing and solving an equation.

13. Sandy has \$130 more in her savings account than she has in her checking account. If she has \$571 in her savings account, how much does she have in her checking account?

14. Diane paid \$24 for a case of 12 bottles of orange juice. What was the cost of each bottle of orange juice?

State whether the number is prime or composite.

15. 23 **16.** 56 **17.** 77

Write in expanded form. Simplify if possible.

18. 7^4 **19.** $(-2)^5$ **20.** r^7

Write each of these products in exponent form.

21. $10 \cdot 10$ **22.** $b \cdot b \cdot b \cdot b \cdot b \cdot b$ **23.** $-4(-4)(-4)$

Multiply. Give the answer in exponent form.

24. $3^3 \cdot 3^3$ **25.** $(-2)^5 \cdot (-2)^3$ **26.** $n^1 \cdot n^4$

Simplify.

27. $2^4 + 2^1$ **28.** $(-3)^2 + (-3)^3$

Use exponents to show the prime factorization of each number.

29. 48 **30.** 80 **31.** 105 **32.** 280

Find the Greatest Common Factor (GCF) of each pair.

33. 16, 20 **34.** 42, 60 **35.** 55, 121

36. Use the formula $D = r \cdot t$ to find the time (t) it took for Brad to go a distance (D) of 125 miles at a rate (r) of 50 mi/h.

Find the Least Common Multiple (LCM) of each pair.

37. 6, 15 **38.** 8, 20 **39.** 18, 30

Cumulative Review

Evaluate.

1. $5y$, for $y = 5$

2. $\frac{3a}{b}$, for $a = 6$, $b = 9$

3. $\frac{3p}{4}$, for $p = 8$

4. $3(10 - x)$, for $x = 7$

Write an equation for each verbal statement.

5. 18 less than a number m is 20.

6. 50 is the result of multiplying -5 by a number f.

Solve.

7. If you use 11 calories per minute bicycling, how many calories would you use on a 20-minute bicycle ride?

8. Sue wants to use 450 calories by swimming. How long will she have to swim if she uses 9 calories each minute?

The formula for the area of a rectangle is $A = lw$; A = area in square centimeters, l = length of the rectangle, w = width of the rectangle. Use the formula to solve the following problem.

9. What is the area of a rectangle with width 25 centimeters and length 30 centimeters?

Find each product.

10. $-6(-9)$

11. $7(2)$

12. $-5(-8)$

13. $3(-1)$

14. $-4(4)$

15. $6(-3)$

Find each quotient.

16. $-42 \div 6$

17. $-24 \div (-8)$

18. $45 \div (-5)$

19. $12 \div (-4)$

20. $-6 \div (-3)$

21. $72 \div (-8)$

Solve and check.

22. $8z = 104$

23. $204 = 17x$

24. $\frac{y}{9} = 16$

25. $-77 = 7t$

26. $-3x = 75$

27. $\frac{j}{6} = -17$

Find each product or quotient.

28. 4.42×1.09

29. -5.5×2.1

30. $-99.44 \div 11$

31. $-3.84 \div (-1.2)$

Solve and check.

32. $-0.5g = 2.60$

33. $1.5z = -6.75$

34. $\frac{s}{0.7} = -3.1$

35. $\frac{p}{-2.2} = -3.4$

Chapter 6
Rational Numbers: Addition and Subtraction

6-1 Fractions and Equivalent Fractions

The symbol $\frac{a}{b}$, where a and b are whole numbers and $b \neq 0$, is called a **fraction**. The number above the bar is the **numerator** and the number below the bar is the **denominator**. A fraction can describe a region or a set. Fractions that show the same amount are called **equivalent fractions**.

This region is divided into equal parts. The fractions $\frac{3}{4}$ and $\frac{6}{8}$ name the same part of the region.

Notice that $\frac{3}{4} = \frac{3 \cdot 2}{4 \cdot 2} = \frac{6}{8}$ and $\frac{6}{8} = \frac{6 \div 2}{8 \div 2} = \frac{3}{4}$.

Property of Equivalent Fractions

Multiplying or dividing both the numerator and denominator of a fraction by the same nonzero integer results in an equivalent fraction.

For all numbers **a, b,** and **c,** **($b \neq 0, c \neq 0$)**

$\frac{a}{b} = \frac{a \cdot c}{b \cdot c}$ and $\frac{a}{b} = \frac{a \div c}{b \div c}$

Example 1

Write an equivalent fraction by replacing the variable with a whole number.

a. $\frac{3}{8} = \frac{x}{24}$ **b.** $\frac{20}{25} = \frac{y}{5}$

Solution **a.** $\frac{3}{8} = \frac{9}{24}$ Since $8 \times 3 = 24$, multiply the numerator by 3.

b. $\frac{20}{25} = \frac{4}{5}$ Since $25 \div 5 = 5$, divide the numerator by 5.

Practice Write an equivalent fraction by replacing the variable with a whole number.

a. $\frac{3}{5} = \frac{x}{60}$ **b.** $\frac{7}{15} = \frac{y}{75}$

If two fractions are equivalent, their **cross products** are equal. And if the cross products are equal, the fractions are equivalent.

$$5 \cdot 36 = 180 \qquad \frac{5}{12} = \frac{15}{36} \qquad 12 \cdot 15 = 180$$

Example 2

Check cross products to decide whether $\frac{15}{25}$ and $\frac{5}{8}$ are equivalent.

Solution

$$\frac{15}{25} \stackrel{?}{=} \frac{5}{8}$$

$15 \cdot 8 \quad 25 \cdot 5$ Find the cross products.

$$120 \neq 125$$

$$\frac{15}{25} \neq \frac{5}{8}$$

Practice Check cross products to decide whether each pair of fractions is equivalent.

a. $\frac{3}{5}, \frac{12}{20}$ **b.** $\frac{7}{12}, \frac{28}{48}$

A fraction is in **lowest terms** when the only common factor of the numerator and denominator is 1. One way to reduce a fraction to lowest terms is to divide the numerator and denominator by the greatest common factor. Another is to factor the numerator and denominator into prime factors and divide common factors.

Example 3

Reduce to lowest terms. $\frac{24}{36}$

Solution

Method 1

$\frac{24}{36} = \frac{24 \div 12}{36 \div 12} = \frac{2}{3}$ The GCF of 24 and 36 is 12. Divide both the numerator and the denominator by 12.

Method 2

$\frac{24}{36} = \frac{2 \cdot 2 \cdot 2 \cdot 3}{2 \cdot 2 \cdot 3 \cdot 3}$ Factor 24 and 36 into prime factors.

$= \frac{\cancel{2} \cdot \cancel{2} \cdot 2 \cdot \cancel{3}}{\cancel{2} \cdot \cancel{2} \cdot 3 \cdot \cancel{3}} = \frac{2}{3}$ Divide common factors.

Practice Reduce to lowest terms. **a.** $\frac{18}{36}$ **b.** $\frac{70}{105}$

Oral Exercises

Give two equivalent fractions for each figure.

1. 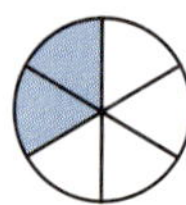

2. 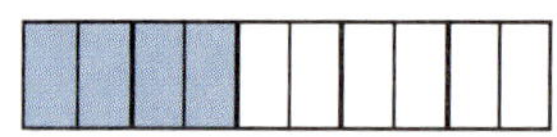

3. 

Exercises

A Write an equivalent fraction by replacing the variable with a whole number.

1. $\frac{7}{15} = \frac{x}{30}$
2. $\frac{1}{2} = \frac{y}{36}$
3. $\frac{18}{30} = \frac{t}{5}$
4. $\frac{4}{9} = \frac{d}{27}$
5. $\frac{16}{64} = \frac{g}{4}$
6. $\frac{2}{3} = \frac{x}{54}$
7. $\frac{5}{6} = \frac{m}{60}$
8. $\frac{56}{80} = \frac{n}{10}$
9. $\frac{13}{15} = \frac{x}{75}$
10. $\frac{5}{18} = \frac{y}{90}$
11. $\frac{49}{140} = \frac{a}{20}$
12. $\frac{156}{240} = \frac{b}{60}$
13. $\frac{7}{12} = \frac{k}{60}$
14. $\frac{8}{9} = \frac{h}{108}$
15. $\frac{72}{150} = \frac{x}{25}$
16. $\frac{25}{60} = \frac{y}{240}$

Check cross products to decide which pairs of fractions are equivalent.

17. $\frac{2}{3}, \frac{4}{9}$
18. $\frac{3}{5}, \frac{9}{15}$
19. $\frac{4}{7}, \frac{8}{14}$
20. $\frac{4}{10}, \frac{6}{15}$
21. $\frac{4}{14}, \frac{6}{21}$
22. $\frac{5}{7}, \frac{35}{49}$
23. $\frac{12}{54}, \frac{2}{9}$
24. $\frac{7}{12}, \frac{3}{4}$

Reduce each fraction to lowest terms.

25. $\frac{40}{52}$
26. $\frac{24}{60}$
27. $\frac{48}{84}$
28. $\frac{66}{102}$
29. $\frac{68}{76}$
30. $\frac{108}{156}$
31. $\frac{36}{54}$
32. $\frac{78}{112}$
33. $\frac{52}{56}$
34. $\frac{105}{126}$
35. $\frac{66}{378}$
36. $\frac{231}{351}$
37. $\frac{9}{21}$
38. $\frac{6}{54}$
39. $\frac{21}{35}$
40. $\frac{14}{56}$
41. $\frac{42}{90}$
42. $\frac{15}{21}$
43. $\frac{63}{81}$
44. $\frac{88}{121}$

B Give two pairs of values for x and y that will make equivalent fractions.

45. $\frac{3}{8}, \frac{x}{y}$
46. $\frac{7}{12}, \frac{x}{y}$
47. $\frac{20}{32}, \frac{x}{y}$
48. $\frac{18}{36}, \frac{x}{y}$
49. $\frac{5}{16}, \frac{x}{y}$
50. $\frac{3}{30}, \frac{x}{y}$
51. $\frac{24}{60}, \frac{x}{y}$
52. $\frac{1}{23}, \frac{x}{y}$

Check cross products to decide which pairs of fractions are equivalent.

53. $\frac{12}{25}, \frac{60}{125}$
54. $\frac{7}{9}, \frac{63}{88}$
55. $\frac{9}{13}, \frac{45}{72}$
56. $\frac{6}{15}, \frac{42}{105}$
57. $\frac{91}{124}, \frac{7}{8}$
58. $\frac{3}{18}, \frac{15}{80}$
59. $\frac{24}{36}, \frac{144}{216}$
60. $\frac{35}{64}, \frac{245}{428}$

C Extending Thinking Skills

61. Is the generalization $\frac{a}{b} = \frac{a + c}{b + c}$ true or false?

62. Find all the ways in which the numbers 2, 4, 8, and 16 can be placed in the squares at right to complete a true statement.

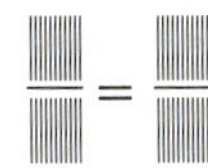

63. Find all the ways in which any four of the numbers 2, 3, 4, 5, 6, 7, 8, 9, and 10 can be placed in the squares to make a true statement.

Mixed Review

Simplify. **64.** $9c - 16c$ **65.** $4m + 2m - m$ **66.** $7x + 5 + 4x$

67. $4(3r) - 10 + 2r$ **68.** $6(y + 4y) + 3y$ **69.** $t + t + t$

70. $p^2 \cdot p^2 \cdot p^4$ **71.** $a \cdot a \cdot a$ **72.** $3^5 \cdot 3^{11}$

Find the greatest common factor (GCF). **73.** 25, 80 **74.** 12, 21

Solve and check. **75.** $14.7 = 9.35 - c$ **76.** $1.5n = -6$

Evaluate for $y = 1.6$. **77.** $y^2 + 4$ **78.** $y^2(y + 2)$

NUMBERS TO ALGEBRA

You can reduce fractional expressions in algebra in the same way you reduce fractions in arithmetic.

Numbers	Algebra
$\frac{6}{15} = \frac{2 \cdot \cancel{3}}{5 \cdot \cancel{3}} = \frac{2}{5}$	$\frac{2a\cancel{n}}{5b\cancel{n}} = \frac{2a\cancel{n}}{5b\cancel{n}} = \frac{2a}{5b}$
$\frac{15}{21} = \frac{\cancel{3} \cdot 5}{7 \cdot \cancel{3}} = \frac{5}{7}$	$\frac{6\cancel{x}}{15\cancel{x}y} = \frac{2 \cdot \cancel{3} \cdot \cancel{x}}{\cancel{3} \cdot 5 \cdot \cancel{x} \cdot y} = \frac{2}{5y}$
$\frac{30}{70} = \frac{\cancel{2} \cdot 3 \cdot \cancel{5}}{\cancel{2} \cdot \cancel{5} \cdot 7} = \frac{3}{7}$	$\frac{4m\cancel{n}}{9\cancel{n}} = \frac{2 \cdot 2 \cdot m \cdot \cancel{n}}{3 \cdot 3 \cdot \cancel{n}} = \frac{4m}{9}$

Reduce to lowest terms. The variables a, b, and c represent distinct whole numbers, not including 0.

1. $\frac{2a}{3a}$ **2.** $\frac{5ab}{25a}$ **3.** $\frac{21a}{24b}$

4. $\frac{15ab}{48b}$ **5.** $\frac{abc}{2bc}$ **6.** $\frac{46ab}{48bc}$

7. $\frac{96a}{24bc}$ **8.** $\frac{18c}{12ac}$ **9.** $\frac{15a}{35a}$

10. $\frac{51ab}{102bc}$ **11.** $\frac{24c}{70ac}$ **12.** $\frac{17a^2}{34ab}$

6-2 Improper Fractions and Mixed Numbers

A tailor uses about $4\frac{1}{2}$ yards of fabric to make a suit.

A fraction is a **proper fraction** if its numerator is less than its denominator. If its numerator is greater than or equal to its denominator, it is an **improper fraction**. For example, $\frac{4}{5}$ is a proper fraction, but $\frac{5}{4}$ is an improper fraction. When an improper fraction is written as an integer and a fraction, it is called a mixed numeral or **mixed number**. As shown below, the improper fraction $\frac{5}{4}$ is the same as the mixed number $1\frac{1}{4}$.

$\frac{5}{4} = 1\frac{1}{4}$

To change an improper fraction to a mixed number, use the fact that a fraction $\frac{a}{b}$ can be interpreted as $a \div b$.

Example 1

Write as an integer or mixed number. $\frac{19}{7}$

Solution

$$\begin{array}{r} 2 \\ 7\overline{)19} \\ \underline{14} \\ 5 \end{array}$$

$\frac{19}{7}$ means $19 \div 7$.

$\frac{19}{7} = 2\frac{5}{7}$ Write the quotient as the integer. Write the remainder over the divisor as the proper fraction.

Practice Write each as an integer or a mixed number.

a. $\frac{11}{3}$ **b.** $\frac{24}{4}$ **c.** $\frac{36}{7}$

Example 2

Write as an improper fraction in lowest terms. $3\frac{1}{7}$

Solution

$3\frac{1}{7}$

$3 \cdot 7 + 1 = 22$ There are $3 \cdot 7$ or 21 sevenths in the 3 whole units. 21 sevenths plus 1 seventh equal 22 sevenths.

$3\frac{1}{7} = \frac{22}{7}$

Practice Write each as an improper fraction in lowest terms.

a. $4\frac{3}{4}$ **b.** $5\frac{1}{3}$ **c.** $7\frac{3}{10}$

Oral Exercises

Give an improper fraction and a mixed number for each.

1. 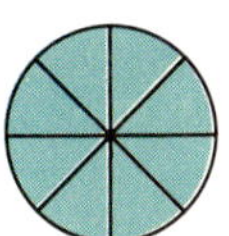

2. 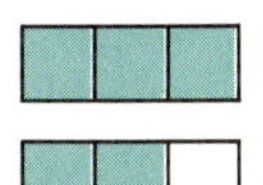

3. 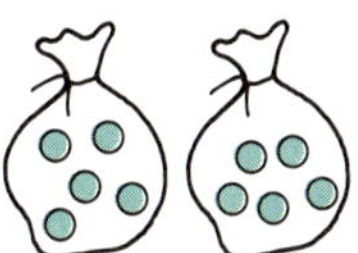 

Exercises

A Write each as an integer or a mixed number.

1. $\frac{25}{6}$ **2.** $\frac{41}{7}$ **3.** $\frac{51}{3}$ **4.** $\frac{17}{11}$

5. $\frac{91}{11}$ **6.** $\frac{238}{10}$ **7.** $\frac{121}{11}$ **8.** $\frac{215}{15}$

9. $\frac{342}{100}$ **10.** $\frac{75}{8}$ **11.** $\frac{80}{16}$ **12.** $\frac{230}{25}$

13. $\frac{290}{25}$ **14.** $\frac{75}{12}$ **15.** $\frac{35}{10}$ **16.** $\frac{440}{100}$

Write each as an improper fraction in lowest terms.

17. $3\frac{7}{8}$ **18.** $4\frac{2}{3}$ **19.** $2\frac{9}{16}$ **20.** $3\frac{6}{15}$

21. $5\frac{7}{9}$ **22.** $7\frac{9}{30}$ **23.** $8\frac{2}{3}$ **24.** $9\frac{7}{11}$

25. $13\frac{7}{10}$ **26.** $15\frac{3}{50}$ **27.** $11\frac{3}{20}$ **28.** $21\frac{7}{8}$

29. $5\frac{3}{51}$ **30.** $7\frac{53}{100}$ **31.** $9\frac{71}{80}$ **32.** $5\frac{31}{40}$

B Evaluate each expression. Write as a mixed number.

33. $\frac{a}{b}$ for $a = 23$ and $b = 5$

34. $\frac{u}{v}$ for $u = 27$ and $v = 11$

35. $\frac{x}{y}$ for $x = 73$ and $y = 17$

36. $\frac{n}{m}$ for $n = 41$ and $m = 12$

37. $\frac{2x}{y}$ for $x = 33$ and $y = 5$

38. $\frac{3a}{2b}$ for $a = 13$ and $b = 7$

C Extending Thinking Skills

39. Find how many ways the numbers 1, 2, 3, 4, and 7 can be placed in the boxes to make a true statement. Numbers may be repeated more than once. The fraction part of the mixed number should be less than 1.

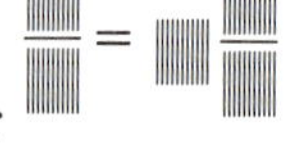

40. Write a generalization for changing any mixed number $a\frac{b}{c}$ to an improper fraction.

Mixed Review

Give the prime factorization of each. **41.** 30 **42.** 27

Evaluate for $a = 1.5$, $b = 2.75$, $c = 3$. **43.** abc **44.** $a(c + b)$

Tell whether the number is prime or composite. **45.** 53 **46.** 15

Write and solve an equation. **47.** A number divided by 5 gives 8.

Solve and check. **48.** $120 - z = 64.37$ **49.** $6m = -36.138$

COMPUTER ACTIVITY

This computer program will reduce the fraction $\frac{A}{B}$ to lowest terms.

```
5 PRINT "TYPE IN THE NUMERATOR AND THE DENOMINATOR OF
YOUR FRACTION SEPARATED BY A COMMA."
10 INPUT N,D
20 T = ABS(N):B=ABS(D)
30 X=INT(T/B):R=T-X*B
40 IF R=0 THEN GOTO 60
50 T=B:B=R: GOTO 30
60 PRINT "THE REDUCED FRACTION IS ";N/B;"/";D/B
70 END
```

Run the program for each fraction.

a. $\frac{2,945}{32,395}$ **b.** $\frac{12,369}{11,994,447}$ **c.** $\frac{1,351,350}{11,781}$

6-3 Rational Numbers

A number that can be expressed in the fractional form $\frac{a}{b}$, where $\boldsymbol{a}$ and $\boldsymbol{b}$ are integers and $\boldsymbol{b \neq 0}$, is called a **rational number**. Each rational number corresponds to *one* set of equivalent fractions and names one point on the number line. For example, in the set $\{\frac{2}{3}, \frac{4}{6}, \frac{6}{9}, \frac{8}{12}, \ldots\}$ each fraction names the same rational number.

The number line below shows points for some rational numbers expressed as fractions or mixed numbers.

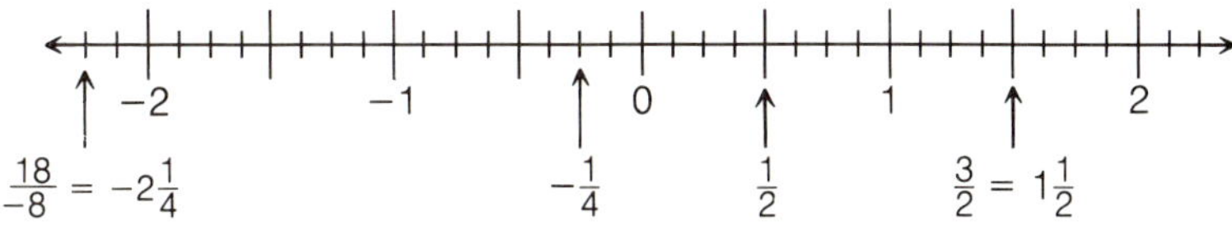

Whole numbers, integers, and certain decimals are rational numbers because they can be expressed as fractions. For example:

$$4 = \frac{4}{1} \qquad -5 = \frac{-5}{1} \qquad 0.3 = \frac{3}{10}$$

The opposite of a negative rational number is a positive rational number. The opposite of a positive rational number is a negative rational number. There are three ways to show a negative rational number.

Example 1

Write the opposite of $\frac{3}{5}$ in three different ways.

Solution

$-\frac{3}{5}, \frac{-3}{5}, \frac{3}{-5}$ The negative sign can precede the entire fraction, precede the numerator, or precede the denominator.

Practice Write the opposite of each in three different ways.

a. $\frac{5}{6}$ **b.** $\frac{7}{3}$ **c.** $\frac{11}{12}$ **d.** $\frac{15}{9}$

Example 2

Graph the following rational numbers.

$-\frac{1}{4}, \frac{3}{4}, -\frac{6}{4}, \frac{6}{4}$

Solution

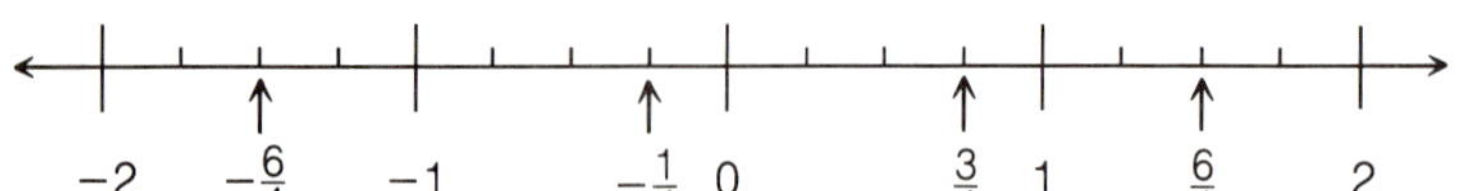

Divide the number line into fourths between integers.

Practice Graph the following rational numbers.

$-\frac{3}{8}, -2, \frac{5}{8}, \frac{1}{8}, \frac{9}{8}$

Oral Exercises

Give the rational number for each point.

1. A B C D

−3 −2 −1 0 1 2 3

2. A B C D

−1 0 1

3. 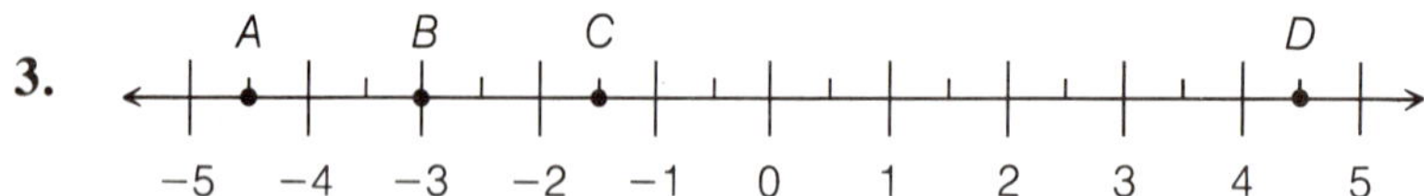

Exercises

A Write the opposite of each in three different ways.

1. $\frac{3}{8}$	**2.** $\frac{2}{9}$	**3.** $\frac{11}{16}$	**4.** $\frac{5}{6}$
5. $\frac{5}{2}$	**6.** $\frac{4}{9}$	**7.** $\frac{3}{2}$	**8.** $\frac{1}{10}$
9. $\frac{3}{7}$	**10.** $\frac{12}{5}$	**11.** $\frac{3}{16}$	**12.** $\frac{6}{5}$
13. $\frac{9}{12}$	**14.** $\frac{23}{100}$	**15.** $\frac{18}{24}$	**16.** $\frac{75}{125}$

Graph the rational numbers.

17. $1\frac{2}{3}, \frac{1}{3}, \frac{2}{3}, 1\frac{1}{3}$

18. $1\frac{2}{5}, \frac{2}{5}, \frac{3}{5}, 2$

19. $-\frac{1}{4}, -1\frac{3}{4}, \frac{4}{4}, -1$

20. $\frac{1}{6}, -\frac{4}{6}, -\frac{5}{6}, \frac{5}{6}$

21. $3\frac{1}{2}, 2, \frac{1}{2}, 1\frac{1}{2}, \frac{5}{2}$

22. $\frac{2}{7}, 1\frac{1}{7}, \frac{4}{7}, \frac{12}{7}$

23. $-\frac{2}{4}, \frac{3}{4}, -\frac{5}{4}, -2, \frac{1}{4}$

24. $1\frac{1}{3}, -\frac{5}{3}, -2, \frac{2}{3}, \frac{8}{3}$

25. $\frac{1}{8}, -\frac{3}{8}, -\frac{5}{8}, \frac{6}{8}, \frac{7}{8}$

26. $\frac{1}{5}, 0, 1, \frac{10}{5}, \frac{4}{5}, \frac{2}{5}$

B Write the opposite of each expression.

27. $\frac{3}{x}$ **28.** $-\frac{2}{y}$ **29.** $-\frac{h}{2}$ **30.** $\frac{t}{7}$

31. $-\frac{6}{n}$ **32.** $\frac{y}{10}$ **33.** $-\frac{12}{m}$ **34.** $-\frac{x}{100}$

Evaluate each expression for the values given.

35. $\frac{x + y}{x}, x = 5, y = -2$

36. $\frac{a + b}{c + d}, a = 4, b = 6, c = -5, d = 12$

37. $\frac{2a + 1}{b}, a = 7, b = 2$

38. $\frac{5x - 2}{3y}, x = -2, y = 4$

C Extending Thinking Skills

Find the pattern and complete each sequence.

39. $\frac{1}{3}, -\frac{1}{5}, \frac{1}{7}, -\frac{1}{9}, \frac{1}{11}$, —, —, —

40. $-\frac{1}{4}, -\frac{1}{2}, -\frac{3}{4}, -1, -1\frac{1}{4}$, —, —, —

Mixed Review

Simplify. **41.** $(3m + 2n) + (m + 6n)$ **42.** $7(m + 2) + (m + 3)$

Solve and check. **43.** $2a = -7.562$ **44.** $r + 2.695 = -8.305$

ESTIMATION

You can think about a number line to estimate what integer is closest to a given fraction or mixed number.

Estimate.

1. $5\frac{3}{8}$ **2.** $-1\frac{7}{8}$ **3.** $-\frac{1}{3}$

4. $1\frac{1}{5}$ **5.** $-4\frac{1}{4}$ **6.** $-4\frac{5}{6}$

6-4 Comparing and Ordering Rational Numbers

You can use a number line to compare rational numbers. On the number line below, -2 is to the left of $-1\frac{1}{2}$; $-\frac{5}{8}$ is to the left of $-\frac{1}{8}$; and $1\frac{7}{8}$ is to the right of $1\frac{1}{8}$.

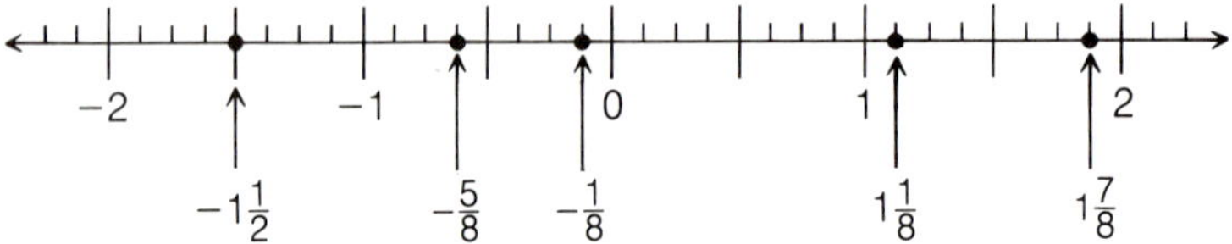

You can show these relationships as:

$$-2 < -1\frac{1}{2} \qquad -\frac{5}{8} < -\frac{1}{8} \qquad 1\frac{7}{8} > 1\frac{1}{8}$$

When two fractions have the same sign, you can compare them by changing them to equivalent fractions with like denominators or to decimals.

Example 1

Write >, <, or = for □. Use equivalent fractions to decide.

$\frac{5}{6} \square \frac{7}{8}$

Solution

$\frac{5}{6} = \frac{20}{24}$ Change $\frac{5}{6}$ and $\frac{7}{8}$ to fractions with like denominators. 24 is the least common multiple of 6 and 8.

$\frac{7}{8} = \frac{21}{24}$

$\frac{5}{6} < \frac{7}{8}$ Since $20 < 21$, $\frac{20}{24} < \frac{21}{24}$, so $\frac{5}{6} < \frac{7}{8}$.

Practice Write <, >, or = for each □.

a. $\frac{3}{5} \square \frac{4}{7}$ **b.** $-\frac{5}{12} \square -\frac{3}{8}$

You can use the fact that $\frac{a}{b}$ means $a \div b$ to change a rational number to a decimal. Since some decimals are repeating or very long, you may choose to round the decimal.

Example 2

Write $<$, $>$, or $=$ for $\square$. Use decimals rounded to the nearest thousandth to decide. $\frac{4}{9} \square \frac{3}{8}$

Solution

$$\begin{array}{r} 0.4444 \\ 9\overline{)4.0000} \\ \underline{3\,6} \\ 40 \\ \underline{36} \\ 40 \\ \underline{36} \\ 40 \\ \underline{36} \\ 4 \end{array} \qquad \begin{array}{r} 0.375 \\ 8\overline{)3.000} \\ \underline{2\,4} \\ 60 \\ \underline{56} \\ 40 \\ \underline{40} \\ 0 \end{array}$$

Annex zeros and divide to the ten thousandths place if necessary. Round to the nearest thousandth. $\frac{4}{9} = 0.444$ and $\frac{3}{8} = 0.375$.

$\frac{4}{9} > \frac{3}{8}$ — $0.444 > 0.375$, so $\frac{4}{9} > \frac{3}{8}$.

Practice Write $<$, $>$, or $=$ for $\square$. Use decimals rounded to the nearest thousandth to decide. **a.** $\frac{5}{8} \square \frac{7}{12}$ **b.** $-\frac{4}{5} \square -\frac{5}{7}$

When two fractions are equivalent, their cross products are equal. You can use this fact to compare positive rational numbers.

Comparing Positive Rational Numbers

To compare two positive rational numbers, compare their cross products. For integers ***a, b, c,*** and ***d,***

$\frac{a}{b} < \frac{c}{d}$ if $ad < bc$ and $\frac{a}{b} > \frac{c}{d}$ if $ad > bc$

Example 3

Write $<$, $>$, or $=$ for $\square$. Use cross products to decide.

$\frac{5}{9} \square \frac{4}{7}$

Solution $\frac{5}{9} \square \frac{4}{7}$

$5 \cdot 7 \quad 9 \cdot 4$ — First find the cross products. The rational numbers compare as their cross products compare.

$35 < 36$

$\frac{5}{9} < \frac{4}{7}$ — $35 < 36$, so $\frac{5}{9} < \frac{4}{7}$.

Practice Write $<$, $>$, or $=$ for each $\square$. Use cross products to decide.

a. $\frac{5}{6} \square \frac{4}{7}$ **b.** $\frac{9}{13} \square \frac{8}{15}$

Oral Exercises

Tell which rational number is greater.

1. $\frac{5}{7}, \frac{6}{7}$ **2.** $-\frac{4}{18}, -\frac{5}{18}$ **3.** $\frac{5}{9}, \frac{4}{9}$ **4.** $-\frac{15}{12}, -\frac{11}{12}$ **5.** $-\frac{5}{2}, -\frac{1}{2}$

Exercises

A Write <, >, or = for each □. Use equivalent fractions to decide.

1. $\frac{2}{5} \square \frac{3}{7}$ **2.** $-\frac{13}{18} \square -\frac{2}{3}$ **3.** $\frac{3}{4} \square \frac{5}{8}$ **4.** $-\frac{3}{8} \square -\frac{5}{17}$

5. $\frac{5}{13} \square \frac{6}{15}$ **6.** $\frac{35}{51} \square \frac{2}{3}$ **7.** $\frac{25}{54} \square \frac{4}{9}$ **8.** $\frac{29}{32} \square \frac{7}{8}$

Write <, >, or = for each □. Use decimals rounded to the nearest thousandth to decide.

9. $-\frac{5}{9} \square -\frac{7}{12}$ **10.** $\frac{4}{5} \square \frac{2}{3}$ **11.** $\frac{4}{9} \square \frac{3}{7}$ **12.** $\frac{17}{30} \square \frac{3}{5}$

13. $\frac{3}{5} \square \frac{7}{10}$ **14.** $-\frac{5}{6} \square -\frac{6}{8}$ **15.** $\frac{11}{12} \square \frac{13}{15}$ **16.** $\frac{7}{9} \square \frac{8}{10}$

17. $-\frac{5}{8} \square -\frac{7}{10}$ **18.** $\frac{2}{3} \square \frac{8}{11}$ **19.** $\frac{9}{16} \square \frac{8}{15}$ **20.** $-\frac{3}{7} \square -\frac{9}{16}$

Write <, >, or = for each □. Use cross products to decide.

21. $\frac{3}{10} \square \frac{1}{3}$ **22.** $\frac{24}{2} \square \frac{12}{1}$ **23.** $\frac{13}{12} \square \frac{8}{7}$ **24.** $\frac{6}{5} \square \frac{15}{12}$

25. $\frac{17}{20} \square \frac{9}{11}$ **26.** $\frac{9}{24} \square \frac{2}{5}$ **27.** $\frac{14}{25} \square \frac{16}{30}$ **28.** $\frac{34}{60} \square \frac{17}{32}$

29. $\frac{5}{8} \square \frac{4}{9}$ **30.** $\frac{9}{13} \square \frac{4}{7}$ **31.** $\frac{13}{15} \square \frac{7}{8}$ **32.** $\frac{5}{9} \square \frac{3}{5}$

B Write in order from least to greatest.

33. $\frac{1}{5}, \frac{1}{3}, \frac{1}{4}$ **34.** $-\frac{3}{4}, -\frac{7}{8}, -\frac{5}{7}$ **35.** $\frac{4}{9}, \frac{6}{12}, \frac{2}{3}$

36. $\frac{2}{5}, \frac{7}{15}, \frac{10}{20}$ **37.** $\frac{5}{6}, \frac{6}{7}, \frac{3}{8}$ **38.** $-\frac{5}{12}, -\frac{6}{15}, -\frac{3}{4}$

Write <, >, or = for each □. The variable stands for a positive integer.

39. $\frac{x}{5} \square \frac{x}{7}$ **40.** $\frac{y}{24} \square \frac{y}{12}$ **41.** $\frac{j}{8} \square \frac{j}{8}$ **42.** $\frac{t}{4} \square t$

43. $\frac{2d}{6} \square \frac{3d}{6}$ **44.** $\frac{5}{a} \square \frac{3}{a}$ **45.** $\frac{4}{2x} \square \frac{4}{3x}$ **46.** $\frac{2a}{3b} \square \frac{6a}{9b}$

C Extending Thinking Skills

47. Write in order from least to greatest. $\frac{5}{6}, \frac{5}{8}, \frac{5}{3}, \frac{5}{2}, \frac{5}{9}, \frac{5}{5}, \frac{5}{12}, \frac{5}{4}$

48. Make an organized list of all rational numbers less than 1 whose numerators and denominators are selected from the numbers 2, 3, 4, 5, 6, 7, 8, 9, and 10.

Mixed Review

Evaluate for $x = 6$. **49.** $x^2 + 19$ **50.** $x(x + 2)$ **51.** $0.5x$

Solve and check. **52.** $-1.35m = -8.37$ **53.** $r - 16.28 = -11.06$

The basic properties for integers also apply to rational numbers. The multiplicative inverse property will be introduced in Chapter 7. The properties below hold for all rational numbers $\frac{a}{b}$, $\frac{c}{d}$, and $\frac{e}{f}$, where $b \neq 0$, $d \neq 0$, and $f \neq 0$.

Basic Property Update

Commutative Properties

$$\frac{a}{b} + \frac{c}{d} = \frac{c}{d} + \frac{a}{b} \qquad \frac{a}{b} \cdot \frac{c}{d} = \frac{c}{d} \cdot \frac{a}{b}$$

Associative Properties

$$\left(\frac{a}{b} + \frac{c}{d}\right) + \frac{e}{f} = \frac{a}{b} + \left(\frac{c}{d} + \frac{e}{f}\right) \qquad \left(\frac{a}{b} \cdot \frac{c}{d}\right) \cdot \frac{e}{f} = \frac{a}{b} \cdot \left(\frac{c}{d} \cdot \frac{e}{f}\right)$$

Identity Properties

$$\frac{a}{b} + 0 = 0 + \frac{a}{b} = \frac{a}{b} \qquad \frac{a}{b} \cdot 1 = 1 \cdot \frac{a}{b} = \frac{a}{b}$$

Additive Inverse Property

$$\frac{a}{b} + \left(-\frac{a}{b}\right) = -\frac{a}{b} + \frac{a}{b} = 0$$

Distributive Property

$$\frac{a}{b}\left(\frac{c}{d} + \frac{e}{f}\right) = \frac{a}{b} \cdot \frac{c}{d} + \frac{a}{b} \cdot \frac{e}{f}$$

CALCULATOR ACTIVITY

You can use a calculator to find the decimal form of a rational number by dividing the numerator by the denominator. To find the decimal form of $\frac{3}{4}$, calculate $3 \div 4$.

		Display
Rational number: $\frac{3}{4}$	3 [÷] 4 [=]	0.75
Rational number: $-\frac{1}{6}$	1 [+/−] [÷] 6 [=]	−0.1666667

Use a calculator to find the decimal form of each rational number.

1. $\frac{4}{5}$ **2.** $-\frac{7}{8}$ **3.** $\frac{13}{16}$ **4.** $\frac{17}{20}$ **5.** $-\frac{7}{25}$

6-5 Adding and Subtracting with Like Denominators

The number line below suggests that $a \cdot \frac{1}{b} = \frac{a}{b}$ when $b \neq 0$.

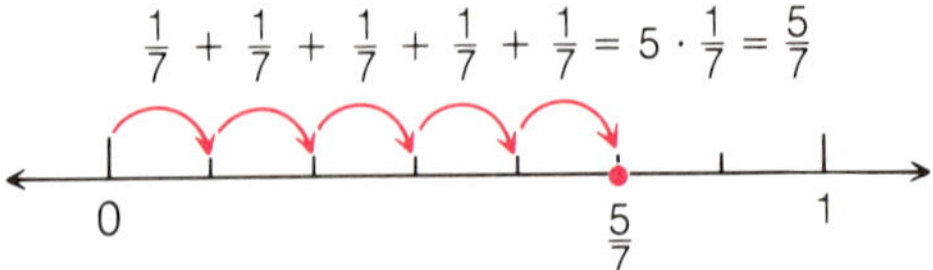

This can be used to explain a method for adding and subtracting rational numbers with like denominators.

$$-\frac{2}{5} + \frac{4}{5} = -2 \cdot \frac{1}{5} + 4 \cdot \frac{1}{5} \qquad a \cdot \frac{1}{b} = \frac{a}{b}$$

$$= (-2 + 4) \cdot \frac{1}{5} \qquad \text{Distributive property}$$

$$= \frac{-2 + 4}{5} \qquad a \cdot \frac{1}{b} = \frac{a}{b}$$

$$= \frac{2}{5}$$

Adding and Subtracting with Like Denominators

To add or subtract rational numbers with like denominators, add or subtract the numerators. Write the sum or difference over the common denominator.

For all integers **a, b,** and **c,** where **c ≠ 0,**

$$\frac{a}{c} + \frac{b}{c} = \frac{a + b}{c} \qquad \frac{a}{c} - \frac{b}{c} = \frac{a - b}{c}$$

Example 1

Subtract. Reduce to lowest terms. $\frac{4}{9} - \frac{7}{9}$

Solution $\frac{4}{9} - \frac{7}{9} = \frac{4 - 7}{9}$ Subtract the numerators. Write the difference over the common denominator.

$= -\frac{3}{9} = -\frac{1}{3}$ Reduce to lowest terms.

Practice Add or subtract. Reduce to lowest terms.

a. $\frac{5}{12} + \frac{4}{12}$ **b.** $-\frac{2}{7} + \frac{4}{7}$ **c.** $-\frac{7}{18} - \frac{13}{18}$

Example 2

Subtract. Reduce to lowest terms. $\frac{13}{25} - \left(-\frac{7}{25}\right)$

Solution

$$\frac{13}{25} - \left(-\frac{7}{25}\right) = \frac{13}{25} + \frac{7}{25}$$ Subtracting $-\frac{7}{25}$ is the same as adding $\frac{7}{25}$.

$$= \frac{13 + 7}{25}$$

$$= \frac{20}{25} = \frac{4}{5}$$

Practice Subtract. Reduce to lowest terms.

a. $\frac{5}{18} - \left(-\frac{4}{18}\right)$ **b.** $-\frac{8}{12} - \left(-\frac{5}{12}\right)$

Oral Exercises

Name the property (commutative, associative, identity, or inverse) shown.

1. $\frac{5}{6} + \left(-\frac{5}{6}\right) = 0$

2. $-\frac{3}{4} + \left(-\frac{1}{4}\right) = -\frac{1}{4} + \left(-\frac{3}{4}\right)$

3. $\frac{12}{10} = 0 + \frac{12}{10}$

4. $1\frac{3}{4} + (-3) = -3 + 1\frac{3}{4}$

5. $0 + \frac{1}{6} = \frac{1}{6}$

6. $\frac{4}{5} + \left(\frac{2}{5} + \frac{3}{5}\right) = \left(\frac{4}{5} + \frac{2}{5}\right) + \frac{3}{5}$

7. $-\frac{3}{2} + \frac{3}{2} = 0$

8. $\left(-\frac{4}{8} + \frac{1}{8}\right) + \frac{3}{8} = -\frac{4}{8} + \left(\frac{1}{8} + \frac{3}{8}\right)$

Exercises

A Add or subtract. Reduce to lowest terms.

1. $\frac{3}{8} + \frac{1}{8}$

2. $-\frac{2}{7} + \frac{3}{7}$

3. $\frac{5}{11} - \frac{2}{11}$

4. $\frac{7}{16} - \frac{3}{16}$

5. $\frac{7}{8} - \frac{9}{8}$

6. $\frac{11}{21} - \frac{5}{21}$

7. $-\frac{7}{11} + \frac{9}{11}$

8. $\frac{23}{27} + \frac{13}{27}$

9. $\frac{48}{13} - \frac{22}{13}$

10. $\frac{12}{7} - \frac{5}{7}$

11. $\frac{7}{19} - \frac{11}{19}$

12. $\frac{3}{13} - \frac{9}{13}$

13. $-\frac{2}{15} - \left(-\frac{13}{15}\right)$

14. $\frac{12}{8} - \left(-\frac{4}{8}\right)$

15. $-\frac{18}{25} - \frac{37}{25}$

16. $-\frac{14}{15} - \frac{1}{15}$

17. $\frac{24}{15} - \left(-\frac{14}{15}\right)$

18. $-\frac{9}{10} - \left(-\frac{9}{10}\right)$

19. $-\frac{18}{24} - \frac{12}{24}$

20. $\frac{27}{60} - \left(-\frac{5}{60}\right)$

21. $\frac{3}{16} - \left(-\frac{12}{16}\right)$

22. $\frac{35}{50} - \frac{45}{50}$

23. $-\frac{21}{24} - \left(-\frac{5}{24}\right)$

24. $\frac{16}{35} - \frac{25}{35}$

25. $-\frac{15}{60} + \frac{35}{60}$

26. $\frac{8}{24} + \frac{16}{24}$

27. $\frac{18}{36} - \left(-\frac{12}{36}\right)$

B Evaluate each expression. Reduce to lowest terms.

28. $a - \frac{3}{8}$ when $a = \frac{7}{8}$

29. $x + \frac{1}{9}$ when $x = \frac{4}{9}$

30. $s + \frac{27}{2}$ when $s = \frac{11}{2}$

31. $y - \frac{9}{14}$ when $y = \frac{13}{14}$

32. $x + y$ when $x = \frac{7}{19}$ and $y = \frac{8}{19}$

33. $u - v$ when $u = \frac{19}{24}$ and $v = \frac{5}{24}$

Solve. Reduce to lowest terms.

34. $\frac{5}{8} + \left(-\frac{7}{8}\right) - \frac{12}{8}$

35. $-\frac{5}{24} - \left(-\frac{13}{24}\right) - \left(-\frac{6}{24}\right)$

36. $\frac{45}{60} - \frac{15}{60} - \left(-\frac{75}{60}\right)$

37. $-\frac{11}{12} - \frac{13}{12} - \left(-\frac{36}{12}\right)$

Write each expression as a fraction. Example: $\frac{12}{m} - \frac{7}{m} = \frac{12 - 7}{m} = \frac{5}{m}$

38. $\frac{5}{y} - \frac{7}{y}$

39. $\frac{6}{z} + \frac{5}{z}$

40. $\frac{12}{s} - \frac{7}{s}$

41. $\frac{27}{x} - \frac{15}{x}$

42. $\frac{123}{t} + \frac{35}{t}$

43. $\frac{67}{u} - \frac{25}{u}$

"Break apart" numbers to find each sum mentally.
Example: To find $5\frac{1}{4} + \frac{3}{4}$, think "$\frac{1}{4} + \frac{3}{4}$ is 1, and $5 + 1$ is 6."

44. $6\frac{1}{3} + \frac{2}{3}$

45. $7\frac{3}{8} + \frac{1}{8}$

46. $26\frac{1}{5} + 4\frac{3}{5}$

47. The total length of a bicycle race course will be $\frac{5}{8}$ mile, and $\frac{3}{8}$ mile is completed so far. What part of the course is not yet completed?

48. A rancher repaired three sections of fencing. The first section was $\frac{1}{10}$ mile long, the second was $\frac{3}{10}$ mile long, and the third was $\frac{4}{10}$ mile long. What was the total length of the fencing the rancher repaired?

C Extending Thinking Skills

49. Find all the whole number values of t that make the equation true.
$\frac{19}{t} + \frac{5}{t} =$ a whole number

50. Find two rational numbers with a sum of 0 and a difference of $\frac{1}{2}$.

51. Find two rational numbers with a sum of $\frac{1}{2}$ and a difference of 0.

Mixed Review

Solve and check. 52. $-27a = 334.8$ 53. $r + 0.414 = 2.396$

Find the greatest common factor (GCF). 54. 32, 96, 48

6-6 Adding and Subtracting with Unlike Denominators

Wrestlers keep accurate records of weight gains and losses. If Jim gained $\frac{5}{8}$ pound one week and $\frac{2}{3}$ pound the next week, he could add $\frac{5}{8}$ and $\frac{2}{3}$ to find his total gain for the two weeks.

To add or subtract rational numbers with unlike denominators, first change them to equivalent fractions with like denominators. This is usually the least common multiple of the denominators, called the **least common denominator**. Add or subtract the numerators and write the sum or difference over the common denominator.

Example 1

Add. Reduce to lowest terms. $\frac{5}{8} + \frac{2}{3}$

Solution

$\frac{5}{8} + \frac{2}{3} = \frac{15}{24} + \frac{16}{24}$ Change each to a fraction with a denominator of 24.

$= \frac{15 + 16}{24}$

$= \frac{31}{24}$

$= 1\frac{7}{24}$

Practice Add. Reduce to lowest terms.

a. $\frac{4}{5} + \frac{5}{12}$ **b.** $\frac{3}{10} + \frac{6}{15}$

Example 2

Subtract. Reduce to lowest terms. $-\frac{5}{6} - \frac{1}{2}$

Solution

$$-\frac{5}{6} - \frac{1}{2} = -\frac{5}{6} - \frac{3}{6}$$ 6 is the least common multiple of 6 and 2.

$$= \frac{-5 - 3}{6}$$

$$= -\frac{8}{6}$$

$$= -1\frac{2}{6} = -1\frac{1}{3}$$ Reduce to lowest terms.

Practice Subtract. Reduce to lowest terms.

a. $\frac{5}{6} - \left(-\frac{1}{8}\right)$ **b.** $-\frac{2}{5} - \frac{3}{6}$

Oral Exercises

Give the least common denominator for each pair of fractions.

1. $\frac{1}{2}, \frac{3}{4}$ **2.** $\frac{2}{3}, \frac{1}{6}$ **3.** $\frac{1}{5}, \frac{3}{10}$ **4.** $\frac{1}{2}, \frac{2}{3}$ **5.** $\frac{1}{3}, \frac{1}{4}$

6. $\frac{2}{3}, \frac{3}{5}$ **7.** $\frac{1}{4}, \frac{3}{8}$ **8.** $\frac{4}{5}, \frac{7}{25}$ **9.** $\frac{5}{6}, \frac{1}{3}$ **10.** $\frac{1}{2}, \frac{7}{10}$

Exercises

A Add or subtract. Reduce to lowest terms.

1. $\frac{1}{2} + \frac{3}{8}$ **2.** $\frac{2}{3} - \frac{1}{4}$ **3.** $\frac{1}{6} - \frac{3}{4}$

4. $\frac{7}{8} - \frac{1}{4}$ **5.** $-\frac{1}{2} + \frac{1}{5}$ **6.** $-\frac{2}{5} - \frac{3}{4}$

7. $-\frac{7}{10} - \frac{1}{2}$ **8.** $\frac{2}{3} - \frac{1}{12}$ **9.** $\frac{3}{4} + \frac{5}{6}$

10. $-\frac{8}{16} + \frac{3}{4}$ **11.** $\frac{3}{4} - \frac{1}{5}$ **12.** $\frac{5}{6} + \frac{7}{10}$

13. $\frac{5}{8} - \left(-\frac{5}{6}\right)$ **14.** $\frac{5}{18} - \left(-\frac{3}{6}\right)$ **15.** $-\frac{11}{12} - \left(-\frac{5}{3}\right)$

16. $-\frac{12}{8} - \frac{2}{3}$ **17.** $-\frac{7}{10} - \left(-\frac{29}{100}\right)$ **18.** $\frac{14}{8} - \left(-\frac{6}{4}\right)$

19. $\frac{7}{8} - \left(-\frac{5}{6}\right)$ **20.** $-\frac{5}{8} + \frac{5}{12}$ **21.** $-\frac{7}{12} - \left(-\frac{4}{9}\right)$

22. $\frac{4}{5} - \left(-\frac{3}{8}\right)$ **23.** $\frac{3}{4} - \frac{4}{7}$ **24.** $-\frac{1}{8} - \left(-\frac{5}{12}\right)$

B Add. Reduce to lowest terms.

25. $-\frac{4}{9}+\frac{2}{3}-\frac{4}{9}$

26. $-\frac{5}{6}-\frac{3}{4}+\frac{1}{2}$

27. $-\frac{2}{3}+\frac{7}{9}+\frac{1}{2}$

28. $-\frac{4}{6}-\left(-\frac{7}{12}\right)-\frac{3}{8}$

29. The high jump record used to be 5 ft $1\frac{1}{4}$ in. Today the record was broken by $\frac{1}{2}$ in. What is the new high jump record?

30. A wrestler lost $\frac{1}{2}$ lb during the morning and another $\frac{3}{4}$ lb during the afternoon. How much weight in all did the wrestler lose that day?

C Extending Thinking Skills

31. Place the digits 2, 3, 4, and 5 in the boxes to make the equation true. $-\frac{\square}{\square}+\frac{\square}{\square}=\frac{7}{20}$

32. Complete the following proof by supplying the missing reasons.

$$\frac{a}{b}+\frac{c}{d}=\frac{a\cdot d}{b\cdot d}+\frac{c\cdot b}{d\cdot b}$$ property of equivalent fractions

$$=\frac{a\cdot d}{b\cdot d}+\frac{c\cdot b}{b\cdot d}$$ why?

$$=a\cdot d\cdot\frac{1}{b\cdot d}+(c\cdot b)\cdot\frac{1}{b\cdot d}$$ $\frac{a}{b}=b\cdot\frac{1}{b}$

$$=(a\cdot d+c\cdot b)\cdot\frac{1}{b\cdot d}$$ why?

$$=\frac{a\cdot d+c\cdot b}{b\cdot d}$$ why?

Mixed Review

Find all the factors of each number. **33.** 25 **34.** 21

Give the absolute value and opposite of each. **35.** -7 **36.** 19

Estimate, then find the value of the variable. **37.** $M = 6.5(68 \div 17)$

Solve and check. **38.** $19.8 = -4c$ **39.** $-11.62 + n = -49.33$

ESTIMATION

You can substitute compatible numbers to estimate the sum or difference of rational numbers by changing them to approximate equivalent fractions. For example, to estimate the sum $\frac{1}{4}+\frac{7}{8}$, think: $\frac{7}{8}$ is about $\frac{3}{4}$, so $\frac{1}{4}+\frac{7}{8}$ is about $\frac{1}{4}+\frac{3}{4}$, or 1.

Estimate each sum or difference.

1. $\frac{7}{8}+\frac{12}{13}$ **2.** $\frac{3}{7}+\frac{5}{8}$ **3.** $\frac{11}{12}-\frac{3}{4}$ **4.** $\frac{14}{15}+\frac{1}{2}$

6-7 Adding and Subtracting with Mixed Numbers

A builder estimated that $4\frac{1}{2}$ cubic yards of concrete were needed for a job. Only $2\frac{2}{3}$ cubic yards were used. You could subtract to check the estimate.

The rules for adding and subtracting rational numbers with like and unlike denominators apply to mixed numbers.

Example 1

Subtract. $\begin{array}{r} 4\frac{1}{2} \\ -2\frac{2}{3} \\ \hline \end{array}$

Solution

$$\begin{array}{rcrcr} 4\frac{1}{2} & = & 4\frac{3}{6} & = & 3\frac{9}{6} \\ -2\frac{2}{3} & = & 2\frac{4}{6} & = & 2\frac{4}{6} \\ \hline & & & & 1\frac{5}{6} \end{array}$$

Find equivalent fractions with like denominators and rename $4\frac{3}{6}$ as $3\frac{9}{6}$.
Subtract the fractions, and then subtract the whole numbers.

Practice Add or subtract. Reduce to lowest terms if necessary.

a. $\begin{array}{r} 3\frac{1}{4} \\ -\ 1\frac{1}{2} \\ \hline \end{array}$ **b.** $\begin{array}{r} 3\frac{4}{5} \\ +\ 5\frac{5}{8} \\ \hline \end{array}$ **c.** $\begin{array}{r} 4\frac{3}{5} \\ +\ 2\frac{3}{5} \\ \hline \end{array}$

Sometimes it helps to change mixed numbers to improper fractions before adding or subtracting.

Example 2

Add and reduce to lowest terms. $-2\frac{2}{3} + 1\frac{1}{6}$

Solution $-2\frac{2}{3} + 1\frac{1}{6} = -\frac{8}{3} + \frac{7}{6}$ Write each mixed number as an improper fraction.

$= -\frac{16}{6} + \frac{7}{6}$ 6 is the least common denominator.

$= \frac{-16 + 7}{6}$

$= -\frac{9}{6} = -1\frac{3}{6} = -1\frac{1}{2}$

Practice Add or subtract. Reduce to lowest terms.

a. $1\frac{1}{2} + \frac{3}{4}$ **b.** $-3\frac{1}{3} - \left(-4\frac{2}{5}\right)$ **c.** $2\frac{3}{8} + 1\frac{7}{8}$

Oral Exercises

Change each mixed number to an improper fraction mentally.

1. $1\frac{3}{5}$ **2.** $-4\frac{1}{2}$ **3.** $-5\frac{3}{4}$ **4.** 4 **5.** $6\frac{2}{3}$

6. $-3\frac{1}{10}$ **7.** $1\frac{7}{12}$ **8.** $2\frac{5}{6}$ **9.** $-3\frac{1}{9}$ **10.** $-7\frac{5}{8}$

Exercises

A Add or subtract. Reduce to lowest terms.

1. $1\frac{2}{3} - \frac{3}{5}$ **2.** $2\frac{2}{5} + 1\frac{1}{5}$ **3.** $2\frac{3}{7} + \frac{1}{3}$

4. $3\frac{1}{6} - \frac{2}{3}$ **5.** $3\frac{3}{5} + \frac{5}{12}$ **6.** $3\frac{7}{8} + 2\frac{1}{3}$

7. $3\frac{3}{8} + 2\frac{5}{8}$ **8.** $5\frac{5}{12} - 3\frac{2}{3}$ **9.** $5\frac{3}{4} + 6\frac{1}{3}$

10. $-3\frac{5}{6} - 2\frac{1}{8}$ **11.** $-4\frac{3}{10} + 7\frac{3}{4}$ **12.** $-1\frac{2}{9} - 1\frac{5}{12}$

13. $-4 - 2\frac{4}{7}$ **14.** $-4\frac{5}{6} + 7$ **15.** $-1\frac{5}{12} - 4\frac{5}{16}$

16. $2\frac{3}{4} - 1\frac{7}{8}$ **17.** $-6\frac{1}{4} + 4\frac{1}{2}$ **18.** $5\frac{3}{8} + 2\frac{3}{4}$

B For Exercises 19–24, estimate, using rounding to the nearest whole number or a **front-end** technique. For example, to find $7\frac{3}{4} + 2\frac{1}{3}$, think: $7\frac{3}{4}$ is closest to 8, $2\frac{1}{3}$ is closest to 2. Estimate: 10. Or think: $7 + 2$ is 9, $\frac{3}{4} + \frac{1}{3}$ is about 1. Estimate: 10.

19. $3\frac{4}{5} - 1\frac{1}{3}$ **20.** $12\frac{5}{8} - \left(-3\frac{2}{5}\right)$ **21.** $-7\frac{1}{2} + 3\frac{1}{4}$

22. $\frac{1}{5} - 4\frac{7}{12} + 6\frac{4}{9}$ **23.** $-5\frac{5}{6} - \left(-\frac{7}{9}\right) + 12$ **24.** $6\frac{2}{3} - 25 - \left(-12\frac{9}{10}\right)$

Estimate each sum using clustering. For example, to find $3\frac{3}{4} + 4\frac{1}{5} + 3\frac{7}{8}$, think "all the numbers cluster around 4, and $3 \cdot 4 = 12$."

25. $4\frac{5}{6} + 5\frac{3}{8} + 4\frac{9}{10}$ **26.** $6\frac{3}{4} + 7\frac{1}{6} + 6\frac{7}{8}$ **27.** $12\frac{1}{5} + 11\frac{7}{8} + 11\frac{9}{10}$

28. A school's record for a race was 4 minutes $23\frac{1}{2}$ seconds. A runner ran this race in 4 minutes $35\frac{3}{10}$ seconds. By how many seconds did the runner miss tying the record?

29. A carpenter cut $5\frac{1}{2}$ inches off one end of a 6-foot-long piece of wood and $3\frac{3}{5}$ inches off the other end. How long was the wood after these two pieces were cut off?

C Extending Thinking Skills

30. Write the rational numbers $\frac{1}{2}$, 1, $1\frac{1}{2}$, 2, $2\frac{1}{2}$, and 3 in the circles so that the sum along each side of the triangle is $4\frac{1}{2}$.

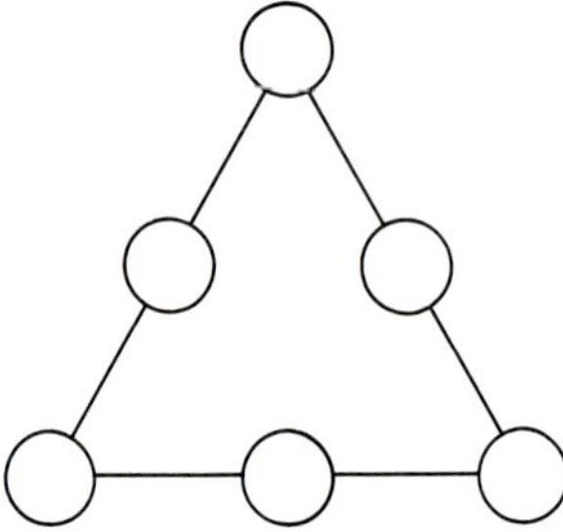

Mixed Review

Find the least common multiple (LCM). **31.** 6, 8, 10, 12

Evaluate for $y = -3$. **32.** $y(y - 4)$ **33.** $y^2 + 3y$

34. $9 - 6y$

MENTAL MATH

You can choose compatible numbers to add or subtract rational numbers mentally. For example, in the equation $2\frac{1}{4} + 3\frac{2}{3} + 4\frac{3}{4}$ you can first add $2\frac{1}{4}$ and $4\frac{3}{4}$ to get 7 and then add 7 and $3\frac{2}{3}$ to get $10\frac{2}{3}$.

Choose compatible numbers to add or subtract mentally.

1. $-5\frac{2}{5} + 7 - 1\frac{3}{5}$ **2.** $6\frac{2}{3} + 4\frac{1}{2} - 2\frac{2}{3}$ **3.** $3\frac{4}{9} + 4\frac{5}{6} + 1\frac{5}{9}$

4. $10\frac{5}{8} - 2\frac{3}{8} - 3$ **5.** $-4\frac{4}{5} + 5\frac{5}{12} - \frac{1}{5}$ **6.** $-5\frac{6}{7} - 7\frac{1}{3} - 2\frac{1}{7}$

More Practice

Add or subtract. Reduce to lowest terms.

1. $\frac{1}{2} + \frac{3}{8}$
2. $\frac{7}{10} + \left(-\frac{7}{10}\right)$
3. $-\frac{2}{9} + \frac{4}{9}$
4. $\frac{3}{4} - \frac{1}{5}$
5. $\frac{4}{5} + \left(-\frac{1}{5}\right)$
6. $1\frac{2}{7} - \frac{3}{7}$
7. $\frac{3}{4} + \frac{1}{2}$
8. $1\frac{5}{12} - \frac{3}{4}$
9. $2\frac{3}{5} - \frac{2}{3}$
10. $\frac{1}{2} - \frac{2}{3}$
11. $\frac{9}{10} - \frac{1}{2}$
12. $-\frac{5}{12} + \frac{3}{4}$
13. $\frac{3}{10} + \left(-\frac{1}{6}\right)$
14. $\frac{4}{9} + 1\frac{2}{3}$
15. $4\frac{1}{2} - 1\frac{2}{3}$
16. $\frac{2}{3} - \left(-\frac{4}{5}\right)$
17. $\frac{5}{6} + \frac{1}{8}$
18. $1\frac{1}{2} + \frac{1}{4}$
19. $\frac{3}{4} - 3\frac{1}{12}$
20. $4\frac{3}{10} - 3\frac{1}{2}$
21. $\frac{2}{5} - \frac{3}{8}$
22. $\frac{8}{9} - \frac{7}{10}$
23. $1\frac{1}{2} + \frac{1}{5}$
24. $\frac{9}{10} + \left(-\frac{1}{2}\right)$
25. $1\frac{3}{7} - \frac{6}{7}$
26. $1\frac{7}{12} - 2\frac{1}{4}$
27. $\frac{3}{4} - \frac{4}{7}$
28. $2\frac{1}{3} - \frac{3}{4}$
29. $\frac{9}{25} + \frac{1}{15}$
30. $\frac{9}{10} + 2\frac{1}{3}$
31. $4\frac{1}{3} - 2\frac{5}{6}$
32. $3\frac{1}{9} + \frac{3}{4}$
33. $1\frac{3}{4} - \frac{5}{8}$
34. $\frac{2}{7} + \left(-\frac{3}{5}\right)$
35. $5\frac{2}{3} - 4\frac{7}{8}$
36. $\frac{5}{16} + \left(-\frac{1}{4}\right)$
37. $-\frac{3}{7} + 1\frac{3}{7}$
38. $6\frac{13}{15} - 5$
39. $3\frac{3}{5} - \frac{2}{3}$
40. $3\frac{3}{4} - 5\frac{1}{4}$
41. $3\frac{5}{9} - \left(-2\frac{3}{5}\right)$
42. $\frac{3}{8} + 2\frac{1}{2}$
43. $2\frac{1}{2} + \left(-3\frac{2}{7}\right)$
44. $\frac{17}{22} - \frac{3}{11}$
45. $-\frac{1}{4} + \frac{5}{6}$
46. $4\frac{1}{3} - 1\frac{1}{3}$
47. $1\frac{2}{3} - \frac{7}{9}$
48. $\frac{3}{4} + \frac{4}{5}$

6-8 The Stock Market

When you buy **shares** of **stock** from a corporation, you become a part owner of the corporation, and are called a shareholder or a stockholder. Anyone can buy stock, but most people have a stockbroker help them buy it. Stock prices are published each day in newspapers. A stock's price is given as a fractional part of a dollar. For example, $19\frac{5}{8}$ means 19 and $\frac{5}{8}$ dollars, or $19.625.

Below is a typical newspaper stock report. The company names are given as abbreviations under the word "stock."

Today's Stock Report

(1)		(2)	(3)		(4)	(5)
High	**Low**	**Stock**	**High**	**Low**	**Last**	**Chg.**
19 3/4	9 1/2	**AWARD**	16 1/4	14	15 5/8	+2 1/4
28	10 7/8	**ConnEt**	16 1/8	13	14 1/8	−1 5/8
62 1/4	47	**NATS**	59 7/8	56 1/2	57 3/4	+1 7/8
45 1/2	22	**PODCo**	33 1/2	29 7/8	31	−3/4
21 1/4	14 7/8	**RICH**	19 3/4	18 3/8	19 5/8	+1/2

(1) High/Low–The highest and lowest selling prices of each share for the year.

(2) Stock–The name of the company.

(3) High/Low–The highest and lowest selling prices of each share for this day.

(4) Last–The price of the last share sold this day. Also called "closing price."

(5) Chg. (Change)–The difference between today's closing price and yesterday's closing price.

Problem Find the price of the last RICH Corporation share sold yesterday.

Solution $19\frac{5}{8} - \frac{1}{2} = 19\frac{1}{8}$ The change (Chg.) was an increase (+) of $\frac{1}{2}$. To find yesterday's last price, subtract $\frac{1}{2}$ from today's last price.

Problems

Solve.

1. PODCo shares went down today compared to yesterday. What was the last price for a share yesterday?

2. AWARD shares went up today compared to yesterday. What was the last price for a share yesterday?

3. What was the closing price of NATS shares yesterday?

4. What was the closing price of ConnEt shares yesterday?

5. What is the difference between the yearly high and low of PODCo shares?

6. What is the difference in the yearly high and low prices for RICH shares?

7. How much would it cost to buy 100 shares of RICH stock at today's high price?

8. About how much would it cost to buy 1500 shares of ConnEt stock at today's high price?

9. Suppose you owned one share in each of the companies listed on page 190. Did the total value of your stock increase or decrease yesterday? By how much?

10. ***Data Search*** Choose any five stocks from a newspaper report. Find the closing price of each stock for the day previous to the day of the report.

What's Your Decision?

Suppose you have $2,000 to invest in stocks. You want to buy at least 20 shares of each stock and you want at least 3 different stocks. Use estimation to decide which of the stocks in the table on page 190 and how many shares of each you would choose for your investment.

6-9 Solving Equations: Using Addition and Subtraction

The steps you have learned for solving equations involving whole numbers, decimals, and integers apply to equations involving all rational numbers.

- Decide which operation (addition or subtraction) has been applied to the variable.
- Use the inverse operation or use the additive inverse property, adding or subtracting the same number on both sides of the equation.

To solve an equation such as $x - \frac{4}{5} = -\frac{3}{10}$, you need to get the variable by itself.

Example 1

Solve and check. $x - \frac{4}{5} = -\frac{3}{10}$

Solution $x - \frac{4}{5} = -\frac{3}{10}$

$$x - \frac{4}{5} + \frac{4}{5} = -\frac{3}{10} + \frac{4}{5}$$ Addition property of equality.

$$x = -\frac{3}{10} + \frac{4}{5}$$

$$= -\frac{3}{10} + \frac{8}{10}$$

$$x = \frac{5}{10} = \frac{1}{2}$$

Check $\frac{1}{2} - \frac{4}{5} \stackrel{?}{=} -\frac{3}{10}$ Replace x with $\frac{1}{2}$ in $x - \frac{4}{5} = -\frac{3}{10}$.

$$\frac{5}{10} - \frac{8}{10} \stackrel{?}{=} -\frac{3}{10}$$

$$-\frac{3}{10} = -\frac{3}{10} \checkmark$$ The solution is $\frac{1}{2}$.

Practice Solve and check.

a. $x + \frac{7}{12} = \frac{1}{4}$ **b.** $y - \frac{5}{6} = -\frac{3}{4}$

c. $-\frac{1}{4} = t - \frac{7}{8}$ **d.** $-\frac{4}{5} + m = \frac{2}{3}$

Example 2

Solve and check. $\frac{5}{6} + a = \frac{4}{9}$

Solution $\frac{5}{6} + a = \frac{4}{9}$

$-\frac{5}{6} + \frac{5}{6} + a = -\frac{5}{6} + \frac{4}{9}$ Add the inverse to both sides.

$a = -\frac{5}{6} + \frac{4}{9}$

$= -\frac{15}{18} + \frac{8}{18}$

$a = -\frac{7}{18}$

Check $\frac{5}{6} + \left(-\frac{7}{18}\right) \stackrel{?}{=} \frac{4}{9}$ Replace a with $-\frac{7}{18}$ in $\frac{5}{6} + a = \frac{4}{9}$.

$\frac{15}{18} + \left(-\frac{7}{18}\right) \stackrel{?}{=} \frac{8}{18}$

$\frac{8}{18} = \frac{8}{18}$ ✓ The solution is $-\frac{7}{18}$.

Practice Solve and check. **a.** $f + \frac{5}{12} = -\frac{3}{8}$ **b.** $\frac{5}{9} = y - \left(-\frac{4}{5}\right)$

Oral Exercises

To solve, would you add or subtract in the first step?

1. $n - \frac{6}{8} = -\frac{2}{3}$ **2.** $y - \frac{5}{2} = -\frac{1}{2}$ **3.** $\frac{3}{4} + b = -\frac{3}{5}$

4. $x - \frac{5}{6} = \frac{7}{12}$ **5.** $-\frac{2}{3} + a = -6$ **6.** $p + \frac{3}{4} = \frac{8}{9}$

7. $t - \frac{7}{10} = -\frac{4}{5}$ **8.** $m - \frac{3}{10} = -\frac{6}{8}$ **9.** $\frac{1}{5} + x = -\frac{3}{8}$

Exercises

A Solve and check.

1. $x - \frac{2}{3} = \frac{4}{9}$ **2.** $t - \frac{4}{3} = -\frac{5}{7}$ **3.** $m - \frac{3}{5} = -\frac{5}{6}$

4. $-\frac{6}{18} + x = \frac{4}{3}$ **5.** $p - \frac{2}{5} = -\frac{5}{6}$ **6.** $y - \frac{5}{3} = \frac{5}{12}$

7. $a - \frac{3}{4} = -\frac{5}{8}$ **8.** $y - \frac{1}{2} = -\frac{7}{10}$ **9.** $-\frac{3}{20} + b = -\frac{2}{5}$

10. $x - \frac{7}{8} = -\frac{5}{12}$ **11.** $p - \frac{14}{25} = -\frac{3}{2}$ **12.** $z - \frac{10}{30} = \frac{2}{5}$

13. $d - \frac{3}{5} = -\frac{1}{10}$

14. $n - \frac{3}{10} = -\frac{2}{50}$

15. $k - \frac{6}{15} = -\frac{12}{9}$

16. $x + \frac{4}{7} = -\frac{2}{5}$

17. $\frac{1}{5} + y = -\frac{1}{8}$

18. $-\frac{6}{24} = \frac{2}{3} + h$

19. $h + \frac{5}{6} = \frac{7}{8}$

20. $\frac{7}{16} + x = -\frac{3}{8}$

21. $\frac{6}{5} = \frac{2}{3} + x$

22. $\frac{9}{16} + y = -\frac{13}{15}$

23. $\frac{3}{7} = h + \frac{4}{5}$

24. $y + \frac{12}{25} = \frac{3}{10}$

25. $\frac{9}{10} + z = -16\frac{3}{8}$

26. $-\frac{5}{16} = \frac{5}{6} + k$

27. $-\frac{9}{10} = \frac{7}{12} + x$

B Solve and check.

28. $x + \left(\frac{5}{8} - \frac{5}{6}\right) = \frac{15}{24}$

29. $\left(-\frac{6}{18} - \frac{3}{4}\right) + y = \frac{2}{9}$

30. $-\frac{4}{15} = \left(-\frac{1}{5} + \frac{1}{2}\right) + h$

31. $\left[-\frac{2}{3} - \left(-\frac{5}{6}\right)\right] + k = -\frac{5}{12}$

32. $\left(\frac{4}{7} - \frac{1}{5}\right) + x = \frac{11}{5}$

33. $-\frac{13}{24} = \left(-\frac{5}{12} + \frac{3}{8}\right) + d$

34. Write two different equations with the solution $\frac{3}{5}$.

35. Write an equation for which the solution $-\frac{7}{12}$ is found by subtracting.

36. Write an equation for which the solution $\frac{11}{16}$ is found by adding.

C Extending Thinking Skills

37. Find 3 rational numbers, each with a numerator of 1, whose sum is $\frac{13}{16}$.

38. Chris's wardrobe is made up of 6 different pairs of trousers, half as many shirts as pairs of trousers, and 2 sweaters, one green and one gray. How many different combinations of trousers, shirt and sweater does Chris have with these items?

Mixed Review

Solve and check. 39. $-36c = 66.6$ 40. $r \div 16 = -0.575$

Find all the factors of the number. 41. 19 42. 9 43. 12

MENTAL MATH

You can use compensation to find certain differences of rational numbers mentally. For example, to find $5 - 3\frac{7}{8}$, think "$5 - 4$ is 1. $\frac{1}{8}$ too much has been subtracted, so it must be added back on. $1 + \frac{1}{8}$ is $1\frac{1}{8}$."

Use compensation to subtract mentally.

1. $8 - 4\frac{3}{4}$
2. $9 - 6\frac{4}{5}$
3. $7\frac{1}{10} - 3\frac{9}{10}$
4. $8\frac{1}{3} - 2\frac{2}{3}$

6-10 Deciding What the Variable Represents

You can use the Problem-Solving Checklist on page 121 to help you solve problems. When your plan involves writing and solving an equation, keep these questions in mind.

- Can you use a variable to represent an unknown number?
- Can you represent other conditions in terms of the variable?
- What is equal?
- Can you write and solve an equation?

Example

The width of a steel rod is $\frac{11}{16}$ inches. The designer says this rod is $\frac{3}{8}$ inch wider than the rod he had originally designed. What was the width of the rod originally designed?

Solution Let x = width of the original rod — Let the variable stand for the width of the original rod.

$x + \frac{3}{8}$ = width of final rod — The width of the final rod is $\frac{3}{8}$ inch wider, or $x + \frac{3}{8}$.

$\frac{11}{16}$ = width of final rod

$$x + \frac{3}{8} = \frac{11}{16}$$

The two expressions for the width of the rod must be equal.

$$x + \frac{3}{8} + \left(-\frac{3}{8}\right) = \frac{11}{16} + \left(-\frac{3}{8}\right)$$

$$x = \frac{5}{16}$$

The original rod was $\frac{5}{16}$ in. wide.

Check $\frac{5}{16} + \frac{3}{8} = \frac{5}{16} + \frac{6}{16} = \frac{11}{16}$ — $\frac{5}{16}$ is less than $\frac{11}{16}$. The answer seems reasonable.

Exercises

A Solve by writing an equation. Check.

1. After cutting $\frac{1}{8}$ inch off the end of a copper pipe, a plumber had the exact length needed to connect a water line. The exact length needed was $\frac{3}{4}$ inch. What was the length of the original piece of pipe?

2. The price of a stereo system increased twice in the last month. The second increase was \$25, for a total increase of \$45.50. What was the first increase?

3. The total length of a race track for bicycles is $\frac{5}{8}$ mile. The first $\frac{1}{5}$ mile is very hilly and the rest is flat. How much of the course is flat?

4. Kim grew a lot during the first 6 months of last year. During the second 6 months she grew only $\frac{1}{8}$ inch. She grew $5\frac{1}{2}$ inches in all last year. How much did she grow during the first 6 months?

5. Al had 48 tapes in his music collection. His older sister Carrie gave him some more tapes. Now he has a total of 73 tapes. How many tapes did Carrie give to Al?

B

6. Rick sold 7 tickets to the talent show during the first week of sales and 5 tickets during the second week of sales. Each ticket cost the same. He turned in a total of \$15. What was the cost of each ticket?

7. A wire had to be wrapped in a plastic coating. The wire was $\frac{7}{12}$ inch wide. Two layers of plastic had to be put over the wire so the total thickness of the plastic would equal the thickness of the wire. The first layer of plastic was $\frac{1}{2}$ inch thick. How thick was the second layer?

8. A machinist usually makes a certain part by welding together two metal strips, one $\frac{1}{8}$ inch thick and the other $\frac{1}{3}$ inch thick. She has a metal strip $\frac{1}{4}$ inch thick that she can use to make this part. How thick a strip must she weld on to make the part the correct thickness?

C Extending Thinking Skills

9. Write a word problem that would be solved using the equation $x + \frac{1}{2} = \frac{5}{8}$.

10. Write a word problem that would be solved using the equation $25 - x = 64$.

Mixed Review

Give the prime factorization of each. **11.** 49 **12.** 34 **13.** 90

Evaluate for $n = 4$. **14.** $5(n + 2) + 12$ **15.** $n(6 - n) + 7$

Write an algebraic expression for the phrase.

16. 14 times the difference of a number and 5.

17. The sum of 64 and a number, divided by 12.

Simplify. **18.** $x \cdot y \cdot x \cdot y$ **19.** $4m + 3m$ **20.** $c + c + c$

Give the least common multiple (LCM). **21.** 3, 6, 7, 4 **22.** 9, 12

PROBLEM SOLVING: STRATEGIES

6-11 Use Logical Reasoning

Some problems must be solved by understanding the given relationships among facts and using known facts and relationships to make conclusions. The problem-solving strategy **Use Logical Reasoning** is a name for this process.

Problem Wally, Kim, José, and Rosalie each like one sport. One plays basketball every day, one plays tennis on weekends, one likes squash, and one coaches a soccer team. Wally's sister likes tennis. Wally hates playing basketball. Kim likes coaching. Which sport does each one prefer?

You can solve this problem by recording the given information in a chart and making conclusions based on it. The charts below show the reasoning you might go through to solve this problem.

	B	T	S	C
W	no	no		
K				
J		no		
R				

Wally's sister plays tennis so Wally and José do not play tennis. Wally does not play basketball.

	B	T	S	C
W	no	no		**no**
K	**no**	**no**	**no**	**yes**
J		no		**no**
R				**no**

If Kim coaches then no one else coaches.

	B	T	S	C
W	no	no	**yes**	no
K	no	no	no	yes
J	**yes**	no		no
R		**yes**		no

Wally must play squash and Rosalie must play tennis. José has to play basketball.

Problem-Solving Strategies

Choose the Operations	**Write an Equation**
Guess, Check, Revise	**Simplify the Problem**
Draw a Picture	**Make an Organized List**
Make a Table	**Use Logical Reasoning**
Look for a Pattern	

This chart lists the strategies presented so far.

Problems

Solve.

1. Ned, Mary, Steve, and Jack live in the towns Millerville, Jefferson, Newville, and Stovertown. None lives in a city that has the same first letter as his or her name. Neither Jack nor Ned has ever been to Millerville. Mary has spent all of her life in Stovertown. Which person lives in which town?

2. Two men and two women each play a different sport. Their names are Elena, Connie, Barry, and Miguel. One plays baseball, one plays soccer, one plays basketball, and one plays football. Connie's brother is part of this group; he plays basketball and he is married to the one who plays soccer. The one who plays football doesn't have any brothers or sisters. Both Miguel and the one who plays baseball are single. Who plays each game?

3. Ricky and his friends are sitting at a large round table playing a game. Ricky's mother gave them a box of 25 oranges to share. The box was passed around the table, and each person took 1 orange until there were no more oranges left. Ricky took the first orange and the last orange and he may have taken more than the first and last orange. How many people could have been sitting at the table?

4. A large circus tent is set up with 12 poles. The poles are arranged in a circle with a separate rope connecting each pair of poles. How many ropes are needed to connect these 12 poles?

5. The varsity baseball team won 5 out of every 7 games it played this year. It lost 24 games. How many games did it win?

6. Walker, Franklin, and King Schools have students in an all-star band. There are 150 band members. Walker school has 300 students and 30 are in the band. Franklin School has 400 students and 60 are in the band. How many students from King School are in the band?

Enrichment

Using a Calculator to Add or Subtract Fractions with Unlike Denominators

You can use a calculator to add or subtract fractions with unlike denominators. The examples show how the calculator solution corresponds to the worked-out solution.

Worked-out Solution

$$\frac{2}{3} + \frac{4}{5} = \frac{2}{3} \cdot \frac{5}{5} + \frac{4}{5} \cdot \frac{3}{3}$$

$$= \frac{2 \cdot 5 + 4 \cdot 3}{3 \cdot 5}$$

$$= \frac{22}{15} = 1\frac{7}{15}$$

Calculator Solution

$$\overset{\substack{n_1 \\ \downarrow}}{\underset{\substack{\uparrow \\ d_1}}{\frac{2}{3}}} + \overset{\substack{n_2 \\ \downarrow}}{\underset{\substack{\uparrow \\ d_2}}{\frac{4}{5}}}$$

To find the numerator:	**Display**
2 [×] 5 [+] 3 [×] 4 [=]	22

To find the denominator:	**Display**
3 [×] 5 [=]	15

Solution $\frac{22}{15} = 1\frac{7}{15}$

Use a calculator to add or subtract.

1. $\frac{12}{13} + \frac{4}{5}$

2. $\frac{5}{9} + \frac{11}{12}$

3. $\frac{32}{60} - \frac{5}{24}$

4. $\frac{7}{10} + \frac{24}{50}$

5. $\frac{7}{8} - \frac{3}{16}$

6. $\frac{23}{24} - \frac{11}{15}$

7. $-\frac{4}{15} - \frac{8}{12}$

8. $-\frac{33}{40} + \frac{17}{20}$

9. $\frac{13}{15} - \frac{3}{10}$

Use a calculator to solve each equation.

10. $x - \frac{7}{9} = \frac{5}{12}$

11. $x + \frac{13}{20} = \frac{7}{18}$

12. $\frac{5}{16} + x = \frac{17}{25}$

13. $x + \frac{5}{8} = -\frac{4}{5}$

14. $x - \frac{1}{10} = \frac{1}{20}$

15. $-\frac{7}{12} + x = -\frac{3}{10}$

Chapter 6 Review

6-1 Write an equivalent fraction by replacing the variable with a whole number.

1. $\frac{5}{6} = \frac{f}{72}$ **2.** $\frac{k}{4} = \frac{13}{52}$ **3.** $-\frac{4}{15} = -\frac{r}{75}$

Reduce each fraction to lowest terms.

4. $\frac{27}{36}$ **5.** $-\frac{42}{91}$ **6.** $\frac{144}{156}$

6-2 Write each as a mixed number.

7. $\frac{19}{3}$ **8.** $-\frac{123}{11}$ **9.** $\frac{187}{30}$

Write each as an improper fraction in lowest terms.

10. $5\frac{1}{7}$ **11.** $-8\frac{2}{5}$ **12.** $4\frac{6}{10}$

6-3 **13.** Graph $-\frac{3}{8}$, $\frac{5}{8}$, -1, and $-1\frac{3}{4}$ on a number line.

6-4 Write $<$, $>$, or $=$ for each $\square$.

14. $\frac{2}{5} \square \frac{6}{15}$ **15.** $-\frac{5}{6} \square -\frac{11}{12}$ **16.** $\frac{9}{13} \square \frac{2}{3}$ **17.** $-\frac{2}{9} \square -\frac{15}{45}$

6-5 Add or subtract. Reduce to lowest terms.

18. $\frac{5}{12} + \frac{5}{12}$ **19.** $-\frac{7}{9} + \frac{5}{9}$ **20.** $-\frac{13}{25} - \left(-\frac{4}{25}\right)$

6-6

21. $\frac{1}{6} + \frac{1}{2}$ **22.** $-\frac{8}{15} - \left(-\frac{1}{5}\right)$ **23.** $-\frac{7}{8} - \left(-\frac{1}{4}\right)$

6-7

24. $2\frac{1}{3} + 1\frac{3}{4}$ **25.** $7\frac{1}{6} - 3\frac{1}{2}$ **26.** $8\frac{1}{5} - \left(-4\frac{1}{2}\right)$

6-8 Solve.

27. Mr. Greyson had $4\frac{1}{2}$ pounds of apples. He used $2\frac{3}{4}$ pounds to make a pie. How many pounds did he have left?

28. Henry and Steve hiked $4\frac{3}{8}$ miles, stopped for an hour, and then hiked $5\frac{1}{4}$ miles farther. How far did they hike?

6-9 Solve and check.

29. $y - \frac{1}{8} = \frac{1}{2}$ **30.** $x + \frac{3}{5} = -\frac{1}{10}$ **31.** $\frac{7}{12} = c - \frac{2}{3}$

6-10

32. Find the solution by writing and solving an equation.

Mr. MacGregor bought 3 yards of string. After tying up his tomato plants, he had $1\frac{3}{8}$ yards of string left over. How much string did he use?

Chapter 6 Test

Write an equivalent fraction by replacing the variable with a whole number.

1. $\frac{6}{7} = \frac{v}{77}$ **2.** $\frac{c}{9} = \frac{49}{63}$ **3.** $-\frac{16}{17} = -\frac{t}{102}$

Reduce each fraction to lowest terms.

4. $\frac{56}{84}$ **5.** $-\frac{12}{90}$ **6.** $\frac{124}{172}$

Write each as a mixed number.

7. $\frac{38}{6}$ **8.** $-\frac{53}{3}$ **9.** $\frac{288}{100}$

Write each as an improper fraction in lowest terms.

10. $2\frac{5}{7}$ **11.** $-4\frac{3}{11}$ **12.** $9\frac{7}{20}$

13. Graph $\frac{3}{8}$, $-\frac{5}{8}$, -1, and $1\frac{1}{2}$ on a number line.

Write $<$, $>$, or $=$ for each $\square$.

14. $\frac{5}{9} \square \frac{2}{3}$ **15.** $-\frac{1}{3} \square -\frac{4}{7}$ **16.** $\frac{8}{7} \square \frac{13}{11}$ **17.** $-\frac{9}{24} \square -\frac{12}{36}$

Add or subtract. Reduce to lowest terms.

18. $\frac{6}{11} + \frac{4}{11}$ **19.** $-\frac{2}{5} + \frac{4}{5}$ **20.** $-\frac{15}{24} - \left(-\frac{7}{24}\right)$

21. $\frac{5}{6} + \frac{2}{3}$ **22.** $-\frac{7}{12} - \frac{1}{4}$ **23.** $-\frac{7}{9} - \left(-\frac{1}{3}\right)$

24. $6\frac{1}{2} + 1\frac{3}{8}$ **25.** $8\frac{1}{4} - 1\frac{1}{2}$ **26.** $9\frac{5}{6} - \left(-2\frac{1}{3}\right)$

Solve.

27. Mr. Cole had $8\frac{1}{2}$ pounds of flour. He gave a neighbor $2\frac{3}{4}$ pounds. How much did he have left?

28. Becky and Linnea rode their bikes $5\frac{3}{4}$ miles, stopped for lunch, then rode $2\frac{3}{8}$ miles more. How far did they ride?

Solve and check.

29. $p - 1\frac{1}{5} = 1\frac{4}{15}$ **30.** $z + \frac{3}{4} = -\frac{1}{6}$ **31.** $\frac{5}{14} = a - \left(-\frac{1}{7}\right)$

32. Find the solution by writing and solving an equation.

Mrs. Chung used $2\frac{1}{2}$ gallons of paint on her bedroom and hallway. If her hallway took $\frac{2}{3}$ gallon of paint, how much did her bedroom take?

Cumulative Review

Write as a decimal.

1. $4(10) + 7(1) + 8\left(\frac{1}{10}\right)$
2. $2(100) + 9\left(\frac{1}{100}\right) + 6\left(\frac{1}{10}\right)$
3. $5(1) + 7\left(\frac{1}{100}\right) + 1\left(\frac{1}{10}\right)$
4. $3\left(\frac{1}{10}\right) + 7\left(\frac{1}{100}\right) + 9\left(\frac{1}{1000}\right)$

Write $<$, $>$, or $=$ for each $\square$.

5. $4.430 \square 4.43$
6. $4.01 \square 4.1$
7. $-2.73 \square -3.12$
8. $6 \square -4$
9. $-2 \square -10$
10. $-5 \square 0$

Round.

11. 83 to the nearest ten
12. 291 to the nearest hundred
13. 7,486 to the nearest thousand
14. 24,576 to the nearest ten thousand

Round to the nearest ten and estimate the value of each variable.

15. $38 + 21 = a$
16. $x = 286 - 57$
17. $12 + 54 = p$

Round to the nearest hundred and estimate the value of each variable.

18. $m = 475 + 391$
19. $402 - 174 = w$
20. $3927 - 301 = f$

Estimate the value of x by rounding.

21. $51.32 - 38.11 = x$
22. $x = 295.2 + 48.8$
23. $r = 67.59 - 16.63$
24. $47.92 + 50.05 = r$

Estimate the product by rounding.

25. 3.73×7.2
26. 7.2×6.8
27. 1.08×6.9

Give the first five nonzero multiples of each number.

28. 4
29. 7
30.

Find all the factors of the given number.

31. 32
32. 42
33. 60

State whether the number is divisible by 2.

34. 48
35. 30
36. 81

State whether the number is divisible by 3.

37. 38
38. 450
39. 522

State whether the number is divisible by 5.

40. 15
41. 510
42. 301

Chapter 7
Rational Numbers: Multiplication and Division

7-1 Multiplying Rational Numbers

In the auditorium seating chart below, the front section contains $\frac{1}{2}$ of the total number of seats. The left section contains $\frac{1}{3}$ of the total number. The *front left* section contains $\frac{1}{2}$ of $\frac{1}{3}$, or $\frac{1}{6}$ of the total number.

Back Left	Back Center	Back Right
Front Left	Front Center	Front Right

This suggests that for all integers a and b, where **($a \neq 0$, $b \neq 0$)**,
$\frac{1}{a} \cdot \frac{1}{b} = \frac{1}{ab}$

This rule, together with properties introduced earlier, can be used to explain the steps in multiplying two rational numbers.

$$\frac{2}{3} \cdot \frac{3}{4} = \left(2 \cdot \frac{1}{3}\right)\left(3 \cdot \frac{1}{4}\right) \qquad a \cdot \frac{1}{b} = \frac{a}{b}$$

$$= (2 \cdot 3)\left(\frac{1}{3} \cdot \frac{1}{4}\right) \qquad \text{Commutative and associative properties}$$

$$= 6 \cdot \frac{1}{12} \qquad \frac{1}{a} \cdot \frac{1}{b} = \frac{1}{ab}$$

$$= \frac{6}{12} \qquad a \cdot \frac{1}{b} = \frac{a}{b}$$

This suggests the following rule.

Multiplying Rational Numbers

To multiply two rational numbers, multiply the numerators and multiply the denominators.

For all rational numbers $\frac{a}{b}$ and $\frac{c}{d}$ **($b \neq 0$, $d \neq 0$),**

$\frac{a}{b} \cdot \frac{c}{d} = \frac{a \cdot c}{b \cdot d}$

Example 1

Multiply. Reduce to lowest terms. $\frac{2}{5}\left(\frac{5}{12}\right)$

Solution

$$\frac{2}{5}\left(\frac{5}{12}\right) = \frac{2(5)}{5(12)} \quad \text{Multiply numerators; multiply denominators.}$$
$$= \frac{10}{60} = \frac{1}{6}$$

Practice Multiply. Reduce to lowest terms.

a. $-\frac{5}{6}\left(-\frac{3}{8}\right)$ **b.** $\frac{2}{3}\left(\frac{8}{9}\right)$

When multiplying mixed numbers, first change them to improper fractions.

Example 2

Multiply. Reduce to lowest terms. $-1\frac{1}{5}\left(-3\frac{1}{2}\right)$

Solution

$$-1\frac{1}{5}\left(-3\frac{1}{2}\right) = \frac{-6}{5}\left(\frac{-7}{2}\right) \quad \text{Change mixed numbers to improper fractions.}$$
$$= \frac{-6(-7)}{5(2)}$$
$$= \frac{42}{10} \quad \text{When both factors are negative, the product is positive.}$$
$$= 4\frac{2}{10} = 4\frac{1}{5}$$

Practice Multiply. Reduce to lowest terms.

a. $2\frac{2}{3}\left(1\frac{1}{5}\right)$ **b.** $3\frac{1}{12}(-2)$

Oral Exercises

Give each mixed number as an improper fraction.

1. $3\frac{1}{2}$ **2.** $-4\frac{2}{3}$ **3.** $1\frac{4}{5}$ **4.** $2\frac{1}{8}$

5. $10\frac{1}{10}$ **6.** $4\frac{3}{4}$ **7.** $-1\frac{5}{8}$ **8.** $6\frac{2}{3}$

State whether the product is positive or negative. Do not compute.

9. $-\frac{7}{8}\left(\frac{1}{2}\right)$ **10.** $\frac{2}{5}\left(\frac{9}{10}\right)$ **11.** $-\frac{3}{5}\left(-\frac{2}{3}\right)$

12. $4\frac{1}{2}\left(-\frac{3}{4}\right)$ **13.** $-\frac{5}{6}\left(-\frac{7}{9}\right)$ **14.** $\frac{4}{9}\left(\frac{35}{100}\right)$

Exercises

A Multiply. Reduce to lowest terms.

1. $\frac{3}{5}\left(\frac{3}{4}\right)$
2. $\frac{3}{5}\left(\frac{5}{7}\right)$
3. $\frac{1}{2}\left(\frac{5}{16}\right)$
4. $-\frac{8}{16}\left(\frac{1}{2}\right)$
5. $-\frac{4}{3}\left(\frac{5}{8}\right)$
6. $-\frac{6}{4}\left(-\frac{3}{5}\right)$
7. $\frac{14}{6}\left(-\frac{3}{10}\right)$
8. $\frac{5}{3}\left(\frac{15}{8}\right)$
9. $\frac{7}{12}\left(\frac{4}{3}\right)$
10. $-\frac{3}{8}\left(-\frac{2}{3}\right)$
11. $-\frac{5}{2}\left(-\frac{5}{10}\right)$
12. $\frac{12}{25}\left(\frac{2}{10}\right)$
13. $\frac{4}{12}\left(\frac{15}{24}\right)$
14. $\frac{24}{26}\left(-\frac{3}{5}\right)$
15. $-\frac{6}{7}\left(-\frac{14}{10}\right)$
16. $-3\frac{1}{10}\left(1\frac{1}{3}\right)$
17. $6\frac{1}{2}\left(2\frac{2}{8}\right)$
18. $4\frac{1}{4}\left(1\frac{2}{5}\right)$
19. $\frac{6}{2}\left(2\frac{1}{4}\right)$
20. $-8\frac{1}{8}\left(-\frac{3}{4}\right)$
21. $-4\frac{5}{6}\left(2\frac{2}{3}\right)$
22. $8\frac{7}{9}\left(-5\frac{2}{5}\right)$
23. $2\frac{3}{4}\left(8\frac{4}{7}\right)$
24. $-1\frac{1}{10}\left(3\frac{2}{10}\right)$
25. $1\frac{3}{4}\left(-\frac{4}{5}\right)$
26. $-2\frac{3}{4}\left(-2\frac{1}{4}\right)$
27. $5\left(4\frac{2}{5}\right)$

B Find the value of each expression. Reduce to lowest terms.

28. $\frac{2}{3}b$ for $b = 1\frac{1}{4}$
29. $-\frac{4}{3}a$ for $a = 12$
30. $1\frac{1}{5}y - \frac{3}{10}$ for $y = -1\frac{3}{5}$
31. $\frac{1}{8}x + 2$ for $x = 3\frac{1}{2}$
32. $1\frac{1}{2}h$ for $h = -\frac{5}{6}$
33. $\frac{2}{3}x + \frac{1}{4}$ for $x = -\frac{5}{6}$

Find the value of x. Reduce to lowest terms.

34. $x = \frac{2}{3}\left(\frac{3}{5} + \frac{6}{15}\right)$
35. $x = \left(\frac{1}{2} + \frac{3}{4}\right)\frac{2}{5}$
36. $x = -\frac{18}{24}(9 - 15)$
37. $x = -\frac{4}{5}(-5 + 8)$
38. $x = \frac{4}{5}\left(\frac{4}{5} + \frac{3}{4}\right)$
39. $x = \frac{3}{8}(6 - 7)$

Solve.

40. A cookbook recommends roasting a turkey at a low temperature $\frac{3}{4}$ hour for each pound. How long should you cook a $10\frac{1}{2}$ pound turkey?

41. Each section of a fence is $6\frac{1}{2}$ ft long. How long is this fence if it has 8 sections?

42. A certain steel bar weighs $2\frac{1}{2}$ pounds per foot. What would be the weight of a piece $3\frac{3}{4}$ ft long?

Estimate each product by rounding to the nearest whole number.

43. $3\frac{4}{5}\left(7\frac{1}{8}\right)$ **44.** $5\frac{1}{6}\left(6\frac{9}{10}\right)$ **45.** $7\frac{3}{4}\left(4\frac{1}{3}\right)$ **46.** $8\frac{1}{7}\left(9\frac{7}{8}\right)$

Estimate each product by substituting compatible numbers.
For example, to estimate $\frac{1}{3}(25)$, think "$\frac{1}{3}$ of 24 is 8."

47. $\frac{1}{5}(39)$ **48.** $\frac{1}{4}(26)$ **49.** $\frac{2}{3}(17)$ **50.** $\frac{1}{10}(79)$

C Extending Thinking Skills

51. To find the value of x in the equations below, look for a pattern. Then write two similar equations with the same solution.

$\frac{1}{3}x = 16, \frac{1}{4}x = 12, \frac{1}{6}x = 8$

52. Look for a pattern to find the next two numbers in this sequence.

$\frac{3}{2}, -\frac{3}{5}, \frac{6}{25}, -\frac{12}{125}$, —, —

53. Marie's age is 4 more than $2\frac{1}{2}$ times her brother's age. If Marie is 24, how old is her brother?

Mixed Review

Simplify. **54.** $(5m + 12) + (4m - 6)$ **55.** $c + t + t + t + c$

Find the greatest common factor (GCF). **56.** 9, 42, 51 **57.** 4, 9

Reduce to lowest terms. **58.** $\frac{16}{100}$ **59.** $-\frac{12}{60}$ **60.** $\frac{27}{51}$

Write each mixed number as an improper fraction.

61. $-6\frac{4}{5}$ **62.** $12\frac{1}{3}$ **63.** $5\frac{7}{16}$ **64.** $-2\frac{7}{8}$

Solve and check. **65.** $19.5x = -1.17$ **66.** $a - 1.06 = -0.98$

67. $n - \frac{1}{2} = \frac{3}{8}$ **68.** $y + \frac{3}{14} = \frac{5}{8}$ **69.** $-\frac{1}{3} = z - \frac{3}{5}$

MENTAL MATH

You can use the distributive property and "break apart numbers" to find the products of rational numbers mentally. For example, to find $8 \cdot 3\frac{1}{4}$, think: "8 times 3 plus 8 times $\frac{1}{4}$ equals 24 plus 2, or 26."

Use the distributive property to find each product mentally.

1. $12 \cdot 2\frac{1}{3}$ **2.** $-16 \cdot 1\frac{1}{4}$ **3.** $20 \cdot \left(-2\frac{3}{10}\right)$ **4.** $\frac{1}{2} \cdot 8\frac{1}{3}$

5. $8\frac{1}{2} \cdot 4$ **6.** $-100 \cdot 1\frac{1}{10}$ **7.** $50 \cdot 2\frac{1}{50}$ **8.** $\frac{1}{4} \cdot 4\frac{1}{2}$

7-2 Dividing Rational Numbers

Two numbers are called **multiplicative inverses** or **reciprocals** of each other if their product is 1. The multiplicative inverse of 3 is $\frac{1}{3}$ since $3 \times \frac{1}{3} = 1$. The multiplicative inverse of $-\frac{3}{4}$ is $-\frac{4}{3}$ since $-\frac{3}{4}\left(-\frac{4}{3}\right) = 1$.

Inverse Property of Multiplication

The product of a rational number and its multiplicative inverse (or reciprocal) is 1.

For every rational number $\frac{a}{b}$ **($a \neq 0$, $b \neq 0$),**

$$\frac{a}{b} \cdot \frac{b}{a} = \frac{b}{a} \cdot \frac{a}{b} = 1$$

We can use this property to develop a rule for dividing two rational numbers.

$$\frac{4}{5} \div \frac{2}{3} = \frac{\frac{4}{5}}{\frac{2}{3}}$$ $\frac{a}{b} \div \frac{c}{d}$ is the same as $\frac{\frac{a}{b}}{\frac{c}{d}}$.

$$\frac{4}{5} \div \frac{2}{3} = \frac{\frac{4}{5} \cdot \frac{3}{2}}{\frac{2}{3} \cdot \frac{3}{2}}$$ $\frac{a}{b} = \frac{a \cdot c}{b \cdot c}$.

$$\frac{4}{5} \div \frac{2}{3} = \frac{\frac{4}{5} \cdot \frac{3}{2}}{1}$$ Inverse property of multiplication.

$$\frac{4}{5} \div \frac{2}{3} = \frac{4}{5} \cdot \frac{3}{2}$$

Dividing Rational Numbers

To divide by a rational number, multiply by its inverse. For rational numbers $\frac{a}{b}$ and $\frac{c}{d}$ **($b \neq 0$, $c \neq 0$, $d \neq 0$),**

$$\frac{a}{b} \div \frac{c}{d} = \frac{a}{b} \cdot \frac{d}{c}$$

Example 1

Divide. Reduce to lowest terms. $\frac{1}{4} \div \frac{2}{6}$

Solution

$$\frac{1}{4} \div \frac{2}{6} = \frac{1}{4} \cdot \frac{6}{2}$$ Dividing by $\frac{2}{6}$ is the same as multiplying by $\frac{6}{2}$.

$$= \frac{6}{8} = \frac{3}{4}$$

Practice Divide. Reduce to lowest terms. **a.** $-\frac{2}{3} \div \frac{1}{6}$ **b.** $\frac{5}{24} \div 5$

Example 2

Divide. Reduce to lowest terms. $-1\frac{3}{4} \div 2\frac{1}{2}$

Solution

$$-1\frac{3}{4} \div 2\frac{1}{2} = -\frac{7}{4} \div \frac{5}{2}$$ Change mixed numbers to improper fractions.

$$= -\frac{7}{4} \cdot \frac{2}{5}$$ Dividing by $\frac{5}{2}$ is the same as multiplying by $\frac{2}{5}$.

$$= -\frac{14}{20} = -\frac{7}{10}$$

Practice Divide. Reduce to lowest terms. **a.** $8 \div \left(-3\frac{3}{4}\right)$ **b.** $3\frac{1}{8} \div 2\frac{1}{12}$

Oral Exercises

Express each as a multiplication problem. Do not solve.

1. $\frac{3}{4} \div \frac{2}{5}$ **2.** $\frac{7}{9} \div \frac{4}{5}$ **3.** $\frac{6}{5} \div \left(-\frac{8}{3}\right)$ **4.** $\frac{5}{8} \div \frac{2}{3}$

5. $-\frac{3}{4} \div 5$ **6.** $12 \div \left(-\frac{1}{2}\right)$ **7.** $\frac{5}{6} \div \frac{1}{3}$ **8.** $\frac{3}{10} \div \left(-\frac{15}{100}\right)$

Exercises

A Divide. Reduce to lowest terms.

1. $\frac{3}{5} \div \frac{1}{5}$ **2.** $\frac{1}{2} \div \frac{3}{4}$ **3.** $\frac{5}{8} \div \frac{7}{8}$ **4.** $\frac{1}{9} \div \left(-\frac{4}{3}\right)$

5. $-\frac{5}{8} \div \frac{3}{2}$ **6.** $\frac{5}{9} \div \left(-\frac{7}{3}\right)$ **7.** $-\frac{3}{10} \div \frac{8}{5}$ **8.** $\frac{9}{12} \div \frac{5}{6}$

9. $-\frac{5}{9} \div \left(-\frac{1}{3}\right)$ **10.** $\frac{5}{12} \div \frac{2}{3}$ **11.** $\frac{5}{4} \div \left(-\frac{5}{8}\right)$ **12.** $-\frac{3}{8} \div 5$

13. $\frac{13}{20} \div \frac{7}{10}$ **14.** $\frac{1}{10} \div \frac{3}{12}$ **15.** $\frac{18}{24} \div \frac{1}{8}$ **16.** $1\frac{1}{2} \div \left(-\frac{3}{4}\right)$

17. $-3\frac{1}{3} \div \left(-\frac{5}{6}\right)$ **18.** $3\frac{1}{3} \div 2\frac{1}{4}$ **19.** $5\frac{2}{3} \div 1\frac{3}{4}$ **20.** $2\frac{1}{4} \div (-6)$

21. $-\frac{4}{5} \div 2\frac{2}{3}$ 22. $-2\frac{1}{2} \div \left(-1\frac{3}{4}\right)$ 23. $\frac{1}{6} \div 3\frac{1}{2}$ 24. $\frac{7}{3} \div \left(-1\frac{3}{7}\right)$

25. $3\frac{1}{10} \div \frac{1}{100}$ 26. $6\frac{1}{4} \div 10\frac{1}{4}$ 27. $-18 \div \left(-2\frac{11}{16}\right)$ 28. $6\frac{2}{3} \div 2\frac{3}{4}$

B Evaluate each expression. Reduce to lowest terms.

29. $\frac{x}{16} - \frac{1}{2}$ for $x = -\frac{3}{8}$ 30. $\frac{-3\frac{1}{3}}{x}$ for $x = \frac{5}{12}$ 31. $\frac{5}{x} + \frac{3}{4}$ for $x = 1\frac{1}{2}$

32. Suppose you walk at a rate of $2\frac{1}{2}$ miles per hour. How long would it take to walk to school and back if the school were $3\frac{1}{2}$ miles from home?

33. Christopher wants to engrave his name on an ID bracelet. There are $1\frac{3}{4}$ inches of space on the bracelet. He can choose from three sizes of letters: $\frac{1}{8}$ inch wide, $\frac{1}{4}$ inch wide, or $\frac{1}{2}$ inch wide. Which size or sizes of lettering could he use for his name?

C Extending Thinking Skills

34. Find all the ways to complete the equation $\frac{x}{y} \cdot \frac{m}{n} = \frac{9}{15}$ where $x < 9$, $m < 9$, $y < 15$, and $n < 15$. Replace each letter with a different whole number.

35. Find two rational numbers with a sum of 1, product of $-\frac{6}{25}$, and quotient of -6.

Mixed Review

Solve and check. **36.** $a \div 1.75 = -16$ **37.** $r + 0.9 = -1.3$

Find the least common multiple (LCM). **38.** 4, 6, 9, 12

ESTIMATION

You can substitute compatible numbers to estimate quotients involving rational numbers.

Example: Choose the best estimate. $14\frac{1}{8} \div 7$ <2 or >2?

Think: $14\frac{1}{8}$ is about 14 and $14 \div 7 = 2$. Since $14\frac{1}{8} > 14$, the quotient will be greater than 2.

Use compatible numbers to choose the best estimate.

1. $7\frac{2}{9} \cdot 2\frac{1}{3}$ <14 or >14? 2. $\frac{2}{5} \cdot 18$ <18 or >18?

3. $12\frac{1}{3} \div 4$ <3 or >3? 4. $8\frac{3}{4} \div 2\frac{1}{4}$ <4 or >4?

5. $22\frac{1}{3} \div 8$ <3 or >3? 6. $24 \div 2\frac{5}{8}$ <8 or >8?

7-3 Solving Equations: Using Multiplication and Division

You can solve equations such as $\frac{3}{4}x = \frac{5}{8}$ by dividing both sides by $\frac{3}{4}$. It is simpler, however, to multiply by the reciprocal of $\frac{3}{4}$. Keep in mind the following steps:

- Decide which operation (multiplication or division) has been applied to the variable.
- Use the inverse operation or use the multiplicative inverse property, multiplying or dividing by the same number on both sides of the equation.

Example 1

Solve and check. $\frac{3}{4}x = \frac{5}{8}$

Solution

$$\frac{3}{4}x = \frac{5}{8}$$

$$\frac{4}{3} \cdot \left(\frac{3}{4}x\right) = \frac{4}{3} \cdot \frac{5}{8}$$ Multiply both sides by the reciprocal of $\frac{3}{4}$ so they remain equal.

$$1 \cdot x = \frac{20}{24}$$ $\frac{4}{3} \cdot \frac{3}{4} = 1.$

$$x = \frac{5}{6}$$

Check

$$\frac{3}{4} \cdot \frac{5}{6} \stackrel{?}{=} \frac{5}{8}$$ Replace x with $\frac{5}{6}$.

$$\frac{15}{24} \stackrel{?}{=} \frac{5}{8}$$

$$\frac{5}{8} = \frac{5}{8} \checkmark$$ The solution is $\frac{5}{6}$.

Practice Solve and check.

a. $\frac{1}{6}f = 4$ **b.** $-\frac{3}{4}y = 1\frac{1}{2}$

c. $6y = \frac{3}{8}$ **d.** $7p = \frac{7}{10}$

Example 2

Solve and check. $-3\frac{1}{2}x = 2\frac{3}{4}$

Solution $-3\frac{1}{2}x = 2\frac{3}{4}$

$-\frac{7}{2}x = \frac{11}{4}$ Change mixed numbers to improper fractions.

$-\frac{2}{7}\left(-\frac{7}{2}x\right) = -\frac{2}{7} \cdot \frac{11}{4}$ Multiply both sides by the reciprocal of $-\frac{7}{2}$.

$1 \cdot x = -\frac{22}{28}$

$x = -\frac{11}{14}$

Check $-\frac{7}{2}\left(-\frac{11}{14}\right) \stackrel{?}{=} \frac{11}{4}$ Replace x with $-\frac{11}{14}$ in $-\frac{7}{2}x = \frac{11}{4}$.

$\frac{77}{28} \stackrel{?}{=} \frac{11}{4}$

$\frac{11}{4} = \frac{11}{4}$ ✓ The solution is $-\frac{11}{14}$.

Practice Solve and check. **a.** $4\frac{1}{3}y = 5$ **b.** $-2\frac{4}{5} = 1\frac{5}{6}h$

Oral Exercises

To solve, what operation would you use in the first step?

1. $\frac{1}{6}y = \frac{2}{3}$ **2.** $\frac{y}{5} = \frac{1}{2}$ **3.** $6b = -\frac{3}{5}$ **4.** $\frac{5}{6}x = \frac{7}{12}$

5. $\frac{2}{3}a = -6$ **6.** $p - 3\frac{3}{4} = \frac{8}{9}$ **7.** $\frac{t}{-7} = \frac{4}{5}$ **8.** $m + \frac{3}{10} = \frac{6}{8}$

Exercises

A Solve and check.

1. $4x = \frac{3}{4}$ **2.** $\frac{t}{4} = \frac{5}{7}$ **3.** $\frac{4}{5}m = 5$ **4.** $6x = \frac{4}{3}$

5. $\frac{1}{5}y = 1$ **6.** $\frac{y}{6} = \frac{5}{12}$ **7.** $\frac{2}{3}h = -6$ **8.** $-\frac{1}{2}y = \frac{7}{10}$

9. $3b = -\frac{2}{3}$ **10.** $-\frac{5}{6}h = -\frac{3}{2}$ **11.** $\frac{p}{14} = \frac{3}{2}$ **12.** $\frac{z}{-10} = \frac{2}{5}$

13. $-\frac{7}{16}x = -\frac{3}{8}$ **14.** $\frac{9}{16}y = \frac{2}{5}$ **15.** $\frac{k}{6} = -\frac{12}{9}$ **16.** $1\frac{2}{3}x = \frac{6}{5}$

17. $-1\frac{3}{8}x = -\frac{3}{4}$ **18.** $4\frac{3}{5}h = 8$ **19.** $4\frac{3}{10} = 2\frac{3}{5}g$ **20.** $1\frac{2}{9} = 18h$

21. $3\frac{1}{3}x = -12$ **22.** $-4f = -3\frac{5}{6}$ **23.** $-\frac{9}{10} = 5\frac{7}{12}x$ **24.** $\frac{y}{12} = 2\frac{3}{10}$

B Solve and check.

25. $\left(\frac{3}{4} + \frac{5}{8}\right)x = 2$ **26.** $-\frac{7}{12}(-6y) = 4$ **27.** $\left(\frac{2}{3}x\right)\frac{1}{2} = 5$

28. $\left(5 - 2\frac{3}{4}\right)x = -2\frac{5}{6}$ **29.** $\left(\frac{1}{2} + \frac{7}{9} - \frac{1}{2}\right)t = 14$ **30.** $5\frac{1}{2}r = 0$

For Exercises 31–33, solve mentally by choosing **compatible numbers**. For example, to solve $x = \frac{1}{5}\left(\frac{7}{8}\right)(5)$, think "$\frac{1}{5}(5)$ is 1; $1\left(\frac{7}{8}\right)$ is $\frac{7}{8}$.

31. $x = \frac{1}{6}\left(2\frac{1}{4}\right)(6)$ **32.** $x = \frac{3}{8}\left(\frac{1}{6}\right)(8)$ **33.** $x = 9\left(2\frac{1}{5}\right)\left(\frac{1}{3}\right)$

C *Extending Thinking Skills*

34. Find a number for which the following is true: $\frac{1}{5}$ of the number added to 28 is triple the number.

35. Mentally find two values of y that make this equation true. $\frac{1}{2}y^2 = 8$.

36. Mentally find two values of x that make this equation true. $8x^2 = 2$.

Mixed Review

Simplify. **37.** $(4c + 2) + (4c - 2)$ **38.** $6(x - 3) + 4x + 2$

Solve and check. **39.** $-16.8 = r \div 2$ **40.** $z + 29 = 317$

COMPUTER ACTIVITY

You can use a computer program to find decimal or integer solutions to equations. To solve the equation $\frac{3}{4}x = 15$, the program computes:

$$x = \frac{4 \cdot 15}{3}$$ Multiply by 4 and divide by 3.

```
10  PRINT "SOLVING EQUATIONS OF THE FORM A/B*N=C"
20  INPUT "ENTER A, B, AND C"; A, B, C
30  IF A=0 OR B=0 THEN GOTO 70
40  N=(B*C)/A
50  PRINT "N="; N
60  GOTO 80
70  PRINT "NEITHER A NOR B CAN EQUAL ZERO."
80  PRINT "DO YOU WANT TO CONTINUE (Y/N)?"
90  INPUT A$:IF A$="Y" THEN 20
100 END
```

Use the program to solve each equation for N.

1. $\frac{15}{29}N = 25$ **2.** $\frac{23}{27}N = -21$ **3.** $\frac{63}{82}N = 136$ **4.** $4\frac{2}{3}N = 215$

5. Modify the program to solve equations such as $37N = \frac{3}{7}$.

6. Modify the program to solve equations such as $\frac{2}{3}N = \frac{4}{5}$.

More Practice

Solve and check. Reduce your answer to lowest terms.

1. $3t = \frac{3}{5}$
2. $\frac{r}{5} = \frac{6}{11}$
3. $3\frac{1}{2}x = 4$
4. $-\frac{k}{9} = \frac{4}{5}$
5. $2\frac{1}{4}z = \frac{4}{9}$
6. $9c = \frac{2}{5}$
7. $6c = \frac{8}{15}$
8. $-\frac{2}{3}f = 1\frac{4}{5}$
9. $\frac{3}{4}m = 6\frac{1}{3}$
10. $\frac{5}{9}w = \frac{10}{17}$
11. $1\frac{1}{2}x = 5$
12. $1\frac{4}{5}y = \frac{3}{4}$
13. $11t = -\frac{9}{10}$
14. $\frac{6}{11}r = \frac{9}{11}$
15. $\frac{a}{3} = \frac{5}{7}$
16. $2\frac{3}{5}k = -4$
17. $3\frac{1}{4}n = -\frac{3}{4}$
18. $-6c = \frac{11}{12}$
19. $-\frac{a}{2} = -\frac{3}{5}$
20. $6\frac{2}{3}x = 15$
21. $\frac{7}{10}k = 1\frac{3}{4}$
22. $-3\frac{1}{8}c = \frac{15}{16}$
23. $\frac{m}{4} = -\frac{2}{9}$
24. $4t = -\frac{2}{5}$
25. $\frac{k}{12} = \frac{7}{8}$
26. $\frac{3}{4} = r + 1\frac{1}{2}$
27. $z - \frac{1}{2} = -\frac{3}{8}$
28. $\frac{5}{6}(m) = -3\frac{3}{4}$
29. $-\frac{4}{5} + c = 1$
30. $k - \frac{7}{8} = 1\frac{1}{3}$
31. $12z = \frac{3}{5}$
32. $\frac{h}{-3} = \frac{11}{15}$
33. $\frac{9}{16}z = -4\frac{2}{3}$
34. $\frac{11}{12}a = -6$
35. $c - 4\frac{1}{3} = \frac{2}{5}$
36. $1\frac{5}{6} = a + \frac{3}{5}$
37. $-5x = 2\frac{1}{8}$
38. $3\frac{1}{3} = z - \left(-\frac{1}{2}\right)$
39. $m + \frac{1}{3} = -\frac{3}{4}$
40. $8a = -\frac{5}{6}$
41. $k - 2\frac{4}{5} = \frac{1}{2}$
42. $\frac{2}{3}x = -9$
43. $2\frac{1}{6}x = 9\frac{1}{2}$
44. $\frac{3}{5} = t + \frac{1}{2}$
45. $\frac{m}{-6} = \frac{8}{15}$
46. $y - \frac{5}{12} = -\frac{3}{4}$
47. $-\frac{4}{9} = c + 2\frac{1}{3}$
48. $6n = \frac{3}{5}$

7-4 Deciding What the Variable Represents

You can use the Problem-Solving Checklist on page 121 to help you solve word problems. When your plan involves writing and solving an equation, keep the following questions in mind.

- Can you use a variable to represent an unknown number?
- Can you represent other conditions in terms of the variable?
- What is equal?
- Can you write and solve an equation?

The variable can often represent the number that the question in the problem is asking you to find. Sometimes, however, the variable must be used to represent another unknown in the problem.

Example

A jazz group gave 2 shows in one night. Attendance at the second show was $1\frac{1}{2}$ times the attendance at the first show. If there were 87 people at the second show, what was the total attendance for the two shows?

Solution

Let f = number at the first show $1\frac{1}{2}f$ = number at the second show	Total attendance is the sum of the numbers for both shows. Let the variable stand for the unknown number at the first show. The number at the second show is $1\frac{1}{2}$ times the number at the first show.
$1\frac{1}{2}f = 87$	The number of people at the second show was 87.
$\frac{3}{2}f = 87$	
$\frac{2}{3} \cdot \frac{3}{2}f = \frac{2}{3} \cdot 87$	Multiply both sides by the reciprocal of $\frac{3}{2}$.
$f = 58$	There were 58 people at the first show.
$58 + 87 = 145$	Add the numbers for both shows to answer the question in the problem.

The total attendance was 145.

Exercises

A Solve by writing an equation.

1. In one year, 120 students enrolled at a technical school. This was $\frac{3}{5}$ of the number of people accepted. How many of those accepted did not enroll?

2. The cost of an adult ticket to a show is $2\frac{1}{2}$ times the cost of a child's ticket. An adult ticket is $3.75. What would the total ticket cost be for 1 adult and 1 child?

3. A cook needed $\frac{1}{3}$ hour cooking time for each pound of turkey. How big was the turkey if it cooked for $5\frac{1}{2}$ hours?

4. A grocery store manager said that $\frac{1}{24}$ of the number of checks received in May were from a certain bank. The store received 96 checks from that bank. How many checks did it receive from other banks?

5. To allow for waste and leftovers, a roofer always orders about $\frac{1}{10}$ more shingles than are needed to cover the exact measurements of a roof. The roofer ordered $2\frac{1}{2}$ extra bundles of shingles for a roof. How many bundles were needed for the exact measurements?

B

6. The odometer on Marta's bicycle read 2375 when she left home. At the end of her trip the odometer read 2453. Marta bicycled for $6\frac{1}{2}$ hours that day. What was her average speed for the trip?

7. If Tim lost $\frac{1}{2}$ lb on Saturday and another $\frac{1}{4}$ lb on Sunday, he would have been down to the wrestling weight his coach wanted for him. His coach wanted him to weigh $105\frac{1}{2}$ lbs. How much did Tim weigh before Saturday?

8. Fran likes to work 20 hours each week. Last week she worked only $4\frac{1}{2}$ hours on Tuesday, $4\frac{1}{2}$ hours on Thursday, and $2\frac{1}{4}$ hours on Friday. Fran earned $54. How much would she earn in a 20-hour work week?

C Extending Thinking Skills

Write a word problem that could be solved using the equation.

9. $\frac{3}{4}x = 8$

10. $\left(\frac{1}{2} + \frac{1}{4}\right)x = 10$

Mixed Review

Solve and check. **11.** $x - \frac{3}{8} = \frac{2}{3}$ **12.** $\frac{4}{11} = c + \frac{1}{2}$ **13.** $y + \frac{1}{4} = \frac{11}{16}$

14. $r + 1.03 = -2.67$ **15.** $-9.86m = 226.78$ **16.** $z - 14.4 = 12.73$

Evaluate for $m = \frac{3}{4}$. **17.** $m + \frac{1}{2}$ **18.** $\frac{2}{5} - m$ **19.** $\frac{3}{16} + m$

PROBLEM SOLVING: APPLICATIONS

7-5 Mathematics and Masonry

A **mason** is a person who builds with stones, bricks, and concrete. Much of the work a mason does involves computation with rational numbers.

Problems

Solve.

1. Figure 1 shows a hollow brick that is used to line the insides of chimneys. What is the overall length of one of these bricks?

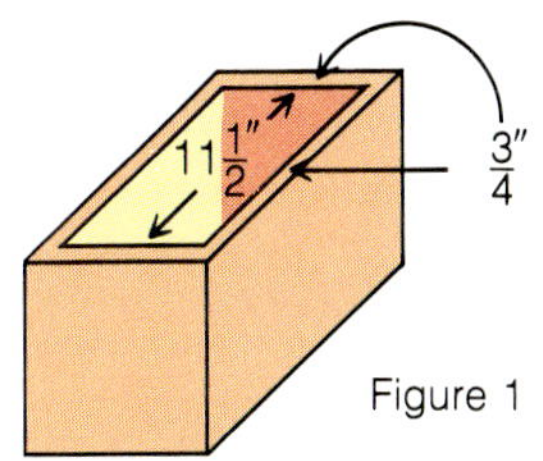

Figure 1

2. The stairway in figure 2 has five risers. What is the rise of these steps?

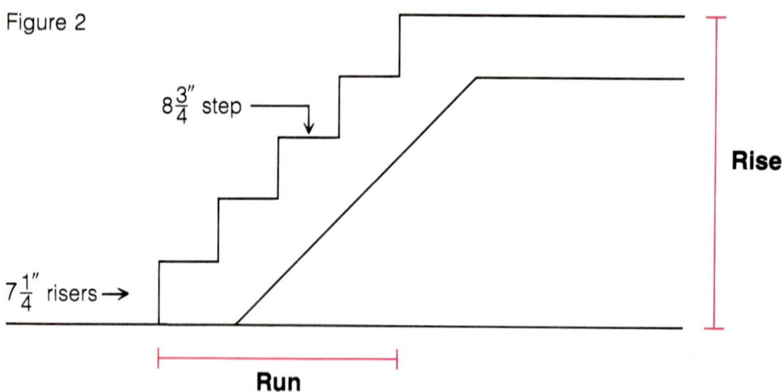

3. The stairway in figure 2 has 4 steps. What is the run of this stairway?

4. A certain stairway has 14 risers. If each riser is $6\frac{5}{8}$ inches high, what is the rise of this stairway?

5. A standard-size brick weighs $2\frac{3}{4}$ pounds. How much would 36 of these bricks weigh?

6. Plans for construction of a patio require 888 square feet of brick. The mason figures that with the size of brick and mortar to be used, about $5\frac{1}{2}$ bricks are needed per square foot. About how many bricks are needed to construct the patio?

7. A mason needs $\frac{5}{8}$ of a cubic yard of mortar to lay 1000 bricks in a wall. About how many cubic yards of mortar would he need to lay 6400 bricks?

8. A standard-size brick is $2\frac{1}{2}$ inches thick. What is the height of a wall made of 6 rows of this brick with $\frac{1}{2}$ inch of mortar at its base and $\frac{1}{2}$ inch of mortar between rows?

9. A standard-size brick is $8\frac{1}{4}$ inches long. How long would a wall be if it had 24 bricks side-by-side, with $\frac{3}{8}$ inch of mortar between bricks?

10. *Data Search* Suppose you were going to cover one wall of your classroom with brick. Find the approximate total cost of the brick you would need for the job.

What's Your Decision?

You have 700 standard-size bricks ($8\frac{1}{4}''$ by $2\frac{1}{2}''$) and plan to build a patio, using $\frac{1}{2}''$ of sand between bricks. You hope to use as many of the bricks as possible. What shape and size patio would you design?

7-6 Rational Numbers and Repeating Decimals

You can write $\frac{3}{8}$ as the **terminating decimal** 0.375, because when you divide 3 by 8 the division process ends with a remainder of 0, or terminates. A **repeating decimal** is a decimal with a set of digits that repeats endlessly. For example, you can write $\frac{15}{33}$ as a repeating decimal.

$$\frac{15}{33} = 0.454545\ldots$$

$$= 0.\overline{45}$$ The bar indicates the set of digits that repeats.

A rational number can be expressed as either a terminating or repeating decimal. A decimal that is neither terminating nor repeating, such as 3.121121112 . . . , names an **irrational number**.

Example

Write $\frac{3}{11}$ as a decimal. Use a bar for a repeating decimal.

Solution

$$\begin{array}{r} 0.2727\ldots = 0.\overline{27} \\ 11\overline{)3.0000} \\ \underline{2\,2} \\ 80 \\ \underline{77} \\ 30 \\ \underline{22} \\ 80 \\ \underline{77} \\ 30 \end{array}$$

Annex zeros and continue dividing until the quotient either terminates or begins to repeat.

Practice Write as a decimal. Use a bar for a repeating decimal. **a.** $\frac{2}{9}$ **b.** $\frac{1}{6}$

Oral Exercises

State whether each is a terminating decimal or repeating decimal, or names an irrational number. For a repeating decimal, identify the digits that repeat.

1. 0.171717 . . . **2.** 0.236 **3.** 3.12121212 . . .

4. 3.123456 . . . **5.** 0.34555 **6.** 2.010010001 . . .

Exercises

A Write as a decimal. Use a bar for a repeating decimal.

1. $\frac{5}{11}$ **2.** $\frac{1}{3}$ **3.** $\frac{7}{20}$ **4.** $\frac{23}{9}$

5. $\frac{1}{15}$ **6.** $\frac{3}{4}$ **7.** $\frac{27}{16}$ **8.** $\frac{7}{18}$

9. $\frac{2}{3}$ **10.** $\frac{5}{8}$ **11.** $\frac{4}{9}$ **12.** $\frac{7}{16}$

13. $\frac{23}{40}$ **14.** $\frac{11}{3}$ **15.** $\frac{9}{24}$ **16.** $\frac{6}{11}$

B Write each as a decimal.

17. $\frac{16}{25}$ **18.** $\frac{48}{11}$ **19.** $\frac{88}{33}$ **20.** $\frac{72}{99}$

21. $\frac{51}{85}$ **22.** $\frac{17}{32}$ **23.** $\frac{65}{18}$ **24.** $\frac{44}{54}$

25. $\frac{5}{12}$ **26.** $\frac{19}{15}$ **27.** $\frac{9}{33}$ **28.** $\frac{16}{6}$

29. Solve for x: $x = 34.\overline{45} - 1.\overline{45}$ **30.** Solve for x: $x = 23.\overline{8} - 2.3\overline{8}$

Write the fractions as decimals to solve. Give an approximate answer if the decimal repeats.

31. A new auditorium has 250 seats. About $\frac{7}{8}$ of the seats have right-hand desks. How many seats have right-hand desks?

32. A consumer guide suggests that people should save about $\frac{1}{6}$ of their earnings. How much money should a person who earns $32,500 a year save?

33. In a school with 360 graduating students, $\frac{3}{4}$ of the students plan to go to college. How many students plan to go to college?

C Extending Thinking Skills

34. Arrange in order from smallest to largest.

$0.44, 0.4, 0.4\overline{3}, 0.\overline{429}, 0.45, 0.4\overline{5}$

35. Write a decimal that neither terminates nor repeats.

36. Find the decimal equivalents for $\frac{1}{11}$, $\frac{2}{11}$, $\frac{3}{11}$, and $\frac{4}{11}$. Look for a pattern in these decimals to give the decimal equivalents for $\frac{5}{11}$, $\frac{6}{11}$, $\frac{7}{11}$, and $\frac{8}{11}$.

Mixed Review

Find the least common multiple (LCM). **37.** 3, 4, 5 **38.** 2, 3, 4

Solve and check. **39.** $a - 3.97 = 2.43$ **40.** $-4c = -16.8$

Find the greatest common factor (GCF). **41.** 8, 16, 34

7-7 More About Exponents

You have used the rule $a^m \cdot a^n = a^{m+n}$ to multiply powers with the same base.

The following suggests a rule for simplifying expressions in the form $\frac{a^m}{a^n}$.

$$\frac{4^5}{4^2} = \frac{\overset{1}{\cancel{4}} \cdot \overset{1}{\cancel{4}} \cdot 4 \cdot 4 \cdot 4}{\underset{1}{\cancel{4}} \cdot \underset{1}{\cancel{4}}} = 4 \cdot 4 \cdot 4 = 4^3$$

Dividing Powers with Like Bases

To find the quotient of two numbers in exponential form with the same base, subtract the exponent of the denominator from the exponent of the numerator. Write this difference as the exponent of the base.

For all values of ***a*** except 0 and for all numbers ***m*** and ***n***, $\frac{a^m}{a^n} = a^{m-n}$

Example 1

Simplify. Write the expression with exponents. $\frac{2^5}{2^3}$

Solution

$\frac{2^5}{2^3} = 2^{5-3} = 2^2$ Since the base is the same, subtract the exponents.

Practice Simplify. Write the expression with exponents.

a. $\frac{5^6}{5^3}$ **b.** $\frac{(-3)^7}{(-3)^4}$ **c.** $\frac{10^4}{10}$

Example 2

Simplify. Write the expression with exponents. $\frac{x^6}{x^2}$

Solution

$\frac{x^6}{x^2} = x^{6-2} = x^4$ Since the base is the same, subtract the exponents.

Practice Simplify. Write the expression with exponents.

a. $\frac{y^8}{y^3}$ **b.** $\frac{m^5}{m}$ **c.** $\frac{z^3}{z^2}$

You can use the rule given on page 221 to simplify the expression $\frac{5^2}{5^4}$:

$$\frac{5^2}{5^4} = 5^{2-4} = 5^{-2}$$

You could also write the following: $\frac{5^2}{5^4} = \frac{\overset{1}{\cancel{5}} \cdot \overset{1}{\cancel{5}}}{\underset{1}{\cancel{5}} \cdot \underset{1}{\cancel{5}} \cdot 5 \cdot 5} = \frac{1}{5 \cdot 5} = \frac{1}{5^2}$

This shows that $\frac{1}{5^2}$ is the same as 5^{-2}. In general, you can use a **negative exponent** to write $\boldsymbol{a^{-m} = \frac{1}{a^m}}$.

Example 3

Write the expression 3^{-2} without exponents.

Solution

$3^{-2} = \frac{1}{3^2} = \frac{1}{9}$ Since the exponent is negative, you can rewrite the expression as $\frac{1}{3^2}$, and $3^2 = 9$.

Practice Write each expression without exponents. **a.** 5^{-3} **b.** 4^{-1}

This rule for dividing powers with like bases also shows that any number to the zero power, $\boldsymbol{a^0}$, is **1**.

Oral Exercises

State each using exponents.

1. $3 \cdot 3 \cdot 3 \cdot 3$ **2.** $\frac{1}{2 \cdot 2 \cdot 2 \cdot 2 \cdot 2}$ **3.** $\frac{1}{5 \cdot 5 \cdot 5}$ **4.** $4 \cdot 4 \cdot 2 \cdot 2 \cdot 2$

Exercises

A Simplify. Write the expression with exponents.

1. $\frac{3^4}{3}$ **2.** $\frac{5^4}{5^2}$ **3.** $\frac{(-4)^3}{(-4)}$ **4.** $\frac{2^6}{2^5}$

5. $\frac{10^5}{10}$ **6.** $\frac{(-4)^7}{(-4)^5}$ **7.** $\frac{8^5}{8}$ **8.** $\frac{(-2)^5}{(-2)}$

9. $\frac{6^2}{6}$ **10.** $\frac{(-3)^8}{(-3)^5}$ **11.** $\frac{x^5}{x^4}$ **12.** $\frac{y^6}{y^5}$

13. $\frac{t^3}{t}$ **14.** $\frac{r^6}{r^4}$ **15.** $\frac{g^5}{g^4}$ **16.** $\frac{y^4}{y}$

17. $\frac{x^6}{x}$ **18.** $\frac{m^4}{m^2}$ **19.** $\frac{n^6}{n^4}$ **20.** $\frac{s^7}{s^2}$

Write the expression without exponents.

21. 4^{-2} **22.** 3^{-3} **23.** $(-2)^{-4}$ **24.** $(-3)^3$

25. 10^{-4} **26.** $(-2)^2$ **27.** $(-5)^{-2}$ **28.** 2^6

B Simplify. Write the expression with exponents.

29. $3^2 \cdot 3^{-5}$

30. $4 \cdot 4^5 \cdot 4^{-3}$

31. $x \cdot x^{-3} \cdot x^3$

32. $\frac{4}{4^4}$

33. $\frac{3^2 \cdot 3^4}{3^5}$

34. $\frac{x^5}{x^2 \cdot x}$

35. $(-3)^{-4} \cdot (-3)^{-1}$

36. $a^{-3} \cdot a^{-4} \cdot a^9$

37. $5^{-2} \cdot 5^{-3} \cdot 5^4$

38. $\frac{z}{z^2 \cdot z^2}$

39. $\frac{(-2)^4(-2)^2}{(-2)^4}$

40. $\frac{5^3 \cdot 5^2}{5^7}$

41. What does n equal in $3^n = 27$?

42. What does n equal in $(-4)^n = \frac{1}{-64}$?

43. Compute $4^{-3} \cdot 4^5$. Then compute $4^5 \cdot 4^{-3}$. Is $\boldsymbol{a^n \cdot a^m = a^m \cdot a^n}$ true for all values of a, n, and m? Why? Name a property that explains the equality.

44. Write $(4x^2)^3$ as an expression with one exponent.

C *Extending Thinking Skills*

Express each as a whole number without exponents.

45. $\frac{1}{3^{-2}}$

46. $\frac{1}{4(4^{-2})}$

47. $\frac{2^{-2}}{2^{-4}}$

48. A poll taker interviewed only 1 person on Monday. On each of the following days, she interviewed 2 more people than on the previous day. How many interviews had she completed by the end of the day on Saturday?

Mixed Review

Evaluate for $y = -1.2$. **49.** $-1.5y$ **50.** $y + 9.35$ **51.** $6.3 - y$

Solve and check. **52.** $r \div 16 = -3$ **53.** $c + 7 = -1.4$

NUMBERS TO ALGEBRA

You can simplify algebraic expressions as you did numerical expressions.

Numbers	Algebra
$\frac{2^4}{3^3} \cdot \frac{3^2}{2^2} = \frac{2 \cdot \not{2} \cdot 2 \cdot 2 \cdot \not{3} \cdot \not{3}}{\not{2} \cdot \not{2} \cdot \not{3} \cdot \not{3} \cdot 3} = \frac{2^2}{3}$	$\frac{2x^3}{5y} \cdot \frac{6y^2}{4x^4} = \frac{\not{2} \cdot \not{x} \cdot \not{x} \cdot \not{x} \cdot \not{2} \cdot 3 \cdot \not{y} \cdot y}{5 \cdot \not{y} \cdot \not{2} \cdot \not{2} \cdot \not{x} \cdot \not{x} \cdot \not{x} \cdot x} = \frac{3y}{5x}$

Simplify.

1. $\frac{x^2}{y^4} \cdot \frac{y^6}{x}$

2. $\frac{4a^3}{5b^5} \cdot \frac{3b}{6a^2}$

3. $\frac{m^4}{n^5} \cdot \frac{6n^7}{5m^5}$

4. $\frac{3x^3}{5y^2} \cdot \frac{y^3}{12x^3}$

5. $xy^2 \cdot x^{-3}y^4$

6. $\frac{ab^5}{c} \cdot \frac{a^3c^4}{b^2}$

7-8 Scientific Notation

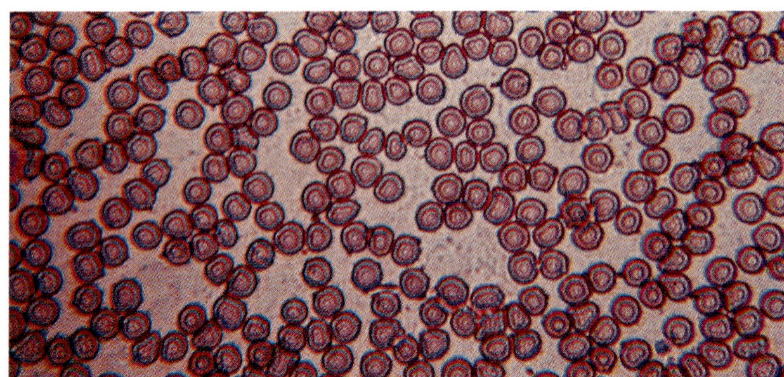

The human body replaces 2.0×10^{11} red blood cells every day. A cell in the body might be as small as 3×10^{-4} inches in diameter.

To simplify work with very large or very small numbers, you can use **scientific notation**. A number written as the product of a power of 10 and a number greater than or equal to 1 but less than 10 is expressed in scientific notation. The number 3.45×10^3 is in scientific notation. The numbers 12.3×10^2 and 124.5 are not in scientific notation.

Example 1

Write 3.23×10^4 in decimal form.

Solution

32,300 Multiplying 3.23 by 10^4 moves the decimal point 4 places to the right.

Practice Write each in decimal form.

a. 1.8×10^{-4} **b.** 6.556×10^2 **c.** 4×10^{-2}

Example 2

Write 1,234,000 in scientific notation.

Solution

1.234×10^6 Move the decimal point 6 places to the left. Multiply by 10^6.

Practice Write each in scientific notation.

a. 4567 **b.** 234,000 **c.** 50,000,000

Example 3

Write 0.000345 in scientific notation.

Solution

3.45×10^{-4} Move the decimal point 4 places to the right. Multiply by 10^{-4}.

Practice Write each in scientific notation.

a. 0.0206 **b.** 0.000008 **c.** 0.2004

Oral Exercises

Tell where the decimal should be placed to express each number in scientific notation.

1. 32,500 **2.** 35 **3.** 0.005
4. 0.6 **5.** 770 **6.** 82.5
7. 430,000 **8.** 18.6 **9.** 0.000050
10. 0.09 **11.** 0.0072 **12.** 25,000

Exercises

A Write each in decimal form.

1. 3.5×10^4 **2.** 6.2×10^{-2} **3.** 4.05×10^5 **4.** 7.0×10^{-5}

Write each in scientific notation.

5. 135 **6.** 23,000 **7.** 345,000 **8.** 8.4
9. 1240 **10.** 650,000 **11.** 4,550,000 **12.** 600
13. 99,000 **14.** 1,000,000 **15.** 0.078 **16.** 0.4
17. 0.000677 **18.** 0.0055 **19.** 0.000001 **20.** 0.05
21. 0.0000405 **22.** 0.000007 **23.** 0.101 **24.** 0.00000003

B Use the rules for multiplying and dividing exponents to write each product or quotient in scientific notation.

25. $(4.0 \times 10^3)(2 \times 10^4)$ **26.** $(3.2 \times 10^{-2})(5 \times 10^{-4})$

27. $\frac{6 \times 10^5}{2 \times 10^4}$ **28.** $\frac{5.2 \times 10^5}{1.3 \times 10^3}$

29. Every 0.4 cubic inch of human blood contains about 5,500,000 red blood cells. Write the number of red blood cells in scientific notation.

30. The red blood cell is one of the smallest cells in the human body. It has a diameter of 0.0003 inch. Write this number in scientific notation.

31. Some cells in the human body are so small that 200,000 could be placed on the head of a pin. Write this number in scientific notation.

C Extending Thinking Skills

32. Solve for y. $(7 \times 10^2)y = 6.3 \times 10^6$

33. Use the digits 1, 2, 3, and 4 and one negative sign to write a number in scientific notation that is as close to 0.01 as possible. $\square.\square\square \times 10^{\square}$

34. Chemical X is made in units weighing 2.5×10^{-2} g. To produce one unit of this chemical, 4×10^{-3} g of chemical A and 5.0×10^{-2} g of chemical B are needed. In the production process, 2.5×10^{-3} g of chemical A and 4.2×10^{-2} g of chemical B are burned off. What amount of each unit of chemical X comes from chemicals other than A and B?

Mixed Review

Reduce each fraction to lowest terms. **35.** $\frac{27}{135}$ **36.** $\frac{48}{192}$ **37.** $\frac{12}{140}$

Solve and check. **38.** $a - \frac{3}{4} = -\frac{5}{8}$ **39.** $h + \frac{13}{15} = 1\frac{1}{3}$

Simplify. **40.** $z \cdot z \cdot 10 \cdot 4 \cdot z$ **41.** $t + 2t + 3t + 4t$

CALCULATOR ACTIVITY

Some calculators allow you to enter numbers in scientific notation. You can use them to work with small or large numbers that would not fit on the calculator's display screen in standard form.

Using a scientific calculator, follow the example below. The EE key tells the calculator you are entering a power of ten. If the number or the exponent is negative, enter the negative sign before you enter the number or the exponent.

Problem in standard notation:
(52,000,000)(230,000,000) = 11,960,000,000,000,000

Problem in scientific notation:
$(5.2 \times 10^7)(2.3 \times 10^8) = 1.196 \times 10^{16}$

Display

5.2  7   2.3  8  1.196 16

Notice that the calculator display shows only 16, rather than 10^{16}, in the product. The answer is written 1.196×10^{16}.

Use a calculator to find each product.

1. $(4.74 \times 10^8)(8.5 \times 10^9)$

2. $(6.33 \times 10^7)(1.9 \times 10^7)$

3. (245,600,000)(700,000)

4. (1,754)(6,570,000,000,000)

5. (1,250,000,000,000)(12,240)

6. (24,400,000,000)(5,500,000,000)

PROBLEM SOLVING: STRATEGIES

7-9 Work Backward

Sometimes a word problem describes a sequence of actions involving numbers, gives the result, and asks for the number started with. A problem of this type can be solved by using a strategy called **Work Backward**.

Problem On Monday Jeff opened a savings account for his summer earnings and deposited all of his first week's earnings. On Tuesday, he deposited \$25 into the account. He withdrew \$23 on Wednesday to buy tapes and another \$15 on Thursday for other expenses. On Friday, he withdrew half of what was left in the account to buy some clothing. He then had \$12.50 remaining in the account. How much money did he deposit on Monday?

To solve this problem you can start with the amount of money Jeff had at the end and work backward, using the inverse operations. The lists below show the data given in the story and indicate how to work backward.

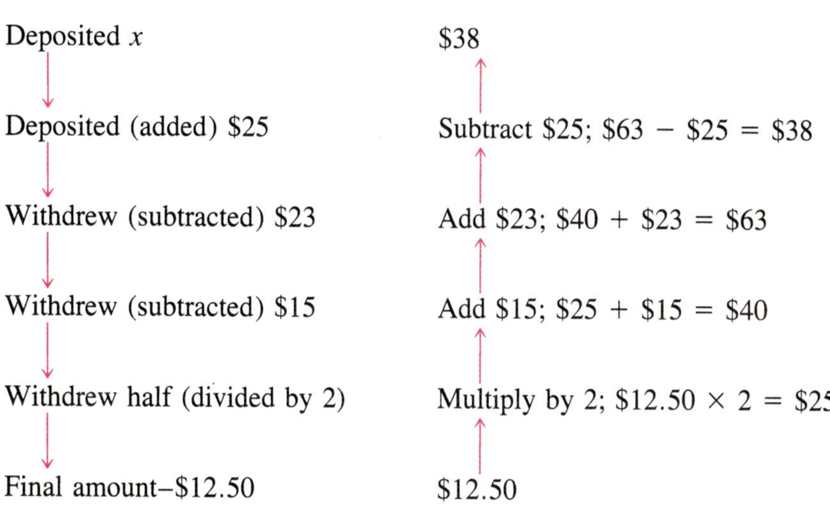

Data in the Story	Work Backward
Deposited x	\$38
↓	↑
Deposited (added) \$25	Subtract \$25; \$63 − \$25 = \$38
↓	↑
Withdrew (subtracted) \$23	Add \$23; \$40 + \$23 = \$63
↓	↑
Withdrew (subtracted) \$15	Add \$15; \$25 + \$15 = \$40
↓	↑
Withdrew half (divided by 2)	Multiply by 2; \$12.50 × 2 = \$25
↓	↑
Final amount–\$12.50	\$12.50

Jeff deposited \$38 on Monday.

Problem-Solving Strategies	
Choose the Operations	Write an Equation
Guess, Check, Revise	Simplify the Problem
Draw a Picture	Make an Organized List
Make a Table	Use Logical Reasoning
Look for a Pattern	Work Backward

This chart shows the strategies presented so far.

Problems

Solve.

1. Ned, Gary, Kris, and Brenda worked at a school car wash on Saturday. One person washed each car. Ned washed twice as many cars as Gary. Gary washed 4 fewer than Kris and Kris washed 5 more than Brenda. If Brenda washed 8 cars, how many cars did these students wash all together?

2. Two jars of chemicals labeled A and B were mixed so that each contained 64 ml at the end. The mixing process involved first pouring from B into A as much liquid as A contained, and finally pouring from A into B as much liquid as B now had. How much liquid was in each jar before they were mixed?

3. Jana spent exactly $1.00 on some snack items at the natural foods store. She bought 11 items on the price list at the right. Which items could she have bought?

Snack Items	
Honey Drops 2 for $0.15	Carob Chews 3 for $0.25
Granola Bars $0.10 each	

4. Suppose you have two pails, one that holds 4L of water and one that holds 9L. There are no markings on either pail to indicate quantities. How can you measure out 6L of water using these two pails?

5. Felipe lives at the corner of 1st and A Streets. Each day he goes to Matty's house at the corner of 5th and F Streets, traveling only east and north. How many days can he go without having to repeat a route?

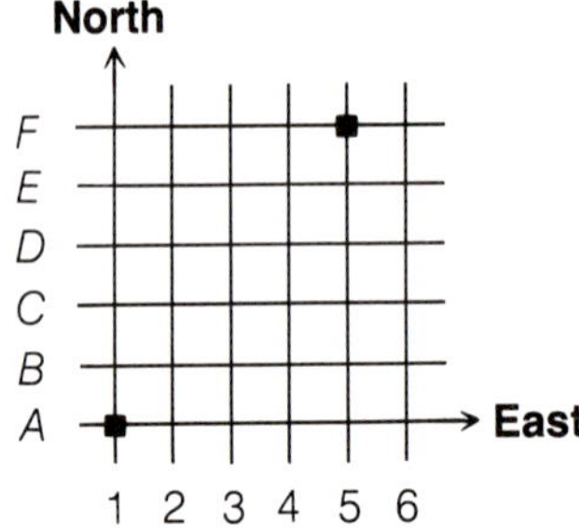

6. A rumor was passed around a town that had a population of 20,550. Each person who heard the rumor passed it on to 4 other people the next day, and then told no one else. One person made up the rumor and told it to 4 people on October 1st. What is the earliest day that everyone in this town might have heard the rumor?

Enrichment

Writing a Repeating Decimal as a Fraction

You can express a terminating decimal as a fraction. For example, $1.235 = \frac{1235}{1000}$.

To write a repeating decimal as a fraction, you can begin by multiplying by 10^n, where n is the number of digits in the repeating decimal part.

Write $0.\overline{36}$ as a fraction.

$x = 0.\overline{36}$ Original equation.

$100x = 36.\overline{36}$ Multiply both sides of the original equation by 10^2 since there are **2** digits in **36**.

$$\begin{array}{rrl} & 100x = & 36.\overline{36} \\ - & x = & 0.\overline{36} \\ \hline & 99x = & 36 \end{array}$$

Subtract the original equation.

$x = \frac{36}{99} = \frac{4}{11}$ Solve for x. Reduce to lowest terms.

The following example involves a single repeating digit.

Write $1.2\overline{3}$ as a fraction.

$x = 1.233333\ldots$ Original equation.

$10x = 12.33333\ldots$ Multiply both sides of the equation by 10, since only 1 digit repeats.

$$\begin{array}{rrl} & 10x = & 12.33333\ldots \\ - & x = & 1.23333\ldots \\ \hline & 9x = & 11.1 \end{array}$$

Subtract the original equation.

$x = \frac{11.1}{9} \cdot \frac{10}{10}$ Solve for x. Multiply by $\frac{10}{10}$ to remove the decimal from the numerator.

$x = \frac{111}{90} = 1\frac{21}{90} = 1\frac{7}{30}$

Write each as a fraction. Reduce to lowest terms.

1. $x = 0.\overline{3}$	**2.** $x = 0.1\overline{6}$	**3.** $x = 0.41\overline{6}$
4. $x = 0.4\overline{25}$	**5.** $x = 1.3\overline{8}$	**6.** $x = 0.5\overline{27}$
7. $x = 1.1\overline{2}$	**8.** $x = 0.6\overline{18}$	**9.** $x = 1.\overline{225}$

Chapter 7 Review

7-1 Multiply. Reduce to lowest terms.

1. $-\frac{4}{9}\left(-\frac{3}{4}\right)$

2. $\frac{6}{7}\left(-\frac{2}{3}\right)$

3. $-1\frac{3}{5}\left(3\frac{4}{7}\right)$

4. $7\frac{1}{2}\left(2\frac{4}{5}\right)$

7-2 Divide. Reduce to lowest terms.

5. $\frac{7}{12} \div \left(-\frac{4}{3}\right)$

6. $-\frac{9}{10} \div \left(-\frac{2}{5}\right)$

7. $4\frac{3}{8} \div 1\frac{3}{4}$

8. $-4\frac{1}{2} \div 6\frac{3}{4}$

7-3 Solve and check.

9. $\frac{4}{5}m = \frac{2}{15}$

10. $\frac{f}{-6} = \left(-\frac{2}{3}\right)$

11. $-5\frac{1}{4}s = 2\frac{4}{5}$

12. $-4\frac{4}{5} = 1\frac{6}{10}n$

7-4 Find the solution by writing and solving an equation.

13. Twenty-one people came to the first electronics class. This was $\frac{7}{8}$ of the number that signed up. How many people signed up?

7-5 Solve.

14. Mario placed dominoes end-to-end to form a line $37\frac{1}{2}$ inches long. If each domino was $2\frac{1}{2}$ inches long, how many were used?

15. If $\frac{1}{4}$ cup of lemon juice is used to make 2 cups of lemonade, how much lemon juice is needed to make 12 cups of lemonade?

7-6 Write each as a decimal. Use a bar for a repeating decimal.

16. $\frac{11}{18}$

17. $\frac{9}{20}$

18. $\frac{2}{9}$

7-7 Simplify. Write the expression with exponents.

19. $\frac{8^5}{8^2}$

20. $\frac{(-5)^8}{(-5)}$

21. $\frac{x^7}{x^5}$

Write each expression without exponents.

22. 4^{-3}

23. $(-6)^{-2}$

24. $\frac{(-8)^3}{(-8)^5}$

7-8 Write each in decimal form.

25. 4.7×10^3

26. 1.9×10^{-2}

27. 3.7×10^{-5}

Write each in scientific notation.

28. 436,000

29. 57,000

30. 80,000,000

31. 0.000722

32. 0.000001

33. 0.05

Chapter 7 Test

Multiply. Reduce to lowest terms.

1. $\left(\frac{5}{12}\right)\left(\frac{3}{8}\right)$

2. $\left(\frac{1}{2}\right)\left(-\frac{4}{5}\right)$

3. $\left(-1\frac{7}{8}\right)\left(4\frac{2}{5}\right)$

4. $\left(-1\frac{1}{5}\right)\left(-2\frac{1}{2}\right)$

Divide. Reduce to lowest terms.

5. $-\frac{8}{9} \div \left(-\frac{4}{5}\right)$

6. $\frac{3}{10} \div \frac{15}{100}$

7. $6\frac{3}{7} \div \left(-1\frac{1}{4}\right)$

8. $-6\frac{1}{4} \div \frac{7}{10}$

Solve and check.

9. $-5y = -\frac{2}{3}$

10. $1\frac{1}{2}v = \frac{7}{10}$

11. $1\frac{1}{3} = -12a$

12. $-6\frac{2}{3} = 3\frac{1}{3}x$

Find the solution by writing and solving an equation.

13. Debbie walked from her house to a bus stop $4\frac{1}{2}$ km away. This was $\frac{1}{3}$ of the total distance to her aunt's house. What was the total distance?

Solve.

14. A stack of 34 identical books is on the teacher's desk. If the stack is $59\frac{1}{2}$ inches high, how thick is each book?

15. A necklace is made of beads that are $\frac{3}{4}$ inch wide. If there are 30 beads with no space between, how long is the necklace?

Write each as a decimal. Use a bar for a repeating decimal.

16. $\frac{21}{40}$

17. $\frac{1}{3}$

18. $\frac{2}{11}$

Simplify. Write each expression with exponents.

19. $\frac{9^8}{9^4}$

20. $\frac{(-2)^6}{(-2)^1}$

21. $\frac{p^9}{p^5}$

Write each expression without exponents.

22. 2^{-4}

23. 3^{-3}

24. $\frac{(-7)^4}{(-7)^6}$

Write each in decimal form.

25. 1.47×10^6

26. 9.0×10^{-3}

27. 2.11×10^{-5}

Write each in scientific notation.

28. 329

29. 85,000

30. 99,000,000

31. 0.08

32. 0.0000101

33. 0.0079

Cumulative Review

Evaluate.

1. $49.07 + h$ for $h = 18.47$

2. $m + 13.73$ for $m = 3.85$

3. $21.8 + v$ for $v = -3.3$

4. $p + 17.32 + 1.94$ for $p = -0.54$

5. $29.1 - f$ for $f = 80.5$

6. $w - 22.71$ for $w = -9.13$

Add or subtract. Reduce to lowest terms.

7. $\frac{2}{13} + \frac{4}{13}$

8. $-\frac{6}{8} + \frac{1}{8}$

9. $-\frac{22}{30} - \left(-\frac{4}{30}\right)$

10. $\frac{1}{3} + \frac{2}{9}$

11. $-\frac{4}{15} - \frac{1}{5}$

12. $-\frac{3}{8} - \left(-\frac{1}{4}\right)$

13. $8\frac{1}{4} + 1\frac{5}{8}$

14. $4\frac{3}{5} - 2\frac{1}{2}$

15. $7\frac{1}{3} - \left(-1\frac{1}{2}\right)$

Solve and check.

16. $m + 23.4 = -16.7$

17. $r - 8.12 = 6.16$

18. $b - \frac{2}{5} = \frac{3}{10}$

19. $t + \frac{1}{3} = -\frac{5}{6}$

20. $\frac{4}{15} = c - \left(-\frac{1}{5}\right)$

Solve by writing an equation.

21. Sally bought a ring on sale for $25.59. This was $6.80 less than the original price. What was the original price?

22. Raul drove 15 more miles on Tuesday than he drove on Monday. If he drove 46 miles on Tuesday, how many miles did he drive Monday?

23. Vince has $210 more in his savings account than he has in his checking account. If he has $616 in his savings account, how much does he have in his checking account?

24. Mrs. Tanaka has 13 envelopes. How many more envelopes does she need if she is sending 56 letters?

Today's Stock Report

High	Low	Stock	High	Low	Last	Chg.
17 1/8	12 5/8	**Zzt**	14 7/8	13 3/4	13 3/4	−1/2
25 1/2	10 1/2	**EEWA**	17 3/8	14 3/8	16 3/4	+1/4

25. What is the difference between the yearly low and today's low for EEWA shares?

26. What was the closing price for Zzt shares yesterday?

Chapter 8

Equations and Inequalities

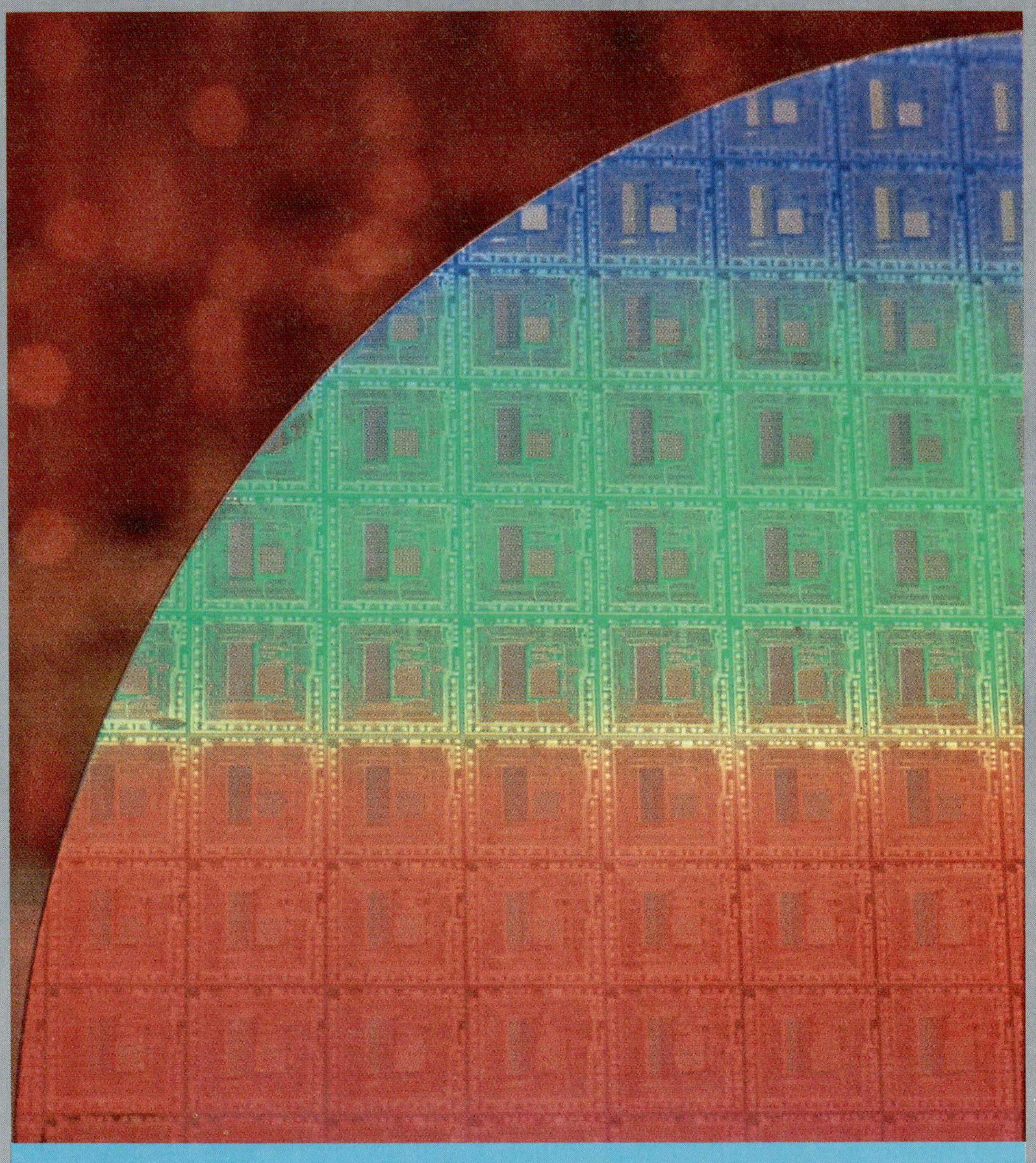

8-1 Solving Equations: Combined Operations

A grocer could solve the equation $0.2n + 8 = 40$ to find the number of 0.2-kg oranges in a crate that weighs 8 kg when empty and 40 kg when full.

You have learned to solve equations in which one operation has been applied to the variable. To solve equations in which more than one operation has been applied to the variable, you will need to observe the order of operations, then undo them, as shown in the table below.

Equation	Order of Operations Applied to the Variable	To Undo These Operations
$3n + 5 = 44$	First n was multiplied by 3. Then 5 was added.	Subtract 5 from each side. Then divide each side by 3.
$\frac{2}{3}b - 4 = 4$	First b was multiplied by $\frac{2}{3}$. Then 4 was subtracted.	Add 4 to each side. Then multiply each side by the reciprocal of $\frac{2}{3}$, or $\frac{3}{2}$.
$6(x + 2) = 30$	First 2 was added to x. Then this sum was multiplied by 6.	Divide each side by 6. Then subtract 2 from each side.
$\frac{y - 7}{3} = 8$	First 7 was subtracted from y. Then this difference was divided by 3.	Multiply each side by 3. Then add 7 to each side.

This leads to steps for solving equations with combined operations.

Solving Equations with Combined Operations

1. Identify the order in which the operations have been applied to the variable.
2. Undo the operations in reverse order by applying the inverse operations or the inverse properties on both sides of the equation.

Example 1

Solve and check. $2n + 8 = 40$

Solution

$$2n + 8 = 40$$
First n was multiplied by 2. Then 8 was added.

$$2n + 8 - 8 = 40 - 8$$
$$2n = 32$$
Since adding 8 was the last operation applied, undo it by subtracting 8 from each side.

$$\frac{2n}{2} = \frac{32}{2}$$
Then divide by 2 to undo multiplying by 2.

$$n = 16$$

Check

$$2(16) + 8 \stackrel{?}{=} 40$$
Replace n with 16 in $2n + 8 = 40$.

$$32 + 8 \stackrel{?}{=} 40$$
$$40 = 40 \checkmark$$
The solution is 16.

Practice Solve and check. **a.** $\frac{3}{4}z + 6 = 18$ **b.** $-y - 5 = 12$ **c.** $6x + 36 = 144$

Example 2

Solve and check. $5(x + 7) = 105$

Solution

$$5(x + 7) = 105$$
First 7 was added to x. Then this sum was multiplied by 5.

$$\frac{5(x + 7)}{5} = \frac{105}{5}$$
Divide each side by 5.

$$x + 7 = 21$$
$$x + 7 - 7 = 21 - 7$$
Subtract 7 from each side.

$$x = 14$$

Check

$$5(14 + 7) \stackrel{?}{=} 105$$
Replace x with 14 in $5(x + 7) = 105$.

$$5(21) \stackrel{?}{=} 105$$
$$105 = 105 \checkmark$$
The solution is 14.

Practice Solve and check. **a.** $\frac{(x + 8)}{6} = 7$ **b.** $-6(n - 7) = 96$

Oral Exercises

To solve, what operation would you use in the first step?

1. $\frac{x}{2} - 4 = -8$
2. $\frac{d}{4} + 8 = 18$
3. $4r + 16 = 28$
4. $9s - 4 = 59$
5. $\frac{x - 14}{8} = -7$
6. $6(x - 2) = 18$

Exercises

A Solve and check.

1. $3b - 5 = 16$
2. $4r + 16 = -80$
3. $9z - 45 = 45$
4. $-x + 46 = 27$
5. $68 = 5n + 43$
6. $37 = 12p - 23$
7. $\frac{y}{4} - 12 = 8$
8. $\frac{c}{8} + 16 = 23$
9. $14 = \frac{a}{24} - 13$
10. $3x + 7 = -38$
11. $\frac{2}{7}n - 18 = 40$
12. $39 = 4y - 45$
13. $4(c + 6) = 56$
14. $6c - 8 = 42$
15. $-45 = 9(s + 12)$
16. $45 = \frac{x}{3} + 36$
17. $0.8a + 3.4 = 7.2$
18. $16 = -b + 3\frac{1}{4}$
19. $\frac{x + 8}{9} = -6$
20. $\frac{p - 7}{12} = -16$
21. $7y - 13 = 50$
22. $\frac{x + 4}{6} = 4$
23. $7(x - 7) = 49$
24. $3x - 6 = 9$

B Solve and check.

25. $3 = \frac{6x + 18}{9}$
26. $\frac{14n + 8}{3} = 26$
27. $\frac{12x - 12}{8} = -9$
28. $\frac{3y - 4}{4} = 2$
29. $\frac{x + 6}{3} = 5$
30. $\frac{3b - 5}{2} = 8$
31. The formula for the perimeter of a rectangle is $P = 2l + 2w$. Find the length (l), when the perimeter (P) is 50 and the width (w) is 9.

C Extending Thinking Skills

32. A taxi fare included a starting fee of \$1.25 plus \$0.55 for each minute of the trip. The total cost for the trip was \$8.40. How many minutes did the trip take?
33. Complete the generalization for solving each type of equation.
a. If $ax + b = c$, then $x =$ __?__ **b.** If $ax - b = c$, then $x =$ __?__

Mixed Review

Evaluate for $n = \frac{2}{3}$. **34.** $n - 1\frac{1}{2}$ **35.** $\frac{4}{5}n$ **36.** $\frac{3}{5} - n$

Solve and check. **37.** $0.8a = -2.4$ **38.** $1.02 + c = -0.85$

PROBLEM SOLVING: WRITING EQUATIONS

8-2 Translating Sentences Involving Combined Operations

You have learned to translate a verbal statement suggesting a single operation into an equation. To solve some problems you need to choose a variable and translate a verbal statement that suggests a combination of operations, as shown below.

Verbal Statement: **Tim's $15 overtime pay** is *$3 less* than **twice his regular pay**.

Equation: $2p - 3 = \mathbf{15}$

Example

Write an equation. Carmen's class of 25 students has only 3 more than twice the number of students in Yoshi's class.

Solution Let s = number of students in Yoshi's class — Choose what the variable represents

$2s + 3 = 25$ — "Twice the number of students" translates to $2s$. "Three more than twice . . ." translates to $2s + 3$. "Is" indicates equality.

Practice Write an equation.

a. When Julio's age is doubled and increased by 5, the result is Eugene's age, or 39.

b. The $65 cost of a pair of shoes is only $4 less than 3 times what shoes cost in 1960.

Oral Exercises

Give an equation.

1. 36 more than 6 times a number gives 84.

2. 14 less than 7 times a number gives 28.

3. The difference of 3 times a number and -9 is -9.

4. The quotient of 6 times a number and 9 is 45.

Exercises

A Write an equation.

1. Emiko's weekly salary, $200, is $25 more than twice Jane's salary.

2. Stefan traveled 300 km, which was 35 km less than half as far as he traveled yesterday.

3. The 67 students in Gloria's class are 4 more than 3 times the number in Vi's class.

4. Nan earned \$56, which was \$8 more than twice Juanita's earnings.

5. Ben's 94 km bike trip on Tuesday was 17 km more than half the length of his trip on Monday.

6. The \$564 collected for the band trip is \$36 more than $\frac{1}{4}$ the amount needed.

7. The election vote turnout of 376 was 56 more than $\frac{3}{4}$ of last year's turnout.

8. If Mr. Yamamoto doubles his old salary and adds his age, 46, the total is \$46,000, his new salary.

B Write a verbal description of each equation.

9. $2x + 3 = 13$ **10.** $4n - 8 = 7$ **11.** $\frac{1}{4}p + 2 = 9$

C Extending Thinking Skills

12. Half an hour ago, it was 3 times as long after noon as it was until midnight. What time is it now?

13. If 4 frogs can catch 4 flies in 4 minutes, how many frogs can catch 100 flies in 100 minutes?

Mixed Review

Solve and check. **14.** $c - 1\frac{2}{3} = \frac{1}{2}$ **15.** $\frac{2}{5}m = 3\frac{3}{4}$

Simplify. **16.** $4(m + 4) - 16$ **17.** $10(t + 30) + 500$

CALCULATOR ACTIVITY

You can use inverse operations and the calculator to solve certain equations quickly.

For example, to solve $3x + 4 = 85$, you might think "The variable x has been multiplied by 3, 4 has been added to this product and the result is 85. Working backward from 85, I'll undo adding 4 by subtracting 4, then undo multiplying by 3 by dividing by 3."

85  [−] 4  [=]  [÷] 3 [=] Display 27 The solution is 27.

Use inverse operations and a calculator to solve.

1. $4x - 17 = 207$ **2.** $\frac{n}{19} + 26 = 39$ **3.** $\frac{p}{15} - 69 = 16$ **4.** $\frac{5a}{12} + 13 = 23$

PROBLEM SOLVING: WRITING EQUATIONS

8-3 Writing Equations to Solve Problems

You can use the Problem-Solving Checklist on page 121 to help you solve problems. When your plan involves writing and solving an equation, keep these questions in mind.

- Can you use a variable to represent an unknown number?
- Can you represent other conditions in terms of the variable?
- What is equal?
- Can you write and solve an equation?

Example

Peter bought a 10-speed bike for \$172. He made a down-payment of \$76 and monthly payments of \$24. How many months did it take him to pay for the bike?

Solution

Let m = the number of monthly payments. — Let m represent the unknown number.

$$24m + 76 = 172$$

The total amount paid can be expressed in two equal ways. Write an equation.

$$24m + 76 - 76 = 172 - 76$$
$$24m = 96$$
$$m = 4$$

Check $24(4) + 76 \stackrel{?}{=} 172$

$$172 = 172 \checkmark$$

The equation solution checks.

It took Peter 4 months to pay for the bicycle.

Estimate: \$76 plus 4 payments of \$25 would be \$176. The answer is reasonable.

Oral Exercises

Give an equation.

1. Rachel's present salary, \$25,000, is \$365 more than twice what it was when she began the job. What was her starting salary?

2. Calvin saved half his allowance, earned \$18, and had a total of \$30. What is his allowance?

3. Mr. Meyer's golf score, 83, was only 5 more than twice his age. How old is Mr. Meyer?

4. Sandy added 16 stamps to her collection and then gave half her stamps to her sister. Then she had 29 stamps. How many stamps did she have at the beginning?

Exercises

A Solve by writing an equation.

1. Three-fourths of the members of a tennis club signed up in advance for a tournament. On the day of the tournament, 9 more entered, making a total of 84. How many members did the tennis club have?

2. Jason earned $6 an hour for a job. He got a bonus of $75, making his total earnings $297. How many hours did he work?

3. The principal of Parkside School reported that there was an average of 27 students in each classroom. Then 56 more students enrolled in the school, making a new total of 704 students. How many classrooms were there?

4. Before giving 12 ounces of flour to a friend, Mrs. Higuera had $\frac{3}{4}$ of a sack of flour. The remaining flour weighed 48 ounces. How many ounces did a full bag weigh?

5. The championship basketball team fell short of getting double its opponents's score by only 3 points. The team scored 81 points. How many points did the opponents score?

B Solve by writing an equation.

6. A tank that was $\frac{3}{4}$ full of liquid fertilizer had 565 gallons pumped out and 832 gallons put in, leaving 2400 gallons in the tank. What would a full tank hold?

7. The temperature dropped by half, decreased by 3°C, and rose 9°C. The thermometer then read 14°C. What was the beginning temperature?

8. The Ortiz family drove at an average rate of 53 mi/h, stopped for food, then drove 78 miles more, in $1\frac{1}{2}$ hours. Their odometer showed they had traveled a total of 343 miles. What was their total driving time?

C Extending Thinking Skills

9. Write a word problem that could be solved using the equation $3x - 4 = 17$.

10. Write a word problem that could be solved using the equation $54 - 2x = 20$.

Mixed Review

Evaluate for $a = 2.5$, $b = 1.4$. **11.** $3(a - b)$ **12.** $a(b + 2)$

Solve and check. **13.** $-2.4a = 3$ **14.** $n + 0.6 = -2.4$

8-4 Simplifying to Solve Equations: Using the Distributive Property

You have learned to use a reversed form of the distributive property to simplify an algebraic expression such as $3x + 4x$ as follows:

$$ba + ca = (b + c)a$$
$$3x + 4x = (3 + 4)x = 7x$$

The distributive property of multiplication over subtraction is stated below.

Distributive Property: Multiplication over Subtraction

For all numbers **a, b,** and **c,** $a(b - c) = ab - ac$

You can use a reversed form of the distributive property of multiplication over subtraction to simplify an algebraic expression such as $7x - 5x$ as follows:

$$ba - ca = (b - c)a$$
$$7x - 5x = (7 - 5)x = 2x$$

Example 1

Solve and check. $5x + 2x = -161$

Solution

$$5x + 2x = -161$$

$$7x = -161$$ Because of the distributive property, $5x + 2x = (5 + 2)x = 7x$.

$$\frac{7x}{7} = -\frac{161}{7}$$ Divide each side by 7, or use the multiplicative inverse property and multiply by $\frac{1}{7}$.

$$x = -23$$

Check

$$5(-23) + 2(-23) \stackrel{?}{=} -161$$ Substitute -23 for x in $5x + 2x = -161$.

$$-115 + -46 \stackrel{?}{=} -161$$

$$-161 = -161 \checkmark$$

Practice Solve and check.

a. $-6x + 19x = 962$ **b.** $\frac{2}{5}y + \frac{4}{5}y = 36$

Example 2

Solve and check. $7x - 5x = 86$

Solution $7x - 5x = 86$

$2x = 86$ Because of the distributive property, $7x - 5x = (7 - 5)x = 2x$.

$\frac{2x}{2} = \frac{86}{2}$

$x = 43$

Check $7(43) - 5(43) \stackrel{?}{=} 86$ Substitute 43 for x in $7x - 5x = 86$.

$301 - 215 \stackrel{?}{=} 86$

$86 = 86 \checkmark$

Practice Solve and check. **a.** $-6n - 4n = 65$ **b.** $72 = 13y - 5y$

Oral Exercises

Use the distributive property to simplify the equation.

1. $4x + 7x = 77$ **2.** $9x + 6x = 30$ **3.** $25x + 75x = 500$

4. $45 = 5x + 4x$ **5.** $60 = 21x - 6x$ **6.** $125 = 65x - 40x$

Exercises

A Solve and check.

1. $5x + 2x = 84$ **2.** $4a + 12a = -48$ **3.** $9c + 8c = 68$

4. $12b + 14b = 52$ **5.** $6n + 9n = 75$ **6.** $-3t + 9t = 144$

7. $24z - 8z = 64$ **8.** $18r - 9r = -108$ **9.** $-9a - 4a = 78$

10. $12y - 3y = 207$ **11.** $25b - 8b = 51$ **12.** $13c - 6c = 98$

13. $65 = 8p + 5p$ **14.** $126 = -14s + 8s$ **15.** $26z + 37z = 315$

16. $21x - 9x = -96$ **17.** $34n - 26n = 136$ **18.** $82t - 69t = 156$

19. $96 = 31d - 19d$ **20.** $288 = -a + 13a$ **21.** $735 = 63r - 28r$

22. $\frac{3}{4}y + \frac{1}{2}y = 24$ **23.** $4.6x + 3.4x = 128$ **24.** $\frac{7}{8}n - \frac{3}{4}n = -6$

B Solve and check.

25. $-5x + 7x + 9x = -88$ **26.** $16n - 9n + 12n = 76$

27. $6.3p + 8.6p - 5.4p = 28.5$ **28.** $-9b + -9b + -9b = -108$

29. $\frac{3}{2}a + \frac{3}{4}a + \frac{3}{8}a = 105$ **30.** $2\frac{1}{2}c + 5\frac{1}{4}c - 3\frac{1}{3}c = 106$

31. Evaluate both $(b - c)a$ and $ba - ca$ for $a = -3$, $b = 6$, and $c = 9$. Choose new values for a, b, and c and evaluate again. Did the expressions have the same value in both cases?

Write equations to solve Exercises 32–34.

32. Alicia bought some \$6 records and an \$18 record-cleaning kit. The total cost was \$60. How many records did she buy?

33. Teri bought 8 tickets to the water slide and spent \$4 on refreshments. The total cost was \$10. What was the cost of each ticket?

34. A family traveled in a car for a number of hours at a speed of 55 mi/h. After stopping for gas, they went 76 miles farther. They traveled a total of 296 miles. How many hours did they travel before stopping for gas?

C Extending Thinking Skills

35. Bill wrote: "For all whole numbers a, b, and c, $a \cdot (b + c) = a + (b \cdot c)$." Check this for $a = 2$, $b = 3$, and $c = 4$, and then for $a = 3$, $b = 5$, and $c = 6$. If you can find one set of values for a, b, and c for which $a \cdot (b + c)$ *does not equal* $a + (b \cdot c)$, you will have found a *counterexample* proving Bill's generalization false! Can you do it?

36. Adam, Bob, Carl, and Dave are brothers. Adam is $\frac{1}{2}$ as old as Carl. Carl is 3 years older than Dave. Dave and Bob together are 17 years old. Bob is 8. Who is the youngest?

Mixed Review

Find the greatest common factor (GCF). **37.** 27, 45, 108

Evaluate for $m = 3.2$, $n = -0.8$. **38.** $3n - m$ **39.** $4(m + n)$

COMPUTER ACTIVITY

This program will solve equations of the form $Ax + B = C$. The values for A, B, and C can be positive or negative rational numbers and are entered as decimals.

```
10 PRINT "THIS PROGRAM WILL SOLVE EQUATIONS OF THE FORM
   AX+B=C"
20 INPUT "TYPE IN INTEGER OR DECIMAL VALUES FOR A, B,
   AND C.";A,B,C
30 PRINT "THE EQUATION IS ";A;"X+";B;"=";C
40 PRINT "THE SOLUTION IS X=";(C-B)/A
50 INPUT "DO YOU WANT TO SOLVE ANOTHER ONE?";A$
60 IF LEFT$(A$,1)="Y" THEN GOTO 20
70 END
```

1. Use the program to solve the equation $2x - 1 = 5$.

2. Use the program to solve the equation $\frac{1}{4}n + \left(-\frac{1}{2}\right) = \frac{3}{8}$.

3. Make up some equations and use the program to solve them.

8-5 More Simplifying to Solve Equations

You learned earlier that terms such as n and $5n$ are called *like terms* because they have the same variable part, n. The terms $-8x$, $0.4x$, and $\frac{2}{3}x$ are also like terms because their variable part, x, is the same. Terms such as $3a$ and $4b$ have different variables and thus are unlike terms. Terms such as $5y$, $5y^2$, and $5xy$ are also unlike terms, since their variable parts are not identical.

To solve some equations you must first simplify expressions by combining all like terms. In the following examples, the commutative, associative, and distributive properties are used to do this.

Example 1

Solve and check. $9x + 5(x + 7) = -49$

Solution

$9x + 5(x + 7) = -49$	Multiply by 5 first, so you will have like terms to combine.
$9x + 5x + 35 = -49$	Distributive property: $5(x + 7) = 5x + 5 \cdot 7$
$14x + 35 = -49$	Distributive property: $5x + 9x = (5 + 9)x = 14x$.
$14x + 35 + (-35) = -49 + (-35)$	Add -35 to each side.
$14x = -84$	
$\frac{14x}{14} = -\frac{84}{14}$	Divide each side by 14.
$x = -6$	

Check

$9(-6) + 5(-6 + 7) \stackrel{?}{=} -49$	Replace x with -6 in $9x + 5(x + 7) = -49$.
$-54 + 5(1) \stackrel{?}{=} -49$	
$-49 = -49$ ✓	The solution is -6.

Practice Solve and check.

a. $2b + 3(b - 7) = 44$ **b.** $4(2y + 9) + 7y = -24$

You can use the commutative and associative properties for addition together to add any three numbers in any order. You can use the commutative and associative properties of multiplication to multiply any three numbers in any order. In the following example, these ideas are used to simplify expressions.

Example 2

Solve and check. $3(5n) + 14 + 6n = 21$

Solution

$$3(5n) + 14 + 6n = 21$$

$$15n + 14 + 6n = 21$$ Associative property: $3(5n) = (3 \cdot 5)n = 15n$.

$$15n + 6n + 14 = 21$$ Commutative and associative properties: $15n + 14 + 6n = 15n + 6n + 14$.

$$21n + 14 = 21$$ Distributive property: $15n + 6n = (15 + 6)n = 21n$.

$$21n + 14 - 14 = 21 - 14$$

$$21n = 7$$

$$\frac{21n}{21} = \frac{7}{21}$$

$$n = \frac{1}{3}$$

Check

$$3\left(5 \cdot \frac{1}{3}\right) + 14 + 6\left(\frac{1}{3}\right) \stackrel{?}{=} 21$$ Replace n with $\frac{1}{3}$ in $3(5n) + 14 + 6n = 21$.

$$3\left(\frac{5}{3}\right) + 14 + 2 \stackrel{?}{=} 21$$

$$5 + 16 \stackrel{?}{=} 21$$

$$21 = 21 \checkmark$$ The solution is $\frac{1}{3}$.

Practice Solve. **a.** $4z + 9 + 3(2z) = 129$ **b.** $-2(7c) - 12 + 5c = 51$

Oral Exercises

Simplify.

1. $3(y + 4)$ **2.** $4(p - 8)$ **3.** $2(b + 9) + 3$

4. $5n + 9 + 3n$ **5.** $7 + 8x - 2x$ **6.** $13 + 6c + 12c$

Exercises

A Solve and check.

1. $5(n + 3) + 5 = -25$ **2.** $4(x - 3) + 8 = 60$

3. $-8a + 6(a + 7) = 1$ **4.** $6c + 4(c + 8) = 48$

5. $10z + 5(z - 12) = 0$ **6.** $7y + 7(y + 3) = -21$

7. $5(4d) + 7 + (-8d) = 88$ **8.** $-3(7a) + 17 + 6a = 82$

9. $4(3c) + 9 + 8c = 109$ **10.** $9b + 6(4b) - 12 = 87$

11. $12r - 8 + 5(3r) = 46$ **12.** $24 + 3(-4s) + 6s = -24$

13. $4t + 3t - 9 = 76$ **14.** $-x + 9 + 7x = 99$

15. $5y - 3y + (-4y) = 96$ **16.** $6(n + 6) + 7n = -55$

17. $5(z + 4) + 6z = 97$ **18.** $-3(2c) + 4(5c) + 11 = 81$

19. $-9 + 4d + 8d = 93$

20. $-4(x - 8) + 20 = -13$

21. $21 + 5(b + 7) = -54$

22. $\frac{4}{5}p - \frac{1}{5}p - 42 = 8$

23. $61 = \frac{1}{3}(6c) + 3c - 9$

24. $24 = 18 + \frac{1}{2}(s + 6)$

B Solve and check.

25. $3(x + 4) + 5(x - 2) = 66$

26. $8(p - 3) + 3p + 7p = 138$

27. $-3(4 + x) + 7(-3x) = 72$

28. $-4(3 + z) + 6z - 12 = -36$

Use a calculator to solve the equations in Exercises 29–30.

29. $678(n + 39) + 457n = 77{,}517$

30. $87(29x) + 43x + 57{,}650 = 1198$

31. If Juana multiplies her age by 6, the result is 156. Mary is 3 times as old as Juana. Write an equation to find Juana's age. Use the solution to find Mary's age.

32. In June, a salesman sold 80 cars. This was 8 more than 3 times the number he sold in May. Write an equation to find how many he sold in May.

C Extending Thinking Skills

33. The sum of what three consecutive page numbers in a book is 264?

34. An apartment manager used 339 metal digits to number apartments consecutively, beginning with 1. How many apartments did he number?

Mixed Review

Write each as a decimal. **35.** $\frac{3}{4}$ **36.** $\frac{7}{8}$ **37.** $\frac{3}{5}$ **38.** $\frac{9}{10}$

Give the prime factorization of each. **39.** 15 **40.** 17 **41.** 28

NUMBERS TO ALGEBRA

The number examples below suggest an important generalization in algebra.

Numbers	Algebra
$-(9 - 5) = 5 - 9 = -4$ $-(2 - 7) = 7 - 2 = 5$ $-\left(\frac{3}{4} - \frac{1}{4}\right) = \frac{1}{4} - \frac{3}{4} = -\frac{1}{2}$	For all numbers a and b, $-(a - b) = b - a$

Use the generalization above to simplify.

1. $-(5 - x)$

2. $-(3 - 2n)$

3. $-(7 - 5t)$

4. $-(4 - 3a) + 7$

5. $-(2b - 6) + 9$

6. $-(12a - 4) + a$

8-6 Solving Equations with Variables on Both Sides

You might solve an equation such as $5h = 12 + 3h$ to help you decide whether to rent a tool at \$5/h or at a base price of \$12 plus \$3/h.

You can solve an equation with like terms on both sides by using the properties of equality to get an equation in which the variable appears on only one side.

Example 1

Solve and check. $5h = 12 + 3h$

Solution $5h = 12 + 3h$

$5h - 3h = 12 + 3h - 3h$ Subtract $3h$ from each side so that all terms with a variable are on the same side of the equation.

$2h = 12$

$\frac{2h}{2} = \frac{12}{2}$

$h = 6$

Check $5(6) \stackrel{?}{=} 12 + 3(6)$ Replace h with 6 in $5h = 12 + 3h$.

$30 \stackrel{?}{=} 12 + 18$

$30 = 30 \checkmark$ The solution is 6.

Practice Solve and check.

a. $2x + 72 = 4x$ **b.** $24 + y = 9y$

Example 2

Solve and check. $6x - 2 = 4x + 3$

Solution

$$6x - 2 = 4x + 3$$ You want to get the variables on one side, numbers on the other.

$$6x - 2 + 2 = 4x + 3 + 2$$ Add 2 to each side.

$$6x = 4x + 5$$

$$6x - 4x = 4x - 4x + 5$$ Subtract $4x$ from each side so all terms with a variable will be on the same side.

$$2x = 5$$

$$\frac{2x}{2} = \frac{5}{2}$$

$$x = \frac{5}{2}$$

Check

$$6\left(\frac{5}{2}\right) - 2 \stackrel{?}{=} 4\left(\frac{5}{2}\right) + 3$$ Replace x with $\frac{5}{2}$ in $6x - 2 = 4x + 3$.

$$15 - 2 \stackrel{?}{=} 10 + 3$$

$$13 = 13 \checkmark$$

Practice Solve and check. **a.** $3y + 4 = 6y + 2$ **b.** $-7a + 8 = 3a - 2$

Oral Exercises

What would you do to get the variable alone on one side of the equation?

1. $5x = 14 - 2x$ **2.** $8b = 18 + 2b$ **3.** $7n = 4n + 12$

4. $9z = 4z - 25$ **5.** $5r = 7r + 24$ **6.** $3p = 8p - 35$

7. $3c + 8 = 7c$ **8.** $4y - 12 = 8y$ **9.** $12n - 18 = 6n$

Exercises

A Solve and check.

1. $9x = 26 - 4x$ **2.** $7n = 15 - 8n$ **3.** $12a = 48 - 4a$

4. $13b = 27 + 4b$ **5.** $16c = 42 + 9c$ **6.** $15y = 72 + 7y$

7. $7r = -5r + 144$ **8.** $7z = 3z - 52$ **9.** $180 - 9s = 9s$

10. $4t = 136 + 9t$ **11.** $5x = 30 - x$ **12.** $54 + 11n = 2n$

13. $121 + 4x = 15x$ **14.** $36 + 9x = 3x$ **15.** $84 + 6x = 18x$

16. $-4a + 3 = 2a + 15$ **17.** $8c - 2 = 5c + 4$ **18.** $12x + 4 = 9x - 11$

19. $9r + 7 = 4r - 8$ **20.** $3s + 7 = -5s - 9$ **21.** $15z - 9 = -3z + 9$

22. $\frac{5}{8}x + 12 = \frac{3}{8}x + 4$ **23.** $\frac{2}{5}n - 3 = \frac{9}{5}n - 5$ **24.** $\frac{5}{6}a + 4 = \frac{2}{3}a + 6$

B Solve and check.

25. $3(x + 4) = -5x - 30$ **26.** $5(b - 3) = 7b - 14$ **27.** $5(r + 6) = -5(r + 3)$

28. $9(z - 6) = 4(z + 12)$ **29.** $6(s + 1) = 4(s + 2)$ **30.** $4(a - 2) = 2(a + 8)$

31. $\frac{1}{3}(x + 6) = \frac{5}{6}x$ **32.** $\frac{1}{2}(y - 16) = \frac{3}{4}y$ **33.** $\frac{3}{8}(n + 24) = \frac{1}{4}n$

Write an equation to solve each problem in Exercises 34–36.

34. Mrs. Greer rented a tool for a base charge of $15 plus $3 per hour. The total rental cost was $33. For how long did she rent the tool?

35. Jeff's checking account charges were $3.00 per month plus $0.15 per check. Jeff was charged $7.50 for the month. How many checks did he write?

36. Christina scored 35 points in each round of a game, plus 46 bonus points. Her total score was 256. How many rounds did she play?

C Extending Thinking Skills

37. If one of the daughters in the Biggs family had been a boy, the number of boys and girls would have been equal. If one of the sons had been a girl, there would have been twice as many girls as boys. How many children were in the family?

38. Each of three large blocks weighs the same. Each of five small blocks weighs the same. Each large block weighs 3 times as much as a small block. All together, the blocks weigh 112 kg. What does a large block weigh?

Mixed Review

Write <, >, or = for each □. **39.** $\frac{5}{9} \square \frac{31}{54}$ **40.** $-\frac{3}{5} \square -\frac{41}{65}$ **41.** $\frac{52}{81} \square \frac{2}{3}$

Solve and check. **42.** $c - 16 = 57$ **43.** $\frac{3}{4}m = 24$ **44.** $r + \frac{1}{2} = -\frac{2}{5}$

Simplify. Write the result with exponents. **45.** $\frac{m^5}{m^2}$ **46.** $\frac{r^3}{r}$

MENTAL MATH

Use a calculator to check whether or not the following equations are true. Then look for a pattern and use it to find the products below mentally.

$29 \cdot 31 = (30 \cdot 30) - (1 \cdot 1)$ $28 \cdot 32 = (30 \cdot 30) - (2 \cdot 2)$
$39 \cdot 41 = (40 \cdot 40) - (1 \cdot 1)$ $38 \cdot 42 = (40 \cdot 40) - (2 \cdot 2)$
$49 \cdot 51 = (50 \cdot 50) - (1 \cdot 1)$ $48 \cdot 52 = (50 \cdot 50) - (2 \cdot 2)$

Find each product mentally.

1. $59 \cdot 61$ **2.** $69 \cdot 71$ **3.** $79 \cdot 81$ **4.** $58 \cdot 62$ **5.** $68 \cdot 72$ **6.** $78 \cdot 82$

8-7 The Cost of Operating a Car

What does it cost to operate a car? The chart below gives ways to estimate the yearly expenses for a car of average size.

Estimated Costs of Owning and Operating a Car

- For a person of average income, the annual cost of owning and operating a car, including financing, might be from 0.10 to 0.15 times his or her annual income.
- The cost of operating a car, including gas, oil, repairs, insurance, and taxes, might be about 17¢ per mile.
- The depreciation, or loss of value, of a car can be estimated for the first three years by subtracting $\frac{20}{100}$ of its original value if it is one year old, $\frac{35}{100}$ if it is two years old, and $\frac{50}{100}$ if it is three years old.

Problems

Solve, using the information above as needed.

1. Estimate the annual cost of operating a car, including financing, for a person earning $28,000 a year.

2. Mr. Young's income was $35,000 last year. His car expenses were $4,823. By how much did his car expenses differ from 0.15 of his income?

3. Sue Brown bought a new car for $8,500. What will its value be after she has owned it for one year?

4. José Lopez drove his car 13,125 miles in one year. What would you expect his expenses, not including depreciation, to be?

5. Marti Berk earns $32,000 a year. Her car expenses were $4,500. Are her expenses within the range given in the chart for her income?

6. Tami Yang bought a new sports car for $14,500. What will be the depreciated value of the car after she has driven it for 3 years?

7. Mrs. Tran bought a new car that cost $9,450. Make a table showing the depreciated value of the car after 1, 2, and 3 years.

8. Carol Glynn drove her new car 15,000 miles the first year. Estimate her operating expenses, not including depreciation, for that year.

9. Ken Harding calculated that the expense, not including depreciation, for operating his car one year was $3,500. Estimate how far he had driven the car.

10. Hector Sanchez's new car cost $10,500. He drove it 15,500 miles the first year. His basic costs were: $97 for repairs, maintenance and accessories, $346 for gas and oil, $295 for insurance, and $328 for taxes. How much per mile, including depreciation, did it cost Hector to operate his car during the first year?

11. ***Data Search*** Find the current value of a new car you would like to buy. Make a chart showing the depreciated value of the car each year for a 3-year period. Then decide what it should cost you to buy the car used in 3 years.

What's Your Decision?

Comparing a Standard and Diesel Automobile

- The diesel engine averages 1.5 times as many miles per gallon of fuel as the standard model.
- The diesel engine model costs $500 more than the standard model.
- Regular fuel costs $1.20 per gallon. Diesel fuel costs $1.25 per gallon.

You are trying to decide whether to buy the diesel or the standard model of a new car. You estimate that you will drive 12,000 miles per year and will keep the car for 4 years. The standard model gets an average of 30 miles to a gallon of gas. Which will you buy?

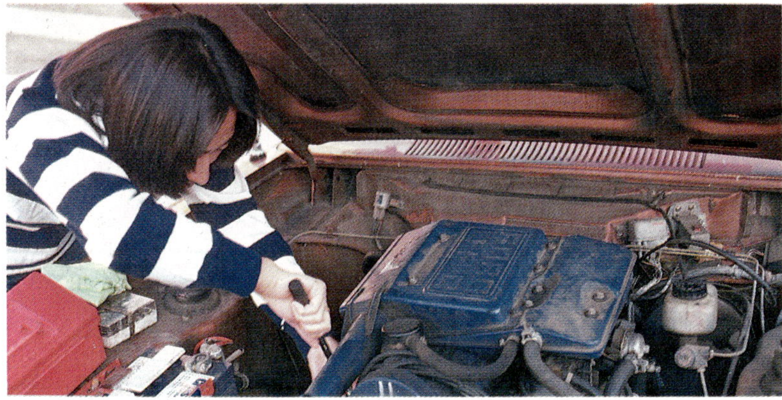

More Practice

Solve and check.

1. $3a - 5 = 19$

2. $-16 = 3c + 2$

3. $(m + 6) \div 12 = 5$

4. $6n - 9n = 36$

5. $3.6 = 10.5 - 3m$

6. $(n + 6) \div 3 = 1.4$

7. $(r + 4) \div 5 = 8$

8. $2(a + 1.7) = 6$

9. $1.43 = 0.4y - 0.6y$

10. $16 - 2n = 10$

11. $6(m - 4) = 24$

12. $19.4 - 0.6c = -16.6$

13. $-9 = 3y + 12$

14. $0.4n = 4 + 0.9n$

15. $(a + 5) \div 0.6 = 10$

16. $3y + 6 = 2y$

17. $4(z + 3) = 4$

18. $(r + 9) \div 4 = 3.5$

19. $2(y + 6) = 12$

20. $4(1 - m) = 6$

21. $11c + 2 = 6c + 12$

22. $-15 - c = 4c$

23. $14 + a = 3a + 2$

24. $9m + 4m + 6 = 32$

25. $6(2 - r) = 15$

26. $m + 4 = -3m$

27. $1.6n + 3.8n = 54$

28. $-63 = 7(x - 9)$

29. $(c + 3) \div 2 = 5$

30. $2.5(z + 4) = 3.75$

31. $5(10 - c) = 125$

32. $14y + 3 = 13.5$

33. $3(a + 2) = 4 + 2a$

34. $144 = 12(c - 2)$

35. $6c + 4c = -30$

36. $4x + 2x = 10 + x$

37. $37 = 14m + 93$

38. $0.5(a + 2) = 2.5$

39. $11r + 4 = 9r + 8$

40. $-16 = 4c + 6$

41. $13k = 19k + 12$

42. $2(a + 6) + 3a = 32$

43. $11z = 20 - 9z$

44. $15r = 3(r + 28)$

45. $25 = 4(m - 3) - 3$

46. $9c + 6 = 15$

47. $(x + 4) \div 6 = -2$

48. $19h + 4h = 126.5$

49. $21 + 4h = 11h$

50. $-6 = 0.75z + 3$

51. $1.2m - 6.5m = 21.2$

52. $26 - 3c = 10c$

53. $4t - 12 = t + 3$

54. $9a - 16 = 5a + 4$

55. $11t - 4 = 40$

56. $6y = 9 + 9y$

57. $(m - 2) \div 7 = 1.5$

58. $46 = 9x - 4x$

59. $8m = 4m - 24$

60. $6r + 9 = 9r - 27$

61. $8.6n - 5n = 9$

62. $19t + 36 = 112$

63. $5x + 6 = 12 + 8x$

64. $(m - 16) \div 2 = 1$

65. $11.5 + 2h = 8.5$

66. $6a + 2(a - 4) = 8$

67. $12m - 4 = 38$

68. $7c + 11c = 162$

69. $11t - 4.5t = 6.5$

70. $180 = 8r + 7r$

71. $19n - 13n = 4.5$

72. $4a + 13 = 5a + 4$

73. $16k + 8k = 312$

74. $5m - 11m = 138$

75. $9t - 2 = 4t + 18$

76. $9 - 14m = -33$

77. $59 - 8w = 3$

78. $11y + 6 = 14y - 27$

79. $12 + 4c = 2c$

80. $(z + 2) \div 2 = -2$

81. $(x - 20) \div 6 = 0.75$

8-8 Solving Inequalities

A booster increases the 4 miles per second orbit speed of a satellite to at least 7 miles per second to send it into outer space. You can write the inequality $4 + b \geq 7$.

An **inequality** is a statement that uses the symbol $>$, $<$, $\geq$ (greater than or equal to), or $\leq$ (less than or equal to) to compare two expressions. You can solve inequalities involving addition or subtraction in the same way you solve equations. The following properties, and similar ones for inequalities involving $<$, are used.

Addition and Subtraction Properties of Inequalities

For all numbers **a, b,** and **c,**

if $a > b$, then $a + c > b + c$ and $a - c > b - c$

Example 1

Solve. $x - 7 \geq -8$

Solution $x - 7 \geq -8$ — Undo subtracting 7 by adding 7 to each side.

$x - 7 + 7 \geq -8 + 7$ — Adding to both sides does not change the direction of the inequality sign.

$x \geq -1$

Practice Solve. **a.** $n + 4 \leq 5$ **b.** $1 > x - \frac{1}{2}$

The display below shows the effects of multiplying or dividing each side of an inequality by a negative number.

$$3 < 4$$
$$-2 \cdot 3 \ ? \ -2 \cdot 4$$
$$-6 > -8$$

When you multiply or divide each side of an inequality by a **negative** number, the inequality sign is **reversed**.

$$6 < 8$$
$$\frac{6}{-2} \ ? \ \frac{8}{-2}$$
$$-3 > -4$$

The following properties and similar ones for inequalities involving $<$ are used when solving inequalities by multiplying or dividing.

Multiplication and Division Properties of Inequalities

For all numbers **a, b,** and **c,** where **c** is positive,

if $a > b$, then $a \cdot c > b \cdot c$ and $\frac{a}{c} > \frac{b}{c}$

For all numbers **a, b,** and **c,** where **c** is negative,

if $a > b$, then $a \cdot c < b \cdot c$ and $\frac{a}{c} < \frac{b}{c}$

Example 2

Solve and check. $-4m > -2$

Solution $-4m > -2$

$$-\tfrac{1}{4}(-4m) < -\tfrac{1}{4}(-2)$$

When you multiply both sides by a negative rational number, you must change the direction of the inequality sign.

$$1 \cdot m < \tfrac{2}{4}$$
$$m < \tfrac{1}{2}$$

Check

To check the computation, replace the inequality sign in $-4m > -2$ with an equal sign and see whether $m = \frac{1}{2}$ is a solution of the resulting equation.

To check whether the inequality sign is correct, see whether a solution to $m < \frac{1}{2}$, such as 0, is also a solution to $-4m > -2$.

$$-4 \cdot 0 \overset{?}{>} -2$$
$$0 > -2 \ \checkmark$$

Practice Solve. **a.** $\frac{3}{4}b > 12$ **b.** $15 < -3p$

Oral Exercises

To solve, what operation would you use?

1. $x + 9 > 13$ **2.** $b - 4 < 8$ **3.** $-3n > 12$ **4.** $15 < y + 7$

5. $\frac{c}{4} < 3$ **6.** $18 > z - 2$ **7.** $25 < 5p$ **8.** $4 > \frac{n}{5}$

Exercises

A Solve and check.

1. $a - 5 < 1$

2. $2 > b + 2$

3. $c - 1 < 4$

4. $-7z < 35$

5. $\frac{1}{3}p > 7$

6. $25 < 5n$

7. $t + 9 < -15$

8. $4 < x - 5$

9. $y + 8 < 2\frac{1}{2}$

10. $d + 1 > 3$

11. $\frac{n}{4} < -1$

12. $\frac{c}{2} > 3$

13. $s - 9 > 0$

14. $-8c > 56$

15. $12 < n + 5$

16. $\frac{3}{8} < n - \frac{5}{6}$

17. $2m \leq \frac{5}{6}$

18. $2\frac{1}{3}b > -6$

B Solve and check.

Write an inequality for each sentence in Exercises 19–21.

19. Three is less than a number x.

20. A number y is greater than negative two.

21. A number is less than or equal to 5 halves.

22. The minimum speed on a highway is 40 mi/h and the maximum speed is 55 mi/h. Write an inequality that describes the situation when a car is:

a. breaking the speed limit **b.** going too slow

Solve the problems in Exercises 23–25 by writing and solving inequalities.

Example: Five more than an integer is less than 27. Find the largest integer that meets this condition.

Solution: $n + 5 < 27$ $n < 22$ The largest integer satisfying this inequality is 21.

23. Six less than an integer n is greater than 25. Find the least possible value for n.

24. Eight times an integer n is less than 48. Find the greatest possible value for n.

25. Louise said she would sell her house only if the sealed bid were more than $4000 above her cost of $92,000. Bids are in multiples of $500. What is the smallest bid that Louise would accept?

C *Extending Thinking Skills*

26. How can you use unmarked 8-liter and 5-liter containers to measure out exactly 7 liters?

27. Solve the inequality $|x - 3| > 5$ for the replacement set $\{-10, -9, \ldots 10\}$

Mixed Review

Evaluate for $x = -0.5$, $y = 0.5$. **28.** $2x^2y$ **29.** $6(x + y)$

30. $1.6x + 3.2y$ **31.** $y(1 - 2x)$ **32.** $x(y - x)$ **33.** $x \div (-y)$

8-9 Solving Inequalities: Combined Operations

You can use the same steps to solve inequalities that involve more than one operation as you used for solving equations with combined operations. Observe the order in which operations are applied to the variable and undo the operations, in reverse order. As with equations, the goal is to get the variable by itself on one side.

Example 1

Solve. $-x + 4 < 6$

Solution $-x + 4 < 6$

$-x + 4 - 4 < 6 - 4$ Subtract 4 from each side. The inequality sign stays the same.

$-x < 2$

$(-1)(-x) > (-1)2$ Multiply each side by -1. Reverse the inequality sign.

$x > -2$

Practice Solve.

a. $\frac{n}{4} - 3 > 2$ **b.** $12 \leq 2a + 3$

To begin to solve an inequality, you often need to simplify an expression by combining like terms. The basic properties help.

Example 2

Solve. $-4b + 6b \geq 5$

Solution $-4b + 6b \geq 5$

$2b \geq 5$ Distributive property: $-4b + 6b = 2b$.

$\frac{1}{2} \cdot 2b \geq \frac{1}{2} \cdot 5$ Multiply each side by $\frac{1}{2}$. The inequality sign stays the same.

$b \geq \frac{5}{2}$

Practice Solve. **a.** $8r - 5r < -12$ **b.** $5(x + 2) > 25$

To solve an inequality with variables on both sides, you can add or subtract a variable expression from each side to get the variable by itself, as with equations.

Example 3

Solve. $5n - 6 < 3n$

Solution $5n - 6 < 3n$

$5n - 6 + 6 < 3n + 6$ Add 6 to each side. The inequality sign stays the same.

$5n < 3n + 6$

$5n - 3n < 3n - 3n + 6$ Subtract 3*n* from each side. The inequality sign stays the same.

$2n < 6$

$\frac{2n}{2} < \frac{6}{2}$ Divide each side by 2. The inequality sign stays the same.

$n < 3$

Practice Solve.

a. $-2b + 5 > 3b$ **b.** $5 + 6c \leq -8c + 3$

Oral Exercises

Is the given number a solution to the inequality?

1. $2z + 3 < 12; 4$ **2.** $\frac{n}{2} - 1 > 20; 50$ **3.** $2b + 3b < 10; 0$

4. $-p + 2 > 0; 3$ **5.** $3(s + 1) < 12; 3$ **6.** $4y - 2y > 9; 5$

7. $6 + 2n < -1; -4$ **8.** $3c - 2c \geq 0; -5$ **9.** $5(r - 1) \leq 9; 3$

Exercises

A Solve.

1. $2a - 1 > 5$ **2.** $3x + 2 < -4$ **3.** $2s + 5 < 3$

4. $n - 3 > 5$ **5.** $4r + 2 > -22$ **6.** $\frac{t}{2} - 8 > 14$

7. $-5 + 3c > 31$ **8.** $\frac{n}{3} - 2 < 4$ **9.** $-5 < -3p + 34$

10. $4y + 7y > -66$ **11.** $9x + 3x < 96$ **12.** $54 < -7c + 4c$

13. $12n - 4n < 64$ **14.** $4x + 6x < 100$ **15.** $15 \leq 14a - 9a$

16. $3(r + 2) > -5$ **17.** $2(n - 6) \geq 4$ **18.** $12 < 5(c + 8)$

19. $7x + 3 < 3x$ **20.** $-9b > 26 + 4b$ **21.** $-24 + 6a > -2a$

22. $-2s + 3 < 5s - 4$ **23.** $9x - 2 \geq -12x + 1$ **24.** $4z - 3 < 10z - 5$

25. $\frac{2}{5}x - 3 > 2$ **26.** $4c + 7 + 3c < -35$ **27.** $\frac{3}{8}n - 5 > \frac{7}{8}n$

B Solve and check.

28. $-3x + \frac{1}{2} < \frac{3}{5}$

29. $-\frac{x}{2} + \frac{3}{8} > -\frac{1}{8}$

30. $-5y - \frac{5}{9} > -2\frac{1}{3}$

31. Write an inequality for "the difference of twice a number and 9 is less than 57."

32. Write an inequality for "12 more than half a number is less than or equal to 30."

33. Write an inequality for "the sum of two thirds of a number and six is less than forty."

34. Five more than twice an integer is less than 51. Write and solve an inequality to find the largest integer that meets this condition.

35. Six less than half an integer is greater than 15. Write and solve an inequality to find the smallest integer that meets this condition.

36. Badminton team A scored 5 less than half of team B's score. Team B scored less than 15 points. What is the greatest score team A could have?

37. Mrs. Taka feels that she should pay no more than $15,000 plus $2\frac{1}{2}$ times her yearly income for a house. What is the smallest yearly income she could have if she is to buy a $90,000 house?

C *Extending Thinking Skills*

38. A sentence with "and" is true if and only if *both* parts of the sentence are true. Give four solutions to this inequality: $x < 10$ **and** $x > 5$

39. A sentence with "or" is true if and only if *one or the other or both* parts are true. Give four solutions to this inequality: $x < -2$ **or** $x > 2$

Mixed Review

Find the least common multiple (LCM). **40.** 4, 10, 15 **41.** 9, 15

Simplify. **42.** $p^3 \cdot p^9 \cdot p$ **43.** $m^2 \cdot n^3 \cdot m^4 \cdot n$

ESTIMATION

You can substitute compatible numbers chosen from 0, $\frac{1}{2}$, and 1, to estimate certain sums. For example, $\frac{1}{12}$ is "close to zero," $\frac{5}{9}$ is "a little greater than $\frac{1}{2}$," $\frac{5}{11}$ is "a little less than $\frac{1}{2}$," $\frac{14}{15}$ is "a little less than 1," and $\frac{11}{10}$ is "a little more than 1."

Estimate whether each sum is more or less than the number given.

1. $\frac{5}{6} + \frac{7}{8}$; 2

2. $\frac{3}{8} + \frac{1}{10} + \frac{4}{5}$; $1\frac{1}{2}$

3. $\frac{7}{8} + \frac{8}{9} + \frac{11}{12}$; 3

4. $\frac{4}{9} + \frac{5}{8} + \frac{7}{12} + \frac{1}{2}$; 2

5. $5\frac{3}{5} + 7\frac{1}{12} + \frac{11}{10}$; 13

6. $\frac{362}{365} + 1\frac{181}{365}$; $2\frac{1}{2}$

PROBLEM SOLVING: STRATEGIES

8-10 Using Several Strategies

You have learned that more than one strategy can be used when solving a problem. In fact, using several strategies is often helpful. For example, **Simplify the Problem, Draw a Picture, Look for a Pattern,** and **Make a Table** are all used to solve the following problem.

Problem How many different squares are there on a patio made of 6 rows of 6 square tiles?

To solve this problem, you might first **simplify** it by starting with fewer squares and **draw** the following pictures.

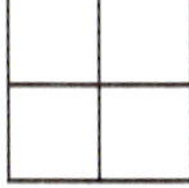

2 by 2

4 1 by 1 squares
1 2 by 2 squares
4 + 1 = 5 squares in all.

3 by 3

9 1 by 1 squares
4 2 by 2 squares
1 3 by 3 squares
9 + 4 + 1 = 14 squares in all.

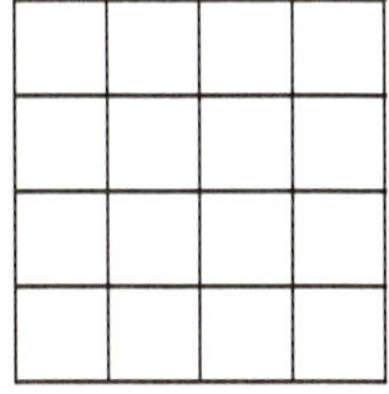

4 by 4

16 1 by 1 squares
9 2 by 2 squares
4 3 by 3 squares
1 4 by 4 squares
16 + 9 + 4 + 1 = 30 squares in all.

Then you could organize the information in a **table** and look for a **pattern**. The total number of squares can be found by squaring the side length and adding this to all the square numbers less than it.

Length of Side	Total Number of Squares
1	1
2	5 = 4 + 1
3	14 = 9 + 4 + 1
4	30 = 16 + 9 + 4 + 1

The total number of different squares on the 6-by-6 square patio is

$$36 + 25 + 16 + 9 + 4 + 1 = 91.$$

This chart shows the strategies presented.

Problem-Solving Strategies	
Choose the Operations	Write an Equation
Guess, Check, Revise	Simplify the Problem
Draw a Picture	Make an Organized List
Make a Table	Use Logical Reasoning
Look for a Pattern	Work Backwards

Problems

Solve.

1. How many different sizes of squares are there on an ordinary checkerboard of 64 squares?

2. What is the largest amount of money you could have in quarters, dimes, nickels, or pennies without being able to make change for $1?

3. Two people on motorcycles leave state parks that are 600 miles apart and travel toward each other. One cycle averages 55 mi/h. The other averages 45 mi/h. They both start at 11 a.m. When should they expect to meet?

4. You have 5 sections of chain and each section has 3 links. The cost to have a link cut is 10¢. The cost to have a link welded is 20¢. How can you join the sections into one continuous chain for less than $1?

5. A prospector wanted to sell 8 pieces of gold. The buyer said he had weighed them and they were all the same weight. The prospector suspected that one of the pieces was heavier than the other 7. He found the heavier piece by using a balance scale and only two weighings. Describe how he did it.

6. A biologist started with 1 microbe in a special liquid. During each hour, the microbe population became 3 times as large as it was the previous hour. How many microbes were there when the biologist stopped the experiment after 6 hours?

Enrichment

Multiplying Binomials

An expression with one term, such as $\mathbf{5x}$, is called a **monomial**. An expression with two terms, such as $\mathbf{4x + 3}$, is called a **binomial**. An expression with three terms, such as $\mathbf{x + xy - 3}$, is called a **trinomial**. A **polynomial** is a monomial or the sum of monomials, such as $\mathbf{2n^2 + 3np + p + 5}$.

You have used the distributive property to multiply a monomial by a binomial when you simplified expressions such as $5(x + 2)$. You can also use the distributive property in two steps to multiply a binomial times a binomial to find a product such as $(x + 2)(y + 3)$.

To use the distributive property in the first step, replace a with $(x + 2)$, replace b with y, and replace c with 3. Then use the distributive property in the second step to simplify $(x + 2)y$ and $(x + 2)3$ to get the final product.

$$a \quad (b + c) = a \; b + a \; c$$

$$\begin{aligned}(x + 2)\;(y + 3) &= (x + 2)y + (x + 2)3 \\ &= xy + 2y + x(3) + (2)(3) \\ &= xy + 2y + 3x + 6\end{aligned}$$

Notice that each term of the second binomial is multiplied by every term of the first binomial. That is, first y is multiplied by x and then by 2, then 3 is multiplied by x and then by 2. This shortcut is shown by the diagram below.

$$(x + 2)(y + 3)$$

$$(x + 2)(y + 3) = xy + 2y + x(3) + (2 \cdot 3)$$

Multiply.

1. $(x + 1)(y + 4)$

2. $(p + 2)(q + 5)$

3. $(b + 3)(c + 1)$

4. $(y + 6)(z + 7)$

5. $(x + 2)(x + 3)$

6. $(t + 1)(t + 5)$

7. $(s + 6)(s + 4)$

8. $(n + 2)(n + 2)$

9. $(a + 10)(a + 9)$

10. $(t + 1)(t + 7)$

11. $(a + 6)(b + 4)$

12. $(n + 3)(m + 8)$

13. $(s + 4)(s + 9)$

14. $(y + 5)[y + (-3)]$

15. $[s + (-4)](s + 4)$

Chapter 8 Review

8-1 Solve.

1. $5h - 12 = 38$

2. $24 = -c + 5$

3. $\frac{f + 2}{7} = -3$

4. $3(y + 1) = 15$

8-2 Write an equation.

5. When Sally's age is multiplied by 5 and increased by 3, the result is Toshi's age, 33.

6. Joaquin's weight, 100 kg, is 2 kg more than twice his sister Abbey's weight. How much does Abbey weigh?

8-3 Solve by writing an equation.

7. Alice scored 22 goals this month. That is 2 fewer than 3 times the number of goals she scored last month. How many goals did she score last month?

8. Gil had a carton of milk that was $\frac{3}{4}$ full. He gave Mr. Fletcher 16 oz, leaving 8 oz in the carton. How many ounces did the carton hold?

8-4 Solve and check.

9. $72 = 4p + 8p$

10. $8c + 7c = -120$

11. $108 = 15r - 6r$

12. $25t - 11t = 70$

8-5 Solve and check.

13. $9c + 5(c + 4) = -92$

14. $3(d - 1) + 4d = 67$

15. $12n - 8 + 4(3n) = 88$

16. $6(y - 8) + 3y = 6$

8-6 Solve and check.

17. $5t + 12 = 7t - 4$

18. $144 - 7t = 5t$

19. $3y + 7 = 4y$

20. $-6r + 1 = -20 + r$

8-7 Solve.

21. A class picnic was attended by 4 less than $\frac{2}{3}$ of the total number of students in the class. Forty-six students came to the picnic. What is the total number of students in the class?

8-8 Solve and check.

22. $p + 10 < 17$

23. $45 > -9p$

8-9 Solve.

24. $15 < 3a + 3$

25. $-6f + 8f < -20$

Chapter 8 Test

Solve.

1. $5t - 1 = 14$
2. $-28 = 3n - 1$
3. $\frac{a + 5}{7} = 4$
4. $3(m - 5) = -27$

Write an equation.

5. The $38 cost of a sweater is $2 more than 3 times the cost of a tie.

6. Brant's age, 37, is 3 less than twice Ricky's age.

Solve by writing an equation.

7. Mike's height is 5 inches less than twice his little sister's height. Mike is 71 inches tall. What is his little sister's height?

8. Cheryl averaged 28 points per game this year. This is 4 more than $\frac{3}{4}$ of last year's average. How many points per game did she average last year?

Solve and check.

9. $18c + 3c = 84$
10. $-55 = 6y + 5y$
11. $20x - 13x = -56$
12. $135 = 22t - 7t$

Solve and check.

13. $3(m + 4) + 6m = 66$
14. $b + 4(b - 9) = 14$
15. $7c - 8 + 3(2c) = 31$
16. $5(x - 8) - 2x = -16$

Solve and check.

17. $7x - 2 = 5x + 16$
18. $14p = 20p - 18$
19. $35 + 6n = 5n$
20. $20r + 7 = 15r + 22$

Solve.

21. Suzy is paid $5 per hour for washing cars. Her total earnings one Saturday came to $39. This included $4 in tips. How many hours did she work that day?

Solve and check.

22. $4 > f - 6$
23. $6r < -12$

Solve.

24. $8b - 5b > 9$
25. $\frac{n}{3} - 4 > 2$

Cumulative Review

Write in expanded form. Simplify if possible.

1. 9^5 **2.** $(-6)^4$ **3.** t^3

Write using exponents.

4. $9 \cdot 9 \cdot 9 \cdot 9$ **5.** $ccccccc$ **6.** $-2(-2)(-2)$

Multiply. Give the answer in exponent form.

7. $4^3 \cdot 4^2$ **8.** $(-5)^7 \cdot (-5)^3$ **9.** $v^3 \cdot v$

Evaluate each expression.

10. $3^3 + 3^1$ **11.** $(-4)^2 + (-4)^2$

Give the prime factorization.

12. 72 **13.** 25

14. 110 **15.** 200

Find the Greatest Common Factor (GCF) of each pair of numbers.

16. 12, 20 **17.** 42, 48 **18.** 45, 120

Find the Least Common Multiple (LCM) of each pair of numbers.

19. 2, 15 **20.** 8, 12 **21.** 12, 30

Write each as a decimal. Use a bar for repeating decimals.

22. $\frac{2}{3}$ **23.** $\frac{7}{8}$ **24.** $\frac{5}{11}$

Simplify. Write the expression with exponents.

25. $\frac{5^8}{5^3}$ **26.** $\frac{(-7)^7}{(-7)^3}$ **27.** $\frac{r^5}{r^8}$

Write the expression without exponents.

28. 2^{-3} **29.** $(-3)^{-2}$ **30.** $\frac{(-6)^5}{(-6)^7}$

Write in scientific notation.

31. 414 **32.** 33,000 **33.** 12,000,000

34. 0.05 **35.** 0.0000225 **36.** 0.0089

Write in decimal form.

37. 2.78×10^4 **38.** 3.0×10^{-5} **39.** 7.08×10^{-3}

Chapter 9

Ratio, Proportion, and Percent

9-1 Ratio

A comparison of one number to another is called a **ratio**.

The instrument ratio helps balance the sound of an orchestra.

Instrument Familes in an Orchestra			
Strings 67	Woodwinds 19	Brass 14	Percussion 11

The ratio of brass instruments to percussion instruments is fourteen to eleven. This ratio can be written as

$$\frac{14}{11}, \quad 14:11, \quad \text{or } 14 \text{ to } 11.$$

A ratio is in **lowest terms** when the only common factor of the two numbers being compared is 1.

Example

Write the ratio $\frac{18}{15}$ as a fraction in lowest terms.

Solution

$\frac{18}{15} = \frac{6}{5}$ Divide 18 and 15 by 3, the greatest common factor.

Practice Write each ratio as a fraction in lowest terms.

a. 9:27 **b.** 35 to 28 **c.** $\frac{36}{24}$

Oral Exercises

Give the ratio. Do not express in lowest terms.

1. cellos to violins
2. double basses to harps
3. English horns to piccolos
4. harps to violins
5. violas to cellos
6. flutes to harps
7. piccolos to bassoons
8. saxophones to clarinets

Strings	Woodwinds
34 violins 10 cellos 12 violas 9 double basses 2 harps	2 oboes 1 English horn 2 flutes 1 piccolo 5 bassoons 6 clarinets 2 saxophones

Exercises

A Write each ratio as a fraction in lowest terms.

1. $\frac{24}{16}$ **2.** 8 to 14 **3.** 16:36 **4.** 26:10

5. 9 to 24 **6.** $\frac{3}{33}$ **7.** 12 to 7 **8.** 30:18

9. 36:24 **10.** 7 to 35 **11.** $\frac{16}{10}$ **12.** $\frac{8}{64}$

13. 28:7 **14.** 10 to 90 **15.** 64 to 36 **16.** 48:144

17. 10 to 36 **18.** 24:60 **19.** 18:36 **20.** 60 to 200

B Write each ratio as a fraction in lowest terms.

21. 2 harps to 10 cellos **22.** 6 clarinets : 2 saxophones

23. 34 violins : 12 violas **24.** 9 double basses to 12 violas

Write each ratio in two other ways.

25. x to y **26.** y to x **27.** $3a$ to b

28. $(s + t)$ to p **29.** $(m + n)$ to z **30.** $(a + b)$ to $(a - b)$

31. A softball team won 12 games and lost 6. What is its ratio of wins to losses?

32. A 120-piece marching band has 7 treble drums and 3 bass drums. What is the ratio of these drums to all instruments in the band?

33. A rock band needed 250 hours of studio work to record an album with 45 minutes of music. What is the ratio of minutes of album music to minutes of work needed?

34. A plane that held a total of 225 passengers had 12 passengers in first class and 113 passengers in "coach." What was the ratio of full seats to empty seats?

35. Six buses took 425 students to a state capital. Four adults were on each bus. What was the ratio of adults to students?

C Extending Thinking Skills

36. How many girls are in a class of 32 students if the ratio of girls to boys is 3:5?

37. A builder used 12 parts sand, 15 parts gravel, 6 parts cement, and 3 parts water in a concrete mix. You can write these relationships as 12:15:6:3. Give the ratio in lowest terms.

Mixed Review

Solve and check. **38.** $9y = 3y - 45$ **39.** $2(a + 6) - 4(a + 1) = 4$

40. $z + 45 < 36$ **41.** $18 > -3c$ **42.** $9 < t + 2$

Write each as a decimal. **43.** $3 \div 8$ **44.** $1 \div 20$ **45.** $3 \div 25$

Evaluate. Reduce to lowest terms. **46.** $\left(\frac{3}{4}\right)\left(\frac{2}{3}\right)$ **47.** $\frac{4}{7} + \frac{1}{2}$ **48.** $\frac{3}{5} \div \frac{7}{15}$

9-2 Proportion

The ratios $\frac{10}{18}$ and $\frac{15}{27}$ can both be written in lowest terms as $\frac{5}{9}$. You can write the equation $\frac{10}{18} = \frac{15}{27}$.

An equation stating that two ratios are equal is called a **proportion**. Notice that the cross products shown by the arrows below in the proportion $\frac{10}{18} = \frac{15}{27}$ are equal.

$$10 \cdot 27 = 270 \qquad \frac{10}{18} = \frac{15}{27} \qquad 18 \cdot 15 = 270$$

Property of Proportions

Two ratios are equal if and only if the cross products are equal.

$\frac{a}{b} = \frac{c}{d}$ **if and only if** $ad = bc$ ($b \neq 0$ and $d \neq 0$)

Example 1

Write = or ≠ for the □. Use the property of proportions.

$\frac{28}{21} \square \frac{8}{6}$

Solution

$$\frac{28}{21} \quad \square \quad \frac{8}{6}$$

$28 \cdot 6 \stackrel{?}{=} 21 \cdot 8$ Find the cross products.

$168 = 168$

$\frac{28}{21} = \frac{8}{6}$ Since the cross products are equal, the ratios are equal.

Practice Write = or ≠ for the □. Use the property of proportions.

a. $\frac{8}{12} \square \frac{12}{15}$ **b.** $\frac{8}{3} \square \frac{16}{6}$

When one of the numbers in a proportion is not known, you can use the property of proportions to write an equation.

Example 2

Solve and check. $\frac{x}{40} = \frac{3}{5}$

Solution $\frac{x}{40} = \frac{3}{5}$

$5 \cdot x = 40 \cdot 3$ Property of proportions.

$5x = 120$

$\frac{5x}{5} = \frac{120}{5}$ Divide each side by 5.

$x = 24$

Check $\frac{24}{40} \stackrel{?}{=} \frac{3}{5}$ Replace x with 24.

$5 \cdot 24 \stackrel{?}{=} 40 \cdot 3$ Property of proportions.

$120 = 120 \checkmark$ The solution is 24.

Practice Solve and check. **a.** $\frac{3}{4} = \frac{m}{20}$ **b.** $\frac{2}{7} = \frac{18}{b}$

Example 3

Use a proportion to solve. The ratio of adults to students on a train is 2 to 11. There are 12 adults on the train. How many students are on the train?

Solution

$\frac{2}{11} = \frac{12}{x}$ ← adults / ← students — To write the proportion, set up each ratio in the same way. Both ratios compare adults to students.

$2 \cdot x = 11 \cdot 12$ Set up an equation by finding the cross products. Then solve the equation.

$x = \frac{11 \cdot 12}{2}$

$x = 66$

There are 66 students on the train.

Practice Use a proportion to solve. Chemical C is made up of chemicals A and B in the ratio of 17 to 5. To make a batch of chemical C with 102 units of chemical A, how many units of chemical B are needed?

Oral Exercises

State the equation you would solve to find the missing number.

1. $\frac{1}{2} = \frac{x}{18}$ **2.** $\frac{n}{48} = \frac{3}{4}$ **3.** $\frac{4}{1} = \frac{24}{t}$ **4.** $\frac{3}{10} = \frac{y}{40}$

5. $\frac{x}{52} = \frac{5}{4}$ **6.** $\frac{16}{n} = \frac{1}{3}$ **7.** $\frac{4}{5} = \frac{m}{65}$ **8.** $\frac{6}{9} = \frac{4}{r}$

Exercises

A Write = or ≠ for each □. Use the property of proportions.

1. $\frac{4}{5} \square \frac{12}{15}$ **2.** $\frac{5}{2} \square \frac{35}{14}$ **3.** $\frac{4}{15} \square \frac{3}{7}$ **4.** $\frac{8}{6} \square \frac{28}{22}$

5. $\frac{9}{16} \square \frac{3}{4}$ **6.** $\frac{8}{15} \square \frac{20}{45}$ **7.** $\frac{3}{2} \square \frac{12}{8}$ **8.** $\frac{17}{34} \square \frac{1}{2}$

9. $\frac{28}{35} \square \frac{4}{5}$ **10.** $\frac{4}{7} \square \frac{32}{56}$ **11.** $\frac{9}{4} \square \frac{63}{28}$ **12.** $\frac{12}{30} \square \frac{10}{25}$

Solve and check.

13. $\frac{24}{x} = \frac{4}{3}$ **14.** $\frac{5}{3} = \frac{y}{42}$ **15.** $\frac{1}{2} = \frac{m}{18}$ **16.** $\frac{t}{14} = \frac{5}{2}$

17. $\frac{12}{27} = \frac{8}{m}$ **18.** $\frac{r}{27} = \frac{8}{18}$ **19.** $\frac{u}{7} = \frac{22}{14}$ **20.** $\frac{12}{30} = \frac{10}{n}$

21. $\frac{4}{5} = \frac{28}{x}$ **22.** $\frac{15}{y} = \frac{10}{8}$ **23.** $\frac{63}{144} = \frac{t}{16}$ **24.** $\frac{8}{15} = \frac{m}{105}$

25. $\frac{7}{x} = \frac{4}{9}$ **26.** $\frac{y}{42} = \frac{15}{18}$ **27.** $\frac{100}{m} = \frac{90}{45}$ **28.** $\frac{18}{y} = \frac{126}{150}$

Use a proportion to solve Exercises 29–32.

29. Four shovels of sand are used for every 5 shovels of gravel in making cement. How many shovels of sand are needed for 25 shovels of gravel?

30. Bob's snack mix contains both peanuts and pecans in a ratio of 8 to 5. How many grams of pecans does he need if he uses 520 g of peanuts?

31. The ratio of Ann's weight to Tina's weight is 5:6. Ann weighs 85 pounds. How much does Tina weigh?

32. The ratio of expenses to income in the Johnsons' business is 5 to 8. What are their expenses for a month in which their income is $9,800?

B Estimate to find two equal ratios from each set. Then write a proportion and use cross products to see whether it is true.

33. $\frac{2}{3}; \frac{10}{18}; \frac{5}{9}$ **34.** $\frac{48}{60}; \frac{56}{75}; \frac{4}{5}$ **35.** $\frac{7}{18}; \frac{42}{126}; \frac{77}{198}$

36. $\frac{5}{12}; \frac{25}{60}; \frac{50}{144}$ **37.** $\frac{24}{125}; \frac{4}{25}; \frac{32}{200}$ **38.** $\frac{6}{15}; \frac{42}{90}; \frac{84}{180}$

39. $\frac{3}{4}; \frac{18}{24}; \frac{28}{35}$ **40.** $\frac{5}{8}; \frac{30}{45}; \frac{40}{64}$ **41.** $\frac{10}{12}; \frac{20}{25}; \frac{15}{18}$

Solve each proportion.

42. $\frac{24}{13} = \frac{x}{91}$ **43.** $\frac{32}{x} = \frac{128}{60}$ **44.** $\frac{15}{8} = \frac{105}{x}$

45. The ratio of full seats to the total number of seats on Mr. Chu's flight is 3 to 7. There are 28 empty seats. How many people are on the plane?

46. The ratio of girls to boys in Maria's school is 3 : 4. The school has 228 boys. How many students does it have all together?

47. Find two values for x and y so that $\frac{x}{12} = \frac{28}{y}$.

C Extending Thinking Skills

48. Eric's school system has 9000 pupils and a teacher-pupil ratio of 1 : 30. How many more or fewer teachers are needed to reduce the teacher-pupil ratio to 1 : 25?

49. It takes 12 minutes to cut a log into 4 pieces. How long will it take to cut a log into 6 pieces?

Mixed Review

Reduce to lowest terms. **50.** $\frac{70}{98}$ **51.** $\frac{27}{144}$ **52.** $\frac{12}{22}$ **53.** $\frac{40}{64}$

Simplify. **54.** $\frac{n^7}{n^2}$ **55.** $\frac{x^4}{x^2}$ **56.** $\frac{(-3)^5}{(-3)^2}$

Solve and check. **57.** $\frac{2}{3}n = \frac{1}{2}$ **58.** $c - \frac{4}{5} = \frac{1}{8}$ **59.** $\frac{1}{2}(t + \frac{1}{3}) = -\frac{1}{6}$

Estimate each product or quotient. **60.** 385×22 **61.** 2.85×16.3
62. $71.2 \div 12.3$ **63.** $83.7 \div 8.5$ **64.** $608 \div 33$ **65.** $124.7 \div 11.1$

NUMBERS TO ALGEBRA

Study the examples to see how proportions involving numbers are related to proportions in algebra.

Numbers	Algebra	
$\frac{8}{5} = \frac{16}{12 - 2}$	$\frac{5}{3} = \frac{10}{x - 1}$	
$8 \cdot (12 - 2) = 5 \cdot 16$	$5 \cdot (x - 1) = 3 \cdot 10$	Property of proportions.
$8 \cdot 12 - 8 \cdot 2 = 5 \cdot 16$	$5x - 5 = 30$	Distributive property.
$96 - 16 = 80$	$5x = 35$	
$80 = 80$	$x = 7$	

Solve each proportion. Check your solution.

1. $\frac{2}{3} = \frac{a + 1}{12}$ **2.** $\frac{n + 1}{9} = \frac{2}{6}$ **3.** $\frac{4}{3} = \frac{32}{x - 1}$

4. $\frac{1}{5} = \frac{x + 2}{25}$ **5.** $\frac{x - 3}{6} = \frac{12}{9}$ **6.** $\frac{5}{4} = \frac{y + 1}{8}$

9-3 Rate

A **rate** is a ratio that involves two different units. A rate is usually given as a quantity per unit, such as kilometers per hour (km/h). You can use division to simplify a rate.

Example 1

Simplify. 176 km/2 h

Solution $\frac{176 \text{ km}}{2 \text{ h}} = 88$ km/h   88 km/1 hr can be written as 88km/h.

Practice Simplify each rate. **a.** 87 km/10 L **b.** 750 words/2 min

Example 2

Solve. A typist types 150 words in two minutes. How many words can he type in 5 minutes?

Solution $\frac{x}{5} = \frac{150}{2}$

$$2x = 150 \cdot 5$$
$$2x = 750$$
$$x = 375$$

He can type 375 words in 5 minutes.

Practice Solve.

How much should Fran get for 3 hours of work at $4.25/hour?

Oral Exercises

Describe a situation in which each rate might be used.

1. km/L **2.** miles/hour **3.** km/hour **4.** revolutions/min

5. beats/min **6.** words/min **7.** dollars/hour **8.** cars/day

Exercises

A Simplify each rate.

1. $56/7 h **2.** 75 km/10 L **3.** 1250 words/5 min

4. 78 cm/6 s **5.** 3,750 km/4 h **6.** 35 days/5 weeks

7. 105 people/35 cars
8. 143 players/11 teams
9. 2128 revolutions/32 min
10. $220/40 h
11. 385 min/7 classes
12. 576 students/24 teachers

Solve.

13. A motorist drove 1200 km on 45 L of gasoline. How many liters are needed to drive 500 km?

14. Apples are on sale at 4 for 60¢. How much will 18 apples cost?

15. What is the hourly rate of a mechanic who charges $160 for 4 hours of labor?

16. A typist can type 275 words in 5 minutes. How many can she type in 12 minutes?

17. What is the rate in beats per minute for a pulse rate of 25 beats per 15 seconds?

B

18. Dana works $5\frac{1}{2}$ hours per day at $4.50 per hour. What does she earn in 5 days?

19. A man bought a crate of apples for $10. The apples cost 90¢/lb and 4 apples equal about 1 pound. About how many apples should the crate contain?

20. How long would it take to lay 8 rows of 18 bricks each at a rate of 4 bricks per minute?

C Extending Thinking Skills

21. If $\frac{a}{b} = \frac{c}{d}$ then $\frac{a + b}{b} = \frac{c + d}{d}$. Show why this is true.

22. A recipe calls for two ounces of butter to every 5 tablespoons of flour. A cube of butter is 4 oz, and there are 4 cubes per pound. How many tablespoons of flour are needed for $4\frac{1}{2}$ pounds of butter?

Mixed Review

Solve and check. 23. $4(m + 2) = 14$ 24. $3.35 = 1 - t$

25. $r + 0.027 = -0.901$ 26. $(x + 5) \div 6 = 102$ 27. $3r = -0.24$

ESTIMATION

Use any estimation techniques you have learned to estimate the following rates.

1. 729 km on 25 L of gasoline. How many km per L is this?
2. 338 words in 5 minutes. What is the typing rate in words per minute?
3. $4.13 for 5 hours parking. What is the hourly parking rate?
4. $37.20 for 9 hours of work. What is the hourly wage?
5. 500 miles in $3\frac{1}{4}$ hours. How many miles per hour is this rate?

PROBLEM SOLVING: WRITING EQUATIONS

9-4 Translating Problems Involving Two Expressions

Some word problems involve two unknowns. An expression for one of the unknowns can be given in terms of the other. To solve such problems, first decide which unknown the variable will represent, then express the other in terms of the variable.

Example 1

Write an expression for each unknown.

Beverly is 3 years older than Celia.

Celia's age? Beverly's age?

Solution

Let c = Celia's age — Since Beverly's age is given in relation to Celia's, make Celia's age the first unknown.

$c + 3$ = Beverly's age — Then express Beverly's age is terms of Celia's.

Practice Sue has 3 times as many books as Dawn. Write an expression for each unknown.

a. The number Dawn has?
b. The number Sue has?

Example 2

Write an equation.

A large bus holds 24 students more than a small bus. The two buses hold 76 students altogether.

Solution

Let s = number a small bus holds — Since the number a large bus holds is given relative to the number a small bus holds, let s represent the number the small bus holds.

$s + 24$ = number a large bus holds — Then express the number the large bus holds in terms of the number the small bus holds.

$s + (s + 24) = 76$ — The two buses together hold 76 students.

Practice Write an equation.

Fred collected twice as many shells as Nick. Together they collected 24.

Oral Exercises

Let m = the number of math books. Give an algebraic expression for each in terms of m.

1. 7 fewer history books than math books
2. 8 times as many English books as math books.
3. $\frac{1}{2}$ as many science books as math books
4. 12 fewer art books than math books

Exercises

A Write an expression for each unknown.

1. Carl had 7 more than Kim: the number Kim had? the number Carl had?
2. 3 times as many cars as bikes: the number of bikes? the number of cars?
3. $\frac{1}{2}$ as many boys as girls: the number of girls? the number of boys?
4. Saturday seats cost double weekday seats: the cost of weekday seats? the cost of Saturday seats?

Write an equation.

5. There are 8 more boys than girls in the 63-member band this year.
6. One side of a record album lasts 98 seconds longer than the other. The total length of the album is 1936 seconds.
7. The second math quiz was worth half as many points as the first quiz. Both quizzes together were worth 110 points.
8. A tape cost \$2.10 more than an album. Together they cost \$13.60.
9. John scored 25 more points in his second bowling game than his first. He had a total of 297 points for the two games.

B Write an equation.

10. A theater has twice as many seats in each row of the middle section as in each row of the two side sections. It has a total of 96 seats per row made up of a middle row and two equal side rows.

C Extending Thinking Skills

Write a word problem that would be solved using the equation.

11. $x + (x + 2) = 18$. **12.** $x + 5x = 36$.

Mixed Review

Simplify. **13.** $2a + 3(a - 6) - 4a$ **14.** $-m - 5(2m + 4) - 8m$

Solve and check. **15.** $22 + 9z = 4$ **16.** $2(x + 1) = 0$

17. $3(14 - n) + 7 = 5n + 1$ **18.** $4(c + 3) = 14c - 3$ **19.** $9y + 16 = 3 - 4y$

9-5 Solving Problems Involving Two Expressions

You can write and solve an equation to find the answer to a word problem in which one unknown can be expressed in terms of another. Keep these questions in mind:

- Can you use a variable to represent an unknown number?
- Can you represent other conditions in terms of the variable?
- What is equal?
- Can you write and solve an equation?

Example

A train engine picked up $3\frac{1}{2}$ times as many cars at the second stop as it picked up at its first stop. Then it had a total of 81 cars. How many cars did it pick up at its second stop?

Solution

Let f = number picked up at the first stop.

$3\frac{1}{2}f$ = number picked up at the second stop — The number of cars picked up at the second stop is given relative to the number picked up at the first stop.

$$f + 3\frac{1}{2}f = 81$$

$$4\frac{1}{2}f = 81$$

$$\frac{9}{2}f = 81$$ Multiply both sides by $\frac{2}{9}$ to get f alone.

$$f = 18$$ The train picked up 18 cars at the first stop.

$$3\frac{1}{2} \cdot 18 = 63$$ The problem asks for the number picked up at the second stop, so find the value of $3\frac{1}{2}f$ when $f = 18$.

The train picked up 63 cars at its second stop. $63 < 81$. The answer is reasonable.

Practice Solve. Mrs. Kang has 4 fewer girls than boys in her art club this year. There are 28 students in the art club this year. How many are girls?

Oral Exercises

Give an equation.

1. Sid paid \$4 more for jeans than for a shirt. The total cost was \$38. How much was each?

2. The deep end of a swimming pool is $\frac{1}{4}$ the length of the shallow end. The total length of the pool is 90 m. How long is each section?

3. Vicky used 15 times as much fertilizer as grass seed on her lawn. Altogether, she used 32 pounds of material. How many pounds of fertilizer did she use?

Exercises

A Solve by writing an equation.

1. An airplane had 65 more occupied seats than empty seats. It had a total of 211 seats. How many seats were occupied?

2. A box of popcorn cost twice as much as a cup of juice. Lyle bought 1 of each and paid $2.25. What was the price of popcorn?

3. A class of 354 graduates has 64 fewer male graduates than female graduates. How many are male and how many are female?

4. Of 410 students graduating, the number planning to get a job is $\frac{1}{4}$ as many as the number planning to go to college. How many students are not planning to go to college?

5. A large bottle of fruit juice contains 4 times as much as the regular size. The total number of ounces in the two sizes is 40. How many ounces are in each size?

B

6. Gilberto bought 2 shirts and a sweater and paid $48. The sweater cost twice as much as each shirt. How much was the sweater and how much was each shirt?

7. Jerry collected twice as many donations as Fred. Tom collected 12 more donations than Fred. Each donation was at least $2. Altogether, the three boys collected 48 donations. How many donations did each boy collect?

8. The weekend rate for a 5-passenger rental car is $\frac{1}{2}$ as much as the weekday rate. Mrs. Cooper rented a car for 3 weekdays and 1 weekend day and paid $171.50. How much more is the cost per day during the week than on the weekend?

C Extending Thinking Skills

9. Write a word problem that could be solved using the equation $x + \frac{1}{2}x = 24$.

10. Write a word problem that could be solved using the equation $x + 2x + 3x = 126$.

Mixed Review

Find the least common multiple (LCM). **11.** 5, 6, 8 **12.** 3, 6, 7

Evaluate for $n = \frac{2}{3}$. **13.** $\frac{1}{5}n + \frac{1}{2}$ **14.** $n - \frac{2}{7}$ **15.** $\frac{9}{10} - n$ **16.** $\frac{n}{4} + \frac{1}{6}$

More Practice

Write each ratio in two other ways.

1. 6 to x **2.** m to $5n$ **3.** $(r + 3)$ to t **4.** $(r + s)$ to $(s + t)$

Write = or ≠ for each □. Use the property of proportions.

5. $\frac{4}{3} \square \frac{9}{7}$ **6.** $\frac{7}{8} \square \frac{42}{48}$ **7.** $\frac{6}{14} \square \frac{33}{77}$ **8.** $\frac{12}{8} \square \frac{26}{18}$

Simplify each rate.

9. 28 days/7 months **10.** 135 mi/3 h **11.** 440 words/5 minutes

Solve.

12. Farmer Hoff raises chickens. He has 216 Rhode Island Reds, 144 Leghorns, and 180 Bantams. **a.** What is the ratio of Rhode Island Reds to Leghorns? **b.** Of Leghorns to Bantams? **c.** Of Bantams to all other chickens?

13. There are 32 students in Mrs. Chu's class. Four students are left-handed. What is the ratio of left-handed students to right-handed students?

14. Acme Industries has 120 employees, including 15 supervisors. What is the ratio of supervisors to all other employees?

15. The ratio of Anaya's age to Raphael's age is 7 : 12. Anaya is 14. How old is Raphael?

16. The ranger at a campground counted tents and camper vans and found that the ratio of tents to vans was 12 : 17. She counted 84 tents. How many vans did she find?

17. A truck driver drove 371 miles in 7 hours. How far did he drive in one hour?

18. Ernesto can assemble 3 circuit boards in 10 minutes. How many boards can he assemble in one hour?

19. Tanisha worked 3 hours and was paid $13.50. At that rate, how long will it take Tanisha to earn $45.00?

20. Nate is 3 years older than Maury. Their combined age is 35. How old is Nate? How old is Maury?

21. Steve sold 12 more tickets than Daniel, and Kyoki sold twice as many as Daniel. They sold 216 tickets in all. How many tickets did each person sell?

9-6 Scale Drawings

In the **scale drawing** below, the dimensions of every object in the drawing are reduced by the same ratio or **scale**. The scale for this drawing is 5 cm to 2 m. This means that an object that has a length of 5 cm in the scale drawing has an actual length of 2 m.

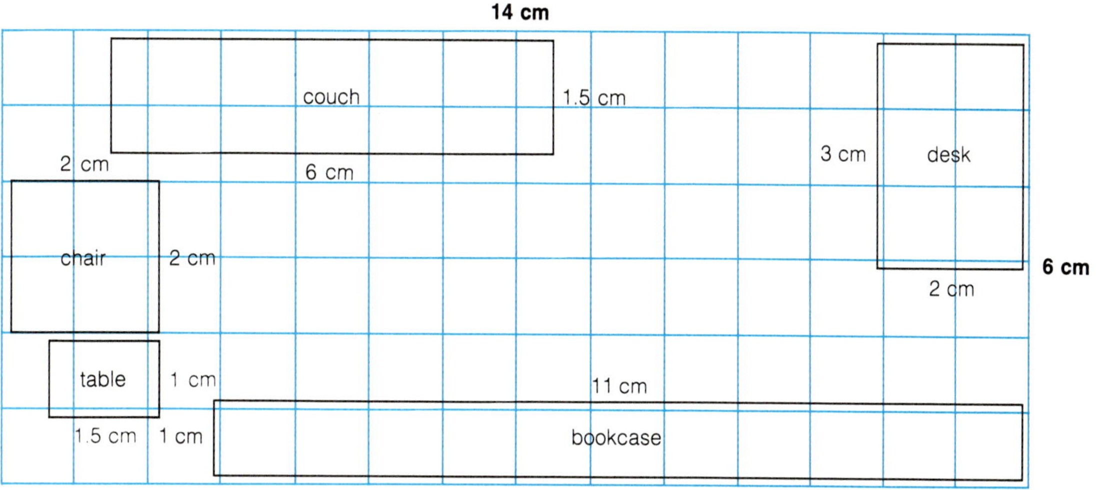

You can use the scale in the drawing to set up a proportion and find the actual dimensions of the objects shown in the picture.

Example 1

Find the actual length of the couch in the scale drawing above.

Solution Let L = actual length of couch

$$\frac{5}{2} = \frac{6}{L} \begin{matrix} \leftarrow \text{cm} \\ \leftarrow \text{m} \end{matrix}$$

The scale is 5 cm to 2 m. The length of the couch in the drawing is 6 cm, and the actual length of the couch is unknown.

$$5 \cdot L = 2 \cdot 6$$

$$L = 2.4$$

The actual length of the couch is 2.4 m.

Practice

Find the actual length and width of the desk in the drawing above.

You can find the scale dimensions of an object if you know its actual dimensions and the scale.

Example 2

The actual dimensions of a park are 825 m (width) and 1350 m (length). Find the width of this park on a scale drawing with a scale of 1 cm = 75 m.

Solution

Let W = scale drawing width of the park

$$\frac{W}{825} = \frac{1}{75} \begin{matrix} \leftarrow \text{cm} \\ \leftarrow \text{m} \end{matrix}$$ The width of the park in the scale drawing is unknown. The actual width is 825 m.

$$75 \cdot W = 1 \cdot 825$$
$$W = 11$$

The width of the park in the scale drawing is 11 cm.

Practice Find the scale dimension for the length of the park.

Oral Exercises

Refer to the scale drawing of the living room on the previous page and give the proportion you would solve to find the actual dimension. The scale for the drawing is 5 cm : 2 m.

1. width of chair
2. length of table
3. width of table
4. length of bookcase
5. width of bookcase
6. width of couch

Exercises

A Refer to the scale drawing to find the actual straight-line distance between each pair of towns. The scale is 1 cm : 150 km.

1. San Anselmo to Easthaven
2. Arcata to Hadleigh
3. Easthaven to Miwok
4. Hadleigh to San Anselmo
5. Arcata to Silver Lake
6. Silver Lake to San Anselmo
7. Miwok to Silver Lake

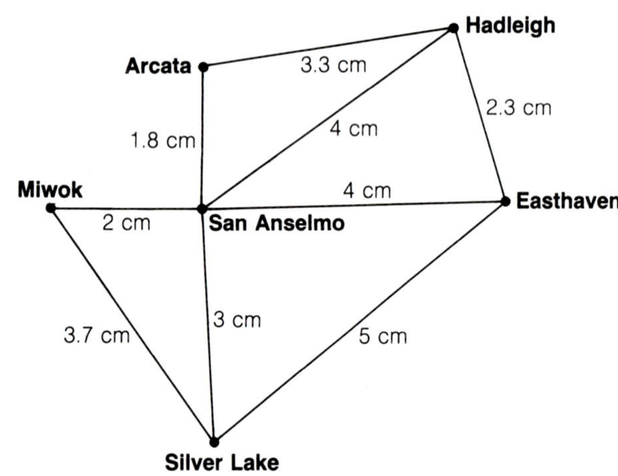

Find the scale dimensions for each if the scale is 5 mm:2 m.

8. Dining Room: 5 m × 4 m

9. Bedroom: 4 m × 5 m

10. Bench: 1.5 m × 1 m

11. Table: 1 m × 3 m

12. Dresser: 2 m × 0.5 m

13. Kitchen table: 1.4 m × 0.66 m

B The scale for this drawing of a patio is 1 cm: 1.25 m. Measure the dimensions of the patio to the nearest millimeter. Then use a proportion to calculate the actual dimensions.

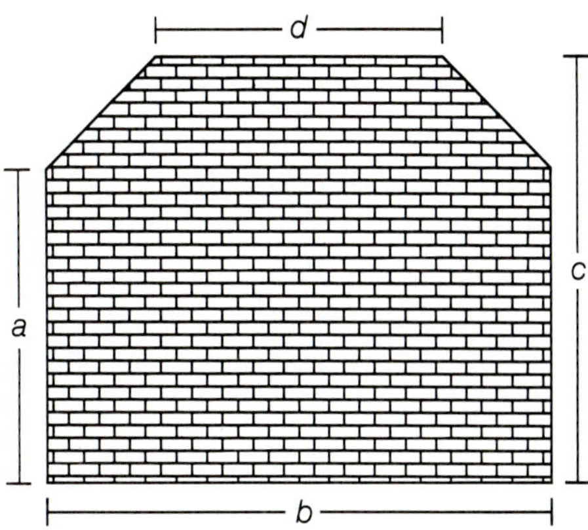

14. dimension a

15. dimension c

16. dimension b

17. dimension d

18. The distance from A to B on the map is 4.2 cm. The distance from B to C is 1.4 cm. B is on a straight road from A to C. The scale on the map is 1 cm: 125 km. What is the actual distance from A to C?

19. On a map with scale 2 cm: 25 km, what would be the dimensions of a 145 km by 80 km rectangle?

C Extending Thinking Skills

20. An insect in a picture is $\frac{1}{2}$ inch long and a label says "enlarged 12 times." What is the insect's actual length?

21. Charles wants to make a scale drawing to represent a driveway 64 ft long. His paper is $8\frac{1}{2}$ inches square. Which of the following scales could he use?

a. 1 in. = 1 ft **b.** $\frac{1}{4}$ in. = 1 ft **c.** $\frac{1}{8}$ in. = 1 ft **d.** $\frac{1}{16}$ in. = 1 ft

22. The length of a rectangle is 5 m more than the width. The ratio of the length to the width is 5 to 4. What are the dimensions of the rectangle? (Let x = the width of the rectangle.)

Mixed Review

Simplify. **23.** $14m + 7m$ **24.** $3c + 9 + (-6c) - 12$ **25.** $t + 3t + 8$

Evaluate for $a = \frac{1}{2}, b = \frac{2}{3}, c = \frac{1}{5}$. **26.** $ab + c$ **27.** $a(2c - b)$

28. $3a - 2b$ **29.** $\frac{ac}{b}$

Simplify. **30.** $\frac{x^5}{x^4}$ **31.** $\frac{5^4}{5^2}$ **32.** $\frac{x^6}{x^4}$ **33.** $\frac{7^5}{7}$

Write each as an improper fraction. **34.** $9\frac{2}{3}$ **35.** $-6\frac{3}{5}$

9-7 Determining the Best Buy

Grocery stores often show unit prices.

The cost of one unit of an item is called the **unit price**. You can find and compare unit prices to determine the better buy. The item with the lower unit price is usually considered the better buy.

A & B Discount	
100 vitamins	2/$1.99
video cassettes	3/$17.50
earrings	2 pair for $5
hand lotion	6 oz/$4.99
cologne	2 oz/$2.99
shampoo	15 oz/$2.99
glass cleaner	32 oz/$1.19

Bob's Super Saver	
100 vitamins	4/$3.75
video cassettes	2/$11
earrings	4 pair for $11
hand lotion	10 oz/$8.10
cologne	3 oz/$3.59
shampoo	24 oz/$5.28
glass cleaner	24 oz/$0.96

Example

Find the unit prices and determine which price advertised above is the better buy for a video cassette.

Solution $\frac{17.50}{3} = 5.8333\ldots \approx 5.84$ Divide the total price by the number of cassettes to find the unit price. Prices are rounded to the next highest cent.

$\frac{11.00}{2} = 5.50$

The price 2 for $11 is better than the price 3 for $17.99.

Problems

Use data from the advertisements on page 282 to find the unit prices and tell which store has the better buy for each.

1. hand lotion **2.** shampoo **3.** cologne

4. glass cleaner **5.** earrings **6.** vitamins

Solve.

7. Jones' store has a price of 3 for $50 on video games. Smith's store is selling 8 video games for $134.50. Which store has the better unit price for video games?

8. Soup is priced at 2 cans for $0.75 at one store. At another store, six cans of the same soup cost $1.98. Find the unit prices to determine the better buy.

9. At A & B Discount, apple juice costs $1.26 for the 1.4 L size. At Bob's Super Saver it costs $1.53 for the 1.8 L size. Which store has the better buy on apple juice?

10. Ground beef is on sale for $1.25/lb. How much could you get for $5?

11. Shampoo at A & B Discount is usually $2.99 for 15 oz. Today, the 10 oz. size is on sale for $2.10. Estimate the cost per ounce. About how much more or less per ounce would the smaller size cost?

12. Squash costs $1.85/kg. Estimate the cost of a squash weighing 0.54 kg.

Use the advertisement below to solve.

13. Mrs. Hamilton bought 2 loaves of wheat bread, 3 loaves of rye bread, 12 muffins, and 15 biscuits on sale. How much did she save off the regular price?

Item	Sale Price	Regular Price
Wheat Bread	2 for $1.25	$0.75 a loaf
Rye Bread	2 for $1.40	$0.90 a loaf
Muffins	6 for $0.75	$0.15 each
Biscuits	6 for $0.54	$0.12 each

14. ***Data Search*** Choose two grocery stores. Find common brands for: $\frac{1}{2}$ gallon whole milk; 20 lbs dog food; 3 cans frozen orange juice; 2 loaves whole wheat bread; 1 whole chicken. Which store has the better buy for each?

What's Your Decision?

You have $10 to spend on items in the advertisements on page 282. What would you buy and from which store?

9-8 Percent

The ratio of a number to 100 is called a **percent**. The word percent means *per one hundred*, and is represented by the symbol %. You can write a percent as a fraction.

Example 1

Write 68% as a fraction in lowest terms.

Solution

$68\% = \frac{68}{100}$ Write the number in front of the % sign over 100.

$= \frac{17}{25}$

Write each as a fraction in lowest terms.

a. 55% **b.** 4% **c.** 21%

Example 2

Write $12\frac{1}{2}\%$ as a fraction in lowest terms.

Solution

$12\frac{1}{2}\% = \frac{12\frac{1}{2}}{100}$ Write the number in front of the % sign over 100.

$= 12\frac{1}{2} \div 100$ $\frac{a}{b}$ is the same as $a \div b$.

$= \frac{25}{2} \div 100$

$= \frac{25}{2} \times \frac{1}{100}$

$= \frac{25}{200}$

$= \frac{1}{8}$ $12\frac{1}{2}\% = \frac{1}{8}$.

Write each as a fraction in lowest terms.

a. $5\frac{1}{2}\%$ **b.** $2\frac{3}{4}\%$ **c.** $6\frac{2}{3}\%$

You can use a proportion to change a fraction to percent.

Example 3

Use a proportion to write $\frac{3}{8}$ as a percent.

Solution

$\frac{3}{8} = \frac{x}{100}$ — 3 is to 8 as what is to 100? Change $\frac{3}{8}$ to a fraction with a denominator of 100.

$100 \cdot 3 = 8 \cdot x$ — Property of proportions.

$300 = 8x$

$\frac{300}{8} = \frac{8x}{8}$

$37\frac{1}{2} = x$

$\frac{3}{8}$ is equal to $37\frac{1}{2}\%$ — The numerator over 100 is the percent. Write the numerator in front of the % sign.

Practice Use a proportion to write each as a percent. **a.** $\frac{24}{25}$ **b.** $\frac{5}{6}$

Oral Exercises

Give each as a percent.

1. $\frac{37}{100}$ **2.** 88 : 100 **3.** 53 to 100 **4.** 40 out of 100

5. 1 : 100 **6.** $\frac{25}{100}$ **7.** $\frac{65}{100}$ **8.** 36 out of 100

9. $\frac{1}{100}$ **10.** 99 : 100 **11.** $\frac{100}{100}$ **12.** $\frac{1\frac{3}{4}}{100}$

Exercises

A Write each as a fraction in lowest terms.

1. 45% **2.** 70% **3.** 5% **4.** 75%

5. 20% **6.** 50% **7.** 10% **8.** 35%

9. 74% **10.** 80% **11.** $1\frac{1}{2}\%$ **12.** 100%

13. 8% **14.** $10\frac{1}{4}\%$ **15.** $5\frac{3}{4}\%$ **16.** $12\frac{1}{2}\%$

17. 63% **18.** $25\frac{1}{5}\%$ **19.** $3\frac{1}{3}\%$ **20.** 48%

21. $9\frac{3}{4}\%$ **22.** 91% **23.** $14\frac{9}{10}\%$ **24.** $1\frac{1}{10}\%$

Use a proportion to write each as a percent.

25. $\frac{3}{4}$ **26.** $\frac{1}{2}$ **27.** $\frac{1}{6}$ **28.** $\frac{4}{40}$

29. $\frac{1}{3}$ **30.** $\frac{50}{50}$ **31.** $\frac{4}{5}$ **32.** $\frac{3}{10}$

33. $\frac{3}{25}$ **34.** $\frac{11}{20}$ **35.** $\frac{5}{8}$ **36.** $\frac{1}{20}$

37. $\frac{5}{6}$ **38.** $\frac{18}{25}$ **39.** $\frac{3}{16}$ **40.** $\frac{7}{8}$

B Solve.

41. If the ratio $2x:100$ is equivalent to 68%, what is x?

42. In a survey of 500 mothers with children under age 18, about 300 worked outside the home. What percentage of those surveyed was this?

43. The Better Business Bureau in Greenville had 85 buyer complaints one year. Twenty of these involved automobile businesses. What percentage of the complaints involved automobile businesses?

44. What percentage of the whole numbers from 1 to 100 are prime numbers? What percentage are composite numbers?

C Extending Thinking Skills

Use estimation to decide which test each student took if the math test had 30 questions and the English test had 50 questions.

45. Wanda had 24 correct and scored 80%.

46. Danny missed 10 and scored 80%.

47. James scored 90%. If he had answered 5 more questions correctly, he would have scored 100%.

Mixed Review

Solve and check. **48.** $3m + 13 = 1 + m$ **49.** $4(3 - t) = 3(1 - t)$

50. $-32 = 16a$ **51.** $6(c + 4.5) = 36.6$ **52.** $14k - 21 = 0$

ESTIMATION

Study the percents to which these commonly-used fractions correspond.

$\frac{1}{5} = 20\%$ $\frac{1}{4} = 25\%$ $\frac{1}{3} = 33\frac{1}{3}\%$

$\frac{1}{2} = 50\%$ $\frac{2}{3} = 66\frac{2}{3}\%$ $\frac{3}{4} = 75\%$

Substitute compatible numbers to estimate the equivalent percent for each.

1. $\frac{24}{49}$ **2.** $\frac{29}{41}$ **3.** $\frac{9}{28}$

4. $\frac{5}{16}$ **5.** $\frac{13}{18}$ **6.** $\frac{5}{24}$

9-9 Percents Greater Than 100 and Less Than 1

A sales clerk had to sell 5 computers to meet his sales goal. He actually sold 6 computers. You could use a proportion to find what percentage of the goal he made.

You have worked with percents between 1 and 100. Percents can also be greater than 100 or less than 1.

Example 1

Use a proportion to write $\frac{6}{5}$ as a percent.

Solution

$$\frac{6}{5} = \frac{x}{100}$$ Change $\frac{6}{5}$ to a fraction with a denominator of 100.

$$100 \cdot 6 = 5 \cdot x$$

$$600 = 5x$$

$$\frac{600}{5} = x$$

$$120 = x$$

$\frac{6}{5}$ is equal to 120% — Notice that the fraction $\frac{6}{5}$ is greater than 1, and the percentage is greater than 100%.

Practice Use a proportion to write each fraction as a percent.

a. $\frac{5}{4}$ **b.** $1\frac{3}{20}$

Example 2

Use a proportion to write $\frac{1}{200}$ as a percent.

Solution

$\frac{1}{200} = \frac{x}{100}$ Change $\frac{1}{200}$ to a fraction with a denominator of 100.

$100 = 200x$

$\frac{100}{200} = \frac{200x}{200}$

$\frac{1}{2} = x$

$\frac{1}{200}$ is equal to $\frac{1}{2}\%$ Since percent means per 100, we can write $\frac{\frac{1}{2}}{100}$ as $\frac{1}{2}\%$.

Practice Use a proportion to write each fraction as a percent.

a. $\frac{3}{400}$ **b.** $\frac{2}{250}$

Example 3

Write 150% as a fraction or mixed number in lowest terms.

Solution

$150\% = \frac{150}{100}$ Write the number in front of the % sign over 100.

$= \frac{3}{2}$

$= 1\frac{1}{2}$

Practice Write each percent as a fraction or mixed number in lowest terms. **a.** 225% **b.** 164%

Example 4

Write $\frac{1}{4}\%$ as a fraction or mixed number in lowest terms.

Solution

$\frac{1}{4}\% = \frac{\frac{1}{4}}{100}$ Write the number in front of the % sign over 100.

$= \frac{1}{4} \times \frac{1}{100}$ $\frac{a}{b} = a \cdot \frac{1}{b}$

$= \frac{1}{400}$

Practice Write each percent as a fraction or mixed number in lowest terms.

a. $\frac{1}{2}\%$ **b.** $\frac{1}{8}\%$

Oral Exercises

Give each ratio as a percent. Which are greater than 100%? Which are less than 100%?

1. $\frac{23}{100}$
2. $\frac{125}{100}$
3. $\frac{2}{3}:100$
4. $\frac{9}{100}$
5. $\frac{\frac{3}{4}}{100}$
6. 200 : 100
7. $\frac{1}{2}$ to 100
8. $\frac{105}{100}$
9. $\frac{1}{5}:100$
10. 300 to 100
11. $\frac{85}{100}$
12. $\frac{9}{10}$ to 100
13. $1\frac{1}{2}$ to 100
14. $\frac{500}{100}$
15. $1\frac{5}{8}:100$
16. $\frac{\frac{1}{10}}{100}$

Exercises

A Use a proportion to write each fraction as a percent.

1. $\frac{175}{100}$
2. $\frac{3}{2}$
3. $2\frac{1}{4}$
4. $\frac{5}{3}$
5. $\frac{6}{3}$
6. $2\frac{1}{2}$
7. $\frac{4}{1}$
8. $3\frac{1}{5}$
9. $\frac{8}{6}$
10. $1\frac{1}{10}$
11. $1\frac{3}{8}$
12. $\frac{26}{20}$
13. $\frac{1}{500}$
14. $\frac{1}{125}$
15. $\frac{3}{1000}$
16. $\frac{1}{400}$
17. $\frac{8}{1000}$
18. $\frac{1}{160}$
19. $\frac{3}{500}$
20. $\frac{4}{600}$
21. $2\frac{1}{5}$
22. $\frac{1}{300}$
23. $\frac{3}{400}$
24. $\frac{5}{1000}$

Write each percent as a fraction, mixed number, or whole number in lowest terms.

25. 110%
26. 250%
27. 300%
28. 108%
29. 175%
30. 500%
31. 200%
32. 1000%
33. $\frac{1}{5}$%
34. $\frac{3}{4}$%
35. $\frac{3}{8}$%
36. $1\frac{1}{4}$%
37. 225%
38. $\frac{7}{10}$%
39. $2\frac{1}{2}$%
40. $1\frac{5}{8}$%

B

41. Bike shop employees set a goal of selling 200 new bikes in a 3-month period. They sold 75 bikes the first month, 130 bikes the second month, and 125 the third month. What percentage of their goal did they reach?

42. A survey of 250 schools showed that 10 schools had more than 30 computers. What percentage of the schools surveyed had more than 30 computers?

43. The Marshalls budgeted \$225 a month for clothing. Last month they spent \$75 for clothing. What percentage of the budgeted amount was spent?

44. Does $x\% + y\% = (x + y)\%$? Use number replacements for x and y to show why the two expressions are or are not equivalent.

45. Does $\frac{x\%}{y\%} = \left(\frac{x}{y}\right)\%$? Use number replacements for x and y to show why the two expressions are or are not equivalent.

C Extending Thinking Skills

46. Within a 10 cm by 10 cm region on a sheet of paper, draw a rectangle with a perimeter of 20 cm and an area that is 16% of the 10 cm by 10 cm region.

47. This large cube is made up of 27 smaller cubes. If the large cube was painted red on all 6 sides, what percentage of the cubes would be painted red on exactly 1 side? 2 sides?

Mixed Review

Find the greatest common factor (GCF). **48.** 8, 64, 92 **49.** 6, 21

Write each as a decimal. Use a bar for a repeating decimal.

50. $\frac{2}{3}$ **51.** $\frac{5}{6}$ **52.** $\frac{7}{8}$ **53.** $\frac{3}{10}$ **54.** $\frac{8}{11}$

Write each as a mixed number. **55.** $\frac{26}{3}$ **56.** $\frac{211}{16}$ **57.** $\frac{67}{8}$

COMPUTER ACTIVITY

This program will write a fraction in the form $\frac{A}{B}$ as a percent.

```
10 PRINT "CHANGE A/B TO A PERCENT."
20 PRINT "WHAT IS A?"
30 INPUT A
40 PRINT "WHAT IS B?"
50 INPUT B
60 PRINT A;"/";B;" IS ";(A/B) * 100;"%."
70 INPUT "DO YOU WANT TO TRY AGAIN? (Y OR N)?";A$
80 IF A$ = "Y" THEN GOTO 10
90 END
```

Use the program to change each to a percent.

1. $\frac{5}{6}$ **2.** $\frac{7}{25}$ **3.** $\frac{65}{80}$

4. $\frac{4}{3}$ **5.** $\frac{12}{48}$ **6.** $\frac{18}{5}$

9-10 Percent and Decimals

When you solve problems involving percent, you will often be working with percents expressed as fractions or percents expressed as decimals. You have learned how to change percents to fractions and fractions to percents. The following examples show how to change a percent to a decimal and a decimal to a percent.

Example 1

Write $25\frac{1}{2}\%$ as a decimal.

Solution $25\frac{1}{2}\% = 25.5\%$

$= \frac{25.5}{100}$ Write as a fraction with a denominator of 100.

$= 0.255$ Change the fraction to a decimal.

Practice Write each as a decimal.

a. 5% **b.** $8\frac{1}{4}\%$ **c.** 125%

Example 2

Write 0.35 as a percent.

Solution $0.35 = \frac{35}{100}$ Change the decimal to a fraction.

$= 35\%$

Practice Write each as a percent.

a. 0.60 **b.** 0.085 **c.** 2.14

Here are three illustrations of a percent expressed as a decimal.

Percent		**Decimal**
68%	$\frac{68}{100}$	0.68
1.8%	$\frac{1.8}{100} \cdot \frac{10}{10} = \frac{18}{1000}$	0.018
12.75%	$\frac{12.75}{100} \cdot \frac{100}{100} = \frac{1275}{10000}$	0.1275

The chart on page 291 suggests shortcuts for changing a percent to a decimal or a decimal to a percent. To change a *percent to a decimal*, move the decimal point in the percent two places to the left and drop the percent symbol. To change a *decimal to a percent*, move the decimal point in the decimal two places to the right and add the percent symbol.

Oral Exercises

Is the equation true or false?

1. $67\% = \frac{67}{100}$ **2.** $41\% = 41$ **3.** $0.78 = 7.8\%$

4. $0.07 = 7\%$ **5.** $\frac{42.5}{100} = 42\frac{1}{2}\%$ **6.** $3\% = 0.3$

7. $100\% = 1$ **8.** $0.62 = 62\%$ **9.** $90\% = 0.90$

10. $425\% = 0.425$ **11.** $1\% = 0.01$ **12.** $105\% = 1.05$

Exercises

A Write each percent as a decimal.

1. 40% **2.** 10% **3.** 5% **4.** 65%

5. 2% **6.** 15% **7.** 150% **8.** 1%

9. 90% **10.** 13% **11.** 100% **12.** 25%

13. $4\frac{1}{2}\%$ **14.** $\frac{1}{4}\%$ **15.** 200% **16.** 80%

17. 12% **18.** $10\frac{1}{2}\%$ **19.** 34% **20.** $2\frac{1}{4}\%$

21. $\frac{3}{4}\%$ **22.** $12\frac{3}{4}\%$ **23.** $5\frac{5}{8}\%$ **24.** $75\frac{3}{4}\%$

Write each decimal as a percent.

25. 0.62 **26.** 0.55 **27.** 0.05 **28.** 0.75

29. 0.8 **30.** 1.25 **31.** 0.001 **32.** 0.95

33. 0.015 **34.** 3.05 **35.** 0.125 **36.** 0.508

37. 1.5 **38.** 0.245 **39.** 0.005 **40.** 0.57

41. 0.465 **42.** 2.4 **43.** 0.075 **44.** 3

45. 4.38 **46.** 2.456 **47.** 0.006 **48.** 0.06

B Solve.

49. A batting average is the number of hits divided by the number of times at bat, expressed as a decimal rounded to the thousandths place. In 1941, Ted Williams got a hit 40.6% of his times at bat. What was Williams' batting average in 1941?

50. In 1927, Babe Ruth hit 60 home runs to set a major league record that held for 34 years. In that same year, Ruth's batting average was 0.356. What percentage of his times at bat in 1927 did Ruth get a hit?

51. In 1985, Willie McGee had 216 hits in 612 at-bats. What was his batting average?

52. In 1985, Dwight Gooden won 24 games and lost 4. What percentage of these games did he win?

53. Change $x\%$ to a decimal where x is a 1-digit number.

54. Change y to a percent where y is a whole number.

C Extending Thinking Skills

Use estimation to find a value for x. Then use a calculator to find the exact value for x.

55. $\frac{x}{16} = 75\%$ **56.** $\frac{x}{20} = 55\%$

57. $\frac{x}{90} = 34\frac{4}{9}\%$ **58.** $\frac{x}{500} = \frac{3}{5}\%$

Mixed Review

Solve and check. **59.** $19(m + 3) = 76$ **60.** $2(r - 5) = 11r + 8$

61. $-15 = 3(9 + m) - 3$ **62.** $14 < 3r + 2$ **63.** $-4c + 2c > -16$

Evaluate for $a = 3$, $b = 4$. **64.** $3(a - b)$ **65.** $b(3a + 2b)$

66. $a \div (2b)$ **67.** $-a(5 - b)$ **68.** $b(b - a)$ **69.** $6(-a)(-b)$

CALCULATOR ACTIVITY

You can change a fraction to a percent by first changing the fraction to a decimal and then changing the decimal to a percent.

Example: Change $\frac{7}{8}$ to a percent.

Fraction		Display	
$\frac{7}{8}$	7  8 	0.875	$0.875 = 87.5\%$

Use a calculator to change each fraction to a percent.

1. $\frac{3}{4}$ **2.** $\frac{3}{10}$ **3.** $\frac{1}{6}$ **4.** $\frac{7}{25}$

5. $\frac{4}{3}$ **6.** $\frac{3}{16}$ **7.** $\frac{3}{20}$ **8.** $\frac{12}{5}$

More Practice

Solve.

1. Feldman's Bakery sells 12 dozen wheat rolls and 10 dozen rye rolls every day. What is the ratio of wheat rolls to rye rolls?

2. The ratio of boys to girls on the Blue Jays soccer team is 5 : 4. There are 15 boys on the team. How many team members are girls?

3. Cindy swims 36 laps of the pool in 45 minutes. At this rate, how many laps will she swim in an hour?

4. Jim is two inches taller than Carlos. Their combined height is 146 inches. How tall is Carlos?

5. The ratio of home-team fans to visiting-team fans at the basketball game is $\frac{5}{3}$. 1250 fans are cheering for the home team. How many are cheering for the visiting team?

6. Anita's sunflower plant sprouted and grew 7 feet tall in just four weeks. How many inches did it grow each day?

7. The Varsity Theater has 220 regular seats and 80 balcony seats. What is the ratio of balcony seats to total seats?

8. Angelo scored 45 more points on his second math quiz than on his first. His combined score was 149. What did he score on the first quiz?

9. The students in Miss Oliveira's class compared lunches. They found that 13 had peanut butter sandwiches, 6 had tuna sandwiches, and 2 had egg salad sandwiches. What was the ratio of tuna sandwiches to all sandwiches?

10. What is the hourly rate of a typist who charges $150 for 12 hours of labor?

11. A double yogurt dish cost $0.95 more than a single dish. Together they cost $3.15. What did each cost?

12. The ratio of Mr. Kovac's age to his son's age is $\frac{5}{2}$. Mr. Kovac's son is eighteen. How old is Mr. Kovac?

13. On Saturday, 96 gallons of green and white paint were sold at O'Hara's House Paints. White paint outsold green paint by 28 gallons. How many gallons of white and how many gallons of green were sold that day?

9-11 Multiple Solutions

You have learned that many problems can be solved by using a combination of strategies. You might first simplify the problem, then draw a picture, make a table, and finally look for a pattern. For many problems, a solution can be found in several different ways. Two people can use completely different strategies but find the same correct solution. In the following example, a problem is solved two ways.

Problem Ms. Malito saves coupons from a service station to get a gift. The station gives 5-point coupons and 3-point coupons. She has exactly 22 coupons, for a total of 86 points. She has fewer than 15 of each type of coupon. How many of each does she have?

Solution 1

One way to solve this problem is to use the **Guess, Check, Revise** strategy. You could guess a number for each type of coupon so that the sum of the two numbers is 22, and check whether they would total 86 points. If they did not, you would revise your guess and continue the process until you found the right combination. The process might be like this.

Try 14 for 3-point coupons and 8 for 5-point coupons: $14 \cdot 3 = 42$, $8 \cdot 5 = 40$, $42 + 40 = 82$ Too low.

Try 12 for 3-point coupons and 10 for 5-point coupons: $12 \cdot 3 = 36$, $10 \cdot 5 = 50$, $36 + 50 = 86$ Correct!

Solution 2

Another way to solve this problem is to **Make a Table** and look for the correct combination.

3-point coupons	**Number**	1	2	3	4	5	6	7	8	9	10	11	**12**	13	14
	Points	3	6	9	12	15	18	21	24	27	30	33	**36**	39	42
5-point coupons	**Number**	1	2	3	4	5	6	7	8	9	**10**	11	12	13	14
	Points	5	10	15	20	25	30	35	40	45	**50**	55	60	65	70

Problem-Solving Strategies	
Choose the Operations	Write an Equation
Guess, Check, Revise	Simplify the Problem
Draw a Picture	Make an Organized List
Make a Table	Use Logical Reasoning
Look for a Pattern	Work Backwards

This chart shows the strategies presented in previous chapters.

Problems

Find two different ways to solve each problem.

1. Jim Westly grows pine trees on a small farm. Twenty of his trees were killed in a very cold winter. That spring he bought the same number of new trees as had survived last winter. Later, he sold all of his trees to 6 customers, each of whom bought 15 trees. How many trees did he originally have?

2. Mrs. Ungar is 28 years old and her daughter, Heather, is 6 years old. How old will Heather be when she is half as old as her mother?

Solve.

3. Fred drove 25 km farther than Tammy. If she had driven twice as far as she did, Fred would have driven only 10 km more than Tammy. How far did each drive?

4. Cesar has $50 to buy tickets to a concert. Seats in the front section cost $7 and seats in the back section cost $5. Cesar bought 8 tickets and spent exactly $50. How many of each kind did he buy?

5. A neighborhood was given 3 numbers to use for 3-digit prefixes on telephone numbers. The numbers were 3, 0, and 9. The only guideline was that the 0 could not be the first number. How many prefixes did the neighborhood have to choose from?

6. An airline reported that on flights from city A to city B, only 2 out of every 5 seats were filled. Each plane holds 250 passengers and each ticket costs $125. How much more money per flight would the airline make if it had every seat filled with a paying passenger?

Enrichment

A Golden Rectangle

Early Greek architects, painters, and sculptors identified what they believed to be the rectangle most pleasing to the human eye. They called it the **Golden Rectangle**. The ratio of the length l to the width w of this rectangle, $\frac{l}{w}$, was called the **Golden Ratio**. The Greeks discovered that the following proportion holds only for a Golden Rectangle:

$$\frac{l}{w} = \frac{l + w}{l}$$

1. Each of the rectangles below is a Golden Rectangle. Measure the length and width of each, to the nearest millimeter. Find the ratio $\frac{l}{w}$ for each. Express each ratio as a decimal, and use them to estimate the Golden Ratio as a decimal.

2. Measure the length and width of each rectangle below to the nearest millimeter and compute the ratio $\frac{l}{w}$ for each. For which rectangle is this ratio closest to the Golden Ratio? Is this rectangle most pleasing to your eye?

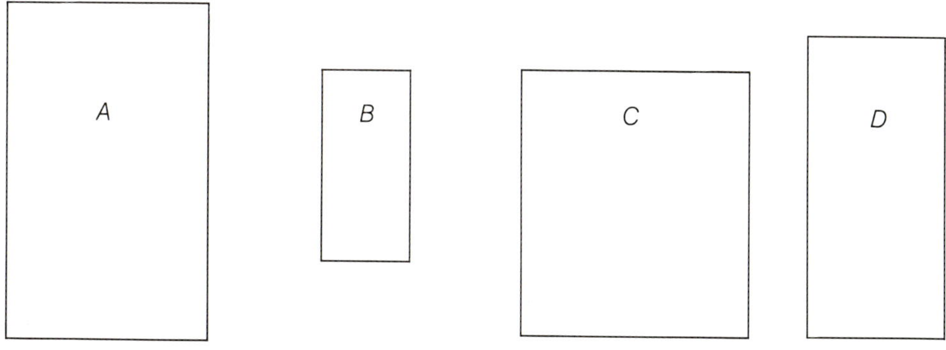

Chapter 9 Review

9-1 Write each ratio as a fraction in lowest terms.

1. 9:21 **2.** 48 to 30 **3.** 70/15

9-2 Solve and check.

4. $\frac{y}{40} = \frac{5}{8}$ **5.** $\frac{4}{7} = \frac{n}{35}$ **6.** $\frac{1}{6} = \frac{5}{k}$

9-3 Simplify the rate.

7. 114 km/3 h **8.** \$120/6 days **9.** 78 kg/6 days

Solve.

10. Ginger walked 20 km in 4 hours. How many kilometers per hour is that?

9-4 Write an equation.

11. Last year Kelly read 3 times as many mysteries as science fiction books. She read 44 of the two types combined. How many did she read of each type?

9-5 Solve by writing an equation.

12. Sayako invited $\frac{1}{2}$ as many boys as girls to her party. She sent out 24 invitations in all. How many did she send to boys and how many to girls?

9-6 Find the scale dimensions of each. The scale is 1 cm = 0.5 m.

13. Counter: 2 m × 0.5 m **14.** Closet: 1.5 m × 0.5 m

9-7 Solve.

15. Which is the better buy, 8 square feet of wrapping paper for \$2.25 or 5 square feet of wrapping paper for \$1.30?

9-8 Write each as a fraction in lowest terms.

16. 14% **17.** 7% **18.** $7\frac{1}{2}\%$

Use a proportion to write each as a percent.

19. $\frac{3}{4}$ **20.** $\frac{9}{25}$ **21.** $\frac{1}{8}$

9-9 Use a proportion to write each as a percent.

22. $\frac{225}{100}$ **23.** $\frac{8}{5}$ **24.** $\frac{3}{400}$

Write each percent as a fraction or mixed number in lowest terms.

25. 275% **26.** $\frac{2}{5}\%$ **27.** $2\frac{3}{4}\%$

9-10 Write as a decimal. **28.** 4% **29.** $8\frac{1}{2}\%$

Write as a percent. **30.** 81 **31.** 0.075

Chapter 9 Test

Write each ratio as a fraction in lowest terms.

1. 8 : 32 **2.** 12 to 15 **3.** $\frac{72}{27}$

Solve and check.

4. $\frac{a}{42} = \frac{3}{7}$ **5.** $\frac{5}{6} = \frac{m}{30}$ **6.** $\frac{3}{4} = \frac{15}{c}$

Simplify the rate.

7. 225 km/3 h **8.** $500/4 days **9.** 186 beats/3 minutes

Solve.

10. Mr. Bertolini charged $60 for 4 hours labor. What is his hourly rate?

Write an equation.

11. Geri's father is 4 times Geri's age. The sum of their ages is 45.

Solve by writing an equation.

12. Peter has taken piano lessons for half as many years as Laura has. The sum of the number of years they have both taken lessons is 12. How many years has each taken lessons?

Find the scale dimensions of each. The scale is 1 cm = 0.5 m.

13. Desk: 1.5 m × 1 m **14.** Patio: 3.5 m × 3 m

Solve.

15. Orange juice costs $2.69 for the 64-ounce size and $1.27 for the 32-ounce size. Which size is the better buy?

Write each as a fraction in lowest terms.

16. 22% **17.** 1% **18.** $4\frac{1}{2}\%$

Use a proportion to write each as a percent.

19. $\frac{1}{4}$ **20.** $\frac{17}{20}$ **21.** $\frac{3}{8}$

22. $\frac{450}{100}$ **23.** $\frac{12}{5}$ **24.** $\frac{25}{500}$

Write each percent as a fraction or mixed number in lowest terms.

25. 325% **26.** $\frac{3}{4}\%$ **27.** $2\frac{1}{2}\%$

Write as a decimal. **28.** 9% **29.** $12\frac{1}{5}\%$

Write as a percent. **30.** 0.20 **31.** 0.025

Cumulative Review

Write an equivalent fraction by replacing the variable with a whole number.

1. $\frac{7}{8} = \frac{b}{96}$ **2.** $\frac{y}{9} = \frac{56}{63}$ **3.** $-\frac{15}{22} = -\frac{f}{110}$

Reduce to lowest terms.

4. $\frac{52}{84}$ **5.** $-\frac{16}{88}$ **6.** $\frac{124}{160}$

Write each as a mixed number.

7. $\frac{41}{6}$ **8.** $\frac{-73}{3}$ **9.** $\frac{149}{100}$

Write each as an improper fraction in lowest terms.

10. $3\frac{1}{7}$ **11.** $-5\frac{3}{12}$ **12.** $4\frac{6}{15}$

Write $<$, $>$, or $=$ for each $\square$.

13. $\frac{7}{9} \square \frac{3}{5}$ **14.** $-\frac{2}{3} \square -\frac{5}{6}$ **15.** $\frac{4}{7} \square \frac{10}{11}$

16. $-\frac{9}{14} \square -\frac{15}{36}$ **17.** $\frac{20}{11} \square \frac{14}{5}$ **18.** $\frac{12}{60} \square \frac{9}{45}$

Solve. Reduce to lowest terms.

19. $\frac{1}{2}\left(\frac{4}{5}\right)$ **20.** $\frac{2}{5}\left(-\frac{3}{8}\right)$

21. $-1\frac{5}{7}\left(4\frac{2}{3}\right)$ **22.** $-2\frac{4}{5}\left(-3\frac{1}{2}\right)$

23. $-\frac{5}{9} \div \left(-\frac{2}{3}\right)$ **24.** $\frac{7}{20} \div \frac{84}{100}$

Solve.

25. $6y - 3 = 15$ **26.** $-22 = 3n - 1$

27. $\frac{m + 4}{5} = 2$ **28.** $3(d - 7) = -27$

Write an equation.

29. The $72 cost of a jacket is $6 more than 6 times the cost of a tie.

Solve by writing an equation.

30. Bill's height is 4 inches more than twice his cousin's height. His cousin is 32 inches tall. How tall is Bill?

Chapter 10
Using Percent

10-1 Finding a Percent of a Number

A customer gave a waiter 15% of the total bill as a tip. The total bill was $60. You can use a proportion or an equation to find the amount of the tip.

You can find a percent of a number by using a proportion or an equation.

Example 1

Use a proportion to solve. 15% of 60

Solution

$\frac{15}{100} = \frac{n}{60}$ You are looking for a number that has the same ratio to 60 as 15 has to 100.

$100 \cdot n = 15 \cdot 60$ Property of proportions.

$\frac{100n}{100} = \frac{15 \cdot 60}{100}$ Divide both sides by 100 to get the variable by itself.

$n = 9$

15% of 60 is 9.

Practice Use a proportion to solve.

a. 5% of 120 **b.** 150% of 60 **c.** 12% of 30

When the percent involves a fraction, you can most easily find the percent of a number using an equation.

Example 2

Use an equation to solve. $12\frac{1}{2}\%$ of 25

Solution $0.125 \times 25 = n$ Think: $12\frac{1}{2}\%$ of 25 is what number?

↓ ↓ ↓ ↓ ↓

$0.125 \times 25 = n$

$3.125 = n$

$12\frac{1}{2}\%$ of 25 is 3.125.

Practice Use an equation to solve.

a. 60% of 130 **b.** $4\frac{1}{2}\%$ of 75 **c.** 120% of 85

Oral Exercises

Give each percent as a decimal and as a fraction in lowest terms.

1. 25% **2.** 50% **3.** 75% **4.** $66\frac{2}{3}\%$ **5.** 1%

6. 100% **7.** 10% **8.** $33\frac{1}{3}\%$ **9.** 90% **10.** 80%

Exercises

A Use a proportion to solve.

1. 20% of 60 **2.** 9% of 360 **3.** 15% of 160 **4.** 4% of 60

5. 90% of 50 **6.** 70% of 8 **7.** 3% of 180 **8.** 25% of 18

9. 28% of 84 **10.** 30% of 412 **11.** 12% of 25 **12.** 25% of 55

Use an equation to solve.

13. 40% of 20 **14.** $12\frac{1}{2}\%$ of 56 **15.** $\frac{1}{2}\%$ of 500

16. 35% of 40 **17.** 0.3% of 126 **18.** 2.5% of 3

19. 15% of 80 **20.** 250% of 100 **21.** 12% of 125

Use a proportion or an equation to solve.

22. 18% of 54 **23.** 9% of 24.5 **24.** 250% of 20

25. $\frac{1}{4}\%$ of 148 **26.** 4.5% of 60 **27.** 0.5% of 12

B Evaluate each expression.

28. 34% of n, $n = 85$ **29.** $x\%$ of 150, $x = 5\frac{1}{2}$ **30.** 150% of h, $h = 20$

Choose compatible numbers to give an estimate for each.
Example: 48% of \$82. Think: "50% of 80 is 40, so 48% of \$82 is about \$40."

31. 20% of \$505 **32.** 5% of \$95 **33.** 78% of \$310

34. A high school had 700 students in its graduating class. Out of this graduating class, 65% of the students went to college. How many students went to college?

35. A salesperson made \$45,500 last year. Her expenses were $67\frac{1}{2}$% of her income. How much money did she have left after expenses?

36. Ruben took 24 shots in last night's basketball game. His shooting percentage was $37\frac{1}{2}$%. Each basket was worth 2 points. How many points did Ruben score?

Some tips are easy to calculate mentally. To find 15% of \$64, you can "break apart" 15% as follows: 10% of \$64 is \$6.40. 5% of \$64 is half of \$6.40, or \$3.20. The tip is \$6.40 plus \$3.20, or \$9.60. Calculate a 15% tip mentally for each bill amount.

37. \$42 **38.** \$15 **39.** \$35 **40.** \$18

C Extending Thinking Skills

Estimate the percentage of each square that is shaded.

41.

42.

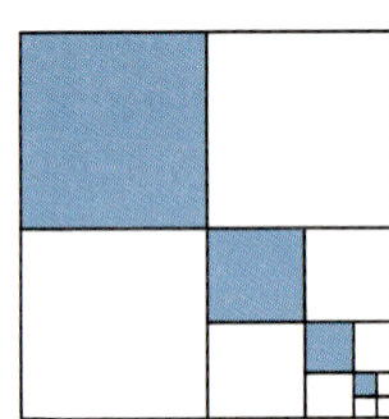

43.

44. Write an equation to show each relationship.

a. a is 45% of b **b.** 5% of g is m

Mixed Review

Solve and check. **45.** $9 + 11c = -13$ **46.** $21 - 3c > 0$

47. $9z + 36 = -9$ **48.** $4(m + 6) + 7 = 3(5m + 2) - 8$

MENTAL MATH

You can substitute compatible numbers and change a percent to a fraction to compute a percent of a number mentally. For example, to find $66\frac{2}{3}$% of 12, you can think, "$66\frac{2}{3}$% is the same as $\frac{2}{3}$, and $\frac{2}{3}$ of 12 is 8."

Compute mentally.

1. 50% of 90 **2.** $33\frac{1}{3}$% of 30 **3.** 200% of 35

4. 25% of 48 **5.** 75% of 20 **6.** 10% of \$80

10-2 Finding What Percent One Number is of Another

Sometimes you may want to find what percent one number is of another. For instance, if you worked at a record store and wanted to compare the number of records and tapes sold of each type of music, you could find what percent each number is of the total number sold.

	Country	Rock	Classical	Jazz	Total Sold
Records	20	78	17	35	150
Tapes	10	66	19	24	120

The chart shows that 24 jazz tapes were sold out of a total of 120 tapes. You can use a proportion to find what percent of the tapes sold were jazz tapes.

Example 1

Use a proportion to solve. 24 is what percent of 120?

Solution $\frac{n}{100} = \frac{24}{120}$ You want to find a number that has the same ratio to 100 as 24 has to 120.

$120 \cdot n = 100 \cdot 24$ Property of proportions.

$\frac{120n}{120} = \frac{100 \cdot 24}{120}$

$n = 20$

24 is 20% of 120. $\frac{20}{100}$ is the same as 20%.

Practice Use a proportion to solve.

a. 30 is what percent of 150?

b. What percent of 120 is 40?

The chart above shows that 78 out of the 150 records sold were rock music. The following example shows how to use an equation to find what percent of the records sold were rock.

Example 2

Use an equation to solve. 78 is what percent of 150?

Solution $78 = p \cdot 150$ Think: 78 is what percent of 150?

$\downarrow\downarrow \quad \downarrow \quad \downarrow\downarrow$

$78 = \quad p \quad \cdot 150$

$\frac{78}{150} = \frac{p \cdot 150}{150}$

$0.52 = p$ Change $\frac{78}{150}$ to a decimal by dividing 78 by 150.

78 is 52% of 150. $0.52 = \frac{52}{100}$ or 52%.

Practice Use an equation to solve.

a. 61 is what percent of 120?

b. What percent of 150 is 20?

Oral Exercises

Tell whether each statement is true or false. If it is false, tell why.

1. 1 out of 10 is 10%.

2. 70 out of 150 is greater than 50%.

3. 60 out of 120 is 50%.

4. 90 out of 75 is greater than 100%.

5. 40 out of 50 is less than 30%.

6. 2 out of 100 is greater than 1%.

Exercises

A Use a proportion to solve.

1. What percent of 20 is 3?

2. 25 is what percent of 125?

3. 27 out of 45 is what percent?

4. 3 is what percent of 24?

5. What percent of 85 is 68?

6. 11 is what percent of 20?

7. 6 is what percent of 80?

8. 4 is what percent of 40?

9. What percent of 125 is 50?

10. 18 is what percent of 60?

Use an equation to solve.

11. What percent of 40 is 8?

12. 60 out of 150 is what percent?

13. What percent of 24 is 8?

14. 18 out of 108 is what percent?

15. 100 is what percent of 300?

16. 39 is what percent of 50?

17. 12 is what percent of 54?

18. What percent of 40 is 13?

19. What percent of 70 is 42?

20. 16 is what percent of 80?

Use a proportion or an equation to solve.

21. What percent of 50 is 40?

22. 17 is what percent of 68?

23. 25 is what percent of 1000?

24. 1 is what percent of 200?

25. 8 is what percent of 64?

26. What percent of 50 is 15?

27. What percent of 65 is 13?

28. 6 is what percent of 15?

B Find each percent in Exercises 29–33. Round to the nearest tenth of a percent.

Example: 24 is what percent of 120?

Solution: $\frac{x}{100} = \frac{24}{120} \longrightarrow x = \frac{24}{120} \cdot 100 = 20$ 24 is 20% of 120.

29. What percent of 2 is 0.5?

30. What percent of 48 is 18?

31. 48 is what percent of 108?

32. What percent of 5 is 1.5?

33. Mr. Perez paid \$3 tax on a \$60 hotel bill. What percent of \$60 was the tax?

34. Of 200 grocery shoppers surveyed, 92 did not have a regular shopping day. What percentage is this?

35. Out of 125 students, 65 received an A or a B on the last math test. What percentage of the students received an A or a B?

36. A math test has 75 total possible points. What percent correct is 68 points?

37. An English test has a total of 120 points. A score of 70% is passing. Dana got 80 points. Did she pass?

38. Of 150 people who went to a play, 40 thought it was excellent, 60 thought it was average, and 50 thought it was poor. What percentage of the people thought the play was better than average?

C *Extending Thinking Skills*

39. Find x and y: x is 50% of y and $x + y = 75$.

40. Find x and y: x is $33\frac{1}{3}$% of y and $3x + y = 120$.

Mixed Review

Write as a decimal. **41.** 25% **42.** 80% **43.** 124% **44.** 19%

Solve and check. **45.** $6(m + 3) = 0$ **46.** $4(9r + 7r) = 256$

ESTIMATION

You can estimate what percent one number is of another by using known fractions. For example, to solve "21 is what percent of 80?" think, "Since $\frac{20}{80}$ is $\frac{1}{4}$ or 25%, $\frac{21}{80}$ is about 25% of 80." Estimate the percent.

1. 25 is what percent of 75?

2. 14 is what percent of 30?

3. 62 is what percent of 90?

4. 76 is what percent of 50?

10-3 Finding a Number When a Percent of it is Known

Packages of computer disks are on sale for 25% off the original price. This is a savings of $15 per package. To find the original price you can use either a proportion or an equation.

Example 1

Use a proportion to solve. 15 is 25% of what number?

Solution $\frac{25}{100} = \frac{15}{n}$ 15 has the same ratio with what number as 25 has with 100?

$$25 \cdot n = 100 \cdot 15$$

$$\frac{25n}{25} = \frac{100 \cdot 15}{25}$$

$$n = 60$$

15 is 25% of 60.

Practice Use a proportion. Round to the nearest tenth if necessary.

a. 45% of what number is 18? **b.** 24 is 12% of what number?

Example 2

Use an equation to solve. 25% of what number is 15?

Solution $0.25n = 15$ Think: 25% of what number is 15?
↓ ↓ ↓ ↓ ↓
$0.25 \cdot n = 15$

$$\frac{0.25n}{0.25} = \frac{15}{0.25}$$

$$n = 60$$

25% of 60 is 15.

Practice Use an equation to solve. Round to the nearest tenth if necessary.

a. 22 is 35% of what number? **b.** 4.5% of what number is 9?

Oral Exercises

State the equation you would use for each problem.

1. 60 is 75% of what number?
2. 40% of what number is 90?
3. 30% of what number is 15?
4. 15 is 150% of what number?
5. 125% of what number is 85?
6. 40 is 35% of what number?

Exercises

A Use a proportion to solve. Round to the nearest tenth if necessary.

1. 75% of what number is 24?

2. 20 is 4% of what number?

3. 40 is 25% of what number?

4. 15 is 6% of what number?

5. 5 is 1% of what number?

6. 56% of what number is 28?

7. 52 is 4% of what number?

8. 150% of what number is 12?

Use an equation to solve. Round to the nearest tenth if necessary.

9. 60 is 20% of what number?

10. 75% of what number is 120?

11. 85 is 30% of what number?

12. 7 is 23% of what number?

13. 5 is 17% of what number?

14. 15% of what number is 12?

15. 4% of what number is 56?

16. 60 is 75% of what number?

Use a proportion or an equation to solve. Round to the nearest tenth if necessary.

17. $4\frac{1}{2}\%$ of what number is 12?

18. 25% of what number is $10\frac{1}{2}$?

19. 4 is 1% of what number?

20. 26 is 50% of what number?

21. 2.25 is $12\frac{1}{2}\%$ of what number?

22. 250% of what number is $\frac{3}{4}$?

23. 150% of what number is 12?

24. 80% of what number is 28?

25. 25 is 40% of what number?

26. 15% of what number is 26?

B Use a calculator for Exercises 27–32. Check the reasonableness of your answer with an estimate.

27. 85% of what number is 350?

28. 28.75 is 75% of what number?

29. $12\frac{1}{2}\%$ of what number is 95.5?

30. 775 is $25\frac{1}{4}\%$ of what number?

31. 130 is 85% of what number?

32. 120% of what number is 25.25?

Solve.

33. The choir at a local high school is the largest in the state. The choir has 192 members. This is 24% of all the students in the school. What is the total number of students in the school?

34. A car race was stopped after 425 miles had been completed. The race was considered official, since 85% of the race had been completed. What was the length of the original race?

35. There are 120 students involved in athletic programs at Washington School this year. This number is 150% of the students involved last year. How many students were in the athletic programs last year?

36. One day 20% of the students in a school went on a field trip. Only 240 students were left in the school. How many students went on the field trip?

37. So far, 135 cubic yards of concrete have been poured for new tennis courts. The job foreman says 75% of the pouring is now completed. What is the total number of cubic yards of concrete that will be used for this job?

C Extending Thinking Skills

38. What is 45% of $3x$ if 30% of x is 45?

39. A jar has 100 ml of water in it and is 20% full. How much water will be in the jar when it is 80% full?

40. Look at the 10×10 block below. Imagine stacking blocks like it and then painting only the outside faces of the stack red. How many blocks would need to be stacked so that $53\frac{1}{3}\%$ of the 1-by-1 blocks had only one face painted red?

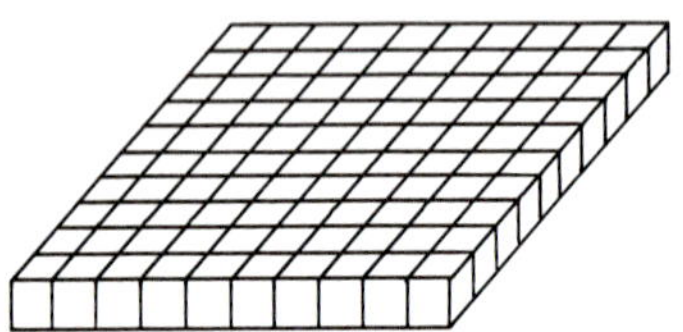

Mixed Review

Write each fraction in lowest terms, then write as a percent.

41. $\frac{6}{8}$ **42.** $\frac{27}{15}$ **43.** $\frac{60}{12}$ **44.** $\frac{45}{75}$ **45.** $\frac{18}{4}$

Solve and check. **46.** $\frac{3}{4}x + \frac{1}{3} = \frac{5}{6}$ **47.** $\frac{2}{5}r - \frac{3}{4} = \frac{1}{2}$ **48.** $-\frac{5}{6} = \frac{2}{3}m + \frac{4}{9}$

CALCULATOR ACTIVITY

You can use the [%] key on a calculator to solve percent problems.

On some calculators, you must push [=] after [%] to get the answer.

Examples:

					Display
a. Find 50% of 300.	50	[×]	300	[%]	150
b. What percent of 50 is 20?	20	[÷]	50	[%]	40 (40%)
c. 30% of what number is 24?	24	[÷]	30	[%]	80

Use the percent key to solve.

1. Find 30% of 64.

2. What percent of 80 is 24?

3. 15% of what number is 30?

4. 35 is what percent of 80?

5. 45% of what number is 54?

6. 85% of 12 is what number?

10-4 Practice Solving Problems

You can use the Problem-Solving Checklist on page 121 to help you solve problems. When your plan involves writing an equation, keep these questions in mind.

- Can you use a variable to represent an unknown number?
- Can you represent other conditions in terms of the variable?
- What is equal?
- Can you write and solve an equation?

Example

Solve by writing an equation. The cost of a small pizza is 75% of the cost of a medium pizza. What is the cost of each size pizza if the total cost for 1 medium and 1 small pizza is $15.05?

Solution Let m = cost of medium pizza

$0.75m$ = cost of small pizza

$$m + 0.75m = 15.05$$
$$1.75m = 15.05$$
$$m = 8.6$$

Since the cost of the small pizza is given relative to the cost of the medium pizza, let m represent the cost of the medium pizza.

A medium pizza costs $8.60.

$$0.75m = (0.75)(8.6) = 6.45$$

A small pizza costs $6.45.

Practice Solve by writing an equation. Linda has 1 more than half as many paper route customers as George. Linda has 35 customers. How many does George have?

Exercises

A Solve by writing an equation.

1. Donna has 3 times as many books as Gloria. Together they have 76 books. How many does Gloria have?

2. Mr. Lee saved $24.00 when he bought a suit on sale at 15% off the regular price. What was the regular price of the suit?

3. A delivery person has 5 more than twice the number of morning customers on his afternoon route. He has 45 customers in the afternoon. How many morning customers does he have?

4. Rick bought 1 record at the regular price and another for 50% of that price. The total price was \$12.24. What was the cost of each record?

5. Karen works as a waitress. One week she worked for 20 hours and got \$64.50 in tips. Her total wages and tips came to \$146.50. What is her hourly wage?

B

6. Martha bought a pair of jeans on sale. The sale price was 50% of the original price. She paid with a \$20 bill and received \$4.25 in change. If there was no tax on the jeans, what was the original price?

7. A salesperson said she would take 10% off the price of a sweater. What was the original price of the sweater if the reduced price was \$24.30?

8. Pat was given a 15% raise. She works 20 hours per week. Her earnings after the raise were \$103.50 per week. How much money did she make per week before her raise?

C Extending Thinking Skills

9. Write a word problem that could be solved using the equation $0.05x = \$16.80$.

10. Write a word problem that could be solved using the equation $2x + 5 = 25$.

Mixed Review

Evaluate for $a = 2$, $b = 3$, $c = 2$. **11.** b^2c^2 **12.** $2ac - 3b$

13. $2b - a$ **14.** $5(c - b) + 3a$ **15.** $10b + ca$

Write without exponents. **16.** 5^3 **17.** 4^{-3} **18.** $\frac{(-6)^4}{(-6)^6}$

10-5 Percent of Increase and Decrease

Ms. Hernandez earned \$500 per week last year. This year she will earn \$530 per week. You can use a proportion to find the percent of increase of Ms. Hernandez's salary.

To find the percent of increase or decrease:

- First subtract to find the amount of increase or decrease.
- Then find what percent of the original price that amount is.

Example 1

Find the percent of increase. Original amount = \$500; new amount = \$530

Solution

Amount of increase = \$530 − 500   amount of increase = new amount − original amount

= \$30

Percent of increase

$\frac{x}{100} = \frac{30}{500}$ To find the percent of increase you need to find what percent 30 is of 500.

$500x = 100 \cdot 30$

$x = 6$

The percent of increase is 6%.

Practice Find the percent of increase.
Original amount = 40; new amount = 45

Example 2

Find the percent of decrease. Original amount = 60; new amount = 45.

Solution

Amount of decrease = 60 − 45   amount of decrease = original amount − new amount

= 15

Percent of decrease

$\frac{x}{100} = \frac{15}{60}$ To find the percent of decrease, you need to find what percent 15 is of 60.

$60x = 100 \cdot 15$

$x = 25$

The percent of decrease is 25%

Practice Find the percent of decrease.
Original amount = 125; new amount = 65

Oral Exercises

State whether the change would be an increase or a decrease.

1. Original price: $65
Sale price: $59

2. Last year's cost: $100
This year's cost: $112

3. During the sale: $75
After the sale: $85

4. 1986 price: $85
1987 price: $105

5. Last year's income: $420
This year's income: $375

6. Price 5 years ago: $12
Price today: $8.50

Exercises

A Find the percent of increase. Round to the nearest tenth if necessary.

1. Original amount = $20
New amount = $30

2. Original amount = $50
New amount = $75

3. Original amount = $120
New amount = $150

4. Original amount = $300
New amount = $360

5. Original amount = $140
New amount = $168

6. Original amount = $345
New amount = $483

7. Original amount = $525
New amount = $609

8. Original amount = $185
New amount = $296

Find the percent of decrease. Round to the nearest tenth if necessary.

9. Original amount = $60
New amount = $15

10. Original amount = $85
New amount = $34

11. Original amount = $80
New amount = $45

12. Original amount = $78
New amount = $39

13. Original amount = \$190
New amount = \$80

14. Original amount = \$135
New amount = \$120

15. Original amount = \$48
New amount = \$32

16. Original amount = \$95
New amount = \$85

B For Exercises 17–19, use the formula below and a calculator to find the percent of increase or decrease. Round each percent to the nearest tenth if necessary.

$$\text{percent of increase or decrease} = \frac{\text{amount of increase or decrease}}{\text{original amount}}$$

17. Original amount = \$750; new amount = \$1000

18. Original amount = \$1250; new amount = \$1000

19. Original amount = \$2995; new amount = \$6500

20. Last year 30 students took a drafting class. This year 35 students are taking the class. What is the percentage of increase in enrollment?

21. Kevin weighed 45 kg last month. This month he weighs 42 kg. By what percentage did his weight decrease?

22. A calculator cost \$25 five years ago. Today the price of the same calculator has decreased by 80%. What is the cost of the calculator today?

23. A gold ring cost \$125 five years ago. There was a 420% increase in the price in the last 5 years. What is the price of that ring today?

24. A computer had 128 K of internal memory when it was first produced. Now its internal memory has been increased by 300%. What is its amount of internal memory now?

C Extending Thinking Skills

25. Last month a clothing store manager decreased prices on all stock by 10%. This month she increased all prices by 10%. What would you pay for a coat this month that had cost \$75 before prices were decreased last month?

26. The original price of an item, increased by a certain percentage, is \$310. Decreased by the same percentage, it is \$190. What is the original price? What is the percentage of increase or decrease?

Mixed Review

Write each as a decimal. Use a bar for a repeating decimal.

27. $\frac{4}{5}$ **28.** $\frac{6}{11}$ **29.** $\frac{8}{3}$ **30.** $\frac{3}{8}$ **31.** $\frac{5}{16}$

Reduce to lowest terms. **32.** $\frac{16}{64}$ **33.** $\frac{35}{112}$ **34.** $\frac{52}{78}$ **35.** $\frac{9}{114}$

Solve and check. **36.** $26a + 2(a + 3) = 146$ **37.** $14r + 3 = 2r - 21$

38. $42 - 13t = 9 - 2t$ **39.** $6(a - 7) + 2 = 50a + 4$

10-6 Discount, Sale Price, and Commission

When you buy an item on sale, you receive a discount from the original price. The **discount** is the amount subtracted from the **regular price**. The **sale price** of an item is the regular price less the discount. A **commission** is the amount a salesperson receives for making a sale. A commission is usually a percentage of the sale price.

Example 1

Find the discount and sale price for the boat in the advertisement above.

Solution

Discount = 15% of \$8500 = 0.15 × 8500 Discount = \$1275	You can find the discount by multiplying the original price by the discount percent.
Sale price = \$8500 − \$1275 Sale price = \$7225	You can find the sale price by subtracting the amount of the discount from the original price.

Practice Find the discount and sale price for each. Round to the nearest cent, if necessary.

a. Regular price = \$2250
Discount = 20%

b. Regular price = \$875
Discount = 12%

Example 2

The sale price of a boat is \$7225. What is the amount of commission for the sale of the boat if the commission is 1.5%? Round to the nearest cent.

Solution

Commission = 1.5% of \$7225	You can find the commission by multiplying the sale price by the commission percent.
= 0.015 × 7225	
Commission = \$108.38	Round 108.375 to the nearest cent.

Practice Find the commission on each. Round to the nearest cent.

a. Sale price = \$600
Commission = 2%

b. Sale price = \$1250
Commission = 2.5%

Oral Exercises

State whether each is true or false.

1. A discount is an amount subtracted from the original amount.
2. The commission is the regular price less the discount.
3. The percent of discount tells the amount of commission.
4. The sale price is less than the regular price.
5. The sale price is the regular price less the discount.

Exercises

A Find the discount and sale price for each. Round to the nearest cent if necessary.

1. Regular price = \$10
Discount = 25%

2. Regular price = \$5
Discount = 10%

3. Regular price = \$12
Discount = 2.75%

4. Regular price = \$30
Discount = 15%

5. Regular price = \$260
Discount = 12.5%

6. Regular price = \$9.85
Discount = 4%

7. Regular price = \$689.95
Discount = 15%

8. Regular price = \$249.95
Discount = 10%

9. Regular price = \$4570
Discount = 12.5%

10. Regular price = \$25,750
Discount = 6%

Find the commission. Round to the nearest cent if necessary.

11. Sale price = \$45
Commission = 3%

12. Sale price = \$125
Commission = 2%

13. Sale price = \$12.95
Commission = $5\frac{1}{2}$%

14. Sale price = \$58.60
Commission = $1\frac{3}{4}$%

15. Sale price = \$1375
Commission = 12%

16. Sale price = \$4575
Commission = 5%

B Use a calculator to help solve Exercises 17–19.

17. How much money would you save if you bought both the screen house and the tent canopy on sale?

18. What is the percentage of discount on the tent canopy?

19. What is the percentage of discount on a tent with a sale price of \$64.95 and regular cost of \$84.95?

Camping Gear
Screen House REG. \$79.95 Today—18% OFF!!
Tent Canopy REG. \$29.95 Today—Save \$9.00

Find the discount, sale price, and commission rounded to the nearest cent.

20. Regular price = \$169
Discount = 30%
Commission = 4%

21. Regular price = \$3,560
Discount = 10%
Commission = 6%

C *Extending Thinking Skills*

22. Mr. Lehr sold 75 pairs of shoes each week for 10 weeks. Ms. Lorenzo sold 1 pair of shoes the first week, 2 pairs the second week, 4 pairs the third week, and so on, doubling the number sold each week. Which salesperson sold the most shoes by the end of the 10 weeks?

23. A store had a 20% discount on every item in stock. Would a customer be better off if the 15% sales tax were applied before or after the discount?

Mixed Review

Write each as a fraction in lowest terms. **24.** 35% **25.** 40% **26.** 125%

Write each as a decimal. **27.** 25% **28.** 140% **29.** 11% **30.** 60%

Evaluate for $a = 6$, $b = 3$. **31.** $\frac{2}{3}(a + b)$ **32.** $\frac{a}{b}$ **33.** $4(a - b)$

Solve and check. **34.** $2(t + 2) < 16$ **35.** $-4r < 12$

COMPUTER ACTIVITY

The program below will compute the discount (D) and the sale price (S) of an item when you input the list price (L) and the percentage of discount (P).

```
10  PRINT "FIND THE SALE PRICE."
20  PRINT "ENTER THE LIST PRICE, L, AND"
30  PRINT "THE PERCENT OF DISCOUNT, D, (IN DECIMAL
    FORM)."
40  INPUT L,P
50  PRINT "THE LIST PRICE IS $";L
60  PRINT "THE PERCENT OF DISCOUNT IS ";P
70  D=P*L
80  S=L-D
90  PRINT "THE DISCOUNT IS $";D
100 PRINT "THE SALE PRICE IS $";S
110 END
```

Use this program to find the discount and sale price for each item.

1. List price, \$375; discount, 10%

2. List price, \$2250; discount, 30%

3. List price, \$9479; discount, 5%

4. List price, \$359; discount, $12\frac{1}{2}$%

Determine which would cost less.

5. A \$95 radio with an 8% discount or a \$110 radio with a 20% discount.

More Practice

Solve.

1. Marilyn deposits 15% of her paycheck into her savings account each week. Her paycheck this week is $215. How much should she deposit into savings?

2. Out of 30 students, 12 had perfect scores on the spelling test last week. What percentage of the students had perfect scores?

3. The library at Bayview School has 4,257 nonfiction books. This is 60% of all the books in the library. What is the total number of books in the library?

4. Steve sold 72 records today. He sold 75% of them in the afternoon. How many records did Steve sell in the morning.

5. Of the 900 students at Harrison Middle School, 360 are in sixth grade, 225 are in seventh, and 315 are in eighth. What percentage of the students are in sixth grade? in seventh? in eighth?

6. McNally's Snack Mix contains peanuts, pecans and almonds. The mix is 35% peanuts. How many ounces of peanuts are in a 12-ounce can?

7. At the Round Hill Apartments, 70 percent of the apartments are rented to families with children. If 35 are rented to families with children, how many apartments are there in all?

8. Last season the Cooley Cougars won 12 football games. This year they won 8 games. What was the percentage of decrease in games won?

9. Jennifer went to the store to buy 48 different items. She found and bought 75% of the items on her list. How many items did she buy?

10. Sol saved $24 by buying his tape player on sale for 40% off the regular price. What was the regular price of the tape player?

11. This year, 455 people went to the Pine City Fourth of July picnic. This number is 140% of the number that went last year. How many people went to the picnic last year?

10-7 Finding Sales Tax

In many places you pay a sales tax when you buy an item. The sales tax is a percentage of the regular price of the item. The tables below show tax rates in certain states and cities for a recent year. If you live in a state that has a sales tax and a city that has a sales tax, both taxes are added to the price of an item you buy.

STATE SALES AND USE TAXES			
STATE	**% RATE**	**STATE**	**% RATE**
California	4.75	S. Dakota	4
Colorado	3	Texas	4.125
Missouri	4.225	Virginia	3
New York	4	Washington	6.5

CITY SALES TAXES			
CITY	**% RATE**	**CITY**	**% RATE**
Anaheim, CA	1.25	New York, NY	4.25
Berkeley, CA	1.75	Rapid City, SD	2
Boulder, CO	2.15	San Antonio, TX	1
Jefferson City, MO	1	Seattle, WA	0.925

Problem Use the tax rate table to find the total cost, including state tax, of a $500 television set bought in Virginia.

Solution

Let T = amount of tax paid

$T = \$500 \times 0.03$ Tax = selling price × tax percent.

$T = \$15$

Let C = total cost of the television set

$C = \$500 + 15$ Total cost = selling price + tax.

$C = \$515$

The total cost of the television set is $515.

Problems

Use the tax rate tables to solve. Round to the nearest cent if necessary.

1. Celia bought a car in Texas for $1200. How much state tax did she pay?

2. What would the New York state sales tax be on a $500 video cassette recorder?

3. A family in Colorado bought a $12,500 camper. How much was the state sales tax?

4. A man in Anaheim, CA, bought a new suit for $125. How much city sales tax did he pay?

5. In the state of Washington, what would the total cost be for a car priced at $7500?

6. A tape deck was on sale in Seattle, WA, for $379. What is the city tax on this tape deck?

7. Mr. Montes paid $10,000 for a boat. This price was 5% less than the original price. Mr. Montes lived in San Antonio, TX. How much city tax would he pay on the boat?

8. A refrigerator originally priced at $875 was on sale for $696.99 in Berkeley, CA. What was the city tax on this refrigerator?

To find the total state and city tax on an item, add the two percentage rates. An item bought in Berkeley, CA, would have a city tax of 1.75% plus a state tax rate of 4.75%. The total tax on the item would be 6.5%.

9. Ms. Flores bought a portable television on sale for $175 in San Antonio, TX. What was the total tax she paid on the item?

10. Ms. Harrison bought 4 new tires for a truck. Each tire was priced at $50. She bought the tires in Boulder, CO. What was the approximate total cost for all of the tires, including tax?

11. The Cho family in Seattle, WA, bought 3 coats that cost $125, $65, and $50. What was the total cost for the coats, including tax?

12. Mr. Sanders of Anaheim, CA, was given $1,250 off the price of a $10,450 van. What was the total price he paid for the van, including tax?

13. *Data Search* Find the total cost, including all taxes, of purchasing a $200 stereo in your home town. If there is no state or local sales tax where you live, use the tax rate for a city or state near you.

What's Your Decision?

Suppose you could choose to live in any of the cities listed in the chart on page 320. You estimate that you will spend $5000 a year on taxable items. Which city would you consider if one of the factors important to you is the amount of sales tax you would pay in that city and state?

10-8 Simple Interest

Interest is a charge for the use of money. When you borrow money, you pay interest for the use of the money. When you place money in a savings account, the bank pays you interest for the use of your money. To find **simple interest**, you multiply the amount of money borrowed or saved by the interest rate and multiply that amount by the time the money is used.

Formula: Simple Interest

$I = Prt$; I = simple interest
P = principal (amount borrowed or saved)
r = interest rate
t = time

Example 1

Find the interest charged and the total amount. Round to the nearest cent.
$300 at 1.5% per month for 6 months

Solution $I = Prt$ — Interest = principal × rate × time
$= 300(0.015)(6)$ — P = \$300, r = 1.5% per month, t = 6 months
$= 27$

The amount of interest is $27.

$A = P + I$ — Total amount = principal + interest
$= 300 + 27$
$= 327$

The total amount of money is $327.

Practice Find the interest and the total amount. Round to the nearest cent.

a. $250 at 10% per year for 3 years. **b.** $75 at 5% per month for 6 months.

An interest rate is given as a percentage for a unit of time such as 5% per year or $1\frac{1}{2}$% per month. When you use the formula for simple interest, the unit of time for the interest rate (r) and the time that the money is earning interest (t) must be the same.

Example 2

Find the interest and the total amount. Round to the nearest cent.
$600 at 12% per year for 6 months.

Solution $P = \$600$

$r = 12\%$ per year

$t = 6$ mos. $= \frac{1}{2}$ year $= 0.5$ year — *r* and *t* must be for the same unit of time. Change months to years.

$I = Prt$

$= 600(0.12)(0.5)$

$= 36$

The amount of interest is $36.

$A = P + I$

$= 600 + 36$

$= 636$

The total amount of money is $636.

Practice Find the interest and the total amount. Round to the nearest cent.

a. $125 at 1% per month for 1 year. **b.** $2000 at 18% per year for 6 months.

Oral Exercises

Replace each variable to make a true statement.

1. $0.75 = x\%$
2. 1 year $= y$ months
3. 4 months $= d$ years
4. $0.45 = t\%$
5. $0.2 = m\%$
6. 3 months $= n$ years
7. 18 months $= d$ years
8. $0.05 = x\%$
9. $0.085 = b\%$
10. 3 years $= t$ months

Exercises

A Find the interest charged and the total amount paid. Round to the nearest cent.

1. $120 at 1% per month for 3 months
2. $95 at 18% per year for 2 years
3. $400 at 1% per month for 6 months
4. $300 at 18% per year for 2 years
5. $500 at 2% per month for 10 months
6. $2500 at 12% per year for 2 years
7. $375 at 1.5% per month for 18 months

8. $2500 at 2% per month for 12 months
9. $425 at 1.5% per month for 18 months
10. $750 at 1% per month for 24 months
11. $695 at $1\frac{1}{4}$% per month for 14 months
12. $200 at $1\frac{1}{2}$% per month for 6 months
13. $400 at 2% per month for 18 months
14. $750 at 10% per year for 3 years
15. $320 at 6% per year for 4 years
16. $1200 at 1% per month for 9 months
17. $700 at 2% per month for 2 years
18. $1000 at 12% per year for 4 months
19. $10,000 at 10% per year for 18 months
20. $100 at 18% per year for 30 months
21. $300 at 15% per year for 9 months
22. $400 at 1% per month for 2 years
23. $90 at 8% per year for 21 months
24. $845 at $1\frac{1}{2}$% per month for 3 years
25. $2000 at $1\frac{1}{2}$% per year for 3 months

B Complete the table for a monthly finance charge of 1.5%. Always round the finance charge to the next whole cent.

Example: October $1500 − 200 = $1300 new amount

$1300(0.015) = $19.50 finance charge

$1300 + 19.50 = $1319.50 balance

	Month	Balance	Payment	New Amt.	Finance Chg.	Balance
	Oct.	$1500	$200	$1300	$19.50	$1319.50
26.	Nov.	$1319.50	$200	$1119.50		$1136.30
27.	Dec.	$1136.30	$200			
	Jan.	$950.35	$200	$750.35	$11.26	$761.61
28.	Feb.		$200			
29.	Mar.		$200			
30.	Apr.	$375.60	$200			
31.	May	$178.24		-0-	-0-	-0-
32.	TOTAL					

In Exercises 33–35, write an equation and solve for the missing value. Round to the nearest tenth of a percent if necessary.

33. $I = \$8.44$; $P = \$75$; $t = 7\frac{1}{2}$ months

34. $I = \$12.50$; $r = 1\%$ per month; $t = 1$ year

35. $I = \$27$; $P = \$450$; $r = 18\%$ per year

C Extending Thinking Skills

36. Write the digits 1, 2, 3, 4, or 5 in the boxes to obtain a simple interest amount of approximately \$13. Use each digit only once.

$I = Prt$

$I = (\blacksquare\blacksquare)(0.\blacksquare\blacksquare)(\blacksquare)$

37. Lucky Larry found an amazing investment plan. For every \$2.50 invested, he had a 360% rate of increase. When he closed his plan, he had a total of \$138. How much did he invest?

Mixed Review

Solve and check. **38.** $\frac{6}{5} = \frac{x}{2}$ **39.** $\frac{n}{15} = \frac{64}{80}$ **40.** $\frac{27}{9} = \frac{54}{t}$

Write an expression for each if there are half as many trucks as cars.

41. Number of cars **42.** Number of trucks

Write an expression for each if $\frac{1}{3}$ of the trucks are red.

43. Number of trucks **44.** Number of red trucks

NUMBERS TO ALGEBRA

You can use the skills you learned for solving equations to write a related formula for $I = Prt$.

Numbers	Algebra
Solve $15 = 100(0.05)t$ for t,	Solve $I = Prt$ for t.
$\frac{15}{100(0.05)} = t$	$\frac{I}{Pr} = t$

Write a related formula.

1. Solve $D = rt$ for t.

2. Solve $V = LWH$ for L.

3. Solve $F = 1.8C + 32$ for C.

4. Solve $p = 2A + B + C$ for A.

10-9 Making Circle Graphs

A **circle graph** is useful for picturing a total amount that is divided into parts. Each part of the circle graph is called a **sector**. A circle graph shows the relationships of the parts to each other and to the total.

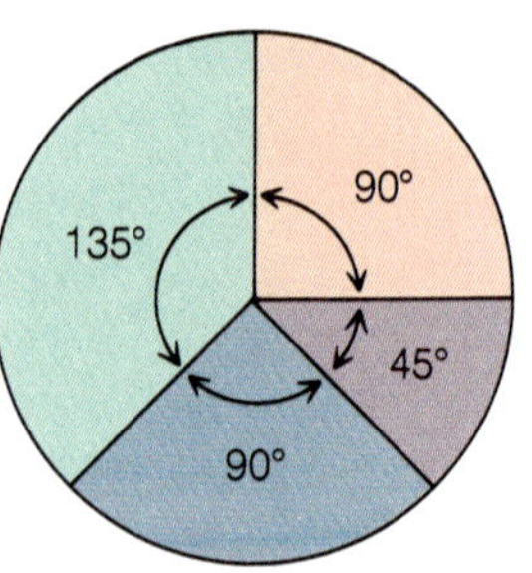

The circle graph at right has four sectors. The measure of the angle for each sector is shown. The sum of the angles of the sectors of a circle equals 360°. To make sectors, you need to draw angles. You can use a protractor to draw angles for sectors.

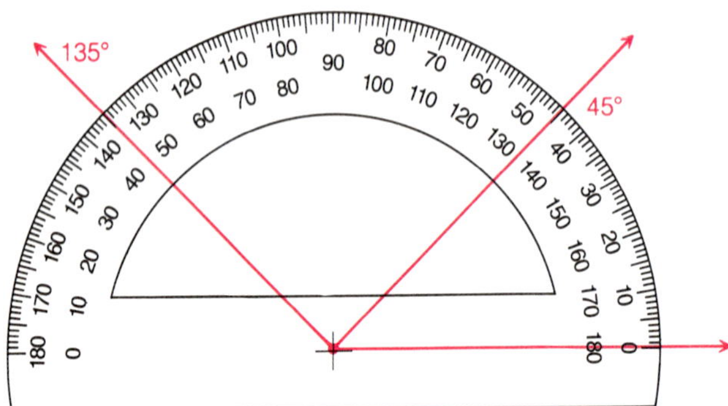

To make a circle graph, follow these steps:

1. Find the total for the data.
2. Express each part as a percent of the total.
3. Find the degrees for each sector.
4. Draw and label the sectors.
5. Title the graph.

Example

Make a circle graph to show the data. Denise's college expenses: \$1500 tuition; \$2250 room and board; \$1250 miscellaneous.

Solution

1500 + 2250 + 1250 = 5000 The circle represents the total expenses.

Tuition: $\frac{1500}{5000} = 0.30 = 30\%$

Room/Board: $\frac{2250}{5000} = 0.45 = 45\%$

Miscellaneous: $\frac{1250}{5000} = 0.25 = 25\%$

Find what percent of the whole each item represents.

Tuition: $0.30 \times 360 = 108°$
Room/Board: $0.45 \times 360 = 162°$
Miscellaneous: $0.25 \times 360 = 90°$

Every circle is made up of 360°. Find what part of the 360° each sector represents.

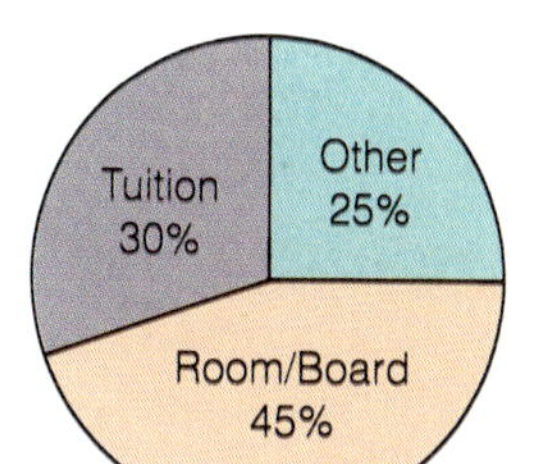

Denise's College Expenses

Use a compass to draw a circle. Use a protractor to draw each angle. Label each sector.

Give the graph a title that clearly indicates what the graph shows.

Practice Make a circle graph. Plans of seniors at Cooper High: Four-year college, 100; work, 55; two-year college, 30; armed services, 10; undecided, 5.

Oral Exercises

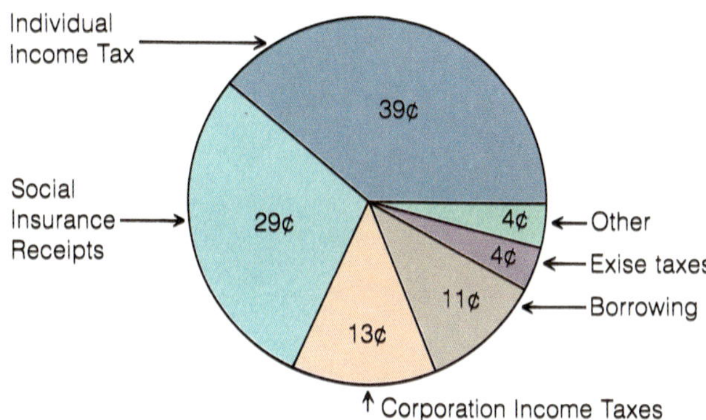

Federal Income for a Given Year (per dollar)

Answer each question about the circle graph.

1. What is the total amount represented in this graph?
2. Do any of the sectors show more than 180°?
3. What is the greatest source of federal income?
4. Which two sources of income together represent more than 50%?
5. Is 39¢ the same as 39% in this graph?

Exercises

A Make a circle graph to show the data.

1. Movies in town over the last six months: adventure, 50%; science fiction, 20%; children's, 15%; comedy, 10%; other, 5%.

2. After-school jobs: restaurants and food stands, 45%; stores, 35%; private homes, 10%; other, 10%.

3. Transportation to school: walk, 45%; bus, 30%; bicycle, 17%; car, 8%.

4. Rainfall, in centimeters: summer, 30 cm; fall, 15 cm; winter, 30 cm; spring, 45 cm.

5. Students' favorite records: popular, 105; soundtrack, 42; comedy, 38; classical, 15.

6. Ms. Bradley's expenses for one month: rent, $424; food, $350; clothing, $150; entertainment, $50; other, $25.

7. Norman's car expenses for one year: payments, $2520; gas, $725; insurance, $450; repairs, $210; registration, $75.

B

8. Make a circle graph to show the monthly electricity use.

	Present Reading (kWh)	Previous Reading (kWh)
Jan–Feb	6781	4993
Mar–Apr	8305	6781
May–Jun	9738	8305
Jul–Aug	0538	9738
Sep–Oct	1163	0538
Nov–Dec	2403	1163

To find the number of kilowatt hours (kWh) used, subtract the previous reading from the present reading (except when the meter passes 9999 and starts at 0000).

C Extending Thinking Skills

9. Make a circle graph, using the numbers 1–20 and the categories below.

a. numbers with 1 or 2 factors

b. numbers with 3 or 4 factors

c. numbers with 5 or 6 factors

Mixed Review

Write each as a fraction in lowest terms. **10.** 8% **11.** 35% **12.** 48%

Solve and check. **13.** $4t - 19 = -7$ **14.** $11(t + 3) = 18t - 2$

PROBLEM SOLVING: STRATEGIES

10-10 Problems without Solutions

For some problems, no solution is possible. In the following example, the strategy **Make an Organized List** is used to determine that there is no solution.

Problem Nancy said she lost 72¢ behind the sofa. Although she wasn't sure what coins she had lost, Nancy knew she did not have a half-dollar and she thought she had lost 5 coins. What 5 coins did Nancy lose that totaled 72¢?

You can use an organized list to make sure you have checked all possibilities. Possible coins to consider are quarters, dimes, nickels, and pennies. Since she had 72¢, she must have had 2 pennies. This reduces the problem to finding 3 coins that total 70¢. The organized list below shows that there are no combinations of quarters, dimes, nickels, and pennies that give 72¢ in 5 coins.

Quarters	Dimes	Nickels	Pennies	Total
3	0	0	2	77¢
2	1	0	2	62¢
1	2	0	2	47¢
1	1	1	2	42¢
1	0	2	2	37¢

If she did not have a half-dollar, Nancy could not have lost 5 coins that totaled 72¢.

Problem-Solving Strategies

Choose the Operations	Write an Equation
Guess, Check, Revise	Simplify the Problem
Draw a Picture	Make an Organized List
Make a Table	Use Logical Reasoning
Look for a Pattern	Work Backwards

This chart shows the strategies presented in previous chapters.

Problems

Solve. If the problem has no solution, show why.

Sandwiches prices include tax	
Hamburger	$1.25
Chicken	$1.65
Pizza	$1.10
Roast Beef	$1.45

1. Ms. Banfield bought 2 different sandwiches from this menu and paid for them with a $5 bill. The clerk said the change was $2.35. Which sandwiches did Ms. Banfield buy?

2. Nicole was in a walkathon for charity. She got 25 people to pledge $0.15 for each kilometer she walked and 45 people to pledge $0.25 for each kilometer she walked. She walked 35 km in the walkathon. How much money did she collect in pledges?

3. Thirty-five people signed up for a 25-km run. The race organizer wants to give each runner a different 4-digit number by using the digits 3, 4, 5, and 6 so that each digit is used once in each number. How many more people could sign up for the race and each be given a different number?

4. Kara found 17 coins in an old pocketbook. She counted a total of $1.15. How many coins of each kind did she find?

5. Will works for the school yearbook. He sets the page numbers for the yearbook by hand. If each digit has to be set separately, and there are 250 pages in the yearbook, how many digits must Will set?

6. A gardener bought 200 m of wire fencing to fit exactly around the outside of a rectangular flower bed. The length of the flower bed is 12 m more than the width. What is the length and width of this flower bed?

7. Jeremy makes 3-legged stools and 4-legged stools. He has 48 legs for stools. He wants to make 12 stools, some of each kind. Can he do this and use all the legs?

Enrichment

Compound Interest

The formula $I = Prt$ can be used to find **compound interest**. When interest is **compounded**, the amount of interest earned in a given time period is added to the principal. Interest is then earned on the new principal. Interest may be compounded annually (every 1 year), semiannually (every $\frac{1}{2}$ year), quarterly (every $\frac{1}{4}$ year), monthly (every $\frac{1}{12}$ year), or daily. The example below shows how to use a calculator to find compound interest.

Suppose $5000 is deposited at an interest rate of 10% per year, compounded semiannually. What will the principal be after 1 year?

		Display	
First $\frac{1}{2}$ Year			
Store 5000 in memory.	5000 [M+]	5000	Principal.
Multiply the principal by the interest rate, 0.1, and the time period, 0.5 year, to find the interest.	5000 [×] 0.1 [×] 0.5 [=]	250	Interest.
Add the interest to the principal amount stored in the memory to get the new principal.	250 [+] [MR] [=]	5250	New principal.
Second $\frac{1}{2}$ Year			
Replace 5000 with 5250 in memory.	[M+]		
Find the interest for the second half-year, using the new principal.	5250 [×] 0.1 [×] 0.5 [=]	262.5	Interest.
Add the interest to the principal.	262.50 [+] [MR] [=]	5512.5	Principal at the end of the year.

The amount after the first six months is $5250. The amount after the full year is $5512.50.

Use a calculator and the formula $I = Prt$ to solve.

1. Amount deposited: $150. Rate of interest: 5% per year compounded semiannually. What will the principal be after 2 years?

2. Amount deposited: $3500. Rate of interest: 6% per year, compounded quarterly. What will the principal be after 2 years?

Chapter 10 Review

10-1 Use a proportion or an equation to solve.

1. 40% of 135

2. 5% of 240

3. 2.5% of 90

10-2 Use a proportion or an equation to solve.

4. What percent of 60 is 12?

5. 42 is what percent of 105?

6. What percent of 120 is 90?

7. 7 out of 28 is what percent?

10-3 Use a proportion or an equation to solve. Round to the nearest tenth if necessary.

8. 35 is 20% of what number?

9. 50% of what number is 51?

10. 60% of what number is 30?

11. 7 is 1% of what number?

10-4 Solve by writing an equation.

12. A skirt costs 80% as much as a sweater. What is the cost of each if the total cost for the skirt and sweater is $45?

10-5 Find the percent of increase or decrease.

13. Original amount = $80; new amount = $96

14. Original amount = $140; new amount = $196

15. Original amount = $150; new amount = $105

10-6 Solve.

16. When Rosa eats at a restaurant, she leaves a tip that is 15% of her bill. How much tip will she leave if the bill is $12.00?

10-7 Find the discount and the sale price for each.

17. Regular price = $25
Discount = 20%

18. Regular price = $1,750
Discount = 4%

Find the commission. Round to the nearest cent if necessary.

19. Sale price = $95
Commission = 3%

20. Sale price = $705.20
Commission = 1.5%

10-8 Find the interest and the total amount. Round to the nearest cent if necessary.

21. $300 at 8% per year for 2 years

22. $160 at 1.5% per month for 7 months

10-9

23. Make a circle graph to show the data. Library books checked out: mystery, 30; fiction, 65; nonfiction, 105; children's, 60; other, 40.

Chapter 10 Test

Use a proportion or an equation to solve.

1. 25% of 64
2. 110% of 50
3. 12.5% of 40

Use a proportion or an equation to solve.

4. What percent of 25 is 7?
5. 26 is what percent of 65?
6. What percent of 152 is 76?
7. 15 out of 150 is what percent?

Use a proportion or an equation to solve. Round to the nearest tenth if necessary.

8. 3 is 5% of what number?
9. 90% of what number is 63?
10. 40% of what number is 34?
11. 66 is 75% of what number?

Solve by writing an equation.

12. James saves $17.40 when he bought a fish tank at 30% off the original price. What was the original price of the fish tank?

Find the percent of increase or decrease.

13. Original amount = $150; new amount = $180
14. Original amount = $70; new amount = $133
15. Original amount = $225; new amount = $45
16. Original amount = $650; new amount = $455

Solve.

17. Pam teaches karate, and 35% of her students are children. If Pam has 180 students, how many are children?

Find the discount and the sale price for each. Round to the nearest cent if necessary.

18. Regular price = $50
Discount = 40%
19. Regular price = $3,550
Discount = 6%

Find the commission. Round to the nearest cent if necessary.

20. Sale price = $70
Commission = 4%
21. Sale price = $73.90
Commission = 8%

Find the interest and the total amount. Round to the nearest cent if necessary.

22. $350 at 15% per year for 6 years
23. $700 at 2% per month for 3 months

24. Make a circle graph to show the data. Greeting cards sold: birthday, 25%; anniversary, 15%; graduation, 10%; special occasion, 30%; other, 20%.

Cumulative Review

Solve. Reduce to lowest terms.

1. $4\frac{1}{8} \div \left(-1\frac{1}{4}\right)$

2. $-3\frac{3}{4} \div 5\frac{5}{8}$

3. $-6x = -\frac{3}{4}$

4. $\frac{2}{3}v = \frac{5}{12}$

5. $2\frac{1}{4} = -12a$

6. $-5\frac{5}{6} = 2\frac{1}{2}x$

Solve by writing an equation.

7. Susanne ran the same distance each day for 5 days. She ran a total of 17 km. How far did she run each day?

8. 21 people attended math class on Friday. This is $\frac{7}{8}$ of the number of people signed up for the class. How many people are signed up for the class?

Solve.

9. $12c + 4c = 80$

10. $-48 = 7v + 5v$

11. $22x - 17x = -65$

12. $150 = 30t - 5t$

13. $7b - 2b = 145$

14. $-96 = 12z - 4z$

15. $3(x - 2) + x = 9$

16. $2y + 4(y + 5) = 80$

17. $2x + 12(x + 2) = 94$

18. $-56 = -4n + 2(n + 7)$

19. $5(d + 4) + 7d = 68$

20. $c + 3(c - 4) = 16$

Find the actual dimensions of the garden. Scale is 2 mm = 0.5 m.

21. Length (l)

22. Width (w)

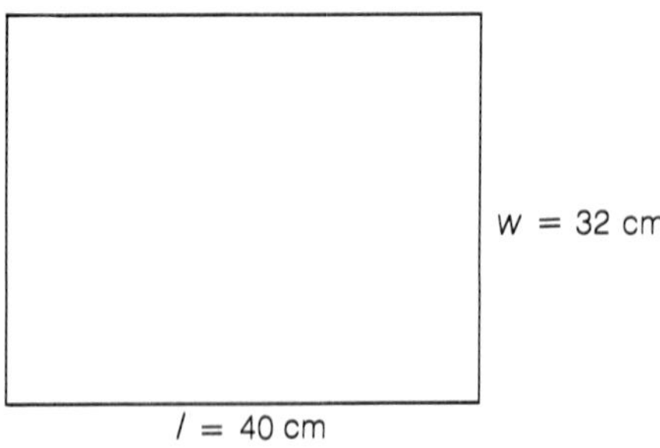

Use the scale of 1 cm = 0.5 m to find the scale dimensions of each.

23. Gate: 1.5 m × 2 m

24. Fence: 7.5 m × 1.5 m

Solve.

25. Blueberries cost $2.69 for the 16-ounce size and $1.42 for the 8-ounce size. Which size is the better buy?

Chapter 11
Equations in Geometry

11-1 Basic Figures

The three basic geometric figures are point, line, and plane.

	Figure	Name	Symbol
A **point** is the simplest geometric figure. It shows a location.	A •	Point A	A
Given any two points, there is only one **line** through the two points.	A B	Line AB	$\overleftrightarrow{AB}$
Three points that are not on the same line determine a **plane**.	A B C	Plane ABC	ABC

Segments and rays are parts of a line.

	Figure	Name	Symbol
A **segment** PQ includes endpoints P and Q and all points between.	P Q	segment PQ	$\overline{PQ}$
A **ray** AB extends in one direction from endpoint A.	A B	ray AB	$\overrightarrow{AB}$

Example

Name a point, a line, a plane, a segment, and a ray on the figure.

Solution W
$\overleftrightarrow{WX}$
WXZ
$\overline{XW}$
$\overrightarrow{YX}$

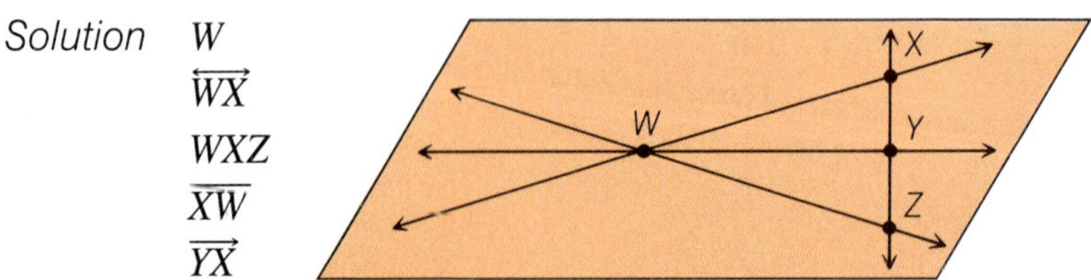

Practice Name another point, line, segment, and ray on the figure.

Oral Exercises

State whether the object suggests a point, a ray, a line, or a plane.

1. tip of an ice pick **2.** top of a desk **3.** the tip of a scissors

4. a flat ceiling **5.** a tightly-stretched string **6.** a laser beam

Exercises

A Use the figure at right for Exercises 1–8.

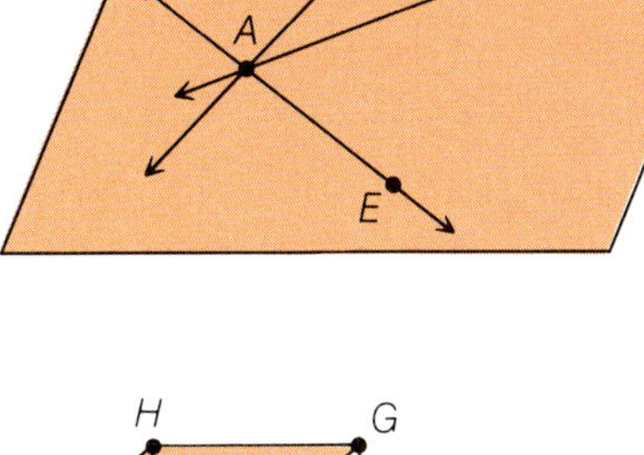

1. Name three points.

2. Name three lines.

3. Name a plane.

4. Name two segments with endpoint C.

5. Name four segments with endpoint A.

6. Name two lines that pass through point C.

7. Name two rays with endpoint D.

8. Name two rays with endpoint B.

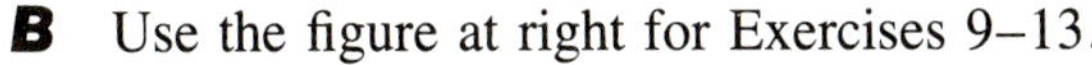

B Use the figure at right for Exercises 9–13.

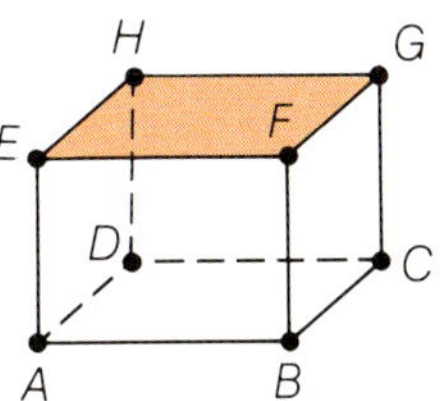

9. Name three segments with endpoint A.

10. Name two planes that include $\overline{EF}$.

11. Name two planes that include $\overline{CG}$.

12. Name twelve different segments.

13. Name six different planes.

C Extending Thinking Skills

14. Copy and complete the third and fourth figures below. Then draw the next two figures to find the next three numbers in the pattern.

3 points
3 lines

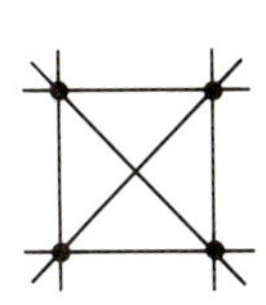

4 points
6 lines

5 points
10 lines

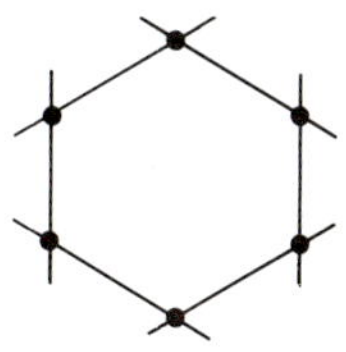

6 points
_?_ lines

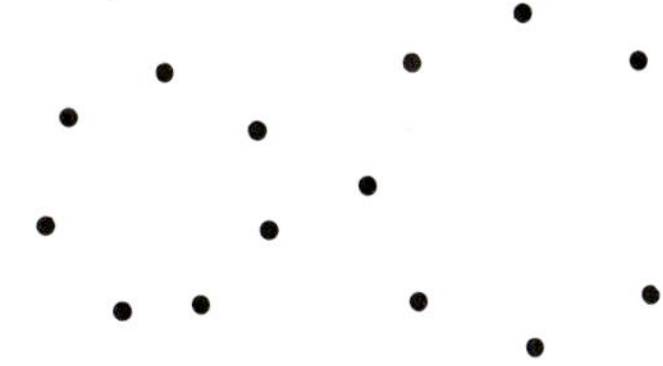

7 points
_?_ lines

8 points
_?_ lines

Mixed Review

Solve and check. **15.** $2(m - 9) + 5m = 6 + m$ **16.** $29.6 - t = -3.9$

17. $2x < 5$ **18.** $3x - 6 > 15$ **19.** $4x + 2 > 10$ **20.** $-2x + 1 < 3$

11-2 Length and Perimeter

To find the length of a segment, choose a unit of length and count the number of times the unit can be laid end-to-end from one endpoint to another.

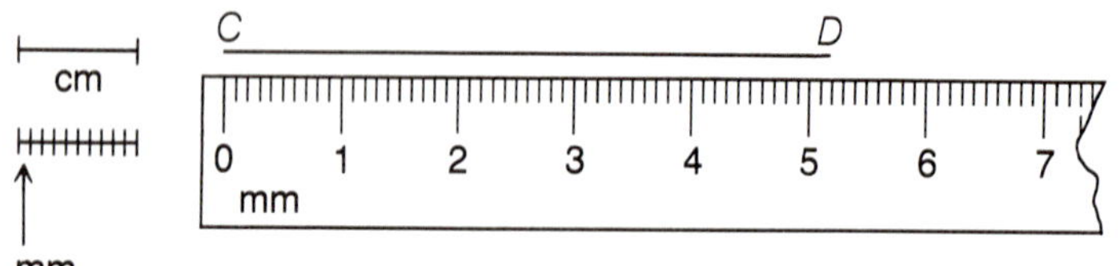

The length of $\overline{CD}$ is equal to 5.2 cm. We write $CD = 5.2$ cm.

Example 1

Estimate the length of $\overline{AB}$ to the nearest centimeter. Use a ruler to check your estimate, and give the length.

Solution

$AB \approx 4$ cm — Mentally picture one centimeter to estimate how many centimeters long $\overline{AB}$ is.

Check $AB = 4.3$ cm — The estimate is about right.

Practice Estimate the lengths. Use a ruler to check, and give the length.

a. $CD = \underline{?}$ cm

b. $DE = \underline{?}$ cm

You can often find an unknown length by solving an equation.

Example 2

Write and solve an equation to find the length of $\overline{CD}$.

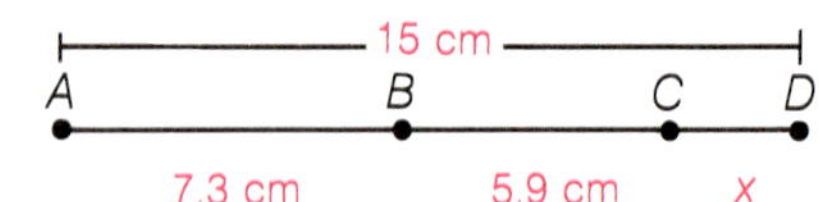

Solution Let $x = CD$. Then — Let x be the unknown length.

$$7.3 + 5.9 + x = 15$$
$$13.2 + x = 15$$
$$-13.2 + 13.2 + x = -13.2 + 15$$
$$x = 1.8$$

$CD = 1.8$ cm

Practice Write and solve an equation to find the length of $\overline{BC}$.

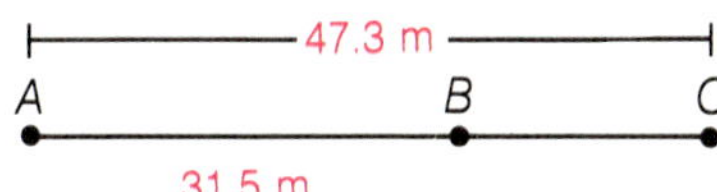

The total distance around a figure is called its **perimeter**. The perimeter of a rectangle is equal to twice its length plus twice its width. The formula is written as $P = 2l + 2w$.

You can find the perimeter of a nonrectangular figure by adding the lengths of the sides.

Example 3

Find the perimeter.

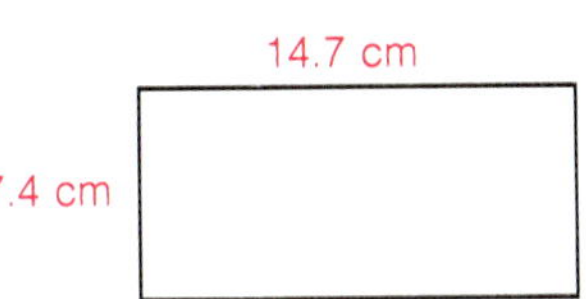

Solution $P = 2l + 2w$

$= 2(14.7) + 2(7.4)$

$= 29.4 + 14.8$

$= 44.2$

The perimeter is 44.2 cm.

Practice Find the perimeter.

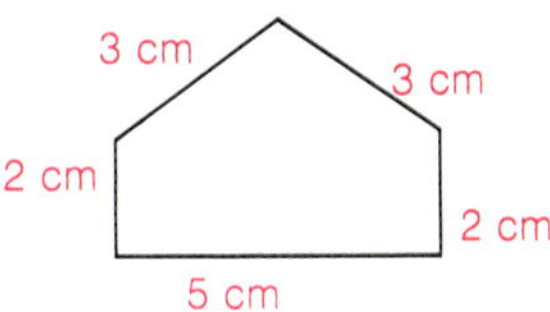

When you know the perimeter of a figure but not the length of one side, you can write and solve an equation to find the unknown length.

Example 4

Write and solve an equation to find the length of $\overline{AB}$.

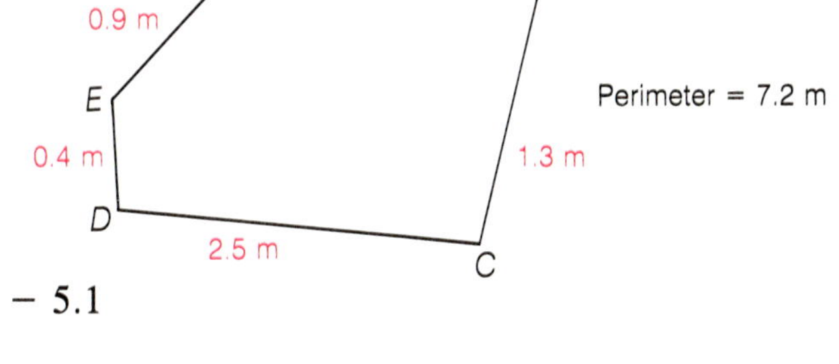

Solution Let $x = AB$.

$$x + 1.3 + 2.5 + 0.4 + 0.9 = 7.2$$
$$x + 5.1 = 7.2$$
$$x + 5.1 - 5.1 = 7.2 - 5.1$$
$$x = 2.1$$

$AB = 2.1$ m

Practice

Write and solve an equation to find the unknown length.

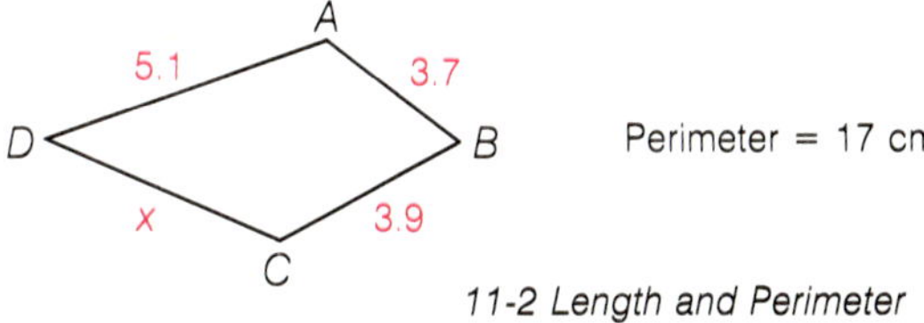

Oral Exercises

Give an equation that is suggested by each figure.

1. 3.5 cm; 2 cm, u

2. 3.4 cm; y, 2.3 cm

3. 3.8 cm; 2.4 cm, z

Exercises

A Estimate the length of each segment to the nearest centimeter. Use a ruler to check your measure, and give the length.

1. $AC = \underline{?}$ **2.** $BD = \underline{?}$ **3.** $CE = \underline{?}$

4. $BC = \underline{?}$ **5.** $BE = \underline{?}$ **6.** $AE = \underline{?}$

Write and solve an equation to find each unknown length.

7. 12.2 mm; A, B, C; x, 5.8 mm

8. 10.9 mm; D, E, F, G; 5.1 cm, y, 3.4 cm

9. 18.3 m; W, X, Y, Z; 9.6 m, 4.7 m, z

10. 32.4 cm; R, S, T, U; $2b$, b, 11.7 cm

Find the perimeter.

11. 12.8 cm; 5.1 cm

12. 5 cm; 6 cm; 4 cm

13. 11 cm; 4 cm; 7 cm; 13 cm

Write and solve an equation to find the unknown length.

14.

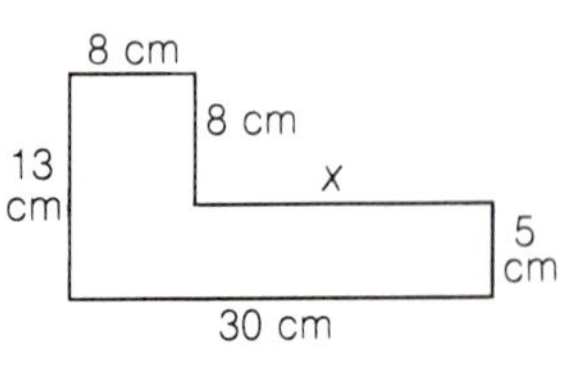

Perimeter = 86

15.

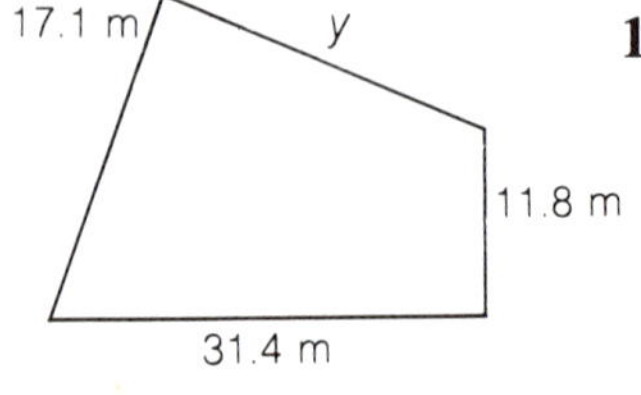

Perimeter = 76.6

16.

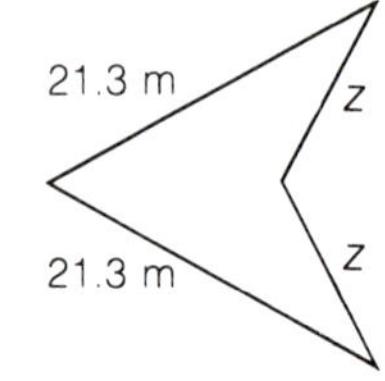

Perimeter = 68.6

B

17. The perimeter of the triangle at right is 14 cm. Write and solve an equation to find the lengths of the sides.

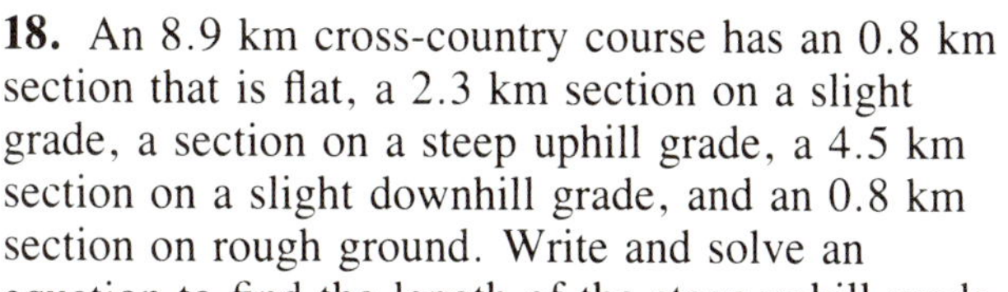

18. An 8.9 km cross-country course has an 0.8 km section that is flat, a 2.3 km section on a slight grade, a section on a steep uphill grade, a 4.5 km section on a slight downhill grade, and an 0.8 km section on rough ground. Write and solve an equation to find the length of the steep uphill grade.

19. A rectangle with a perimeter of 96 cm has a length 3 times its width. Write and solve an equation to find the lengths of the sides.

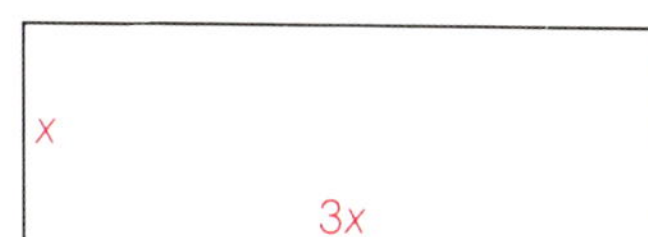

20. A field has sides of length 519.3 m, 391.4 m, and 791.6 m. Its perimeter is 2141.5 m. Write and solve an equation to find the length of the fourth side.

C Extending Thinking Skills

Write and solve equations to find x and y in each figure below. Then find the perimeter of the figure. Assume all angles are right angles.

21.

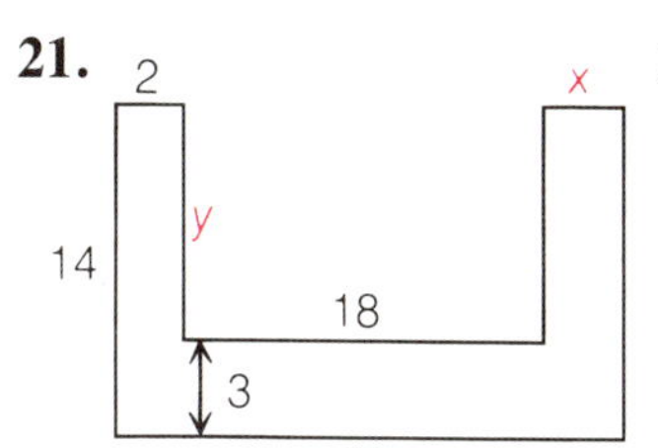

22.

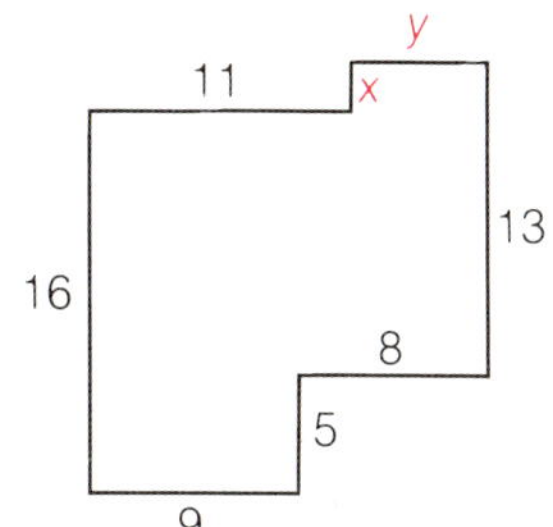

23.

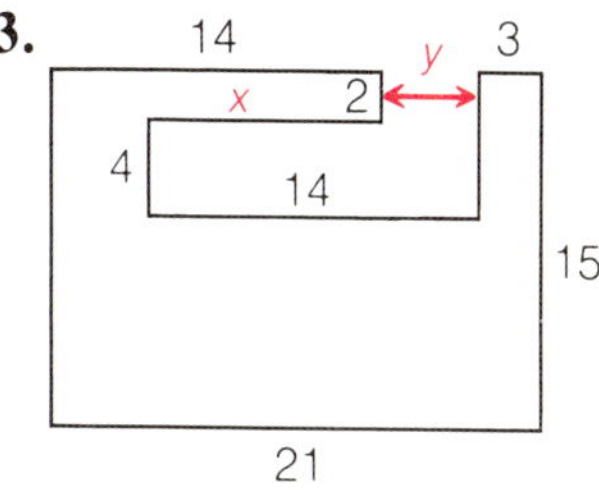

Mixed Review

Write as a decimal. **24.** $9\frac{1}{4}$ **25.** $\frac{6}{5}$ **26.** $-\frac{3}{10}$ **27.** $2\frac{5}{8}$

Write as a mixed number. **28.** $\frac{11}{3}$ **29.** $\frac{14}{5}$ **30.** $\frac{9}{4}$

Evaluate for $a = 2$, $b = 1.5$, $c = 1.8$ **31.** $2a - bc$ **32.** $-a(b - c)$

Write each percent as a fraction or mixed number in lowest terms.
33. 140% **34.** 250% **35.** 108% **36.** 70% **37.** 37%

Write an equation to find each. **38.** 60% of 12 **39.** 0.5% of 60
40. 16 is what percent of 40? **41.** 27 is what percent of 18?

11-3 Angles and Angle Measures

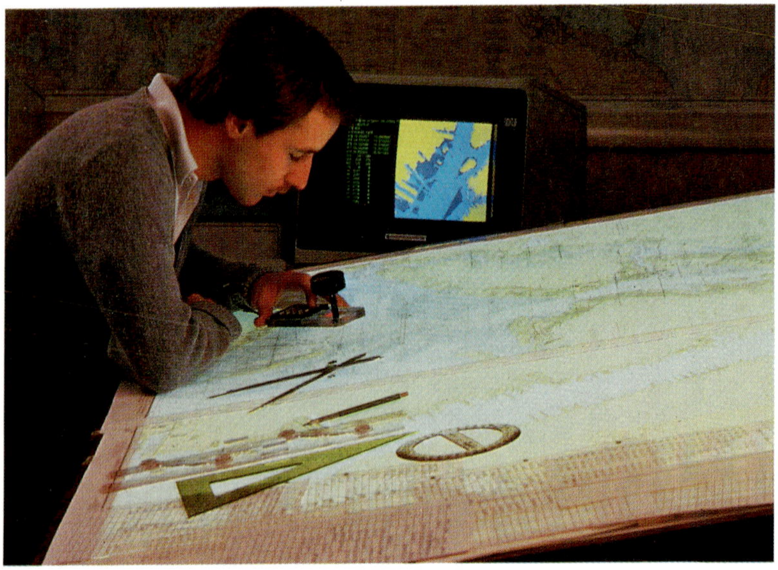

A navigator uses angles and angle measures to plot a ship's course.

Figure	Name	Symbol
An **angle** is two rays with a common end-point called the **vertex**. Each ray is called a side of the angle. 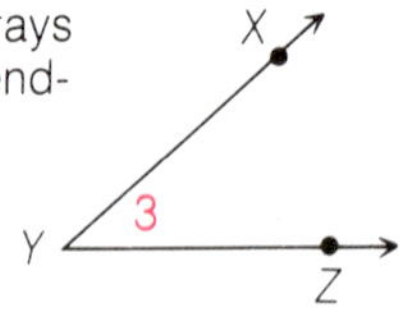	angle *XYZ* or angle *Y* or angle 3	$\angle XYZ$ or $\angle Y$ or $\angle 3$

A **protractor** is used to measure angles. The unit of angle measure is the **degree** (°). To measure an angle, place the arrow of the protractor at the vertex of the angle and the baseline of the protractor along one side of the angle. Then read the number of degrees from the other side of the angle. In the drawing at the right, the measure of $\angle ABC$ is 50°. We write: $m\angle ABC = 50°$.

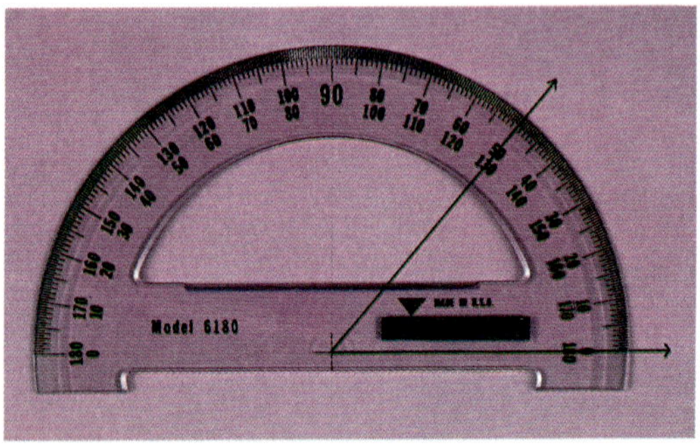

Angles are classified into three groups according to their measures. The measure of an **acute angle** is less than 90°. The measure of a **right angle** is 90°. The measure of an **obtuse angle** is greater than 90°.

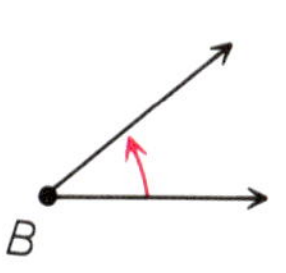

Acute Angle
$m\angle B < 90°$

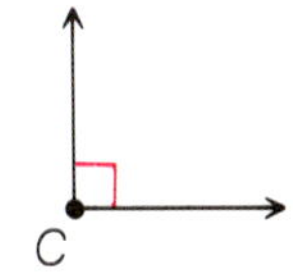

Right Angle
$m\angle C = 90°$

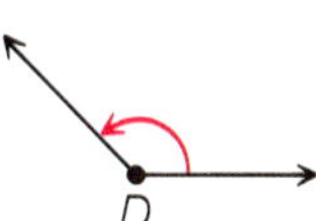

Obtuse Angle
$m\angle D > 90°$

Example 1

In the figure, name: **a.** one acute angle **b.** one obtuse angle

Solution
a. $\angle CAB$ **b.** $\angle ACB$

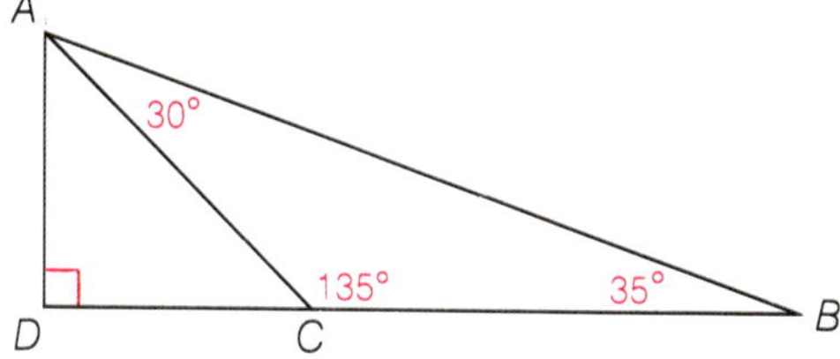

Practice In the figure, name:
a. two other acute angles
b. a right angle

Example 2

Write and solve an equation to find $m\angle ABD$.

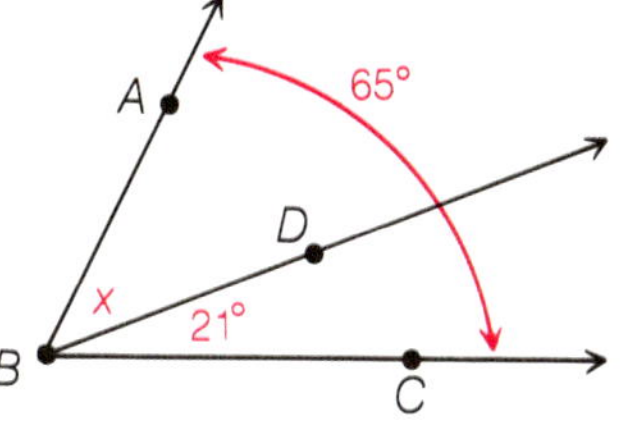

Solution $m\angle ABC = m\angle ABD + m\angle DBC$

$$65 = x + 21$$
$$65 - 21 = x + 21 - 21$$
$$44 = x$$

$m\angle ABD = 44°$

Practice For the figure above, write and solve an equation to find each.
a. $m\angle DBC$ if $m\angle ABD$ is 28° **b.** $m\angle ABD$ if $m\angle DBC$ is 49°

Two angles are **complementary** if the sum of their measures is 90°. Two angles are **supplementary** if the sum of their measures is 180°.

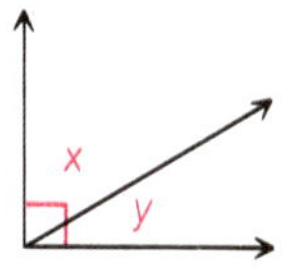

Complementary angles
$x + y = 90$

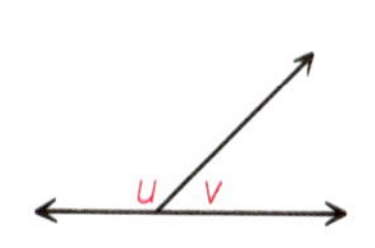

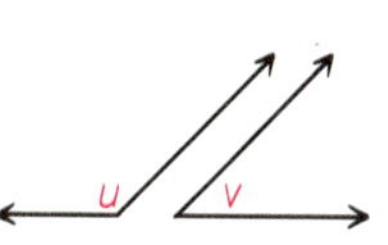

Supplementary angles
$u + v = 180$

Example 3

Write and solve an equation to find the complement of a 49° angle.

Solution $x + 49 = 90$ Let x = the measure of the complement. The sum of the measures of an angle and its complement is 90°.

$x + 49 - 49 = 90 - 49$

$x = 41$ The complement of a 49° angle is a 41° angle.

Practice Write and solve an equation to find:

a. the supplement of a 119° angle **b.** the complement of a 48° angle

Oral Exercises

State whether an angle with the given measure is acute, right, or obtuse.

1. 10° **2.** 90° **3.** 175° **4.** 1° **5.** 95°

6. 80° **7.** 18° **8.** 100° **9.** 89° **10.** 130°

Exercises

A Use the figure at right for Exercises 1–5.

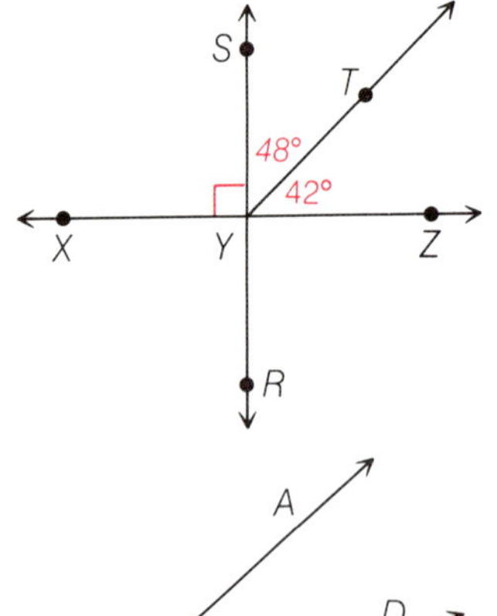

1. Name an acute angle.

2. Name an obtuse angle.

3. Name two right angles.

4. Name a pair of complementary angles.

5. Name a pair of supplementary angles.

Write and solve an equation to find:

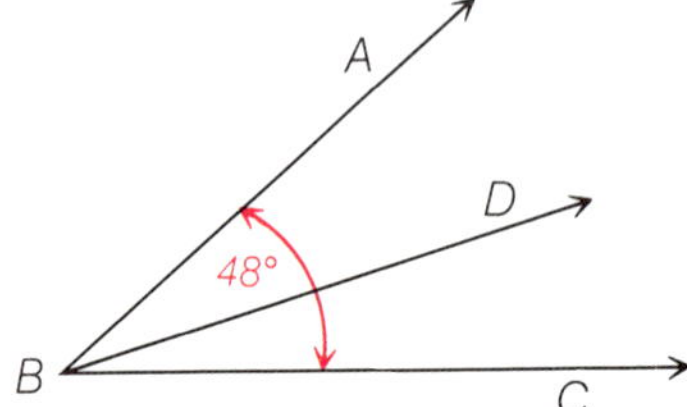

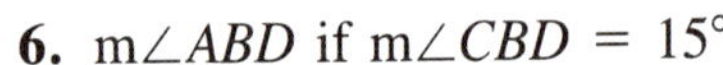

6. m∠ABD if m∠CBD = 15°

7. m∠CBD if m∠ABD = 31°

8. m∠ABD if m∠CBD = 21°

9. m∠CBD if m∠ABD = 35°

10. m∠ABD if m∠CBD = 19.2°

11. m∠CBD if m∠ABD = 27.5°

Write and solve an equation to find:

12. the complement of a 23° angle

13. the complement of a 53° angle

14. the supplement of a 123° angle

15. the supplement of a 153° angle

16. the supplement of a 23° angle

17. the complement of a 17° angle

B

18. If m∠A = x, what is the measure of the complement of ∠A?

19. If m∠B = x, what is the measure of the supplement of ∠B?

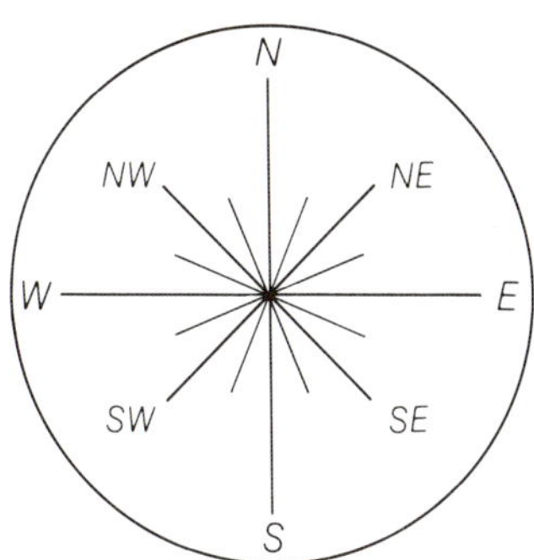

20. Draw four angles of different measures. Estimate their measures. Check your estimates with a protractor.

21. What is the measure of the angle between east and northeast?

22. What is the measure of the angle between northeast and north-northeast?

23. Two supplementary angles have measures of $2x$ and $3x$. Write and solve an equation to find the measure of the angles.

24. Two complementary angles have measures of y and $5y$. Write and solve an equation to find the measure of angle y.

C *Extending Thinking Skills*

25. A ship travels in a direction 12° east of due north until it reaches a lighthouse. It then turns 30° to the left. How many degrees from due north is the ship now traveling?

26. After a ship travels due east for several hours, it turns 21 degrees to the left. How many degrees east of north is the ship now traveling?

Mixed Review

Write as a fraction in lowest terms. **27.** 40% **28.** 35%

Solve and check. **29.** $4.5n + 16.3 = 21.7$ **30.** $-6.2m + 18.3 = 6m$

ESTIMATION

Use the 60°, 45°, and 30° angles to estimate the measures of the angles below.

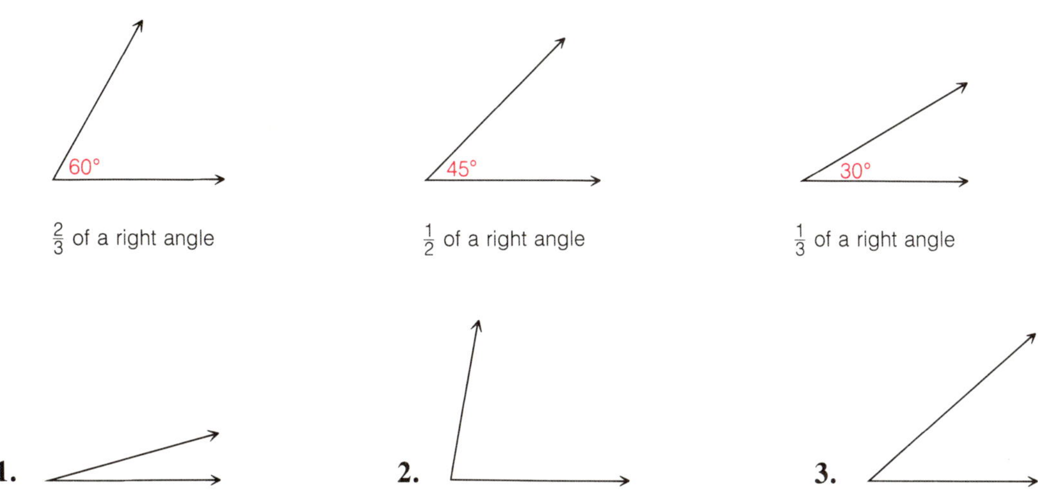

11-4 Parallel and Perpendicular Lines

Two lines in the same plane are **parallel** if they have no points in common. Two segments or rays in the same plane are parallel if the lines containing them are parallel. Lines in the same plane that are not parallel are called **intersecting** lines. Lines that intersect to form right angles are called **perpendicular** lines.

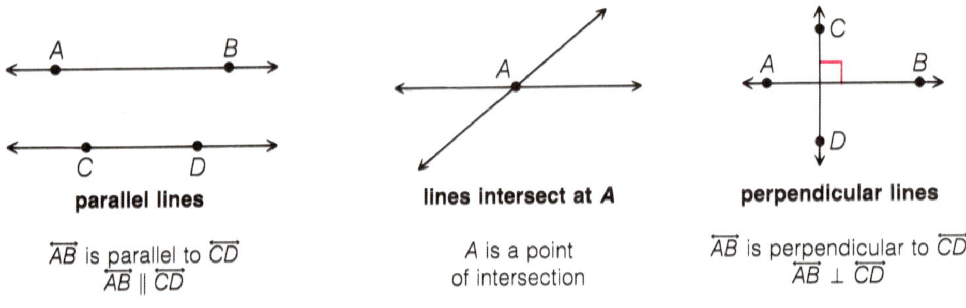

parallel lines

$\overleftrightarrow{AB}$ is parallel to $\overleftrightarrow{CD}$
$\overleftrightarrow{AB} \parallel \overleftrightarrow{CD}$

lines intersect at *A*

A is a point of intersection

perpendicular lines

$\overleftrightarrow{AB}$ is perpendicular to $\overleftrightarrow{CD}$
$\overleftrightarrow{AB} \perp \overleftrightarrow{CD}$

Two intersecting lines form two pairs of **vertical angles**. In the figure at right, $\angle 2$ and $\angle 4$ are vertical angles, and $\angle 1$ and $\angle 3$ are vertical angles.

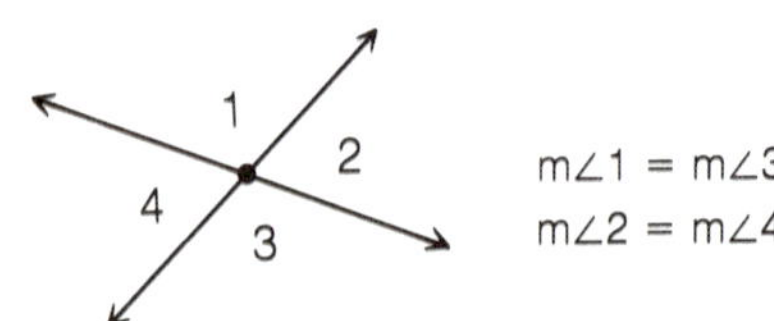

Measure of Vertical Angles

Vertical angles have the same measure.

When lines intersect, you can sometimes use vertical angles to find the measure of an angle not given.

Example 1

Find $m\angle 1$ on the figure at right.

Solution $m\angle 1 = 29°$ $\angle 1$ is vertical to an angle of 29°. Vertical angles have the same measure.

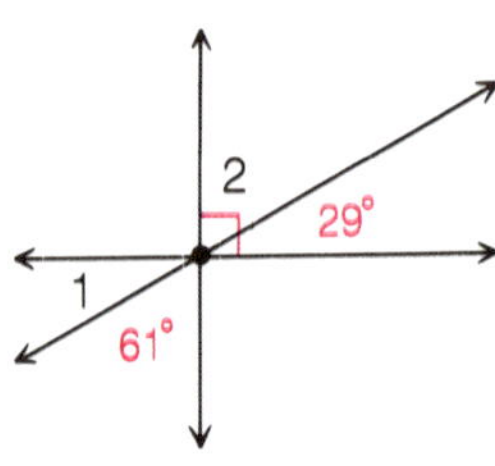

Practice Find $m\angle 2$ on the figure at right.

A line that intersects two other lines is called a **transversal**. When a transversal intersects a pair of parallel lines, the pairs of **corresponding angles** formed have the same measure.

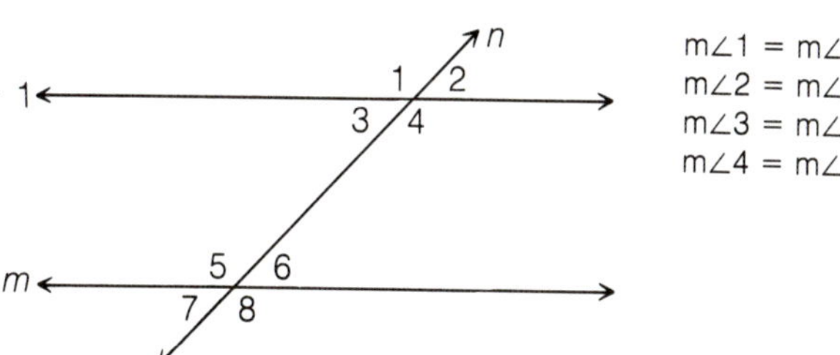

Corresponding angles in this figure are ∠1 and ∠5, ∠2 and ∠6, ∠3 and ∠7, and ∠4 and ∠8.

Measures of Corresponding Angles

Where a transversal intersects a pair of parallel lines, corresponding angles have the same measure.

Example 2

Lines *a* and *b* are parallel. Find the measures of ∠1, ∠2, and ∠3.

Solution

m∠1 + 121 = 180	∠1 is supplementary to the angle measuring 121°
m∠1 = 59°	
m∠2 = 121°	Vertical angles have equal measures.
m∠3 = 59°	Corresponding angles have equal measures.

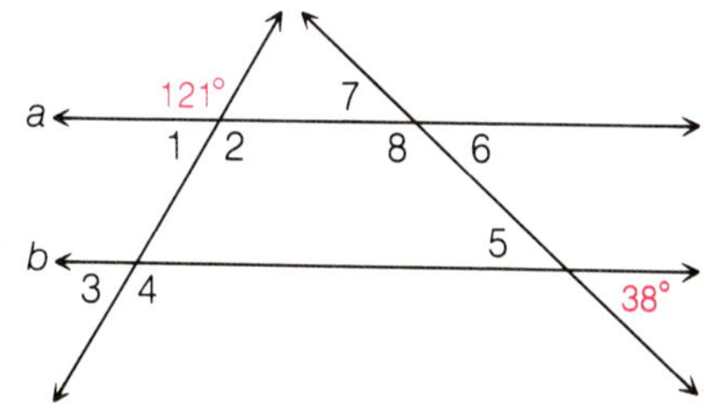

Practice Find the measures of ∠5, ∠6, ∠7, and ∠8.

Oral Exercises

1. Name a pair of parallel lines.
2. Name a pair of perpendicular lines
3. Name an angle that is vertical to ∠4
4. Name an angle corresponding to ∠3
5. Name an angle corresponding to ∠5

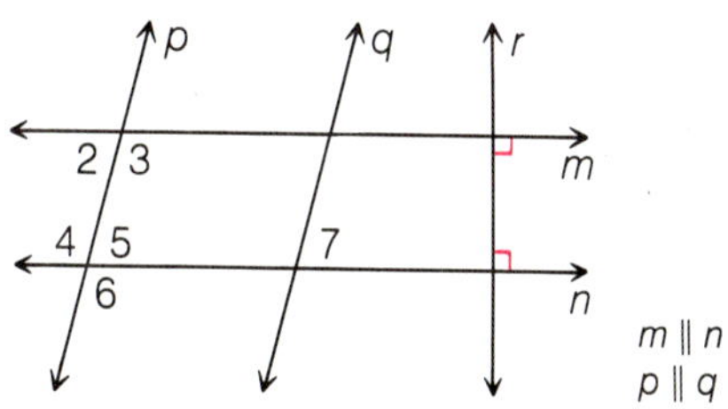

Exercises

A Find the measures of ∠1, ∠2, ∠3, and ∠4.

1.

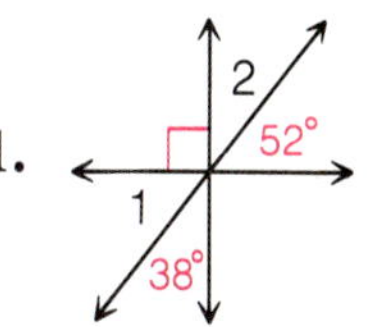

2.

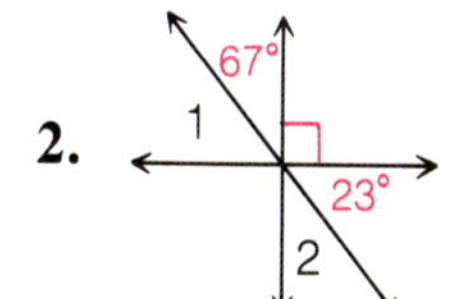

3.

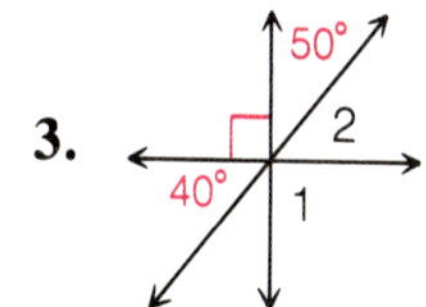

4. 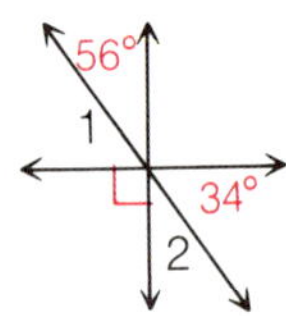

5. 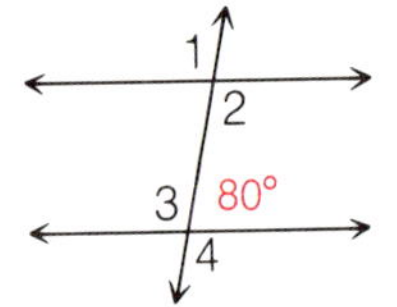

6. 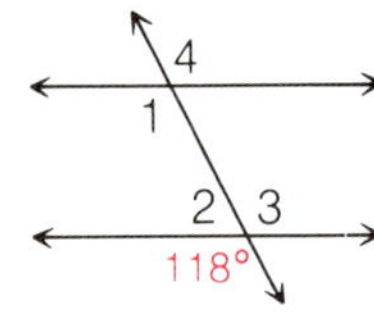

7. 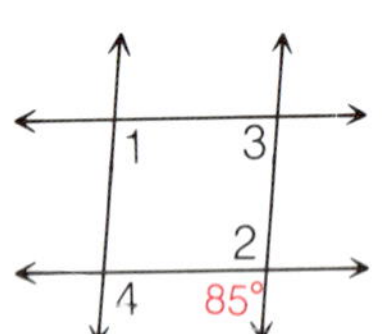

8. 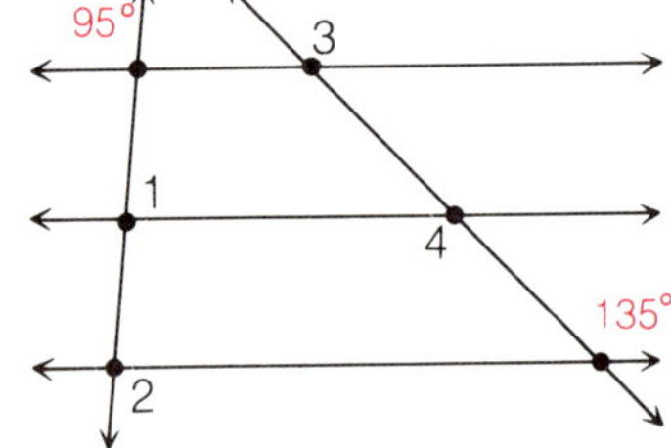

B Write and solve an equation to find the measure of $\angle ABC$.

9. 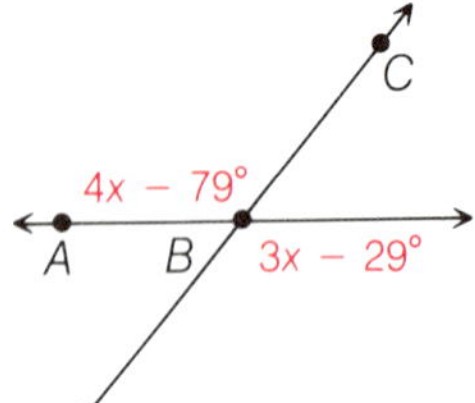

10. 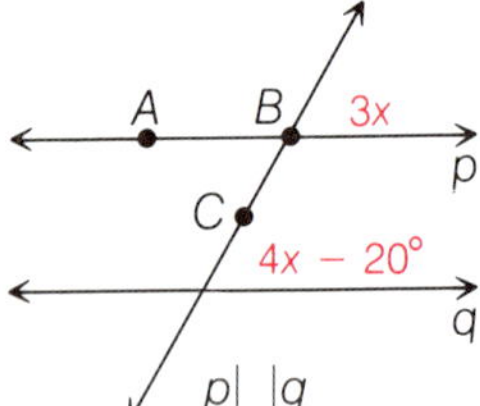

11. 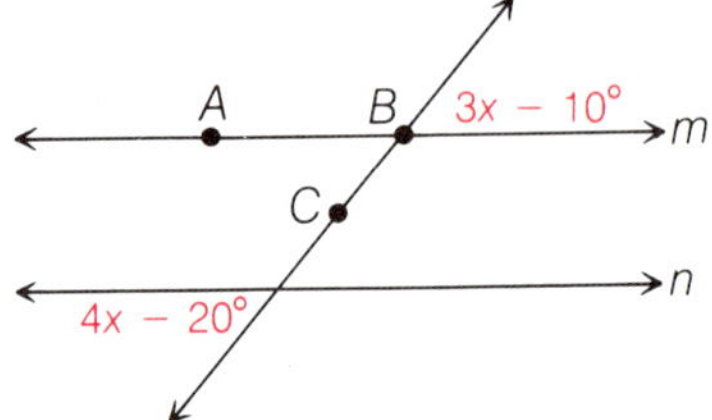

C Extending Thinking Skills

12. In the plan for a fence gate at right, what are the measures of angles 1, 3, and 4?

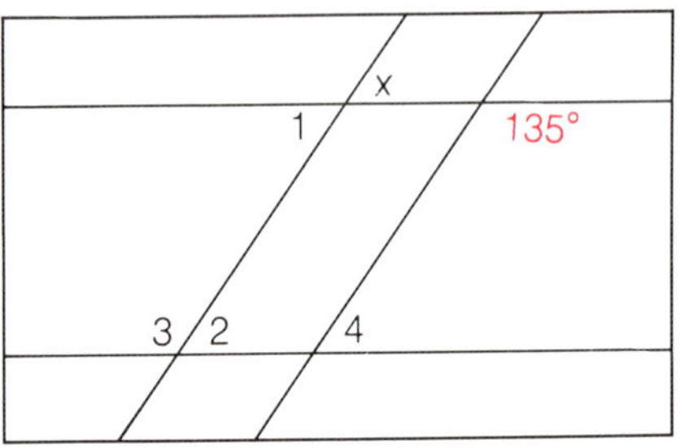

13. Angles 1 and 2 are called **alternate interior angles**.
$m\angle 1 = m\angle x$ (why?)
$m\angle x = m\angle 2$ (why?)
Formulate a generalization about alternate interior angles: If 2 lines are parallel, alternate interior angles are _?_.

Mixed Review

Use a proportion to write as a percent. **14.** $\frac{4}{5}$ **15.** $\frac{1}{8}$

16. What percent of 16 is 12? **17.** What percent of 45 is 27?

11-5 Triangles

A **triangle** is a figure in a plane, made up of three segments meeting at endpoints. In the triangle at right, $\overline{AB}$, $\overline{BC}$, and $\overline{AC}$ are called the **sides**. Points A, B, and C are called **vertices**.

The symbol for triangle *ABC* is $\triangle ABC$.

Triangles are classified by the measures of their angles or the lengths of their sides.

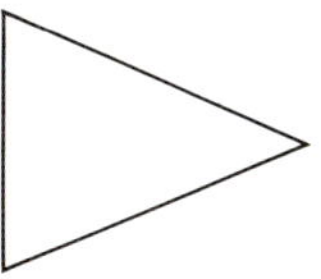

Acute
all acute angles

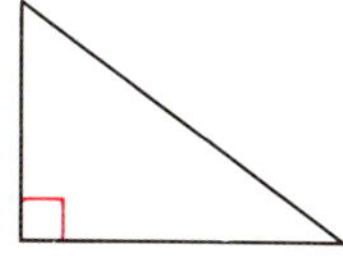

Right
one right angle

Obtuse
one obtuse angle

Equilateral
all sides equal in length

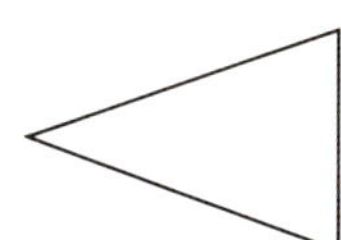

Isosceles
at least two sides equal in length

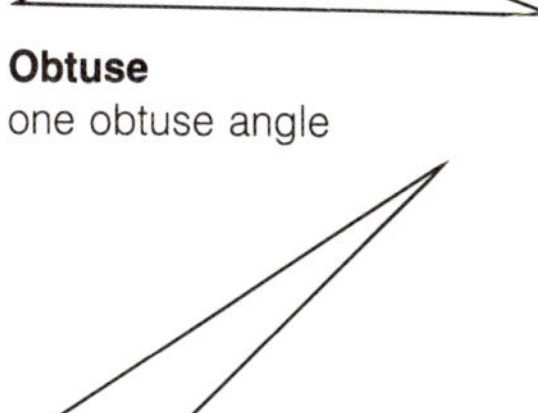

Scalene
no two sides equal in length

Example 1

Classify $\triangle ABC$ and $\triangle DEF$ by the measures of the angles and the lengths of the sides.

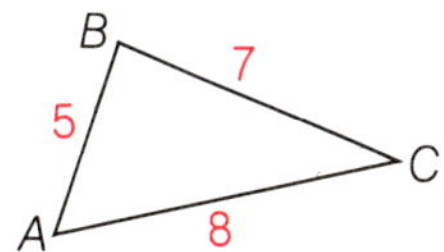

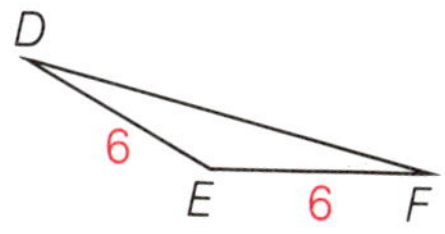

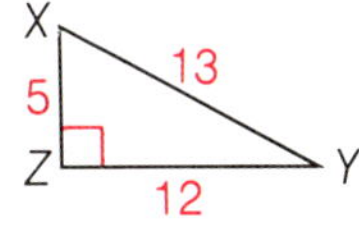

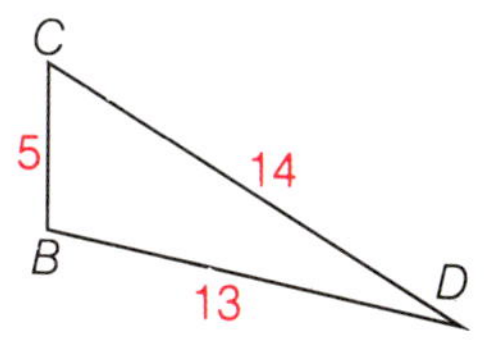

Solution

$\triangle ABC$ is acute and scalene. All angles are acute and no two sides are equal in length.

$\triangle DEF$ is obtuse and isosceles. Angle E is obtuse; two sides are equal in length.

Practice Classify $\triangle XYZ$ and $\triangle BCD$ above by the measures of their angles and the lengths of the sides.

The picture below suggests an important property of triangles.

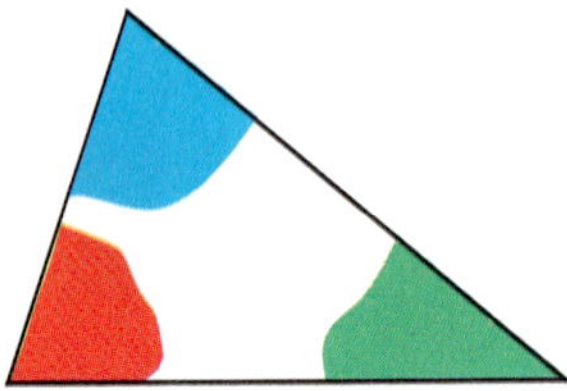

Sum of the Angle Measures of a Triangle

The sum of the angle measures in any triangle is 180°.

$m\angle A + m\angle B + m\angle C = 180°$

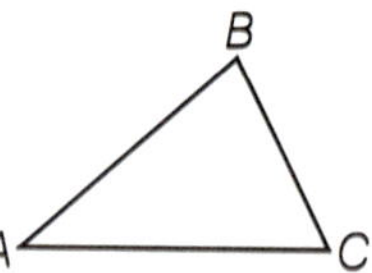

Example 2

Write and solve an equation to find m∠A.

Solution $x + 30 + 130 = 180$

$x + 160 = 180$

$x = 20$

$m\angle A = 20°$.

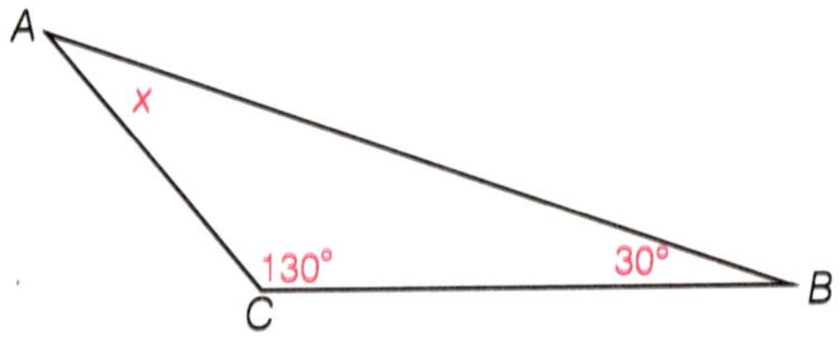

Practice Two angles of a triangle have measures 37° and 92°. Write and solve an equation to find the measure of the third angle.

Oral Exercises

On the figure at right, name the following:

1. An obtuse triangle.
2. Three right triangles.
3. Two acute triangles.

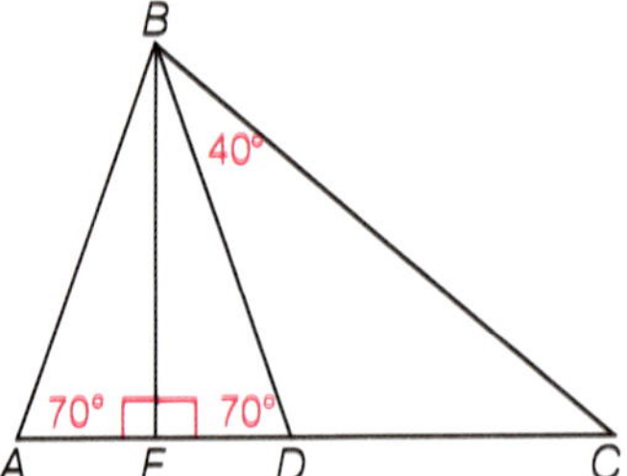

Exercises

A Classify each triangle by the measures of its angles and the lengths of its sides.

1. 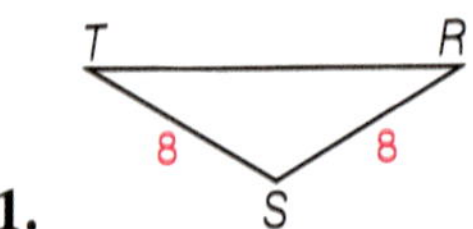

2. 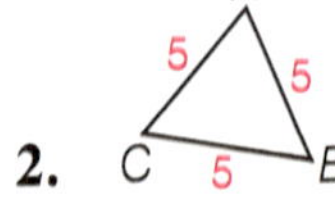

3. 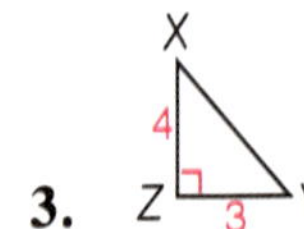

4. 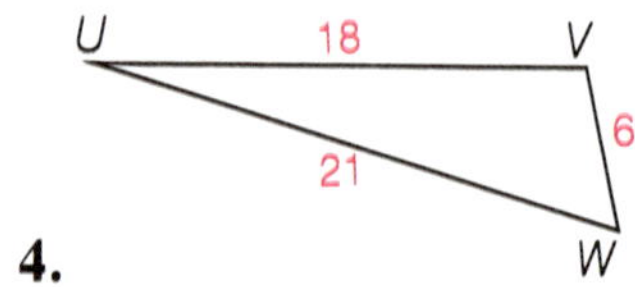

Write and solve an equation to find $m\angle A$.

5. 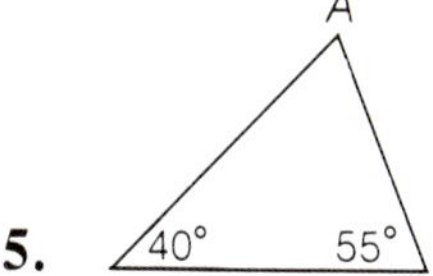

6. 61° 58° A

7. 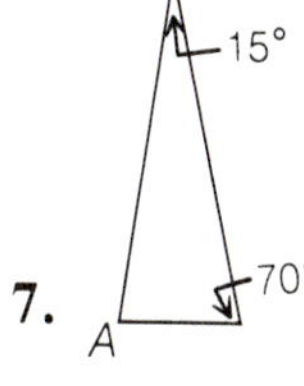

8. 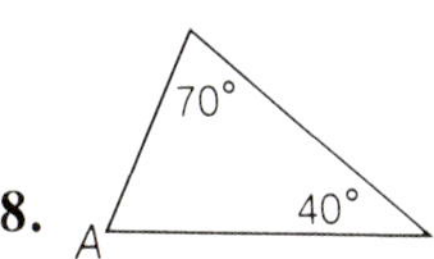

Write and solve an equation to find the measure of the third angle.

9. Two angles of a triangle have measures of 70° and 32°.

10. Two angles of a triangle have measures of 119° and 25°.

B Write and solve an equation to find the measure of each angle.

11. 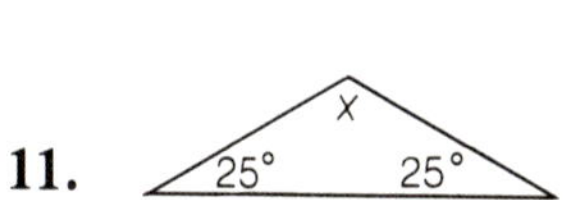

12. 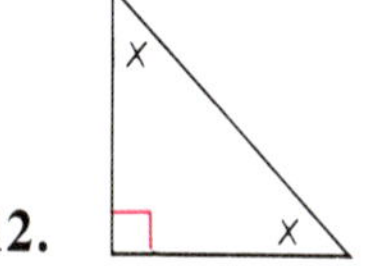

13. 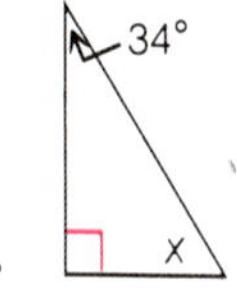

14. 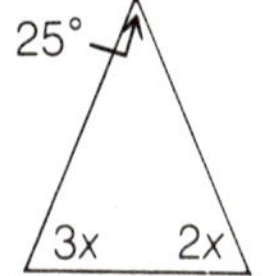

C Extending Thinking Skills

Find the pattern and use the variable n to complete the following: $x = \underline{\ ?\ }$

15. 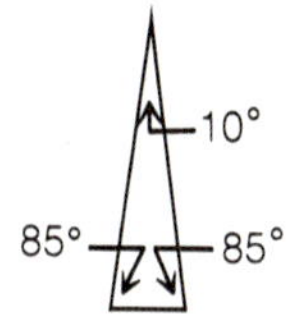

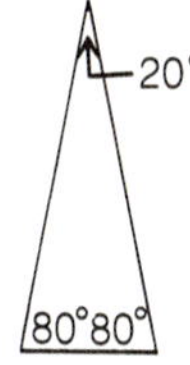

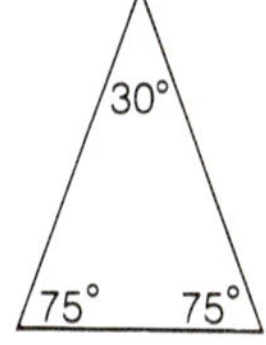

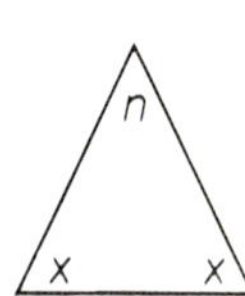

Mixed Review

Solve and check. **16.** $-16c > 32$ **17.** $4m + 6 < 2m + 12$

18. What percent of 20 is 4? **19.** What percent of 20 is 17?

CALCULATOR ACTIVITY

You can use the key sequence below to solve an equation such as $x + 45 + 73 = 180$.

Display

       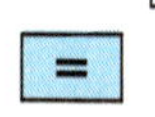 

45 [+] 73 [=] [+/−] [+] 180 [=] 62

Use a calculator to solve.

1. $x + 48 + 23 = 180$ **2.** $x + 56 + 112 = 180$ **3.** $x + 84 + 27 = 180$

11-6 Polygons

A **polygon** is a plane figure formed by three or more segments that intersect only at their endpoints so that exactly two segments meet at each endpoint. A polygon is named according to the number of its sides.

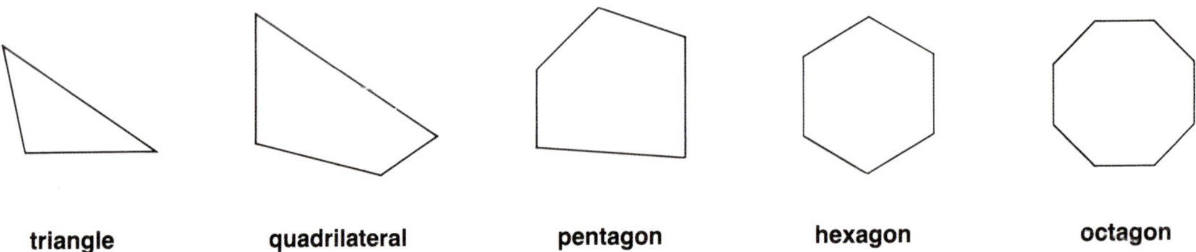

In a **regular polygon**, all sides and all angles have the same measure. The hexagon and octagon above are regular polygons.

A **quadrilateral** is a polygon with four sides. Some quadrilaterals have specific names.

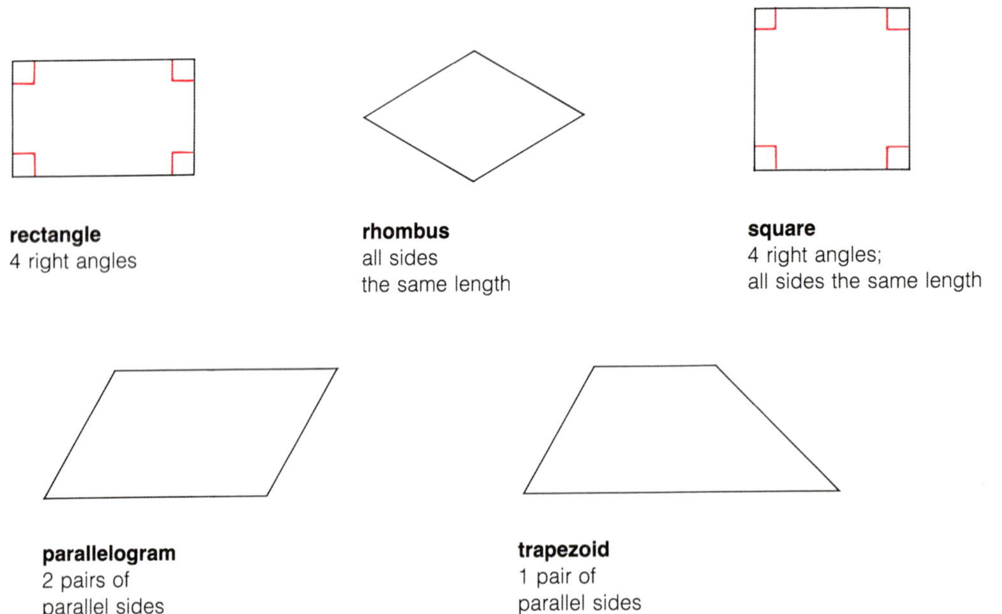

Example 1

Name each polygon and indicate whether it is regular. Use specific names for quadrilaterals.

a.

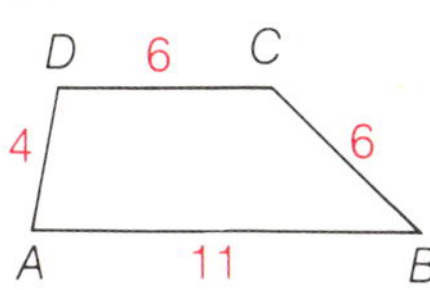

b.

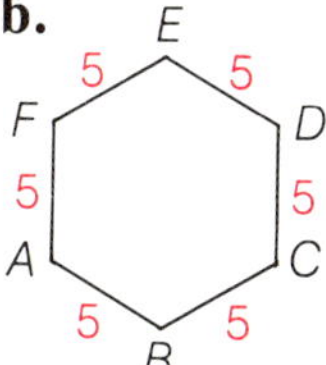

Solution

a. *ABCD* is a trapezoid. Quadrilateral with only one pair of parallel sides.

b. *ABCDEF* is a regular hexagon. All angles and all sides are equal in measure. It is regular.

Practice Name each polygon and indicate whether it is regular. Use specific names for quadrilaterals.

a.

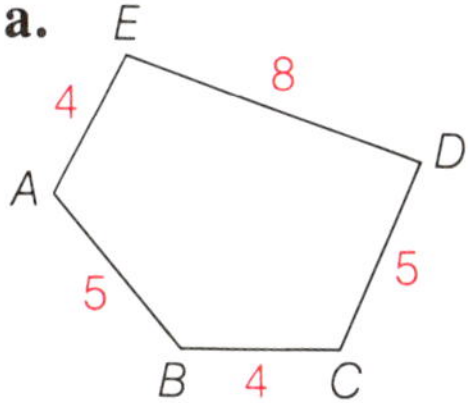

b.

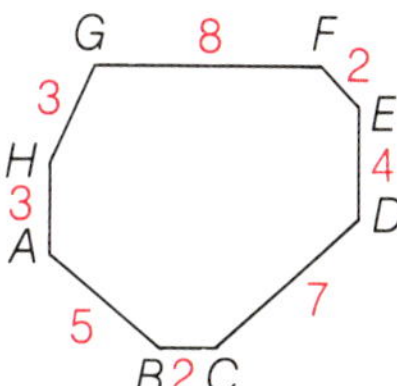

The figure below shows an important property of quadrilaterals.

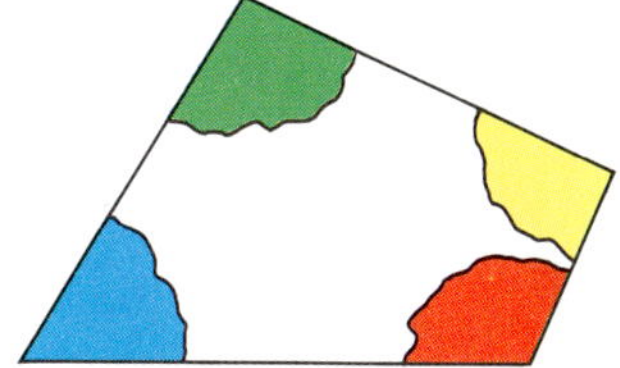

Sum of the Angle Measures of a Quadrilateral

The sum of the measures of the angles in any quadrilateral is 360°.

$$m\angle A + m\angle B + m\angle C + m\angle D = 360°$$

D C A B

Example 2

Write and solve an equation to find $m\angle A$.

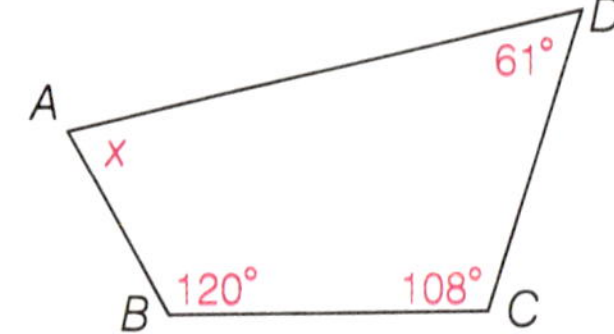

Solution

$$x + 120 + 108 + 61 = 360$$ The sum of the measures of the angles in a quadrilateral is 360°.

$$x + 289 = 360$$ Combine terms.

$$x + 289 - 289 = 360 - 289$$

$$x = 71$$

$m\angle A = 71°$.

Practice Write and solve an equation to find $m\angle A$.

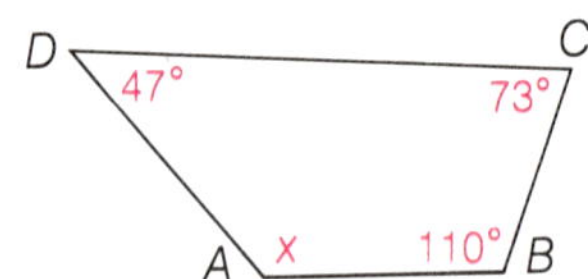

Oral Exercises

Name a polygon that has:

1. 5 sides **2.** 4 sides **3.** 6 sides **4.** 3 sides **5.** 8 sides

6. When is a polygon a regular polygon?

7. What is another name for a regular triangle.

8. What is another name for a regular quadrilateral?

Exercises

A Name each polygon and indicate whether it is regular. Use any special names for quadrilaterals.

1.
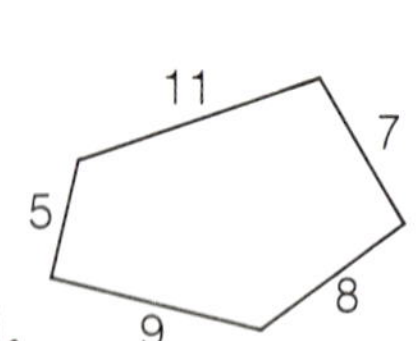

2.
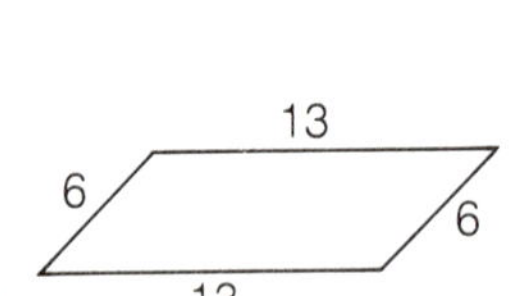

3.
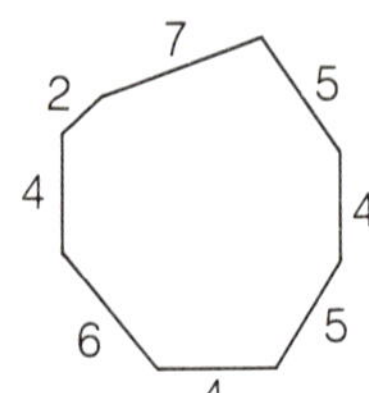

4.
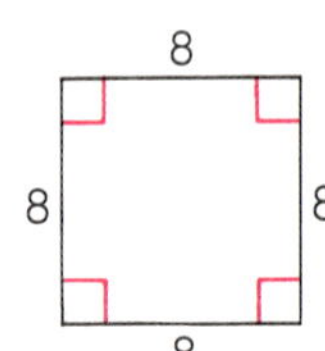

Write and solve an equation to find $m\angle A$.

5.
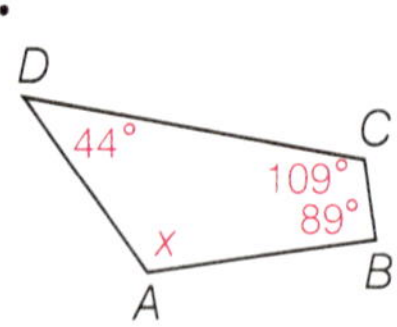

6.
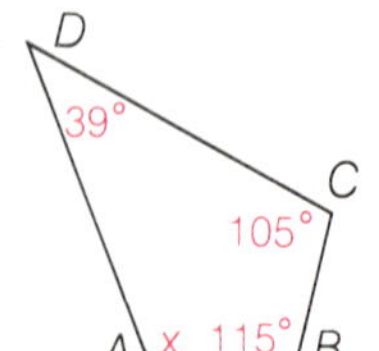

7.
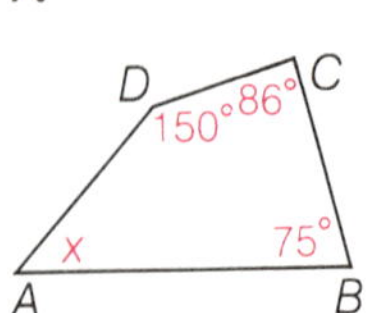

8.
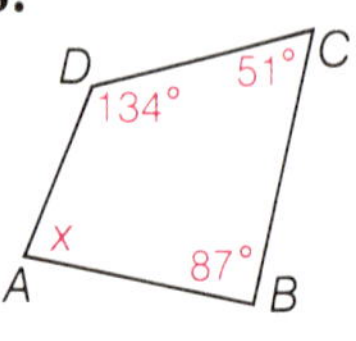

B Write and solve an equation to find each angle measure.

9. 10. 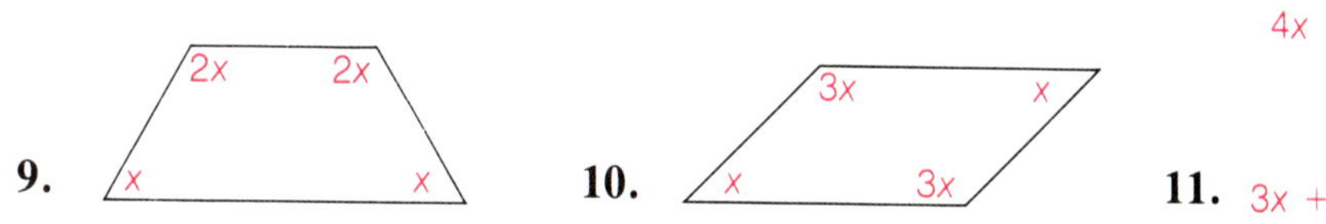

11. 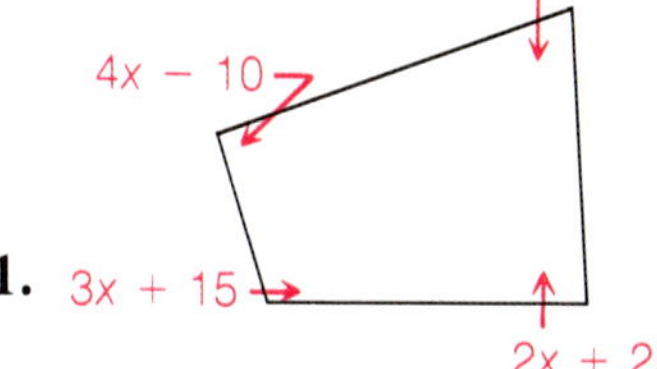

12. Name a quadrilateral that is not regular but has all sides the same length.

13. Name a quadrilateral that is not regular but has all angles the same measure.

C Extending Thinking Skills

14. Draw a quadrilateral, a pentagon, and a hexagon. Find the number of diagonals from a single vertex needed to divide each figure into triangles. What generalization can you make from your answer?

Mixed Review

Give the greatest common factor (GCF). **15.** 20, 32, 8 **16.** 15, 21, 36

17. What percent of 70 is 105? **18.** What percent of 200 is 1?

NUMBERS TO ALGEBRA

You can find a general formula for the sum of the measures of the angles of a polygon with n sides by generalizing from the number patterns shown below.

Numbers			Algebra
			Polygon with n sides
3 sides 1 × 180	4 sides 2 × 180	5 sides 3 × 180	n sides $(n - 2) \times 180$

1. Find the sum of the angle measures of a polygon with 6 sides.
2. Find the sum of the angle measures of a polygon with 12 sides.
3. Find the sum of the angle measures of a polygon with 150 sides.

11-7 Using a Road Map

A road map gives information about distances between cities. On the map below, the interstate highway is shown in blue. Notice the red arrowheads at exits 18 and 33. About halfway between these two arrowheads is a red number 40. This means the distance between the arrowheads is 40 miles. Notice the small numbers in black between each pair of exits. Between exits 23 and 28 is a small black 8. This means the distance between these two exits is 8 miles.

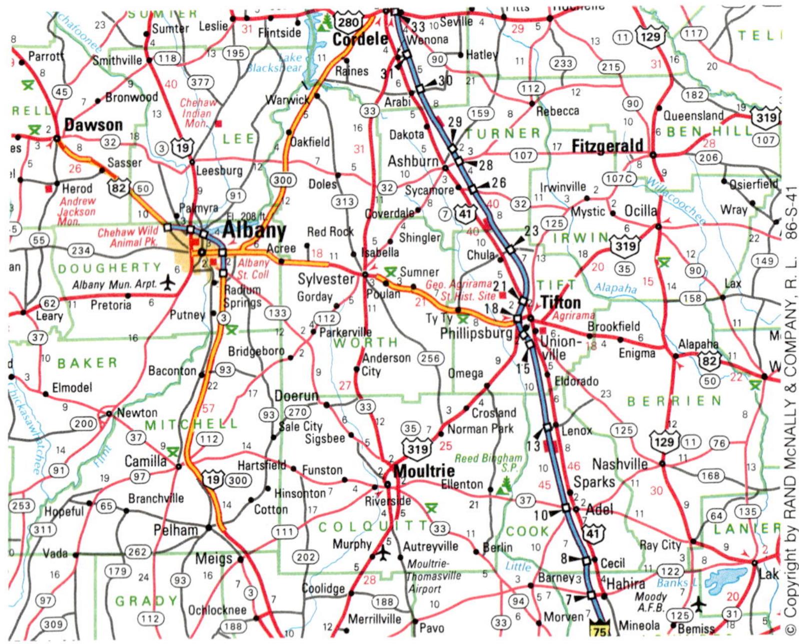

Problems

Solve. Use the map and the formula Distance = rate × time as needed.

1. How far is it from Moultrie to Sylvester along highway 33? (Note the red arrows at these towns and the red numbers between them.)

2. How far is it from Tifton to Ocilla on Highway 319?

3. How far is it from Albany to Tifton on Highway 82?

4. How far will a car traveling at 55 mi/h drive in $1\frac{1}{2}$ hours?

5. Would a car traveling at 55 mi/h be able to drive from exit 18 to exit 33 in less than 45 minutes?

6. How long does it take to travel 125 miles at 55 mi/h?

7. The distance from San Francisco to New York is about 2800 miles. About how long will it take for a jet to fly from San Francisco to New York at an average speed of 620 mi/h?

8. A truck driver averages 50 mi/h. If he drives $10\frac{1}{2}$ hours a day, about how many days will it take him to travel 1500 miles?

9. A family drove a distance of about 3000 miles from Boston, MA, to Los Angeles, CA. They averaged 500 miles a day. Traveling costs were $35 a day for food and $40 for a motel each night. If it cost $0.17 per mile to operate their car, what was their total expense for the trip?

Use the mileage chart to answer problems 10–12.

	Chicago	Dallas	St. Louis	Wash., D.C.
Chicago		921	289	709
Dallas	921		655	1307
St. Louis	289	655		862
Wash., D.C.	709	1307	862	

10. How many miles is it from Washington, D.C. to Dallas and back?

11. How many miles is it from Dallas to St. Louis and back?

12. How many more miles is it to travel through St. Louis on the way from Dallas to Chicago than to go directly?

13. ***Data Search*** For a driver averaging 50 miles per hour, how long would it take to drive from Kansas City, Missouri, to Denver, Colorado?

What's Your Decision?

Suppose you are planning to travel from New Orleans, LA, to Detroit, MI on interstate highways. To travel the minimum number of miles, what route should you take? If you average 50 miles per hour, how many hours will you drive?

11-8 Circles and Circumference

A **circle** is the set of all points in a plane that are a fixed distance from a point called the **center**. Any segment that joins the center to a point on the circle is called a **radius** (***r***) of the circle. The **diameter** (***d***) of the circle is a segment that passes through the center and has endpoints on the circle.

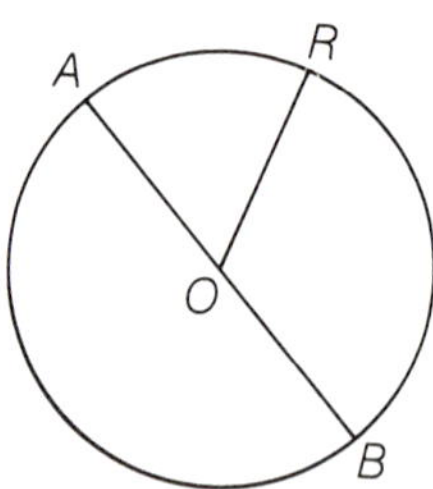

O is the center
$\overline{OR}$ is a radius
$\overline{AB}$ is a diameter

The distance around a circle is called the **circumference** (***C***) of the circle. The ratio $\frac{C}{d}$ is the same number for all circles, and is represented by the Greek letter π. The number $\pi \approx 3.14$.

Formula: Circumference of a Circle

The circumference of a circle is π times the diameter, or 2 times π times the radius.

$$C = \pi d \quad \text{or} \quad C = 2\pi r$$

Example 1

Find the circumference of a circle with diameter 4 cm. Use 3.14 for π.

Solution $C = \pi d$

$C \approx 3.14 \times 4$ Substitute 3.14 for π and 4 for d.

$C \approx 12.56$ cm

Practice Find the circumference of a circle with the given diameter or radius.

a. diameter = 3.2 cm **b.** radius = 8.2 cm

Example 2

Find the radius of a circle with circumference 9 cm. Use 3.14 for π.

Solution $C = 2\pi r$

$9 \approx 2(3.14)r$ Substitute 9 for C and 3.14 for π.

$r \approx \frac{9}{6.28} \approx 1.43$

Practice **a.** Find the radius of a circle with circumference 12 m.

b. Find the diameter of a circle with circumference 18 cm.

Oral Exercises

For the figure at right:

1. name the center.
2. name three radii.
3. give the length of a radius.
4. name a diameter.
5. name another diameter.
6. give the length of a diameter.

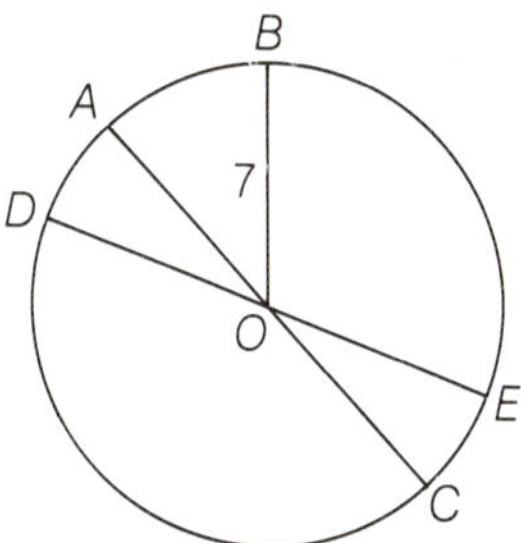

Exercises

A Find the circumference of a circle with the given diameter or radius. Use 3.14 for π.

1. diameter = 5 cm **2.** diameter = 12 cm **3.** diameter = 20 cm
4. diameter = 4.8 cm **5.** radius = 6.1 m **6.** radius = 8.3 m

Find the diameter of a circle with the given circumference (C) or radius (r).

7. $C = 5$ cm **8.** $C = 8$ mm **9.** $C = 12$ m
10. $r = 35.7$ cm **11.** $C = 4.6$ m **12.** $r = 99.8$ m

Find the radius of a circle with the given circumference (C) or diameter (d).

13. $C = 9$ cm **14.** $C = 4$ m **15.** $C = 15$ cm
16. $d = 452.8$ cm **17.** $C = 14.8$ m **18.** $d = 32.84$ m

B Use 3.14 for π in Exercises 19–23.

19. Estimate the circumference of a 28-inch diameter bicycle wheel. Find the circumference with a calculator.

20. How many feet does a bicycle travel with each revolution of a 28-inch diameter wheel? How many revolutions does the wheel make to travel one mile (5280 feet/mile)?

Find the perimeter of each figure. All curves are parts of circles.

21.

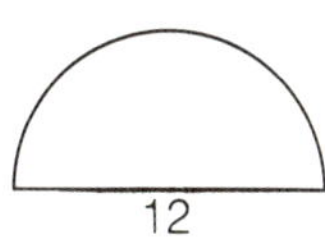

22.

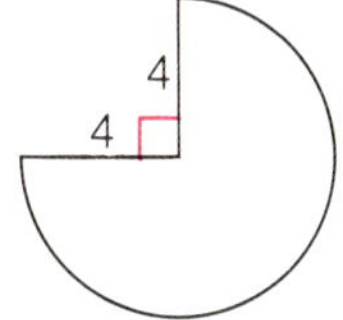

23.

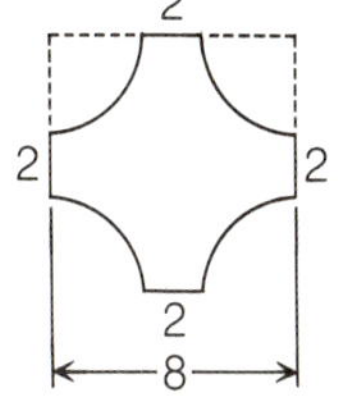

C Extending Thinking Skills

24. If the radius of a circle doubles, by how much does the circumference increase?

25. The radius of the earth is approximately 6380 kilometers. Imagine that a steel ring is looped tightly around the equator. Suppose the steel ring is made 6 meters longer. Will this make the ring loose enough so that:

an ant could walk under the ring?

a finger would fit under the ring?

a cat could walk under the ring?

a truck could be driven under the ring?

Mixed Review

Solve. There are 36 students in Mrs. Ward's class. 20 students are boys. 6 students are left-handed.

26. What is the ratio of boys to girls?

27. How many more boys than girls are in the class?

28. What percentage of the students are left-handed?

29. What is the ratio of left-handed to right-handed students?

COMPUTER ACTIVITY

This program calculates an approximation for π by calculating the perimeter of a polygon that is inscribed in the circle.

```
10  PRINT "HOW MANY SIDES DO YOU WANT
    THE APPROXIMATING POLYGON TO HAVE?"
20  INPUT S
30  LET NM=INT(S/4)
40  LET AR=0:X0=0:Y=1:X=0:ST=1/NM
50  FOR N=1 TO NM
60  LET X1=X0+N*ST:LET Y1=SQR(1-X1*X1)
70  LET L=SQR((X1-X)*(X1-X)+(Y1-Y)*(Y1-Y))
80  LET AR=AR+L
90  LET X=X1:Y=Y1
100 NEXT N
110 PRINT "PI IS APPROXIMATELY ";2*AR
120 END
```

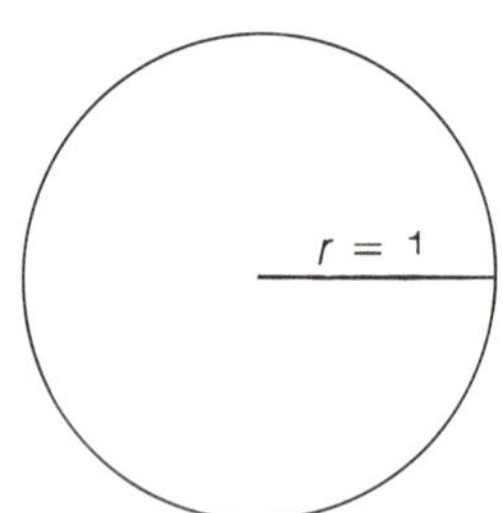

The circumference is π. The perimeter of this polygon is approximately π.

About how many sides are required for the approximation of π to round to:

1. 3.14

2. 3.141

3. 3.1415

11-9 Congruent Figures

Two figures are **congruent** if they are identical in size and shape. Segments are congruent if they have the same length. Angles are congruent if they have the same measure. The symbol $\cong$ means "is congruent to."

Imagine that one congruent polygon is lifted and placed upon the other. The matching vertices are called **corresponding vertices,** and the matching sides are called **corresponding sides**. In the figures below, vertex A corresponds to vertex G and $\overline{CD}$ corresponds to $\overline{EH}$.

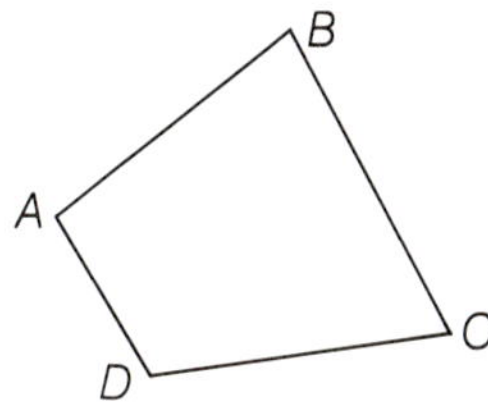

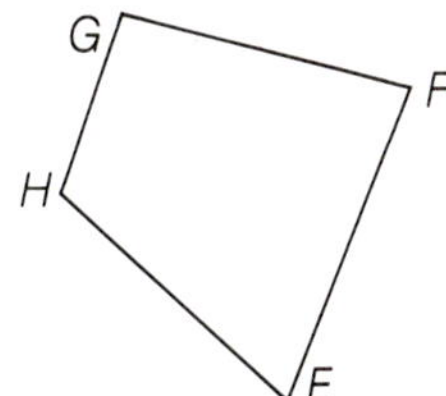

For any two congruent figures, corresponding vertices are congruent and corresponding sides are congruent. When naming two figures as congruent, list corresponding vertices in the same order. For example, if $\triangle ABC \cong \triangle DEF$, then A and D, B and E, C and F are corresponding vertices.

Example 1

$\triangle ABC \cong \triangle DEF$. Complete each statement.

$\angle A \cong \underline{\ ?\ }$ $\quad \overline{AB} \cong \underline{\ ?\ }$

$\angle B \cong \underline{\ ?\ }$ $\quad \overline{AC} \cong \underline{\ ?\ }$

$\angle C \cong \underline{\ ?\ }$ $\quad \overline{BC} \cong \underline{\ ?\ }$

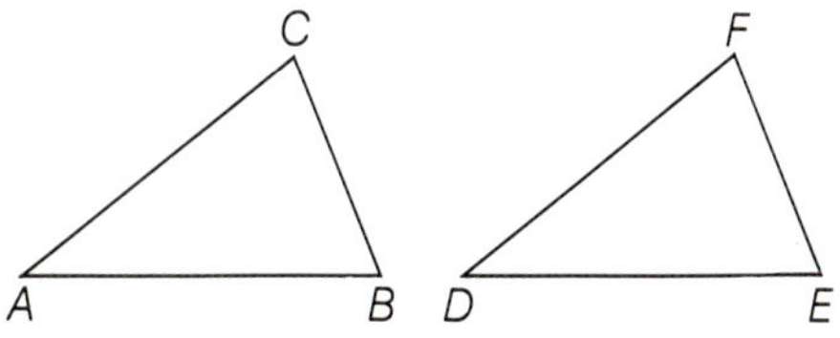

Solution $\angle A \cong \angle D$, $\angle B \cong \angle E$, $\angle C \cong \angle F$, $\overline{AB} \cong \overline{DE}$, $\overline{AC} \cong \overline{DF}$, $\overline{BC} \cong \overline{EF}$.

Practice Write all statements about congruent angles and sides.
$ABCDEF \cong GHIJKL$

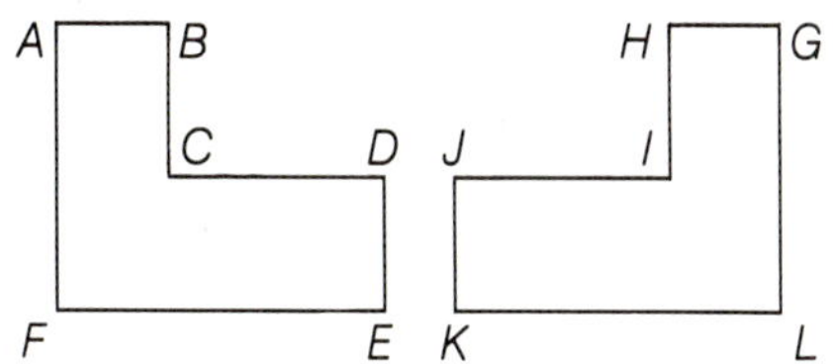

When two triangles are congruent, they have six pairs of congruent parts. To be sure that two triangles are congruent, you do not need to show that all six congruence statements are true. You can use any of the following three congruence properties to decide. The red marks in the figures below show the corresponding sides and angles.

Congruence Properties

1. **Side-Angle-Side (SAS)**
   If two sides and the included angle (the angle between the two sides) of one triangle are congruent to two sides and the included angle of another triangle, then the two triangles are congruent.

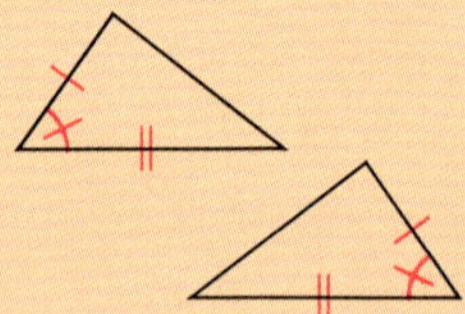

2. **Side-Side-Side (SSS)**
   If the three sides of one triangle are congruent to the three sides of another triangle, then the two triangles are congruent.

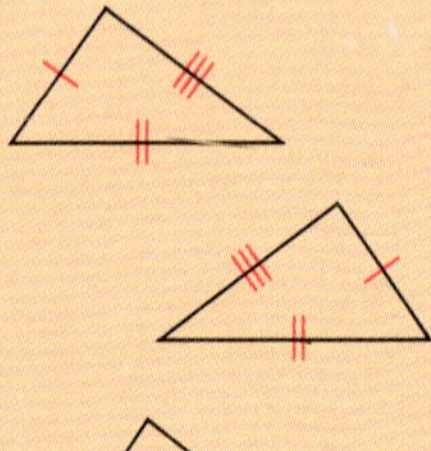

3. **Angle-Side-Angle (ASA)**
   If two angles and the included side of one triangle are congruent to two angles and the included side of another triangle, then the two triangles are congruent.

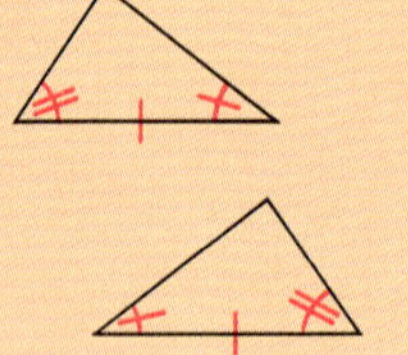

Example 2

Use SAS, SSS, or ASA property to show that the pair of triangles at right is congruent.

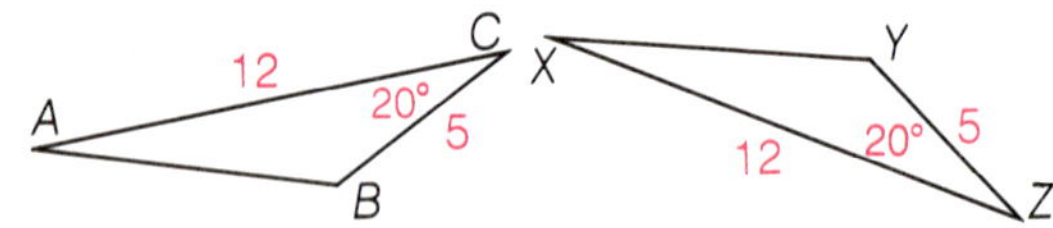

Solution $\overline{AC} \cong \overline{XZ}$

$\angle C \cong \angle Z$

$\overline{BC} \cong \overline{YZ}$ Since lengths of two sides and the included angle are given, use the SAS property.

$\triangle ABC \cong \triangle XYZ$ by the SAS property.

Practice Use the SAS, SSS, or ASA property to show that the pair of triangles is congruent.

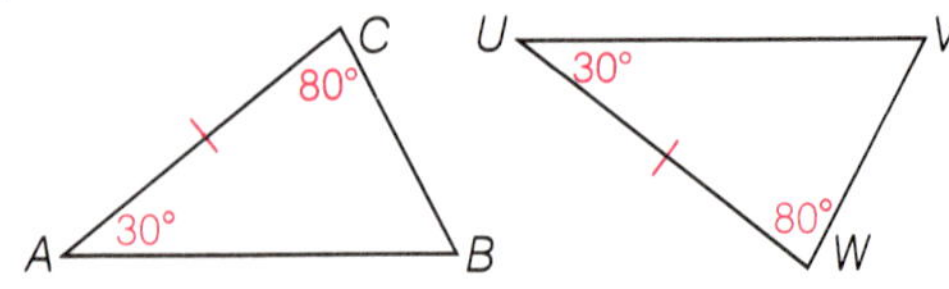

Oral Exercises

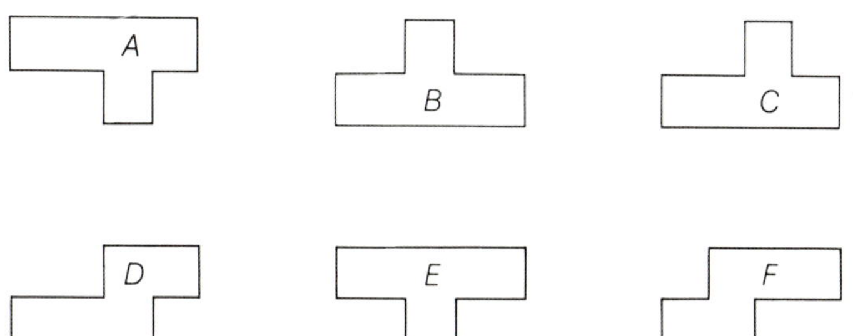

1. Which polygon seems to be congruent to polygon A?
2. Which polygon seems to be congruent to polygon E?
3. Which polygon seems to be congruent to polygon D?

Exercises

A $\triangle RST \cong \triangle UVW$. Complete each statement.

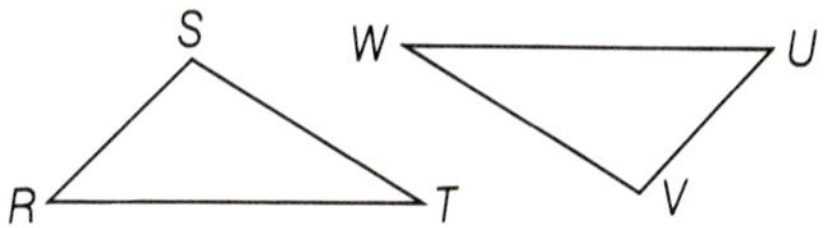

1. $\angle R \cong$ _?_
2. $\overline{RS} \cong$ _?_
3. $\angle W \cong$ _?_
4. $\overline{VW} \cong$ _?_

ABCDEF is congruent to *RSTUVW*. Complete each statement.

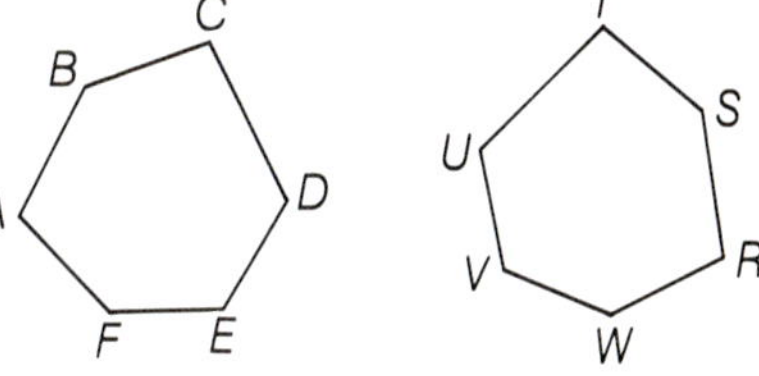

5. $\angle A \cong$ _?_
6. $\angle U \cong$ _?_
7. $\overline{EF} \cong$ _?_
8. $\overline{ST} \cong$ _?_
9. $\angle S \cong$ _?_
10. $\angle E \cong$ _?_
11. $\overline{CD} \cong$ _?_
12. $\angle D \cong$ _?_
13. $\overline{RS} \cong$ _?_
14. $\overline{AB} \cong$ _?_

Use the SAS, SSS, or ASA property to show that each pair of triangles is congruent.

15.

16.

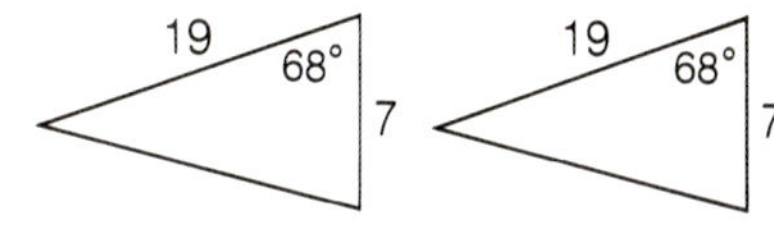

17.

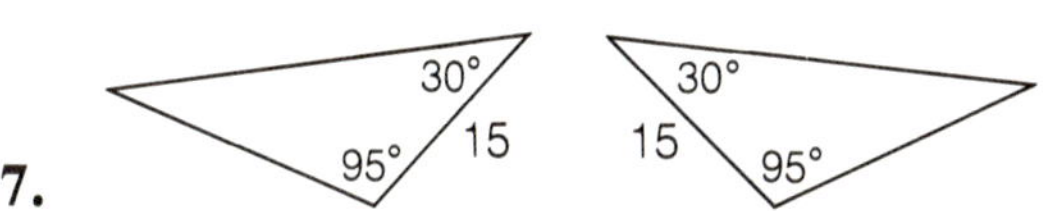

18.

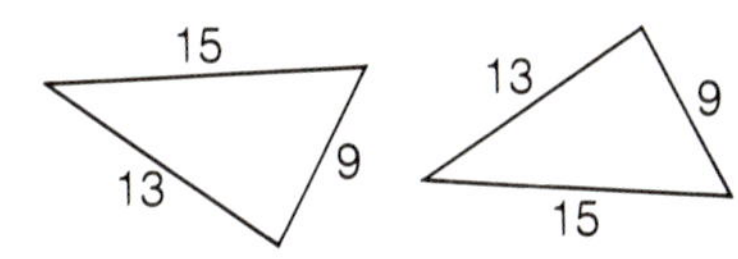

B The figure at right is a regular hexagon.

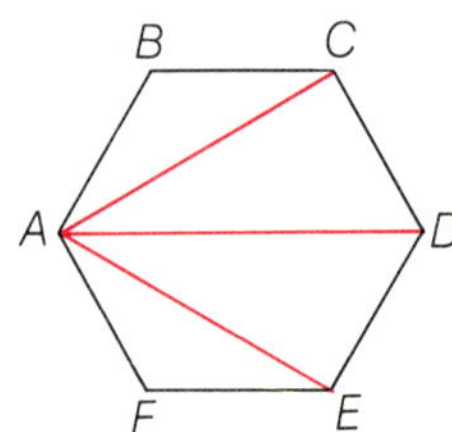

19. Name a triangle congruent to $\triangle ABC$. What congruence property shows this?

20. Name a triangle congruent to $\triangle ACD$. What congruence property shows this?

C Extending Thinking Skills

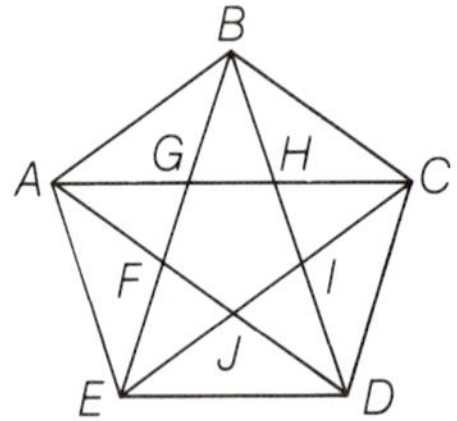

The five-pointed star is drawn in a regular pentagon.

21. Name all the triangles that are congruent to $\triangle ABD$.

22. List five triangles in this figure that are not congruent to each other.

Mixed Review

Write as a decimal. Use a bar for a repeating decimal.

23. $\frac{3}{16}$ **24.** $\frac{2}{3}$ **25.** $\frac{5}{12}$ **26.** $\frac{2}{5}$ **27.** $\frac{2}{11}$

Solve and check. **28.** $45c - 17 = 140.5$ **29.** $5m \div 6 = 10$

30. $m + 1.7m = 0.54$ **31.** $r - 16 = -373$ **32.** $26t - 14 = 18.5$

Write as a fraction in lowest terms. **33.** $2\frac{1}{2}\%$ **34.** 84%

Write as a percent. **35.** $\frac{45}{10}$ **36.** $\frac{7}{12}$ **37.** $1\frac{2}{5}$ **38.** $\frac{1}{8}$

ESTIMATION

Use estimation to decide whether each pair of triangles is congruent.

1.

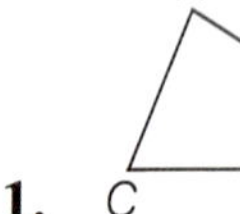

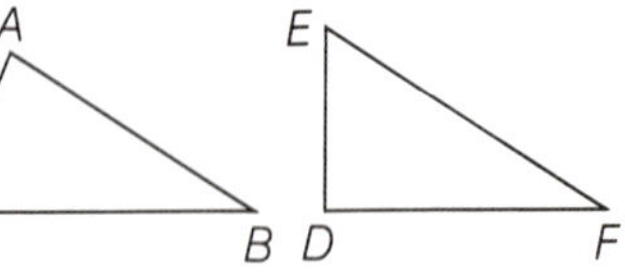

2.

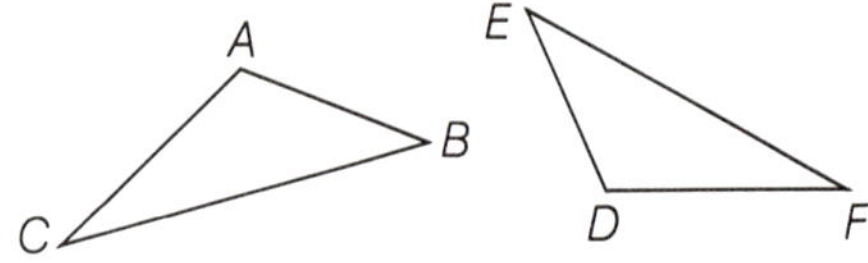

3.

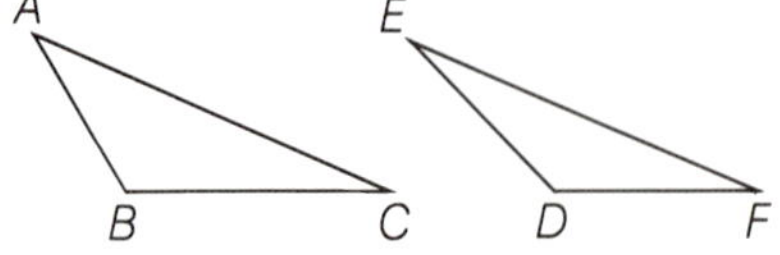

4.

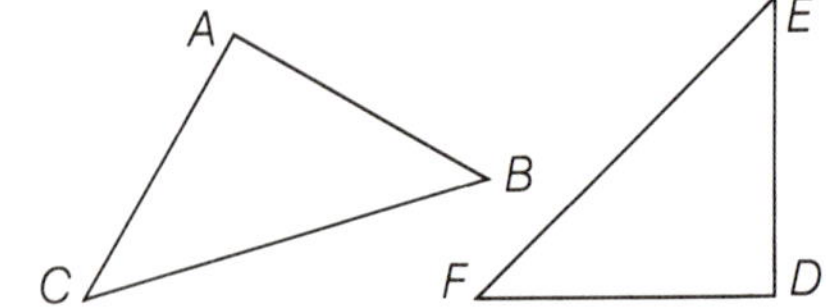

11-10 Practice Solving Problems

Problems

A Solve by writing an equation.

1. This week Lisa worked only 25% of the hours she usually works in a week. She worked 9 hours this week. How many hours does she usually work in a week?

2. Tammy bought 2 tapes for the same price. With a "rebate" of \$1.50, the total cost for both came to \$7.50. What was the original cost for each tape?

3. The length of one side of a rectangular lot is $2\frac{1}{2}$ times as long as the width. How long is each side if the perimeter is 56 m?

4. One angle of a triangular-shaped sign is 45°. The second angle is 2 times the measure of the third angle. What are the measures of the three angles?

B

5. Sally worked at a restaurant for 5 hours on Saturday and earned \$7.50 in tips. The total of her wages and tips was \$31.25. What is her hourly wage?

6. Arnie and Alicia each collected the same number of aluminum cans in a clean-up project. When they turned their cans in, they were told they had collected 25% of the total number of cans brought in that day. Arnie and Alicia each collected 158 cans. What was the total number of cans brought in that day?

7. A child's theater ticket costs 25% less than an adult's ticket. A family paid \$22 for 2 adult's tickets and 1 child's ticket. How much is a child's ticket?

8. The cost to develop film at a store decreases for more than one roll. The second roll costs 10% less than the first roll and the third roll costs 20% less than the first roll. The cost for 3 rolls is \$23.76. What is the cost for 1 roll?

C Extending Thinking Skills

9. Write a word problem that would be solved using the equation $\frac{2}{3}x = 4$.

10. Write a word problem that would be solved using the equation $x - 15 = 120$.

Mixed Review

Solve and check. **11.** $4.5t + 1.9t = 3.2$ **12.** $-16 = 21m + 5$

13. $14x = 4x - 30$ **14.** $r + 63 = 8r$ **15.** $17c + 4c = 84$

11-11 Geometric Constructions

To do a geometric construction, you use only a compass and straightedge. Below are some basic constructions.

Example 1

Construct a copy of $\overline{AB}$.

Solution

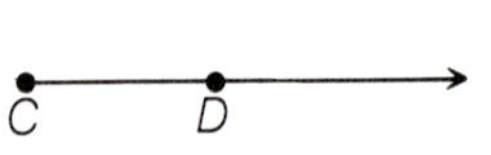

Use a straightedge to draw $\overrightarrow{CD}$.

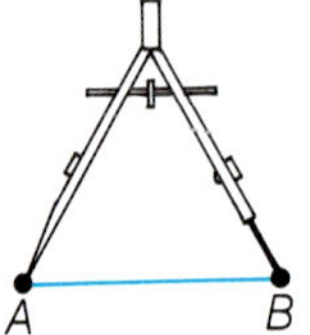

Place the sharp tip of the compass at A and the writing tip at B.

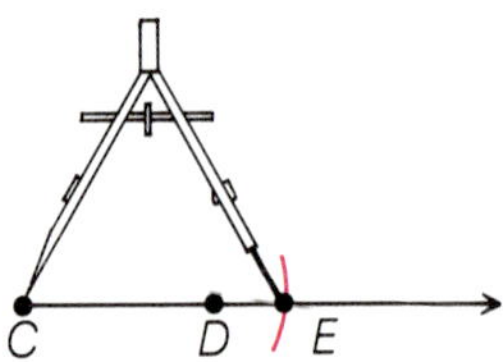

With the same setting, place the sharp tip of the compass at C and draw an arc. Label point E. $\overline{CE} \cong \overline{AB}$.

Practice Draw a segment and construct a copy of the segment.

Example 2

Construct a copy of $\angle ABC$.

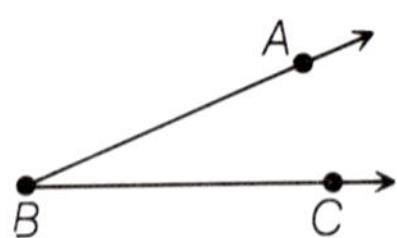

Solution

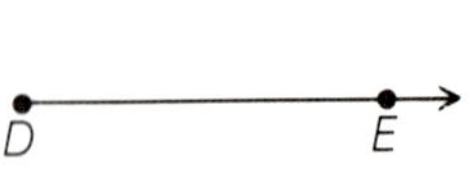

Use a straightedge to draw $\overrightarrow{DE}$.

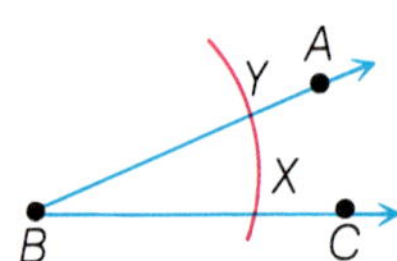

With the sharp tip of the compass at B, draw an arc on $\angle ABC$. Label points X and Y.

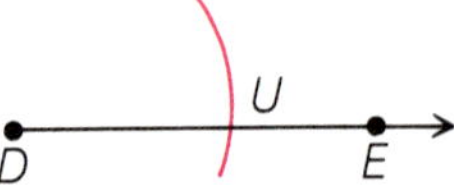

With the same setting, place the sharp tip of the compass at D and draw an arc. Label point U.

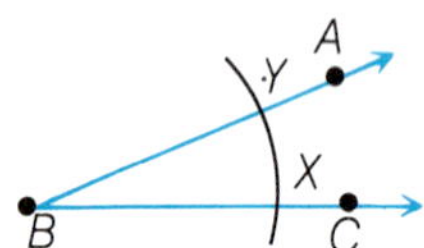

Place the sharp point on X and the writing point on Y.

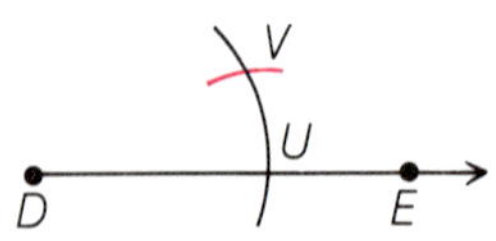

With the same setting, place the sharp point at U and draw an arc. Label point V.

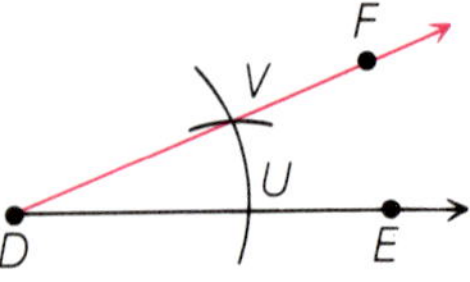

Draw ray DF through point V. $\angle EDF \cong \angle CBA$

Practice Draw an angle and construct a copy of it.

Example 3

Construct a line perpendicular to the given line through point P.

Solution

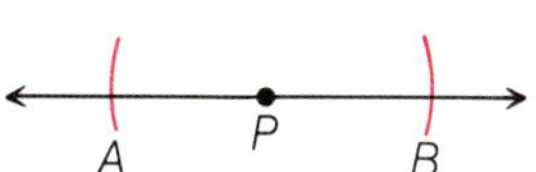

Place the sharp point of the compass at P and draw 2 arcs with the same setting, intersecting the line at A and B.

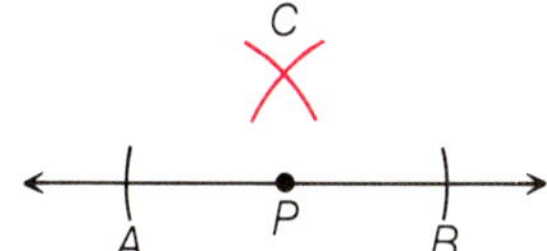

Place the sharp point at A, open it to beyond P, and draw an arc. With the same setting place the sharp point at B and draw an arc intersecting the first arc. Label point C.

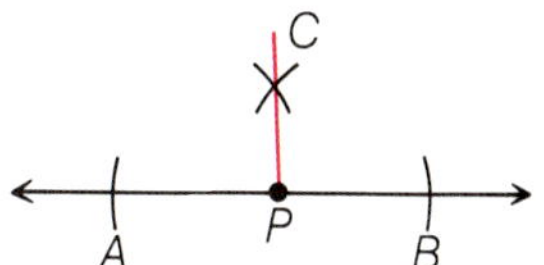

Draw line PC. It is perpendicular to line AB.

Practice Draw a line and locate a point on the line. Construct a line perpendicular to the line through the given point on the line.

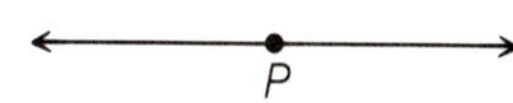

Example 4

Construct a triangle with side lengths a, b, and c.

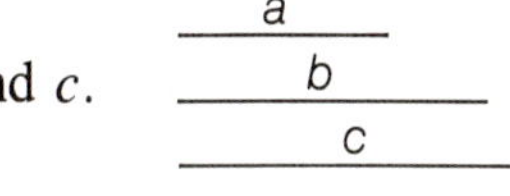

Solution

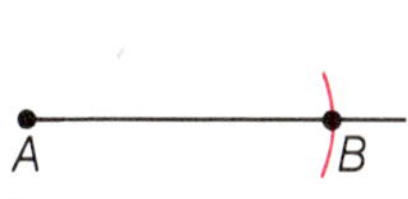

Draw a ray and copy the segment of length b.

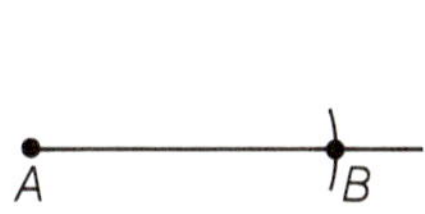

Set the compass opening by length c. Then place the sharp point at A and draw an arc.

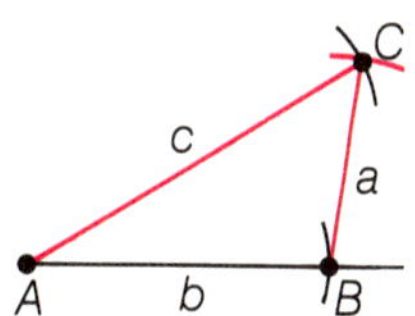

Set the compass opening by length a. Then place the sharp point at B and draw an arc to form point C. Draw segments $\overline{AC}$ and $\overline{BC}$.

Practice Construct an equilateral triangle.

An **angle bisector** is a ray that divides an angle into two congruent angles.

Example 5

Draw an angle ABC and bisect it.

Solution

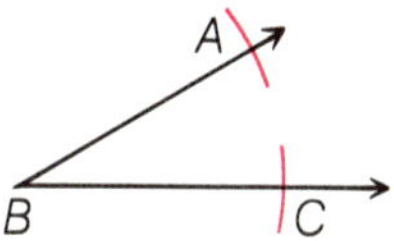

Place the sharp point of the compass at B and draw an arc intersecting the sides of the angle at A and C.

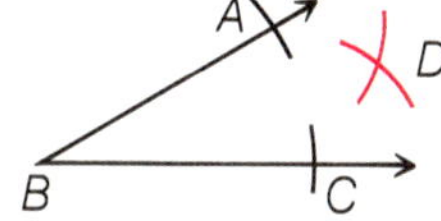

Open the compass more than half the distance from C to A and draw arcs from A and C. Label the point D.

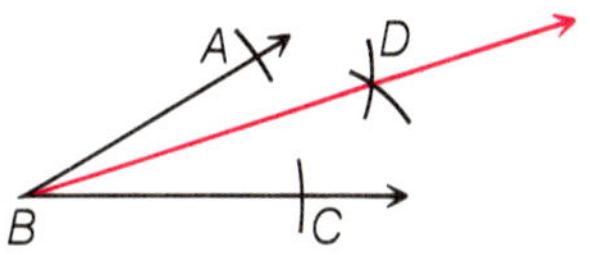

Draw ray $\overrightarrow{BD}$. It is the bisector of the angle.

Practice Construct a right angle and bisect it to form a 45° angle.

Exercises

A Copy the segments and construct a perpendicular at point M.

1. 

2. A M

3. M A

Copy the angle and construct a bisector.

4. 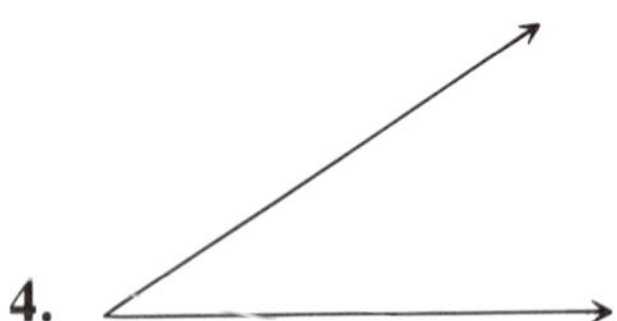

5. 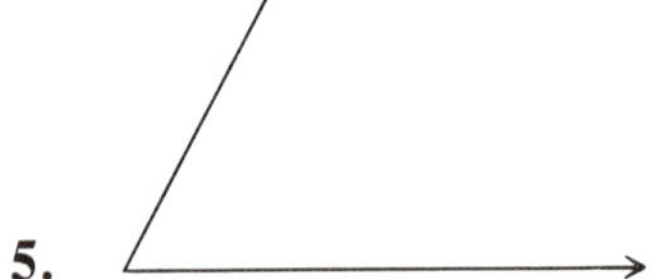

6. 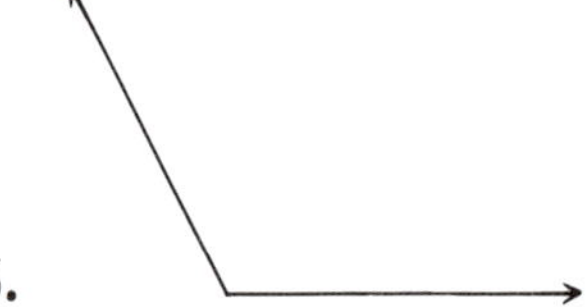

Construct a triangle with sides the lengths of the segments given.

7.

8.

9.

B Construct.

10. a 45° angle

11. a 30° angle

12. a 60° angle

13. a $22\frac{1}{2}°$ angle

14. a 15° angle

15. a $7\frac{1}{2}°$ angle

16. a square

17. an isosceles right triangle

18. a pair of perpendicular lines

C Extending Thinking Skills

19. Draw a circle. Construct points A, B, C, D, E, F on it to make a regular hexagon.

20. Draw a circle. Construct points A, B, C, D, E, F, G, H on it to make a regular octagon.

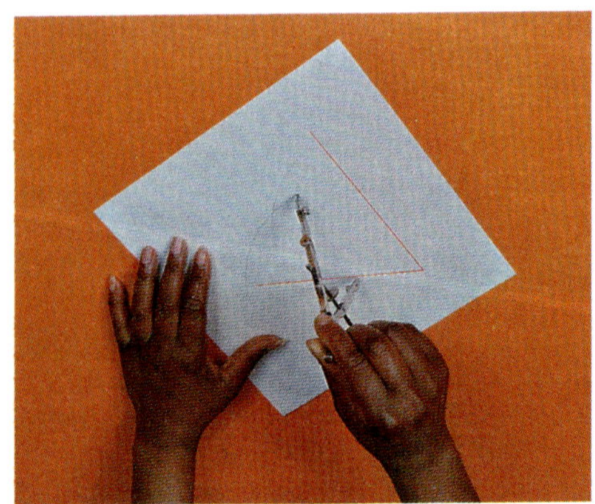

Mixed Review

Solve and check. **21.** $2x + 10 = 4x$

22. $14 - 9x = -4$

23. $36 = 15c - 24$

24. What percent of 90 is 65?

25. 38 is 200% of what number?

11-12 Problems with More than One Answer

Some problems have more than one answer. You need to check solutions carefully to see whether a problem could have other answers. Consider the following.

Problem Some members of the school band were thirsty after a parade. They stood in a circle and passed around 31 cups of lemonade. Each person in order took 1 cup until no cups were left. The tuba player took the first and the last cup. He may have had more. How many band members were in the group?

You could use the **Guess, Check, Revise** strategy to find a solution. You might guess that there were 20 members in the group. When you checked this guess, you would see that if the tuba player took the first cup, the cups would be gone before he could take the last cup. Since about half the number of members as cups would work, you might revise the guess to 15. You could **Draw a Picture** and verify that 15 is an answer.

T(first)
| | | | | | | | | | | | | | | Each of 15 members gets a cup.

T
| | | | | | | | | | | | | | | Each of 15 members gets another cup.

T(last)
| The tuba player gets the last cup. Total: 31 cups.

To be sure your solution is correct, you must check to see whether any other answers are possible. The problem above has several answers. You can **Make a Table** of answers and **Look for a Pattern** to help you describe a solution.

Number of Band Members	2	3	4	5	6	7	8	9	10	. . .	15	. . .	30
Is this a solution?	yes	yes	no	yes	yes	no	no	no	yes	no	yes	no	yes

Any number that is a factor of 30 will work. There could have been 2, 3, 5, 6, 10, 15, or 30 band members in the group.

Problem-Solving Strategies	
Choose the Operations	Write an Equation
Guess, Check, Revise	Simplify the Problem
Draw a Picture	Make an Organized List
Make a Table	Use Logical Reasoning
Look for a Pattern	Work Backwards

This chart shows the strategies presented so far.

Problems

Solve. Check to see whether the problem has more than one answer.

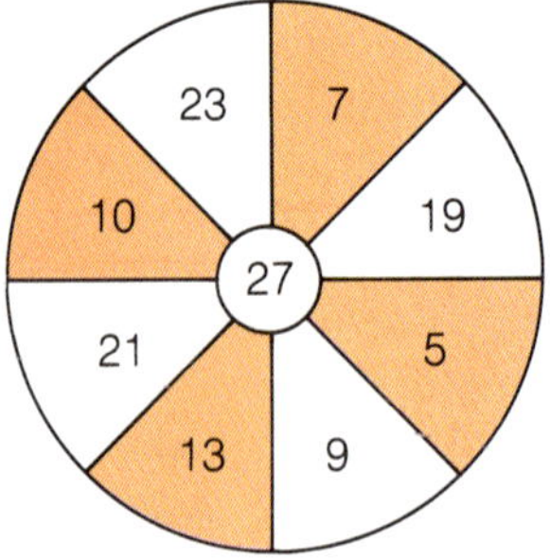

1. In a dart contest, Jennifer hit the dart board with 4 darts. Each dart hit a different number. Her total was 58. Which numbers did she hit?

2. Several pairs of guinea pigs each gave birth to two new pairs (a second generation). Then each of those new pairs gave birth to two new pairs (a third generation). There were 48 pairs of guinea pigs in the fourth generation. How many pairs were in the first generation?

3. A boy asked a girl for her telephone number. She described it as follows: "It contains all the digits 1–7. Each digit is used only once. The 3 numbers in the first part (prefix) are in order from smallest to largest and add up to 14. The numbers in the second part (suffix) are in order from smallest to largest and add up to 14. The number does not begin with 1." Using this information, could he figure out her phone number?

4. Five different-sized singing groups were needed for a musical program. The director formed the first group. Then she doubled the number of people in the first group and added one to make the second group. She doubled the number of people in the second group and added one more to make the third group. She used the same procedure for the fourth and fifth groups. The fifth group had 95 people in it. How many were in the first group?

5. A cashier often gave change for $1 so people could use the soda machine. Just for fun, he tried to find all the ways to do this, using no more than 4 of any coin and no coin smaller than a nickel or bigger than a quarter. How many ways are there?

6. Ned had a higher bowling score than Jane, and Jane had a lower score than Marty. Jeff had a higher score than both Ned and Marty. Dee had a lower score than Marty but a higher score than Ned. Who had the highest score?

Enrichment

Symmetry

A figure has **reflectional symmetry** if, when it is traced and folded in half, one half falls exactly on the other half. The line on which the figure is folded is called **line of symmetry**. A figure has **rotational symmetry** if a tracing of it can be turned, or rotated, around a point less than a full revolution and fall exactly upon itself.

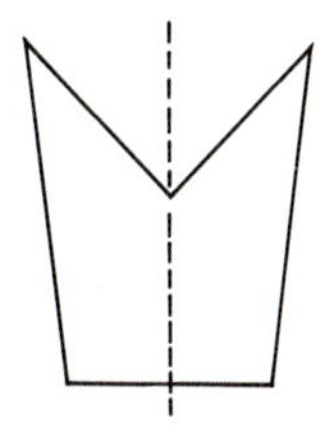

one line of symmetry

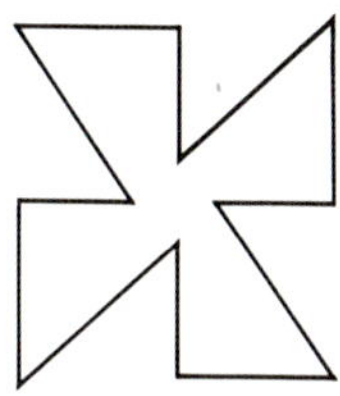

rotational symmetry

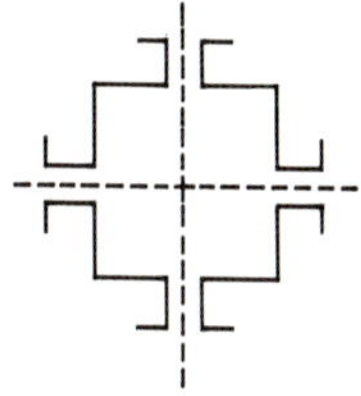

two lines of symmetry and rotational symmetry

Trace each figure and draw all lines of symmetry.

1. 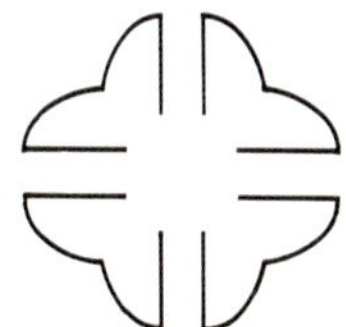

2. 

3. 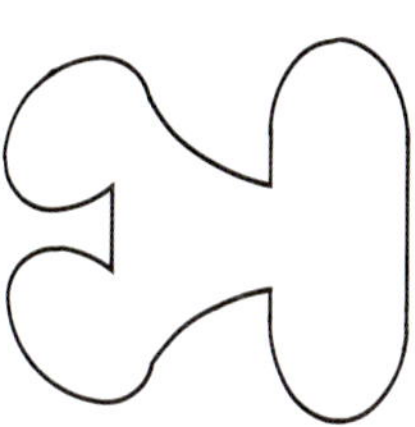

Which figures have rotational symmetry?

4. 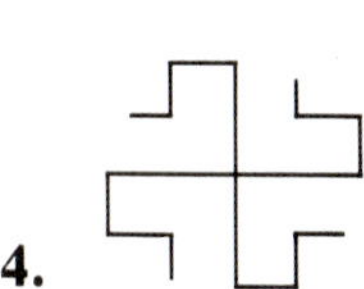

5. 

6. 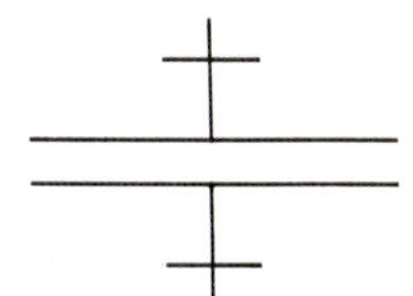

Trace each figure and draw all lines of symmetry. If the figure has rotational symmetry, how many degrees is the smallest rotation that turns the figure onto itself?

7. 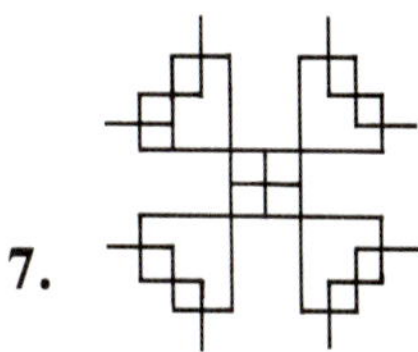

8. 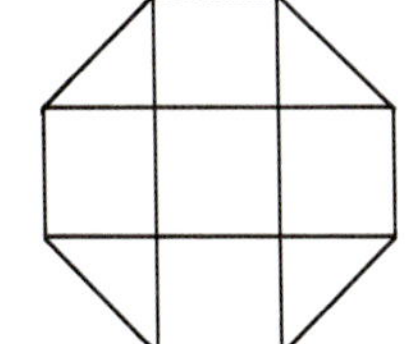

9. 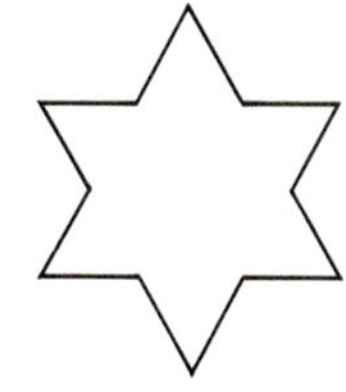

Chapter 11 Review

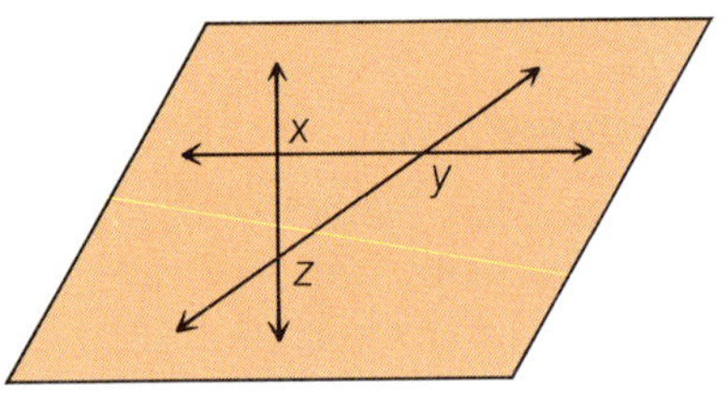

11-1 Refer to the figure for Exercises 1–3.

1. Name a point.
2. Name a line.
3. Name a segment that includes point Z.

11-2 Estimate the length of each segment to the nearest centimeter.

4. $\overline{AB}$ 5. $\overline{AC}$

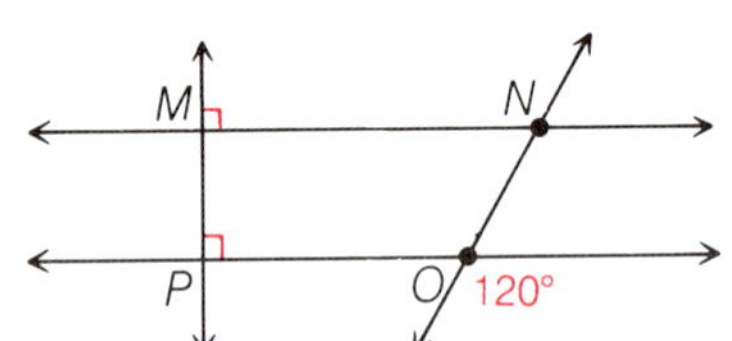

11-3–11-4 Refer to the figure for Exercises 8–11.

6. Name an acute angle.
7. Name an obtuse angle.
8. Find the measure of angle PON.

11-5 Classify each triangle by the measures of its angles and the lengths of its sides.

9. $\triangle RST$ has all 60 degree angles and all sides are equal in length.
10. $\triangle LMN$ has one right angle and two sides equal in length.

11-6 Name the polygon.

11. 

12. 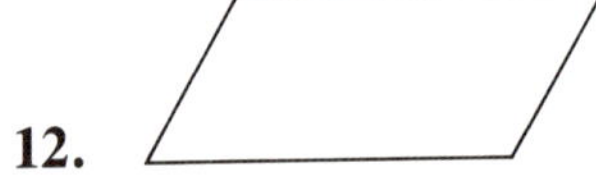

11-7 Solve. Use the formula *Distance* = *rate* × *time*.

13. If a driver averages 50 miles per hour, how long would it take to drive 215 miles?

11-8 Find the circumference of a circle with the given diameter or radius. Use 3.14 for π.

14. diameter = 3.5 m 15. radius = 6 cm

11-9 Use the SAS, SSS, or ASA property to show that the pair of triangles is congruent.

16.

11-10 Solve by writing an equation.

17. Bob and Betty each sold 17 ads for the school paper. Together they sold 40% of the total number of ads in the paper. How many ads were in the paper?

Chapter 11 Test

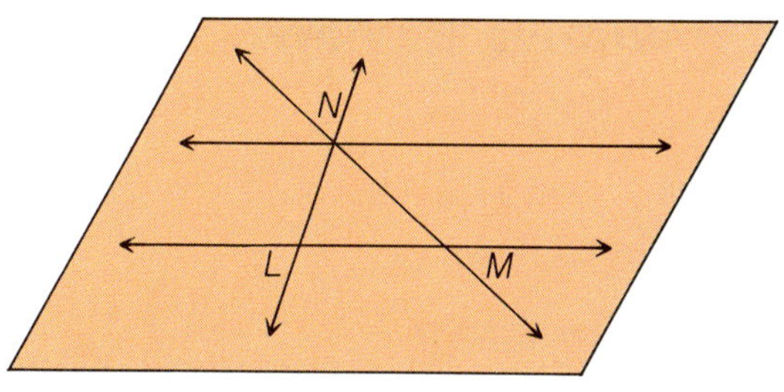

Refer to the figure for Exercises 1–3.

1. Name a point.

2. Name a line.

3. Name a segment that includes point L.

Estimate the length of each segment to the nearest centimeter.

4. $\overline{TU}$ **5.** $\overline{SU}$

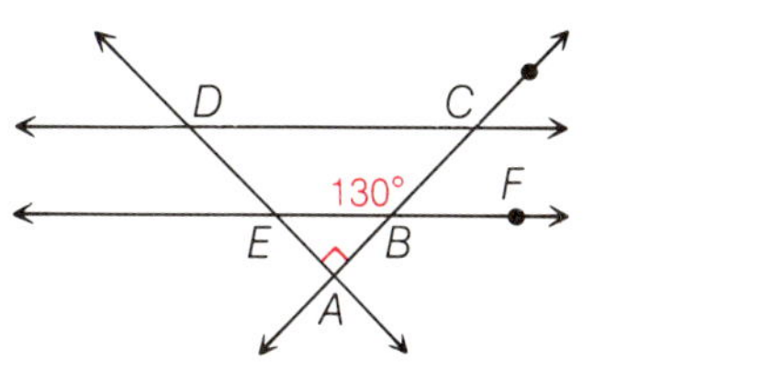

Refer to the figure for Exercises 8–11.

6. Name an acute angle.

7. Name an obtuse angle.

8. Find the measure of $\angle CBF$.

Classify each triangle by the measures of its angles and the lengths of its sides.

9. $\triangle EFG$ has a 90 degree angle and no sides are equal in length.

10. $\triangle VWX$ has an obtuse angle and two sides equal in length.

Name the polygon.

11. 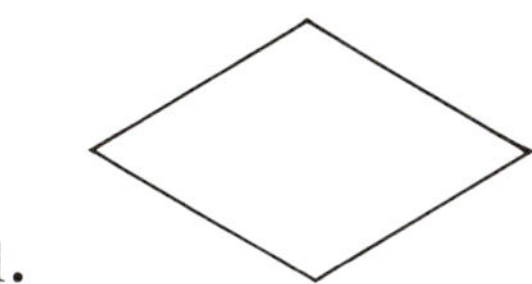

12. 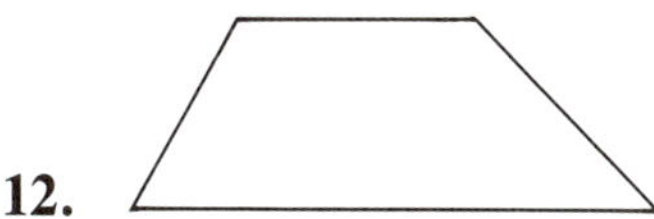

Solve. Use the formula *Distance* = *rate* × *time*.

13. Albert averaged 11 miles per hour on a $3\frac{1}{2}$ hour bicycle ride. How many miles did he ride?

Find the circumference of a circle with the given diameter or radius. Use 3.14 for π.

14. diameter = 7 cm

15. radius = 3.2 m

Use the SAS, SSS, or ASA property to show that the pair of triangles is congruent.

16. 17 cm, 42°, 11 cm 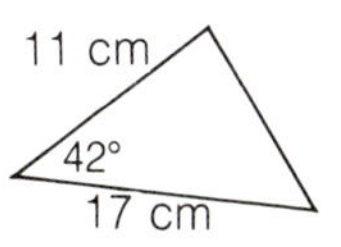

Solve by writing an equation.

17. Sandy attended 65% of the high school basketball games. If she attended 13 games, what was the total number of games played by the basketball team?

Cumulative Review

Solve.

1. $4x - 2 = 2x + 16$
2. $12f = 16f - 16$
3. $25 + 6d = 5d$
4. $30k + 8 = 22k + 24$

Solve each inequality.

5. $7 > p - 6$
6. $6m < -48$
7. $9n - 5n > 20$
8. $\frac{w}{3} - 6 > 12$
9. $1 - 3x < 10$
10. $2x - 3x > -8$

Write each ratio in lowest terms.

11. 7:17
12. 30 to 40
13. $\frac{72}{18}$

Solve. Check your answers.

14. $\frac{a}{35} = \frac{2}{7}$
15. $\frac{7}{8} = \frac{y}{56}$
16. $\frac{2}{3} = \frac{16}{p}$

Solve by using a proportion.

17. The ratio of Amy's height to Rita's height is 11 to 9. Amy is 66 inches tall. How tall is Rita?
18. The ratio of trumpets to trombones in a band is 4 to 3. The band has 16 trumpets. How many trombones does it have?

Simplify each rate using a proportion.

19. 159 km/3 h
20. $600/5 days
21. 192 beats/3 min

Solve.

22. Paul charges $90 for 5 hours of labor. What is his hourly rate?
23. Shari drove 204 miles on 6 gallons of gas. How many miles per gallon did she get?

Solve by using a proportion or writing an equation.

24. 25% of 84
25. 120% of 50
26. 12.5% of 72

Find the percent.

27. What percent of 20 is 9?
28. 25 is what percent of 125?
29. What percent of 96 is 24?
30. 18 out of 120 is what percent?

Find the missing number. Round to the nearest tenth if necessary.

31. 7 is 5% of what number?
32. 80% of what number is 64?
33. 25% of what number is 19?
34. 36 is 75% of what number?

Chapter 12

Area and Volume Formulas

12-1 Area of Rectangles and Parallelograms

The **area** of a region is the number of unit squares needed to cover the region. The unit square used to measure the area of the rectangle below is a square centimeter. Since 15 square centimeters (cm^2) are used to cover the rectangle, its area is 15 cm^2.

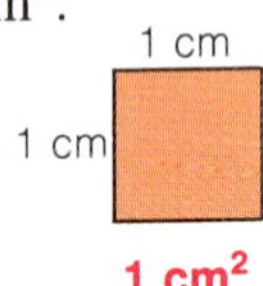

1 cm^2

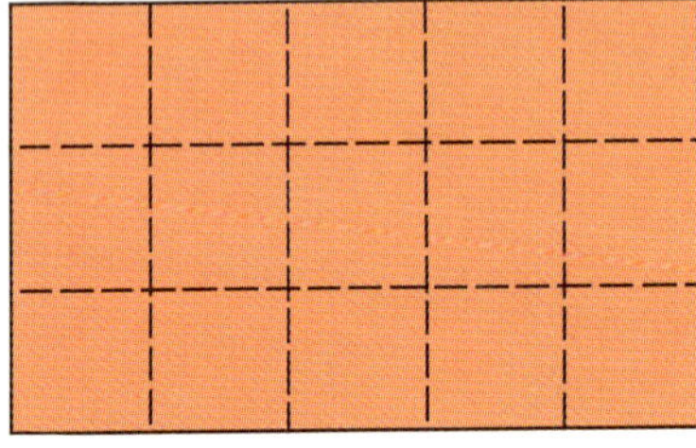

Area = 15 cm^2

In this rectangle, there are 3 rows of 5-unit squares. Note that the product of the length and the width of the rectangle gives its area, $5 \times 3 = 15$, and the area is 15 cm^2. This suggests the following formula for the area of a rectangle.

Formula: Area of a Rectangle

The area of a rectangle is equal to the length times the width.

$A = lw.$

Example 1

Find the area of the rectangle.

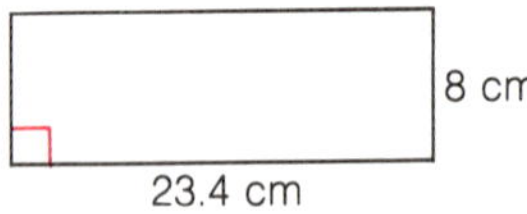

Solution

$A = lw$

$A = 23.4 \times 8$ Replace l with 23.4 and w with 8.

$A = 187.2$ The area is 187.2 cm^2.

Practice Find the area of the rectangle.

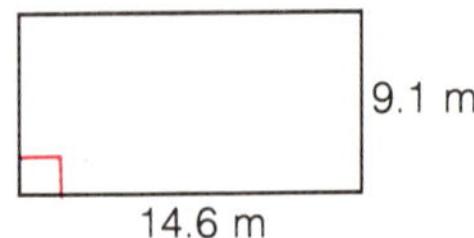

The formula for the area of a parallelogram is similar to that for a rectangle. The length of one side of a parallelogram is called the *base* (b). The perpendicular distance between a pair of parallel bases is called the *height* (h). Any parallelogram can be cut into two pieces and rearranged to form a rectangle. The area of the parallelogram is equal to the area of the resulting rectangle.

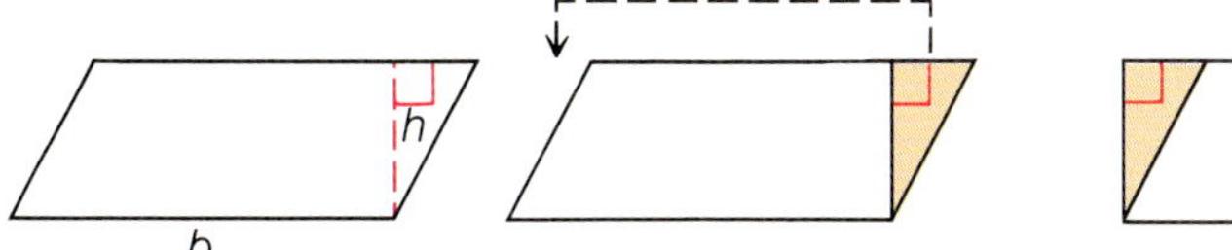

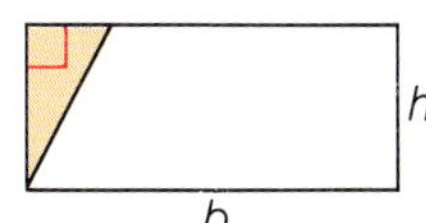

This suggests the following formula.

Formula: Area of a Parallelogram

The area of a parallelogram is equal to the base times the height.

$A = bh$

Example 2

Find the area of the parallelogram.

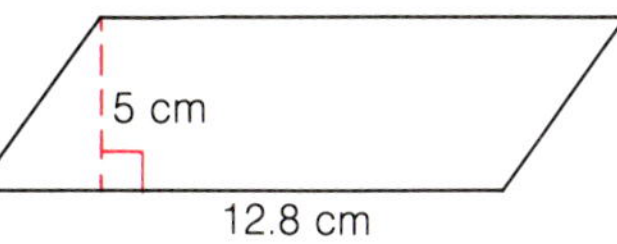

Solution $A = bh$

$A = 12.8 \times 5$ Replace b with 12.8 and h with 5.

$A = 64$ The area is 64 cm^2.

Practice Find the area of a parallelogram with the dimensions given.

a. 24 m long and 9 m high **b.** 48.3 cm long and 51.5 cm high

Oral Exercises

Give the dimensions you would use to find the area.

1.

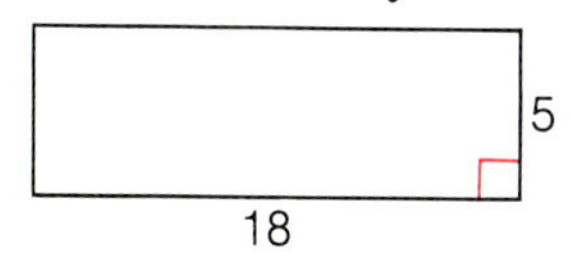

2.

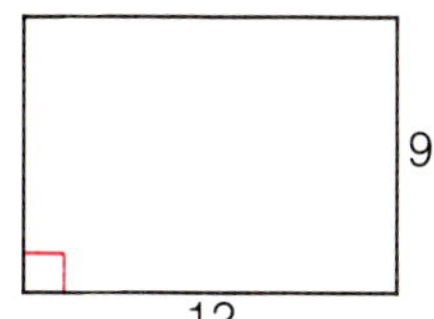

3.

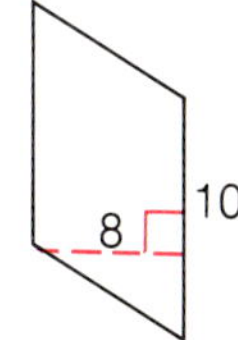

4.

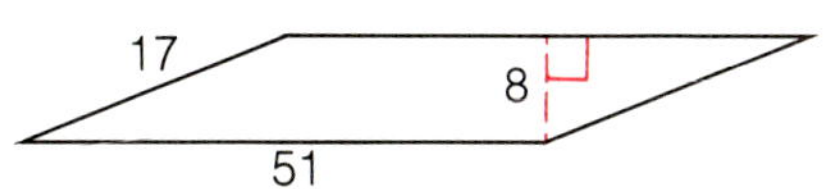

5.

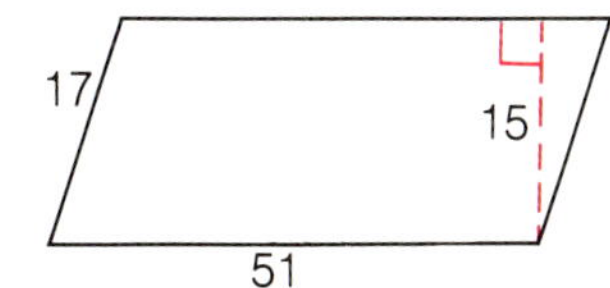

Exercises

A Find the area of each figure. Assume all units are centimeters.

1. 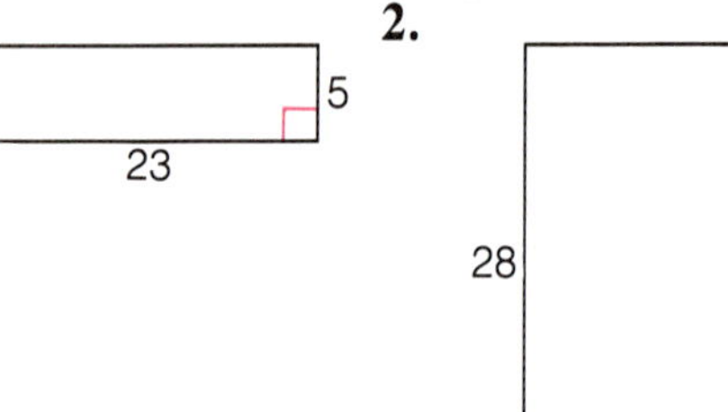

2.

3. 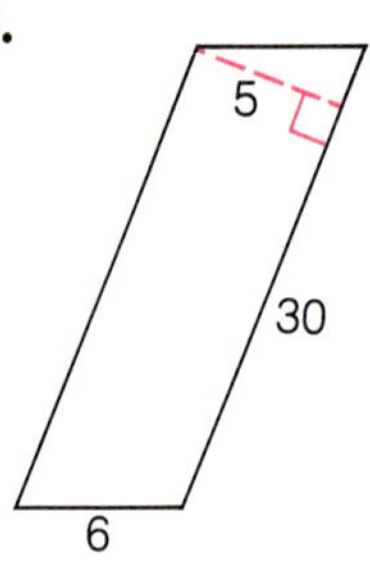

4. 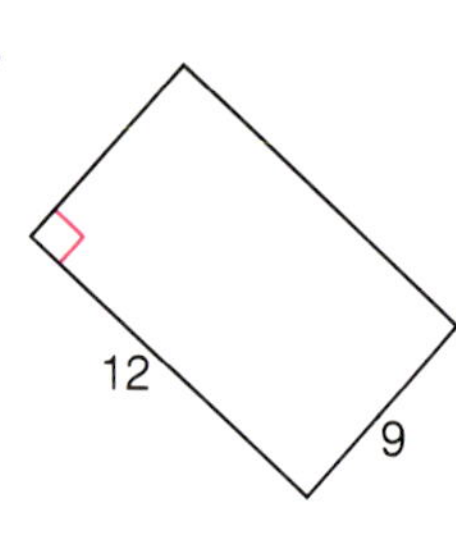

5. 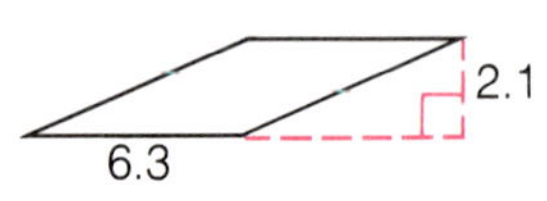

6. 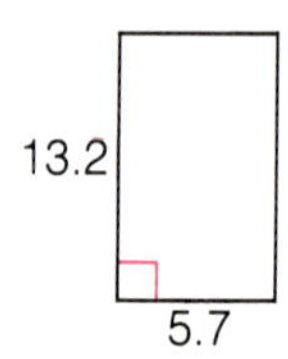

7. 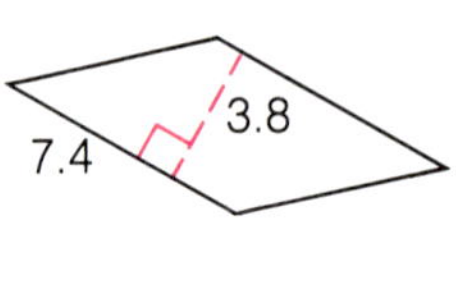

Find the area of a parallelogram with the dimensions given.

8. base = 14.3 cm, height = 5.8 cm

9. base = 123 mm, height = 18 mm

10. base = 1.56 km, height = 0.23 km

11. base = 2.51 m, height = 6.89 m

12. b = 21.3 m, h = 12 m

13. b = 73 cm, h = 14.1 cm

B Find the area of each parallelogram. All units are centimeters.

14. 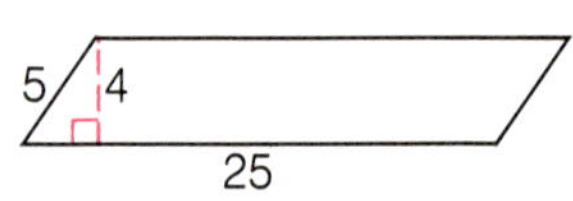

15. 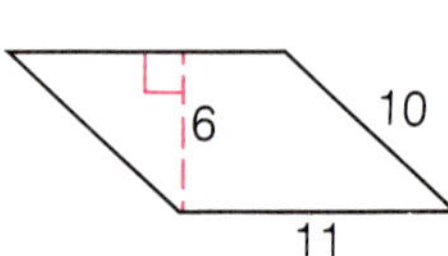

16. 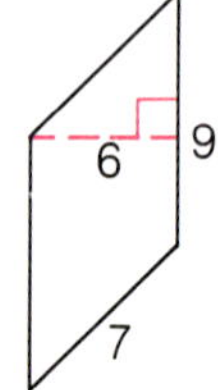

Find the base or height of a parallelogram with the dimensions given.

17. area = 4851 cm^2, height = 21 cm

18. area = 172.2 m^2, base = 12.3 m

19. area = 43.8 m^2, base = 36.5 m

20. area = 24.91 mm^2, height = 5.3 mm

Any unit of length can be converted to a unit of area. The length units inch, foot, and yard become the area units square inch (in^2), square foot (ft^2), and square yard (yd^2). To calculate area, you must use the same unit for length and width. Use the smaller unit in your answer.

21. A rectangle has length of 12.5 in. and width of 0.5 ft. What is its area?

22. A rectangle has area 45 in^2. If its length is 9 inches, what is its width?

23. A gallon of paint covers about 450 ft^2. How many gallons are needed to paint the walls of a room that is 32 ft long, 16 ft wide, and 12 ft high? (The windows and doors take up 33 ft^2.)

24. Carpet costs $18/$yd^2$. What is the cost to carpet a room 12 ft by 16 ft?

C Extending Thinking Skills

25. A rectangle has a length of 25 cm and a perimeter of 70 cm. Find its area.

26. Complete the table to find which rectangle with perimeter 100 has the largest area. What generalization can you make from your answer?

perimeter	100	100	100	100	100	100	100
width	5	10	15	20	?	?	35
length	45	40	?	?	?	?	?
area	225	400	?	?	?	?	?

Mixed Review

Evaluate for $n = -\frac{1}{3}$. **27.** $2n + \frac{1}{2}$ **28.** $\frac{4}{5}n$ **29.** $-6n$ **30.** $\frac{3}{4} - n$

31. 16 is what percent of 24?

32. 28 is what percent of 24?

33. 15 is what percent of 24?

34. 21 is what percent of 24?

CALCULATOR ACTIVITY

You can estimate the area of a square by rounding the length of one side before squaring the length. This gives a different result than you would get if you squared the exact length of one side first and then rounded the answer.

1. Use a calculator to complete this table for finding the area of a square.

Length of side	square, then round		round the side, then square	
23.4	547.56	548	23	529
117.3				
259.2				
98.7				

2. Which method gives the more accurate area?

12-2 Area of Triangles and Trapezoids

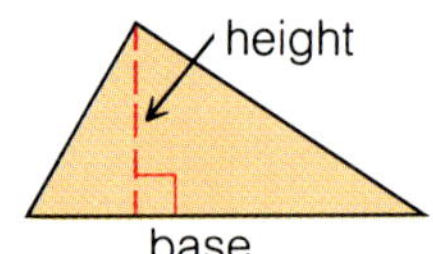

Any side of a triangle can be called a **base.** The **height** is the perpendicular distance from a vertex to the base.

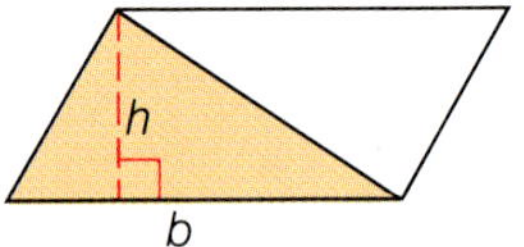

Study the figures at right. Since two congruent triangles can form a parallelogram, the area of the triangle must be one half the area of the parallelogram that has the same base and height.

Formula: Area of Triangle

The area of a triangle is equal to $\frac{1}{2}$ the base times the height.

$$A = \frac{1}{2}bh$$

Since any side of a triangle can be a base, each triangle has three bases and three heights. When calculating the area of a triangle, you must use the correct height for the chosen base.

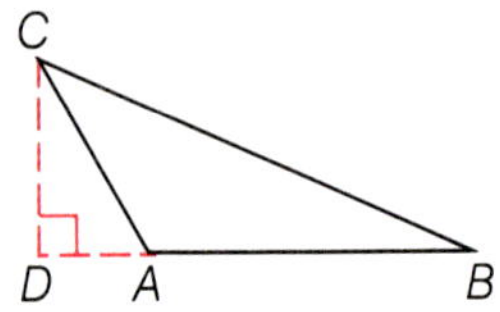

$\overline{AB}$ is a base
$\overline{CD}$ is a height

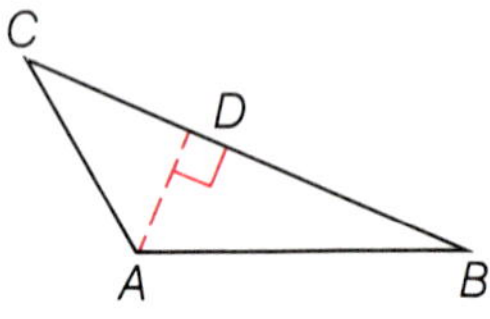

$\overline{BC}$ is a base
$\overline{AD}$ is a height

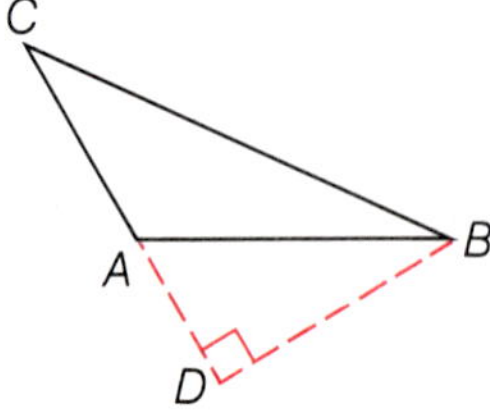

$\overline{AC}$ is a base
$\overline{BD}$ is a height

Example 1

Find the area of the triangle.

Solution $A = \frac{1}{2}bh$

$A = \frac{1}{2}(23 \times 12)$ Replace *b* with 23 and *h* with 12.

$= 138$

The area is 138 cm^2.

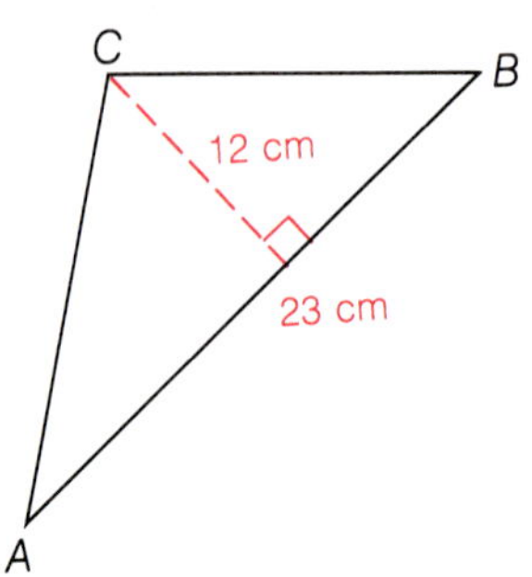

Practice Find the area of each triangle.

a.

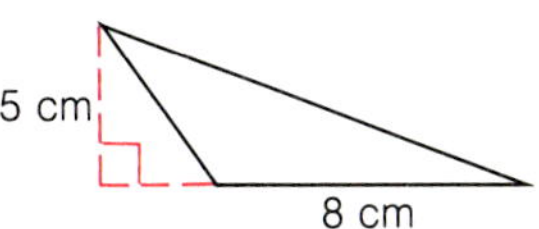

b.

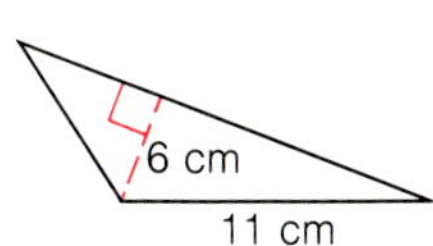

You learned earlier that a trapezoid is a quadrilateral with one pair of parallel sides, called bases. Since two congruent trapezoids can form a parallelogram, the area of one of the trapezoids is one half the area of the resulting parallelogram.

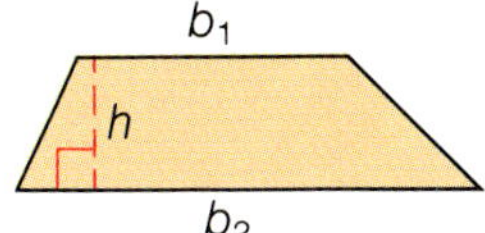

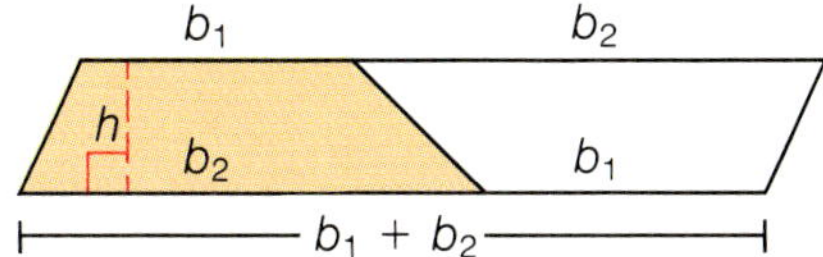

If the bases of the trapezoid have lengths b_1 and b_2, the parallelogram formed has a pair of sides with length $b_1 + b_2$.

Formula: Area of a Trapezoid

The area of a trapezoid is equal to $\frac{1}{2}$ the height times the sum of the bases.

$$A = \frac{1}{2}h(b_1 + b_2)$$

Example 2

Find the area of the trapezoid.

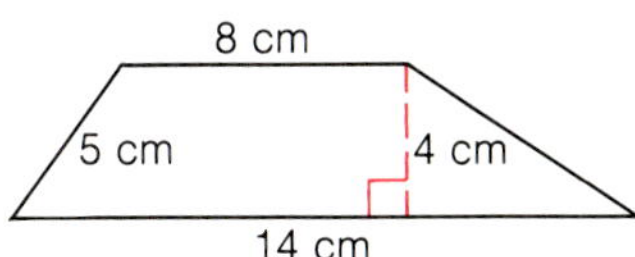

Solution $A = \frac{1}{2}h(b_1 + b_2)$

$A = \frac{1}{2}(4)(8 + 14)$

$= 44$

Notice that 5 is not the height, since the side is not perpendicular to the two bases.

The area is 44 cm^2.

Practice Draw a trapezoid and label it with the lengths given. All units are meters. Find the area.

a. $b_1 = 9$, $b_2 = 23$, $h = 29$ **b.** $b_1 = 5$, $b_2 = 28$, $h = 14$

Oral Exercises

Select the base or height that you could use with the given base or height.

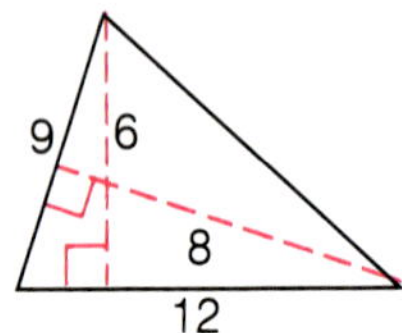

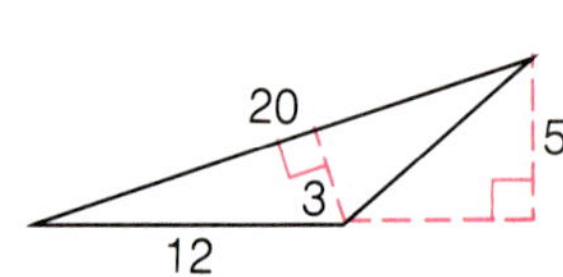

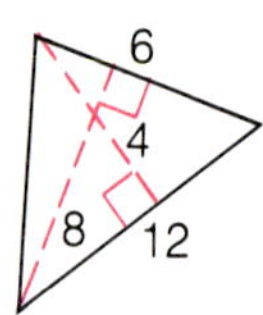

1. base = 12, height = ?
height = 8, base = ?

2. height = 3, base = ?
base = 12, height = ?

3. base = 12, height = ?
base = 6, height = ?

Exercises

Find the area of each triangle. All units are centimeters.

1.

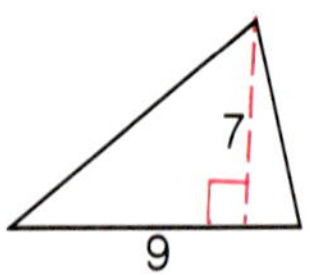

2.

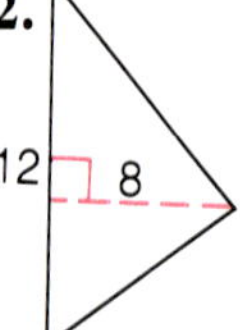

3.

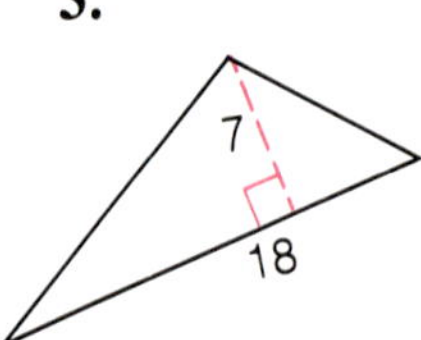

4.

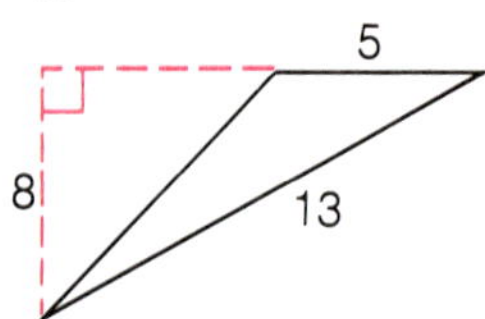

Draw a triangle and label it with the base and height given. Find the area.

5. b = 12 cm; h = 5 cm
6. b = 15 m; h = 8 m
7. b = 5 m; h = 18 m
8. b = 23 m; h = 9 m
9. b = 18 m; h = 2 m
10. b = 34 cm; h = 2 cm
11. b = 15 cm; h = 17 cm
12. b = 40 m; h = 23 m
13. b = 48 cm; h = 73 cm

Find the area of each trapezoid. All units are meters.

14.

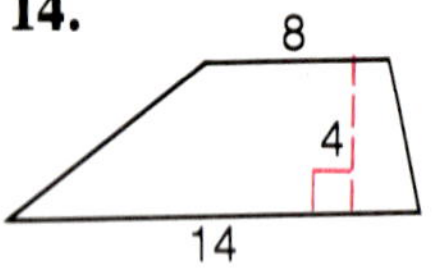

15.

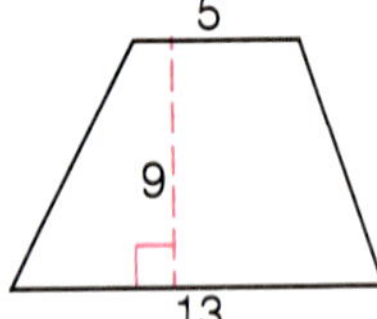

16.

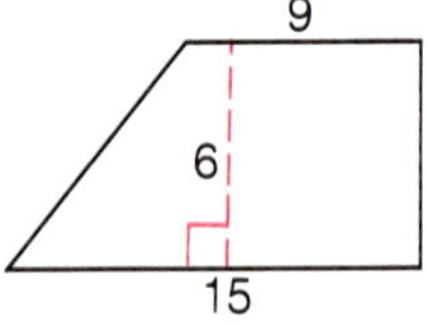

Draw a trapezoid and label it with the lengths given. Find the area.

17. b_1 = 8 cm, b_2 = 15 cm; h = 5 cm
18. b_1 = 9 cm, b_2 = 17 cm; h = 5 cm
19. b_1 = 5 m, b_2 = 8 m; h = 18 m
20. b_1 = 9 cm, b_2 = 16 cm; h = 12 cm
21. b_1 = 4 m, b_2 = 1.2 m; h = 0.23 m
22. b_1 = 24 m, b_2 = 4 m; h = 2 m

B

23. A triangle has area 30 cm^2 and a height of 5 cm. Find the length of the base.

24. A triangle has area 50 m^2 and a base of 20 meters. Find the height.

25. A trapezoid has bases of 15 cm and 48 mm. The area is 79.2 cm^2. Find the height.

26. A trapezoid has nonparallel sides of length 7 cm and 9 cm and a perimeter of 40 cm. One base is twice as long as the other base. Find the lengths of the bases.

C Extending Thinking Skills

27. Use an equilateral triangle as the unit of area to find the pattern. Complete the next three columns of this table. What is the area of an equilateral triangle with side length n?

Side length	1	2	3			
Area	1	4	9			

Mixed Review

Solve and check. **28.** $3.4t + 5.2 = -3.3$ **29.** $3(y + 2) = 3$

30. Evaluate the formula $2a + 3(b + 4)$ for $a = 17$, $b = 9$.

NUMBERS TO ALGEBRA

Replacing variables in a formula with specific numbers can help you see how to solve a formula for one variable in terms of the other variables. The example below shows how to solve the formula $A = \frac{1}{2}bh$ for h by using numbers for a triangle with an area of 45 square units and a base of 9 units.

Numbers		**Algebra**	
$A = \frac{1}{2}bh$		$A = \frac{1}{2}bh$	
$45 = \frac{1}{2}(9)h$	Replace *A* with 45 and *b* with 9.		
$2(45) = 9h$	Multiply both sides by 2.	$2A = bh$	Multiply both sides by 2.
$\frac{2(45)}{9} = h$	Divide both sides by 9 to solve for *h*.	$\frac{2A}{b} = h$	Divide both sides by *b* to solve for *h*.

1. Solve the formula $A = bh$ for h. **2.** Solve the formula $P = 2l + 2w$ for w.

12-3 Area of Circles

A city engineer uses the formula $A = \pi r^2$ to calculate the amount of water that a pipe carries.

The circumference, C, of a circle with radius r is found by using the formula $C = 2\pi r$. This formula is used to develop a formula for the area of a circle.

In the figure below, a circle of radius r has been divided into pie-shaped pieces. The pieces have been rearranged into a parallelogram-like shape. This "parallelogram" has a height r and a base that is about half the circumference of the circle. Therefore, the approximate area is $(\pi r)r$, or πr^2. Since the area of the "parallelogram" would be the same as the area of a circle, the area of the circle is also πr^2.

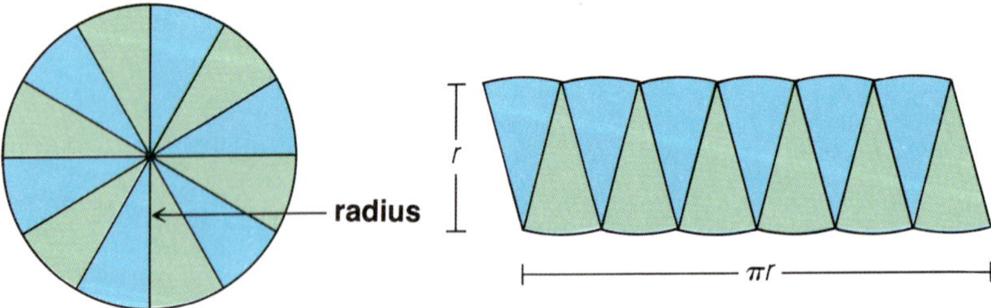

Formula: Area of a Circle

The area of a circle is equal to π times the radius squared.

$$A = \pi r^2$$

Example

Find the area of a circle with radius 5 cm.

Solution $A = \pi r^2$

$\approx (3.14)5^2$ Replace π with 3.14 and r with 5.

$A \approx 78.5$ The area is approximately 78.5 cm^2.

Practice Find the area of the circle. **a.** radius = 3 ft **b.** diameter = 8 m

Oral Exercises

Give the radius and diameter of each figure.

1.

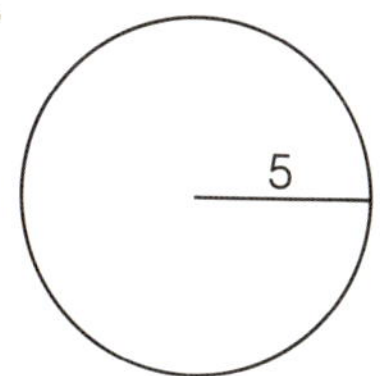

2.

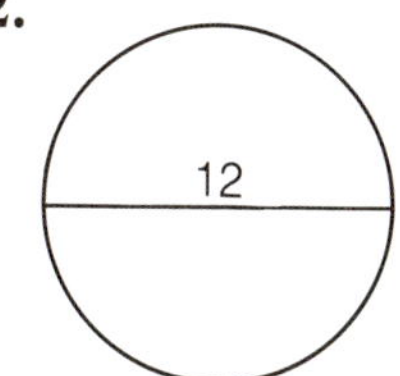

3.

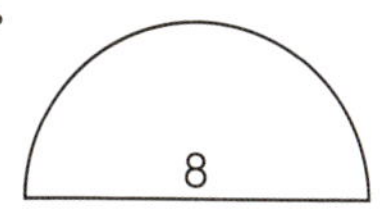

4.

Exercises

A Find the area of each circle. Use 3.14 as an approximation for π.

1. $r = 5$ cm **2.** $r = 8$ cm **3.** $d = 10$ cm **4.** $r = 25$ m

5. $d = 4.8$ cm **6.** $r = 3.9$ m **7.** $d = 500$ m **8.** $r = 250$ cm

9. $r = 50$ cm **10.** $r = 4.8$ m **11.** $d = 3$ m **12.** $d = 12$ mm

B

13. Estimate, then give the area of a microcomputer disk with diameter of:

a. 8 inches **b.** 5 inches **c.** $3\frac{1}{2}$ inches

14. Estimate whether the area of an 8-inch disk is about 2 times, 3 times, 4 times, or 5 times the area of a $3\frac{1}{2}$-inch disk. Check your estimate with a calculation.

Find the area of each shaded region. Express the answer in terms of π. Assume that semicircular regions are half-circles.

15.

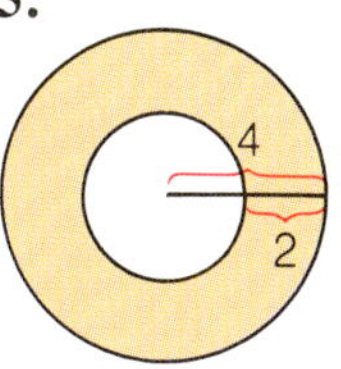

16.

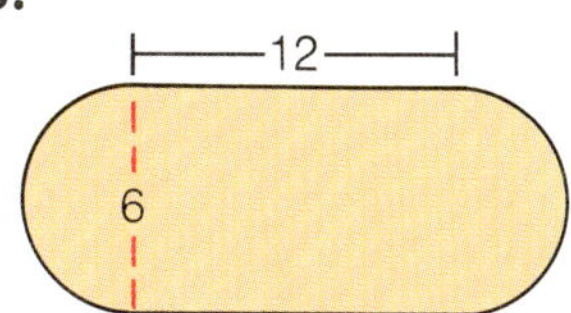

17.

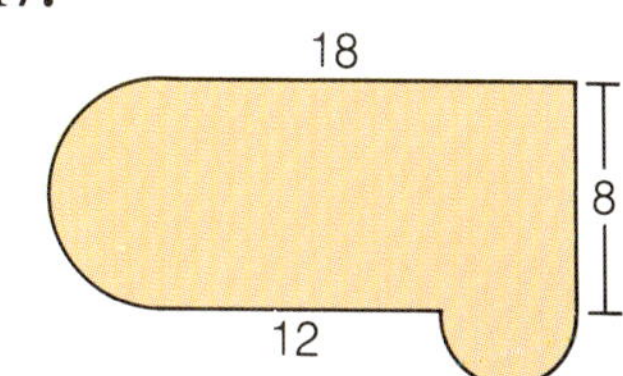

Use a calculator to find the area of the circle in Exercises 18–23.

18. $r = 523.6$ cm **19.** $r = 83.5$ m **20.** $r = 14.2$ cm

21. $d = 25.2$ cm **22.** $d = 4.5$ m **23.** $d = 18.8$ cm

C Extending Thinking Skills

24. Mr. Green divides a square-mile field into quarters with a circular irrigation system on each quarter. Ms. Peabody has one large circular irrigation system. Guess which farmer irrigates the greater percentage of land. Check your guess with a calculation.

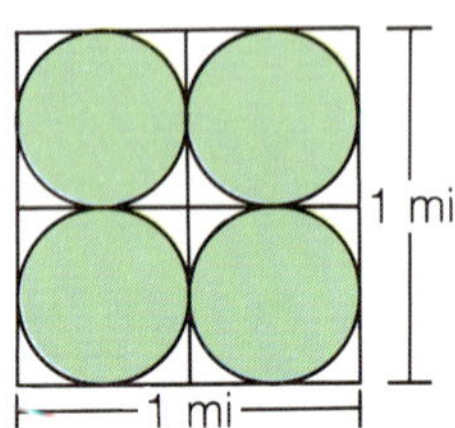

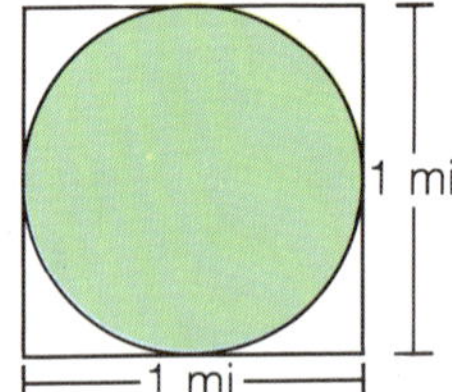

Mixed Review

Solve by writing an equation. Leonetti's Fruit Market is selling apples for 25¢/lb and oranges for 35¢/lb.

25. What is the cost of 3 lbs of apples and 3 lbs of oranges?

26. How many lbs of apples can you buy for $3.50?

Write as a fraction in lowest terms. **27.** 24% **28.** 15% **29.** 11%

Give the least common multiple (LCM). **30.** 2, 3, 4, 8 **31.** 2, 4, 6, 12

Evaluate for $x = 2$, $y = 24$. **32.** x^2y **33.** $3(x - y)$ **34.** $x(y - 1)$

Solve and check. **35.** $1.4 - n = 0.28$ **36.** $4m + 9 = m$ **37.** $6(y + 1) = 6$

ESTIMATION

Estimate the ratio of the area of the smaller circle to the area of the larger circle. Then check your estimate by calculating.

1.

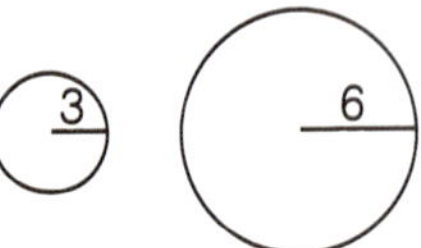

2.

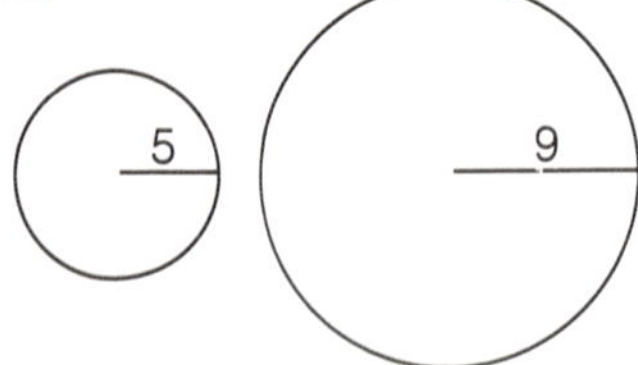

3.

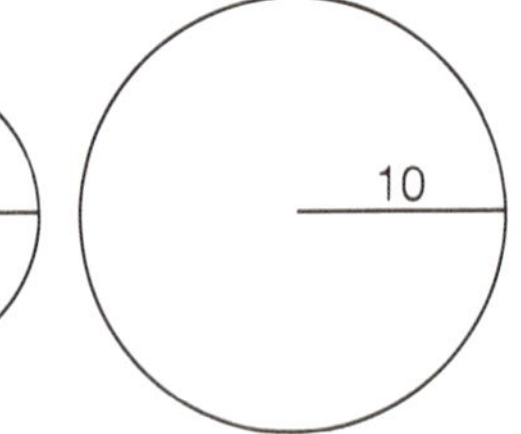

12-4 Area of Figures of Irregular Shape

An architect will often design a floor plan for a house that is irregular in shape. To find the area of such a figure, divide it into smaller regions that have familiar shapes. Find the area of each region and then add the areas together.

Example

Find the area of the figure.

Solution

$A_T = \frac{1}{2}(8)(12 + 17)$ First find the area A_T of the trapezoid, using the formula $\frac{1}{2}h(b_1 + b_2)$.

$= 116$ square units

$A_{SC} = \frac{1}{2}\pi\left(\frac{5}{2}\right)^2$ Next find the area A_{SC} of the semicircle. The area of a semicircle is $\frac{1}{2}$ the area of the whole circle. The radius is $\frac{5}{2}$.

$\approx \frac{25}{8}(3.14) = 9.8125$ square units

$A = A_T + A_{SC} \approx 116 + 9.8125 = 125.8125$ square units.

Practice Find the area of each figure. All units are meters.

a.

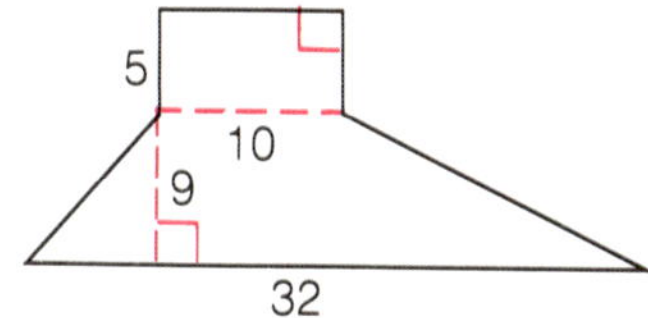

b.

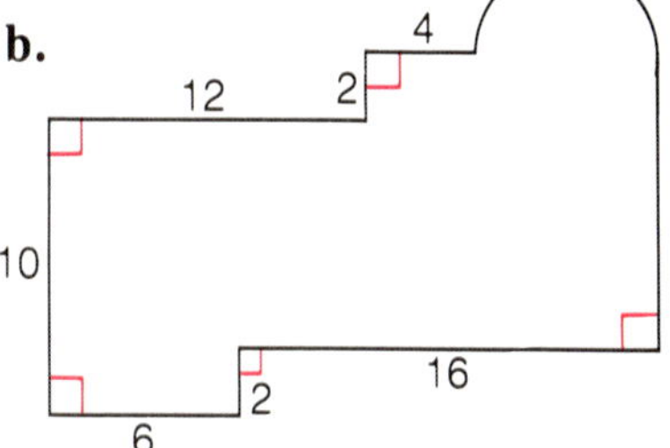

Oral Exercises

First name the shapes into which each figure could be divided. Then find lengths x and y in each figure.

1.

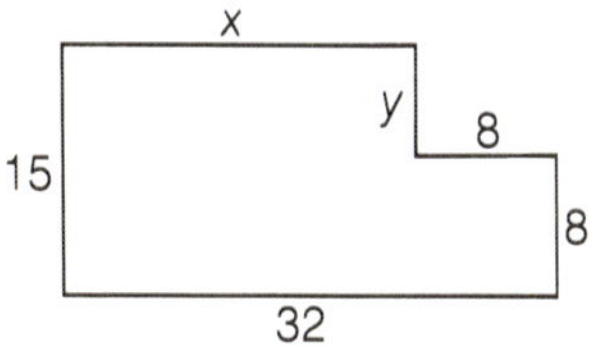

2.

Exercises

A Find the area of each figure. All units are meters.

1.

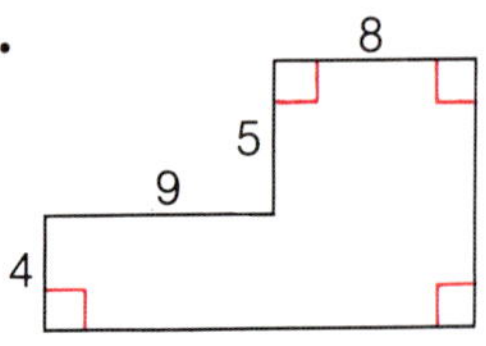

2.

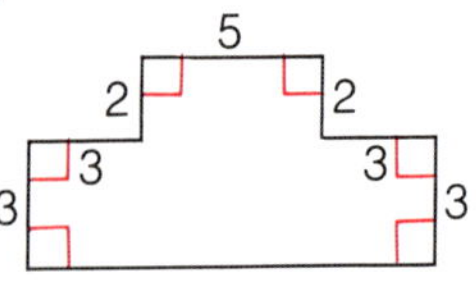

3.

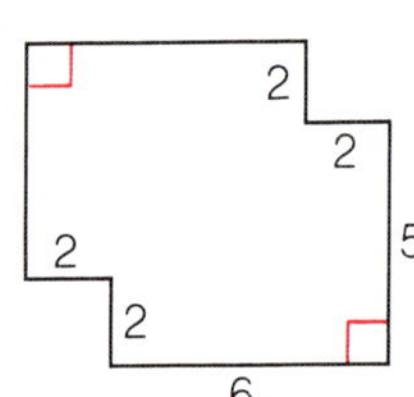

4.

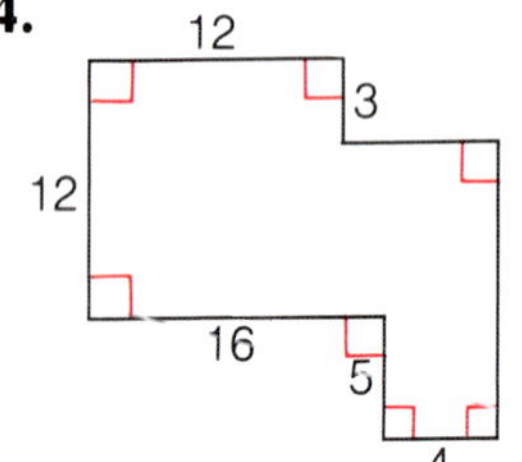

5.

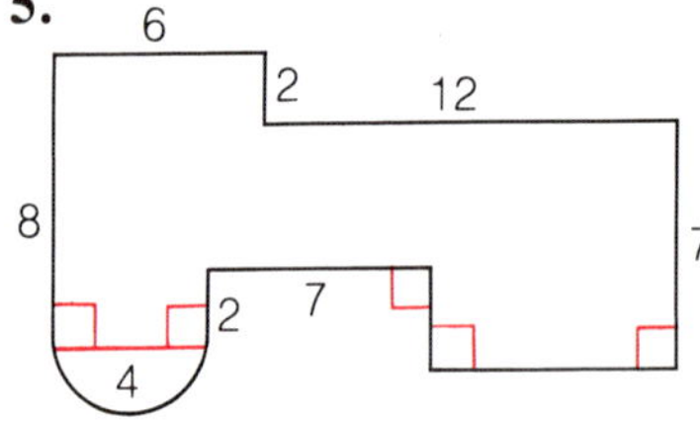

6.

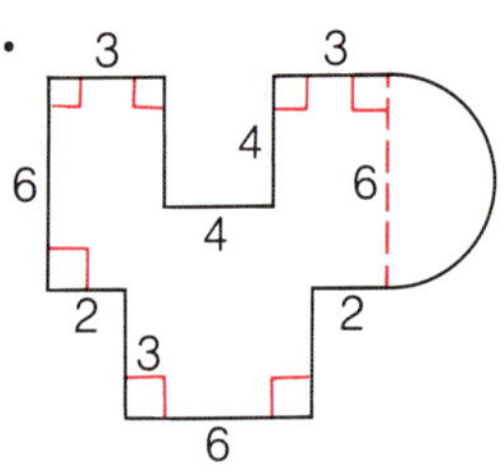

B Find the area of each figure. All units are feet.

7.

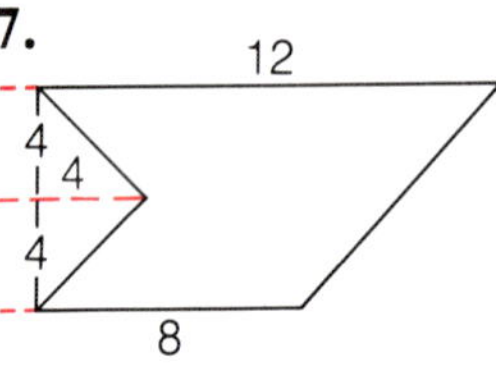

8.

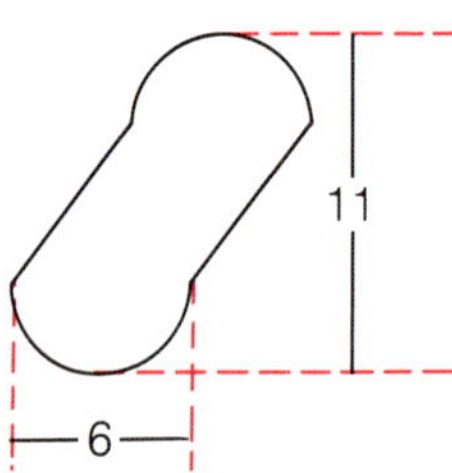

9.

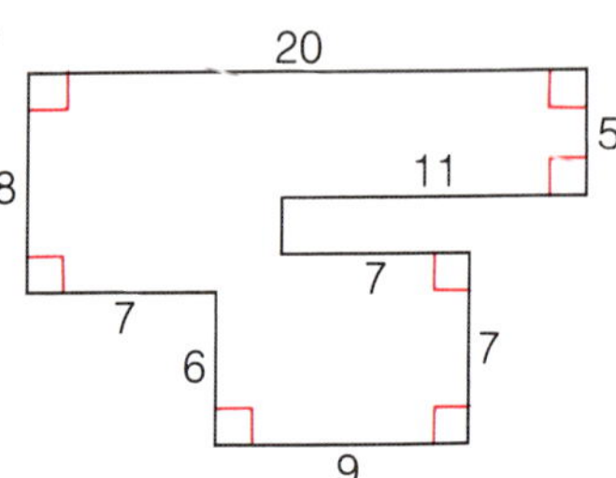

C Extending Thinking Skills

Find the area of each shaded region. All units are meters.

10.

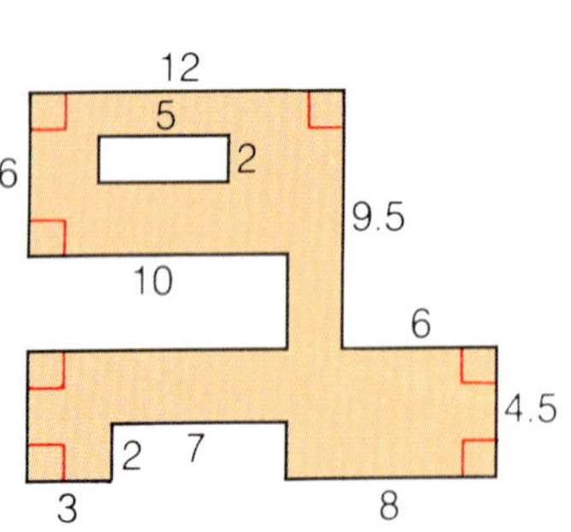

11.

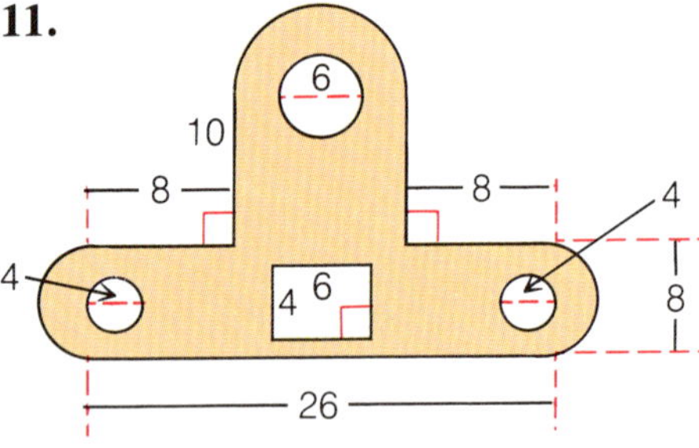

Mixed Review

Write as a decimal. **12.** 16% **13.** 12.5% **14.** 120% **15.** 7%

Solve and check. **16.** $4(2n + 1) = 10$ **17.** $0.3n + 16.5 - 3n = 3$

12-5 Practice Solving Problems

Problems

Solve by writing an equation.

A

1. Joanna broke the old high-jump record, set in 1980, by $1\frac{3}{4}$ in. The new record is 6 ft $5\frac{1}{2}$ in. What was the old record?

2. Mr. Bertolini saved $48 on a tape deck by buying it at 30% off the regular price. What was the regular price of the tape deck?

3. Popcorn costs $0.25 more than a cup of juice. What is the price of each if they cost $1.65 together?

4. Teresa bought 3 pairs of hiking shorts. Each pair cost the same. The sales tax on the 3 pairs of shorts came to $2.25. The total cost, including tax, was $39.75. What was the cost of each pair of shorts?

5. Lynn got a $4 rebate for buying two hair dryers. Each cost the same. The cost for both dryers after the rebate was $21. What was the cost for one?

B

6. Patrick worked 6 hours on Monday and 8 hours on Wednesday. He did not work the rest of the week. A total of $13 was taken out of his paycheck that week for taxes and insurance. His "take home" pay was $39.50. What was his hourly wage?

7. An airline has a holiday special. When 2 people travel together, the cost of the second ticket is $\frac{1}{2}$ the price of a full-fare ticket. Jayne paid a total of $210 for 2 tickets. What was the price of a full-fare ticket?

C Extending Thinking Skills

8. Write a word problem that would be solved using the equation $0.5x + 1.25 = 7.5$.

9. Write a word problem that would be solved using the equation $x + 2x + 3x = 120$.

Mixed Review

Use a proportion to find: **10.** 12% of 20 **11.** 15% of 120 **12.** 110% of 30

Solve and check. **13.** $a + 2.5a = -7$ **14.** $3n < 10 - 2n$

12-6 Volume of Prisms and Cylinders

The **volume** of a solid is the number of cubic units needed to occupy the amount of space the solid occupies. The rectangular solid at right has 8 cubic centimeters in the base layer and a height of 2 layers, making a volume of $8 \times 2 = 16$ cubic centimeters. This is written 16 cm^3.

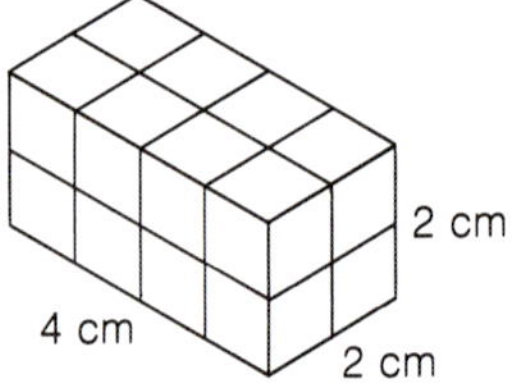

A **prism** is a solid that has a pair of bases that are congruent and parallel; its sides are parallelograms. A prism with triangles as bases is called a triangular prism. A prism with hexagons as bases is called a hexagonal prism.

Formula: Volume of a Prism

The volume of a prism is equal to the area of a base times the height.

$$V = Bh$$

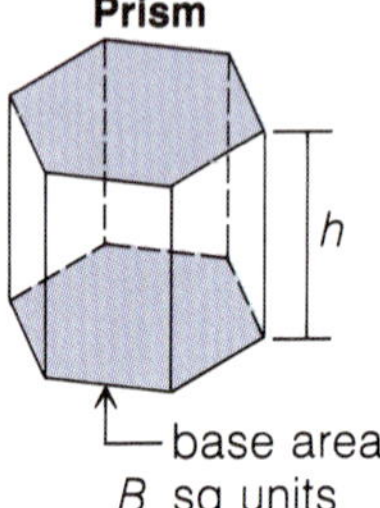

Example 1

Find the volume of the triangular prism.

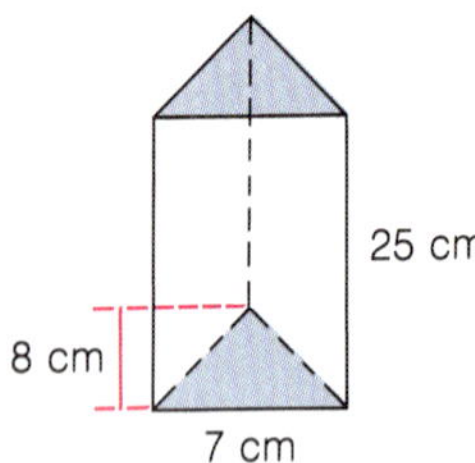

Solution

$V = Bh$

$= \frac{1}{2} \times 7 \times 8 \times 25$ *The bases are triangles.* $B = \frac{1}{2} \times 7 \times 8$.

$V = 700 \text{ cm}^3$

The volume of the prism is 700 cm^3.

Practice Find the volume of the prism at right.

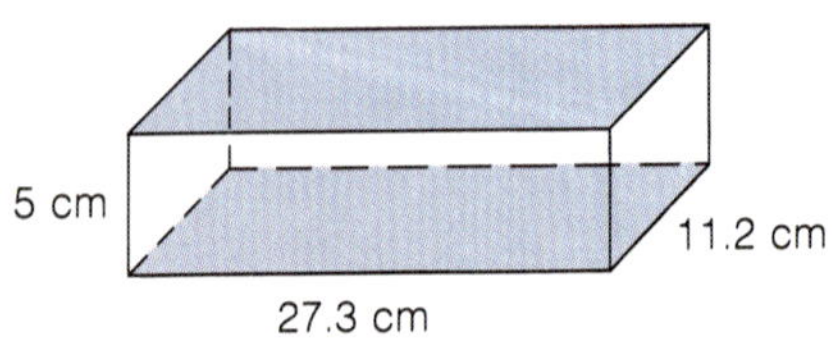

A **cylinder** has a pair of parallel and circular bases with the same radius.

Formula: Volume of a Cylinder

The volume of a cylinder is equal to the area of the base (πr^2) times the height.

$$V = \pi r^2 h$$

Cylinder

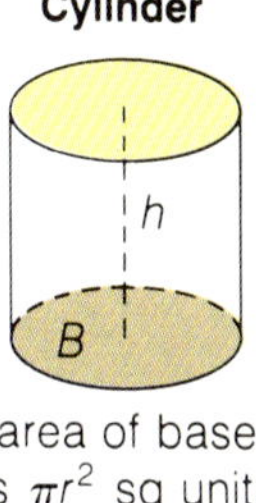

area of base is πr^2 sq units

Example 2

Find the volume of the cylinder at right. Use 3.14 for π.

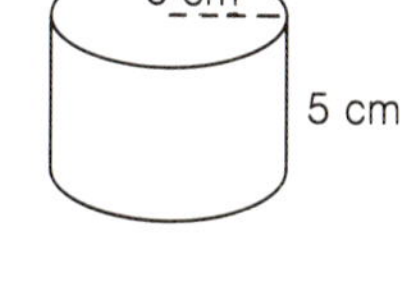

Solution $V = \pi r^2 h$

$\approx (3.14) \times 6^2 \times 5$

$V \approx 565.2$

The volume is approximately 565.2 cm^3.

Practice Find the volume of a cylinder with the dimensions given.

a. $r = 10$ cm, $h = 8$ cm **b.** $r = 5$ cm, $h = 1.8$ cm

Oral Exercises

Give the height of each prism.

1.

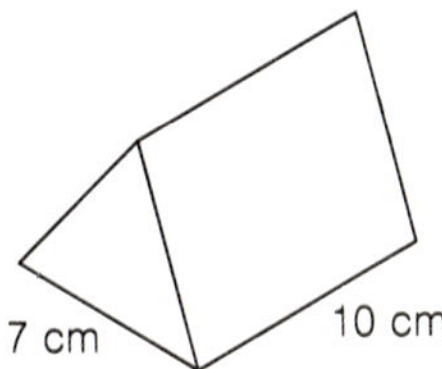

2.

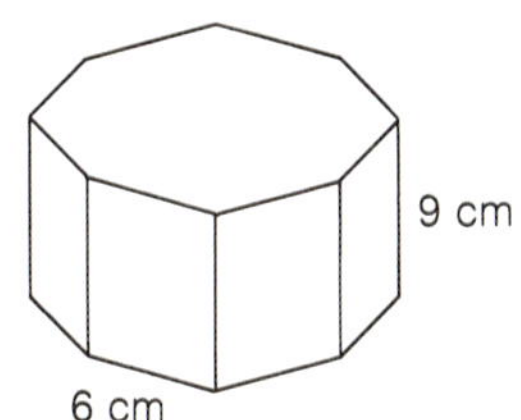

3.

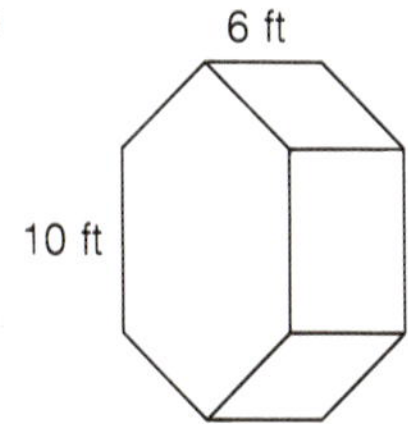

Give the radius and height of each cylinder.

4.

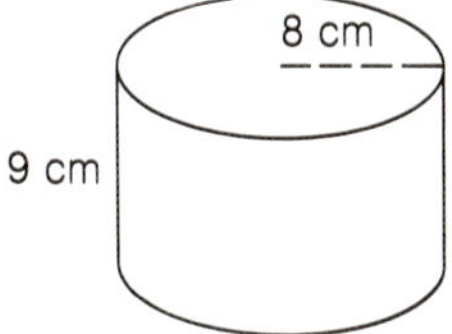

5.

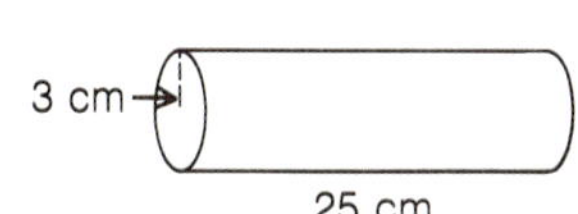

6.

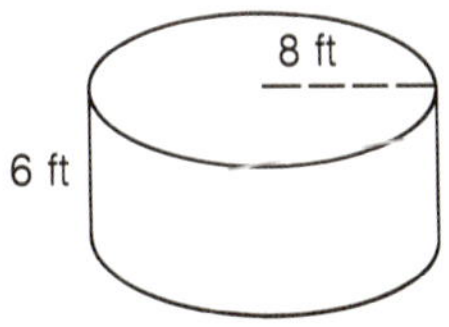

Exercises

A Find the volume of each prism or cylinder. Use 3.14 for π.

1.

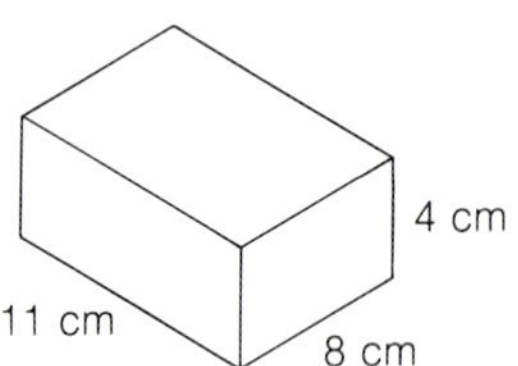

2.

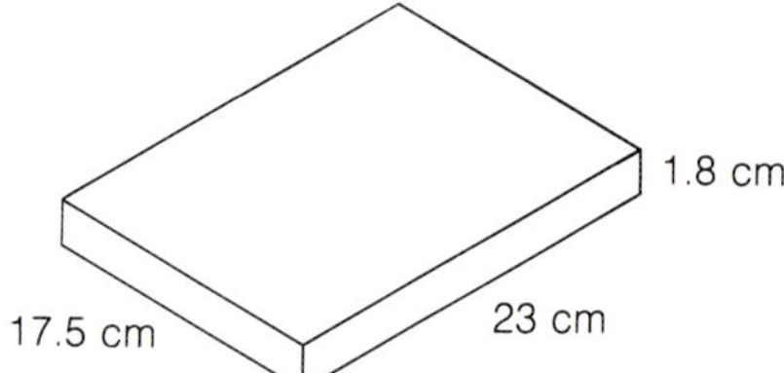

3.

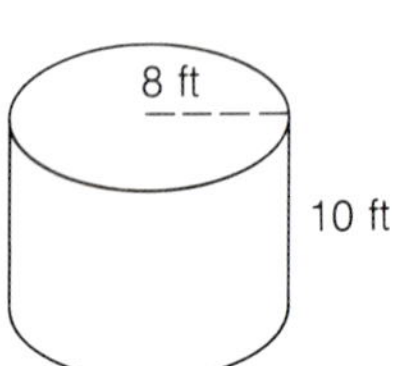

4.

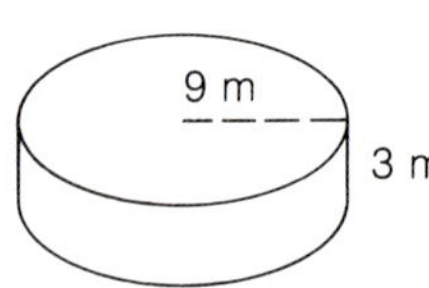

5. $B = 25 \text{ cm}^2$
$h = 12 \text{ cm}$

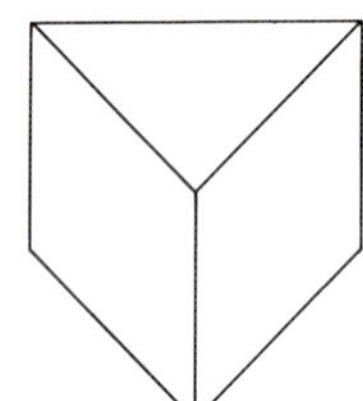

6. $B = 192 \text{ in}^2$
$h = 24 \text{ in}$

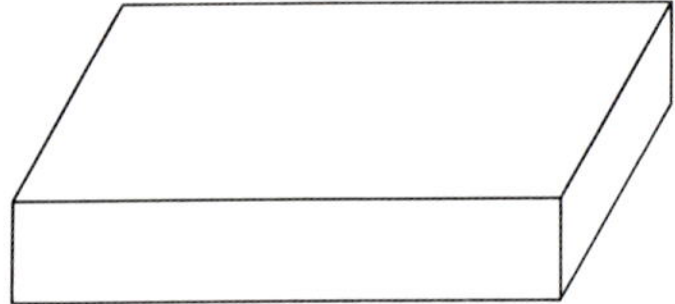

7. $B = 126 \text{ ft}^2$
$h = 4 \text{ ft}$

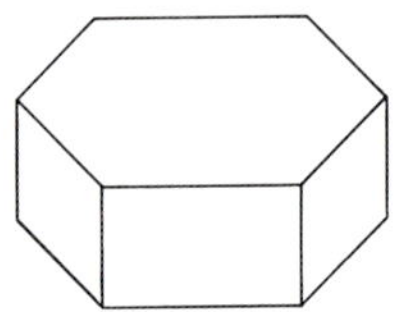

B For Exercises 8–19, be sure to use consistent units when computing. Express the answer in the smaller unit. Use the formula $V = lwh$ to find the volume of a rectangular prism with the dimensions given.

8. $l = 5$ m, $w = 12$ cm, $h = 18$ cm

9. $l = 25$ cm, $w = 8$ dm, $h = 36$ cm

10. $l = 23.4$ cm, $w = 12.3$ cm, $h = 12.6$ cm

11. $l = 7$ m, $w = 2.3$ m, $h = 1.8$ m

Find the volume of a cylinder with the dimensions given. Use 3.14 for π.

12. $r = 12$ cm, $h = 8$ cm

13. $r = 11$ m, $h = 19$ m

14. $r = 2$ m, $h = 3$ m

15. $r = 4$ dm, $h = 12$ dm

16. $r = 2.4$ cm, $h = 3.1$ cm

17. $r = 56$ cm, $h = 2$ m

18. $r = 8$ m, $h = 40$ cm

19. $r = 3$ cm, $h = 2$ dm

20. Find the base area of a cylinder with volume 500 cm^3 and height 5 cm.

21. Find the height of a prism with volume 125 m^3 and a base area of 5 m^2.

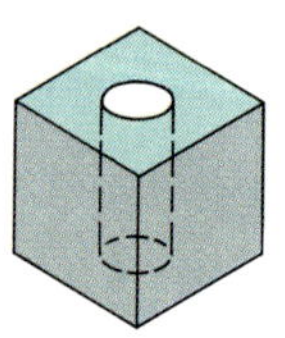

22. A cylindrical hole with radius 4 cm is cut through a solid cube whose edges are 10 cm long. What is the total volume of this solid?

C Extending Thinking Skills

Mentally count unit cubes to find the volume of each figure. The hidden back view of each looks like the corner of a box.

23.

24.

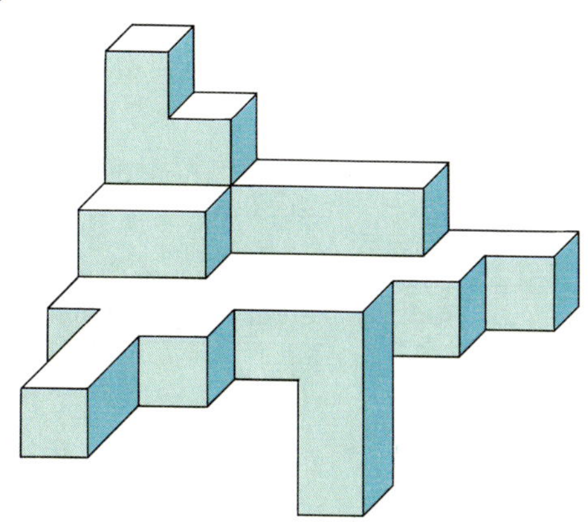

Mixed Review

Give the greatest common factor (GCF). **25.** 18, 42, 90 **26.** 15, 72, 111

Write as a decimal. **27.** $3\frac{4}{5}$ **28.** $-1\frac{3}{4}$ **29.** $\frac{15}{12}$ **30.** $\frac{1}{3}$

Write as a percent. **31.** $\frac{16}{5}$ **32.** $\frac{24}{8}$ **33.** $-\frac{3}{4}$ **34.** $\frac{7}{10}$

Solve and check. **35.** $30 = 5(x - 2)$ **36.** $9 = 2.5 + y$ **37.** $3t + 0.25 = 1$

Reduce. **38.** $\frac{9}{6}$ **39.** $\frac{35}{7}$ **40.** $\frac{16}{64}$

ESTIMATION

Estimate the volume of each cylinder by rounding π down to 3 and rounding r^2 or h up. For example, for a cylinder with $r = 7$ and $h = 10$, volume $= \pi r^2 h \approx 3 \times 50 \times 10 = 1500$. Estimated volume: 1500 cubic units.

1.

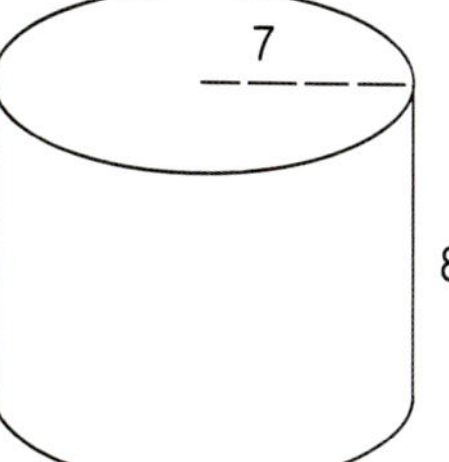

2.

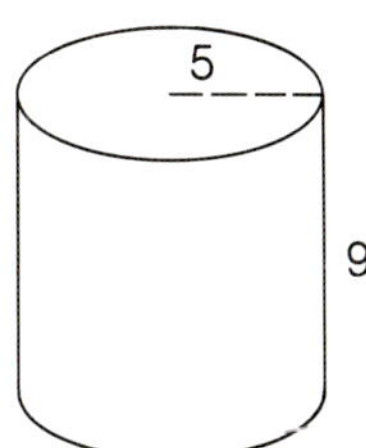

3.

3

7

12-7 Building a House

The table below gives costs of some building materials and services for building a house.

Building Materials and Services	
Item	**Cost**
Excavation	\$ 1.30/cubic yard
Carpet	12.00/square yard
Concrete	45.00/cubic yard
Wallpaper	18.00/roll
Roofing plywood	8.85 per 4 × 8 foot sheet

To find costs for materials and services, you need to find the area or volume of the space being built. You may need to change the units of a dimension to make them consistent.

Example

How many cubic yards of concrete are needed to pour a floor 81 feet long, 42 feet wide, and 4 inches thick?

Solution $V = lwh$

$= 81 \times 42 \times \frac{1}{3}\ \text{ft}^3$ — Express 4 inches as $\frac{1}{3}$ foot. Replace the l with 81, w with 42, and h with $\frac{1}{3}$.

$= 1{,}134\ \text{ft}^3$

$= \frac{1{,}134}{27}\ \text{yd}^3$ — There are 27 ft^3 in one yd^3. To change cubic feet into cubic yards, divide by 27.

$= 42\ \text{yd}^3$

The volume is 42 yd^3.

Problems

Use the data in the table above to solve.

1. An excavator digs a hole 34 feet by 120 feet by 4 feet for the foundation of a building. How many cubic yards of earth are moved? What is the cost?

2. What is the cost for a concrete floor 56 ft long, 40 ft wide, and 4 inches thick?

3. How many cubic yards of concrete are needed for a wall 48 inches high, 125 feet long and 10 inches thick? How much will the concrete cost?

Use this figure for Exercises 4 and 5.

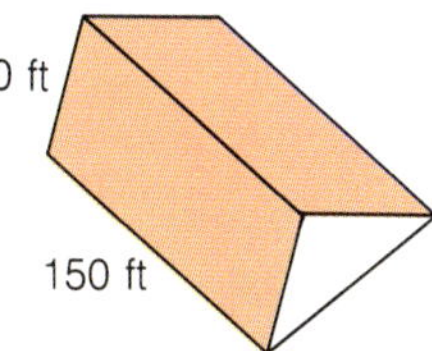

4. A roof is 40 feet from edge to peak and 150 feet long. What is the area of the roof (the shaded region on both sides)?

5. How much will the plywood for the roof in Problem 4 cost?

6. Wallpaper comes in rolls 20 inches wide and 24 feet long. How much will the wallpaper cost for a wall 8 feet high by 12 feet wide? The wall has no windows or doors.

7. Estimate the cost of carpeting a two-story house with a rectangular foundation that measures 30 feet by 42 feet.

8. *Data Search* Find the cost of a gallon of interior paint at a store near your school. Estimate the cost of the paint needed for two coats of paint on the walls of your classroom.

What's Your Decision?

The Malone family wants to carpet a room that is shaped as shown. The carpet salesman says they need to order 30 square yards. At $12/yd this would cost them $360. They find a pre-cut carpet piece that is 12 ft by 19 ft for $250. Should the Malones buy the pre-cut piece and save $110, or order the 30 square yards? Why?

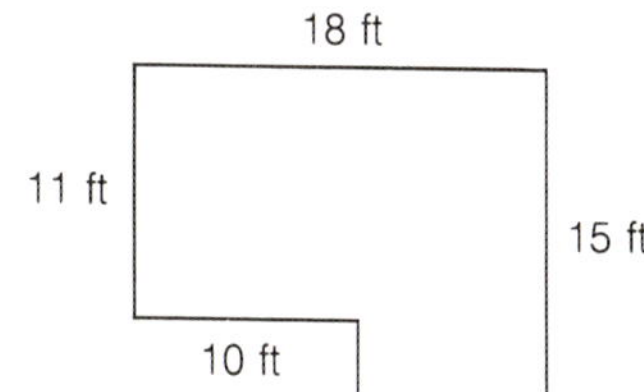

12-8 Volume of Pyramids and Cones

A **pyramid** has a polygon as a base and triangular sides. A **cone** has one circular base. The height of a pyramid or a cone is the perpendicular distance from its vertex to its base.

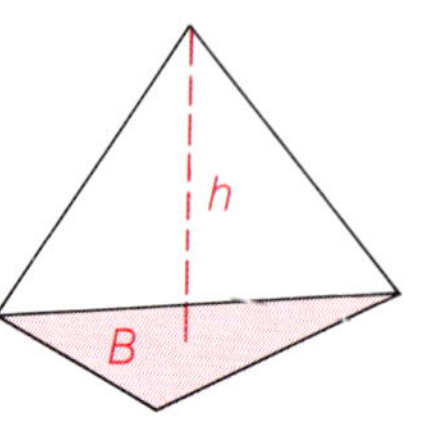

Pyramid

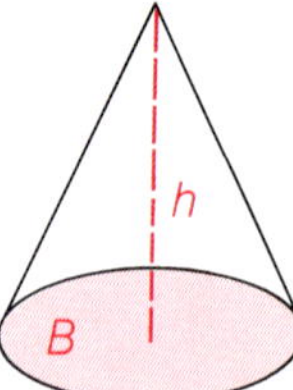

Cone

The volume of a cone or a pyramid can be found by the same formula.

Formula: Volume of a Pyramid or Cone

The volume of a pyramid or a cone is equal to one-third the area of the base times the height.

$$V = \frac{1}{3}Bh$$

Example

Find the volume of a cone with radius 4 cm and height 8 cm.

Solution $V = \frac{1}{3}Bh$ — The volume of a cone is $\frac{1}{3}$ the area of the base times the height.

$\approx \frac{1}{3} \times 3.14 \times 4^2 \times 8$ — The area of the base is πr^2. Substitute 3.14 for π and 4 for r. Substitute 8 for h.

$= \frac{401.92}{3}$

$= 133.97$

The volume is 133.97 cm^3.

Practice Find the volume of a pyramid or cone with the base area or radius and the height given.

a. $B = 27 \text{ cm}^2$, $h = 22$ cm

b. $r = 6$ m, $h = 5$ m

Oral Exercises

Is the statement true or false?

1. A cube is a pyramid.
2. The volume of a cone is $\frac{1}{3}$ the area of the base times the height.
3. Some pyramids have rectangular sides.
4. All pyramids have round bases.
5. A pyramid always has a square base.

Exercises

A Find the volume of each figure.

1. 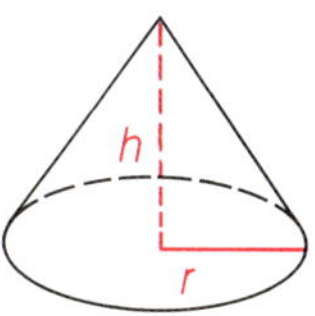

$r = 5$ cm
$h = 8$ cm

2. 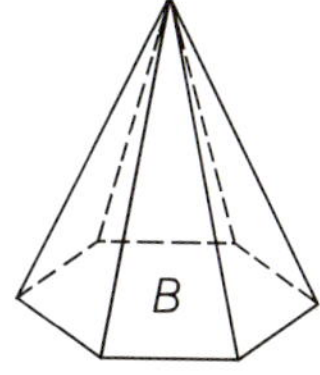

$B = 14\text{ cm}^2$
$h = 10$ cm

3. 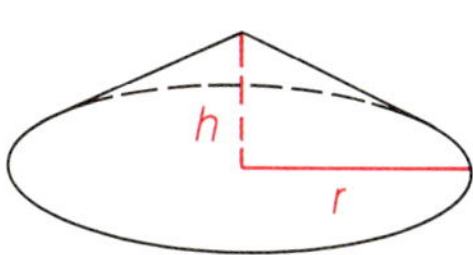

$r = 9$ cm
$h = 4$ cm

4. 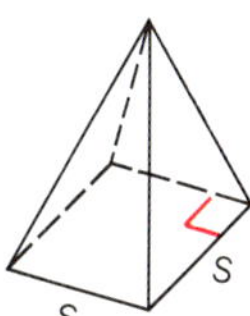

$s = 9$ cm
$h = 12$ cm

5. 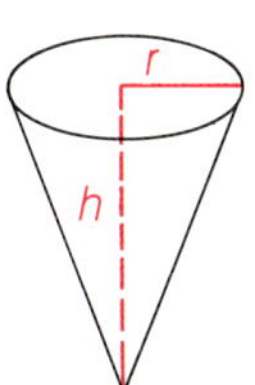

$r = 4$ in
$h = 9$ in

6. 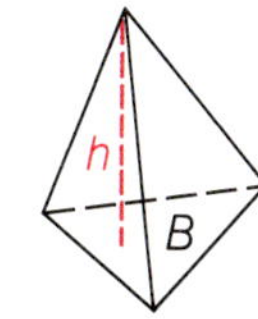

$B = 9\text{ cm}^2$
$h = 5$ cm

Find the volume of a cone with the radius and height given. Round your answer to the nearest tenth.

7. $r = 11$ cm, $h = 8$ cm
8. $r = 12$ m, $h = 4$ m
9. $r = 5$ dm, $h = 9$ dm
10. $r = 4$ cm, $h = 8$ cm
11. $r = 5$ cm, $h = 12$ cm
12. $r = 4$ cm, $h = 124$ cm
13. $r = 4$ mm, $h = 24$ mm
14. $r = 5$ m, $h = 10$ m

Find the volume of a pyramid with the base area and height given. Round your answer to the nearest tenth.

15. $B = 25\text{ cm}^2$, $h = 19$ cm
16. $B = 96\text{ m}^2$, $h = 23$ m
17. $B = 47\text{ m}^2$, $h = 12$ m
18. $B = 12\text{ cm}^2$, $h = 5$ cm
19. $B = 46\text{ cm}^2$, $h = 45$ cm
20. $B = 31\text{ cm}^2$, $h = 6$ cm
21. $B = 270\text{ m}^2$, $h = 47$ m
22. $B = 75\text{ m}^2$, $h = 12$ m

B In the table below, B represents the area of the base, h the height, and V the volume of a pyramid. Find the unknown variable in each column.

		23.	24.	25.	26.	27.	28.	29.
Base area	B	12π	35	?	?	36	5.3	?
height	h	6	?	12	32	12	?	4.5
volume	V	?	105	288	160π	?	63.6	10.35

30. What is the height of a prism if the volume is 162 m^3 and the area of the base is 9 m^2?

31. A cone and a cylinder have the same base. If the cone's height is 6 times the height of the cylinder, how much greater is the volume of the cone?

Use the formula $V = \frac{4}{3}\pi r^3$ to find the **volume of a sphere** with the dimensions given. Give your answers in terms of π.

32. $r = 8$ cm **33.** $r = 6$ cm **34.** $r = 7$ m **35.** $r = 5.1$ m

C Extending Thinking Skills

These spheres are in pyramid-shaped stacks. Find the pattern and give the next 3 numbers.

36.

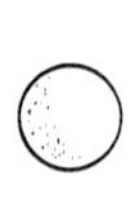

1

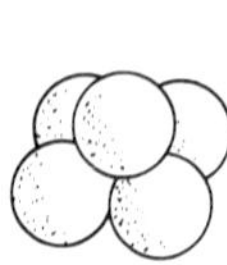

5

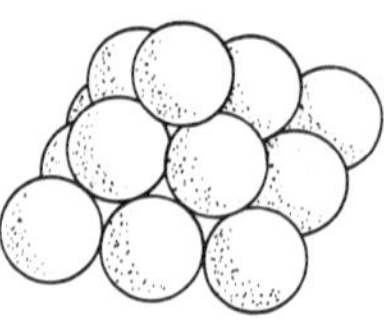

14

37.

1

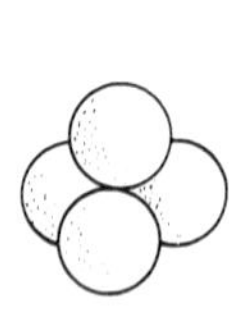

4

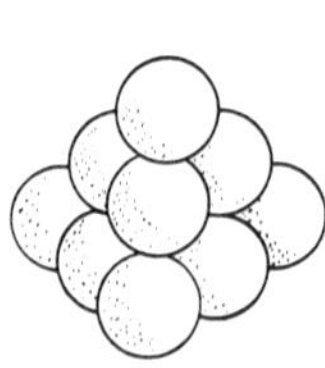

10

Mixed Review

Write as a decimal. **38.** 8% **39.** 135% **40.** 420% **41.** 19.4%

Write in scientific notation. **42.** 16,500 **43.** 0.00016 **44.** 42,300,000

Solve and check. **45.** $y \div \left(-\frac{3}{4}\right) = \frac{3}{2}$ **46.** $\frac{4}{5}c = \frac{1}{20}$ **47.** $2x + 5 = -12$

12-9 Surface Area

The cylinder and prism shown below have been cut apart and laid flat. The surface area of each is equal to the area of the corresponding flat regions.

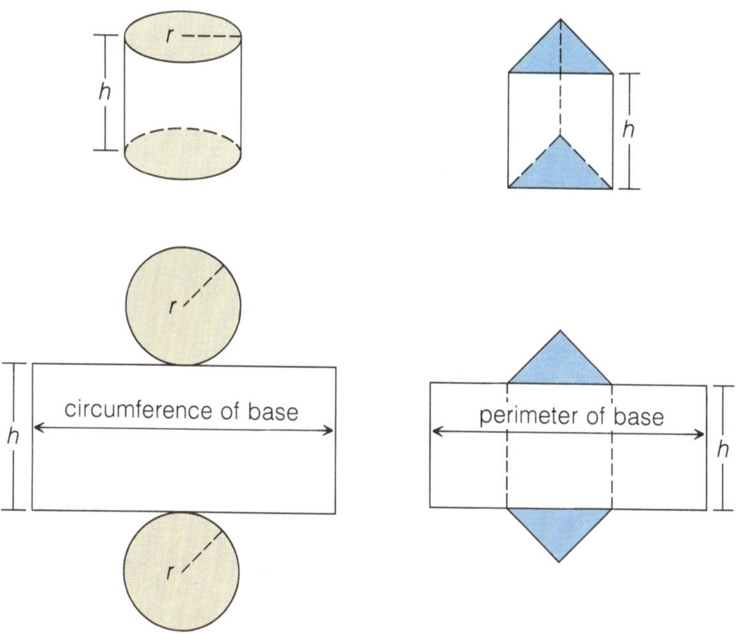

For a prism or a cylinder, surface area is equal to the area of the bases plus the area of the sides.

Example 1

Find the surface area of the cylinder at right. Use 3.14 for π.

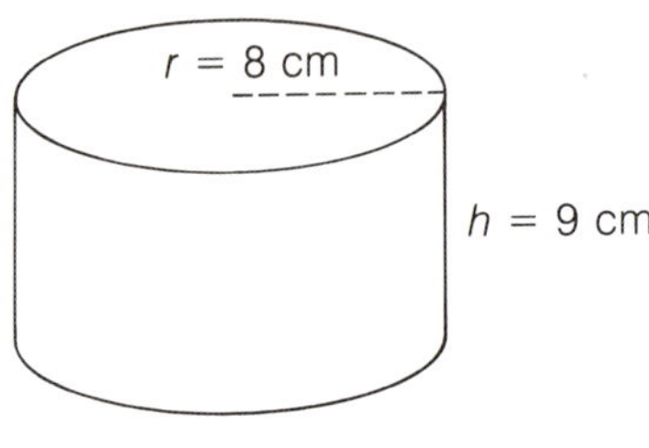

Solution Area of one base $= \pi 8^2$
$\approx 3.14 \times 64$
≈ 200.96

Area of sides $=$ circumference of base $\times$ height
$= 2\pi \times 8 \times 9 \approx 2 \times 3.14 \times 8 \times 9 \approx 452.16$

Surface area $=$ area of bases $+$ area of sides
$\approx 2 \times 200.96 \text{ cm}^2 + 425.16 \text{ cm}^2 \approx 854.08 \text{ cm}^2$

Practice Find the surface area of a cylinder with the radius and height given.

a. $r = 5$ cm, $h = 12$ cm **b.** $r = 8$ m, $h = 15$ m

Example 2

Find the surface area of the rectangular prism at right.

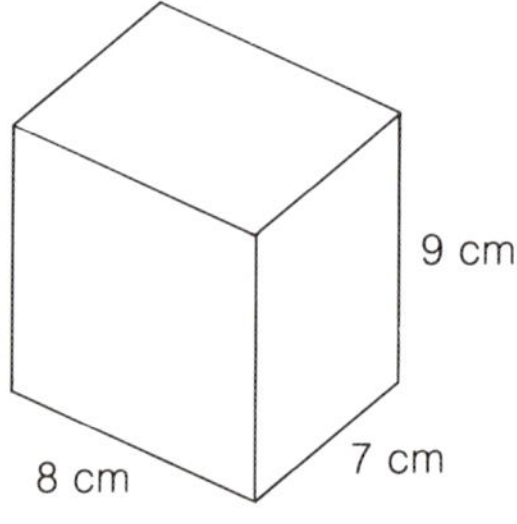

Solution

Area of one base $= 8 \times 7 = 56$

Area of sides $=$ (perimeter of base) $\times 9$
$= 30 \times 9$
$= 270$

Surface area $=$ area of the bases $+$ area of the sides
$= 2 \times 56 \text{ cm}^2 + 270 \text{ cm}^2 = 382 \text{ cm}^2$

Practice Find the surface area of the prism at right.

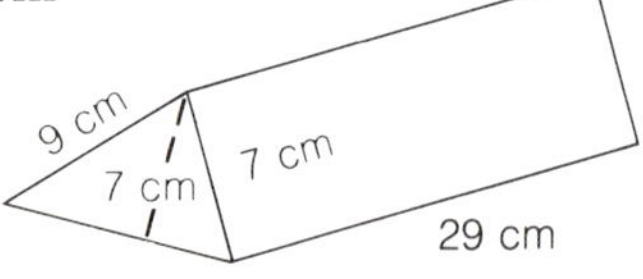

Oral Exercises

Give the height and the perimeter or circumference of the base for each figure.

1.

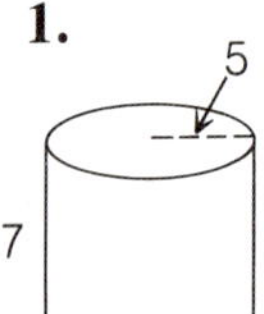

2.

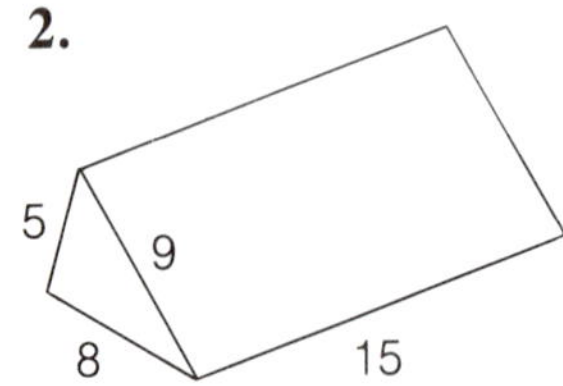

3.

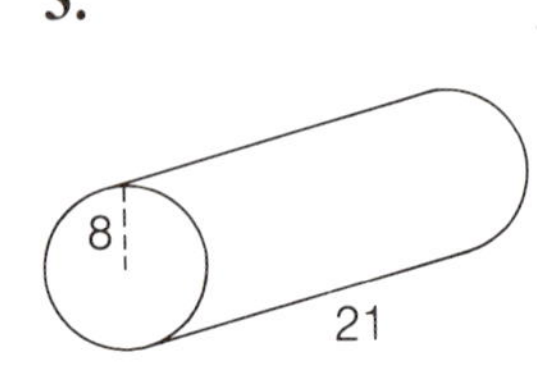

4.

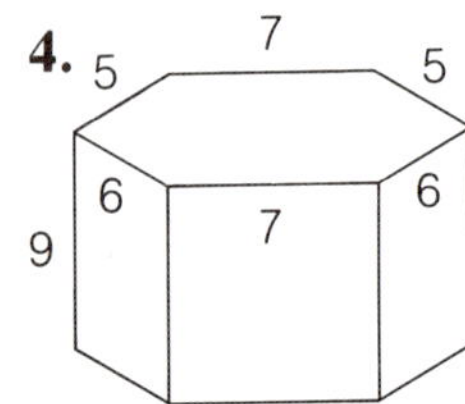

Exercises

A Find the surface area of each cylinder.

1.

6 cm

8 cm

2.

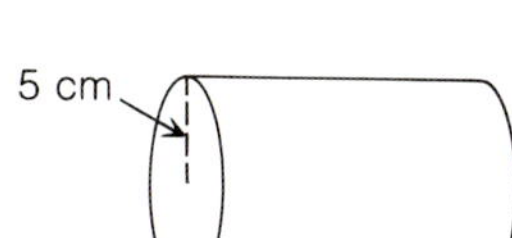

3.

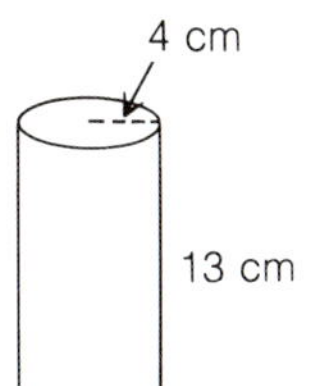

4.

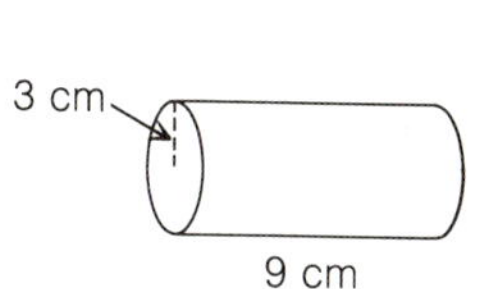

Find the surface area of a cylinder with the radius and height given.

5. $r = 8$ cm $h = 12$ cm	**6.** $r = 3$ cm $h = 5$ cm	**7.** $r = 9$ m $h = 3$ m	**8.** $r = 2.1$ m $h = 8.3$ m
9. $r = 5$ dm $h = 9$ dm	**10.** $r = 11$ cm $h = 25$ cm	**11.** $r = 12$ m $h = 30$ m	**12.** $r = 8$ cm $h = 4$ cm

Find the surface area of each prism.

13.

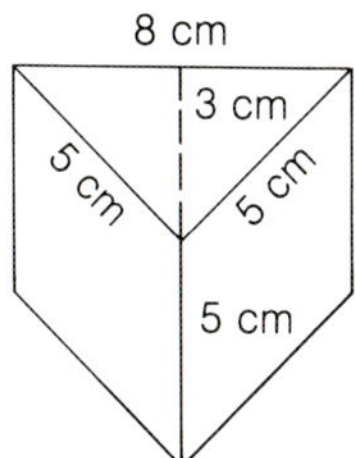

14.

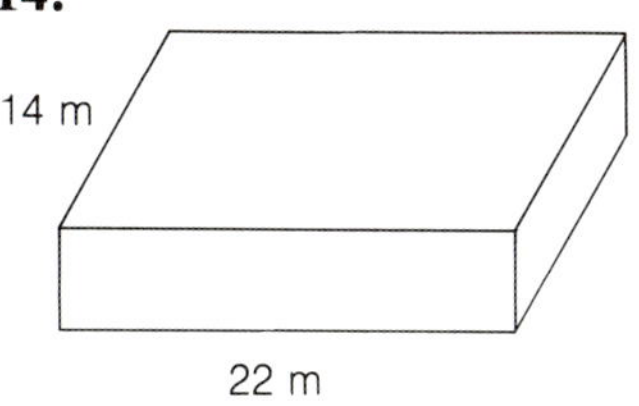

15.

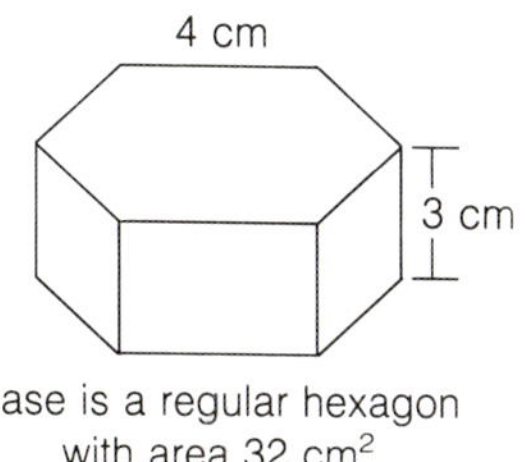

base is a regular hexagon with area 32 cm^2

B

16. A cylinder with height 8 cm has a volume of 288π cm^3. What is its surface area?

17. A cylinder with radius 16 cm has a volume of 2560π cm^3. What is its surface area?

18. A prism with a square base has a height of 9 m and a volume of 576 m^3. What is its surface area?

The surface area of a sphere is equal to 4π times the radius squared. The formula is $A = 4\pi r^2$. Use this formula for Exercises 19–20.

19. A spherical satellite that is 2 m in diameter is covered with a thin layer of a reflective material. What is the surface area of this satellite?

20. A spherical storage tank with a 30-foot radius is to be painted. If the paint covers 350 square feet per gallon, how many gallons of paint are needed?

C Extending Thinking Skills

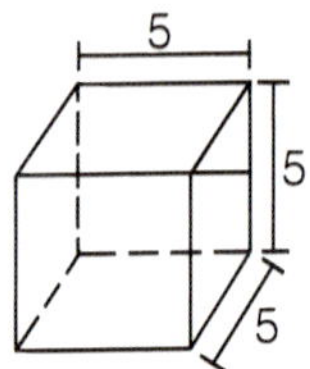

21. The hollow cube at right has a removable top and is to be painted on all surfaces, inside and out. If each edge is 5 feet long, how many square feet of surface will be painted?

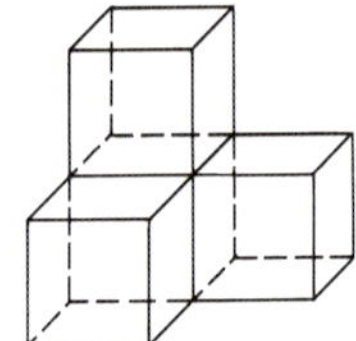

22. The solid at right is made up of 4 cubes glued together. If an edge of each cube is 2 feet, how many square feet of surface can be painted?

Mixed Review

Write as a fraction in lowest terms. **23.** 36% **24.** 65% **25.** 26%

Solve by writing an equation. **26.** In 1970, a haircut cost \$2.50. Now it costs \$7.00. What is the percentage of increase in the price?

27. 11 is 25% of what number? **28.** 12 is 150% of what number?

Solve and check. **29.** $24c + 17 = 65$ **30.** $14 = -r + 2$ **31.** $6x = 16 - 2x$

COMPUTER ACTIVITY

This program will ask you to input a number for the radius of a sphere. It will then calculate the volume and surface area of the sphere.

```
10 REM: CALCULATING VOLUME AND SURFACE AREA OF SPHERES
20 PRINT "TYPE A DECIMAL NUMBER THAT IS THE RADIUS OF A
   SPHERE"
30 INPUT R
40 LET V=4/3*3.14*R*R*R
50 LET S=4*3.14*R*R
60 PRINT "THE VOLUME OF A SPHERE OF RADIUS ";R;" IS ";V
70 PRINT
80 PRINT "THE SURFACE AREA OF A SPHERE OF RADIUS ";R;
   " IS ";S
90 END
```

1. Use the program to find the volume and surface area of these planets:
a. Mercury, radius 1516 miles **b.** Mars, radius 2108 miles
c. Earth, radius 3963 miles

2. Find the lines in the program that use the formulas for volume and surface area of a sphere. Write the formulas.

PROBLEM SOLVING: STRATEGIES

12-10 Using Special Insight

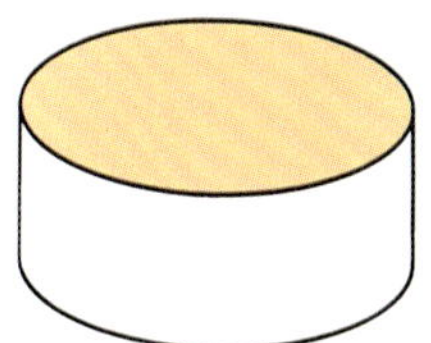

Solving some problems requires special insight. If you use the strategies and your first attempts are not successful, try thinking about the problem in a different way. A new point of view may help a solution idea to pop into your head. Try the following problem.

Problem A waitress had always used 4 straight cuts to cut a cylinder of cheese into 8 identical pieces. One day, she suddenly realized that she could do it with only 3 straight cuts! How did she do it?

When looking for a solution to the problem, you might first think about cutting the cheese with 4 cuts, as in figure A below. Then you might think about ways to make 3 straight cuts across the top, as in figure B. After several unsuccessful tries, you might try to think about the problem in a different way. Perhaps, suddenly, you will decide to try horizontal cuts as well as vertical cuts, and find the solution shown in figure C.

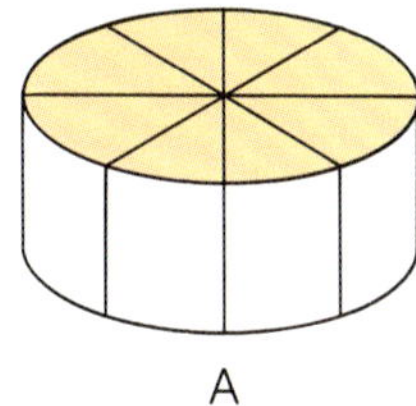

A

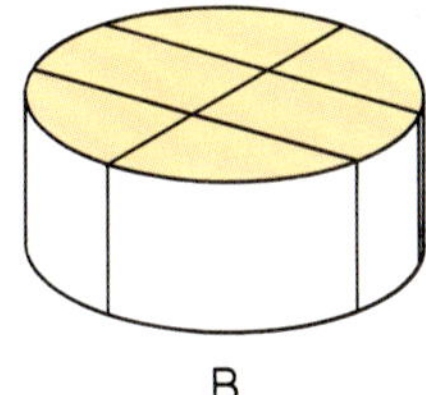

B

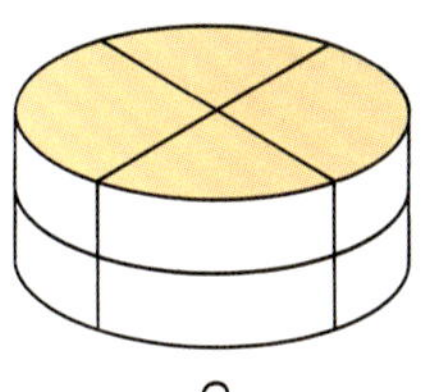

C

Problem-Solving Strategies

Choose the Operations	Write an Equation
Guess, Check, Revise	Simplify the Problem
Draw a Picture	Make an Organized List
Make a Table	Use Logical Reasoning
Look for a Pattern	Work Backwards

This chart shows the strategies presented.

Problems

Solve. Allow yourself time to think about problems in different ways.

1. Copy these nine dots. Draw four connected straight lines through all nine dots without lifting your pencil or retracing any part of a line.

2. Place these 12 toothpicks together to form six squares. Make a drawing of your answer.

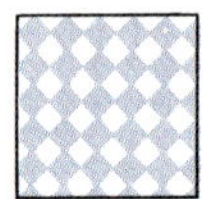

3. How can these two square quilts be cut and sewn back together to form one square quilt with twice the area of one quilt?

4. A very honest teenager said "Two days ago I was 13, but next year I'll be 16." When is the teenager's birthday?

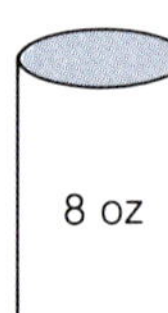

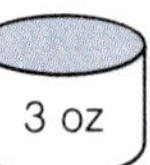

5. You have an 8-ounce can and a 3-ounce can, with no markings on either can. How can you measure out 4 ounces of juice using only these two cans?

6. Where should you put the fences to divide this field into 4 congruent fields that are the same shape as the original field?

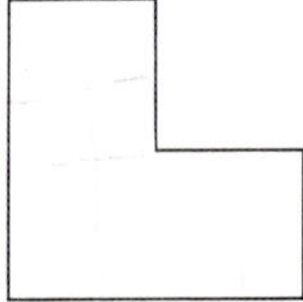

Enrichment

Pick's Formula for Area

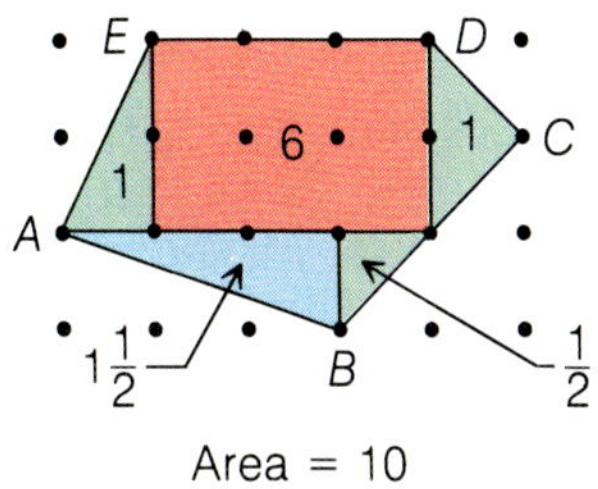

The area of polygon *ABCDE* can be found by dividing it as shown and adding together the areas of the smaller regions.

Another way to find the area of this polygon is to use Pick's Formula. The formula uses the number of dots on the boundary (***b***) and the number of dots in the interior (***i***) of the polygon.

The shaded part of the table below has been filled in for polygon *ABCDE*.

Polygon	***b***	***i***	$\frac{b}{2} + i$	**Area**
ABCDE	8	7	11	10
Exercise 1	10	?	?	?
Exercise 2	?	?	9	?
Exercise 3	?	?	?	5

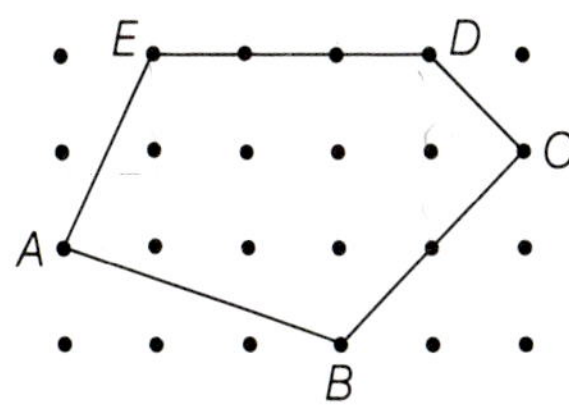

Complete the table above for the polygons in Exercises 1–3 and discover Pick's Formula.

1. 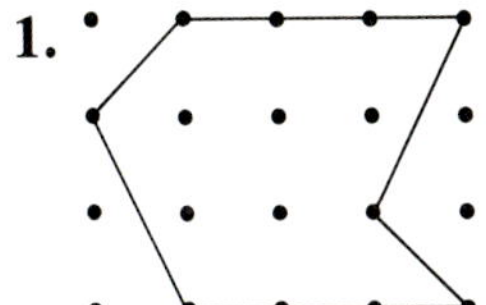

2. 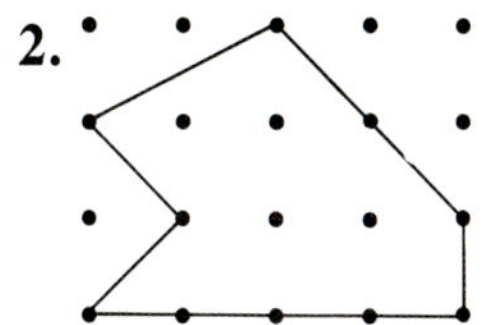

3. 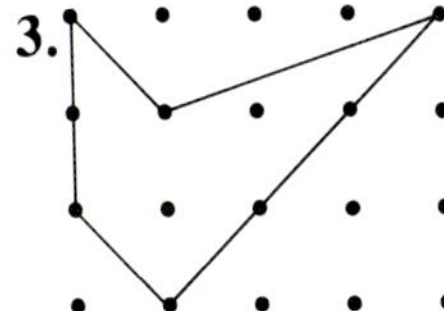

Use Pick's Formula to find the areas of each.

4. 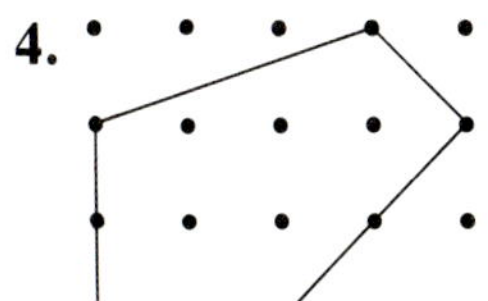

5. 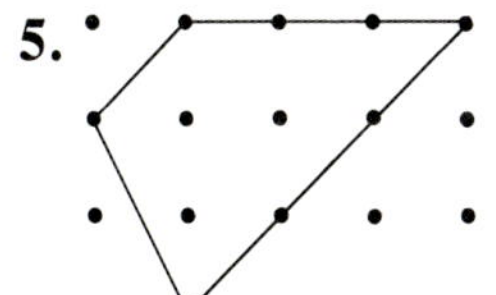

6. 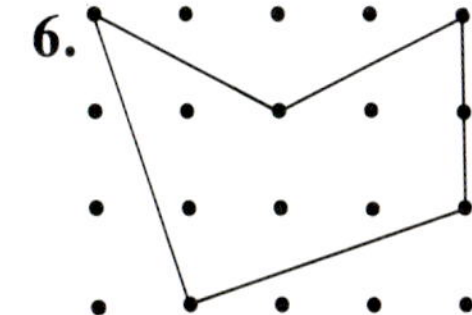

Chapter 12 Review

12-1–12-2 Find the area of each figure.

1. Rectangle with length 8 mm, width 25 mm

2. Triangle with base 16 cm, height 16 cm

Find the area of each quadrilateral.

3. Parallelogram with base = 14.4 m, height = 6.8 m

4. Trapezoid with $b_1 = 16$ cm, $b_2 = 12$ cm, $h = 7$ cm

12-3 Find the area of each circle. Use 3.14 for π.

5. $r = 9$ m

6. $d = 3.4$ km

12-4 Find the area of the figure.

7. 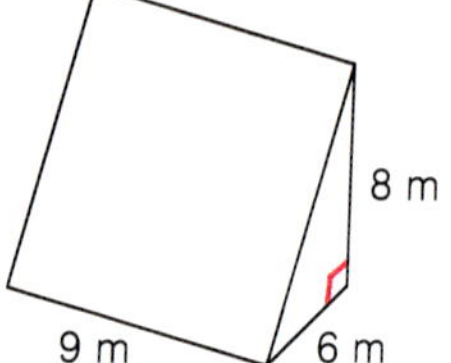

12-5 Solve by writing an equation.

8. Irene bought 3 adult tickets and one child's ticket for $16.50. If the child's ticket cost $3.00, what was the cost of each adult ticket?

12-6 Find the volume of the prism or cylinder. Use 3.14 for π.

9. 8 m, 9 m, 6 m

10. 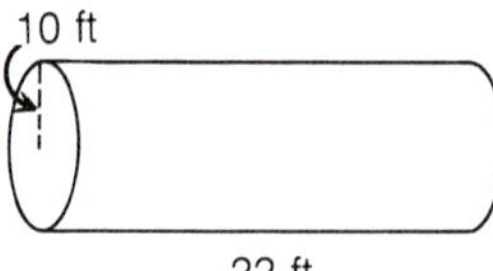

12-7 Solve each problem.

11. How many cubic yards of concrete are needed for a patio 42 feet long, 27 feet wide, and 6 inches thick?

12-8 Find the volume. Use 3.14 for π.

12. A cone with a radius of 11 feet and a height of 4 feet

13. A pyramid with a base area of 32 dm^2 and a height of 16 dm

12-9 Find the surface area. Use 3.14 for π.

14. A cylinder with a radius of 8 cm and a height of 30 cm

15. 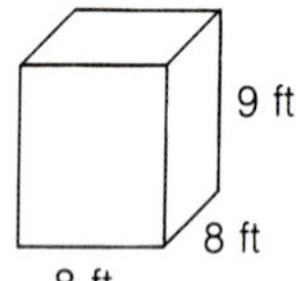

Chapter 12 Test

Find the area of each figure.

1. Rectangle with length 7 cm, width 36 cm

2. Triangle with base 34 m, height 8 m

Find the area of each quadrilateral.

3. Parallelogram with base = 146 mm, height = 36 mm

4. Trapezoid with b_1 = 18 m, b_2 = 7 m, h = 12 m

Find the area of each circle. Use 3.14 for π.

5. r = 4 m

6. d = 30 km

Find the area of the figure.

7. 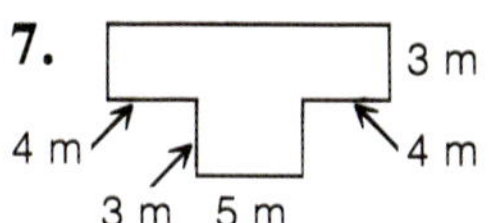

Solve by writing an equation.

8. Brian saved $40 on a suit at a 25%-off sale. What was the regular price of the suit?

Find the volume of the prism or cylinder. Use 3.14 for π.

9. 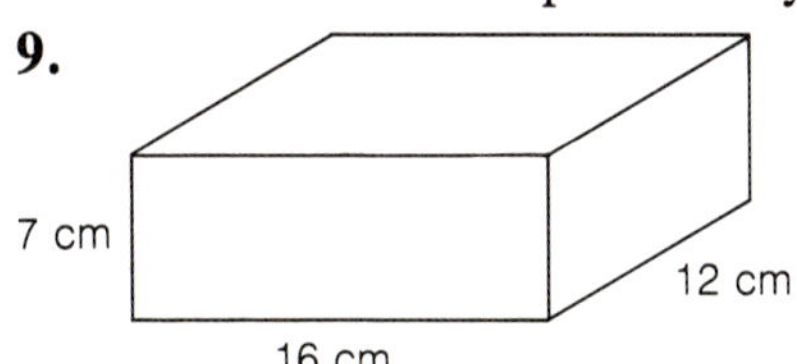

10. 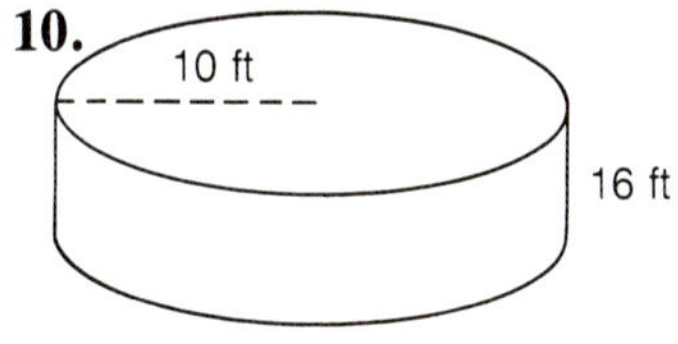

Solve each problem.

11. If concrete costs $45 per cubic yard, how much will it cost for concrete for a foundation 48 feet long, 30 feet wide, and 8 inches thick?

Find the volume. Use 3.14 for π.

12. A cone with a radius of 7 inches and a height of 15 inches

13. A pyramid with a base area of 80 square m and a height of 22 m

Find the surface area. Use 3.14 for π.

14. A cylinder with a radius of 6 feet and a height of 24 feet

15. 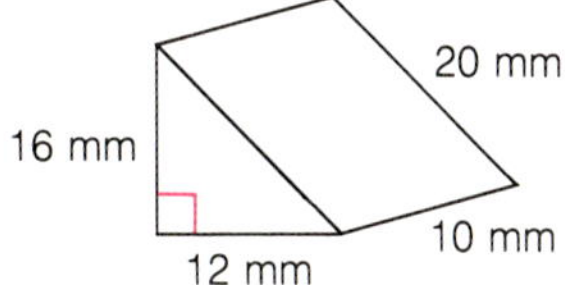

Cumulative Review

Write each as a fraction in lowest terms.

1. 34%　　**2.** 5%　　**3.** $8\frac{1}{2}\%$

Use a proportion to write each fraction as a percent.

4. $\frac{2}{5}$　　**5.** $\frac{13}{20}$　　**6.** $\frac{5}{8}$

7. $\frac{625}{100}$　　**8.** $\frac{14}{5}$　　**9.** $\frac{25}{250}$

Write each percent as a fraction or mixed number in lowest terms.

10. 275%　　**11.** $\frac{3}{4}\%$　　**12.** $12\frac{1}{2}\%$

Write each as a decimal.

13. 7%　　**14.** $22\frac{1}{5}\%$　　**15.** 425%

Write each as a percent.

16. 0.60　　**17.** 0.085　　**18.** 8.98

Find the percent of increase.

19. Original amount = \$120; new amount = \$180

20. Original amount = \$90; new amount = \$108

Find the percent of decrease.

21. Original amount = \$85; new amount = \$68

22. Original amount = \$276; new amount = \$69

Solve.

23. Juan bought a computer program for \$240.00. If the sales tax was 5.5%, what was the total amount that Juan paid?

24. Bill bought a camera priced at \$125. The sales tax was 6%. What was the total cost of the camera?

Use the figure at right for Exercises 25–29.

25. Name a point.

26. Name a line.

27. Name a plane.

28. Name a segment that includes point B.

29. Name a ray with vertex A.

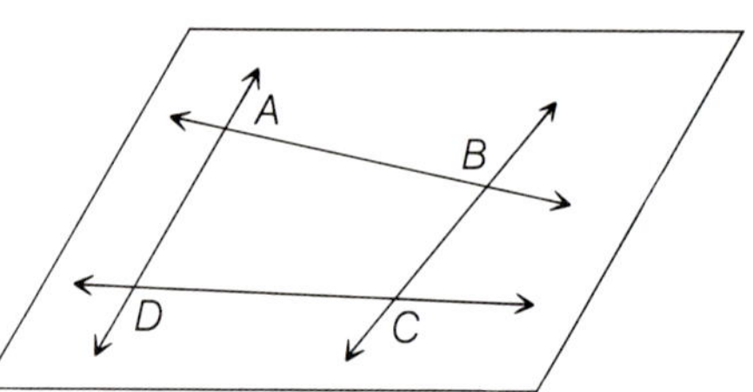

Chapter 13

Probability, Statistics, and Graphs

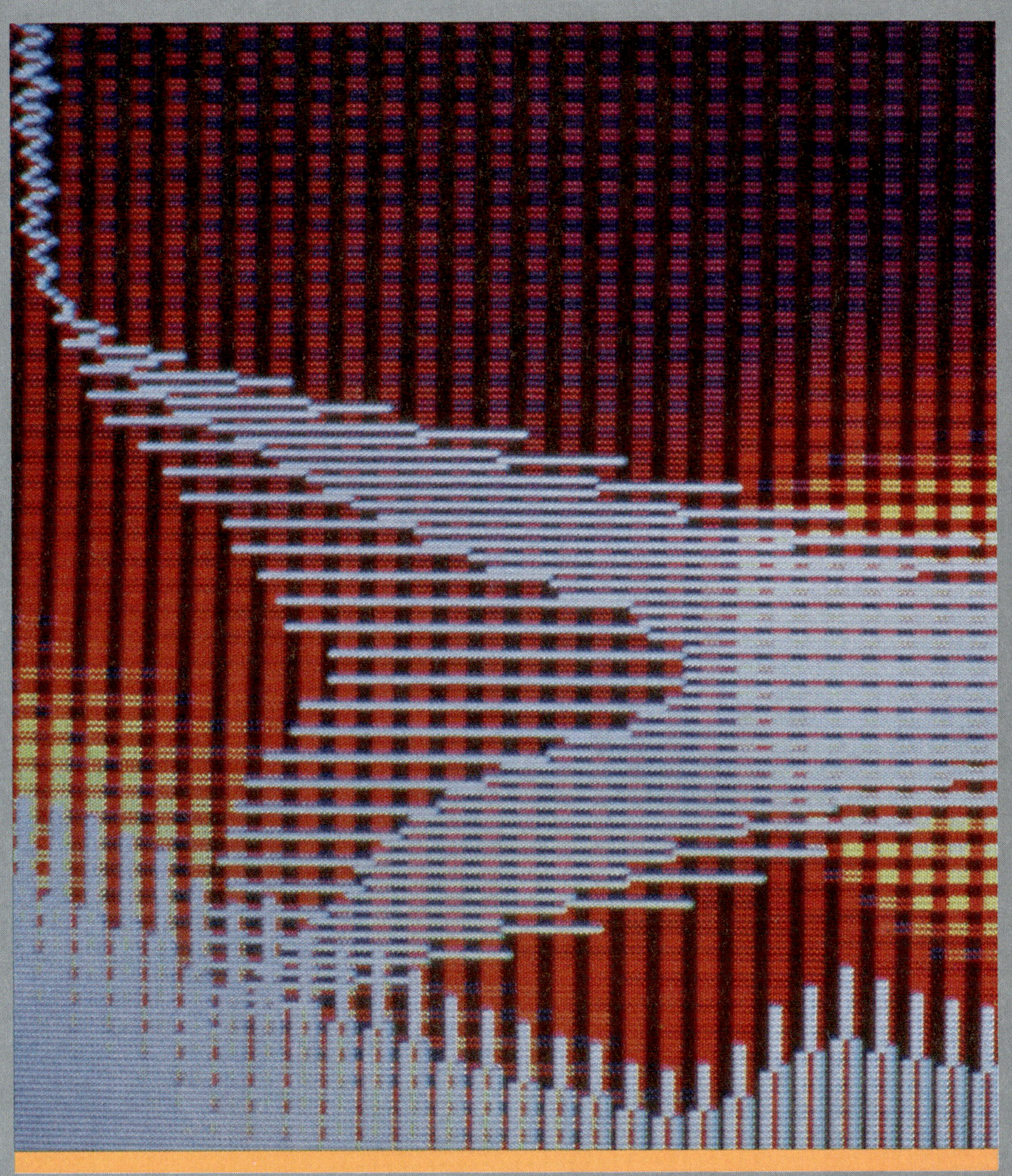

13-1 Counting Principle

A school is having an election for student council president, vice-president, and secretary. The ballot below shows one possible **outcome** of the election. One way to show all the possible outcomes is to make a tree diagram as shown below. Each choice for president can be matched with two choices for vice-president. And each choice for president and vice-president can be matched with 2 choices for secretary. Each "branch" shows a possible outcome.

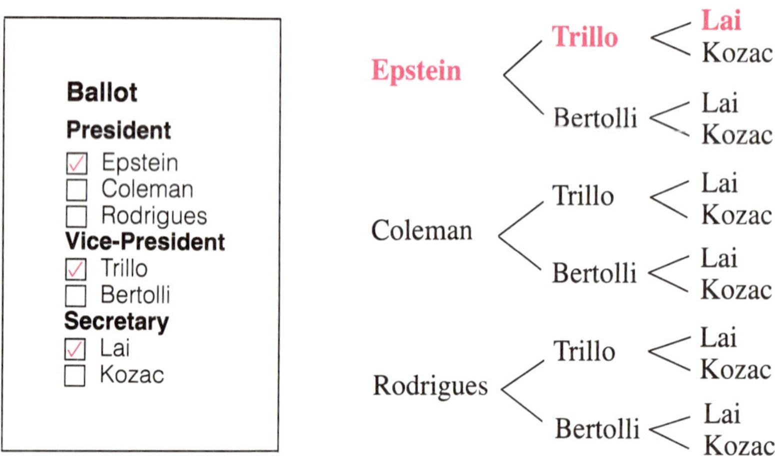

This election has 12 possible outcomes.

Since there are 3 choices for president, 2 choices for vice-president, and 2 choices for secretary, there are $3 \times 2 \times 2 = 12$ possible outcomes for the election. When you multiply to find the total number of outcomes, you are using the **counting principle.**

Counting Principle

To find the total number of choices for an event, multiply the number of choices for each part.

Example

Use the counting principle to solve.

A singer has 4 blouses and 5 pairs of jeans to use in concerts. How many different ways can she dress for a concert?

Solution $4 \times 5 = 20$ The total number of choices equals the product of the number of blouses and the number of pairs of jeans.

She has 20 choices for her outfit.

Practice Use the counting principle to solve.

Reggie needs to get glasses. He can choose from 3 different colors for the frame, and 4 tints for the glass. How many different kinds of glasses could Reggie select?

Oral Exercises

Use the tree diagram showing total possible outcomes for a Frozen Yogurt Special to answer questions 1–2.

1. How many choices are there for: size? yogurt flavor? topping? a small yogurt special? a large yogurt special? a yogurt special?

2. What equation can you use to find the total number of choices?

Exercises

A Use the counting principle to find the total number of outcomes.

1. Select 1 sandwich and 1 drink. Sandwiches: hamburger, chicken, cheese. Drinks: juice, milk, tea.

2. Select 1 shirt and 1 tie. Shirts: white, blue, yellow, cream. Ties: striped, light blue, navy.

3. Select 1 exterior car color and 1 interior car color. Exterior colors: white, blue, tan, red. Interior colors: cream, black, red, blue, light green.

4. Select 1 club and 1 sport. Clubs: debate, drama, art, math. Sports: tennis, golf, volleyball.

5. Select 1 section of the airplane and 1 seat location. Sections: first class, business, coach. Locations: window, middle, aisle.

6. Select 1 watch style and 1 watchband. Watch style: digital, standard, Roman numerals. Watchband: metal, leather, canvas.

7. Select 1 ticket for a level and section in a theater. Level: main floor, balcony. Section: front, middle, back.

8. Select a 2-digit football jersey number. First digit: 5, 6, 7, 8, 9. Second digit: any number from 0 through 9.

9. Select a 2-digit basketball jersey number. Choose any of the numbers 0 through 9 for each digit.

10. Select colors for a room. Wall colors: white, yellow, pink, blue. Rug colors: white, yellow, red, blue, brown.

B Find the total number of outcomes.

11. Select 1 president, 1 vice-president, and 1 secretary. President: Sunji, Carlos. Vice-president: Denise, Kim, Kerry, Celia. Secretary: Mark, Inez.

12. Select 1 telephone style, 1 color, and 1 format. Style: wall, desk, antique. Color: green, white, tan, black, brown. Format: touch-tone, rotary.

13. Select 1 size of hamburger, 1 topping, and 1 bun. Sizes: single, double, triple. Toppings: mushrooms, pickles, onions, lettuce. Bun: regular, whole wheat.

14. The winners of each conference in the National Basketball Association play to determine the champion. There are 11 teams in the Eastern Conference and 12 teams in the Western Conference. How many outcomes are possible for the two teams that play for the championship?

C Extending Thinking Skills

15. Ms. Ortega wants a one-way airline ticket from Chicago to San Francisco with a stop in Denver. She wants a minimum of 1 hour and a maximum of 3 hours between flights. How many choices for flights does she have?

Flight Number	CHICAGO TO DENVER Depart	Arrive
#63	7:05 a.m.	8:20 a.m.
#1122	8:15	9:30
#34	10:10	11:25
#125	12:01 p.m.	1:16 p.m.
#456	1:40	2:55

Flight Number	DENVER TO SAN FRANCISCO Depart	Arrive
#1156	7:50 a.m.	8:51 a.m.
#92	8:50	9:51
#8	9:50	10:51
#54	12:50 p.m.	1:51 p.m.
#32	1:50	3:30

Mixed Review

Solve and check. **16.** $6(2m + 3) = 78$ **17.** $4c + 2c = 5c + 2$

What percent of 50 is: **18.** 40? **19.** 75? **20.** 15?

13-2 Permutations

A **permutation** is an arrangement of objects in a particular order. The tree diagram at right shows permutations of 3 books. Any of the three books can be chosen for the first position. Either of the two books left can be chosen for the second position. One book is left for the third position. Using the counting principle, there are $3 \times 2 \times 1 = 6$ permutations of the books. The product $3 \times 2 \times 1$ can be written as **3!** This is read as "**3 factorial**."

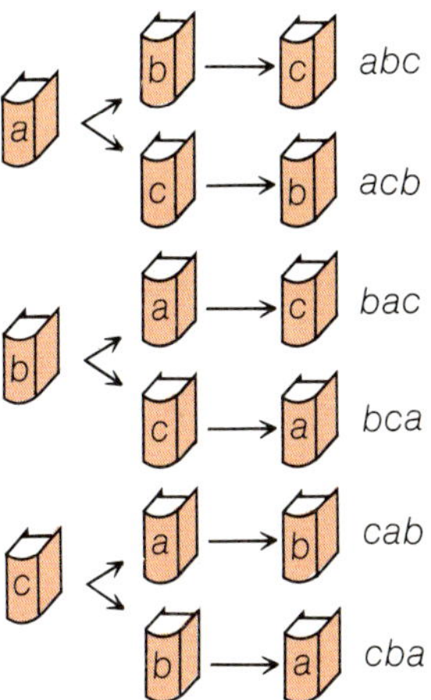

Permutations

To find the number of permutations of ***n*** objects, find the product of the numbers **1** through ***n***.

$n! = n \times (n-1) \times \ldots \times 3 \times 2 \times 1$

Example 1

Find the number of permutations of the letters A, B, C, D.

Solution $4! = 4 \times 3 \times 2 \times 1$
$= 24$

Since there are 4 letters, the number of permutations is equal to 4 factorial.

Practice Find the number of permutations. **a.** Tom, Dick, Harry **b.** 1, 3, 5, 7, 9

The list at right shows the arrangement of two numbers that can be made from the numbers 2, 4, 6, and 8. The list shows all the permutations of two numbers with 2 as the first number, then the permutations with 4 as the first number, and so on. There are 4 choices for the first number. Then, after the first number is chosen, there are 3 choices for the second number. Using the counting principle, $4 \times 3 = 12$ two-digit numbers can be made. You can use the steps below to find the total number of ways to order part of a group.

24 26 28
42 46 48
62 64 68
82 84 86

Permutations of n Objects Taken r at a Time

To find the number of permutations of ***n*** objects taken ***r*** at a time, carry out the product $n(n-1)(n-2)\ldots$ to ***r*** factors.

Example 2

Find the number of permutations. Five students ran in a 100-meter dash. In how many ways could first, second, and third place be won?

Solution

$5 \times 4 \times 3 = 60$ You want to find the number of permutations of 5 objects taken 3 at a time. There are 5 choices for first place, 4 choices for second, and 3 choices for third.

The prizes could be awarded in 60 ways.

Practice Find the number of permutations. Four people applied for 2 jobs, painter and carpenter. In how many ways could the jobs be filled?

Oral Exercises

Use $n! = n \times (n - 1) \times \ldots \times 3 \times 2 \times 1$ to restate each expression.

1. $5!$

2. $6!$

3. $11!$

4. $1 \times 2 \times 3 \times 4 \times 5 \times 6 \times 7$

5. $1 \times 2 \times 3 \times \ldots \times 9 \times 10$

6. $1 \times 2 \times 3 \times \ldots \times 19 \times 20$

Exercises

A Find the number of permutations.

1. 1, 2

2. Sue, Kim, Heather

3. 12, 14, 16

4. math, history, English, art

5. quick, Jane, run

6. m, u, s, i, c

7. Ace, King, Queen

8. North, South, East, West

9. 10, 20, 30, 40

10. m, i, l, k

11. Lincoln, Washington, Jefferson

12. winter, spring, summer, fall

13. 0, 1, 2, 3, 4, 5, 6, 7, 8, 9

14. Huey, Dewey, Louie, Donald

15. Harpo, Chico, Groucho, Zeppo

16. soup, salad, potatoes, turkey, pie

Solve.

17. How many 3-letter arrangements can be made from the letters A, B, C, D, E?

18. How many 3-song arrangements can be made from a list of 7 songs?

B Solve.

19. How many 2-letter arrangements are possible from the 26 letters? You can use the same letter twice in an arrangement.

20. How many 2-digit track jersey numbers can be made from 3, 5, 7, and 9? You can use the same number twice in an arrangement.

21. How many ways can first, second, and third place be given to 10 players?

22. How many 6-digit zip codes would be possible if no digit could be repeated?

23. In how many ways can 6 track teams be assigned to 6 lanes on a track?

24. A band, a float, and an antique car are to be in a parade. In how many different ways can they be arranged in the parade?

25. How many different license plates are possible with 2 letters followed by 4 numbers if no letter or number is used twice?

C Extending Thinking Skills

26. How many different 3-digit telephone area codes are possible if the first digit cannot be a 0 or a 1?

27. How many different 7-digit phone numbers are possible in each area code if the following restrictions apply: the first digit cannot be a 0 or a 1, the middle digit in the prefix cannot be a 0 or a 1, and the 3-digit prefix cannot be 555 or 911?

Mixed Review

Simplify. **28.** $(6 + 3t) + 15$ **29.** $m + 6m - 4m$ **30.** $12 + 3c - 9$
31. $26n - 19n + 2n$ **32.** $3 + 6r - 12$ **33.** $4x + 3y + 2x - 9y$

Give the circumference. Use 3.14 for π. **34.** radius = 4 **35.** diameter = 5

Solve and check. **36.** $3(x + 4) - 3 = 15$ **37.** $0.4c + 0.7c = 22$
38. $14 = 2t - 8$ **39.** $6m = m - 10$ **40.** $27 + 6(y - 2) = 3$

NUMBERS TO ALGEBRA

You can use variables to write expressions for consecutive numbers.

Numbers	Algebra
The next 3 even numbers after 4.	The next 3 even numbers after an even number n.
4, 6, 8, 10	n, $(n + 2)$, $(n + 4)$, $(n + 6)$

Write expressions for each of the following.

1. The next 4 consecutive whole numbers after whole number n.
2. The 2 whole numbers just before a whole number x.
3. The 2 even numbers just before an even number y.
4. Numbers that are 5, 10, and 15 times greater than a whole number m.

13-3 Combinations

Tanya's class must select 2 students out of 5 candidates as class representatives. How many different pairs can be selected from the 5 candidates?

Candidates (choose 2)
(A) Alvarez (B) Barnes (C) Carlsen (D) Dickinson (E) Ebel

You learned in the last lesson that there are $5 \cdot 4 = 20$ ways to select 2 out of 5 people. Here are the 20 ways.

AB	**AC**	**AD**	**AE**
BA	**BC**	**BD**	**BE**
CA	**CB**	**CD**	**CE**
DA	**DB**	**DC**	**DE**
EA	**EB**	**EC**	**ED**

Alvarez–Barnes (AB) and Barnes–Alvarez (BA) are both included in the list above. Since the *order* of the students does not matter, you need to divide the total number of permutations by the number of permutations of 2 people ($2! = 2 \cdot 1 = 2$). The list below shows all 10 ways in which 2 out of the 5 people can be selected. An arrangement of objects in which the *order of the objects does not matter* is called a **combination**.

AB	**AC**	**AD**	**AE**
	BC	**BD**	**BE**
		CD	**CE**
			DE

You can use the following steps to find the number of combinations.

Combinations

To find the number of combinations of n objects taken r at a time:

- Find the number of permutations of n objects taken r at a time.
- Divide this number by the number of permutations of r objects.

Example

Find the number of combinations. 3 bracelets from 5.

Solution

$$\frac{5 \cdot 4 \cdot 3}{3 \cdot 2 \cdot 1} = \frac{5 \cdot 4 \cdot \cancel{3}}{\cancel{3} \cdot 2 \cdot 1} = 10$$

Find the number of permutations of 5 objects taken 3 at a time. Divide that by the number of permutations of 3 objects.

There are 10 combinations of bracelets.

Practice Find the number of combinations.

a. 5 ties from a box of 7 ties.

b. 2 cards from a pile of 8 different cards.

Oral Exercises

Tell whether each is a permutation or a combination. Do not solve.

1. Ways 5 pictures can be arranged in a row on a wall.

2. Ways 3 people can be selected from a group of 5.

3. Ways first and second violin players can be chosen from 6 players.

4. Ways 4 sweaters can be chosen out of 7.

5. Ways 5 chairs can be arranged in a row.

6. Possible finishing orders of 7 people in a race if there are no ties.

7. Ways 3 representatives can be selected from 21 students.

Exercises

A Find the number of combinations.

1. 2 letters from A, B, C

2. 3 people from Blake, Carol, Annie, Phil

3. 3 numbers from 10, 20, 30

4. 2 symbols from #, $, ?, %, *

5. 3 letters from M, A, T, H

6. 2 colors from red, orange, green, blue

7. 2 digits from 0 through 5

8. 3 numbers from 1, 2, 3, 4, and 5

9. 1 digit from 0 through 9

10. 4 people from Carl, Jim, Sue, Tim

11. 1 shirt from a box of 8 shirts

12. 5 colors from a list of 5 choices

13. 7 people from 9 people

14. 4 records from a list of 7

15. 2 blouses from 8 blouses

16. 5 movies from 8 in town

17. 6 books from 10 books

18. 4 cheerleaders from a group of 10

19. 3 shirts from a box of 12

20. 5 stamps from a book of 12

B

21. A planning committee for a talent show is to have 4 members. Twelve apply for the committee. How many committee selections are possible?

22. There are 10 movies in town but you have money to see only 3. How many choices of 3 movies do you have?

23. A shoe store has 8 kinds of running shoes. The window holds only 6 shoes. How many different displays can be put in the window?

24. The winner of a contest can select any 5 record albums from a collection of 10. How many choices for 5 albums does the winner have?

C Extending Thinking Skills

25. How many teams of 4 boys and 3 girls can be made from 5 boys and 7 girls?

26. A table tennis club has 10 members. How many games would be played if each member played each other member 1 time?

27. If seventy different committees of the same size could be formed from a group of 8 people, how many people would be on a committee?

Mixed Review

Solve and check. **28.** $\frac{6}{7} = \frac{n}{14}$ **29.** $\frac{5}{8} = \frac{20}{x}$ **30.** $\frac{20}{48} = \frac{y}{12}$

31. $-18 = 0.45t$ **32.** $1.3 - x = 2.1$ **33.** $6.3 = 2.1m$

What percent of 40 is: **34.** 15? **35.** 10? **36.** 56?

Evaluate for $x = 2$, $y = 4$. **37.** $2xy$ **38.** $4x - 2y$ **39.** $x(x - y)$

40. $3x - 2y + 9$ **41.** $6(x - 9) + 3y$ **42.** $4.5x - 2.1y$

43. Give the perimeter of a square with a side with length of 4.5 cm.

13-4 Probability

A die has sides numbered 1 through 6. If you toss a die once there are 6 possible outcomes: 1, 2, 3, 4, 5, or 6. Each outcome is **equally likely**. Since there are 6 equally likely outcomes, the **probability** of each outcome is $\frac{1}{6}$. If there are n equally likely outcomes from an activity, the probability of each outcome is $\frac{1}{n}$. An outcome or a combination of outcomes is called an **event**.

Probability

To find the probability of an event **A**, written **P(A)**, divide the number of ways for the event to occur by the total number of possible outcomes.

Example 1

Find the probability of each for one toss of a die.

a. $P(\text{even number})$ **b.** $P(\text{a number} < 6)$ **c.** $P(\text{a number} > 6)$

Solution

a. $P(\text{even number}) = \frac{3}{6} = \frac{1}{2}$ There are 3 even numbers. There are 6 possible outcomes. Reduce $\frac{3}{6}$ to $\frac{1}{2}$.

b. $P(\text{a number} < 6) = \frac{5}{6}$

c. $P(\text{a number} > 6) = \frac{0}{6} = 0$ It is impossible to throw a number greater than 6. The probability of an impossible event is 0.

Practice Find the probability of each for one toss of a die.

a. $P(\text{a multiple of } 2)$ **b.** $P(0 < \text{a number} < 7)$ **c.** $P(\text{not an even number})$

If two events cannot occur at the same time, they are **mutually exclusive**. In one toss of a die, the events "an even number" and "an odd number" are mutually exclusive, since no number is both even and odd. The events "a number > 3" and "an even number" are not mutually exclusive, since 4 and 6 are both greater than 3 and even. This relationship is stated in the following formula.

Formula: Mutually Exclusive Events

If two events are **mutually exclusive**, the probability of one or the other occurring is equal to the sum of the probabilities of each one occurring. If A and B are mutually exclusive events,

$$P(\text{A or B}) = P(\text{A}) + P(\text{B})$$

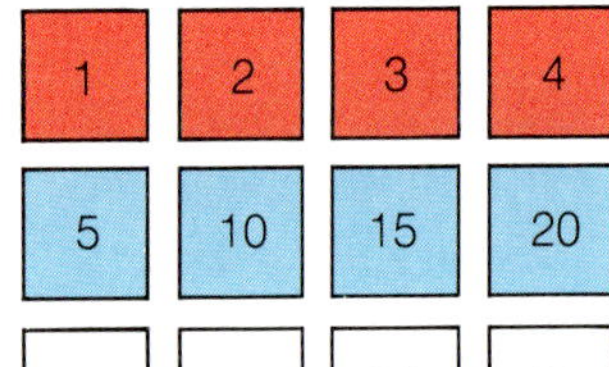

Example 2

Find the probability of each.

a. P(red or white) **b.** P(red or a multiple of 10)

Solution

a. $P(\text{red or white}) = \frac{1}{3} + \frac{1}{3} = \frac{2}{3}$

The events are mutually exclusive. $P(\text{red}) = \frac{1}{3}$ and $P(\text{white}) = \frac{1}{3}$

b. $P(\text{red or a multiple of 10}) = \frac{1}{3} + \frac{6}{12} = \frac{4}{12} + \frac{6}{12} = \frac{10}{12} = \frac{5}{6}$

The events are mutually exclusive. $P(\text{red}) = \frac{1}{3}$ and $P(\text{multiple of 10}) = \frac{6}{12}$

Practice Find the probability of each, using the picture above.

a. $P(\text{number} < 4 \text{ or number} > 20)$

b. P(prime number or a multiple of 10)

Oral Exercises

Suppose you closed your eyes and pushed one button on the telephone at random. What is the probability of pushing each?

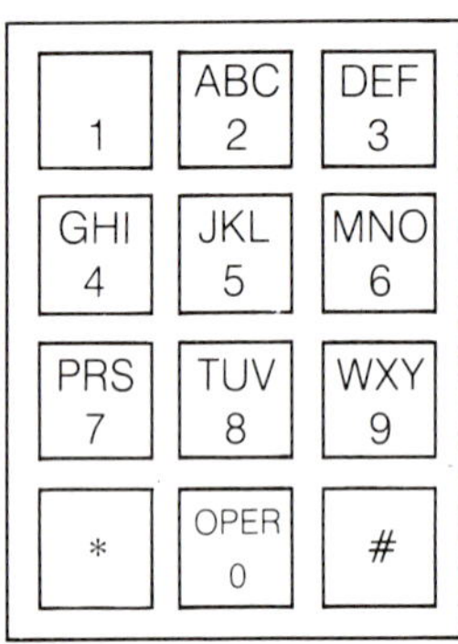

1. 0 (zero) **2.** an even number
3. an odd number **4.** a number less than 5
5. a prime number **6.** a factor of 4
7. a vowel **8.** a consonant
9. the letter Z **10.** a button with no number

Exercises

A Suppose you draw 1 card from a deck of 52 playing cards. Find each probability.

1. P(red card) **2.** P(black card) **3.** P(ace)
4. P(heart) **5.** P(5) **6.** P(queen)

7. P(king of diamonds) 8. P(ace of hearts) 9. P(not a black card)
10. P(red 7) 11. P(not a heart) 12. P(black face card)

Suppose there are 15 balls in a bag. All are the same size. Four are red, 6 are white, and 5 are blue. You select one ball from the bag. Find each probability.

13. P(red) 14. P(white) 15. P(blue)
16. P(not blue) 17. P(not white) 18. P(not red)

Use the spinner at right. Find each probability.

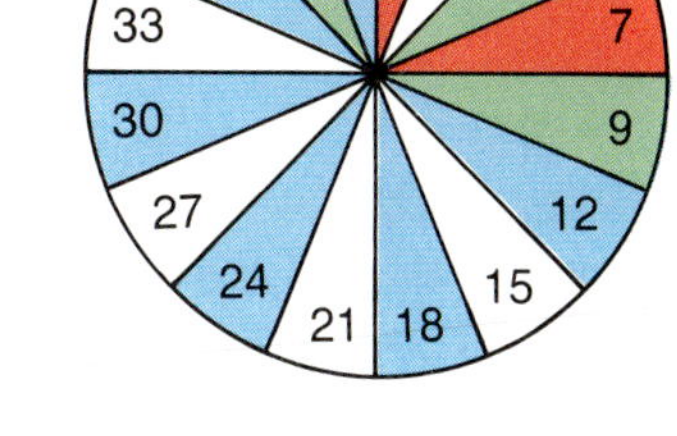

19. P(blue or white)
20. P(blue or prime)
21. P(multiple of 5 or multiple of 4)
22. P(odd or blue)
23. P(even or green)
24. P(green or blue or white)
25. P(multiple of 10 or green or red)

B Solve.

26. One postcard will be drawn out of 500 received for a ticket to a concert. You mailed 25 postcards. What are your chances of getting the ticket?

27. Janis and 4 of her friends are among 40 candidates for a visit to Washington, D.C. One student will be selected at random. What is the probability that the student selected will be Janis or one of her friends?

28. A radio station is giving away 20 prizes: 8 movie tickets, 5 albums, 4 cassettes, and 3 concert tickets. Each prize has a number from 1 to 20. You have to pick a number from 1 to 20 to determine which prize is yours. What is the probability you will get an album or a cassette?

29. Lisa and her brother are among 12 girls and 18 boys nominated for band positions. One girl and one boy will be selected at random. What is the probability Lisa or her brother will be selected?

C Extending Thinking Skills

30. One die has a blank face instead of a 1-dot face. Another die has a blank face instead of a 4-dot face. What is the probability of rolling a sum of 7 with the dice?

31. A lost-and found office had 3 identical jackets. One was yours. You and two others arrived to claim your jackets. The clerk handed out the three jackets at random. What is the probability each of you got your own jacket?

Mixed Review

Give the least common multiple (LCM). **32.** 3, 5, 6 **33.** 4, 6, 9

Solve and check. **34.** $2m - 6 < -2$ **35.** $4(c + 1) = 28$ **36.** $6 = 0.8t$

37. $19 - 3y = 3y + 1$ **38.** $x + 3 = 2x$ **39.** $3m - 5m = 16$

13-5 Independent and Dependent Events

Suppose you first spin the spinner with numbers and then the spinner with letters. The outcome of the first spin does not influence the outcome of the second. The events are **independent**.

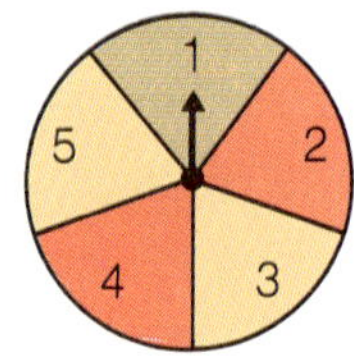

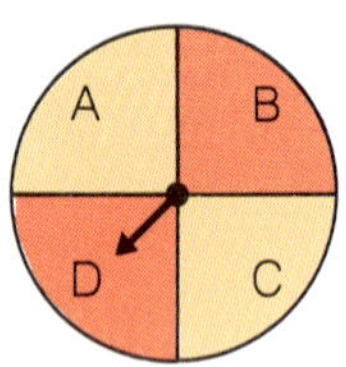

Formula: Independent Events

When two events are independent, the probability of both occurring is equal to the product of the probabilities of each event occurring.

P(A and B) = P(A) × P(B)

Example 1

For the two spinners above, find P(even number and vowel).

Solution

$P(\text{even number}) = \frac{2}{5}$ $\qquad$ $P(\text{vowel}) = \frac{1}{4}$

$P(\text{even number and vowel}) = \frac{2}{5} \times \frac{1}{4} = \frac{1}{10}$ Since the two events are independent, multiply their probabilities.

Practice Find each probability for the spinners above.

a. P(odd number and consonant) **b.** $P(\text{number} < 5 \text{ and a B})$

Suppose you select 1 ball and then another from a bag filled with 8 yellow balls and 4 green balls. The probability that the second ball you select is yellow depends on whether you replaced the first ball before selecting the second. If you did replace it, the two events are independent. If you did *not* replace it, the probability would depend on the outcome of the first draw. When an event's outcome is influenced by the outcome of a previous event, it is a **dependent event**.

To find the **probability of dependent events**, find the probability of the first event. Then, taking the first event into consideration, find the probability of the second event. Repeat this for each dependent event. Then multiply the probabilities.

Example 2

For the bag of marbles at right, find P(red then yellow).

Solution

$P(\text{red}) = \frac{4}{12}$ — 4 out of 12 marbles are red.

$P(\text{then yellow}) = \frac{8}{11}$ — If a red marble is selected first, only 11 marbles remain in the bag. 8 of these are yellow.

$P(\text{red then yellow}) = \frac{4}{12} \times \frac{8}{11}$ — Multiply the probabilities of the two events.

$= \frac{32}{132} = \frac{8}{33}$

Practice For the bag shown above, find each probability.

a. P(yellow then red) **b.** P(yellow then yellow)

Oral Exercises

State whether the pairs of activities are dependent or independent events.

1. Tossing heads on 1 coin and tails on another coin.

2. Taking 1 white sock from a drawer and then, without replacing it, taking another.

3. Seeing a blue motorcycle yesterday and a blue motorcycle today.

4. Picking a king of clubs from a deck and then, without replacing it, picking a king of hearts from the same deck.

5. Throwing a 5 with a die and then throwing a 4 on the second throw of the same die.

Exercises

A Find the probability for the spinner and for the cube numbered 1–6. Assume that the first outcome is for the spinner and the second is for the cube.

1. P(8 and 3)

2. P(14 and odd)

3. P(multiple of 4 and even)

4. P(12 and a number <6)

5. P(even and odd)

6. P(a number >12 and a number >4)

7. P(multiple of 5 and 5)

8. P(multiple of 6 and a number <2)

9. P(even and even)

10. P(a number >10 and a number <6)

11. P(odd and odd)

12. P(divisible by 7 and prime)

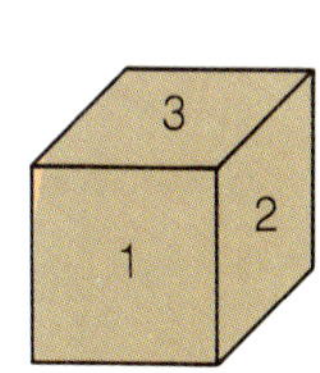

Suppose you have a standard deck of 52 playing cards. You select two cards at random without replacing the first. Find the probability of each.

13. *P*(king of spades then ace of hearts)
14. *P*(red card then black card)
15. *P*(red card then a red card)
16. *P*(ace then an ace)
17. *P*(heart then a diamond)
18. *P*(spade then a spade)
19. *P*(a 4 then a queen)
20. *P*(4 of hearts then 3 of hearts)
21. *P*(a king then a jack)
22. *P*(queen then queen)
23. *P*(heart then another heart)
24. *P*(club then a diamond)

B Solve.

You have a drawer with 3 white shirts, 4 gray shirts, 5 green shirts, and 4 blue shirts. You reach in and select three shirts at random without replacing them. Find each probability.

25. *P*(white then gray then green)
26. *P*(blue then green then gray)
27. *P*(green then green then blue)
28. *P*(blue then blue then blue)

Suppose you replace each shirt each time in the situation above. Find each probability.

29. *P*(white then blue then green)
30. *P*(gray then blue then green)
31. *P*(green then blue then gray)
32. *P*(gray then gray then gray)

C Extending Thinking Skills

The probability that person A will pass gym class is $\frac{5}{6}$, that B will pass is $\frac{3}{4}$, and that C will pass is $\frac{2}{3}$. If the probability that A will pass gym is $\frac{5}{6}$, then the probability A will not pass gym is $\frac{1}{6}$. Find each probability.

33. all 3 will *not* pass the course
34. A and C will pass but B will not
35. A and B will pass but C will not
36. C will pass but A and B will not pass

Mixed Review

Write as a percent. **37.** $\frac{3}{5}$ **38.** $1\frac{3}{8}$ **39.** $\frac{9}{15}$ **40.** $\frac{11}{4}$

Give the greatest common factor (GCF). **41.** 6, 24, 51

CALCULATOR ACTIVITY

Use a calculator to help you give each probability as a percent. Round to the nearest whole percent.

1. Of 60 previous days with atmospheric conditions like today's, it has rained on 35. What is the probability of rain today?

2. Of 150 previous days with atmospheric conditions like today's, it has rained on 20. What is the probability of rain today?

13-6 Practice Solving Problems

Exercises

A Solve by writing an equation.

1. A bricklayer makes \$15.75 an hour. She makes 3 times as much per hour as she did when she started. What was her starting hourly wage?

2. Fred's pay was 4 times his assistant's. Together, they earned \$675 for building a greenhouse. How much did each earn?

3. A shovel was priced at \$3.74 less than a saw. A carpenter bought one shovel and one saw and paid \$24.50. What was the price of the shovel?

4. The length of a garage is 3 times the width. The perimeter is 144 ft. What is the length and width?

5. Students raised money to visit a museum. This year, they earned \$50 more than twice the amount they raised last year. This year they collected \$1000. How much more did they collect this year than last year?

B

6. Three boys saved a total of \$75 for carpentry tools. Tim saved \$10 more than Kyle, and Jeff saved \$5 more than Kyle. How much did each boy save?

7. The area of the floor in a closet is 36 ft^2. The length of the closet is 4 times the width. What is the length and width of the closet?

8. A worker repaired a fireplace. Since he did the job on a Saturday, his fee was \$20 plus twice his normal hourly wage. He did the job in 5 hours and charged \$87.50. What was his regular hourly wage?

C Extending Thinking Skills

9. Write a word problem that could be solved by the equation $2x - 5 = 43$.

10. Write a word problem that could be solved by the equation $x + 3x = 58$.

Mixed Review

Write $<$, $>$, or $=$ for each $\square$. **11.** $-0.633 \square -0.632$ **12.** $-0.4 \square 0.5$

Solve and check. **13.** $0.45c = 1.8$ **14.** $t - 0.6t = 3.6$

13-7 Frequency Tables, Range, and Mode

Some students wanted to know the most common starting salary paid by restaurant chains in their city. They surveyed 33 restaurants and recorded their data in this **frequency table**.

Hourly Wage	Tally	Frequency
$3.35	卌	5
$3.50	卌 卌 I	11
$3.75	卌 I	6
$4.00	卌 II	7
$4.10	IIII	4

The **range** of a set of data is the difference between the greatest and the least numbers in the set.

$$\begin{array}{rl} \$4.10 & \leftarrow \text{greatest hourly wage} \\ -\ 3.35 & \leftarrow \text{least hourly wage} \\ \hline \$0.75 & \leftarrow \text{range} \end{array}$$

The **mode** is the number or item that appears most frequently. Eleven restaurants pay $3.50 an hour, so the mode is $3.50.

Example

Make a frequency table for the data. Find the range and mode. Student admission prices to 20 movie theaters: $3, $2.75, $3, $3.50, $2.25, $2.75, $3, $4, $3.50, $3, $3, $3.50, $2.25, $3.50, $3, $3, $2.25, $3, $4, $3.

Solution

Ticket Price	Tally	Frequency
$2.25	III	3
$2.75	II	2
$3.00	卌 IIII	9
$3.50	IIII	4
$4.00	II	2

Range = $4.00 − $2.25 = $1.75

Greatest price is $4; lowest price is $2.25.

Mode = $3.00

$3 occurs most frequently in the table.

Practice Make a frequency table for the data. Find the range and mode. Ages of girls on a soccer team: $16\frac{1}{2}$, 17, 15, 16, $15\frac{1}{2}$, $16\frac{1}{2}$, $17\frac{1}{2}$, 17, $15\frac{1}{2}$, $16\frac{1}{2}$, $16\frac{1}{2}$, 18, $16\frac{1}{2}$, $17\frac{1}{2}$, $16\frac{1}{2}$, $16\frac{1}{2}$, 16, 16, 17, 16, $16\frac{1}{2}$.

Oral Exercises

In a survey, English students asked people to try to say five tongue twisters. They made a frequency table showing which ones people were able to say.

Tongue Twister	Tally	Frequency
1. The sinking steamer sunk.	𝍸 𝍸 𝍸 𝍸 𝍸	
2. Rubber baby buggy bumpers	𝍸 𝍸 𝍸 𝍸 𝍸 𝍸 𝍸 I	
3. Toy boat (repeat 6 times)	𝍸 𝍸 𝍸 𝍸 𝍸 𝍸 𝍸 𝍸 I	
4. The sixth sick sheik's sixth sheep's sick.	𝍸 𝍸 III	
5. She sells seashells by the seashore.	𝍸 𝍸 𝍸 𝍸 𝍸 𝍸 𝍸 𝍸 𝍸 II	

1. How many people were able to say each tongue twister?

2. Which tongue twister could the most people say?

3. Which tongue twister could the fewest people say?

Exercises

A Make a frequency table for each set of data. Find the range and mode.

1. Runs scored in baseball games: 1, 1, 1, 1, 1, 2, 2, 2, 2, 2, 2, 2, 3, 3, 3, 4, 4, 4, 4, 5, 5, 5, 6, 6, 7, 7, 7, 7, 8, 8, 8, 9, 9, 10.

2. High temperature, in degrees Celsius: 25, 25, 26, 26, 26, 27, 29, 29, 30, 31, 31, 31, 31, 31, 31, 32, 32, 32, 33, 33, 34, 35, 35.

3. Grades on a math test: 72, 73, 73, 73, 73, 73, 73, 76, 76, 80, 80, 84, 84, 84, 84, 84, 86, 88, 88, 88, 90, 90, 98, 100.

4. Games won: 45, 46, 46, 46, 46, 46, 54, 62, 62, 62, 62, 63, 63, 65, 65, 65, 65, 70, 70, 70, 70, 70, 70, 76, 79.

5. Miles run: 14, 14, 14, 16, 17, 17, 17, 17, 20, 20, 20, 20, 20, 34, 34, 34.

6. Ages of airplane pilots: 37, 37, 38, 38, 38, 39, 39, 40, 40, 40, 42, 43, 43, 43, 45, 45, 50, 50, 50, 52, 52, 52, 52, 52, 52, 52, 53, 55.

7. Chalk length in mm: 39, 76, 27, 98, 18, 52, 21, 76, 45, 98, 19, 76, 93, 76.

8. High school seniors in several schools: 175, 210, 124, 150, 275, 110, 210, 325, 265, 173, 423, 212, 314, 226, 239, 219.

9. Percent correct on a test: 65%, 45%, 58%, 82%, 90%, 76%, 82%, 97%, 69%.

10. Students on the honor roll: 65, 43, 67, 56, 80, 54, 43, 72, 54, 47, 43, 64, 80.

11. People on a waterslide each hour: 35, 45, 24, 34, 50, 32, 19, 28, 34, 17, 28, 27, 36, 41, 16, 29, 24, 35, 32, 41, 36, 35, 29, 34, 27, 38, 42, 37, 28, 28, 34, 44.

12. Skiers on the slopes: 42, 27, 16, 15, 22, 23, 34, 17, 28, 33, 30, 34, 41, 26, 22, 30, 18, 35, 31, 21, 23, 22, 40, 36, 37, 34, 28, 33, 2, 22, 18, 36, 23, 16, 22, 34, 27, 42, 17, 22, 40, 12, 22, 32, 19, 25.

B

13. Make a frequency table for the data. Use intervals of \$2, with \$1.00–2.99 as the first interval. Find the range and mode.

Videocassette rental fees of different stores: \$4.50, \$1.99, \$5.75, \$1, \$1.50, \$5, \$1, \$2, \$3, \$3.80, \$2, \$2.75, \$5, \$4.25, \$5, \$2.50, \$3.75, \$2, \$3, \$2, \$2.75, \$2.60, \$2, \$3.25, \$4, \$3.10, \$1.69, \$3, \$2, \$6, \$3.25, \$2, \$3.50, \$4.75, \$4, \$2.50.

C Extending Thinking Skills

14. Add two numbers so that the mode changes. 18, 18, 18, 17, 16, 16, 15, 14

15. Add one of the numbers 20 through 24 so that the mode does not change. 24, 24, 24, 23, 23, 22, 22, 21, 21, 20, 20

16. Add two numbers so the range becomes 8. 9, 8, 8, 7, 6, 6, 6, 5, 3, 3, 3, 3, 2, 2

Mixed Review

Solve and check. **17.** $9 < 2c + 1$ **18.** $4.5y = -18$ **19.** $-6t = 3$

20. $a \div 4 = 9$ **21.** $11y + 16 = -17$ **22.** $12m = 10m + 12$

ESTIMATION

Find the range and mode for the data shown in the graph. Estimate the frequency of each response.

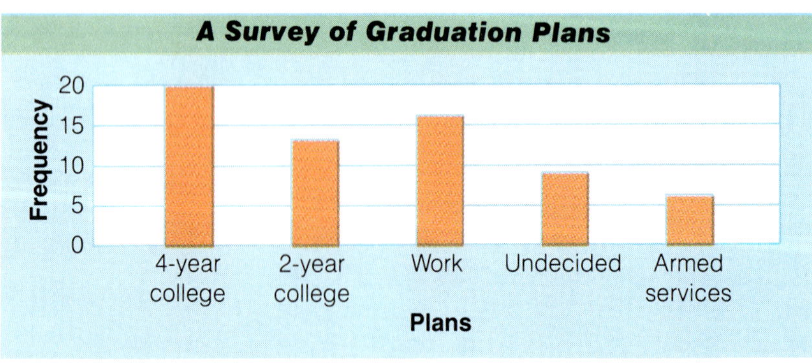

13-8 Mean and Median

In section 13-7, you learned how you find the mode. Two other measures used to determine which number in a list of numbers is "most typical" are **mean** and **median**. To find the **mean** or **average** of a list of numbers, find the total and divide by the number of items. The **median** is the middle number in a list of numbers arranged in order. If there are two middle numbers, the median is the mean of the two middle numbers.

Advertising by Restaurant Chains	
Restaurant	**Amount Spent in 3 Months**
A	\$45 million
B	\$20 million
C	\$15 million
D	\$11 million
E	\$11 million
F	\$ 6 million

Example

Find the mean and median for the numbers in the chart above.

Solution

$$\text{Mean} = \frac{45 + 20 + 15 + 11 + 11 + 6}{6}$$ Find the sum of the 6 numbers and divide by 6.

$$= \frac{108}{6}$$

$$\text{Mean} = 18$$ The mean is 18 million dollars.

45 20 15 11 11 6 List the numbers in order.

$$\text{Median} = \frac{15 + 11}{2}$$ The median is the mean of the two middle numbers.

$$\text{Median} = \frac{26}{2} = 13$$ The median is 13 million dollars.

Practice Find the mean and median. Round to the nearest tenth if necessary. 11, 14, 12, 12, 16, 18, 10, 20, 22

Oral Exercises

Tell whether each is true or false.

1. The mean and median are always the same.
2. An equal number of numbers in a list are above and below the median.
3. The mean is always one of the numbers in a list of numbers.
4. The median is always one of the numbers in a list of numbers.
5. Mean and average are the same.
6. Items should be in order to find the mean.
7. Items should be in order to find the median.
8. If there is 1 middle number in a list, it is the median.
9. To find the mean, find the total and divide by the number of items.

Exercises

A Find the mean and median for each set of numbers. Round to the nearest tenth if necessary.

1. 4, 2, 3, 4, 6, 8, 2
2. 10, 14, 9, 12, 14, 13, 8
3. 23, 25, 20, 18, 26, 28, 22, 23
4. 24, 35, 20, 16, 45, 50
5. 42, 60, 42, 42, 60, 40, 70, 45, 45
6. 12, 56, 43, 34, 58, 62, 71
7. 12, 8, 8, 24, 15, 3, 4, 9, 10, 16
8. 100, 125, 145, 132, 150, 143
9. 6, 8, 2, 6, 8, 10, 8, 2, 4, 8, 8, 2, 10, 2, 8, 4, 6, 6, 8, 10
10. 20, 40, 50, 10, 20, 30, 30, 10, 10, 30, 40, 50, 70, 40, 30, 20
11. 125, 250, 225, 75, 75, 200, 275, 175, 100, 200, 125, 250, 150
12. 500, 250, 250, 750, 200, 350, 400, 150, 600, 350, 100, 200

Find the mean and median. Round answers to the nearest hundredth if necessary.

13. 2.6, 3.8, 7, 4.5, 4.6, 7.8, 5.1, 8.1, 4.6, 5.6, 6.2
14. 7.5, 1.25, 6, 8.25, 11, 12.2, 14, 6.5, 14
15. 0.8, 0.25, 0.006, 0.26, 0.08, 0.045, 0.007
16. 5, 3, 6, 4, 7, 8, 9, 10, 3, 18, 24, 26, 30, 14, 14, 14, 25, 36
17. 2.8, 3.5, 4.07, 5.009, 4, 3.2, 2.25, 3.86, 1.4
18. 273, 485, 233, 225, 486, 387, 250, 239, 428

Solve. Round answers to the nearest hundredth if necessary.

19. Jared made \$2, \$5, \$4, \$5, \$1, and \$3 by doing odd jobs. What was the average amount he received?

20. The Falcons scored the following numbers of runs in their games last week: 6, 4, 1, 8, 2, 5, 4. Find the mean and median number of runs scored.

21. Carrie bowled 5 games. Her scores were 95, 110, 88, 102, and 130. What was her average score?

22. The math teachers at Jefferson School are 24, 23, 35, 40, 42, 50, 32, and 36 years old. What is the median age for these teachers?

B

23. Restaurants in Middletown paid different starting hourly wages. A new restaurant opened and wanted to offer a starting wage greater than the median wage paid by others. What would be the lowest wage the new restaurant could offer? Wages: \$3.65, \$4.50, \$4.25, \$5.00, \$3.65, \$4.75

24. In 29 at-bats in a World Series, Roberto Clemente had 7 singles, 2 doubles, 1 triple, and 2 home runs. What was his batting average for the World Series? Batting average is the number of hits divided by the times at bat. Round the decimal to the thousandths place.

C Extending Thinking Skills

25. Estimate the mean for the following numbers mentally. 87, 195, 213, 230, 298, 305, 479, 550

26. Derek's score on each math exam increased by 5 points from the previous exam. The mean for the 5 exams he took was 70. What were his exam scores?

Mixed Review

What percent of 24 is: **27.** 16? **28.** 9? **29.** 12? **30.** 21?

Evaluate for $x = 3$, $y = 4$. **31.** $\frac{x}{y}$ **32.** $\frac{2x}{3y}$ **33.** $\frac{x}{3} + \frac{y}{2}$ **34.** $\frac{1 - x}{1 - y}$

Solve and check. **35.** $12 = 3m + 15$ **36.** $m - 0.3m = 2.1$

Write <, >, or = for each □. **37.** $\frac{2}{3} \square \frac{18}{25}$ **38.** $-\frac{5}{16} \square -\frac{3}{16}$ **39.** $\frac{9}{4} \square \frac{53}{24}$

40. $1.106 \square 1.016$ **41.** $1 - 0.73 \square 0.27$ **42.** $-0.62 \square -0.63$

PROBLEM SOLVING: APPLICATIONS

13-9 Managing a Computer Store

A manager of a computer store keeps data on sales of computers and of computer materials. The data are often shown in graphs.

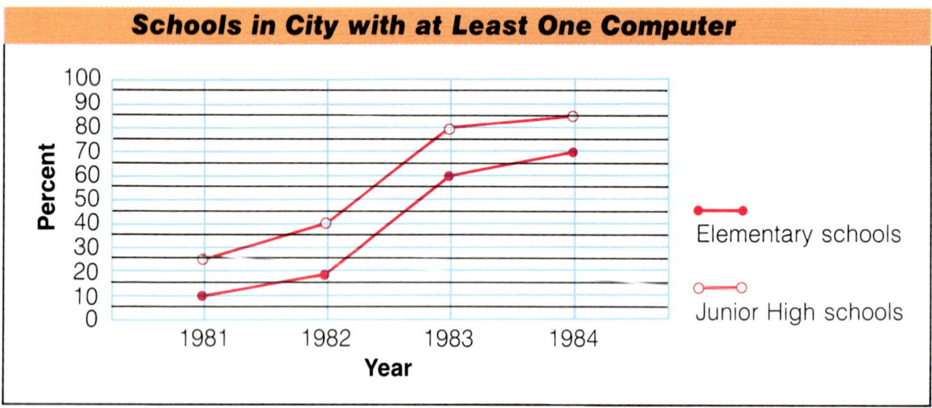

Problems

Use the graphs to solve.

1. What percentage more junior high schools than elementary schools had at least 1 computer in 1983?

2. By how many percentage points did the elementary schools having at least 1 computer increase from 1981 to 1984?

3. By how many percentage points did the junior high schools having at least 1 computer increase from 1981 to 1984?

4. What was the mean percentage of elementary and junior high schools having at least 1 computer in 1981?

5. What was the mean percentage of elementary and junior high schools having at least 1 computer in 1984?

6. How many fewer computers costing less than $500 were sold in 1984 than were sold in 1983?

7. How many more computers costing $500 to $1000 than computers costing more than $1000 were sold in 1984?

8. What was the total number of computers sold in 1983? In 1984?

9. What was the mean number of computers sold in 1983? What was the mean number sold in 1984?

10. What was the approximate percentage of increase in sales of computers costing more than $1000 from 1983 to 1984?

11. What was the approximate percentage of decrease in sales of computers costing less than $500 from 1983 to 1984?

12. How much more money was made on game software than on business software?

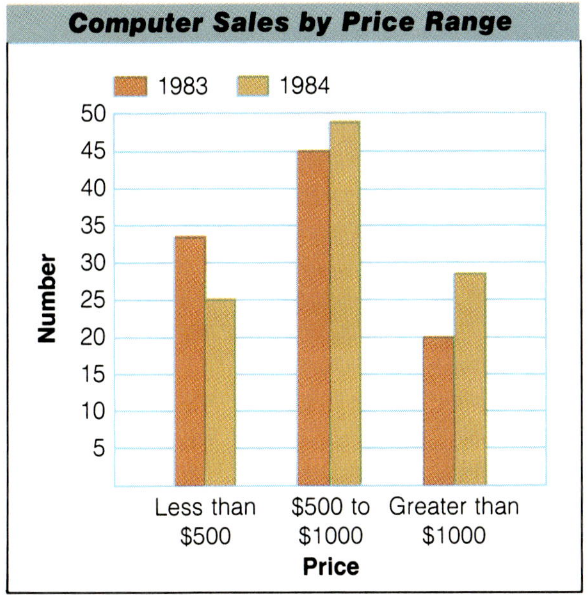

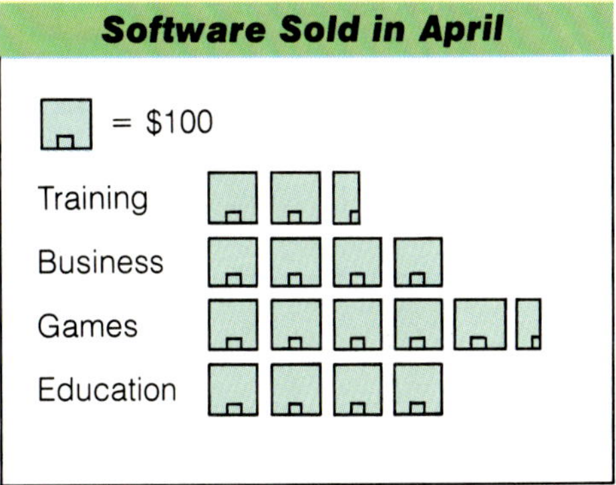

13. How much less money was made on training software than on education software?

14. What were the average sales for computer software in April?

15. ***Data Search*** Find the cost of 5 different computers in a computer store in your city. Find the average cost of the computers.

What's Your Decision?

Your school wants to buy 20 new computers. The regular price at two stores is the same, $1500 per computer. Store A will give the school 5 computers at no charge if it buys 15 at the regular price. Store B will give the school 15% off the cost of each computer. A 5% sales tax must be paid at either store. Where should your school buy the computers?

13-10 Making Bar Graphs and Line Graphs

Bar graphs and line graphs are useful for comparing data. You can use these steps to make bar graphs and line graphs.

1. Determine the scale.
   - Find the greatest and least values for the data.
   - Select a scale to fit your data.
2. Draw and label the horizontal and vertical sides of the graph.
3. Plot the points for the line graph or draw the bars for the bar graph.
4. Give the graph a title.

Example 1

Make a line graph for the data. Room rates at Pines Motel: 1940, \$4.75; 1950, \$8.75; 1960, \$13.40; 1970, \$25.40; 1980, \$39.75.

Solution Greatest amount = \$39.75

Least amount = \$4.75

Let the scale = \$5 per mark

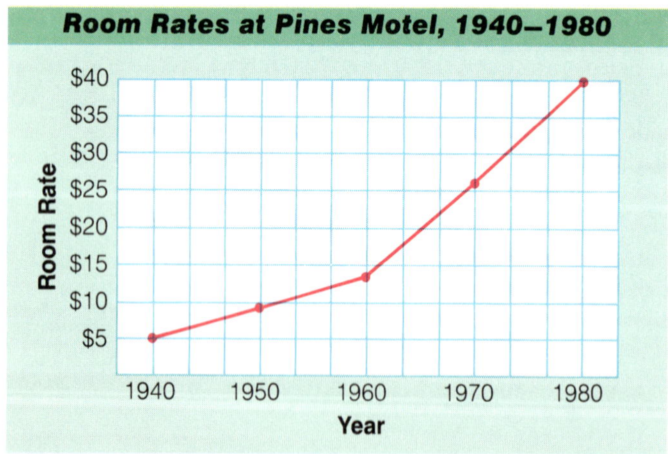

Practice Make a line graph for the data. Median heights of boys: age 11, 142 cm; age 12, 150 cm; age 13, 158 cm; age 14, 163 cm; age 15, 169 cm; age 16, 176 cm; age 17, 177 cm.

Example 2

Make a bar graph for the data. Airline tickets sold on one day: Northeast, 9; Southeast, 3; Midwest, 6; Southwest, 4; Rockies, 3; West Coast, 7.

Solution Greatest number = 9

Least number = 3

Let the scale = 1 ticket per mark

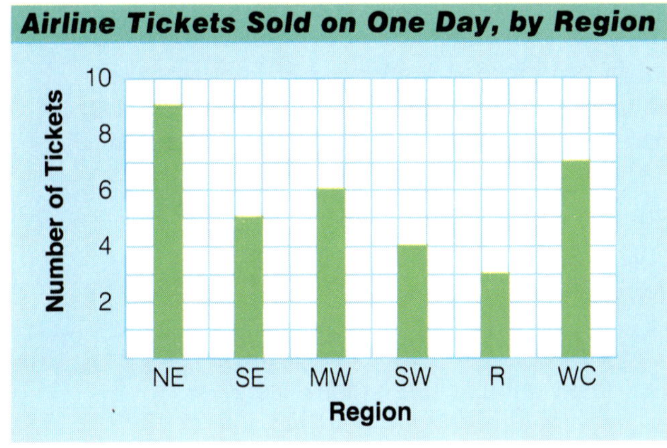

Practice Make a bar graph for the data. Take-offs and landings at busy airports each year: Chicago, 600,000; Atlanta, 580,000; Los Angeles, 480,000; Denver, 475,000; Dallas, 440,000.

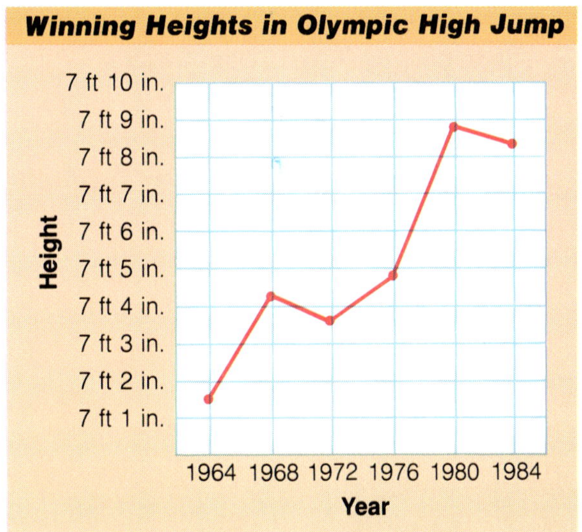

Oral Exercises

Use the graph to answer the questions.

1. How many inches does each mark on the vertical scale represent?

2. How many years does each mark on the horizontal scale represent?

3. In what year was the highest jump? The lowest jump?

4. Between which years did the winning height drop?

5. Between which years was the change in the winning height greatest?

Exercises

A Make a bar graph for the data in Exercises 1 and 2.

1. Number of students using a computer lab at lunchtime. Monday, 7; Tuesday, 6; Wednesday, 4; Thursday, 5; Friday, 5. Let each mark on the scale represent 1 student.

2. Average wind velocities, in miles per hour: Boston, 12.5; Chicago, 10.3; Honolulu, 11.8; San Francisco, 10.5; Washington, D.C., 9.4. Let each mark on the scale represent 0.5 mi/h.

Make a line graph for the data in Exercises 3 and 4.

3. Average monthly rainfall in a town, in centimeters: January, 1.8; February, 2.2; March, 4.0; April, 7.6; May, 8.2; June, 5.4; July, 3.6; August, 2.8; September, 4.2; October, 4.2; November, 2.6; December, 2.0. Let each mark on the scale represent 0.4 cm.

4. Price of gold, per ounce: 1972, $59; 1973, $98; 1974, $160; 1975, $161; 1976, $125; 1977, $148; 1978, $194; 1979, $308; 1980, $613; 1981, $460; 1982, $376. Let each mark on the scale represent $50.

B

5. Make a line graph for the data. Then make another line graph, using the same data but changing the scale so the graph is almost a straight line.

Leaded Regular Gasoline Prices, 1973–1982									
1973	1974	1975	1976	1977	1978	1979	1980	1981	1982
$0.40	$0.53	$0.57	$0.59	$0.62	$0.63	$0.86	$1.19	$1.31	$1.26

C Extending Thinking Skills

6. Make up a story that could explain the changes in the graph below.

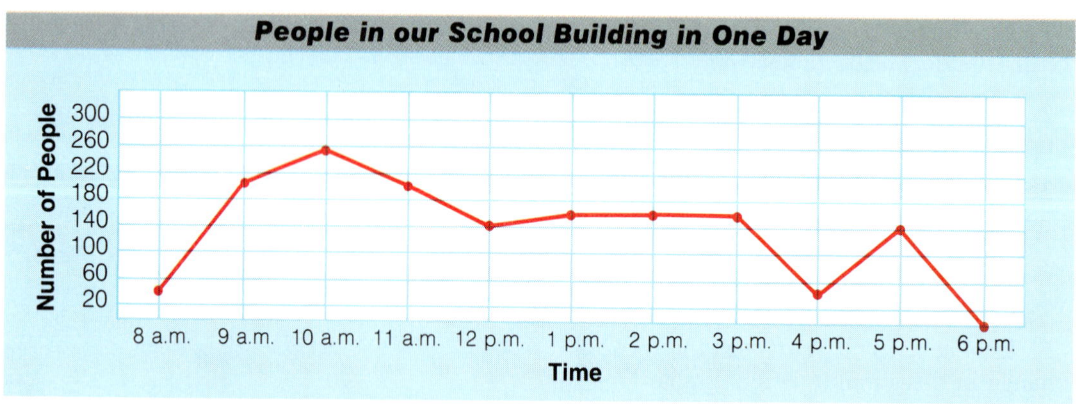

Mixed Review

Simplify. **7.** $16n + 3n - 9 - 10n$ **8.** $2(a + 6) - 8$

Solve and check. **9.** $2t = 16 - 2t$ **10.** $3c = c + 5$ **11.** $-42 = 6y$

12. $2m < 3m + 1$ **13.** $t + 2t = 21$ **14.** $-18 = 6 + 4n$

15. $\left(\frac{3}{16}\right)y = -\frac{3}{4}$ **16.** $r - \frac{1}{2} = \frac{5}{16}$ **17.** $\frac{m}{6} = \frac{25}{15}$ **18.** $\frac{2}{3} = z + \frac{4}{5}$

A square has one side = 6 m. **19.** Give the perimeter. **20.** Give the area.

21. Give the perimeter of a regular pentagon with one side = 7.5 cm.

22. Give the perimeter of an equilateral triangle with one side = 11 m.

ESTIMATION

Estimate the winning times for this race for the next three years.

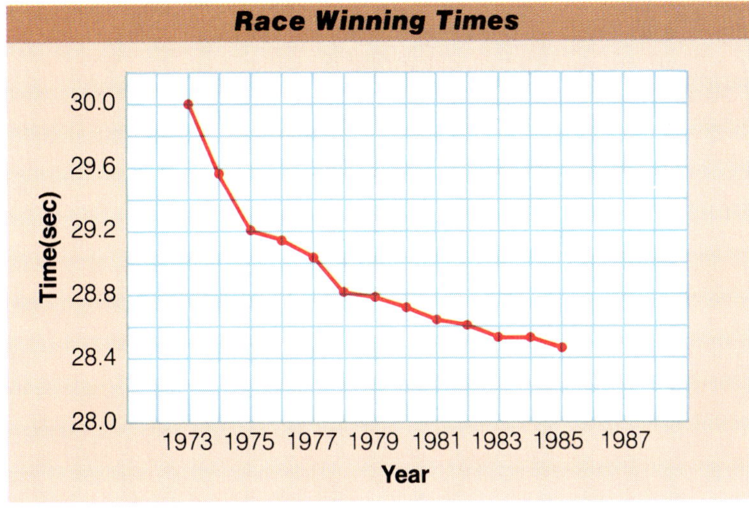

13-11 Making Pictographs

You can follows these steps to make a pictograph.

1. Determine the scale:
   - Find the greatest and least values for the data.
   - Select a scale to fit the data.
2. Round the data; draw and label the pictures for the graph.
3. Show the scale for the graph.
4. Give the graph a title.

Example

Make a pictograph for the data. Coins made at the Denver Mint in 1982: half-dollars, 6 million; quarters, 120 million; dimes, 54 million; nickels, 19 million; pennies, 60 million.

Solution Greatest number = 120. Least number = 6.

Let = 10 million coins and = 5 million coins.

Rounded data: Half-dollars, 5 — 6 is closer to 5 than to 10.
Quarters, 120
Dimes, 55 — 54 is closer to 55 than to 60.
Nickels, 20 — 19 is closer to 20 than to 15.
Pennies, 60

Coins Made at Denver Mint in 1982

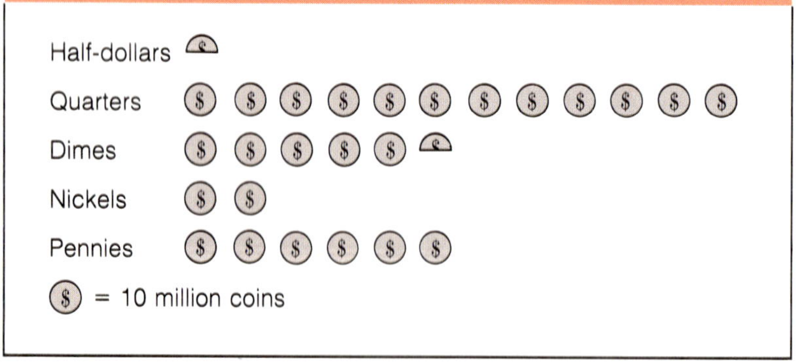

Half-dollars

Quarters

Dimes

Nickels

Pennies

= 10 million coins

Practice Make a pictograph for the data. Favorite breakfast meals: cereal, 88; eggs, 39; pancakes, 129; toast, 138; fruit, 70.

Oral Exercises

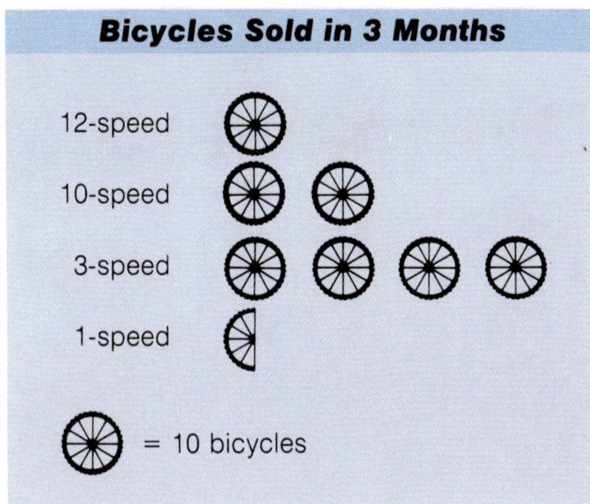

1. What does each wheel represent?
2. What does each half-wheel represent?
3. Which type of bicycle was sold most?
4. How many 3-speed bikes were sold?
5. How many 1-speed bikes were sold?
6. How many 10-speed bikes were sold?

Exercises

A Make a pictograph for the data.

1. Favorite sports at the Simmonsville Racquet Club: racquetball, 18 members; tennis, 32 members; handball, 12 members; squash, 10 members. Let each picture represent 4 people.

2. Campers on Labor Day weekend: Camp Pine, 125; Camp Timber, 75; Tent City, 150; Mountain Trees, 105. Let each picture represent 25 campers.

3. Favorite forms of exercise: running, 125 people; walking, 58 people; swimming, 29 people; bicycling, 46 people; exercise class, 15 people.

4. Populations of cities: New York, 7,072,000; Tokyo, 8,336,000; Mexico City, 9,191,000; Sydney, 3,281,000; London, 6,696,000; Bombay, 8,227,000; Nairobi, 1,048,000; Moscow, 7,831,000. Let each picture represent 1 million people.

5. Size (in acres) of National Parks in Alaska: Wrangell-St. Elias, 8,945,000; Gates of the Arctic, 7,500,000; Denali, 4,700,000; Katmai, 3,716,000; Glacier Bay, 3,225,000; Lake Clark, 2,875,000; Kobuk Valley, 1,750,000. Let each picture represent 1 million acres.

B

6. Use the graph on campers during Labor Day weekend (Exercise 2) to find the mean number of people at a camp.

7. Use the graph on populations of cities (Exercise 4) to find the mean and median number of people living in the cities.

C Extending Thinking Skills

8. Make up two different sets of data that, when rounded, would be shown by the graph below.

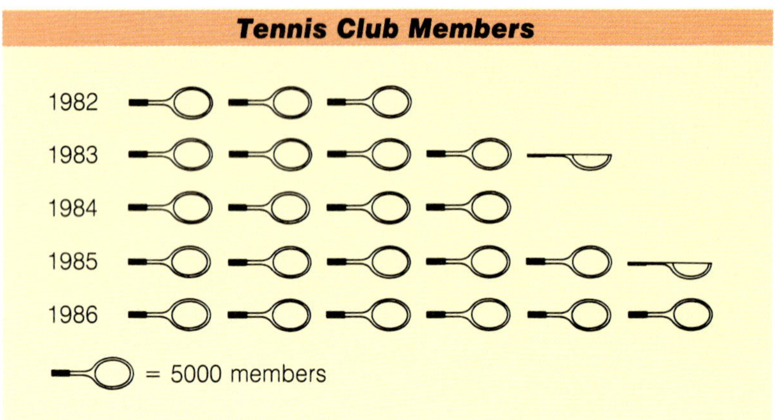

Mixed Review

Write <, >, or = for each □. **9.** $-0.33 \square -0.32$ **10.** $9.01 \square 9.1$
11. $3(n - 4) \square 3n - 3(4)$ **12.** $6(2) \square -6(-2)$ **13.** $ab \square ba$
Solve and check. **14.** $9.6n + 1.4n = 27.5$ **15.** $3.5c = 14.7$
What percent of 64 is: **16.** 36? **17.** 20? **18.** 72? **19.** 4?

COMPUTER ACTIVITY

The program below will compute the mean temperature for a week (7 days).

```
10 PRINT "MEAN TEMPERATURE FOR THE LAST WEEK"
20 PRINT "ENTER SEVEN TEMPERATURES."
30 INPUT T1,T2,T3,T4,T5,T6,T7
40 AV=(T1+T2+T3+T4+T5+T6+T7)/7
45 PRINT "THE MEAN TEMPERATURE WAS "; AV
50 IF AV>65 THEN GOTO 80
60 PRINT "PLEASE GET WARMER!"
70 GOTO 90
80 PRINT "GREAT WEATHER!"
90 END
```

1. Use the program to find the mean temperature for the last week.

2. Change the program to find the mean temperature for 3 days.

3. Change the program to find the mean score on 5 math tests.

13-12 Practice Solving Problems

Most problems are solved by some combination of strategies. Notice how strategies are used in the example below.

Problem Amanda wants to lay out a patio in a design like the one shown below. She has 50 bricks to use. How many bricks should she place in the middle row to use the greatest number of bricks?

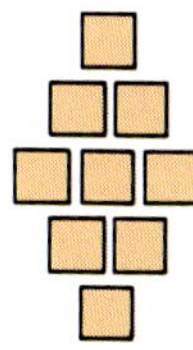

To solve, you can first **simplify the problem** to find the total bricks used if 1 brick is in the middle row, then the total with 2 bricks in the middle row, 3 bricks in the middle row, and so on. You can **draw a picture** to determine the number of bricks used each time. You can **make a table** to record this information, then **look for a pattern**.

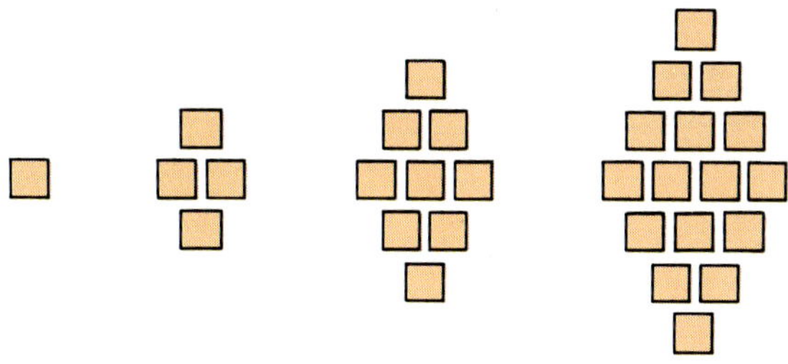

Number in Middle Row	1	2	3	4	5	6	7
Total Number of Bricks Used	1	4	9	16	25	36	49

The total number of bricks used is equal to the square of the number in the middle row. If there were 7 in the middle row, 49 would be used in all.

To use the greatest number of bricks, Amanda should place 7 bricks in the middle row.

This chart shows the strategies presented.

Problem-Solving Strategies

Choose the Operations	Write an Equation
Guess, Check, Revise	Simplify the Problem
Draw a Picture	Make an Organized List
Make a Table	Use Logical Reasoning
Look for a Pattern	Work Backwards

Problems

Solve.

1. What is the greatest number of pieces into which a pizza can be cut with 5 straight cuts if the pieces cannot be stacked for cutting?

2. A box holding 40 pencils weighs 135 g. The same box holding 20 of the same pencils weighs 75 g. What is the weight of the box?

3. In how many different ways can a football team score 18 points?

touchdown = 6 points	field goal = 3 points
point after a touchdown = 1 point	safety = 2 points

4. Three boys were playing a game. They decided to play 3 more rounds. The player with the most points at the end of 3 rounds would be the winner. For each round there would be one loser and two winners, and the loser would have to double the points each winner had by giving his own points away. Each boy won twice and lost once. The game ended in a tie, with each boy having 40 points. How many points did each boy have before the last 3 rounds?

5. Jane, Al, and Sally were selling school sweatshirts to raise money for a class trip. Al sold 1 less shirt than Jane, and Sally sold half as many shirts as Jane. Together the three sold 89 shirts. How many did each sell?

6. Ms. Davies gave a math quiz with 20 questions. She gave 2 points for each correct answer and subtracted 3 points for each incorrect answer. Yolanda answered all 20 questions and got a score of 0. How many did she get right and how many did she get wrong?

7. A drink in a vending machine costs 50¢. The machine takes nickels, dimes, and quarters. How many different ways could you pay for a drink?

8. A restaurant has 2 types of tables. One type seats 4 people and one type seats 6. One night, 114 people were eating at 24 tables in the restaurant, and no table with people had empty seats. How many tables of each type were used?

Enrichment

A Probability Experiment

George Buffon (1707–1788), a French biologist, created the *Buffon Needle Problem.* In Buffon's house, the joints between the floorboards made parallel lines. Buffon took a needle shorter than the width of a board and dropped it on the floor over and over again. Each time, he recorded whether the needle crossed a line or did not cross a line. His results are, oddly enough, related to the number π.

You can conduct a similar experiment. On a large sheet of paper, draw 5 parallel lines 3 cm apart. Drop a piece of toothpick 2 cm long on the paper from a height of about 50 cm, giving it a slight twist as you drop it. Record whether the toothpick lands across a line or between the lines. Repeat this 50 times.

Let l represent the length of the toothpick, b the distance between lines, and P the probability the toothpick will fall across a line (number of times the toothpick fell across a line divided by the number of tosses). Buffon concluded that the following formula gives a formula for π.

$$\pi = \frac{2l}{bP}$$

Using the length of the toothpick and the distance between lines given above,

$$\pi = \frac{2l}{bP} = \frac{2 \cdot 2}{3 \cdot P} = \frac{4}{3P}$$

1. Conduct this experiment and calculate a value for π. How close did you come to 3.14, an approximate value for π?

2. Suppose the toothpick fell across a line on 21 out of 50 tosses. How close is the value to the true value of π?

3. Change the distance between lines to 9 cm and the length of the toothpick to 4 cm and repeat this experiment. How do the results compare to the first experiment?

Chapter 13 Review

13-1 Use the counting principle to find the total number of outcomes.

1. Selection: 1 size and 1 flavor
Sizes: 6 ounces, 12 ounces
Flavors: strawberry, peach, apple

13-2 Find the number of permutations.

2. f, l, a, v, o, r **3.** 2, 4, 6, 8, 10

13-3 Find the number of combinations.

4. 7 people try out for a part in a play. How many ways can the actor and an understudy be chosen?

5. Select 2 records from a rack of 6 records.

13-4 There are 14 names in a hat. 8 are boys' names and 6 are girls' names. You select one name without looking. Find each probability.

6. P(boy) **7.** P(not boy) **8.** P(boy or girl)

13-5 Find the probability of each for one toss of two dice.

9. P(1 and 6) **10.** P(3 and odd)

13-6 Solve by writing an equation.

11. Carla paid a total of $34.88 for a scarf and a pair of gloves. The scarf cost $2.90 less than the gloves. What was the cost of the scarf?

13-7–13-8 Use the data to solve problems 12–15. Plant height in cm: 16, 18, 22, 22, 23, 25.

12. Find the range. **13.** Find the mode.

14. Find the median. **15.** Find the mean.

13-9 **16.** Make a line graph for the data. Library books loaned: Monday, 12; Tuesday, 8; Wednesday, 25; Thursday, 18; Friday, 21.

13-10 Use the bar graph to solve.

17. How many tickets did the seventh grade class sell?

18. Which class sold the most tickets?

19. Which class sold about 48 tickets?

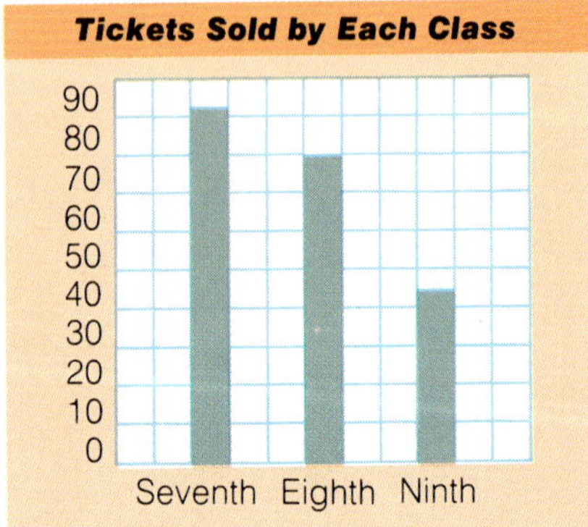

13-11 Make a pictograph for the data.

20. Trees on schoolgrounds: maple, 9; birch, 15; pine, 6; oak, 12.

Chapter 13 Test

Use the counting principle to find the total number of outcomes.

1. Selection: 1 date and 1 show time
Dates: June 10, June 11, June 17, June 18, June 24, June 25
Times: 6:00 p.m., 8:00 p.m., 10:00 p.m.

Use a formula to find the number of permutations.

2. c, o, m, p, u, t, e, r

3. left, right, forward, back

Use a formula to find the number of combinations.

4. 6 dogs are in a contest. How many ways can the winner and runner-up be chosen?

5. Select 3 kites from a display of 8 kites.

There are 10 tennis balls in a bag. 2 are green, 3 are white, and 5 are yellow. You select one ball from the bag without looking. Find each probability.

6. P(yellow)

7. P(not green)

8. P(green or white)

Find the probability of each for one toss of two dice.

9. P(2 and 5)

10. P(a number $>$ 5 and an even number)

Solve by writing an equation. **11.** The length of a room is 4 times its width. The perimeter is 155 ft. Find the dimensions of the room.

Use the data to solve problems 12–15.

Team members' ages: 20, 20, 20, 22, 23, 25, 25, 26, 26.

12. Find the range.

13. What is the mode?

14. What is the median?

15. Find the mean.

16. Make a bar graph for the data. Mountain heights in feet: McKinley, 20,320; Whitney, 14,494; Mauna Kea, 13,796; Granite Peak, 12,799; Rainier, 14,410.

Use the line graph to answer each question.

17. During which month were Jean's scores highest?

18. Between which months did Jean's scores drop?

19. Between which months was the change in Jean's score the greatest?

20. Make a pictograph for the data. Records sold: Monday, 12; Tuesday, 20; Wednesday, 18; Thursday, 26; Friday, 22.

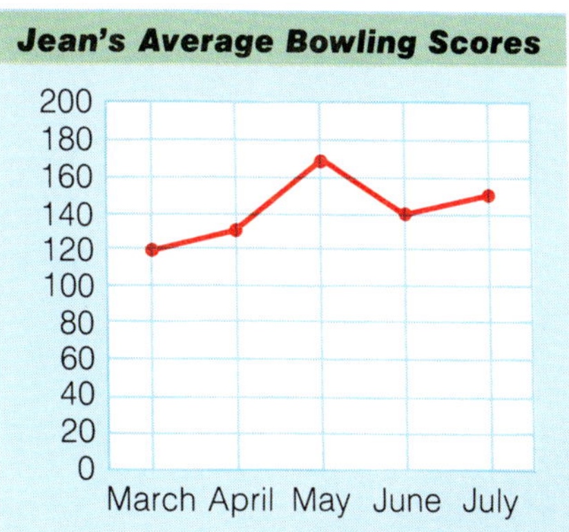

Cumulative Review

Find the discount and the sale price. Round to the nearest cent if necessary.

1. Regular price = \$60
   Discount = 30%

2. Regular price = \$1200
   Discount = 9%

Find the commission. Round to the nearest cent if necessary.

3. Sale price = \$66
   Commission = 4%

4. Sale price = \$90
   Commission = 8%

Find the interest and the total amount. Round to the nearest cent if necessary.

5. \$750 at 15% per year for 3 years
6. \$600 at 2% per year for 4 months

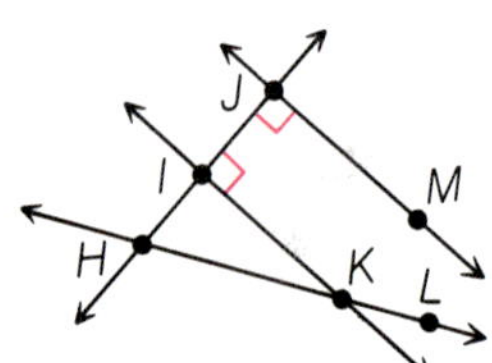

Refer to the figure for Exercises 7–10.

7. Name an acute angle.
8. Name an obtuse angle.
9. Name a right angle.
10. Name a pair of parallel lines.

Classify each triangle according to the measures of its angles and the lengths of its sides.

11. $\angle CDE$ has a 90-degree angle and two sides equal in length.
12. $\angle PQR$ has a 112-degree angle and no two sides equal in length.

13. Name the polygon.

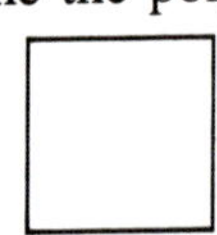

14. Write and solve an equation to find the measure of $\angle M$.

Find the area of each figure.

15. A rectangle with width 9 ft and length 22 ft.
16. A triangle with base 14 m and height 5 m.

17. a parallelogram with base = 212 mm, height = 40 mm
18. a trapezoid with $b_1 = 16$ m, $b_2 = 8$ m, $h = 12$ m

Find the area of a circle with the given radius or circumference. Use 3.14 as an approximation for π.

19. $r = 6$ m
20. $d = 1.5$ km

21. Find the area of the figure at right.

7 cm
6 cm
3 cm
15 cm

Chapter 14

Square Roots and Special Triangles

14-1 Square Roots

The **square root** of 36 is 6 since $6 \cdot 6 = 36$. In general, the square root of a number x is the number y if $y^2 = x$. The symbol $\sqrt{\ }$, called a **radical sign**, is used to indicate the square root. We write $\sqrt{36} = 6$.

Each positive number has two square roots. For example, 64 has square roots of 8 and -8 since $8^2 = 64$ and $(-8)^2 = 64$.

8 is the positive square root of 64, written as $\sqrt{64} = 8$.

-8 is the negative square root of 64, written as $-\sqrt{64} = -8$.

Example 1

Find $\sqrt{49}$.

Solution $\sqrt{49} = 7$

Practice Find the square root.

a. $-\sqrt{25}$ **b.** $\sqrt{64}$

Whenever the square root of a number is not an integer it is an *irrational* number. This means the square root cannot be written as a fraction, but can be approximated as a decimal. For example, $\sqrt{7} \approx 2.646$.

Example 2

Between what two consecutive integers does $\sqrt{18}$ lie?

Solution $4 < \sqrt{18} < 5$ Since $4^2 = 16$ and $5^2 = 25$, $\sqrt{18}$ is between 4 and 5.

Practice Between what two consecutive integers does each square root lie?

a. $\sqrt{28}$ **b.** $\sqrt{53}$

When numbers are added or subtracted under a single radical sign, carry out the operation before finding the square root.

Example 3

Evaluate each expression. **a.** $\sqrt{81} - \sqrt{36}$ **b.** $\sqrt{29 + 7}$

Solution

a. $\sqrt{81} - \sqrt{36} = 9 - 6$
$= 3$

Find the square root of each number before subtracting.

b. $\sqrt{29 + 7} = \sqrt{36}$
$= 6$

Since both numbers are under the same radical sign, add before finding the square root.

Practice Evaluate each expression. **a.** $\sqrt{49} + \sqrt{121}$ **b.** $\sqrt{121 - 40}$

Oral Exercises

State whether the following are true or false.

1. $\sqrt{25} = 5$ **2.** $\sqrt{9} = 3$ **3.** $\sqrt{36} = -6$ **4.** $-\sqrt{16} = 4$

5. $\sqrt{36} = 6$ **6.** $\sqrt{16} = -4$ **7.** $-\sqrt{25} = -5$ **8.** $\sqrt{49} = 7$

Exercises

A Find the square root.

1. $\sqrt{25}$ **2.** $-\sqrt{81}$ **3.** $\sqrt{4}$ **4.** $\sqrt{9}$ **5.** $\sqrt{144}$

6. $\sqrt{64}$ **7.** $-\sqrt{16}$ **8.** $-\sqrt{4}$ **9.** $\sqrt{16}$ **10.** $\sqrt{100}$

Between what two consecutive integers does each square root lie?

11. $\sqrt{7}$ **12.** $\sqrt{12}$ **13.** $\sqrt{17}$ **14.** $-\sqrt{5}$ **15.** $\sqrt{43}$

16. $\sqrt{39}$ **17.** $-\sqrt{42}$ **18.** $\sqrt{38}$ **19.** $\sqrt{29}$ **20.** $-\sqrt{41}$

21. $\sqrt{24}$ **22.** $\sqrt{37}$ **23.** $\sqrt{85}$ **24.** $\sqrt{57}$ **25.** $\sqrt{112}$

Evaluate each expression.

26. $\sqrt{25} + \sqrt{81}$ **27.** $\sqrt{41 - 5}$ **28.** $\sqrt{55 - 6}$

29. $\sqrt{74 + 26}$ **30.** $\sqrt{81} - \sqrt{100}$ **31.** $\sqrt{221 - 100}$

32. $\sqrt{23 + 58} - \sqrt{36}$ **33.** $\sqrt{81 - 17} - \sqrt{81}$ **34.** $\sqrt{16 + 9} - \sqrt{9}$

35. $\sqrt{12 + 13} + \sqrt{49}$ **36.** $\sqrt{81} - \sqrt{45 - 20}$ **37.** $\sqrt{64} - \sqrt{36 + 28}$

B Write <, >, or = in place of □ to make a true statement.

38. $\sqrt{25} + \sqrt{36}$ □ $\sqrt{25 + 36}$ **39.** $\sqrt{81} - \sqrt{4}$ □ $\sqrt{81 - 4}$

40. $\sqrt{16 - 9}$ □ $\sqrt{16} - \sqrt{9}$ **41.** $\sqrt{16 + 9}$ □ $\sqrt{16} + \sqrt{9}$

A square root can be multiplied by another number. For example, $6\sqrt{25} = 6 \times 5 = 30$. In Exercises 42–43, write $<$, $>$, or $=$ in place of $\square$ to make a true statement.

42. $2\sqrt{16} \square \sqrt{32}$ **43.** $3\sqrt{9} \square \sqrt{27}$

44. Evaluate the expression $3\sqrt{a} + \sqrt{b}$ for $a = 25$ and $b = 81$.

45. Evaluate the expression $\sqrt{\frac{a}{b}}$ for $a = 243$ and $b = 3$.

C Extending Thinking Skills

Find the pattern and give the next two terms in the sequence. Then complete the nth term.

46. $\sqrt{2^4} = 4$, $\sqrt{3^4} = 9$, $\sqrt{4^4} = 16$, __?__, __?__, $\sqrt{n^4} =$ __?__

47. $\sqrt{2^6} = 8$, $\sqrt{3^6} = 27$, $\sqrt{4^6} = 64$, __?__, __?__, $\sqrt{n^6} =$ __?__

Mixed Review

Use the figure at right for Exercises 48–52.

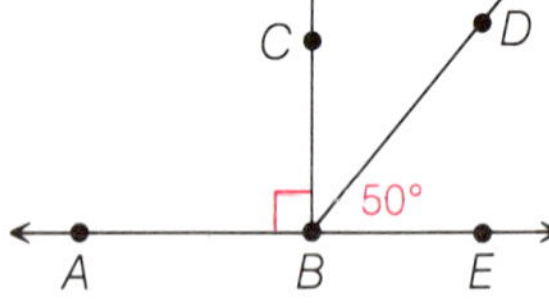

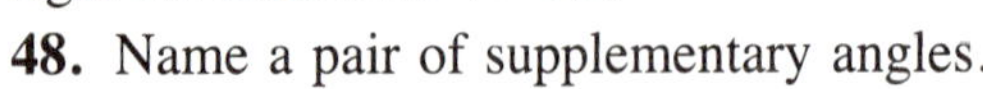

48. Name a pair of supplementary angles.

49. Name a pair of complementary angles.

50. Name a right angle.

Write an equation to find the measure of: **51.** $\angle CBD$ **52.** $\angle ABD$

Give the area. **53.** A rectangle with height = 6 cm, width = 11 cm

Give the mean, median, and mode. **54.** 11, 13, 12, 11, 9, 14, 11

NUMBERS TO ALGEBRA

Check to see that the number examples are true. Then replace a and b with other perfect squares to test the generalization given.

Numbers	Algebra
$\sqrt{4} \cdot \sqrt{9} = \sqrt{4 \cdot 9}$ $\sqrt{4} \cdot \sqrt{16} = \sqrt{4 \cdot 16}$ $\sqrt{9} \cdot \sqrt{16} = \sqrt{9 \cdot 16}$	For non-negative numbers $\boldsymbol{a}$ and $\boldsymbol{b}$, $\sqrt{a}\sqrt{b} = \sqrt{ab}$

Use the generalization above to express each product as an integer.

1. $\sqrt{2} \cdot \sqrt{32}$ **2.** $\sqrt{18} \cdot \sqrt{2}$ **3.** $\sqrt{3} \cdot \sqrt{48}$ **4.** $\sqrt{5} \cdot \sqrt{20}$

5. $\sqrt{2} \cdot \sqrt{50}$ **6.** $\sqrt{8} \cdot \sqrt{18}$ **7.** $\sqrt{3} \cdot \sqrt{27}$ **8.** $\sqrt{6} \cdot \sqrt{24}$

14-2 Finding Square Roots

Engineers evaluate formulas such as $t = \sqrt{\frac{d}{16}}$ to calculate the time for an object to travel d feet.

To find approximations of square roots, you can use square root tables or a calculator with a $\sqrt{}$ key.

Example 1

Use the table to find an approximation for $\sqrt{13}$.

Solution $\sqrt{13} \approx 3.606$

Look down the left column of the table to find 13. Then look across to the square root column to read 3.606.

Number n	Square Root $\sqrt{n}$	Square n^2
1	1	1
2	1.414	4
3	1.732	9
4	2	16
5	2.236	25
6	2.449	36
7	2.646	49
8	2.828	64
9	3	81
10	3.162	100
11	3.317	121
12	3.464	144
13	3.606	169
14	3.742	196
15	3.873	225
16	4	256

Practice Use this table to find an approximate value for each.

a. $\sqrt{15}$ **b.** $\sqrt{11}$

Example 2

Use a calculator with a $\sqrt{\ }$ key to find an approximation for $\sqrt{34}$.

Solution 5.83095

Input	Display
34 [√] [=]	5.83095

Practice Use a calculator with a $\sqrt{\ }$ key to find an approximation for each.

a. $\sqrt{53}$ **b.** $\sqrt{43.7}$

Oral Exercises

Give the closest integer estimate for each square root.

1. $\sqrt{12}$ **2.** $\sqrt{17}$ **3.** $\sqrt{24}$ **4.** $\sqrt{39}$ **5.** $\sqrt{15}$

6. $\sqrt{27}$ **7.** $\sqrt{80}$ **8.** $\sqrt{50}$ **9.** $\sqrt{10}$ **10.** $\sqrt{99}$

Exercises

A Use the table on page 509 to find each square root.

1. $\sqrt{2}$ **2.** $\sqrt{5}$ **3.** $\sqrt{14}$ **4.** $\sqrt{17}$ **5.** $\sqrt{19}$

6. $\sqrt{27}$ **7.** $\sqrt{10}$ **8.** $\sqrt{47}$ **9.** $\sqrt{93}$ **10.** $\sqrt{39}$

11. $\sqrt{32}$ **12.** $\sqrt{18}$ **13.** $\sqrt{28}$ **14.** $\sqrt{76}$ **15.** $\sqrt{87}$

Use a calculator with a $\sqrt{\ }$ key to find an approximation for each square root. Round your answer to the nearest thousandth.

16. $\sqrt{46}$ **17.** $\sqrt{93}$ **18.** $\sqrt{421}$ **19.** $\sqrt{57}$

20. $\sqrt{948}$ **21.** $\sqrt{95.8}$ **22.** $\sqrt{84.25}$ **23.** $\sqrt{8392}$

24. $\sqrt{38.9}$ **25.** $\sqrt{42.93}$ **26.** $\sqrt{38.64}$ **27.** $\sqrt{57.23}$

B Square the number in parentheses. Write $<$, $>$, or $=$ for $\square$.

28. $(3.606)^2 \square 13$ **29.** $(1.414)^2 \square 2$ **30.** $(1.732)^2 \square 3$

31. $(2.828)^2 \square 8$ **32.** $(3.317)^2 \square 11$ **33.** $(3.873)^2 \square 15$

34. $(5.764)^2 \square 33$ **35.** $(4.444)^2 \square 20$ **36.** $(6.602)^2 \square 44$

37. Find the time (t) in seconds it takes for a parachutist to free-fall the distance (d) 3600 feet. Use the formula $t = \sqrt{\frac{d}{16}}$.

Evaluate each formula.

38. $r = \sqrt{\frac{a}{\pi}}$ for $a = 121\pi$.

39. $D = \sqrt{a^2 + b^2 + c^2}$ where $a = 3$, $b = 7$, and $c = \sqrt{63}$.

C Extending Thinking Skills

40. Choose nonzero whole numbers for a, b, and c so that $\sqrt{a} \cdot \sqrt{b} = \sqrt{c}$.

41. Find two solutions to $\sqrt{x} = x$.

Mixed Review

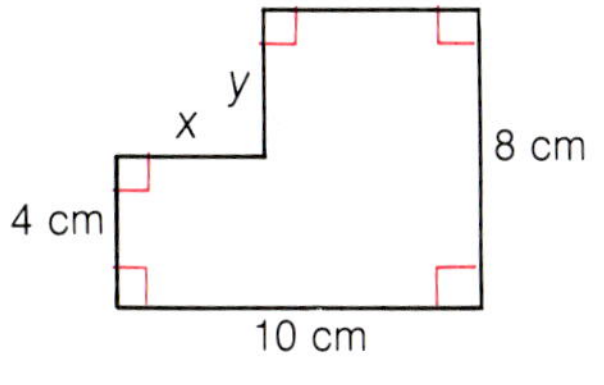

Use the figure at right for Exercises 42–45.
Write and solve an equation to find each.

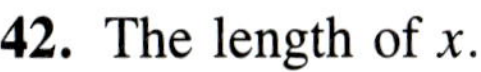

42. The length of x.

43. The length of y.

44. The perimeter of the figure.

45. The area of the figure.

Give the probability of drawing from a standard deck of 52 playing cards:

46. a diamond **47.** the king of spades **48.** a red ten

Solve and check. **49.** $5m - 2m = 27$ **50.** $4.5c + 6.9c = 45.6$

51. $11 = 9x + 6.5$ **52.** $3t = 12 - 5t$ **53.** $21m + 16 = 79$

CALCULATOR ACTIVITY

On a calculator without a $\sqrt{}$ key, you can find an approximate square root of a number by using a method of averaging. The method is explained below for $\sqrt{38}$.

- Locate the square root between a pair of consecutive integers. $6 < \sqrt{38} < 7$
- Select an estimated square root. $\sqrt{38} \approx 6.2$
- Divide by the estimate. Find the quotient to one more place than is desired in the final answer. $6.2\overline{)38.000}$ = 6.129
- Find the average of the estimated square root and the quotient from the division. $\dfrac{6.2 + 6.129}{2} = 6.164$
- Use this average as a new divisor. Continue this process until the quotient and the divisor agree in the hundredths place. $6.164\overline{)38.00000}$ = 6.164

Use the method of averaging to find an approximate square root.

1. $\sqrt{6}$ **2.** $\sqrt{11}$ **3.** $\sqrt{31}$ **4.** $\sqrt{18}$ **5.** $\sqrt{42}$

14-3 Solving Equations: Using Square Roots

To solve equations of the form $x^2 = 25$, you need to use the property shown by the examples below.

$$\sqrt{5^2} = \sqrt{25} = 5 \qquad \sqrt{7^2} = \sqrt{49} = 7$$

The general property is stated as follows.

The Square Root Property

For any number x, $\sqrt{x^2} = |x|$.

When both sides of an equation are positive, you can find the square root of both sides and the equality is maintained.

Example 1

Solve and check. $x^2 = 25$

Solution

$x^2 = 25$

$\sqrt{x^2} = \sqrt{25}$ — Undo squaring by finding the square root of both sides.

$|x| = \sqrt{25}$ — Use the property $\sqrt{x^2} = |x|$ on the left side.

$x = 5$ or $x = -5$

Check $5^2 = 25$ and $(-5)^2 = 25$

Practice Solve and check. **a.** $x^2 = 49$ **b.** $x^2 = 100$

Example 2

Solve and check. $w^2 = 17$

Solution

$w^2 = 17$

$\sqrt{w^2} = \sqrt{17}$

$|w| = \sqrt{17}$

$w = \sqrt{17}$ or $w = -\sqrt{17}$ — When $\sqrt{w^2}$ is not an integer, write the answer using the $\sqrt{\ }$ symbol.

Check $(\sqrt{17})^2 \stackrel{?}{=} 17$ Replace x with $\sqrt{17}$ and $-\sqrt{17}$ in $x^2 = 17$.

$(-\sqrt{17})^2 \stackrel{?}{=} 17$

$17 = 17$ √

Practice Solve and check. **a.** $x^2 = 121$ **b.** $x^2 = 39$ **c.** $x^2 = 73$

Oral Exercises

State whether or not the equation has integer solutions.

1. $x^2 = 16$ **2.** $x^2 = 64$ **3.** $x^2 = 85$ **4.** $x^2 = 48$ **5.** $x^2 = 25$

6. $x^2 = 121$ **7.** $x^2 = 144$ **8.** $x^2 = 81$ **9.** $x^2 = 65$ **10.** $x^2 = 36$

Exercises

A Solve and check.

1. $x^2 = 16$ **2.** $x^2 = 36$ **3.** $x^2 = 81$ **4.** $x^2 = 47$

5. $x^2 = 121$ **6.** $x^2 = 38$ **7.** $x^2 = 56$ **8.** $x^2 = 121$

9. $x^2 = 132$ **10.** $x^2 = 144$ **11.** $x^2 = 53$ **12.** $x^2 = 99$

13. $x^2 = 113$ **14.** $x^2 = 75$ **15.** $x^2 = 55$ **16.** $x^2 = 33$

B Solve and check.

17. $x^2 - 25 = 0$ **18.** $x^2 + 7 = 43$ **19.** $x^2 + 11 = 111$ **20.** $x^2 + 15 = 40$

21. $x^2 - 9 = 40$ **22.** $x^2 + 34 = 70$ **23.** $x^2 + 3 = 52$ **24.** $x^2 - 8 = 41$

C Extending Thinking Skills

Find two solutions to each equation.

25. $x^2 = x$ **26.** $x^2 = x + 2$ **27.** $x^2 = -x$ **28.** $x^4 = 16$

Mixed Review

What percent of 60 is: **29.** 33? **30.** 45? **31.** 12? **32.** 20?

Solve and check. **33.** $16t + 13t = 15t + 28$ **34.** $4.2c - 11 = 1.6$

ESTIMATION

To estimate a square root of a number that is not an integer, you can choose compatible numbers. For example, $\sqrt{26} \approx \sqrt{25} = 5$, so $\sqrt{26} \approx 5$.

Use compatible numbers to estimate these square roots.

1. $\sqrt{37}$ **2.** $\sqrt{80}$ **3.** $\sqrt{99}$ **4.** $\sqrt{10}$ **5.** $\sqrt{15}$

14-4 Pythagorean Theorem

The longest side of a right triangle, the side opposite the right angle, is called the **hypotenuse**. The two shorter sides are called the **legs** of the triangle.

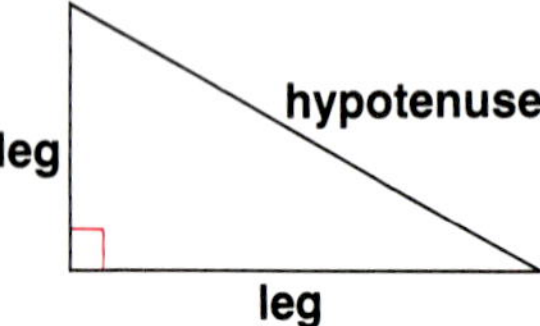

The triangle in the figure below has sides that are 3, 4, and 5 units long. The areas of the squares that have been constructed on each side show that the square of the hypotenuse is equal to the sum of the squares of the two legs.

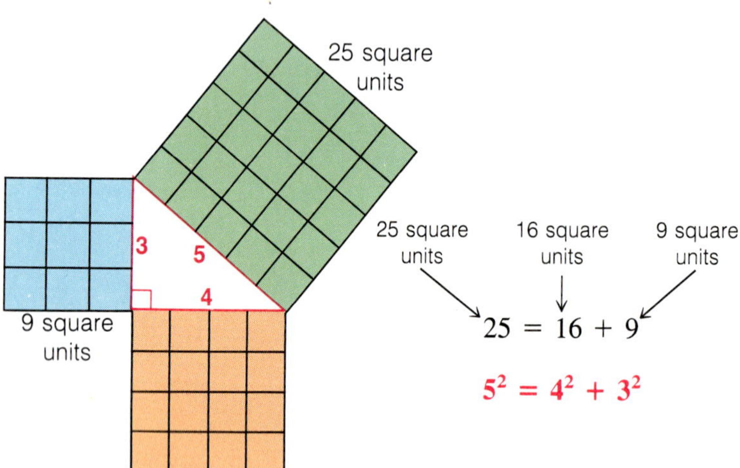

This suggests the following theorem.

The Pythagorean Theorem

In a right triangle, the square of the length of the hypotenuse is equal to the sum of the squares of the lengths of the two legs. If ***c*** is the length of the hypotenuse and ***a*** and ***b*** are the lengths of the two legs,

$$c^2 = a^2 + b^2$$

Example 1

Find the length of the hypotenuse. Express your answer in radical form.

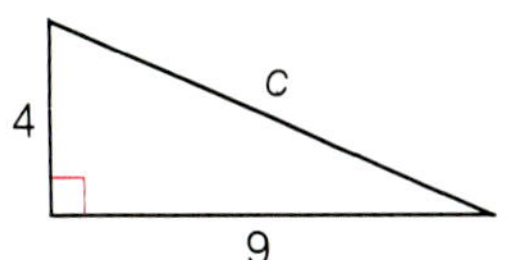

Solution $c^2 = a^2 + b^2$ Use the Pythagorean theorem.

$c^2 = 4^2 + 9^2$ Substitute 4 for *a* and 9 for *b*.

$c^2 = 16 + 81$ Square terms and add.

$c^2 = 97$

$c = \sqrt{97}$ Since *c* represents a length, its value is the positive square root. The length of the hypotenuse is $\sqrt{97}$.

Practice Draw a right triangle with hypotenuse *c* and legs *a* and *b*.

a. Find length *c* if $a = 5$ and $b = 8$.

b. Find length *c* if $a = 7$ and $b = 15$.

Example 2

Find the length of leg *a*. Express your answer in radical form.

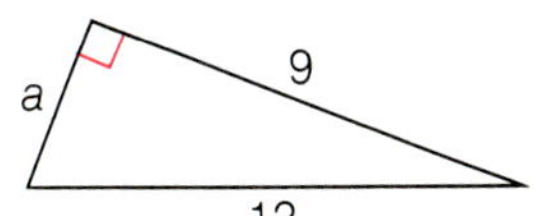

Solution $a^2 + b^2 = c^2$ Use the Pythagorean theorem.

$a^2 + 9^2 = 12^2$ Substitute 9 for *b* and 12 for *c*.

$a^2 + 81 - 81 = 144 - 81$

$a^2 = 63$

$a = \sqrt{63}$ The length of leg *a* is $\sqrt{63}$.

Practice Draw a right triangle with hypotenuse *c* and legs *a* and *b*.

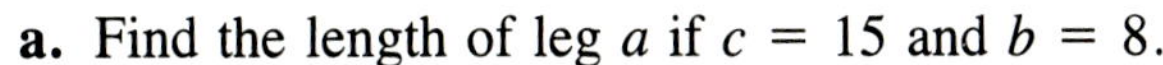

a. Find the length of leg *a* if $c = 15$ and $b = 8$.

b. Find the length of leg *a* if $b = 6$, $c = 14$.

Oral Exercises

State the equation given by the Pythagorean Theorem.

1.

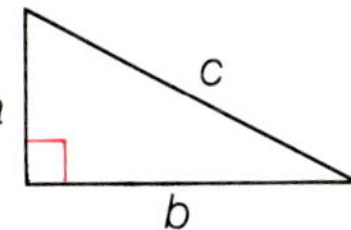

2.

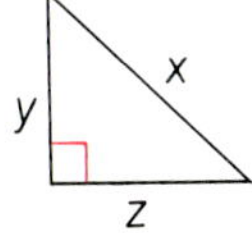

3.

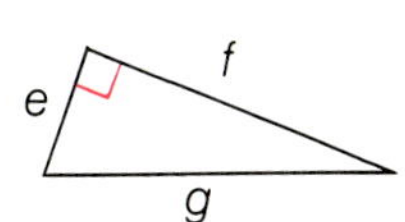

4.

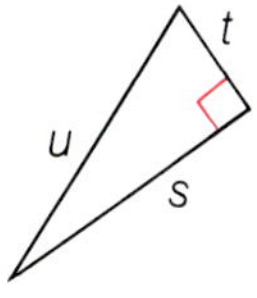

Which statements about legs *a* and *b* and hypotenuse *c* of a right triangle are true and which are false?

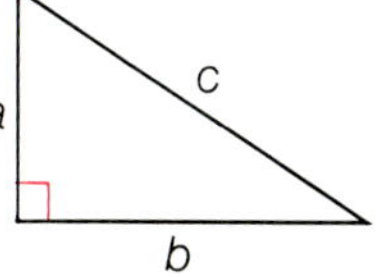

5. $c^2 = a^2 + b^2$ **6.** $a^2 = b^2 + c^2$ **7.** $b^2 = c^2 - a^2$

8. $a^2 = b^2 - c^2$ **9.** $b^2 = a^2 - c^2$ **10.** $a^2 = c^2 - b^2$

Exercises

A Find the length of the hypotenuse.

1.

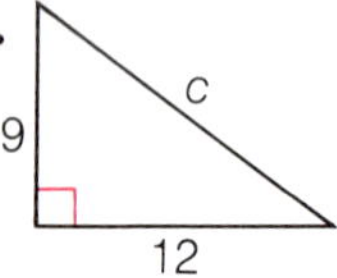

2.

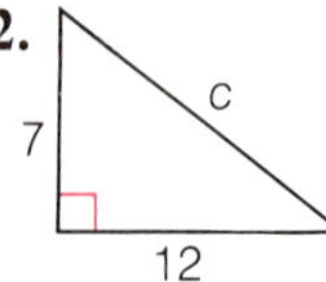

3.

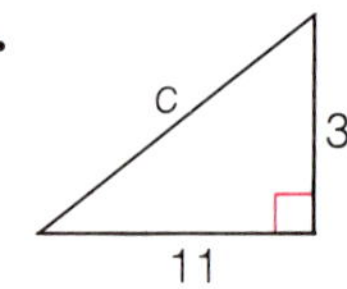

4.

Draw a right triangle with legs a and b and hypotenuse c to use for Exercises 5–12. Find the length of c. If c is not an integer, express in radical form.

5. $a = 8$ and $b = 12$. Find c.

6. $a = 8$ and $b = 15$. Find c.

7. $a = 12$ and $b = 5$. Find c.

8. $a = 9$ and $b = 40$. Find c.

9. $a = 10$ and $b = 16$. Find c.

10. $a = 15$ and $b = 6$. Find c.

11. $a = 12$ and $b = 20$. Find c.

12. $a = 7$ and $b = 9$. Find c.

Find the missing length of leg a.

13.

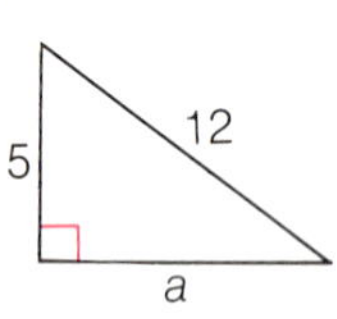

14.

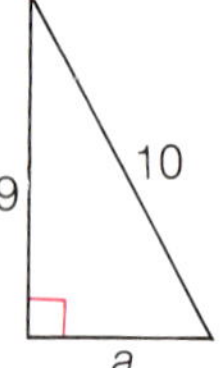

15.

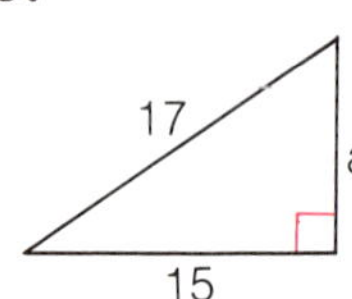

16.

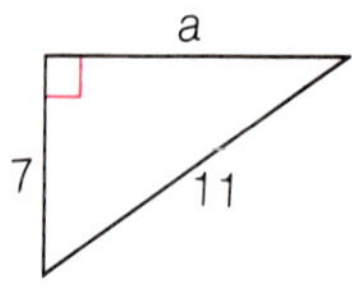

Draw a right triangle with legs a and b and hypotenuse c to use for Exercises 17–24. Find the length.

17. $a = 6$ and $c = 13$. Find b.

18. $a = 10$ and $c = 20$. Find b.

19. $b = 13$ and $c = 15$. Find a.

20. $b = 6$ and $c = 12$. Find a.

21. $a = 18$ and $c = 23$. Find b.

22. $a = 12$ and $c = 15$. Find b.

23. $b = 5$ and $c = 14$. Find a.

24. $b = 8$ and $c = 20$. Find b.

B Solve.

25. The base of a 32-foot ladder is 10 feet from the building. How high above the ground is the top of the ladder?

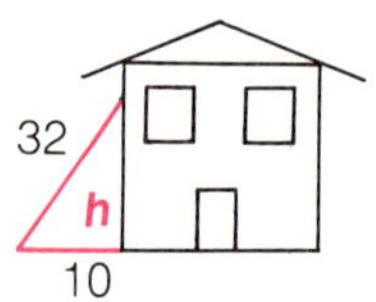

26. Movers are trying to take a large table through a door with these dimensions. They want to know the length of diagonal $\overline{AB}$. What is the length?

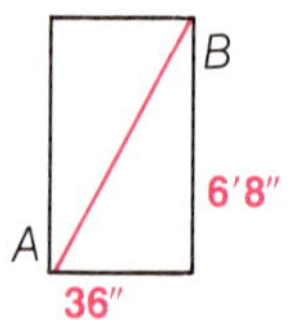

27. A road climbs 800 feet as you travel a horizontal distance of 3 miles. How much longer is the road surface than the horizontal distance? (5280 ft = 1 mile)

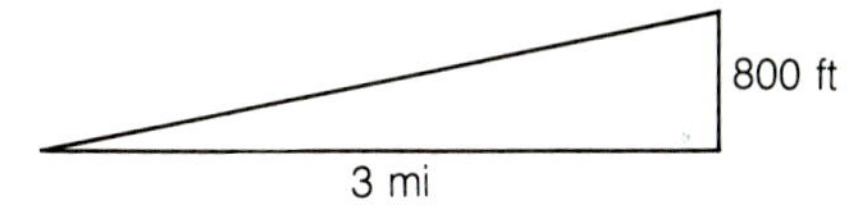

28. A building 36 feet wide has a roof that rises 4 feet vertically for each 12-foot horizontal change. The roof has a 2-foot overhang. How long is length *AB*?

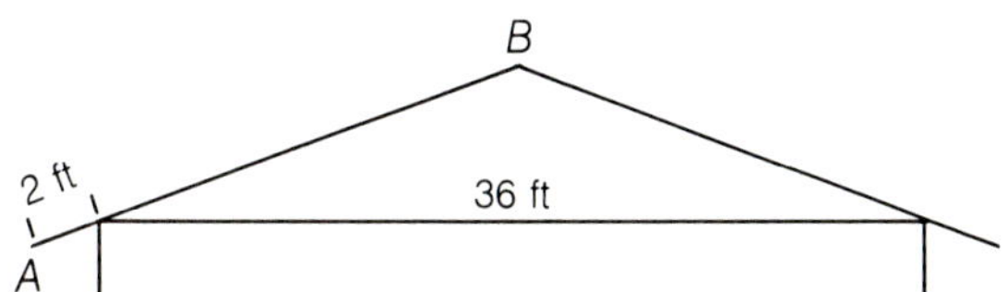

Three whole numbers a, b, and c are called **Pythagorean triples** if $c^2 = a^2 + b^2$. For example, 3, 4, and 5 are Pythagorean triples since $5^2 = 3^2 + 4^2$. Which of these are Pythagorean triples?

29. 40, 50, 60 **30.** 5, 12, 13 **31.** 7, 15, 21 **32.** 8, 15, 17

33. 9, 11, 17 **34.** 7, 24, 25 **35.** 20, 21, 29 **36.** 9, 29, 36

C Extending Thinking Skills

Suppose that u and v are any two whole numbers. Let x, y, and z be the following three numbers: $x = 2uv$, $y = u^2 - v^2$, $z = u^2 + v^2$.

For which of these values of u and v are x, y, and z Pythagorean triples?

37. $u = 4, v = 1$ **38.** $u = 4, v = 3$ **39.** $u = 5, v = 2$ **40.** $u = 6, v = 5$

Mixed Review

Simplify. **41.** $6t + 9 - 4t - 1$ **42.** $9c - 6c - 12$ **43.** $2n + 4n + 12$

Solve and check. **44.** $3.6y = 5y - 0.7$ **45.** $9x + 6 = 8.7$

MENTAL MATH

These equations show a way to square mentally a 2-digit number ending in 5. Study the pattern.

$$25 \cdot 25 = (20 \cdot 30) + 25 = 625$$
$$35 \cdot 35 = (30 \cdot 40) + 25 = 1225$$
$$45 \cdot 45 = (40 \cdot 50) + 25 = 2025$$

Use mental math to find each product.

1. $55 \cdot 55$ **2.** $65 \cdot 65$ **3.** $75 \cdot 75$ **4.** $85 \cdot 85$ **5.** $95 \cdot 95$

14-5 Sports Playing Areas

Many sports are played on rectangular areas. The table below lists the dimensions commonly used for several sports.

Playing Area Dimensions	
Sport	**Dimensions**
Boxing	20 ft × 20 ft
Karate	26 ft × 26 ft
Wrestling	39 ft 3 in × 39 ft 3 in
Judo	52 ft 6 in × 52 ft 6 in
Basketball	28 yd × 15 yd 9 in
Ice Hockey	200 ft × 100 ft
U.S. Football	120 yd × 53 yd
Soccer	110 yd × 80 yd

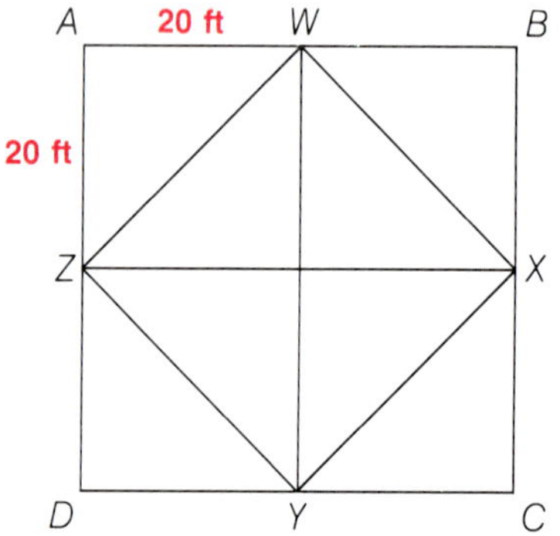

Problems

Use the data from the table to solve.

1. This gymnasium floor has overlapping areas drawn to allow for several different sports. The square *ABCD* is divided into quarters for use as four boxing areas. Is the square *WXYZ* large enough for karate?

2. Suppose that in the figure above, $AW = AZ = 39$ ft 3 in and the square is used for wrestling. Is square *WXYZ* large enough to be used for judo?

3. Suppose that in the figure above, $AW = AZ = 26$ ft and the square is used for karate. Is square *WXYZ* large enough to be used for wrestling?

4. When a basketball court *QRST* is laid out, *QRST* must be a rectangle. A way of checking this is to measure the diagonals *QS* and *RT* to make sure they are the same length. How long are these diagonals?

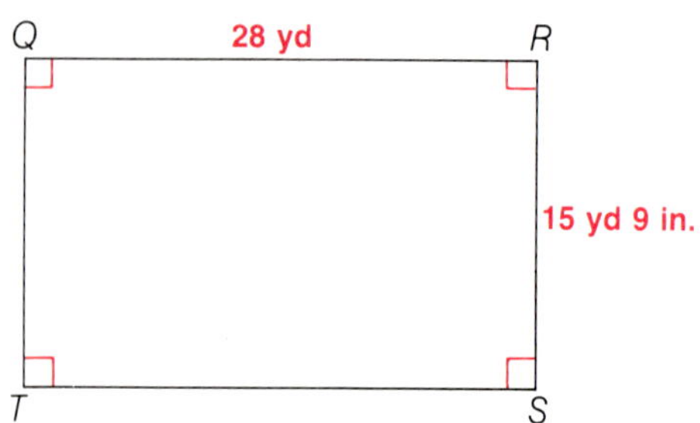

5. What is the length of the diagonal of a soccer field? (This is the longest possible kick that would keep the ball in play.)

6. How many basketball courts could fit on a football field?

7. A football field *ABCD* and a soccer field *WXYZ* are to be laid out in overlapping fashion, as shown (O is the center of both fields). The people painting the lines want to know the length *AW*. What is it?

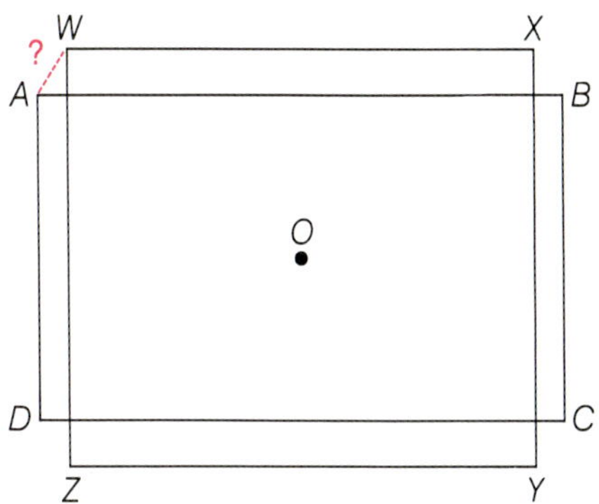

8. The ratio of length to width for the ice hockey field is 2 to 1. Which playing field listed in the table has the greatest length to width ratio?

9. *Data Search* Find the cost of grass seed in your area and estimate the cost of grass seed for a soccer field and a football field.

What's Your Decision?

A school board bought a piece of land with the dimensions shown. On the land, they want to lay out football and soccer practice fields and 6 basketball courts. How would you arrange these playing fields on the land?

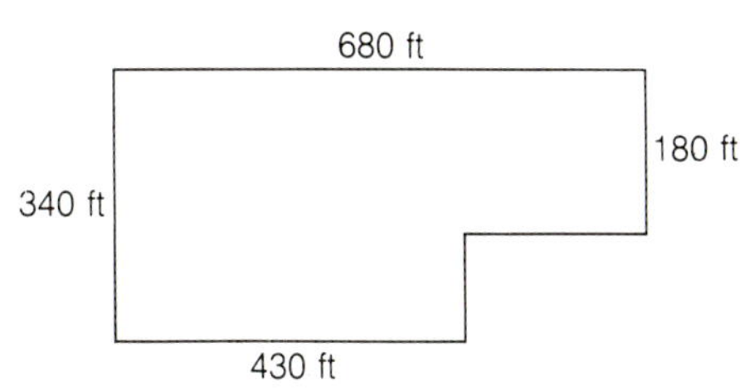

14-6 Similar Triangles

Triangles that are the same shape but not necessarily the same size are called **similar triangles**. Two triangles that are similar have matching congruent angles, called corresponding angles. Corresponding angles are shown by matching arc symbols.

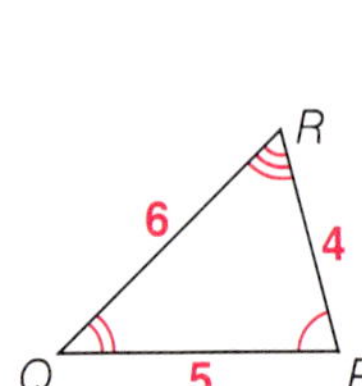

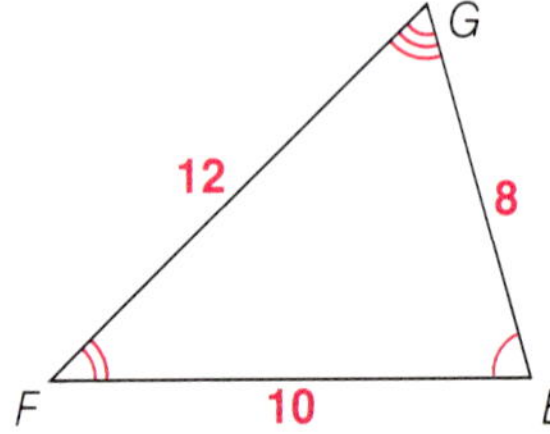

Corresponding angles
$\angle P$ and $\angle E$
$\angle Q$ and $\angle F$
$\angle R$ and $\angle G$

The symbol ~ means *is similar to*. We write $\triangle \boldsymbol{PQR} \sim \triangle \boldsymbol{EFG}$. Lengths of corresponding sides of similar triangles are proportional. In the figures above, the three ratios of corresponding sides all equal $\frac{1}{2}$.

$$\frac{QR}{FG} = \frac{6}{12} = \frac{1}{2} \qquad \frac{PR}{EG} = \frac{4}{8} = \frac{1}{2} \qquad \frac{PQ}{EF} = \frac{5}{10} = \frac{1}{2}$$

You can use this idea to find lengths of sides of similar triangles.

Example

$\triangle QPR \sim \triangle YZX$. Use a proportion to find r.

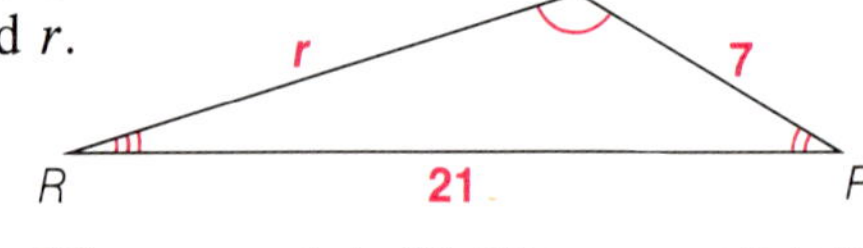

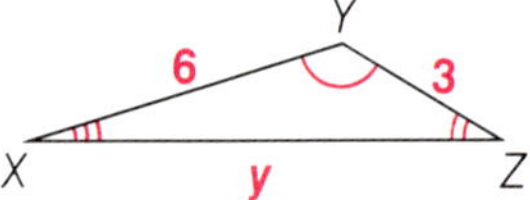

Solution

$\frac{PQ}{ZY} = \frac{QR}{YX}$ — PQ corresponds to ZY. QR corresponds to YX. Lengths of corresponding sides are proportional.

$\frac{7}{3} = \frac{r}{6}$ — Substitute lengths of sides in the proportion.

$7 \cdot 6 = 3 \cdot r$

$42 = 3r$

$14 = r$

Practice $\triangle ABC \sim \triangle XYZ$

Use a proportion to find:

a. x **b.** y

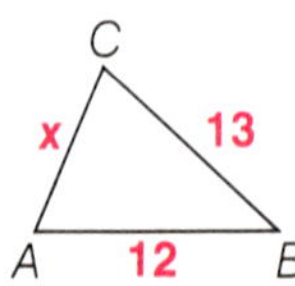

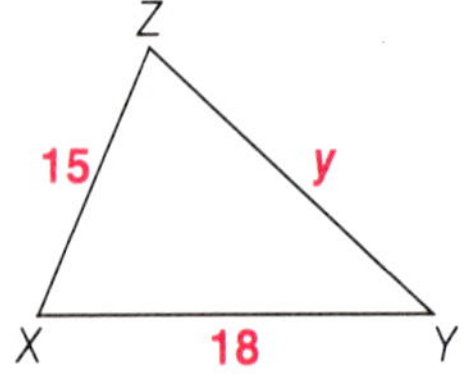

Oral Exercises

Name the corresponding angles and sides for these similar triangles.

1.

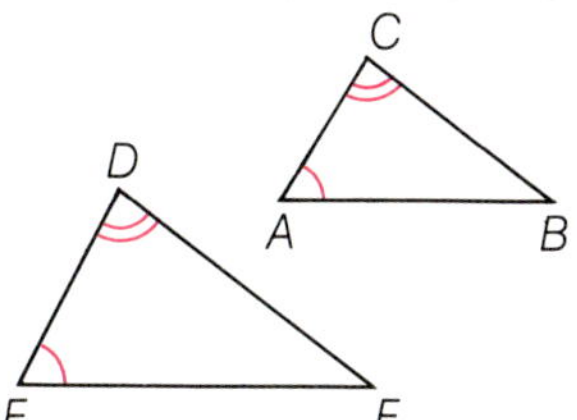

2.

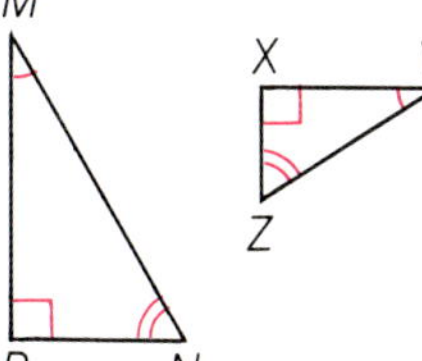

3.

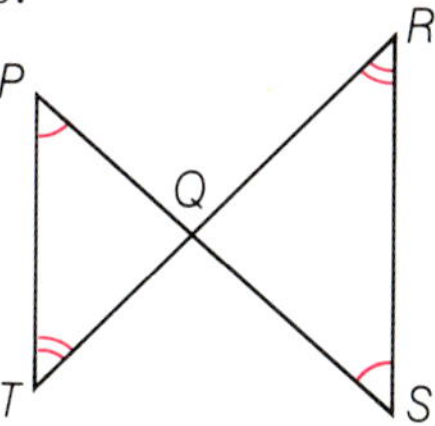

Exercises

A Use proportions to find the unknown lengths for these similar triangles.

1.

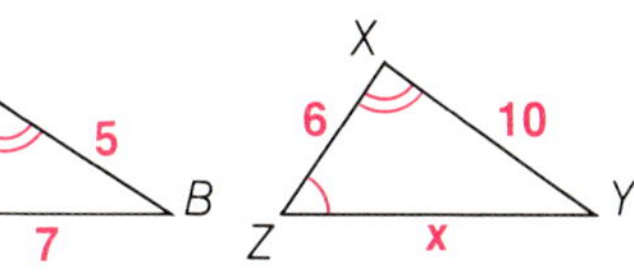

2.

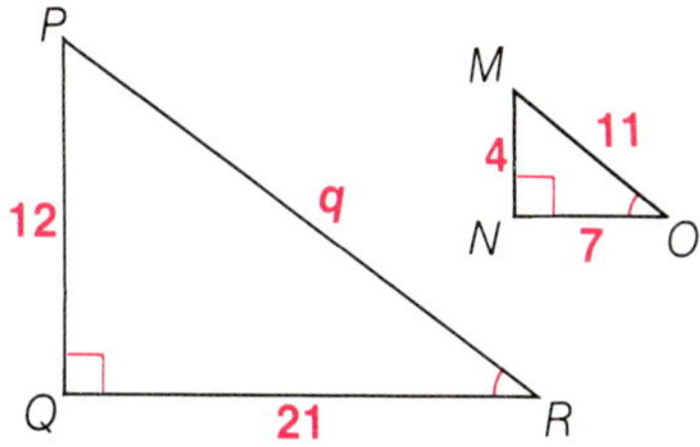

3.

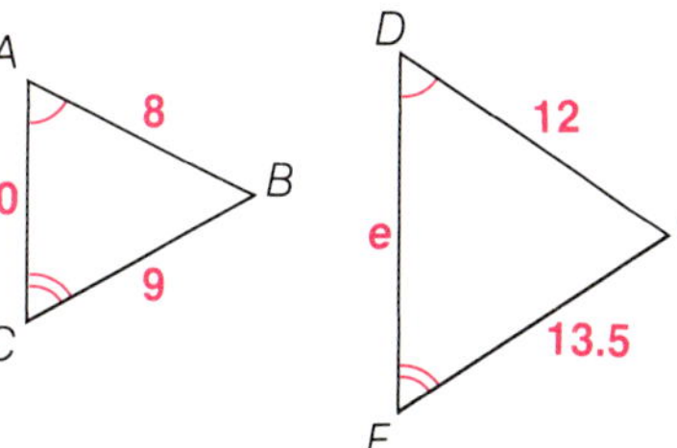

4.

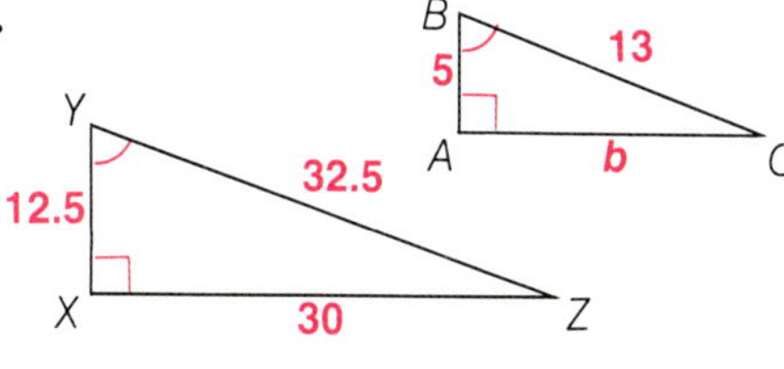

B Use a proportion to find the unknown length for these similar triangles.

5.

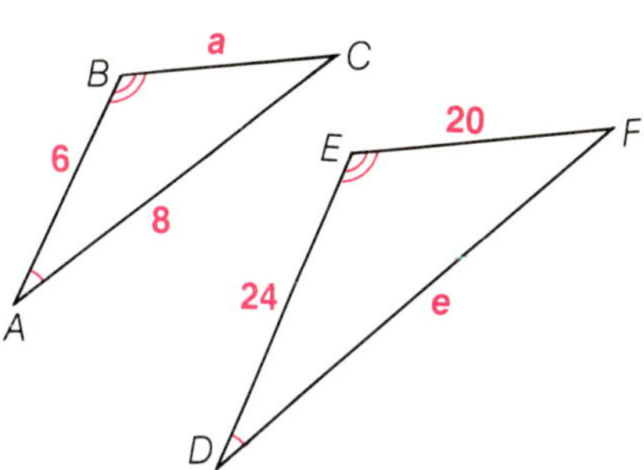

6.

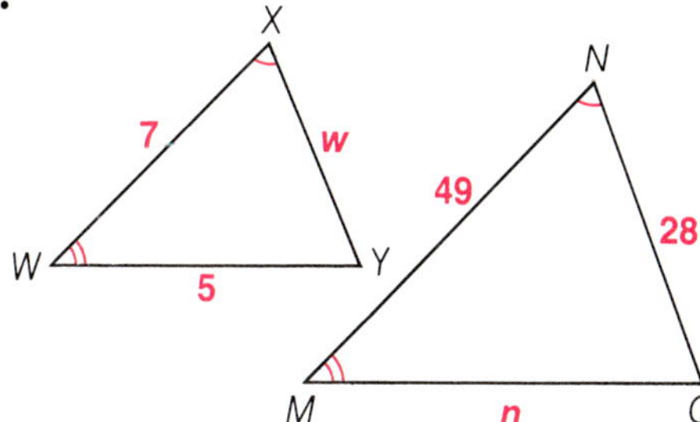

7. 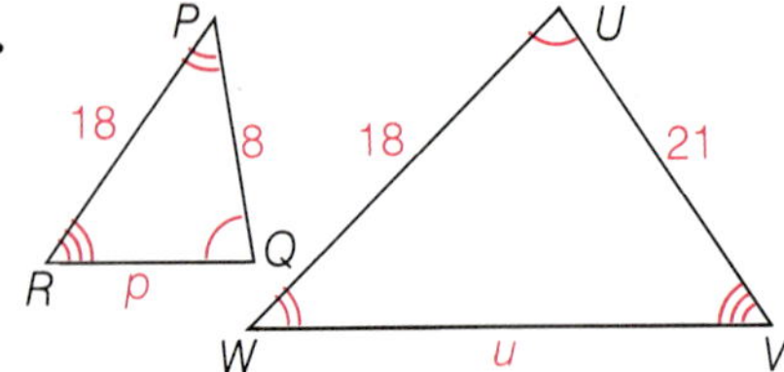

8. 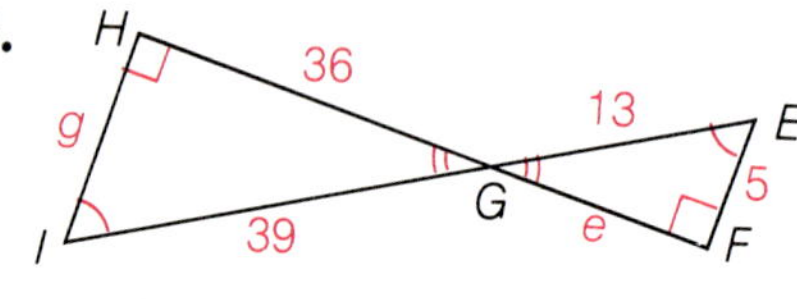

9. Find the distance (d) across the pond.

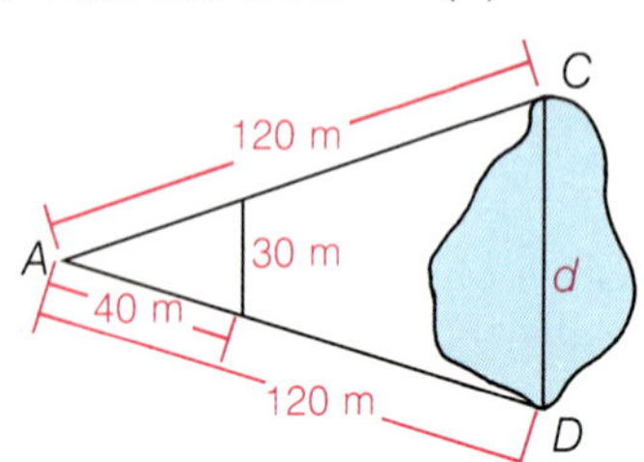

10. Find the height (h) of the wall.

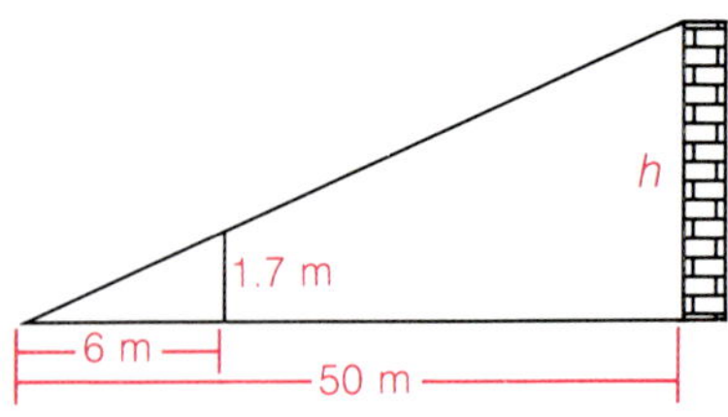

11. A surveyor needs to find the length AB, but the garage is in the way. $\triangle ABC \sim \triangle DEC$. What is the length of AB?

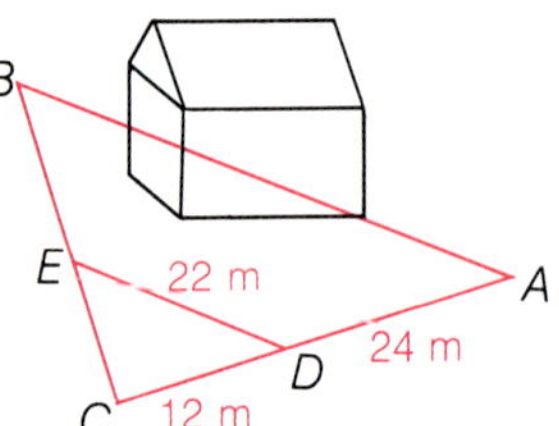

C Extending Thinking Skills

12. Triangle ABC at right is similar to a larger triangle PQR (not shown). The ratio of corresponding sides is 2 : 1. What is the area of each triangle?

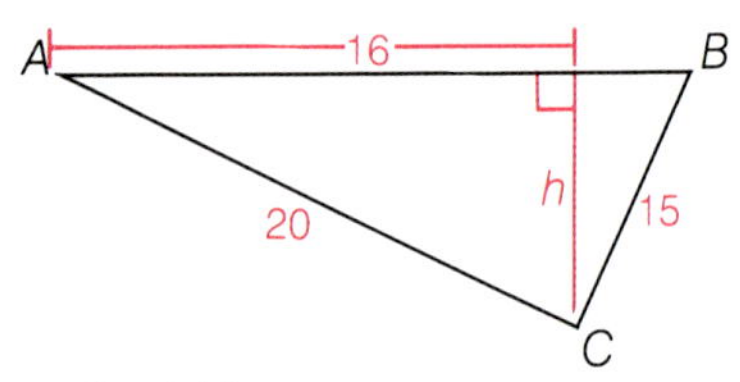

13. This table shows the areas of rectangles of given lengths and widths.

length	2	4	8	. . .	x	$2x$
width	3	6	12	. . .	y	$2y$
area	6	24	96	. . .	xy	$4xy$

Complete the following generalization. If the length and width of a rectangle are both doubled, the area of the rectangle is increased by a factor of __?__

Mixed Review

Reduce to simplest terms. **14.** $\frac{18}{84}$ **15.** $\frac{52}{65}$ **16.** $\frac{45}{63}$ **17.** $\frac{54}{6}$

Solve and check. **18.** $4n + 9n = 10 + 12n$ **19.** $2.4y = y + 7$

14-7 Special Triangles

The two acute angles of an isosceles right triangle are both 45° angles. An isosceles right triangle is called a **45°-45° right triangle**.

You can use the Pythagorean theorem to show that the length of the hypotenuse of the 45°-45° right triangle ABC is $\sqrt{2}$ when the legs are length 1.

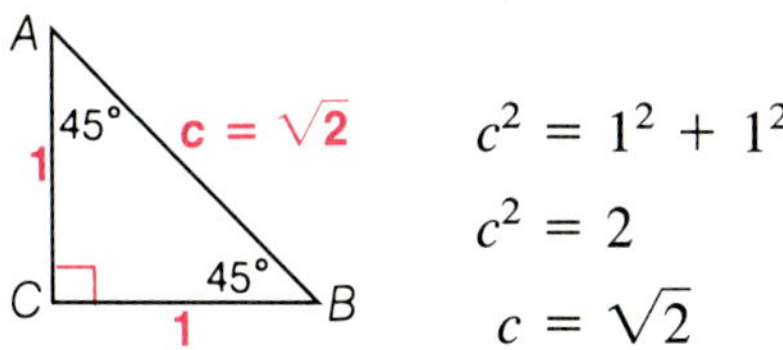

$$c^2 = 1^2 + 1^2$$
$$c^2 = 2$$
$$c = \sqrt{2}$$

A line drawn diagonally across a baseball infield divides it into two congruent, isosceles right triangles.

$\triangle DEF$ below is a 45°-45° right triangle with legs $\boldsymbol{a}$ units long. We use the fact that $\triangle ABC \sim \triangle DEF$ to write the proportion below.

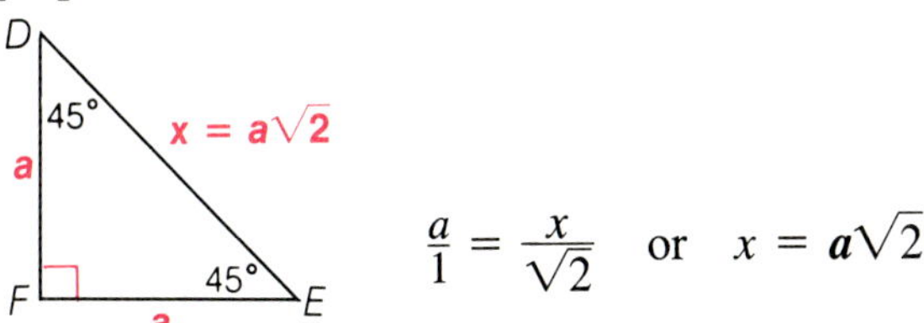

$$\frac{a}{1} = \frac{x}{\sqrt{2}} \quad \text{or} \quad x = \boldsymbol{a}\sqrt{2}.$$

45°-45° Right Triangle

If a 45°-45° right triangle has legs $\boldsymbol{a}$ units long, then the hypotenuse is $\boldsymbol{a\sqrt{2}}$ units long.

Example 1

Find length x.

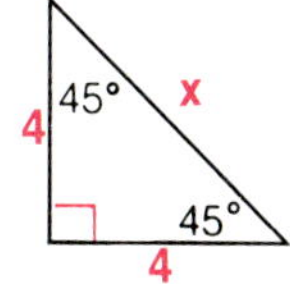

Solution $x = 4\sqrt{2}$ x is equal to the length of the leg times $\sqrt{2}$.

Practice Draw a 45°-45° triangle. Find the length of the hypotenuse if the length of each leg is 5.

An altitude of an equilateral triangle bisects an angle and a base to form two right triangles. Each of these triangles has a 30° angle and a 60° angle and is called a **30°-60° right triangle**.

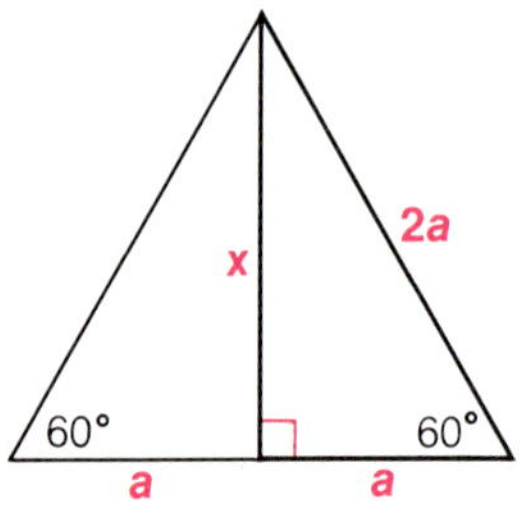

The short leg of the 30°-60° right triangle is half as long as the hypotenuse. If the hypotenuse is length $2a$, the short leg has length a.

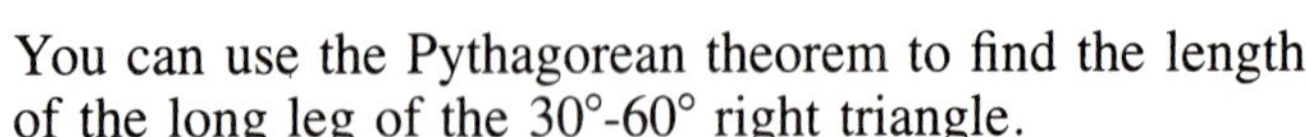

You can use the Pythagorean theorem to find the length of the long leg of the 30°-60° right triangle.

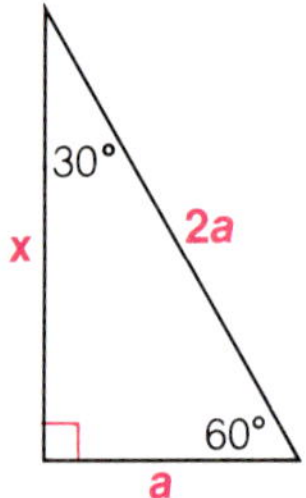

$$(2a)^2 = x^2 + a^2$$
$$4a^2 = x^2 + a^2$$
$$3a^2 = x^2$$
$$\sqrt{3}a = x$$

30°-60° Right Triangles

If a 30°-60° right triangle has a shorter leg a units long, then the longer leg is $a\sqrt{3}$ units long and the hypotenuse is $2a$ units long.

Example 2

Find lengths x and y.

Solution $x = \frac{8}{2} = 4$ The short leg of a 30°–60° right triangle is half the length of the hypotenuse.

$y = 4\sqrt{3}$ The long leg of a 30°–60° right triangle is $\sqrt{3}$ times the length of the short leg.

Practice Draw a 30°-60° right triangle. Find the lengths of the legs if the hypotenuse is 5.

Oral Exercises

Is it possible for a right triangle to have side lengths as shown?

1.

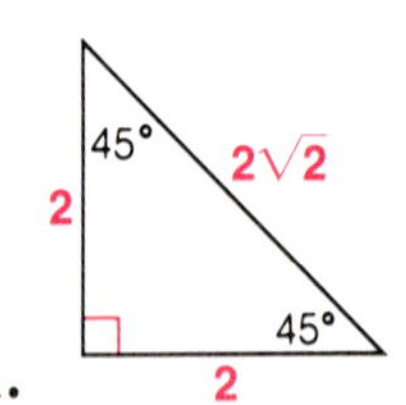

2.

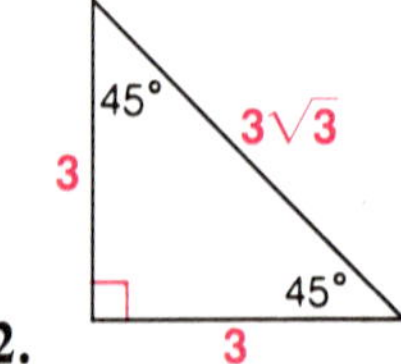

3.

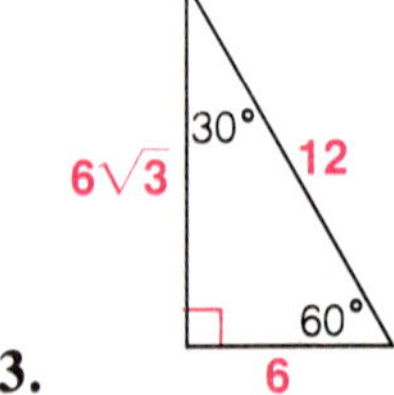

4.

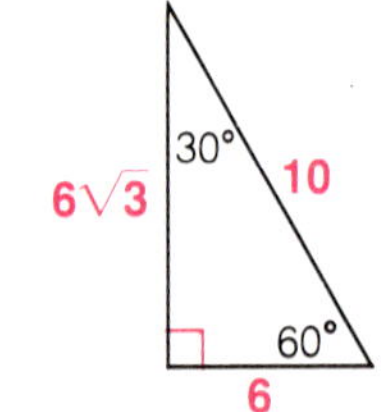

Exercises

A Find the unknown lengths.

1. 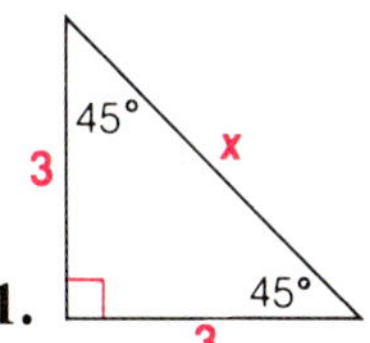

2. 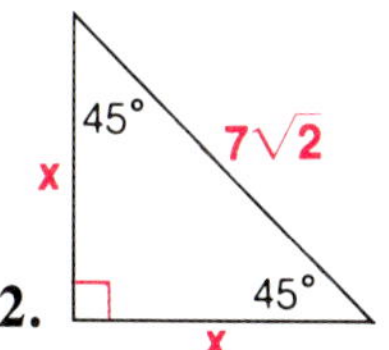

3. 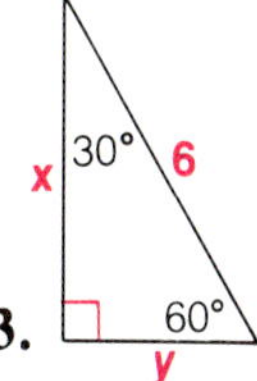

4. 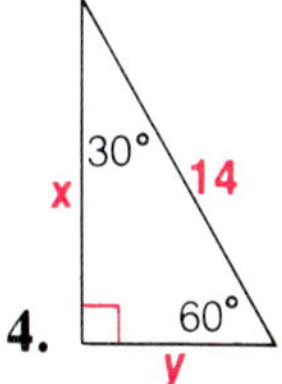

Draw a 45°–45° right triangle for Exercises 5–6.

5. Find the length of the hypotenuse if the length of each leg is 5.
6. Find the length of the hypotenuse if the length of each leg is 4.3.

Draw a 30°–60° right triangle for Exercises 7–8.

7. Find the lengths of the legs if the length of the hypotenuse is 25.
8. Find the lengths of the legs if the length of the hypotenuse is $2\sqrt{3}$.

B Solve. Use the approximations $\sqrt{2} \approx 1.414$ and $\sqrt{3} \approx 1.732$.

Refer to the planter box at right for Exercises 9 and 10. The end of a planter box is shaped like a trapezoid, with dimensions as shown.

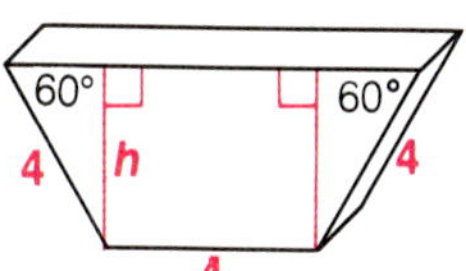

9. Find the height of the planter.
10. Find the length of the upper edge of the end of the planter.
11. On a baseball diamond, the distance between bases is 90 ft. Find the approximate distance from home plate to second base.
12. The end of a tent is shaped like an equilateral triangle. If the base of the tent is 5 feet across, how high is the tent?
13. *ABCD* is a rhombus with all sides of length 8. Diagonals *AC* and *BD* bisect the angles and are perpendicular to each other. Find the length of each diagonal.

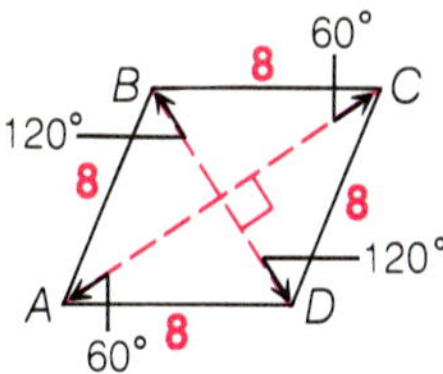

C Extending Thinking Skills

14. Triangle *ABC* is drawn on the surface of a box whose length, width, and height are all 1. What is the length of *AB*?
15. What is the area of $\triangle ABC$?

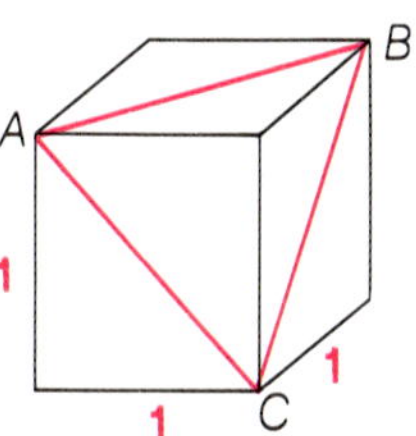

Mixed Review

Solve and check. **16.** $35 = 5c + 2c$ **17.** $m + 16 = 17$

18. $10 + 2m = 13$ **19.** $t + 6t = -42$ **20.** $14 - 2m = 18$

14-8 Trigonometric Ratios

You can use trigonometric ratios to find a length that cannot be measured directly.

When you want to find a distance that cannot be measured directly, such as the height of a building, you can use an indirect method of measurement. One such method is to use trigonometric ratios.

Trigonometric ratios are ratios of lengths of sides of right triangles. Three of these ratios are called the **sine,** the **cosine,** and the **tangent.** They are defined for an acute angle *A* in a right triangle as follows.

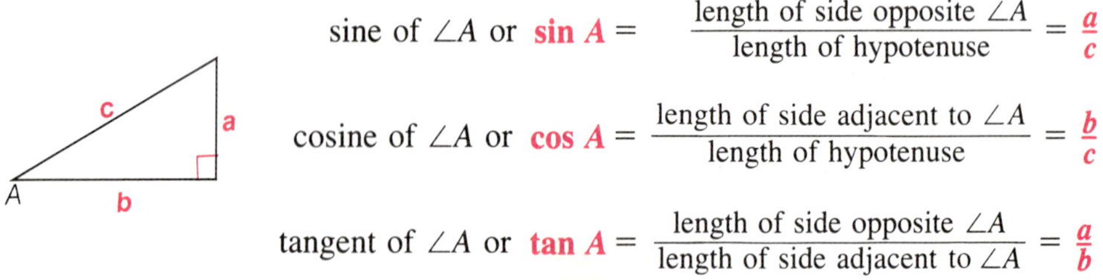

$$\text{sine of } \angle A \text{ or } \sin A = \frac{\text{length of side opposite } \angle A}{\text{length of hypotenuse}} = \frac{a}{c}$$

$$\text{cosine of } \angle A \text{ or } \cos A = \frac{\text{length of side adjacent to } \angle A}{\text{length of hypotenuse}} = \frac{b}{c}$$

$$\text{tangent of } \angle A \text{ or } \tan A = \frac{\text{length of side opposite } \angle A}{\text{length of side adjacent to } \angle A} = \frac{a}{b}$$

Since ratios of corresponding sides of similar triangles are equal, these three ratios have the same value for any acute angle congruent to angle *A*.

Example 1

Find sin A, cos A, and tan A for $\angle A$.

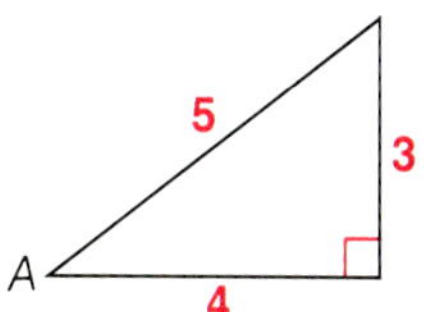

Solution

$\sin A = \frac{3}{5}$ Sine is the length of the opposite side divided by the length of the hypotenuse.

$\cos A = \frac{4}{5}$ Cosine is the length of the adjacent side divided by the length of the hypotenuse.

$\tan A = \frac{3}{4}$ Tangent is the length of the opposite side divided by the length of the adjacent side.

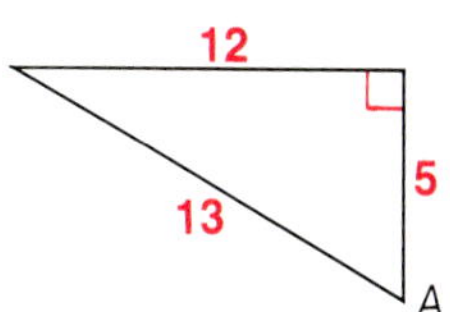

Practice Find sin A, cos A, and tan A for $\angle A$.

Example 2

The measure of angle A is 37° at a point 155 feet from the base of the flagpole. Tan 37° ≈ 0.75. Find the height of the flagpole.

Solution $\tan 37° = \frac{h}{155}$

$h = 155(\tan 37°)$

$h \approx 155(0.75)$

≈ 116.25 ft. Substitute the value of tan 37°.

B
h
A 37°
C
155 ft

Practice Find the length of AB in the figure above.

Oral Exercises

State whether each equation is true or false.

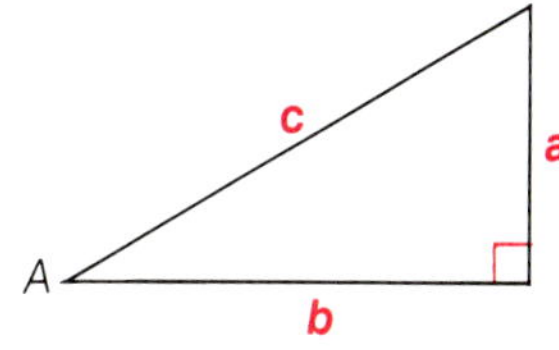

1. $\sin A = \frac{a}{b}$ **2.** $\cos A = \frac{b}{c}$ **3.** $\tan A = \frac{b}{a}$

4. $\sin A = \frac{a}{c}$ **5.** $\cos A = \frac{b}{a}$ **6.** $\tan A = \frac{a}{b}$

Exercises

A Find sin A, cos A, and tan A for $\angle A$.

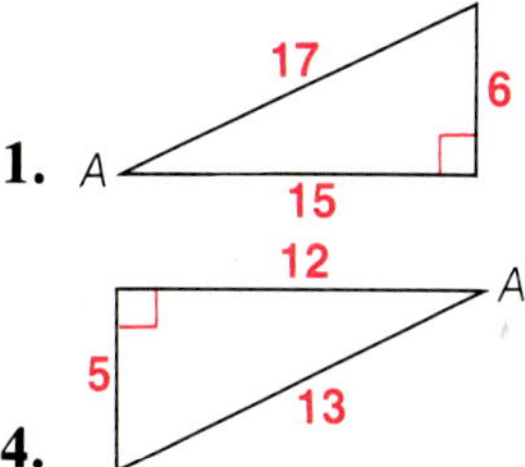

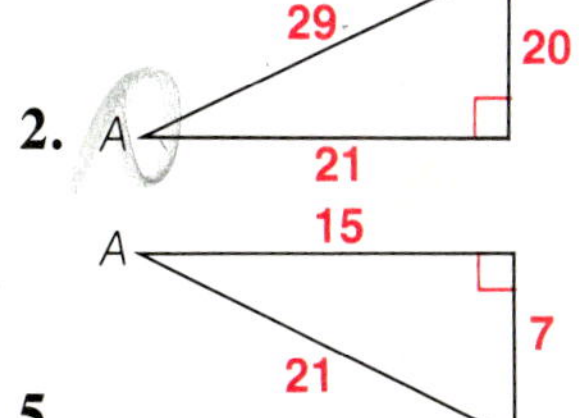

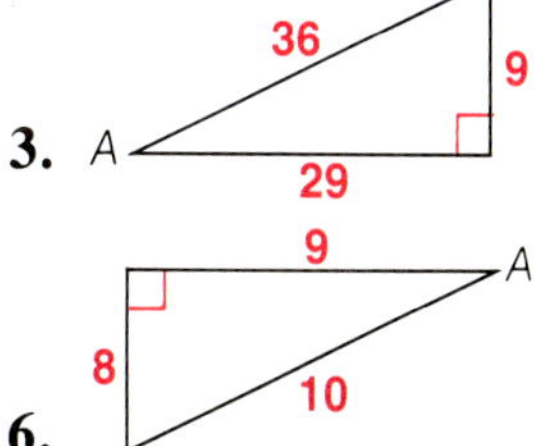

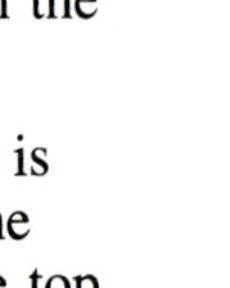

7. The angle from the ground to the top of the World Trade Center in New York City is 48° at a distance of 1220 ft from the building. Tan 48° ≈ 1.11. Find the height of the building.

8. Sears Tower in Chicago is 1454 ft tall. Suppose point A is 1000 ft from the base of the tower. What is the tangent of the angle at A formed by the ground and the line of vision to the top of the tower?

9. A surveyor measured BC to be 125 ft. Sin 29° ≈ 0.48. Find the distance AB across the lake.

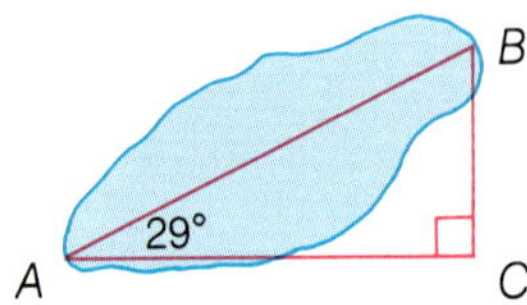

10. A surveyor wants to find the distance between mountain peaks A and B. He finds a point C, 228 ft from point A, so that $\angle ACB$ is a right angle. The measure of $\angle BAC$ is 89°. Find the distance AB if cos 89° ≈ 0.017.

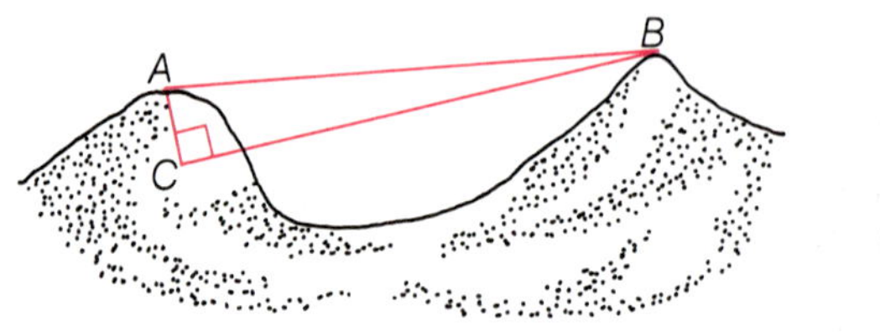

B Draw a 45°–45° right triangle with legs of length 2. Draw a 30°–60° right triangle with a short leg of length 1. Find the lengths of all other sides. Use these figures to find the trigonometric ratios in Exercises 11–18. Leave your answer in radical form.

11. sin 30° **12.** tan 45° **13.** cos 60° **14.** tan 30°

15. cos 45° **16.** sin 60° **17.** sin 45° **18.** tan 60°

Find sin A, cos A, and tan A for $\angle A$. Use the Pythagorean Theorem to find x.

19.
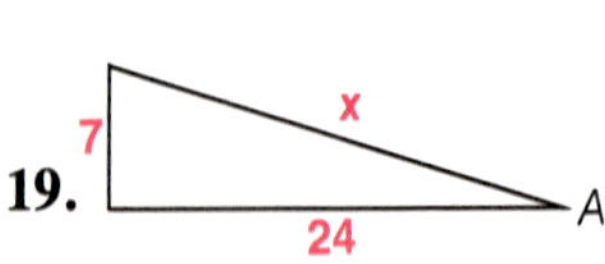

20.
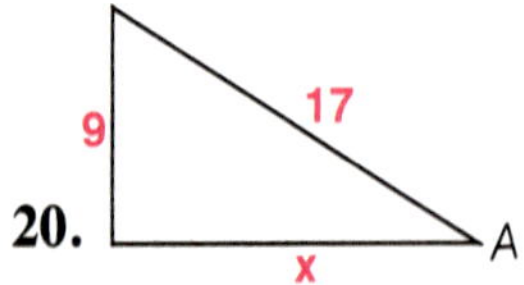

21.
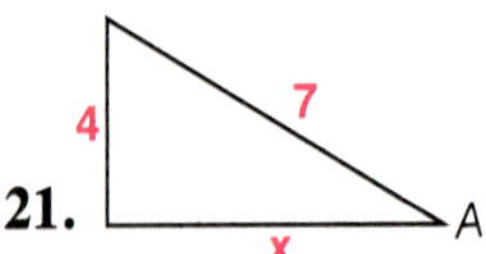

Use your answers to Exercises 11–18 to evaluate each expression.

22. $5 + x \sin 30° \text{ for } x = 4$

23. $y \cos 45° \text{ for } y = 4\sqrt{2}$

24. $x \tan 45° + 2x \sin 30° \text{ for } x = 5$

25. $5x \sin 30° \text{ for } x = 12$

C *Extending Thinking Skills*

Use the results from Exercises 11–18 to solve the equations.

26. $\sin x = \frac{1}{2}$

27. $\cos x = \frac{\sqrt{3}}{2}$

28. $\tan x = \sqrt{3}$

29. $\sin 2x = \frac{\sqrt{3}}{2}$

30. $\tan 2x = 1$

31. $\cos 3x = \frac{1}{2}$

Mixed Review

Use the counting principle to find the total number of choices.

32. Select one soup and one salad from 4 soups and 5 salads.

Give the area. **33.** A square with one side = 4 cm.

34. A circle with diameter = 6 cm. Use 3.14 for π.

35. A triangle with base = 7 in, height = 8 in.

Give the mean. **36.** 12, 15, 17, 12, 13 **37.** 6, 2, 5, 4, 6, 0, 6

Give the least common multiple (LCM). **38.** 4, 5, 6, 12 **39.** 2, 3, 4, 8

Solve and check. **40.** $3m - 12 = -6$ **41.** $9y - 6y = 12$

42. $10 = 4c - 2c$ **43.** $9 - 3c = 0$ **44.** $12 + 3n = 9$

COMPUTER ACTIVITY

This program will list the values of the trigonometric ratios for all angles from 1 degree to 45 degrees.

```
10 PRINT TAB(1)"ANGLE";"SINE(A)"; TAB(19)"COSINE(A)";
   TAB(31)"TANGENT(1)"
20 PRINT
30 FOR N=1 TO 45
40 PRINT N;" DEG ";SIN(N*3.14159/180);"  ";
   COS(N*3.14159/180);"  ";TAN(N*3.14159/180)
50 NEXT N
60 END
```

1. Load and run this program.
2. Change the program to find the ratios for all angles from 1 degree to 90 degrees. Load and run the new program.

14-9 Practice Solving Problems

A Solve by writing an equation.

1. A field is in the shape of a right triangle. The length of the longest side of the field is twice the length of the shortest side. The other side is 149 m long. The perimeter of the field is 407 m. How long is each side?

2. The total cost of a bicycle is \$140. Glenda put \$20 down on the bicycle and will pay the rest in 3 equal payments. How much will each payment be?

3. The Redbirds were only 2 points short of getting double the Gray Sox score in a basketball game. The Redbirds scored 86 points. How many points did the Gray Sox score?

4. Bob rode his bike from his house to a house 5 miles north. He rode at the rate of $\frac{1}{4}$ mile per minute. How far from home was he after 20 minutes?

5. A board 6 m long is to be cut into 2 pieces. The length of one piece must be 0.5 m more than twice the length of the other. How long should each piece be?

6. Mary made \$4.75 an hour and \$15 in overtime pay the first week of her job. Her total salary for the week was \$181.25. How many regular hours did she work?

B Solve by writing an equation.

7. A carpenter measured the sides of a triangular wooden frame for a house. Each side measured one foot more than the previous side. The perimeter of the frame was 51 feet. How long was each side of the frame?

8. 50% of the cost of a television set was \$60 more than 25% of its cost. How much did the television cost?

C Extending Thinking Skills

9. Write a word problem that could be solved by the equation $25x - 15 = 65$.

10. Write a word problem that could be solved by the equation $x + 12 = 4x$.

Mixed Review

Solve and check. **11.** $9x + 3x = 48$ **12.** $r = 16 + 3r$ **13.** $x + 3x = 8$

Write the prime factorization, using exponents. **14.** 504 **15.** 495

14-10 Practice Solving Problems

Problem-Solving Strategies	
Choose the Operations	Write an Equation
Guess, Check, Revise	Simplify the Problem
Draw a Picture	Make an Organized List
Make a Table	Use Logical Reasoning
Look for a Pattern	Work Backwards

This chart shows the strategies presented in previous chapters.

Problems

Solve.

1. The owner of a car rental business buys gasoline at $1.05 per gallon. Each of the 25 rental cars holds 15 gallons. If the tank in each car is between empty and one-quarter full, about how much would it cost to fill all 25 cars with gasoline?

2. A shipment of 3 boxes of machine parts weighed a total of 65 kg. The heaviest box weighed 3 times as much as the second box, which was 3 times heavier than the lightest box. How much did each box weigh?

3. The owner of a furniture factory set up a plan for training new employees. The first training session was to be for 1 employee. Each of the following sessions was to hold 2 more people than the previous one. The factory had 30 new employees. How many training sessions were needed?

4. Three baseball teams played each other one time at home and one time away. The Blue Birds never defeated the Lions. The Spartans never lost a home game. The Spartans lost 2 games. Find how many of these games each team won and lost.

5. A printer who made envelopes and stationery for Companies A, B, and C mixed up the shipments. Each company received another company's envelopes and yet another company's stationery. Company A received Company C's stationery. Whose envelopes and whose stationery did each company receive?

6. By mistake, three groups are all scheduled to meet at the same time on the same day. They are the Debate Club, the Student Council, and the Math Club. Every member of every club cannot attend, because some students belong to more than one of the clubs. Half of the Math Club and all of the Debate Club belong to the Student Council. Five students are members of all three groups. There are 28 members of the Math Club, 11 members of the Debate Club, and 35 members of the Student Council. The Student Council's meeting is official only if 60% of its members attend. If none of the Math Club and Debate Club members who also belong to the Student Council attend the Student Council meeting, will the Student Council meeting be official?

7. A secret-service agent has been told to find all possible routes from the airport to the state capitol building. Each route has to be studied and the safest one selected. The figure below shows the streets from the airport to the capitol. All streets are one-way, as shown by the arrows. How many different routes are possible?

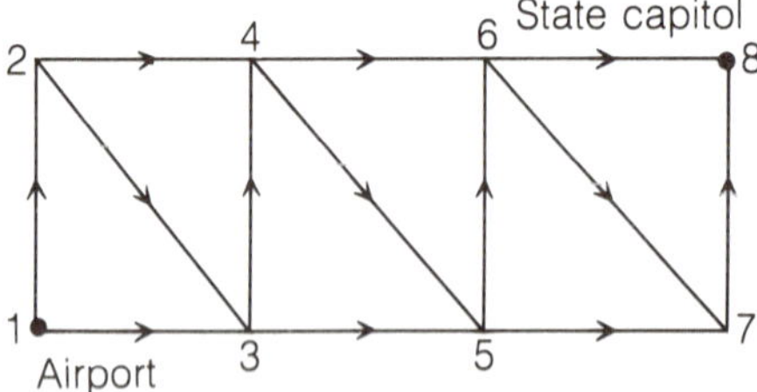

8. Ms. Wells had a stack of math papers to grade. She graded $\frac{1}{4}$ of the papers during lunch break. She graded $\frac{1}{2}$ of what was left after school. She took the rest of the papers home with her and graded only $\frac{1}{6}$ of those. She had 20 papers left to grade the next morning. How many papers did she have in the beginning?

9. At Peter's Pizza Pan, customers can order thin or deep-dish pizza with whole-wheat or regular crust. They can choose either one or two of the following toppings: pepperoni, sausage, mushrooms. How many different pizzas could a customer order?

10. A paint salesperson visits a store every 8th working day. Another salesperson visits the same store every 6th working day. The store is open Monday through Saturday. Today is Tuesday, May 2nd. Both visited the store today. On what date will they both visit the store again? Can one of them change his schedule and never meet the other in the store again? Explain.

Enrichment

Sequences and Square Roots

Because the number $\sqrt{2}$ is an irrational number, it cannot be written exactly as a decimal or a fraction. The terms of the sequence below are approximations of $\sqrt{2}$. Each term of the sequence is a closer approximation than the term before it.

$$\frac{3}{2}, \frac{7}{5}, \frac{17}{12}, \frac{41}{29}, \frac{99}{70}, \ldots$$

$$\frac{99}{70} \longrightarrow \frac{99 + 2(70)}{99 + 70} = \frac{239}{169}$$

You can use a calculator to confirm that the square of each term of this sequence is as shown.

$$\left(\frac{3}{2}\right)^2 = 2.25 \quad \left(\frac{7}{5}\right)^2 = 1.96 \quad \left(\frac{17}{12}\right)^2 = 2.0069 \quad \left(\frac{41}{29}\right)^2 = 1.9988$$

$$\left(\frac{99}{70}\right)^2 = 2.00020$$

You can see that $\frac{99}{70}$ is approximately $\sqrt{2}$.

Find the next term in each sequence. Then use a calculator to find what square root each sequence approximates.

1. $\frac{4}{3}, \frac{10}{7}, \frac{24}{17}, \frac{58}{41}, \frac{140}{99}, \ldots$
2. $\frac{3}{2}, \frac{9}{5}, \frac{24}{14}, \frac{66}{38}, \frac{180}{104}, \ldots$
3. $\frac{4}{3}, \frac{13}{7}, \frac{34}{20}, \frac{94}{54}, \frac{256}{148}, \ldots$
4. $\frac{2}{1}, \frac{5}{3}, \frac{14}{8}, \frac{38}{22}, \frac{104}{60}, \ldots$

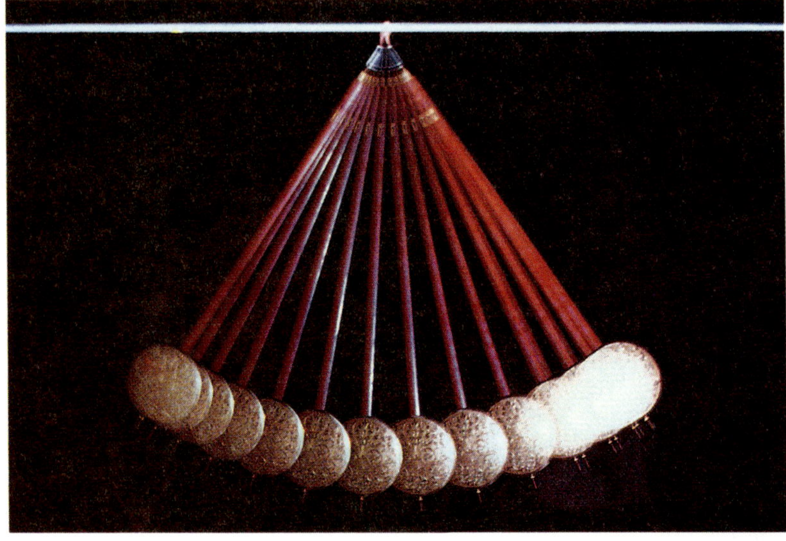

For a pendulum with length L, the time (T) of one period is given by the formula $T = 2 \cdot \sqrt{L}$.

Chapter 14 Review

14-1 Between what two consecutive integers does each square root lie?

1. $\sqrt{33}$ **2.** $\sqrt{75}$

Evaluate each expression.

3. $\sqrt{81} - \sqrt{49}$ **4.** $\sqrt{140 - 19}$

14-2 Use a calculator with a $\sqrt{}$ key to find an approximation for each square root.

5. $\sqrt{7}$ **6.** $\sqrt{117}$

14-3 Solve and check. **7.** $x^2 = 169$ **8.** $x^2 = 12$

14-4 Find the length of a to the nearest hundredth.

9.

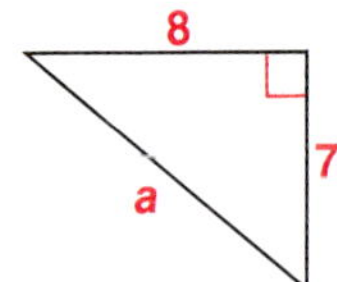

10.

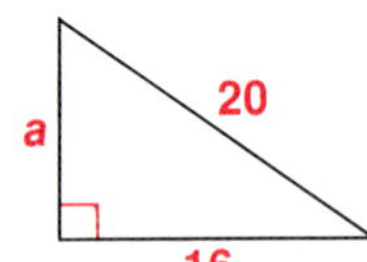

14-5 Solve. **11.** A standard-size base in baseball is 15 inches long and 15 inches wide. What is the length of the diagonal of a base?

14-6 Use proportions to find the unknown length for these similar triangles.

12.

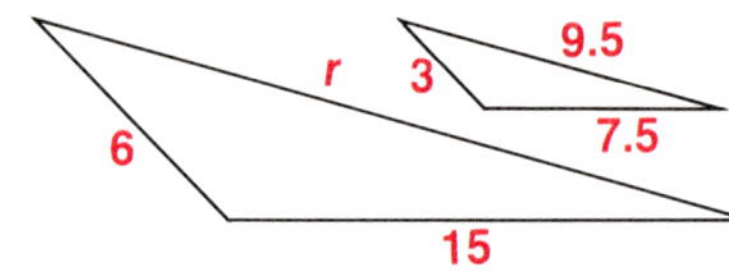

13.

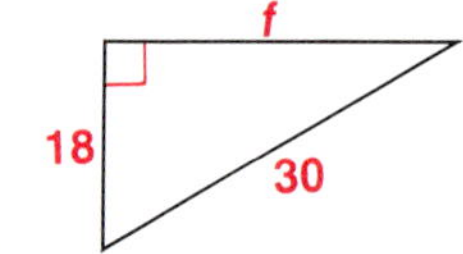

8
6
10

14-7 Find the unknown length.

14.

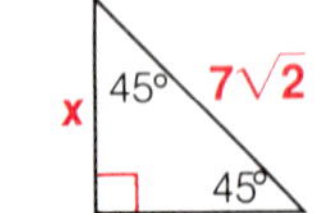

15.

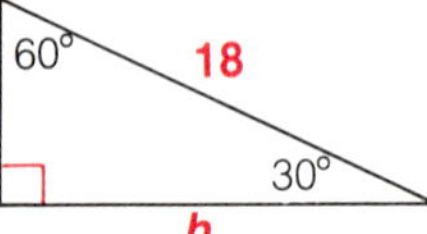

14-8 Find each ratio for $\angle A$.

16. $\sin A$

17. $\cos A$

18. $\tan A$

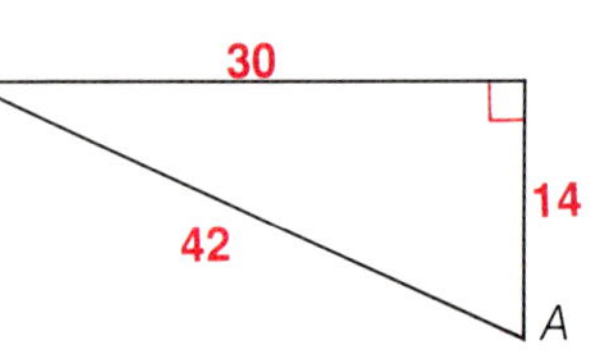

14-9 Solve by writing an equation. **19.** A garden with an area of 870 square feet is to be divided into 2 sections. One section will be 50 square feet larger than the other. What will be the area of each section?

Chapter 14 Test

Between what two consecutive integers does each square root lie?

1. $\sqrt{61}$ **2.** $\sqrt{18}$

Evaluate each expression.

3. $\sqrt{25} - \sqrt{100}$ **4.** $\sqrt{33 + 16}$

Use a calculator with a $\sqrt{}$ key to find an approximation for each square root.

5. $\sqrt{11}$ **6.** $\sqrt{96}$

Solve and check. **7.** $x^2 = 1$ **8.** $x^2 = 43$

Find the length of a to the nearest hundredth.

9.

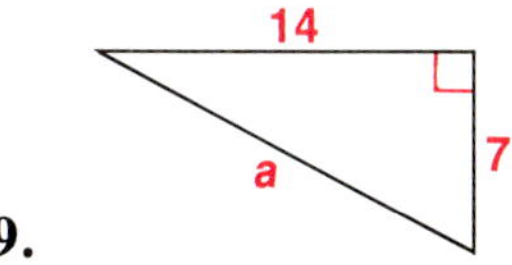

10.

Solve. **11.** A window is 6 feet wide and 4 feet high. What is the length of the diagonal of the window?

Use proportions to find the unknown lengths for these similar triangles.

12.

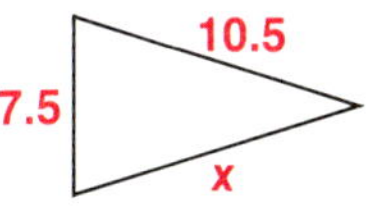

13.

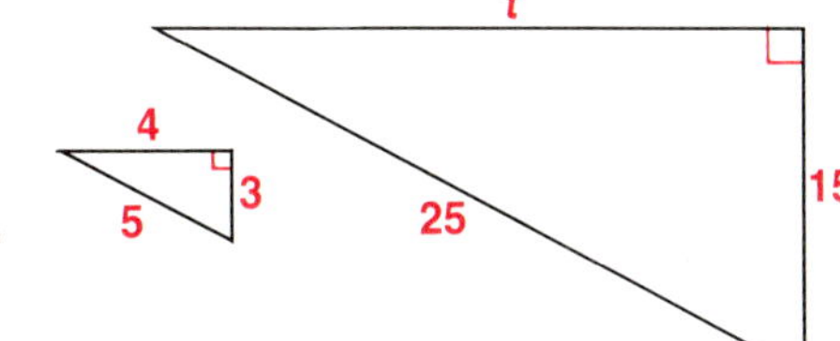

Find the unknown length.

14.

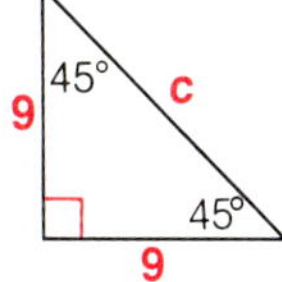

15.

Find each ratio for $\angle A$.

16. sin A

17. cos A

18. tan A

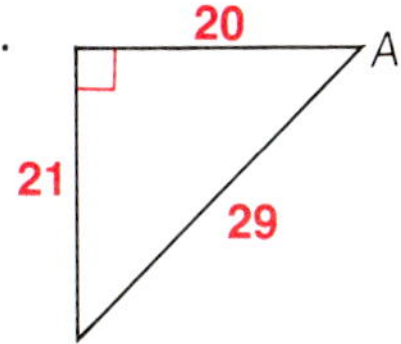

Solve by writing an equation. **19.** The Wilson family drove 623 miles to visit relatives. They drove 51 miles more than $\frac{1}{2}$ of the distance on the first day. How far did they drive the second day?

Cumulative Review

Solve the problem. Use the formula Distance = rate × time.

1. An airplane averaged 470 miles per hour on a $4\frac{1}{2}$ hour flight. How far did it fly?

Find the circumference of a circle with the given diameter or radius. Use 3.14 for π.

2. diameter = 8 cm

3. radius = 1.2 m

Use the SAS, SSS, or ASA property to show that each pair of triangles is congruent.

4.

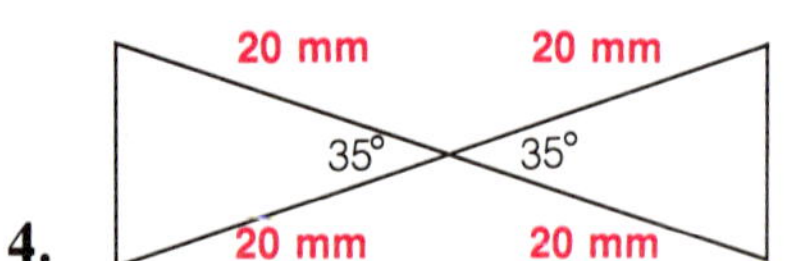

5.

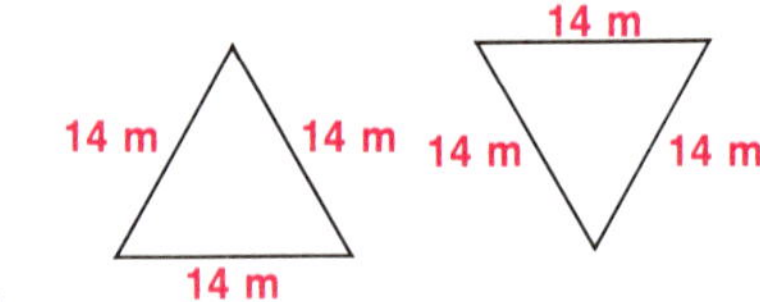

Solve by writing an equation. **6.** Mr. Dunlop bought 15% of the total number of tickets sold to a concert. If Mr. Dunlop bought 180 tickets, how many tickets were sold in all?

Find the volume of the prism or cylinder. Use 3.14 for π.

7.

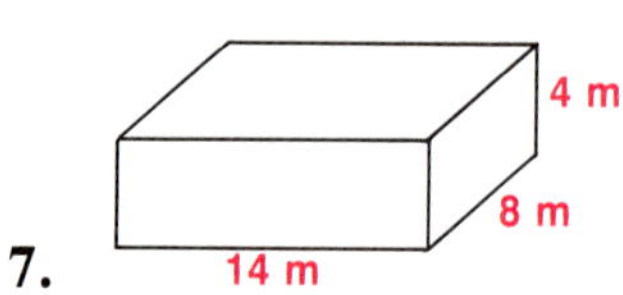

8.

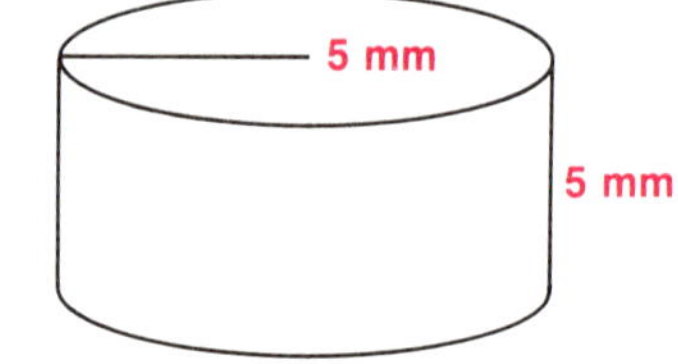

Solve.

9. How many cubic yards of concrete are needed for a driveway 54 feet long, 12 feet wide and 6 inches thick?

There are 12 tennis balls in a bag: 4 are green, 3 are white, 5 are yellow. You select one ball from the bag without looking. Find each probability.

10. P(yellow)

11. P(not green)

12. P(green or white)

You throw a die twice. Give the probability of each.

13. P(3 and 4)

14. P (first throw > 4, second throw an even number)

There are 9 balls in a bag: 5 red and 4 blue. Find each probability if you pull one ball from the bag and then pull another ball from the bag without replacing the first.

15. P(red then blue)

16. P(blue then blue)

Chapter 15
Graphs of Equations and Inequalities

15-1 Graphing on the Number Line

The **real numbers** are the numbers represented by the points on the number line. Solutions to inequalities are graphed on the number line.

Example 1

Solve $2x - 5 < 1$. Graph the solutions on a number line.

Solution $2x - 5 < 1$ — To solve the inequality, you need to get x by itself on one side.

$2x - 5 + 5 < 1 + 5$ — Add 5 to both sides of the inequality.

$\frac{2x}{2} < \frac{6}{2}$ — Divide both sides by 2.

$x < 3$

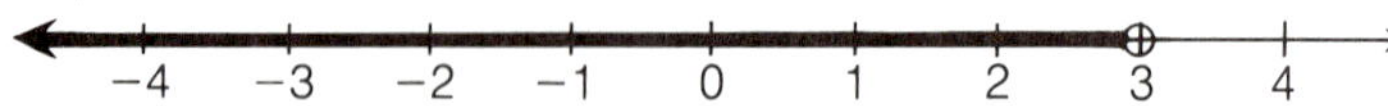

This solution is "all real numbers less than 3." Shade the number line to the left of 3. The open circle means the number 3 is not included.

Practice Solve. Graph the solutions on a number line.

a. $3x + 2 > -6$ **b.** $3x + 4 < 7$

Example 2

Solve $-2x + 1 \leq 5$. Graph the solutions on a number line.

Solution $-2x + 1 \leq 5$

$-2x + 1 - 1 \leq 5 - 1$ — Subtract 1 from both sides of the inequality.

$-2x \leq 4$

$\frac{-2x}{-2} \geq \frac{4}{-2}$ — Divide both sides by −2. Reverse the inequality sign.

$x \geq -2$

Use a closed circle on the graph to show that −2 is included in the solution.

Practice Solve. Graph the solutions on a number line.

a. $-3x + 7 \leq 13$ **b.** $-2x + 5 \geq 3$

Oral Exercises

Give an inequality for each solution shown.

1.

2.

3.

Exercises

A Solve. Graph the solutions on a number line.

1. $x < 3$ **2.** $x > -1$ **3.** $x \leq 2$ **4.** $x \geq -2$

5. $4x > 2$ **6.** $-3x \geq -1$ **7.** $-x > -5$ **8.** $\frac{1}{5}x < 1$

9. $x + 2 \leq -3$ **10.** $x - 5 \leq -4$ **11.** $-x + 5 < 2$ **12.** $3x + 5 \geq -4$

13. $2x + 3 \leq 5$ **14.** $x - 2 > -4$ **15.** $5x - 3 \leq -12$ **16.** $-2x + 1 \geq 5$

17. $\frac{1}{4}x - 1 \geq -17$ **18.** $-2x - 5 \leq 3$ **19.** $\frac{1}{3}x + 1 < 4$ **20.** $-3x + 5 < -4$

B Solve. Graph the solutions on a number line.

Example: $-2 < x \leq 4$. Solution:

The solution is all numbers both greater than −2 and less than or equal to 4.

21. $-1 < x \leq 3$ **22.** $1 \leq x \leq 3$ **23.** $-2 < x < 3$ **24.** $-3 \leq x < -1$

25. $0 \leq x < 2$ **26.** $-3 < x \leq 4$ **27.** $-1 \leq x \leq 2$ **28.** $-3 < x \leq 0$

C Extending Thinking Skills

29. Graph on a number line all real numbers that satisfy both $-2 < x \leq 3$ *and* $1 \leq x < 4$.

30. Determine the graph of the solutions to $|x - 5| < 3$.

Mixed Review

Evaluate for $a = 3$, $b = -1$. **31.** $2(a - b)$ **32.** $a - 3b$ **33.** $b(ba)$

Solve and check. **34.** $21t - 15t = 4t + 8$ **35.** $7y = 6 + 2y$

15-2 Graphing on the Coordinate Plane

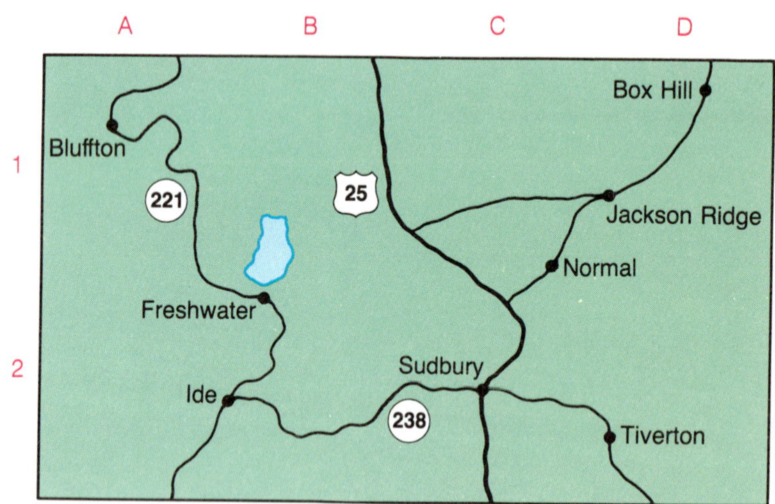

A letter and number pair is used to identify a position on this map. The town of Sudbury is located near the point with coordinates C-2.

In a **rectangular coordinate system**, two perpendicular number lines, called **axes**, intersect at a point called the **origin**. The horizontal axis is called the ***x*-axis** and the vertical axis is called the ***y*-axis**. These two axes allow each point to be named by an **ordered pair** of numbers called the **coordinates** of the point.

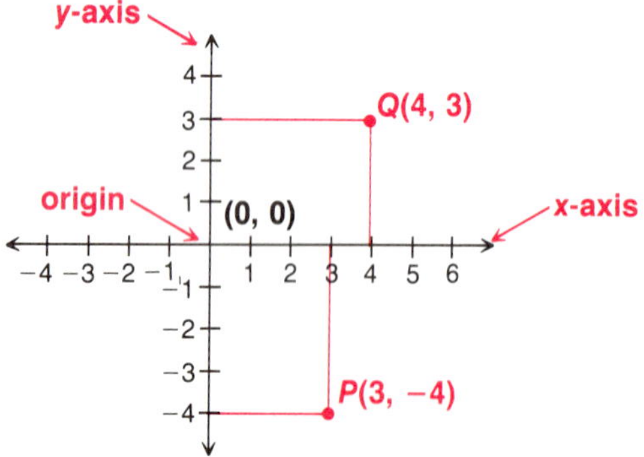

The coordinates of the origin are (0, 0). The coordinates of point P are $(3, -4)$ and the coordinates of point Q are $(4, 3)$. The ***x*-coordinate** of point P is 3 and the ***y*-coordinate** of point P is -4.

Example 1

Give the coordinates of points A, B, and C.

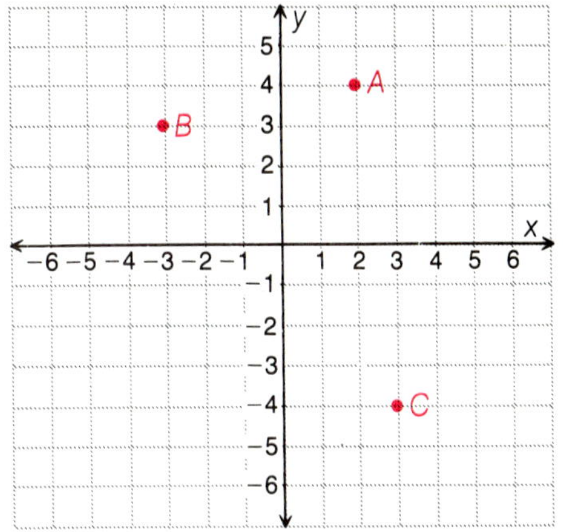

Solution

$A(2, 4)$

$B(-3, 3)$

$C(3, -4)$

Practice Give the coordinates of points D, E, F, and G.

Example 2

Graph points $A(2, 3)$, $B(-3, 5)$, and $C(4, -1)$.

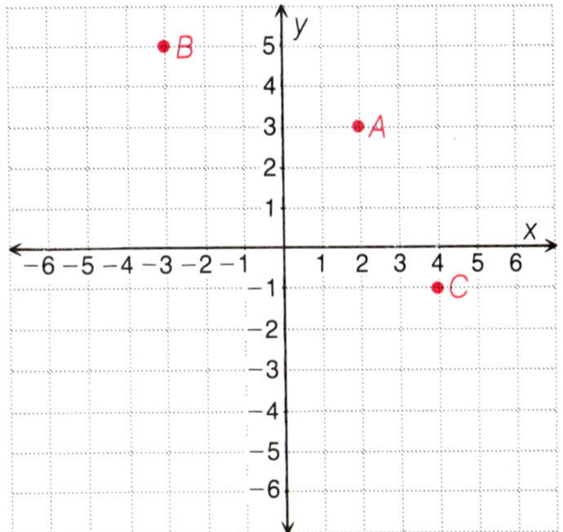

Solution

To graph point A at (2, 3), begin at the origin and move 2 units to the right and 3 units up.

To graph point B at (−3, 5), begin at the origin and move 3 units to the left and 5 units up.

To graph point C at (4, −1), begin at the origin and move 4 units to the right and 1 unit down.

Practice Graph points $D(-2, -3)$, $E(0, 4)$, and $F(3, 5)$.

Oral Exercises

State the x-coordinate and the y-coordinate for each point.

1. (3, −4) **2.** (−5, 4) **3.** (−1, 4)

4. (2, −3) **5.** (−12, −7) **6.** (−3, 0)

Describe the moves from the origin you would make to graph these points.

7. (−2, 5) **8.** (3, 5) **9.** (4, −2)

10. (1, −1) **11.** (7, −6) **12.** (0, 4)

Exercises

A Give the coordinates of each point.

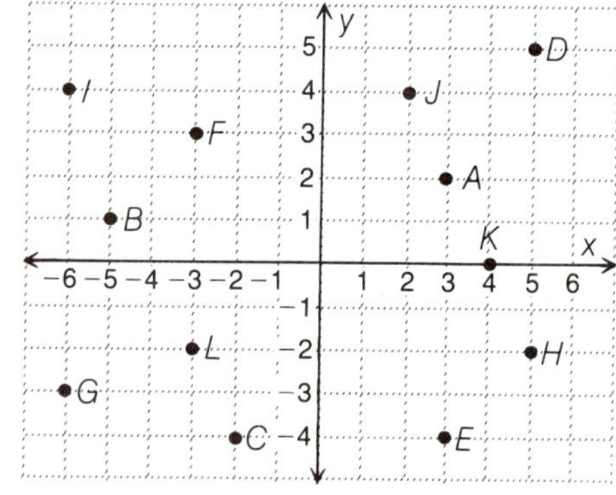

1. *A*	**2.** *B*
3. *C*	**4.** *D*
5. *E*	**6.** *F*
7. *G*	**8.** *H*
9. *I*	**10.** *J*
11. *K*	**12.** *L*

Graph each point.

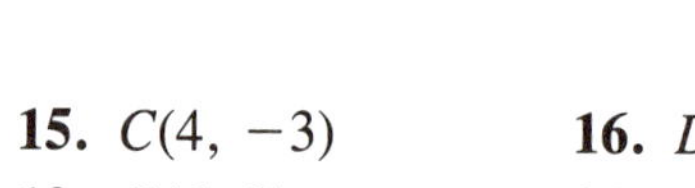

13. $A(3, 5)$	**14.** $B(-2, 7)$	**15.** $C(4, -3)$	**16.** $D(4, -4)$
17. $E(-2, -3)$	**18.** $F(-5, 1)$	**19.** $G(6, 3)$	**20.** $H(1, -5)$
21. $I(-4, -4)$	**22.** $J(2, 3)$	**23.** $K(0, 4)$	**24.** $L(-3, 0)$

B Name the coordinates for each point.

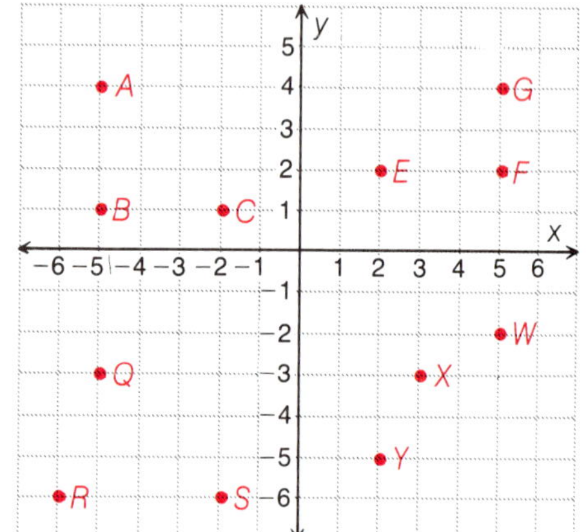

25. The point *D* that makes *ABCD* a square.

26. The point *H* that makes *EFGH* a rectangle.

27. The point *T* that makes *QRST* a parallelogram.

28. The point *Z* that makes *WXYZ* a rhombus.

On a single pair of axes draw a continuous line from point *A* to points *B*, *C*, *D*, *E*, and *F* for each of Exercises 29–37. What do you discover?

29. $A(-6, 9)$; $B(-5.5, 11)$; $C(-5, 10)$; $D(-4.5, 11)$; $E(-4, 9)$

30. $A(-3, 9)$; $B(-2, 11)$; $C(-1, 9)$; $D(-1.5, 10)$; $E(-2.5, 10)$

31. $A(1, 11)$; $B(3, 11)$; $C(2, 11)$; $D(2, 9)$

32. $A(4, 11)$; $B(4, 9)$; $C(4, 10)$; $D(6, 10)$; $E(6, 11)$; $F(6, 9)$

33. $A(-1.5, 7)$; $B(-0.5, 7)$; $C(-1, 7)$; $D(-1, 5)$; $E(-1.5, 5)$; $F(-0.5, 5)$

34. $A(3, 7)$; $B(1, 7)$; $C(1, 6)$; $D(3, 6)$; $E(3, 5)$; $F(1, 5)$

35. $A(-2, 3)$; $B(-4, 3)$; $C(-4, 1)$; $D(-4, 2)$; $E(-3, 2)$

36. $A(-1, 3)$; $B(-1, 1)$; $C(1, 1)$; $D(1, 3)$

37. $A(2, 1)$; $B(2, 3)$; $C(4, 1)$; $D(4, 3)$

C Extending Thinking Skills

38. Graph the pairs of points (2, 1) and (1, 2); (−2, 3) and (3, −2); (3, −4) and (−4, 3); (2, 4) and (4, 2); (3, 5) and (5, 3); (−4, −2) and (−2, −4). From the pattern formed, make a generalization about the way the graphs of (a, b) and (b, a) are related.

39. Find an ordered pair (x, y) that is a solution to $|x - 2| + |y - 3| = 0$.

Mixed Review

Evaluate each expression. **40.** $\sqrt{169 - 144} + \sqrt{9}$ **41.** $\sqrt{(104 - 79)} + \sqrt{16}$

Give the mean and mode. **42.** 4, 9, 4, 8, 6 **43.** 17, 12, 15, 11, 12, 14, 16, 12

NUMBERS TO ALGEBRA

You can find the distance between a point and the origin O (0, 0) by using the Pythagorean theorem. In the example below, we demonstrate the method for the specific point $A(4, 3)$ and for the general point $A(x, y)$.

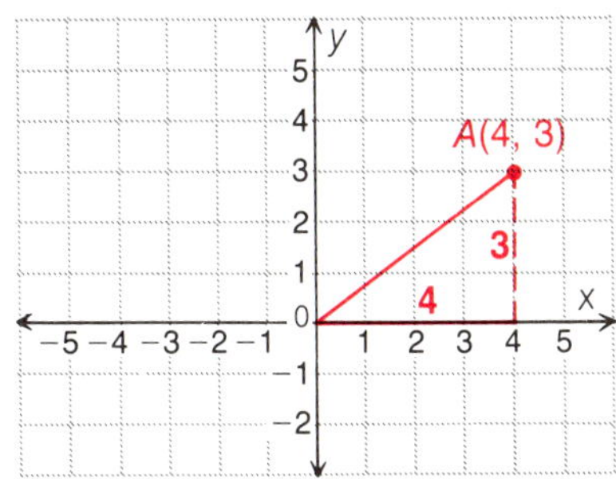

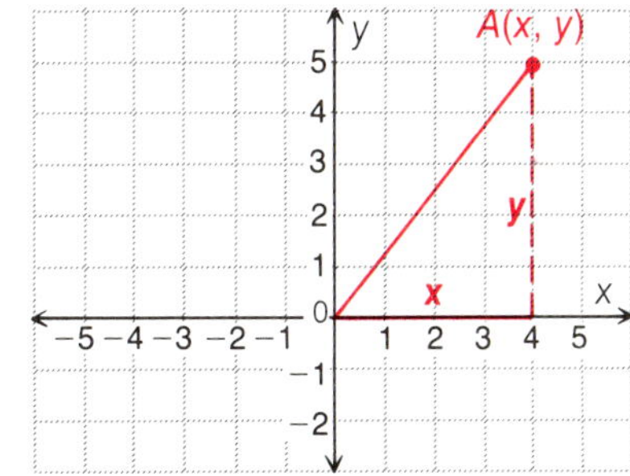

$$OA = \sqrt{4^2 + 3^2}$$
$$= \sqrt{25}$$
$$= 5$$

$$OA = \sqrt{x^2 + y^2}$$

Find the distance between the origin O (0, 0) and each point A.

1. $A(5, 12)$ **2.** $A(8, 15)$ **3.** $A(8, 6)$ **4.** $A(2, 3)$

15-3 Graphing Linear Equations

The graph of each of the equations $y = 2x + 1$, $2x + y = 5$, and $3x - 4y = 17$ is a line. Any equation that can be written in the form $y = ax + b$, where a and b are numbers and x and y are variables, is called a **linear equation**. An ordered pair is a solution for a linear equation if the equation is true when the coordinates of the ordered pair are substituted for x and y.

Example 1

Which of the ordered pairs (2, 7) and (−1, 2) is a solution for the linear equation $y = 3x + 1$?

Solution

$$y = 3x + 1$$
$$7 \stackrel{?}{=} 3(2) + 1$$ To determine whether (2, 7) is a solution, substitute 2 for x and 7 for y.
$$7 \stackrel{?}{=} 6 + 1$$
$$7 = 7$$

(2, 7) is a solution.

$$y = 3x + 1$$
$$2 \stackrel{?}{=} 3(-1) + 1$$ To determine whether (−1, 2) is a solution, substitute −1 for x and 2 for y.
$$2 \stackrel{?}{=} -3 + 1$$
$$2 \neq -2$$

(−1, 2) is not a solution.

Practice Which of the ordered pairs (2, −3) and (−2, −2) is a solution to the linear equation $y = 4x - 11$?

A linear equation has an infinite number of solutions. To find solutions for an equation such as $y = 2x + 1$, substitute a number for x and solve for y.

Substitute 1 for x	Substitute 2 for x	Substitute 3 for x
↓	↓	↓
$y = 2x + 1$	$y = 2x + 1$	$y = 2x + 1$
$y = 2(1) + 1$	$y = 2(2) + 1$	$y = 2(3) + 1$
$y = 3$	$y = 5$	$y = 7$
(1, 3) is a solution.	(2, 5) is a solution.	(3, 7) is a solution.

You can use a table to show a set of solutions for a linear equation.

Example 2

Make a table of solutions for $y = 2x + 3$ when $x = -2, -1, 0, 1, 2$, and 3.

Solution $y = 2x + 3$

x	y
−2	−1
−1	1
0	3
1	5
2	7
3	9

Substitute each value of x into the equation and solve for the corresponding value of y. Enter this value of y into the table beside the value of x.

Practice Make a table of solutions for $y = 2x - 3$ for $x = -3, -2, -1, 0$, and 1.

When the ordered pairs found in a solution table are graphed, the graphed points fall on a straight line. By drawing the line through this set of graphed points, you *graph the linear equation*. The line represents *all* solutions to the equation.

Example 3

Make a table of solutions for $y = x + 1$. Graph the equation.

Solution $y = x + 1$

x	y
−2	−1
−1	0
0	1
1	2
2	3
3	4

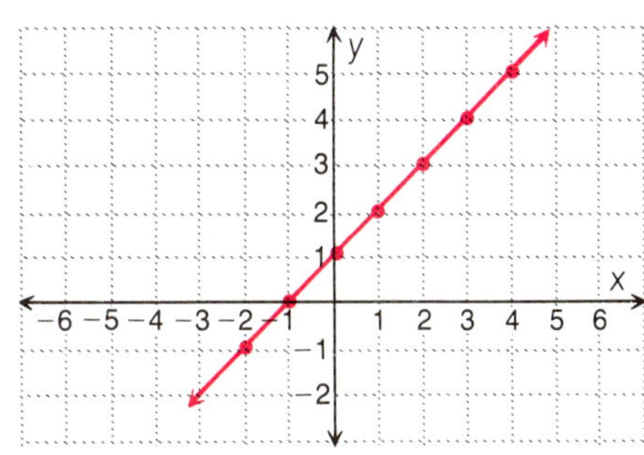

Practice Make a table of solutions for $y = 2x - 1$. Graph the equation.

Oral Exercises

These equations are written in the form $y = ax + b$. Give the values of a and b for each equation.

1. $y = 3x + 5$ **2.** $y = 2x - 4$ **3.** $y = -x + 17$ **4.** $y = 3x + 5$

5. $y = -x + 6$ **6.** $y = -2x + 3$ **7.** $y = 5x + 7$ **8.** $y = -x$

Exercises

A Which of the ordered pairs is a solution for the equation?

1. (2, 3) or (3, 9) for $2x + y = 7$

2. (1, 5) or (2, 6) for $3x - y = 0$

3. (−3, 4) or (3, −4) for $3x + 2y = -1$

4. (5, 7) or (7, 8) for $x - 2y = -9$

For each equation, make a table of solutions for $x = -2, -1, 0, 1, 2, 3$, and 4.

5. $y = 2x - 1$ **6.** $y = 3x + 2$ **7.** $-2x + 5 = y$ **8.** $y = -x + 3$

9. $y = 4x - 7$ **10.** $y = -2x + 3$ **11.** $y = x - 12$ **12.** $y = 2x - 5$

Make a table of solutions and graph each linear equation.

13. $y = x + 1$ **14.** $y = 2x - 3$ **15.** $y = -x + 2$ **16.** $y = 3x - 4$

17. $y = x + 3$ **18.** $y = -x - 2$ **19.** $y = -2x + 1$ **20.** $y = -x + 3$

B Rewrite the equation in the form $y = ax + b$. Make a table of solutions and graph the equation.

21. $4x + y = 4$ **22.** $-2x + y = 6$ **23.** $2x + y = 8$ **24.** $y - 2x = 1$

25. $3x = 2y + 4$ **26.** $3y + 6x = 6$ **27.** $2x = 4y$ **28.** $3x - 4y = 8$

C Extending Thinking Skills

29. Find an ordered pair that is a solution to both $x + y = 2$ and $x - y = 0$.

30. At what points does the graph of $\frac{x}{2} + \frac{y}{3} = 1$ cross the x- and y-axes?

Mixed Review

Write each as a fraction. **31.** 60% **32.** 11% **33.** 75% **34.** 240%

Solve and check. **35.** $0.75m + 4 = 13$ **36.** $3t + 11t - 16 = 12$

COMPUTER ACTIVITY

This program prints 20 solutions to a linear equation.

```
10  PRINT "THIS PROGRAM GIVES 20 SOLUTIONS TO A"
20  PRINT "LINEAR EQUATION OF THE FORM Y = AX + B"
30  PRINT
40  INPUT "CHOOSE A VALUE FOR A AND A VALUE FOR B:";A, B
50  PRINT "X";TAB(12);"Y=";A;"X + ";B
60  PRINT
70  FOR N=1 TO 20
80  PRINT N;TAB(16);A*N+B
90  NEXT N
100 END
```

1. Type and run the program for the equation $y = 3x + 5$.

2. Type and run the program for $y = 17x - 236$.

15-4 Practice Solving Problems

Problems

A Solve by writing an equation.

1. Ms. Ericson bought a used car for $175 more than half its original price. She paid $2465 for the car. What was its original price?

2. Sally has 8 more than twice as many coins in her collection as she did when her grandmother gave her the first coins in her collection. She now has 120 coins. How many did her grandmother give her?

3. A gasoline station charges $1.16 per gallon and $2.50 for a car wash. Celia's total charge for gas and a wash was $12.94. How many gallons of gasoline did she buy?

4. An amusement park had $\frac{1}{3}$ as many customers on Sunday as on Saturday. The total number of customers for the two days was 1648. How many customers did the park have on each of the two days?

5. Mr. Walton weighed 186 pounds. He planned a diet that would help him lose 2 pounds per week. He wanted to get his weight down to 160 pounds. How many weeks should he plan to diet?

B

6. A taxi driver charges $1.25 plus $1.75 for each mile traveled. To pay his cab fare and a $2 tip, Mr. Bush gave the driver $16. How far did he travel?

7. Tim and Ginny work in different restaurants. They both worked the same number of hours and earned the same amount last week. Tim worked for $6 per hour and could keep no tips. Ginny worked for $4 an hour, but was allowed to keep tips totaling $76. How many hours did each work?

8. A three-member relay team ran the relay in 186 seconds. Lisa ran her lap in 9 seconds less than Sara. Kay took 3 seconds more than Sara to run her lap. What was the lap time for each runner?

C Extending Thinking Skills

9. Write a word problem that could be solved using the equation $\frac{1}{2}x + 3 = 75$.

10. Write a word problem that could be solved using the equation $x + 7 = 12$.

Mixed Review

Give the greatest common factor (GCF). **11.** 78, 54, 24 **12.** 9, 27, 15

Solve and check. **13.** $19 - 4m = 11$ **14.** $t + 0.9t = 9.5$

15-5 Direct and Inverse Variation

A car driven 40 km/h will travel 40 km in 1 hour, 80 km in 2 hours, 120 km in 3 hours, and so on. You can show this with the equation $d = 40t$, where d is distance, 40 is rate, and t is time. In this situation, as the value of one variable *increases at a constant rate,* the value of the other variable *also increases at a constant rate*. The second variable **varies directly** with the first.

Suppose a car is to travel 40 km. Traveling at the rate of 40 km/h, it would take 1 hour. At 80 km/h, it would take $\frac{1}{2}$ hour, at 120 km/h it would take only $\frac{1}{3}$ hour, and so on. You can show this relationship as $t = \frac{40}{r}$ or $rt = 40$, where t is time, 40 is distance, and r is rate. In this situation, as the value of one variable *increases* at a constant rate, the value of the other variable *decreases* and the product of the variables is a constant. The second variable **varies inversely** with the first variable. Direct and inverse variation are defined as follows.

Direct Variation

A variable y **varies directly with** x if there is a positive number k such that $y = kx$.

Inverse Variation

A variable y **varies inversely with** x if there is a positive number k such that $y = \frac{k}{x}$ or $xy = k$.

Example 1

Does y vary directly with x? If it does, find the value of k.

x	y
1	3
2	6
3	9
4	12

Solution $3 = k(1)$ The pair (1, 3) satisfies $y = kx$ if $k = 3$.

$6 = 3(2)$ Check to see whether other pairs satisfy $y = 3x$.

$9 = 3(3)$

$12 = 3(4)$ The pairs (2, 6), (3, 9), and (4, 12) do satisfy $y = 3x$.

y varies directly with x, and $k = 3$.

Practice Does y vary directly with x? If it does, find the value of k.

a.

x	y
1	5
2	10
3	15
4	20
5	25

b.

x	y
1	-2
2	-4
3	-6
4	-8
5	-10

Example 2

Does y vary directly with x? If it does, find the value of k.

x	y
1	2
2	3
3	6
4	9
5	12

Solution

$2 = k(1)$ The pair (1, 2) satisfies $y = kx$ if $k = 2$.

$3 \neq 2(2)$ Check to see whether other pairs satisfy $y = 2x$.

$6 = 2(3)$

$9 \neq 2(4)$

$12 \neq 2(5)$ The pairs (2, 3), (4, 9), and (5, 12) do not satisfy $y = 2x$.

y does not vary directly with x.

Practice Does y vary directly with x? If it does, find the value of k.

x	y
1	5
2	7
3	9
4	3
5	6

Example 3

Does y vary inversely with x? If it does, find the value of k.

x	y
1	24
2	12
3	8
4	6
5	$\frac{24}{5}$

Solution

$24 = \frac{k}{1}$ The pair (1, 24) satisfies $y = \frac{k}{x}$ if $k = 24$.

$12 = \frac{24}{2}$ Check to see whether other pairs satisfy $y = \frac{24}{x}$.

$8 = \frac{24}{3}$

$6 = \frac{24}{4}$

$\frac{24}{5} = \frac{24}{5}$ All pairs do satisfy $y = \frac{24}{x}$.

y varies inversely with x, and $k = 24$.

Practice Does y vary inversely with x? If it does, find the value of k.

a.

x	y
1	5
2	4
3	3
4	2
5	1

b.

x	y
1	1
2	$\frac{1}{2}$
3	$\frac{1}{3}$
4	$\frac{1}{4}$

Oral Exercises

For each question, state whether y varies directly with x, y varies inversely with x, or neither case is true.

1. $y = 2x$ **2.** $xy = 5$ **3.** $xy = 14$ **4.** $y = 4x$

5. $x = \frac{1}{y}$ **6.** $x = \frac{y}{5}$ **7.** $y = \frac{3}{x}$ **8.** $y = \pi x$

Exercises

A Does y vary directly with x? If it does, find the value of k.

1.

x	y
1	1
2	2
3	3
4	4
5	5

2.

x	y
1	2
2	4
3	6
4	8
5	10

3.

x	y
1	2
2	4
3	5
4	6
5	7

4.

x	y
1	4
2	8
3	12
4	16
5	20

5.

x	y
1	−2
2	4
3	−6
4	8
5	−10

Does y vary inversely with x? If it does, find the value of k.

6.

x	y
1	12
2	10
3	8
4	6
5	4

7.

x	y
1	120
2	60
3	40
4	30
5	24

8.

x	y
1	12
2	6
3	4
4	3
5	$\frac{12}{5}$

9.

x	y
1	2
2	1
3	$\frac{2}{3}$
4	$\frac{1}{2}$
5	$\frac{2}{5}$

10.

x	y
1	20
2	10
3	5
4	3
5	1

B

11. A car averages 25 miles per gallon of gas. Does the total number of miles traveled vary directly or inversely with the number of gallons of gas used?

12. A truck driver drives 150 miles between rest stops. Does his average speed vary directly or inversely with the time it takes to travel the 150 miles?

13. The tax on Mr. Jones's income is 20%. Does the amount of tax he pays vary directly or inversely with the amount he earns?

C Extending Thinking Skills

14. Copy and complete the table at right so that y varies directly with x.

15. Copy and complete the table at right so that y varies inversely with x.

16. A variable y varies directly with the square of a variable x if $y = kx^2$ when a constant k is a positive number. Complete the table at right so that y varies directly with the square of x.

x	y
1	?
2	?
3	?
4	80

Mixed Review

Compute. **17.** 1.2×25 **18.** $36 + (-25)$ **19.** 3.6×25

20. $3^2 + 3^3$ **21.** $3^2 \cdot 3^3$ **22.** 4.16×10^3 **23.** 2^{-2}

Solve and check. **24.** $12.4 = 36m - 5.6$ **25.** $3c - 1.7c = 3.12$

CALCULATOR ACTIVITY

The constant multiplier 29 can be stored in the memory to make completing this table of direct variations easier. The key sequence below puts the constant 29 in the memory, then calculates the first entry of the table.

Use the following key sequence:

29 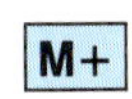

30 

Display
870

$y = 29x$

x	y
30	870
60	?
90	?
120	?
150	?
180	?
210	?

1. Use the key sequence above to continue completing the table.

2. Use a calculator to complete a table of direct variation for $y = 123x$. Use values of x with multiples of 35 up to 280.

3. Find a key sequence that includes the MR key to complete a table for the inverse variation described by $y = \frac{123}{x}$.

15-6 Slope and Intercepts

A roof that increases 4 feet vertically for every 12 feet of horizontal distance has a slope of $\frac{4}{12}$.

The **slope** of a line gives the idea of the steepness of a line. The slope is **the change in *y* divided by the change in *x***. The change in *y* is called the **rise**. The change in *x* is called the **run**. To find the slope of a line, choose any two points on the line and calculate the change in the *y*-coordinate and *x*-coordinate for these points.

From A to B:

$$\text{slope} = \frac{\text{change in } y}{\text{change in } x} = \frac{2}{4} = \frac{1}{2}$$

From B to C:

$$\text{slope} = \frac{\text{change in } y}{\text{change in } x} = \frac{3}{6} = \frac{1}{2}$$

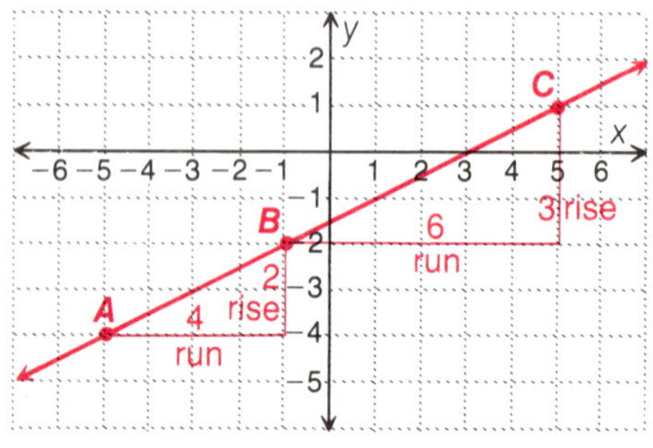

Example 1

Graph the line that contains the points $A(-2, 3)$ and $B(6, -3)$. Find the slope.

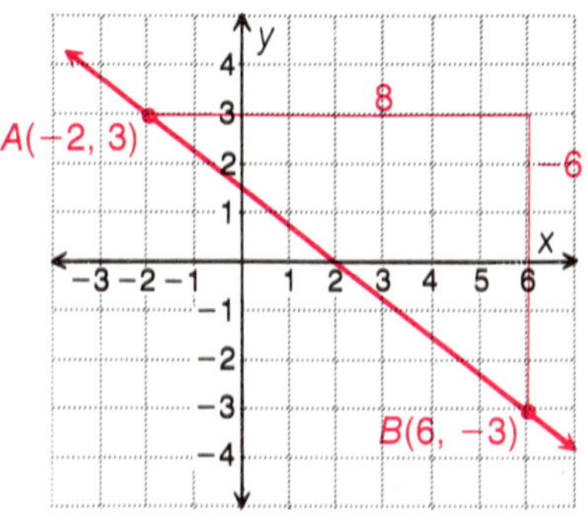

Solution

$$\text{slope} = \frac{\text{change in } y}{\text{change in } x}$$ Subtract in the same order.

$$\text{slope of } \overleftrightarrow{AB} = \frac{-3 - 3}{6 - (-2)}$$

$$= \frac{-6}{8} = -\frac{3}{4}$$

Practice Graph the line that contains the points given. Find the slope.

a. $A(1, 2)$ and $B(4, 8)$ **b.** $C(-3, 1)$ and $D(5, 3)$

You can find the slope of the line for a linear equation by using any two points that make the equation true.

Example 2

Find the slope of the line $y = 3x - 1$.

Solution

When $x = 1$, $y = 3(1) - 1 = 2$ Find two points by using any two values of x and calculating the corresponding values of y. (1, 2) is on the graph.

When $x = 2$, $y = 3(2) - 1 = 5$ (2, 5) is on the graph.

$$\text{slope} = \frac{\text{change in } y}{\text{change in } x}$$

$$= \frac{5 - 2}{2 - 1} = \frac{3}{1} = 3$$ Make sure you begin with the same point in calculating both the change in y and the change in x.

Practice Find the slope of the line.

a. $y = -2x + 1$ **b.** $2x - 3y = 6$

The ***x*-intercept** is the x-coordinate of the point where the line crosses the x-axis. The ***y*-intercept** is the y-coordinate where the line crosses the y-axis. Since all points on the y-axis have an x-coordinate of 0, you find the y-intercept by letting $x = 0$. Since all points on the x-axis have y-coordinate of 0, you find the x-intercept by letting $y = 0$.

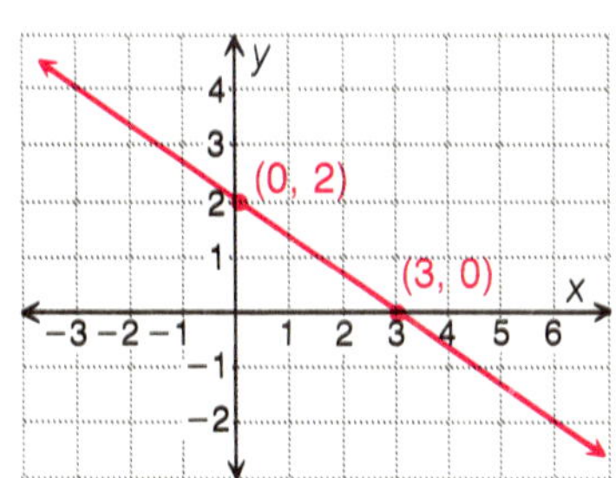

The line is the graph of $2x + 3y = 6$.

The x-intercept is 3.

The y-intercept is 2.

Example 3

Find the x- and y-intercepts for the line $3x + 2y = 12$.

Solution

Let $y = 0$. $3x + 2(0) = 12$ The y-coordinate of the x-intercept is 0. So let $y = 0$ and solve for x.

$3x = 12$

$x = 4$

The x-intercept is 4. The pair (4, 0) satisfies the equation $3x + 2y = 12$.

Let $x = 0$. $3(0) + 2y = 12$ The x-coordinate of the y-intercept is 0. So let $x = 0$ and solve for y.

$2y = 12$

$y = 6$

The y-intercept is 6. The pair (0, 6) satisfies the equation $3x + 2y = 12$.

Practice Find the x- and y-intercepts. **a.** $-2x + y = 6$ **b.** $3x - 2y = 10$.

Oral Exercises

For each line, give the slope, the x-intercept, and the y-intercept.

1.

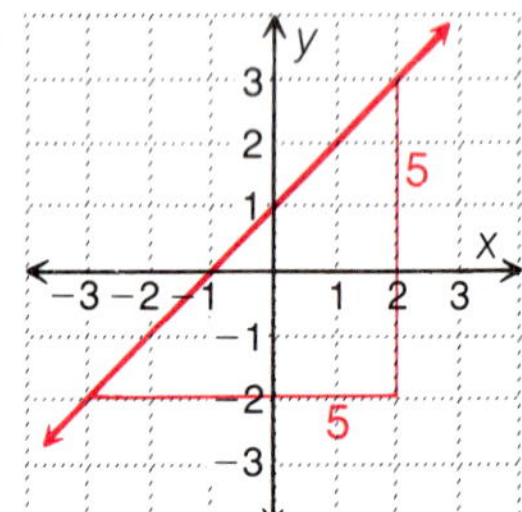

2.

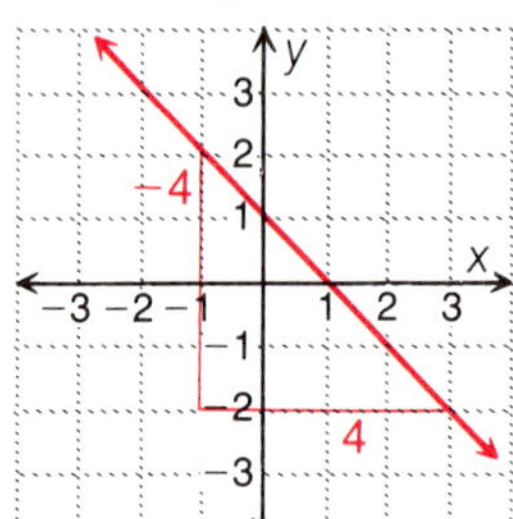

3.

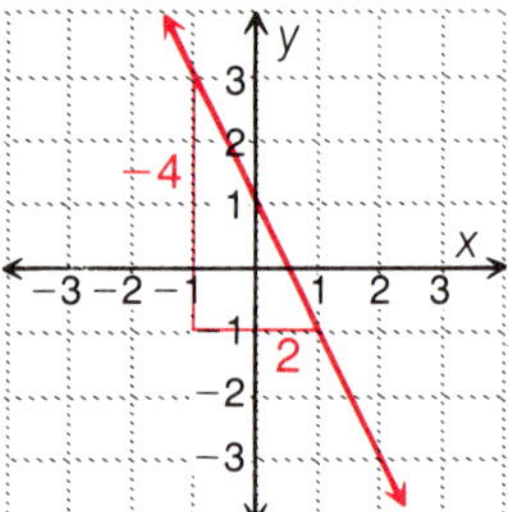

Exercises

A Graph the line that contains the given points and find the slope.

1. $A(1, 1), B(4, 3)$ **2.** $A(1, 3), B(5, 8)$ **3.** $A(-2, -3), B(4, 6)$

4. $A(-3, -1), B(3, 1)$ **5.** $A(-2, 2), B(2, -2)$ **6.** $A(-1, 3), B(1, -3)$

7. $A(-2, 8), B(3, -2)$ **8.** $A(-2, 3), B(4, -6)$ **9.** $A(8, 4), B(1, 3)$

10. $A(3, 5), B(-2, -3)$ **11.** $A(-4, -6), B(-1, 3)$ **12.** $A(3, -5), B(-3, 8)$

Find the slope of each line.

13. $y = 2x - 1$ **14.** $y = -3x + 7$ **15.** $2x - y = 5$ **16.** $3x + 2y = 24$

17. $x + 3y = 6$ **18.** $2x - 5y = 10$ **19.** $2x - 7 = y$ **20.** $3y = 2x - 5$

Find the x- and y-intercepts.

21. $x + y = 5$ **22.** $2x + y = 4$ **23.** $x - 3y = 6$ **24.** $2x - 3y = 24$

25. $4x + 5y = 20$ **26.** $3x - 4y = 12$ **27.** $-y + 2x = 5$ **28.** $5x + 3y = 15$

B Graph the equation. How do the numbers in the equation relate to the slope?

29. $y = 2x - 3$ **30.** $y = -3x + 5$ **31.** $y = \frac{1}{2}x + 1$

32. A long grade on a highway through the mountains has a vertical rise of 7 ft for each 100 ft of horizontal distance. How many feet of rise are there in one mile (5280 ft.) of horizontal change?

33. A ladder is to reach a point 30 feet above the ground. How far from the building should its base be if its slope is 2.5?

C Extending Thinking Skills

34. Suppose a line through (1, 2) has slope 3. Find values for b, c, and d so that $(2, b)$, $(3, c)$, and $(4, d)$ are points on the line.

Mixed Review

Give the least common multiple (LCM). **35.** 2, 4, 7 **36.** 4, 6, 8

Solve and check. **37.** $3t = 15 - 2t$ **38.** $406 - 5y = 371$

ESTIMATION

The graph of the equation that gives the relationship between temperature in degrees Fahrenheit and degrees Celsius is a line with slope $\frac{5}{9}$. That means a change in temperature of 9°F is a change of 5°C.

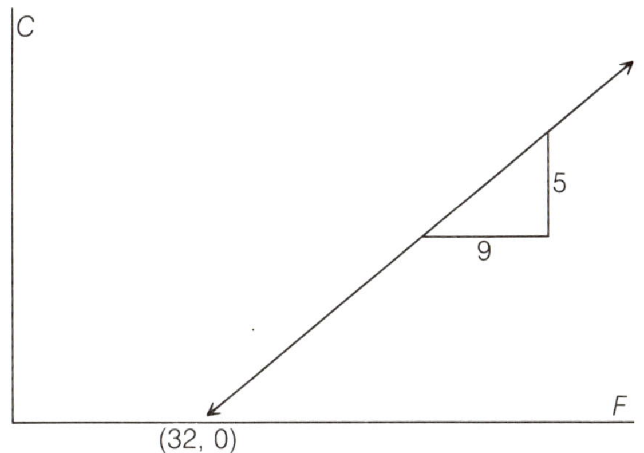

F	C	
change by 9	change by 5	
32	0	← water freezes
41	5	
50	10	
59	15	
68	20	
77	25	

Use the table above to estimate each temperature in degrees Celsius.

1. 55°F ≈ _?_°C **2.** 70°F ≈ _?_°C **3.** 45°F ≈ _?_°C **4.** 23°F ≈ _?_°C

PROBLEM SOLVING: APPLICATIONS

15-7 School Newspaper Advertising

The staff of the school newspaper sells advertising to help pay printing costs. The pages are set up in 3 columns. Each column is 4 inches wide and 14 inches long. A "column inch" is an area 1 column wide by 1 inch long.

Classified Ads	6 lines per column inch	\$ 0.10 per line
Merchant Ads	less than half page half page full page	\$ 0.60 per column inch \$12.00 \$22.00
Ads for School Activities		no charge

Problems

1. How much would 1 column of classified ads earn for the paper?

2. How much would a 2-inch classified ad earn for the paper?

3. How much is earned by 8 inches of classified ads?

4. How much more is earned by a full page of classified ads than by two half-page merchant ads?

5. How much is earned by a merchant ad 3 inches long by 2 columns wide?

6. How much is earned by a merchant ad 4 inches long by 3 columns wide?

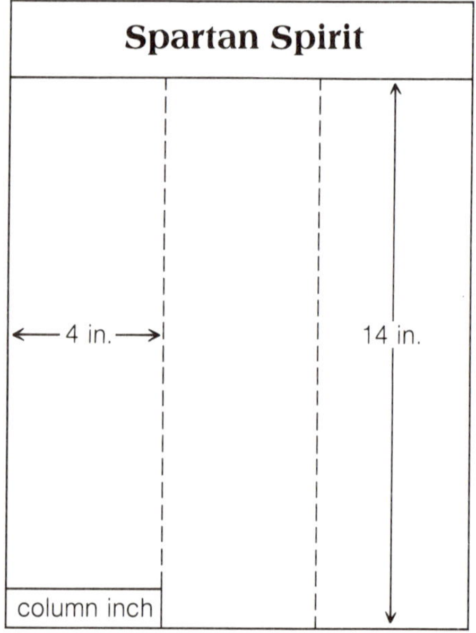

7. How much would the page of ads shown at right earn for the paper?

8. How much more would the page at right earn if the merchant ad 4 inches long by 1 column wide were replaced with a 4-inch classified ad?

9. The typesetter charges the *Spartan Spirit* $3.00 more to prepare a page of classified ads than it charges to prepare one full-page merchant ad. After paying the extra typesetting cost, how much more has the paper earned from a full page of classified ads than from a full-page merchant ad?

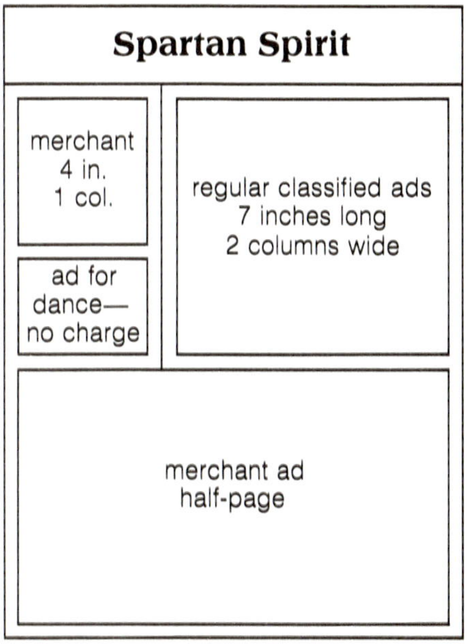

10. The *Spartan Spirit* provides a free ad 4 inches long by 2 columns wide for the school dance on the day of each of 5 home football games. It also provides a half-page ad for the Junior Prom and two half-page ads for the Senior Prom. How much would these ads cost at the merchant advertising rates?

11. The circulation of the *Spartan Spirit* (the number of copies printed and distributed) is 1550. How much per copy does a merchant pay for a full-page ad?

12. Data Search Find the cost of a full-page merchant ad in a local newspaper. Find the circulation of the paper. How much per copy does a merchant pay for a full-page ad?

Spartan Spirit

merchant
4 in.
1 col.

regular classified ads
7 inches long
2 columns wide

ad for
dance—
no charge

merchant ad
half-page

What's Your Decision?

The six-page *Spartan Spirit* is published 17 times per school year. About 50% of the space is devoted to ads that earn money. Printing costs are increasing by $50 per issue. The following ideas for reducing the budget deficit have been proposed:
a. increase the paid advertising space to 60% per issue; **b.** raise advertising rates 15%; **c.** print only 13 issues per year; **d.** charge each of the 1500 students $1.50 for a year's subscription. As the *Spartan Spirit* Managing Editor, which idea would you prefer? Why?

15-8 Graphing Systems of Equations

Two equations with the same two variables are called a **system of equations**. Any ordered pair that is a solution to both equations is called a solution of the system of equations. To find a solution of a system, find the point of intersection of the graphs of the two equations.

Example

Graph the equations to solve the system. Check the solution.

$$x + y = 2$$
$$-x + 2y = 1$$

Solution

Graph each equation on the same coordinate system.

Decide what point lies on both lines.

The solution appears to be (1, 1).

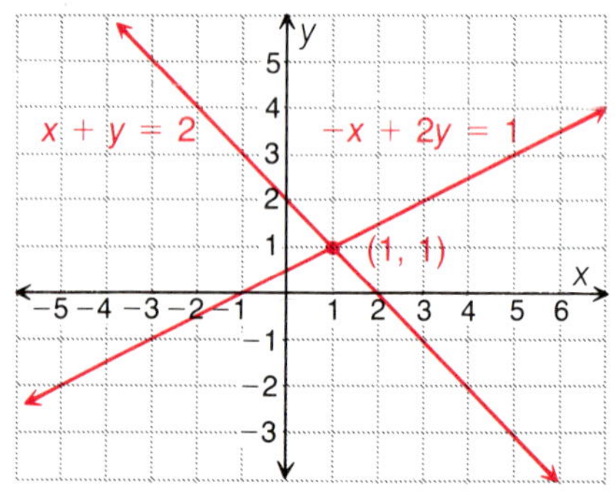

Check

$x + y = 2$ $\quad -x + 2y = 1$

$1 + 1 = 2\surd$ $\quad -1 + 2(1) = 1\surd$

Check to see that the point you have selected satisfies both equations. The solution is (1, 1).

Practice Graph the equations to solve the system. $x - y = 1$
$x + y = 3$

Oral Exercises

Is the ordered pair given a solution for the system of equations?

1. (1, 2) $\quad 2x + y = 4$
$3x - 2y = -1$

2. (−2, 3) $\quad 2x + y = 1$
$-x + 2y = 8$

3. (3, 1) $\quad x + 2y = 5$
$2x - y = 2$

4. (2, −1) $\quad -3x + y = -7$
$3x + 5y = 1$

Exercises

A Graph the equations to find a solution for the system. Check the solution.

1. $x - y = 1$
$x + 2y = 1$

2. $x + y = 2$
$2x - y = 1$

3. $x - y = 0$
$2x + y = 6$

4. $x + y = 0$
$x - y = -2$

5. $2x - y = -1$
$x + y = -2$

6. $2x + y = 5$
$-2x + y = 1$

7. $x + y = 3$
$x - y = 1$

8. $-2x + y = -4$
$2x + y = 0$

9. $x - 2y = 1$
$2x - y = 5$

B

A system of equations has *no solutions* if the lines of the system have the same slope, making the lines parallel. A system of equations has an *infinite number of solutions* if the graphs of the two linear equations are the same line. Decide whether each system has no solutions, an infinite number of solutions, or a one-point solution.

10. $3x - 2y = 2$
$4y - 6x = -4$

11. $2x + y = 3$
$2x + y = 5$

12. $3x + 2y = 6$
$4y - 12 = -6x$

13. What value of k will make $2x + 3y = k$ and $4x + 6y = k$ have the same set of solutions?

14. Translate to a system of equations and solve. The sum of two numbers is 6 and their difference is 2. Find the two numbers.

C Extending Thinking Skills

15. Cheap-at-the-Price Rent-a-car charges $20 a day and $0.15 per mile. More-for-Your-Money Rent-a-car charges $15 a day and $0.20 per mile. Which company charges the least for 75 miles in one day? For what mileage is the cost the same?

16. Guess and check to find the value of k that makes (1, 2) a solution of the system. $3x - y = 1$
$-x + ky = 3$

Mixed Review

Find the volume. Use 3.14 for π. **17.** A cylinder with radius 4 cm, height 5 cm
18. A cube with one side = 9 in. **19.** A cone with radius 5 m, height 9 m.
What percent of 36 is: **20.** 12? **21.** 27? **22.** 4? **23.** 54?
Solve and check. **24.** $12t - 10t = 26$ **25.** $495 = 27m + 90$
26. $1640 + 32x = 360$ **27.** $9y + 4.75 = 31.3$ **28.** $3c - 2.4c = 3$

15-9 Graphing Inequalities

The graph of a linear equation such as $y = x + 2$ divides the plane into two regions, one above the line and the other below the line. The line is the **boundary** of the two regions.

Point (1, 4) is a solution to $y > x + 2$, and is a point in the region **above** the line.

Point (1, 3) is a solution to $y = x + 2$, and is a point **on** the line.

Point (1, 2) is a solution to $y < x + 2$, and is a point in the region **below** the line.

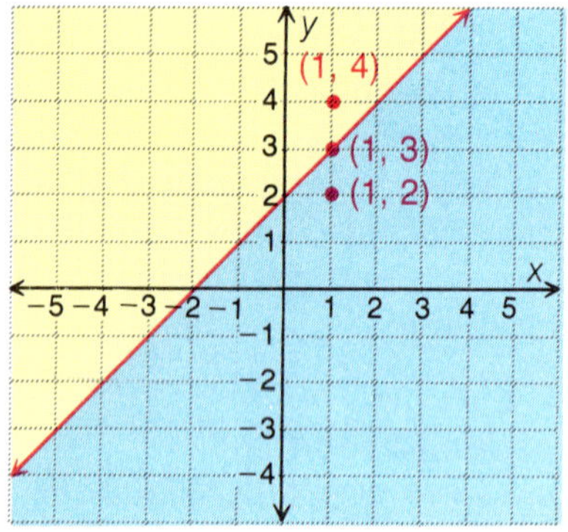

The region above the line is the set of all points that are solutions to the inequality $y > x + 2$. The region below the line is the set of all points that are solutions to the inequality $y < x + 2$. To graph a linear inequality, shade the graph to indicate the region that represents the solutions. If the inequality is $\leq$ or $\geq$, the boundary line is part of the region and is drawn as a solid line. If the inequality is $<$ or $>$, the boundary line is *not* a part of the region, and is drawn as a dashed line.

Example

Graph the inequality $y < x - 1$.

Solution

First, graph the boundary line $y = x - 1$.

The graph is the region below the line $y = x - 1$.

Since the inequality is $<$, draw the boundary line as a dashed line rather than a solid line.

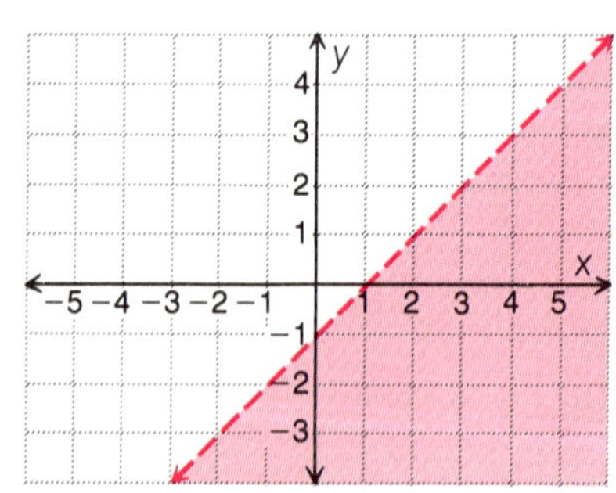

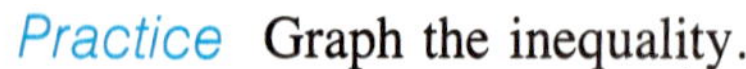

Practice Graph the inequality.

a. $y > 2x - 1$ **b.** $y \leq \frac{1}{2}x + 1$

Oral Exercises

When the inequality is graphed, will the boundary line be drawn as a solid line or a dashed line?

1. $y < 4x - 5$ **2.** $3x + 2 > y$ **3.** $-x \geq 4 + y$

4. $-2 - y \geq x$ **5.** $3x - 2y > 1$ **6.** $y - 7 < \frac{1}{2}x$

Exercises

A Graph the inequality.

1. $y < 3x - 2$ **2.** $y \geq -x + 2$ **3.** $y > -2x + 1$

4. $x \geq 1$ **5.** $y < 5$ **6.** $y < \frac{1}{2}x + 3$

7. $y < 2x - 5$ **8.** $x + 4 \geq y$ **9.** $y < 3 - x$

B Graph the inequality.

10. $2x + 3y \geq 6$ **11.** $3(x + 2y) \geq 6$ **12.** $x < 2y + 1$

13. $3 \leq \frac{6}{x}$ **14.** $2x + 7 > y - 3x$ **15.** $4y - 3x < 12$

16. Jim and Sally are a two-person relay team in a bicycle marathon. Jim averages 20 mi/h, and Sally averages 18 mi/h. The team with the current record rode 872 miles. Write an inequality that must be satisfied for Jim and Sally to set a new record if Jim rides x hours and Sally rides y hours.

17. Suppose corn seeds cost \$5/lb and wheat seeds cost \$7/lb. A farmer has a budget of \$500 for seeds. She plants x pounds of corn and y pounds of wheat. Write an inequality that must be satisfied for her to stay within the budget.

C Extending Thinking Skills

To find the solution for a system of linear inequalities, you graph each inequality and identify the region common to both graphs. Graph each system of linear inequalities.

Example: Graph the system $x \geq 1$
$y \leq 2$

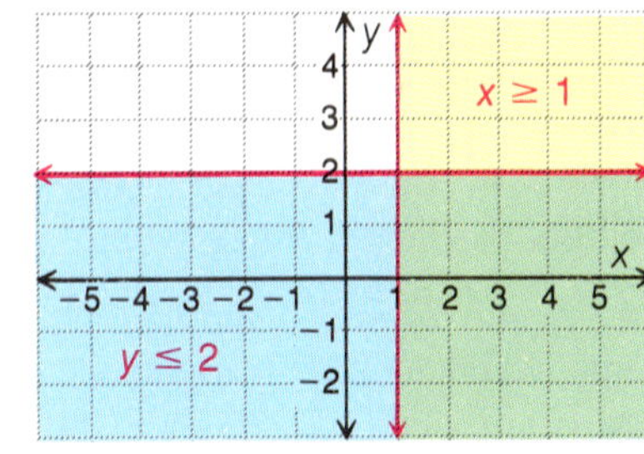

Graph each system of linear inequalities.

18. $x \leq 3$
$y \geq -1$

19. $y \leq x + 2$
$y \leq -x + 1$

20. $y \geq \frac{1}{2}x - 2$
$y \leq -2x + 6$

Mixed Review

21. Find the diameter and area of a circle with radius = 6 in. Use 3.14 for π.

Solve and check. **22.** $13t + 16 = 3$ −1 **23.** $4m + 17 - 7m + 5m = 21$

15-10 Practice Solving Problems

Problem-Solving Strategies	
Choose the Operations	Write an Equation
Guess, Check, Revise	Simplify the Problem
Draw a Picture	Make an Organized List
Make a Table	Use Logical Reasoning
Look for a Pattern	Work Backwards

This chart shows the strategies presented in previous chapters.

Problems

Solve.

1. A meeting room has a floor area of 625 ft^2 and an 8-foot high ceiling. Office guidelines recommend at least 200 ft^3 per person. What should be the maximum number of people allowed to meet in this room?

2. A car rental agency charges $21.50 per day plus $0.13 a mile. Mrs. Higby needs to rent a car for 1 day. Her company will pay up to $50 per day for a rental car. What is the maximum number of miles she can drive in one day and stay below the $50 limit?

3. Doctors knew that a flu virus could spread very rapidly. They estimated that each person who had it would give it to 4 other people every day. On April 12th, the first case of the flu was reported. If the flu spread as the doctors predicted, when would about 20,000 people have had the flu?

4. Angie, Brenda, and Clara weighed themselves 2 at a time. Brenda and Clara weighed 208 lb together. Angie and Brenda weighed 222 lb, and Angie and Clara weighed 216 lb. How much did each one weigh?

5. A rich man left his money to two nieces and a nephew. To the older niece he gave half of his money. He gave the younger niece $\frac{1}{3}$ what he gave the older niece. He gave the nephew twice as much as he gave the younger niece. He gave the nephew $3.5 million. How much did he give to all three?

6. A grocer is arranging grapefruit in his produce department so that it will form a pyramid. He forms the base of the pyramid using 64 grapefruit, with 8 grapefruit on each side. How many will he need to build the whole pyramid?

Enrichment

Telephone Rate Function

A telephone directory lists various rates for long-distance calls. The table below lists daytime rates for direct-dialed calls at $0.58 for the first minute and $0.39 for each additional minute. It shows a relationship between the length of a call in minutes and the cost of the call. The pairs of points in the table are graphed on the right.

time/min	total cost
0.5	$0.58
1	0.58
1.5	0.97
2	0.97
2.5	1.36
3	1.36
3.5	1.75
4	1.75
4.5	2.14
5	2.14

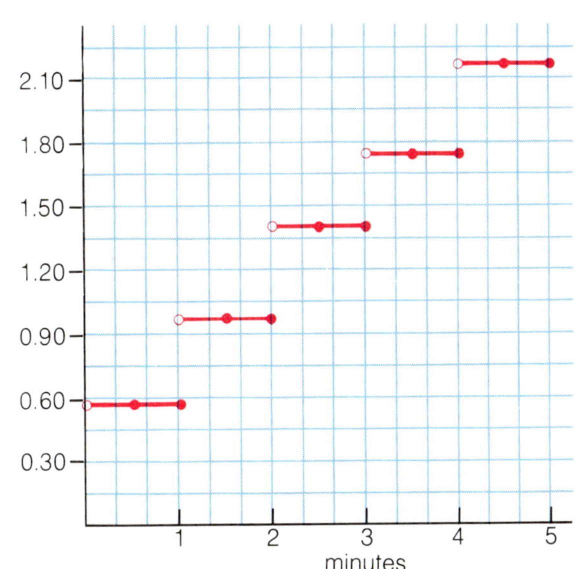

The cost of a call stays the same for any part of a minute. For example, from the beginning of the call to the end of the first minute, the cost is $0.58. On the graph, this is a horizontal line from 0 to 1. As soon as the call goes over 1 minute in length, the cost jumps to $0.97, and the line on the graph also jumps. The graph shows a jump at the end of each minute.

1. Evenings from 5 p.m. to 11 p.m., rates are reduced to $0.34 for the first minute and $0.24 for each additional minute. Complete a table of values and make a graph showing the relationship between time and cost.

2. All day Saturday and Sunday, rates for direct-dialed calls are reduced to $0.23 for the first minute and $0.16 for each additional minute. Complete a table of values and make a graph.

3. For calls handled by the operator, a $1.55 charge is added to the regular charges. Complete a table of values and make a graph for Saturday and Sunday calls handled by the operator. Refer to Exercise 2 for the regular charges.

Chapter 15 Review

15.1 Graph the solution on a number line.

1. $x < 0$

2. $x + 1 \geq 0$

15.2 Give the coordinates of each point.

3. R

4. U

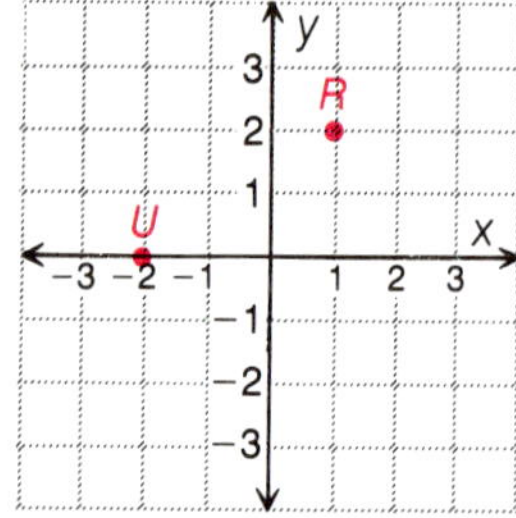

Graph the points on a pair of axes.

5. $V(-1, 1)$

6. $W(0, -2)$

15.3 7. Which of the ordered pairs (4, 9) or (3, 5) is a solution for the linear equation $y = 2x + 1$?

Make a table of solutions for the equation.

8. $y = -x - 1$ Use $x = -2, -1, 0, 1, 2, 3$.

15.4 Solve. **9.** Ms. Pierce bought a coat for \$30 more than half its original price. If she paid \$110 for the coat, what was the original price?

15.5 Does y vary directly with x? If it does, find the value of k.

Does y vary inversely with x? If it does, find the value of k.

10.

x	y
1	4
2	8
3	12
4	16
5	20

11.

x	y
1	2
2	4
3	−6
4	−8
5	−10

12.

x	y
1	20
2	10
3	$6.\overline{6}$
4	5
5	4

13.

x	y
1	15
2	7.5
3	5
4	3.75
5	3

15.6 Find the slope of the line.

14. A line that contains the points $C(-2, -2)$, $D(2, 2)$

15. $y = 5x + 2$

Find the intercepts for the line $2x + y = 4$.

16. x-intercept

17. y-intercept

15.7 Solve. **18.** Cabins at Duck Lake rent for \$250 for the first week and \$25 for each additional day. How much would it cost to rent a cabin for 10 days?

15.8 19. Graph the equations to solve the system. $-x + 2y = 0$, $x + y = 3$

15.9 20. Graph the inequality $y \geq 2x - 1$. Is point $(0, -3)$ a solution?

Chapter 15 Test

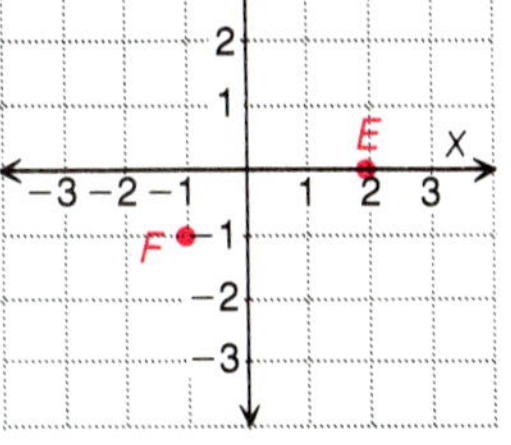

Graph the solution on a number line.

1. $x > -2$

2. $2x - 1 > -1$

Give the coordinates of each point.

3. E

4. F

Graph the points on a pair of axes.

5. $G\ (0, 1)$

6. $H\ (2, 2)$

7. Which of the ordered pairs $(-3, -6)$ or $(-3, 6)$ is a solution for the linear equation $2x + y = 0$?

Make a table of solutions for the equation.

8. $y = -x + 3$ Use $x = -2, -1, 0, 1, 2, 3$.

Solve. **9.** Bob sold a radio at a garage sale for $17. This was $3 more than $\frac{1}{7}$ of its original price. What was the original price of the radio?

Does y vary directly with x? If it does, find the value of k.

10.

x	y
1	3
2	4
3	5
4	6
5	7

11.

x	y
1	5
2	10
3	15
4	20
5	25

Does y vary inversely with x? If it does, find the value of k.

12.

x	y
1	24
2	12
3	8
4	6
5	4.8

13.

x	y
1	3
2	2
3	1
4	0
5	−1

Find the slope of the line.

14. A line contains the points $A(-1, 2)$, $B(2, -4)$

15. $3x + 4 = y$

Find the intercepts for the line $9 + 3y = x$.

16. x-intercept

17. y-intercept

Solve. **18.** A house-painting company charges $180 to paint two rooms, and $80 for each additional room. How much would it cost to have 5 rooms painted?

19. Graph the equation to solve the system $x + 2y = 1$, $x - y = -2$

20. Graph the inequality $y < (2 - x)$. Is point $(4, -1)$ a solution?

Cumulative Review

For problems 1–4, use 3.14 for π.

1. Find the volume of a cone with a radius of 6 inches and a height of 19 inches.
2. Find the volume of a pyramid with a base area of 64 square m and a height of 20 m.
3. Find the surface area of a cylinder with a $r = 4$ ft, $h = 11$ ft.
4. Find the surface area of the figure at right.

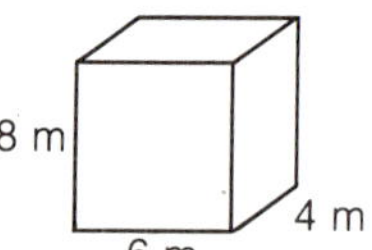

Use the counting principle to find the total number of outcomes.

5. Selection: 1 color and 1 size. Colors: Blue, Red, Orange, Green, Black; Sizes: Small, Medium, Large, Extra Large

Find the number of permutations.

6. t, u, e, s, d, a, y
7. stop, start, slow, fast

Solve. **8.** 5 drawings are entered in a drawing contest. How many ways can a winner and a runner-up be chosen?

Find the number of combinations. **9.** 3 books from a shelf of 9 books.

Use the data to solve problems 10–13.

Points scored by Pamela in basketball games: 14, 14, 10, 18, 15, 14, 13

10. Find the range.
11. Find the mode.
12. Find the median.
13. Find the mean.

Between what two consecutive integers does each square root lie?

14. $-\sqrt{93}$
15. $\sqrt{34}$

Use a calculator with a $\sqrt{\ }$ key to find an approximation for each square root.

16. $\sqrt{28}$
17. $\sqrt{80}$

Find the length of a.

18.

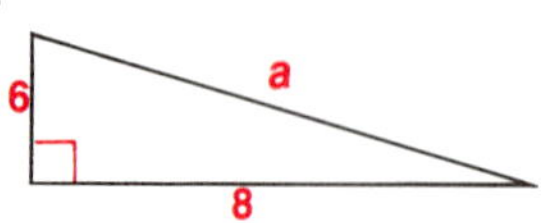

19.

5
a
8

Find each ratio for angle A.

20. sin A
21. cos A
22. tan A

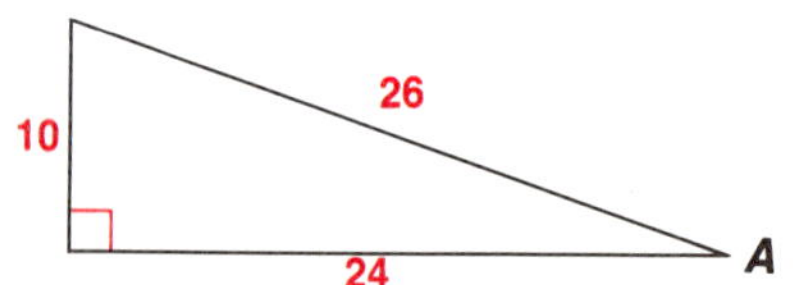

Table 1: Squares and Square Roots

N	N^2	$\sqrt{N}$	N	N^2	$\sqrt{N}$
1	1	1	51	2,601	7.141
2	4	1.414	52	2,704	7.211
3	9	1.732	53	2,809	7.280
4	16	2	54	2,916	7.348
5	25	2.236	55	3,025	7.416
6	36	2.449	56	3,136	7.483
7	49	2.646	57	3,249	7.550
8	64	2.828	58	3,364	7.616
9	81	3	59	3,481	7.681
10	100	3.162	60	3,600	7.746
11	121	3.317	61	3,721	7.810
12	144	3.464	62	3,844	7.874
13	169	3.606	63	3,969	7.937
14	196	3.742	64	4,096	8
15	225	3.873	65	4,225	8.062
16	256	4	66	4,356	8.124
17	289	4.123	67	4,489	8.185
18	324	4.243	68	4,624	8.246
19	361	4.359	69	4,761	8.307
20	400	4.472	70	4,900	8.367
21	441	4.583	71	5,041	8.426
22	484	4.690	72	5,184	8.485
23	529	4.796	73	5,329	8.544
24	576	4.899	74	5,476	8.602
25	625	5	75	5,625	8.660
26	676	5.099	76	5,776	8.718
27	729	5.196	77	5,929	8.775
28	784	5.292	78	6,084	8.832
29	841	5.385	79	6,241	8.888
30	900	5.477	80	6,400	8.944
31	961	5.568	81	6,561	9
32	1,024	5.657	82	6,724	9.055
33	1,089	5.745	83	6,889	9.110
34	1,156	5.831	84	7,056	9.165
35	1,225	5.916	85	7,225	9.220
36	1,296	6	86	7,396	9.274
37	1,369	6.083	87	7,569	9.327
38	1,444	6.164	88	7,744	9.381
39	1,521	6.245	89	7,921	9.434
40	1,600	6.325	90	8,100	9.487
41	1,681	6.403	91	8,281	9.539
42	1,764	6.481	92	8,464	9.592
43	1,849	6.557	93	8,649	9.644
44	1,936	6.633	94	8,836	9.695
45	2,025	6.708	95	9,025	9.747
46	2,116	6.782	96	9,216	9.798
47	2,209	6.856	97	9,409	9.849
48	2,304	6.928	98	9,604	9.899
49	2,401	7	99	9,801	9.950
50	2,500	7.071	100	10,000	10

Table 2: Values of Trigonometric Functions

Degrees	Sin	Cos	Tan	Degrees	Sin	Cos	Tan
0°	0.0000	1.0000	0.0000				
1°	0.0175	0.9998	0.0175	46°	0.7193	0.6947	1.0355
2°	0.0349	0.9994	0.0349	47°	0.7314	0.6820	1.0724
3°	0.0523	0.9986	0.0524	48°	0.7431	0.6691	1.1106
4°	0.0698	0.9976	0.0699	49°	0.7547	0.6561	1.1504
5°	0.0872	0.9962	0.0875	50°	0.7660	0.6428	1.1918
6°	0.1045	0.9945	0.1051	51°	0.7771	0.6293	1.2349
7°	0.1219	0.9925	0.1228	52°	0.7880	0.6157	1.2799
8°	0.1392	0.9903	0.1405	53°	0.7986	0.6018	1.3270
9°	0.1564	0.9877	0.1584	54°	0.8090	0.5878	1.3764
10°	0.1736	0.9848	0.1763	55°	0.8192	0.5736	1.4281
11°	0.1908	0.9816	0.1944	56°	0.8290	0.5592	1.4826
12°	0.2079	0.9781	0.2126	57°	0.8387	0.5446	1.5399
13°	0.2250	0.9744	0.2309	58°	0.8480	0.5299	1.6003
14°	0.2419	0.9703	0.2493	59°	0.8572	0.5150	1.6643
15°	0.2588	0.9659	0.2679	60°	0.8660	0.5000	1.7321
16°	0.2756	0.9613	0.2867	61°	0.8746	0.4848	1.8040
17°	0.2924	0.9563	0.3057	62°	0.8829	0.4695	1.8807
18°	0.3090	0.9511	0.3249	63°	0.8910	0.4540	1.9626
19°	0.3256	0.9455	0.3443	64°	0.8988	0.4384	2.0503
20°	0.3420	0.9397	0.3640	65°	0.9063	0.4226	2.1445
21°	0.3584	0.9336	0.3839	66°	0.9135	0.4067	2.2460
22°	0.3746	0.9272	0.4040	67°	0.9205	0.3907	2.3559
23°	0.3907	0.9205	0.4245	68°	0.9272	0.3746	2.4751
24°	0.4067	0.9135	0.4452	69°	0.9336	0.3584	2.6051
25°	0.4226	0.9063	0.4663	70°	0.9397	0.3420	2.7475
26°	0.4384	0.8988	0.4877	71°	0.9455	0.3256	2.9042
27°	0.4540	0.8910	0.5095	72°	0.9511	0.3090	3.0777
28°	0.4695	0.8829	0.5317	73°	0.9563	0.2924	3.2709
29°	0.4848	0.8746	0.5543	74°	0.9613	0.2756	3.4874
30°	0.5000	0.8660	0.5774	75°	0.9659	0.2588	3.7321
31°	0.5150	0.8572	0.6009	76°	0.9703	0.2419	4.0108
32°	0.5299	0.8480	0.6249	77°	0.9744	0.2250	4.3315
33°	0.5446	0.8387	0.6494	78°	0.9781	0.2079	4.7046
34°	0.5592	0.8290	0.6745	79°	0.9816	0.1908	5.1446
35°	0.5736	0.8192	0.7002	80°	0.9848	0.1736	5.6713
36°	0.5878	0.8090	0.7265	81°	0.9877	0.1564	6.3138
37°	0.6018	0.7986	0.7536	82°	0.9903	0.1392	7.1154
38°	0.6157	0.7880	0.7813	83°	0.9925	0.1219	8.1443
39°	0.6293	0.7771	0.8098	84°	0.9945	0.1045	9.5144
40°	0.6428	0.7660	0.8391	85°	0.9962	0.0872	11.4301
41°	0.6561	0.7547	0.8693	86°	0.9976	0.0698	14.3007
42°	0.6691	0.7431	0.9004	87°	0.9986	0.0523	19.0811
43°	0.6820	0.7314	0.9325	88°	0.9994	0.0349	28.6363
44°	0.6947	0.7193	0.9657	89°	0.9998	0.0175	57.2900
45°	0.7071	0.7071	1.0000	90°	1.0000	0.0000	

Chapter 1 Extra Practice

Evaluate each numerical expression.

1. $(23 + 8) - 14$
2. $12 + (16 - 7)$
3. $9 - (21 + 13)$
4. $44 + (17 - 9)$
5. $(38 + 7) - 12$
6. $(46 - 9) + 27$

Evaluate each algebraic expression.

7. $b - 2$ for $b = 11$
8. $8 + v$ for $v = 5$
9. $3 + (x - 4)$ for $x = 7$
10. $(21 - t) + 2$ for $t = 4$
11. $r + z$ for $r = 13$, $z = 4$
12. $(a + 7) - 8$ for $a = 6$

Write as an algebraic expression.

13. 7 decreased by b
14. 3 added to p
15. 6 more than r

Write an expression for each question.

Chip rides his horse 11 miles every day. How far will he ride if

16. he rides 3 miles less?
17. he rides m miles farther?

Use the basic properties. Write an equivalent expression.

18. $z + 0$
19. $(2 + r) + 6$
20. $4 + b$

Solve the equation for the replacement set given.

21. $g - 8 = 5$ {12, 13, 14, 15}
22. $6 + b = 17$ {9, 10, 11, 12}

Solve and check.

23. $n - 18 = 7$
24. $x + 8 = 13$
25. $t - 9 = 4$
26. $43 + s = 72$
27. $t - 35 = 63$
28. $212 = x - 27$
29. $b + 345 = 567$
30. $111 = r - 343$
31. $654 = 321 + a$

Solve.

32. Robin played tennis 2 hours less today than she did yesterday. She played for 3 hours today. How many hours did she play yesterday?

33. Bruce has 7 magazine subscriptions. All but 4 of them were gifts from his family. How many subscriptions did he get as gifts?

Round to the nearest ten and estimate the value of the variable.

34. $a = 26 + 47$
35. $67 + 234 = b$
36. $z = 257 - 79$

Round to the nearest hundred and estimate the value of the variable.

37. $r = 968 + 497$
38. $p = 423 + 1254$
39. $2873 - 952 = t$

Use front-end estimation to estimate the value of the variable.

40. $768 + 269 + 548$
41. $4584 - (1955 + 2462)$

Chapter 2 Extra Practice

Simplify.

1. $72 \div (5 + 3)$
2. $9 \div [(4 + 1) - 2]$
3. $(5 \times 6) \div (7 + 3)$

Evaluate.

4. $3d$ for $d = 9$
5. $\frac{6w}{9}$ for $w = 3$
6. $a(4 + b)$ for $a = 7$
7. $\frac{8x}{z}$ for $z = 2$
8. $(f - g)$ for $f = 9$, $g = 4$
9. $t(10 - v)$ for $v = 9$

Write as an algebraic expression.

10. 9 divided by s
11. 4 less than twice r
12. 7 multiplied by x

Use the commutative property to write an equivalent expression.

13. rd
14. $m(3)$
15. $6s$

Use the associative property to write an equivalent expression.

16. $13(3x)$
17. $(11b)t$
18. $(r6)7$

Use the distributive property to write an equivalent expression.

19. $d(4 + 7)$
20. $2(n + 9)$
21. $(x + 5)6$

Use the basic properties to simplify.

22. $12(3d)$
23. $5x(4)$
24. $17(a + 9)$
25. $4b + 3b$
26. $15z + z$
27. $24r - 7r$

Solve.

28. $9n = 63$
29. $\frac{56}{x} = 8$
30. $\frac{t}{4} = 6$

Solve and check.

31. $6x = 72$
32. $121 = 11d$
33. $\frac{d}{13} = 4$
34. $207 = 23f$

Solve.

35. Nancy used 280 calories while exercising for 35 minutes. How many calories did she use each minute?

36. Formula: $V = lwh$. V is the volume of a box in cubic centimeters, l is the length of the box in centimeters, w is the width of the box in centimeters, and h is the height of the box in centimeters. What is the volume of a box with length 5 cm., width 6 cm., and height 8 cm.?

Use rounding and choose compatible numbers to estimate the value of each variable.

37. $\frac{420}{38} = x$
38. $\frac{561}{82} = z$
39. $\frac{2493}{52} = t$

Chapter 3 Extra Practice

Find the absolute value.

1. $|-23|$
2. $|-14|$
3. $|1|$

Use inequality symbols. Order from least to greatest.

4. 7, −6, 3
5. 0, 4, −12
6. 3, −3, −33

Find the sum.

7. $-5 + (-5)$
8. $-4 + 8$
9. $-9 + 3$
10. $12 + (-6)$
11. $14 + -5$
12. $-17 + 6$

Evaluate.

13. $-15 + x$ for $x = -1$
14. $s + (-8)$ for $s = 19$

Subtract.

15. $9 - 14$
16. $-5 - 7$
17. $2 - 21$
18. $8 - (-5)$
19. $-26 - 5$
20. $14 - (-3)$

Evaluate.

21. $x - 9$ for $x = 4$
22. $-17 - n$ for $n = -8$

Solve and check.

23. $b + 37 = 15$
24. $25 + x = -2$
25. $r - 47 = 35$
26. $43 = 78 + c$
27. $d - (-56) = 77$
28. $f + (-24) = 68$

Solve.

29. Tom has $235 in his checking account and $450 in bills to pay. How much does he need to deposit to keep his account from being overdrawn?

Find the product.

30. $9(6)$
31. $7(-3)$
32. $-4(-8)$
33. $-7(2)$
34. $8(-6)$
35. $-9(-4)$

Find the quotient.

36. $-9 \div 3$
37. $-56 \div (-7)$
38. $121 \div (-11)$
39. $92 \div (-4)$
40. $-57 \div 3$
41. $-18 \div (-6)$

Solve and check.

42. $75 = -3n$
43. $-9y = 72$
44. $12 = -\frac{x}{3}$
45. $55 = -b$
46. $-k = -1$

Write an equation.

47. 17 multiplied by a number q is 85.
48. 34 less than a number p is 71.

Chapter 4 Extra Practice

Write as a decimal.

1. $8(10) + 6(1) + 3\left(\frac{1}{100}\right)$

2. $7\left(\frac{1}{100}\right) + 3\left(\frac{1}{1000}\right) + 2(1)$

Write <, >, or = for each □.

3. 3.23 □ 3.32

4. 7.41 □ 7.414

5. 5.05 □ 5.050

Estimate the value of x by rounding.

6. $x = 49.82 + 27.89$

7. $x = 64.79 + 575.13$

8. $x = 99.64 - 64.82$

9. $x = 749.86 - 244.91$

Add or subtract.

10. $4.87 + 3.9$

11. $13.56 + 24.94 - 17.31$

12. $-5.3 + 8.44$

13. $72.4 + (-6.9) + 21.78$

14. $-21.65 + (-4.2)$

15. $74.68 - (-29.38)$

Solve and check.

16. $c - 2.96 = 3.84$

17. $13.62 + d = -4.85$

18. $m - 8.34 = -2.79$

19. $-41 + b = 17.32$

Estimate the product by rounding.

20. 30.21×4.7

21. 4.12×24.89

22. 0.79×19.8

Find the product.

23. 4.2×11.83

24. 6.7×-5.92

25. 14.3×-0.03

26. -3752×0.001

Solve.

27. A tennis court is 12.3 meters long. How many centimeters long is the court?

28. Kim's dog weighs 5500 grams. How many kilograms does it weigh?

Solve and check.

29. $3.6r = 194.4$

30. $-0.04x = 16$

31. $1.7s = 16.66$

32. $\frac{b}{0.23} = 5.9$

33. $\frac{f}{-1.4} = 13.8$

34. $\frac{d}{4.2} = -3.7$

Solve by writing an equation.

35. Ivan got a \$13.79 discount on a baseball glove with an original price of \$54.98. How much did he pay for the glove?

36. Alan has 54.3 meters of insulation. He needs a total of 100 meters to insulate his attic. How much more insulation does he need to get?

Chapter 5 Extra Practice

Give the first five nonzero multiples of each number.

1. 7 **2.** 20 **3.** 60

Find all the factors of the given number.

4. 18 **5.** 42 **6.** 81

Tell whether the number is divisible by 2, by 3, and by 5.

7. 98 **8.** 12345 **9.** 86

10. 156 **11.** 272 **12.** 985

Find the solution by writing and solving an equation.

13. Gloria is making 96 sandwiches for a party. Sandwich rolls come in packages of 8. How many packages does she need to buy?

14. Alfred has $250 more in his savings account than in his checking account. If he has $735 in his savings account, how much does he have in his checking account?

State whether the number is prime or composite.

15. 57 **16.** 79 **17.** 96

Write in expanded form. Simplify if possible.

18. 2^5 **19.** $(-4)^3$ **20.** r^7

Write using exponents.

21. $6 \cdot 6 \cdot 6 \cdot 6$ **22.** $b \cdot b \cdot b \cdot b \cdot b$ **23.** $(-8)(-8)(-8)$

Multiply. Give the answer in exponent form.

24. $x^2 \cdot x^3$ **25.** $7^4 \cdot 7^1$ **26.** $(-4)^4(-4)^5$

Simplify.

27. $2^4 + 2^6$ **28.** $(-6)^2 + (-6)^3$

Use exponents to show the prime factorization of each number.

29. 72 **30.** 210 **31.** 54 **32.** 225

Find the Greatest Common Factor (GCF) of each pair of numbers.

33. 42, 91 **34.** 21, 27 **35.** 70, 182

36. Formula: $D = r \cdot t$. D is the distance in miles, r is rate in mi/hour, and t is time of ride in hours. Find how far Hank drove his truck in $4\frac{1}{2}$ hours at 53 mi/hour.

Find the Least Common Multiple (LCM) of each pair of numbers.

37. 5, 12 **38.** 18, 24 **39.** 7, 11

Chapter 6 Extra Practice

Write an equivalent fraction by replacing the variable with a whole number.

1. $\frac{4}{9} = \frac{x}{54}$ **2.** $\frac{m}{7} = \frac{35}{49}$ **3.** $-\frac{3}{11} = \frac{p}{66}$

Reduce each fraction to lowest terms.

4. $\frac{24}{36}$ **5.** $-\frac{11}{99}$ **6.** $\frac{105}{133}$

Write each as a mixed numeral.

7. $\frac{21}{8}$ **8.** $-\frac{41}{13}$ **9.** $\frac{246}{25}$

Write each as an improper fraction in lowest terms.

10. $6\frac{7}{9}$ **11.** $-4\frac{3}{8}$ **12.** $-5\frac{8}{10}$

13. Graph $-\frac{6}{4}, \frac{2}{3}, \frac{1}{4}$, and $\frac{3}{2}$ on a number line.

Write >, <, or = for each □.

14. $\frac{4}{8}$ □ $\frac{3}{7}$ **15.** $-\frac{2}{3}$ □ $-\frac{5}{9}$ **16.** $\frac{26}{39}$ □ $\frac{2}{3}$ **17.** $\frac{7}{11}$ □ $\frac{3}{4}$

Add or subtract. Reduce to lowest terms.

18. $\frac{6}{13} + \frac{3}{13}$ **19.** $-\frac{8}{18} + \frac{14}{18}$ **20.** $-\frac{8}{20} - \frac{7}{20}$

21. $\frac{1}{4} + \frac{1}{5}$ **22.** $\frac{4}{7} - \frac{1}{2}$ **23.** $-\frac{3}{8} - \left(-\frac{2}{5}\right)$

24. $3\frac{5}{6} - 2\frac{3}{8}$ **25.** $-5\frac{3}{4} + 1\frac{5}{12}$ **26.** $4\frac{2}{5} - 7\frac{3}{7}$

27. Mr. Drucker walked $2\frac{7}{8}$ miles, stopped for a drink, then walked $3\frac{1}{6}$ miles more. How far did he walk?

28. Alita had $6\frac{1}{2}$ buckets of paint. After she painted the living room, she had $2\frac{2}{3}$ buckets of paint left. How much did she use?

Solve and check.

29. $x - \frac{3}{8} = \frac{5}{12}$ **30.** $\frac{3}{7} + y = -\frac{3}{14}$ **31.** $\frac{9}{10} = b - \frac{2}{5}$

Find the solution by writing and solving an equation.

32. Ms. Gomez bought 5 yards of material to sew a dress. When she was finished, she had $1\frac{5}{12}$ yards of material left. How much material did she use to make the dress?

Chapter 7 Extra Practice

Multiply. Reduce to lowest terms.

1. $-\frac{3}{8}\left(\frac{4}{5}\right)$

2. $-\frac{5}{9}\left(-\frac{3}{5}\right)$

3. $-2\frac{3}{4}\left(-3\frac{4}{7}\right)$

4. $6\frac{4}{9}\left(-\frac{3}{4}\right)$

Divide. Reduce to lowest terms.

5. $\frac{5}{12} \div \left(-\frac{3}{4}\right)$

6. $\frac{-7}{10} \div \left(-\frac{5}{7}\right)$

7. $4\frac{1}{2} \div \left(-2\frac{3}{4}\right)$

8. $-6\frac{4}{7} \div 7\frac{2}{3}$

Solve and check.

9. $-\frac{x}{5} = -\frac{18}{30}$

10. $\frac{1}{4}y = \frac{7}{8}$

11. $-4\frac{1}{5} = 1\frac{2}{5}m$

12. $\frac{2}{3}z = \frac{-5}{7}$

Find the solution by writing and solving an equation.

13. Maria lives $4\frac{8}{10}$ miles from school. She rode her moped $\frac{2}{3}$ of the way there before she ran out of gas. How far did she have to walk to get to school?

Solve.

14. If $\frac{2}{3}$ cup of soy sauce is used to make 2 cups of teriyaki sauce, how much soy sauce is used to make 10 cups of teriyaki sauce?

15. Gil placed 28 dominoes end-to-end to form a line 63 inches long. How long was each domino?

Write each as a decimal. Use a bar for repeating decimals.

16. $\frac{3}{8}$

17. $\frac{4}{9}$

18. $\frac{7}{25}$

Simplify. Write the expression with exponents.

19. $\frac{9^7}{9^3}$

20. $\frac{(-6)^6}{(-6)^4}$

21. $\frac{x^8}{x^5}$

Write each expression without exponents.

22. 2^{-6}

23. $\frac{5^3}{5^7}$

24. $\frac{(-3)^5}{(-3)^3}$

Write each in decimal form.

25. 3.9×10^4

26. 2.4×10^{-2}

27. 5.38×10^{-5}

Write each in scientific notation.

28. 4270

29. 67,000

30. 200,000,000

31. 0.0035

32. 0.0001001

33. 0.246

Chapter 8 Extra Practice

Solve.

1. $4d - 3 = 45$

2. $33 = -2x + 3$

3. $5(7 + w) = -10$

4. $\frac{a - 11}{9} = -3$

Write an equation.

5. Paul has 24 marbles, which is 4 more than twice as many marbles as Eric has. How many marbles does Eric have?

6. Erica's age, 7, is 1 less than twice Brian's age. How old is Brian?

Solve by writing an equation.

7. Mr. Fritz has been a teacher for 17 years. That is 5 fewer than twice the number of years Mrs. Weiner has been a teacher. How many years has Mrs. Weiner been a teacher?

8. Steve had a box of spaghetti that was $\frac{2}{3}$ full. He used 4 oz, leaving 12 oz in the box. How many ounces did the box hold?

Solve and check.

9. $2x + 7x = 54$

10. $-121 = 8p + 3p$

11. $108 = 17w - 5w$

12. $-11b - 12b = -92$

Solve and check.

13. $3(x + 2) + 6x = 60$

14. $12d + (4 - 5d) = -52$

15. $8m + 6 - 2(3m) = 16$

16. $c + 5(3c - 5) = 23$

17. $3p + 2(p - 4) + 16 = 38$

18. $6r - 6 - 2(-2r) = 74$

Solve and check.

19. $156 - 9t = 4t$

20. $11z + 7 = 31 - z$

21. $6y + 11 = 5y$

22. $-6 + r = -20 -$

Solve the problem.

23. Margaret invited 3 more than $\frac{4}{5}$ of her class to a party. She invited 63 people to her party. How many people are in her class?

Solve and check.

24. $5d > 40$

25. $-3 + r < 12$

Solve.

26. $17 < 4a - 3$

27. $-7b + 10b > -18$

Chapter 9 Extra Practice

Write each ratio as a fraction in lowest terms.

1. 72 to 88 **2.** 12:21 **3.** $\frac{68}{16}$

Solve and check.

4. $\frac{9}{x} = \frac{27}{42}$ **5.** $\frac{y}{11} = \frac{30}{66}$ **6.** $\frac{3}{8} = \frac{27}{c}$

Simplify the rate.

7. $75/5 days **8.** 217 km/3.5 h **9.** 396 steps/18 floors

Solve.

10. Florida and New York are 2100 km apart. If it takes 3 hours to fly this distance, how fast does the plane travel?

Write an equation.

11. Connie wants to tile her bedroom floor and her kitchen floor. Her bedroom is twice as large as her kitchen. If Connie needs 144 tiles for both rooms, how many are used in each room?

Solve by writing an equation.

12. Juan had half the number of Bs on his report card as he had As. He was taking 6 courses all together, and got no lower than a B. How many of each grade did he get?

Find the scale dimensions of each if the scale is 1 cm = 0.5 m.

13. desk: 1 m × 2 m **14.** bookcase: 1.5 m × 2.5 m

Solve.

15. Grape juice costs $1.99 for the 32 ounce bottle and $2.69 for the 48 ounce bottle. Which size is the better buy?

Write each as a fraction in lowest terms.

16. 22% **17.** 4% **18.** 8.5%

Use a proportion to write each as a percent.

19. $\frac{5}{8}$ **20.** $\frac{7}{25}$ **21.** $\frac{9}{5}$

Write each percent as a fraction or mixed number in lowest terms.

22. 175% **23.** $\frac{4}{5}\%$ **24.** $3\frac{1}{2}\%$

Write as a decimal. **25.** $14\frac{1}{4}\%$ **26.** 350%

Write each as a percent. **27.** 0.072 **28.** 9.68

Chapter 10 Extra Practice

Use a proportion or an equation to solve.

1. 60% of 185 **2.** 5% of 80 **3.** 4% of 55

Use a proportion or an equation to solve.

4. What percent of 90 is 27?

5. 63 is what percent of 105?

6. What percent of 160 is 120?

7. 9 out of 36 is what percent?

Use a proportion or an equation to solve. Round to the nearest tenth if necessary.

8. 14 is 7% of what number?

9. 40% of what number is 35?

10. 15% of what number is 45?

11. 22 is 25% of what number?

Solve by writing an equation.

12. A pair of jeans costs 75% as much as a pair of corduroy pants. The total cost for the jeans and cords is $42. What is the cost of each?

Find the percent of increase or decrease.

13. Original amount = $75; new amount = $60.

14. Original amount = $60; new amount = $75.

Solve.

15. When Juanita was on vacation, it rained 35% of the time. She was on vacation for 20 days. How many days did it rain?

Find the discount and sales price for each. Round to the nearest cent if necessary.

16. Regular price = $45
Discount = 40%

17. Regular price = $2,450
Discount = 6%

Find the commission.

18. Sale price = $11,250
Commission percent = 4%

19. Sale price = $225
Commission percent= 6%

Find the interest and total amount. Round to the nearest percent if necessary.

20. $600 at 15% per year for 3 years.

21. $800 at 12% per year for 4 months.

22. $300 at 3% per month for 6 months.

23. Make a circle graph to show the data in the table.
Rackets Sold:

Badminton	Racquetball	Squash	Tennis	Other
5%	31%	19%	43%	2%

Chapter 11 Extra Practice

Refer to the figure for Exercises 1–5.

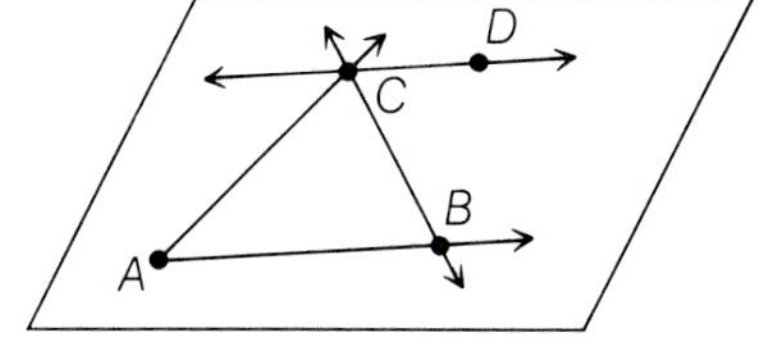

1. Name a point.
2. Name a line.
3. Name a plane.
4. Name a segment that includes point C.
5. Name a ray.

Estimate the length of each segment to the nearest centimeter.

6. $\overline{XY}$ 7. $\overline{XZ}$

Refer to the figure for Exercises 8–11.

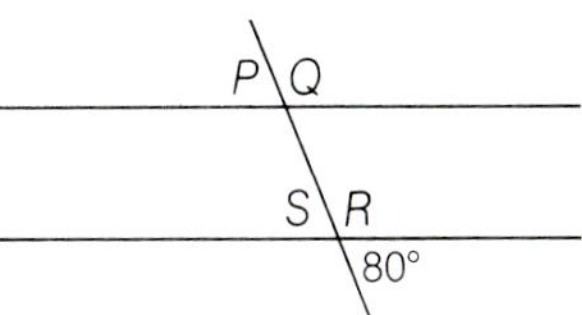

8. Name an acute angle.
9. Name an obtuse angle.
10. Find the measure of angle R.

Classify each triangle by the measures of its angles and the lengths of its sides.

11. $\triangle ABC$ has a 120 degree angle and two sides equal in length.
12. $\triangle RST$ has three sides equal in length and three acute angles.

Name the polygon.

13. 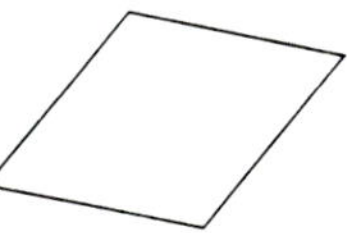

14. 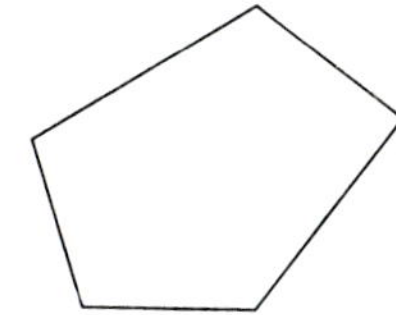

Solve. Use the formula *Distance* = *rate* × *time*.

15. Hans drove $4\frac{1}{2}$ hours and traveled 243 miles. What was his average speed?

Find the circumference of a circle with the given diameter or radius. Use 3.14 for π.

16. radius = 4.3 cm 17. diameter = 7 m

Use the SAS, SSS, or ASA property to show that each pair of triangles is congruent.

18. 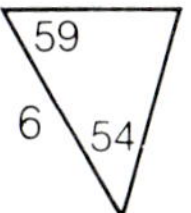

19. 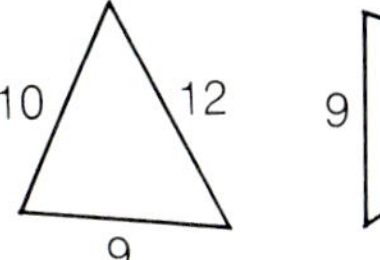

Solve by writing an equation.

20. Joan and Harold each sold 23 tickets to the school play. Together they sold 40% of the total number of tickets sold to the play. How many tickets were sold in all?

Chapter 12 Extra Practice

Find the area of each figure.

1. Rectangle with length 15 m, width 6 m

2. Triangle with base 38 ft, height 8 ft

Find the area of each quadrilateral.

3. Parallelogram with base = 11.2 m, height = 9.4 m

4. Trapezoid with $b_1 = 9$ cm, $b_2 = 5.5$ cm, $h = 13$ cm

Find the area of each circle. Use 3.14 for π.

5. $r = 6$ cm

6. $d = 5.8$ m

Find the area of the figure.

7.

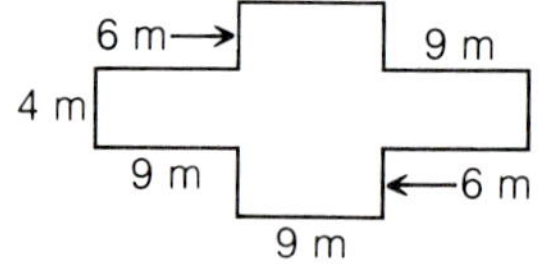

Solve by writing an equation.

8. Linda bought 4 medium-sized drinks and 1 large drink for $3.20. If the large drink cost $0.80, how much did each medium-sized drink cost?

Find the volume of the prism or cylinder. Use 3.14 for π.

9.

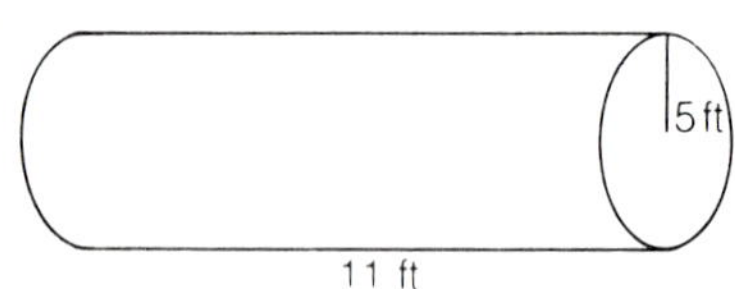

10.

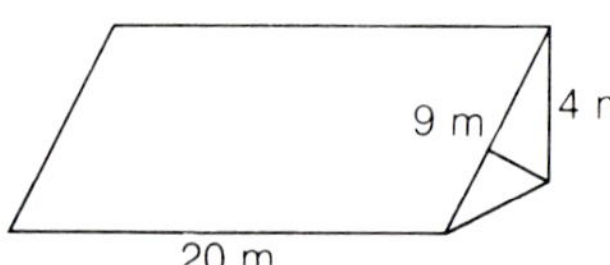

Solve.

11. Concrete is on sale for $30 per cubic yard. How much will it cost to buy concrete to cover a foundation 38 feet long, 30 feet wide, and 6 inches thick?

Find the volume. Use 3.14 for π.

12. Cone with a radius of 6 cm and a height of 14 cm

13. Pyramid with a base area of 45 square feet and a height of 12 feet

Find the surface area. Use 3.14 for π.

14. Cylinder with a radius of 2 m and a height of 7 m

15.

5 cm
9 cm
14 cm

Chapter 13 Extra Practice

Use the counting principle to find the total number of outcomes.

1. Select 1 tennis racket. Composition: wood, metal, graphite, fiberglass. Head size: small, midsize, oversize. Grip size: $4\frac{3}{8}$, $4\frac{1}{2}$, $4\frac{5}{8}$.

Find the number of permutations.

2. m, a, t, h

3. 1, 2, 4, 5, 7, 8

Find the number of combinations.

4. You may be scheduled to work 4 days out of a 7-day work week.

5. Select 2 blouses from 5 possible choices.

There are 18 marbles in a bag. 6 are clear, 4 are black, and 8 are red.

6. P(black)

7. P(not clear)

8. P(clear or red)

Find the probability of each for one toss of two dice.

9. P(total of 2)

10. P(a number < 3, a number > 3)

Solve by writing an equation.

11. The length of a yard is 3 times its width. It takes 104 ft. of fencing to surround the yard. Find the dimensions of the yard.

Use this data to solve Exercises 12–15.
Test grades: 71, 75, 75, 78, 82, 83, 86, 89, 93

12. Find the range.

13. What is the mode?

14. What is the median?

15. Find the mean.

16. Make a bar graph for the data. Distance from Orlando in miles: Miami, 220; New York, 1050; Raleigh, 600; Syracuse, 1230.

Use the line graph to answer each question

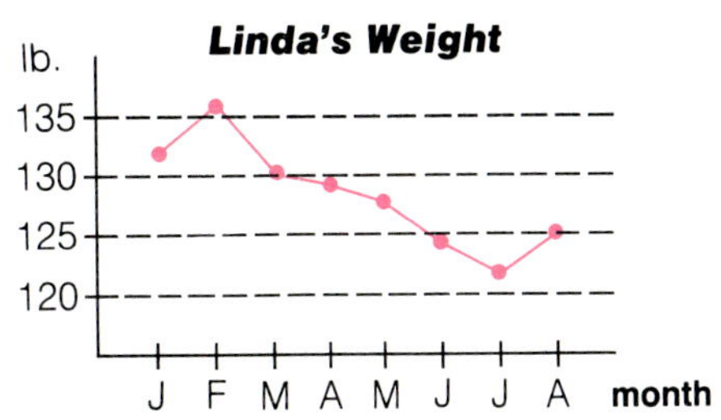

17. During which month was Linda's weight the lowest?

18. Between which months did Linda's weight increase?

19. Between which months was the change in Linda's weight the greatest?

20. Make a pictograph for the data. Cars sold: January, 75; April, 150; July, 120; October, 90.

Chapter 14 Extra Practice

Between what two consecutive integers does each square root lie?

1. $\sqrt{45}$ **2.** $\sqrt{88}$

Evaluate each expression.

3. $\sqrt{36} - \sqrt{25}$ **4.** $\sqrt{(155 - 11)}$

Use a calculator with a $\sqrt{\ }$ key to find an approximation for each square root.

5. 10 **6.** 234

Solve and check. **7.** $x^2 = 196$ **8.** $x^2 = 15$

Find the unknown length.

9.

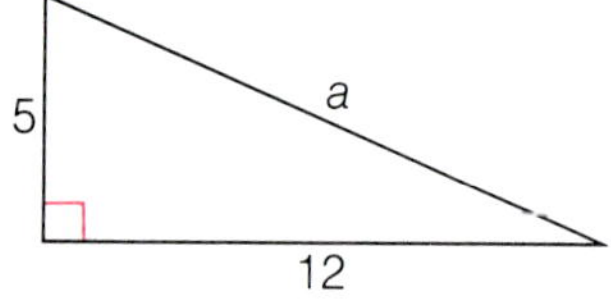

10.

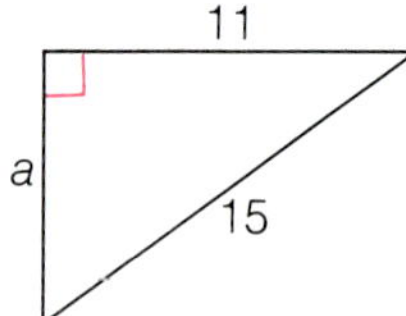

Solve.

11. A television screen is 7 inches tall and 9 inches wide. What is the length of the diagonal of the screen?

Use proportions to find the unknown lengths for these similar triangles.

12.

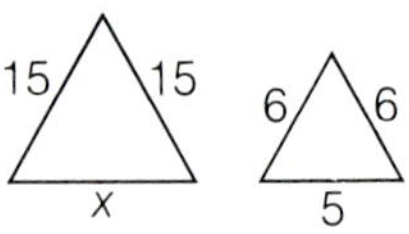

13.

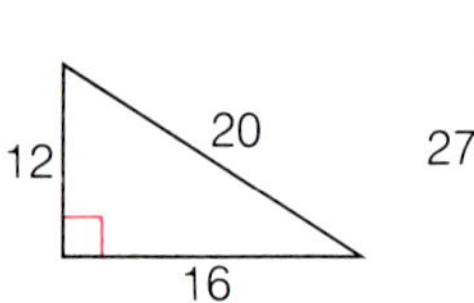

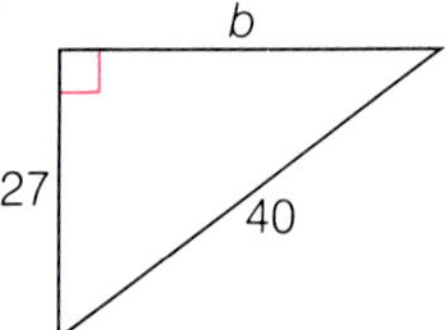

Find the unknown length.

14.

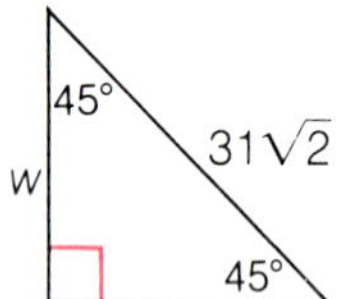

15.

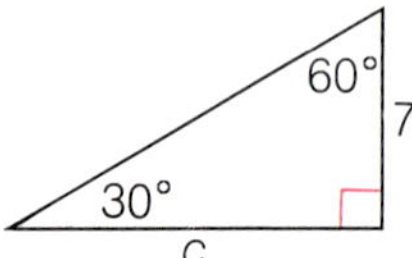

Find each ratio for $\angle X$.

16. cos X

17. sin X

18. tan X

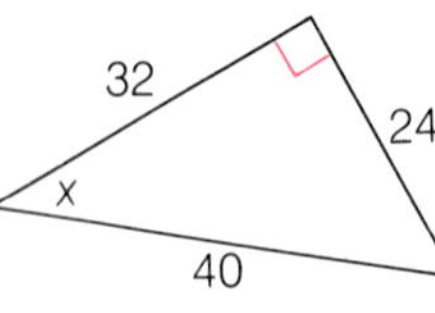

Solve by writing an equation.

19. Rick, Ray and Rose picked apples. Rose picked twice as many apples as Ray, Ray picked twice as many apples as Rick. In all, they picked 21 bushels of apples. How many bushels of apples did Rose pick?

Chapter 15 Extra Practice

Graph each solution on a number line.

1. $x \geq 0$

2. $2x - 2 < -6$

Give the coordinates of each point on the graph at right.

3. A

4. B

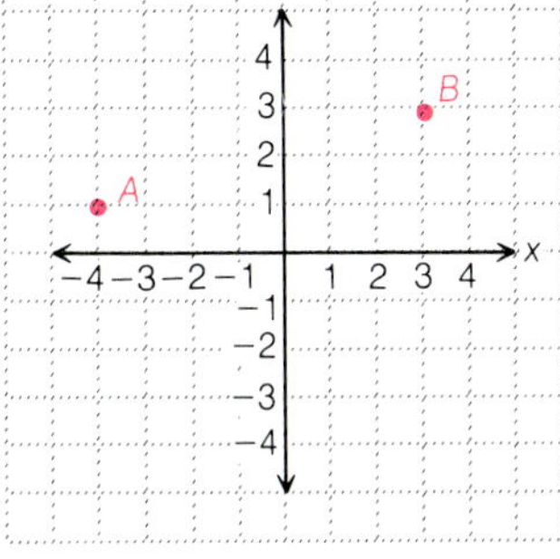

Graph the point on a pair of axes.

5. $C(2, -3)$

6. $D(-1, -1)$

7. Which of the ordered pairs $(-2, 3)$ or $(-3, -2)$ is a solution for the linear equation $2x - 3y = 0$?

Make a table of solutions for the equation.

8. $y = -2x + 1$ Use $x = -2, -1, 0, 1, 2, 3$

Solve. **9.** Mr. Himes bought a camera on sale for $115. This was $25 more than 40% of its original price. What was the original price of the camera?

Does y vary directly with x? If it does, find the value of k.

10.

x	y
1	2
2	4
3	6
4	8
5	10

11.

x	y
1	2
2	3
3	4
4	5
5	6

Does y vary inversely with x? If it does, find the value of k.

12.

x	y
1	9
2	7
3	5
4	3
5	1

13.

x	y
1	12
2	6
3	4
4	3
5	2.4

Find the slope of the line.

14. $3 - 7x = y$

15. A line contains the points $A(3, 4)$, $B(-2, -6)$.

Find the intercepts for the graph of $8 + 4y = x$.

16. x-intercept

17. y-intercept

Solve.

18. Ace Carpet Cleaners charges $75 to clean 3 rooms and $20 for each additional room. How much would it cost to have 8 rooms cleaned?

19. Graph the equation to solve the system. $x + y = 3$, $y - 3x = 3$.

20. Graph the inequality $y > x + 4$. Is point $(2, 2)$ a solution?

Glossary

Absolute value The absolute value of a number is its distance from 0 on a number line.

Acute angle An angle that has a measure less than 90°.

Additive identity Zero. When zero is added to a number, the result is that same number.

Additive inverse property *See* Inverse Property

Algebraic expression An expression that contains at least one variable; for example, $n + 7$.

Angle Two rays with a common endpoint called the vertex.

Area The measure of a plane region in terms of square units.

Associative property The sum or product of three or more numbers is the same regardless of grouping:

$(a + b) + c = a + (b + c)$ or
$(a \cdot b) \cdot c = a \cdot (b \cdot c)$

Base (geometry) Any side of a polygon may be referred to as a base.

Base (numbers) In exponential notation a^n, a is the base.

Circle All the points in a plane that are a fixed distance from a point called the center.

Circumference The distance around a circle.

Combination A selection of a group of objects from a set without regard to order.

Common factor Any number that is a factor of each of the numbers in a set of numbers.

Commutative property The sum or product of any two numbers is the same regardless of the order in which they are added or multiplied:

$a + b = b + a$ or $a \cdot b = b \cdot a$

Complementary angles Two angles whose measures have a sum of 90°.

Composite number Any whole number greater than 1 that has more than two factors.

Cone A solid with exactly one circular base and exactly one vertex, not in the same plane as the base.

Congruent Two geometric figures are congruent if they have the same size and shape.

Coordinate plane A plane containing two intersecting perpendicular number lines; used for graphing ordered number pairs.

Coordinates An ordered pair of numbers matched with a point in the coordinate plane.

Corresponding angles A pair of angles with equal measure, formed by the intersection of a transversal and a pair of parallel lines, with interiors on the same side as the transversal.

Corresponding parts The matching sides and angles in a pair of congruent figures.

Cosine ratio For an acute angle A in a right triangle, the ratio of the length of the adjacent side to the length of the hypotenuse.

Counting principle To find the total number of choices for an event, multiply the number of choices for each part.

Cross products For fractions $\frac{a}{b}$ and $\frac{c}{d}$, the products ad and bc.

Cylinder A solid having two congruent, circular bases in parallel planes.

Decimal system The place-value numeration system that uses the digits 0 through 9, and groups by tens.

Denominator For a fraction $\frac{a}{b}$, b is the denominator.

Dependent event An event whose outcome is influenced by the outcome of a previous event.

Diameter A segment that passes through the center of a circle and has endpoints on the circle.

Distributive property Connects multiplication and addition of whole numbers:

$a(b + c) = a \cdot b + a \cdot c$

Divisible A number is divisible by a second number if the quotient of the first divided by the second is a whole number and the remainder is 0.

Equation A statement of equality between two expressions.

Equivalent expressions Two algebraic expressions are equivalent if (and only if) they have the same value for any number that replaces the variable.

Even numbers All whole numbers that are multiples of 2.

Expanded form (factored form) A number represented as the product of factors.

Factor A number that is multiplied by another number to yield a product.

Factor completely To express a number as the product of prime factors.

Formula An equation that shows a relationship between two or more variables.

Fraction A symbol in the form $\frac{a}{b}$, where a is the numerator and b is the denominator and $b \neq 0$.

Greatest common factor (GCF) The Greatest Common Factor of two numbers is the greatest whole number that is a factor of both numbers.

Grouping symbols Parentheses ( ), brackets [ ], and the fraction bar (a division symbol) are grouping symbols, and indicate the order in which operations should be done.

Height In any geometric figure, the perpendicular distance from a vertex to a base.

Hypotenuse The longest side of a right triangle, opposite the right angle.

Identity property For addition, the sum of an addend and zero is the addend:

$a + 0 = 0 + a = a$

For multiplication, the product of a factor and one is the factor:

$a \cdot 1 = 1 \cdot a = a$

Improper fraction A fraction whose numerator is greater than or equal to its denominator.

Independent event An event whose outcome is not influenced by the outcome of a previous event.

Inequality A statement that uses the symbols $>$ (greater than), $<$ (less than), $\geq$ (greater than or equal to), or $\leq$ (less than or equal to), to compare two expressions.

Integers The whole numbers and their additive inverses.

Inverse property For addition, the sum of any number and its additive inverse is 0:

$a + -a = 0; -a + a = 0.$

For multiplication, the product of any rational number and its multiplicative inverse is 1:

$\frac{a}{b} \cdot \frac{b}{a} = \frac{b}{a} \cdot \frac{a}{b} = 1$

Irrational number A real number that cannot be expressed as the quotient of two integers. Irrational numbers have nonrepeating decimal representations.

Least common multiple (LCM) The smallest nonzero number that is a multiple of two or more given numbers.

Like terms Terms having exactly the same variables with exactly the same exponents.

Line A set of points determined by two points, and extending endlessly in both directions.

Linear equation An equation that can be written in the form $y = ax + b$.

Lowest common denominator The least common multiple of the denominators of two or more fractions.

Lowest terms A fraction is in lowest terms when the only common factor of the numerator and the denominator is 1.

Mean The average; the sum of a set of numbers divided by the number of members in the set.

Median The middle number in a list of numbers given in order.

Metric system The system of measurement that uses the meter as the basic unit of length, the liter as the basic unit of capacity, and the gram as the basic unit of mass.

Mixed number A numeral that has a whole number part and a fraction part.

Mode In a list of numbers, the number that occurs most frequently.

Multiple The product of two whole numbers is a multiple of each of the whole numbers.

Multiplicative identity One. When a number is multiplied by one, the result is that same number.

Multiplicative inverse property *See* Inverse Property

Numerator For each fraction $\frac{a}{b}$, a is the numerator.

Obtuse angle An angle with measure greater than 90° and less than 180°.

Odd numbers All whole numbers that are not multiples of 2.

Ordered pair A pair of numbers in a particular order; the coordinates of a point in a plane.

Parallel lines Lines in the same plane that do not intersect.

Parallelogram A quadrilateral with both pairs of opposite sides parallel.

Percent Literally, "per one hundred"; represented by the symbol %.

Perimeter The sum of the lengths of the sides of a polygon.

Permutation An arrangement of objects in a particular order.

Perpendicular lines Two intersecting lines that form right angles.

Pi (π) The ratio of the circumference of a circle to its diameter. The decimal for π is unending and does not repeat. $\pi = 3.14159. . . .$

Place value The value given to the place a digit occupies in a numeral. In the decimal system, each place of a numeral has ten times the value of the place to its right.

Plane The geometric figure determined by three points that are not on the same line.

Point The simplest geometric figure; it shows a location.

Polygon A closed plane figure formed by three or more segments that intersect only at their endpoints so that exactly two segments meet at each point.

Power A product in which each factor is identical; for example, 32 is the fifth power of 2.

Prime factorization The expression of a composite number as the product of prime factors.

Prime number A whole number greater than 1 that has exactly two factors, itself and 1.

Prism A solid that has a pair of parallel, congruent bases and rectangular sides that are parallelograms.

Probability The ratio of the number of times a certain outcome can occur to the number of total possible outcomes.

Proper fraction A fraction whose numerator is less than its denominator.

Property of equivalent fractions Multiplying or dividing both the numerator and denominator of a fraction by the same nonzero integer results in an equivalent fraction:
for all numbers a, b, and c, $(b \neq 0, c \neq 0)$,
$\frac{a}{b} = \frac{a \cdot c}{b \cdot c}$ and $\frac{a}{b} = \frac{a \div c}{b \div c}$

Proportion An equation stating that two ratios are equal.

Pyramid A solid that has three or more triangular sides and a polygon as a base.

Pythagorean theorem In a right triangle, the square of the length of the hypotenuse is equal to the sum of the squares of the lengths of the other two sides.

Quadrilateral A four-sided polygon.

Radical sign The symbol $\sqrt{\ }$ is called a radical sign and is used to indicate a square root.

Radius Any segment that joins the center to a point on a circle.

Range The difference between the greatest number and the least number in a set of data.

Rate A ratio that compares two different units.

Ratio A comparison of one number to another, expressed as a quotient.

Rational number Any number that can be written in the form $\frac{a}{b}$ where a and b are integers, $b \neq 0$.

Ray A part of a line that has one endpoint and extends endlessly in one direction.

Real numbers The rational numbers and the irrational numbers. There is a real number for each point of the number line.

Reciprocal Two numbers are reciprocals if their product is 1. A reciprocal is also called a multiplicative inverse.

Rectangle A quadrilateral with two pairs of parallel sides and four right angles.

Regular polygon A polygon in which all sides have the same measure and all angles have the same measure.

Repeating decimal A decimal with a sequence of digits that repeats endlessly.

Replacement set The set of numbers from which replacements for the variable in an equation are selected.

Right angle An angle that measures 90°.

Right triangle A triangle with a right angle.

Scientific notation A system of writing a number as the product of a power of 10, and a number greater than or equal to one but less than 10.

Segment Part of a line; two points and all the points between them.

Simplify an expression To replace an algebraic (or numerical) expression with the simplest equivalent expression.

Sine ratio For an acute angle A in a right triangle, the ratio of the length of the opposite side to the length of the hypotenuse.

Slope The ratio of rise to run in the graph of any linear equation.

Solution set The collection of all the solutions to a given equation.

Sphere The set of all points in space at a fixed distance from a point called the center.

Square (geometry) A quadrilateral with sides of equal length and four right angles.

Square (numbers) The product of a number multiplied by itself is called the square of that number.

Square root If $a^2 = b$, then a is a square root of b.

Supplementary angles Two angles whose measures have a sum of 180°.

Tangent ratio For an acute angle A in a right triangle, the ratio of the length of the opposite side to the length of the adjacent side.

Terminating decimal A decimal with a finite number of digits; for example, 0.375.

Terms The parts of an algebraic expression that are separated by an addition or subtraction sign.

Transversal A line that intersects two or more lines.

Trapezoid A quadrilateral with one pair of parallel sides.

Triangle A three-sided polygon.

Trigonometric ratios Ratios of lengths of sides of right triangles. Three of these ratios are called the sine, the cosine, and the tangent.

Variable A letter or other symbol used to reserve a place for a number in an expression or equation.

Vertex The point that the two rays of an angle have in common.

Vertical angles The two pairs of angles formed by the intersection of two lines.

Volume The measure of a solid region in terms of cubic units.

Whole number Any number in the set $\{0, 1, 2, 3, 4, 5, \ldots\}$.

***x*-axis** The horizontal axis in a rectangular coordinate plane system.

***x*-coordinate** The first number in an ordered pair; used to plot a point in a coordinate plane system.

***y*-axis** The vertical axis in a rectangular coordinate plane system.

***y*-coordinate** The second number in an ordered pair; used to plot a point in a coordinate plane system.

Zero property of multiplication The product of any number and zero is zero:
For all whole numbers a, $a(0) = 0$, $0(a) = 0$.

Selected Answers

Chapter 1 Expressions and Equations: Addition and Subtraction

1-1 pages 2–5

Practice **1a.** 9 **b.** 16 **c.** 14 **2a.** 24 **b.** 11 **3a.** 14 **b.** 4
Exercises **1.** 15 **3.** 0 **5.** 35 **7.** 30 **9.** 46 **11.** 15 **13.** 39 **15.** 5 **17.** 1 **19.** 10 **21.** 12 **23.** 33 **25.** 74 **27.** 50 **29.** 4, 6, 68 **31.** 4 **33.** 27 **35.** 90 **37.** 4 **39.** 31 **41.** 1 **43.** 2 **45.** 132 **47.** 38 **49.** 17 **51.** 8 **53.** 3 **55.** 22 **57.** yes **59.** $x = 9$; $y = 7$ **61.** 245 **63.** 101 **65.** 617 **67.** 859 **69.** 311 **71.** 348 **73.** 113 **75.** 2,242 **77.** 7,349 **79.** 1,099 **81.** 24,359 **83.** 10,836 **85.** 39,033 **87.** 8,835 **89.** 1,719 **91.** 2,556 **93.** 55,798 **95.** 4,164
Calculator Activity **1.** 3,775 **3.** 2,355

1-2 pages 6–8

Practice **1a.** $10 - 6$ **b.** $9 - 4$ **c.** $8 + 7$ **d.** $8 + 7$ **2a.** $n + 5$ **b.** $n - 8$ **c.** $n + 7$ **d.** $n - 5$ **e.** $n - 3$ **3a.** $23 + 9$ **b.** $23 + y$ **c.** $23 - 14$ **d.** $23 - t$
Exercises **1.** $8 + 6$ **3.** $9 + 7$ **5.** $6 + 7$ **7.** $12 + 8$ **9.** $x + 6$ **11.** $n + 7$ **13.** $r + 8$ **15.** $y - 5$ **17.** $n - 9$ **19.** $n + 6$ **21.** $n + 16$ **23.** $n - 126$ **25.** $64 + 9$ **27.** $64 - 16$ **29.** $45 + 7$ **31.** $45 - 4$ **33.** $75 + 45$ **35.** $75 - 37$ **37.** $n + 1$ **39.** $n + 2$ **41.** $x + y = 31$, $x - y = 3$; $x = 17$, $y = 14$ **43.** 993 **45.** 436 **47.** 728, 524, 376
Mental Math **1.** 343 **3.** 325 **5.** 7,633

1-3 pages 9–12

Practice **1a.** $x + 45$ **b.** $5{,}138 + a$ **c.** $t + 479$ **2a.** $n + (145 + 68)$ **b.** $(125 + 75) + a$ **c.** $(m + 123) + 77$ **d.** $118 + (12 + c)$ **3a.** t **b.** a **c.** z **d.** n
Exercises **1.** $4 + y$ **3.** $n + 12$ **5.** $b + 137$ **7.** $y + 507$ **9.** $n + (2 + 8)$ **11.** $t + (9 + 7)$ **13.** $z + (16 + 34)$ **15.** $(17 + 8) + b$ **17.** $(38 + 12) + r$ **19.** y **21.** $7 + n$, comm. **23.** $n + (7 + 3)$, assoc. **25.** $23 + p$, comm. **27.** $s + 8$, comm. **29.** $x + y$, identity; or $(0 + x) + y$, assoc.; or $0 + (y + x)$, comm. **31.** $x = 0$ **33.** $z = 34$ **35.** yes, $b - a$ can be evaluated, $8 - 15 = -7$; no, commutative property is not true for subtraction because $7 \neq -7$ **37.** 198 **39.** 1,492 **41.** 299 **43.** 3 **45.** 1 **47.** 189 **49.** 1,519 **51.** 157 **53.** 26 **55.** 15 **57.** 1

1-4 pages 13–14

Practice **1a.** $n = 6$ **b.** $2 = b$ **c.** $y = 4$ **2a.** no solution **b.** no solution
Exercises **1.** $n = 9$ **3.** $n = 4$ **5.** $z = 9$ **7.** no solution **9.** $n = 20$ **11.** $p = 8$ **13.** no solution **15.** no solution **17.** all whole numbers **19.** answers will vary. Example: $m + 1 = 15$ **21.** $7 - 6$ **23.** 220, 230, 240

1-5 pages 15–17

Practice **1a.** $a = 3$ **b.** $n = 8$ **c.** $y = 8$ **2a.** $a = 36$ **b.** $y = 16$ **c.** $d = 14$
Exercises **1.** $n = 6$ **3.** $x = 2$ **5.** $c = 9$ **7.** $p = 5$ **9.** $t = 13$ **11.** $c = 11$ **13.** $n = 8$ **15.** $a = 6$ **17.** $n = 30$ **19.** $b = 70$ **21.** $x = 3$ **23.** $y = 19$ **25.** $a = 21$ **27.** $n = 13$ **29.** $n = 75$ **31.** $n = 756$ **33.** $c = 7{,}489$ **35.** $r = 5{,}365$ **37.** 7,500 buttons **39.** $431,400 **41.** 37,364 **43.** $y = 96 + 35$; $y = 131$ **45.** $x = 13$, $y = 11$ **47.** 100 **49.** $y + 28$
Mental Math **1.** 73 **3.** 102 **5.** 765

1-6 pages 18–20

Practice **1a.** $x = 317$ **b.** $x = 36$ **2a.** $m = 234$ **b.** $y = 235$
Exercises **1.** $n = 46$ **3.** $a = 38$ **5.** $c = 78$ **7.** $x = 115$ **9.** $x = 150$ **11.** $x = 197$ **13.** $c = 252$ **15.** $c = 864$ **17.** $n = 89$ **19.** $a = 187$ **21.** $x = 177$ **23.** $n = 966$ **25.** $a = 756$ **27.** $n = 6{,}659$ **29.** $a = 283$ **31.** $x = 156$ **33.** $y = 66$ **35.** $2{,}475 = 1{,}697 + n$; $n = 778$ **37.** $y = 6$; $n = 4$; $x = 11$ **39.** $b + a$ **41.** 1,313 **43.** 1,304 **45.** $y = 16$

1-7 pages 22–23

Problems **1.** $1,840 **3.** $1,576 **5.** $9,277 **7.** $10,404 **9.** AM/FM stereo radio and power steering

1-8 pages 24–26

Practice **1a.** 14,000 **b.** 72,000 **21.** 1,700 **b.** 6,500
Exercises **1.** $x \approx 150$ **3.** $y \approx 170$ **5.** $x \approx 960$ **7.** $n \approx 1{,}200$ **9.** $z \approx 1{,}600$ **11.** $c \approx 6{,}000$ **13.** $n \approx 1{,}500$ **15.** $x \approx 15{,}000$ **17.** $a \approx 80{,}000$ **19.** $x \approx 3{,}500$ **21.** $c \approx 40{,}000$ **23.** 94,000 mi **25.** 9,000 mi **25.** $F, G, H, I, J, K, L, M, N, O$ **29.** 325 **31.** $78 + (65 + 135)$ **33.** $x = 27$ **35.** $n = 92$ **37.** 1,022 **39.** 21,352

Chapter 1 Review page 30

1. 33 **2.** 12 **3.** 26 **4.** 35 **5.** 29 **6.** 10 **7.** 8 **8.** 4 **9.** 9 **10.** 11 **11.** 5 **12.** 8 **13.** $z + 1$ **14.** $p + 9$ **15.** $v - 2$ **16.** $9 + m$ **17.** $9 - 2$ **18.** $c + (1 + 3)$ **19.** $5 + k$ **2.** w or $w + 0$ **21.** 10 **22.** 8 **23.** 9 **24.** 13 **25.** 9 **26.** 11 **27.** 67 **28.** 86 **29.** 72 **30.** 0 **31.** 112 **32.** 22 km **33.** 17 **34.** 16,000 **35.** 2,000 **36.** 9,000 **37.** 1,500 **38.** 400 **39.** 2,800 **40.** 1,300 **41.** 7,500

Chapter 1 Cumulative Review page 32

1. 2 **3.** 34 **5.** $p \approx 19{,}000$ **7.** $k + 3$ **9.** $15 + 22$ **11.** $5 + r$ **13.** 6 or $0 + 6$ **15.** $a = 12$ **17.** $g = 10$ **19.** $a = 23$ **21.** $x = 19$ **23.** $n = 107$ **25.** $r = 215$ **27.** 22 hours **29.** $v \approx 80$ **31.** $d \approx 70$ **33.** $h \approx 200$ **35.** 15 **37.** 7

Chapter 2
Expressions and Equations: Multiplication and Division

2-1 pages 34–37
Practice **1a.** 3 **b.** 16 **2a.** 33 **b.** 26 **c.** 36 **3a.** 324 **b.** 9 **4a.** 5 **b.** 1 **c.** 2
Exercises **1.** 19 **3.** 6 **5.** 16 **7.** 2 **9.** 536 **11.** 49 **13.** 32 **15.** 50 **17.** 1,088 **19.** 4 **21.** 225 **23.** 60 **25.** 2 **27.** 4 **29.** 9 **31.** 66 **33.** 4 **35.** 50 **37.** 10 **39.** 54 **41.** 1,384 **45.** $25 = m$ **47.** $27 - x$ **49.** 6,500
Calculator Activity **1.** 569 **3.** 208 **5.** 40

2-2 pages 38–40
Practice **1a.** $24 \div 6$ **b.** $2 \cdot 8$ **c.** $12 \cdot 7$ **2a.** $6n$ **b.** $2n$ **c.** $n \div 5$ **3a.** $5t + 2n$ **b.** $7(n + 4)$ **4a.** $645 \cdot 8$ **b.** $645h$ **c.** $645 \div 5$ **d.** $645 \div b$
Exercises **1.** $8 \cdot 7$ **3.** $2 \cdot 46$ **5.** $48 \div 4$ **7.** $9n$ **9.** $15n$ **11.** $6x$ **13.** $n \div 5$ **15.** $35 + 2x$ **17.** $2n - 12$ **19.** $3r - 24$ **21.** $5n + 4$ **23.** $36(9)$ **25.** $36 \div 4$ **27.** $48(4)$ **29.** $48 \div 12$ **31.** $2n + 2$ **33.** $2n + 3$ **35.** Rams 38, Dolphins 13 **37.** $454 = n$ **39.** $r = 71$ **41.** $x + (7 + 3)$

2-3 pages 41–45
Practice **1a.** yx **b.** $6z$ **c.** $p(24)$ **2a.** $n(12 \cdot 7)$ **b.** $(25 \cdot 4)a$ **c.** $6(ab)$ **3a.** 0 **b.** n **c.** 0 **4a.** $6(r + 4) = 6r + 24$ **b.** $(5 + 3)n = 5n + 3n$
Exercises **1.** $4y$ **3.** dc **5.** $b(68)$ **7.** $r(15)$ **9.** $n(3 \cdot 8)$ **11.** $(8 \cdot 5)a$ **13.** y **15.** 1 **17.** $4x + 12$ **19.** $6y + 9y$ **21.** $30 + 5s$ **23.** $5z + 15$ **25.** yes **27.** 13 **29.** 36 **31.** no **37.** 29,165 **39.** 5,192 **41.** 19 **43.** 17 **45.** 23 **47.** 225 **49.** 841 **51.** 630 **53.** 505 **55.** 23,066
Numbers to Algebra **1.** $2(a + b)$ **3.** $6(n + 7)$ **5.** $p(3 + n)$

2-4 pages 46–48
Practice **1a.** $30x$ **b.** $63b$ **c.** $96y$ **2a.** $n + 32$ **b.** $z + 20$ **c.** $r + 32$ **3a.** $11n$ **b.** $40b$ **c.** $41z$ **d.** $6x$
Exercises **1.** $208c$ **3.** $48p$ **5.** $56x$ **7.** $81y$ **9.** $138b$ **11.** $1{,}564z$ **13.** $x + 16$ **15.** $b + 32$ **17.** $n + 23$ **19.** $b + 83$ **21.** $y + 203$ **23.** $12a$ **25.** $16z$ **27.** $23y$ **29.** $123c$ **31.** $30a$ **33.** $56c$ **35.** $35x$ **37.** 1 **39.** $\frac{2(x + 7 - 2) - 10}{2} = \frac{2x}{2} = x$ **41.** 25 **43.** 373
Mental Math **1.** 68 **3.** 92 **5.** 258

2-5 pages 49–51
Practice **1a.** 36 **b.** 8 **c.** 27 **2a.** 5 **b.** 54 **c.** 8
Exercises **1.** 9 **3.** 7 **5.** 36 **7.** 30 **9.** 5 **11.** 240 **13.** 30 **15.** 20 **17.** 12,500 **19.** 500 **21.** 4 **23.** 2 **25.** 6,615 **27.** 3,198 **29.** 121,156 **31.** $56,475 **33a.** 1,176 **b.** 1,272 **c.** 2,125 **35.** 4 **37.** 1 **39.** 19 **41.** 27
Estimation **1.** 900 **3.** 3,600 **5.** 800

2-6 pages 52–54
Practice **1a.** 13 **b.** 24 **2a.** 72 **b.** 32
Exercises **1.** 8 **3.** 11 **5.** 23 **7.** 12 **9.** 6 **11.** 3 **13.** 192 **15.** 205 **17.** 192 **19.** 512 **21.** 1,944 **23.** 2,622 **25.** 12 **27.** 17 **29.** 326 **31.** 9,747 **33.** 3 **35.** 4,860 **37.** 70 **39.** 204 **41.** 1,776 **43.** $(6 \cdot 9) + 13$ **45.** 22

2-7 page 56
Problems **1.** 270 **3.** 910 **5.** 385 **7.** lose

2-8 pages 57–58
Practice **1a.** 135 **b.** 150 **2.** 420
Exercises **1.** 140 **3.** 86 **5.** 272 **7.** 51 mi **9.** $277 **11.** 16 **13.** 4 **17.** $g = \frac{P - f}{2}$ **19.** 19

2-9 pages 59–60
Practice **1a.** 72,000 **b.** 30 **2a.** 80 **b.** 40
Exercises **1.** 2,400 **3.** 1,600 **5.** 32,000 **7.** 50,000 **9.** 3 **11.** 5 **13.** 40 **15.** 80 **17.** 480,000 **19.** 50 **21.** 80 **23.** 5 **25.** 7 **27.** 40 **29.** estimate: 3,000; exact: 3,234 **31.** $8,400 **33.** estimate: 9; exact: 8.68932 hours **35.** $\geq 3{,}350$ and $<3{,}450$ **37.** 85 **39.** 66

Chapter 2 Review page 64
1. 8 **2.** 7 **3.** 22 **4.** $\frac{24}{y}$ **5.** $6c + 24$ **6.** 12 **7.** $2x$ **8.** $m \div 4$ **9.** $5b$ **10.** $4f$ **11.** ba **12.** $x(14)$ **13.** $(12 \cdot 3)p$ **14.** $7(tk)$ **15.** $v(3 \cdot 6)$ **16.** $4h + 24$ **17.** $7w + w$ **18.** $45 + 5n$ **19.** $20 + r$ **20.** $27m$ **21.** $24x$ **22.** $9y$ **23.** $11a$ **24.** $30p$ **25.** 6 **26.** 5 **27.** 35 **28.** 15 **29.** 51 **30.** 120 **31.** 184 **32.** 270 **33.** 300 mi **34.** 16,000 **35.** 200 **36.** 50

Cumulative Review page 66
1. 17 **3.** 37 **5.** 75 **7.** 9,000 **9.** 7,000 **11.** 200 **13.** 16,000 **15.** 300 **17.** 12,000 **19.** 9 **21.** $4 + f$ **23.** $981 + c$ **25.** $4z$ **27.** $a + 279$ **29.** $(m + 16b) + 580$ **31.** $44s$ **33.** $k + 7k$ **35.** $18 + 6p$ **37.** $54y$ **39.** $6v$ **41.** $45h$

Chapter 3
Integers

3-1 pages 68–71
Practice **1.** X: -9, Y: 4 **2a.** 9 **b.** 85 **3a.** $-16 < -8 < 6$ **b.** $-3 < 0 < |-6| < 9$
Exercises **1.** 2 **3.** 5 **5.** 8 **7.** 5 **9.** 123 **11.** 36 **13.** 199 **15.** 1 **17.** $-21 < 2$ **19.** $-6 < -1 < 4$ **21.** $-9 < -6 < -2 < -1$ **23.** $-24 < -23 < 8$ **25.** $-13 < -4 < 6 < 12 < |-18|$ **27.** -124 **29.** -12 **31.** 8 **33.** negative **35.** 0 **37.** negative **39.** 32, 47, 62 **41.** a square **43.** 189 **45.** 120 **47.** $99x$ **49.** 1 **51.** 6

3-2 pages 72–74
Practice **1a.** -30 **b.** 64 **c.** -60 **2a.** 2 **b.** 16 **c.** -25 **3a.** -20 **b.** 12
Exercises **1.** -12 **3.** -15 **5.** 4 **7.** 19 **9.** 8 **11.** 8 **13.** -6 **15.** 1 **17.** -9 **19.** -24 **21.** -12 **23.** 26 **25.** 52 **27.** -5 **29.** 201 **31.** 6 **33.** 20
Numbers to Algebra **1.** -8 **3.** 24

3-3 pages 75–77
Practice **1a.** −5 **b.** −10 **c.** −11 **d.** 6 **2a.** 12 **b.** 14 **c.** −7 **3a.** −6 **b.** 6
Exercises **1.** 6 **3.** −6 **5.** −6 **7.** −14 **9.** −22 **11.** 13 **13.** 25 **15.** 14 **17.** 8 **19.** −6 **21.** −8 **23.** 14 **25.** −49 **27.** 81 **29.** −15 **31.** −6 **33.** 16 **35.** −13 **37.** 2 **39.** −17, 15, 93 **41.** 1 **43.** −2 **45.** 23 **47.** 3 − 2 = 1, but 2 − 3 = −1 **49.** 14,776 ft **53.** 27 **55.** −2 **57.** 2
Calculator Activity **1.** −431 **3.** 192 **5.** 13,511

3-4 pages 79–81
Practice **1a.** −66 **b.** −118 **c.** −129 **2a.** 28 **b.** −16 **c.** −101 **3a.** −58 **b.** 69
Exercises **1.** −111 **3.** −253 **5.** 78 **7.** −85 **9.** 309 **11.** −1712 **13.** −16 **15.** 145 **17.** −148 **19.** 442 **21.** 180 **23.** 200 **25.** −209 **27.** −311 **29.** −73 **31.** 581 **33.** −121 **35.** $y - 78 = -29$; $y = 49$ **37.** $A = 17$, $B = 7$ **39.** −7 **41.** $2(7 + n)$
Mental Math **1.** 28 **3.** 210

3-5 pages 82–83
Problems **1.** $46 **3.** $88; $663 **5.** $159 **7.** Overdrawn by $200

3-6 pages 84–86
Practice **1a.** 54 **b.** 56 **c.** 45 **2a.** −20 **b.** −48 **c.** −36 **d.** −21
Exercises **1.** 63 **3.** 32 **5.** 36 **7.** 14 **9.** 56 **11.** −45 **13.** 0 **15.** −81 **17.** 18 **19.** −48 **21.** 460 **23.** 1248 **25.** 7448 **27.** −4464 **29.** −120; odd; negative **31a.** negative **b.** positive **33.** −168 **35.** −10,800 **37.** −5040 **39.** −255 **41.** −41 **45.** −28°C **47.** −1,255,616 **49a.** 12, −24, 15 **b.** −10, −14, −18 **51.** −59 **53.** 43
Mental Math **1.** 687,000 **3.** −57,900 **5.** 9,600

3-7 pages 87–88
Practice **1a.** 5 **b.** 5 **c.** 9 **2a.** −6 **b.** −5 **c.** −8
Exercises **1.** 7 **3.** 5 **5.** −9 **7.** −8 **9.** −9 **11.** 6 **13.** −9 **15.** 6 **17.** −18 **19.** −13 **21.** −25 **23.** −8 **25.** 3 **27.** 7 **29.** 8 **31.** −6 **33.** no **35.** −9 **37.** −2,400 **39.** $a = 8$, $b = -2$ **41.** 5 a.m. **43.** 57 **45.** $108c$ **47.** $13 + t$

3-8 pages 89–91
Practice **1a.** −17 **b.** −26 **2a.** −432 **b.** −200 **3a.** 15 **b.** −36
Exercises **1.** −12 **3.** 15 **5.** −23 **7.** 12 **9.** −153 **11.** 186 **13.** −270 **15.** −506 **17.** −6 **19.** −63 **21.** 46 **23.** −5082 **25.** −16 **27.** −36 **29.** 18 **31.** 6 **33.** 6 **35.** $7a = -224$, $8a = -512$, $9a = -1152$ **37.** 68, −68 **39.** 7 **41.** 216 **43.** 108 **45.** 11
Computer Activity **1.** 6, −3

3-9 pages 93–94
Practice **1a.** $x - 9 = 54$ **b.** $y + 47 = -112$ **2a.** $55h = 220$ **b.** $n \div 9 = 12$
Exercises **1.** $n - 17 = 101$ **3.** $n + 35 = 372$ **5.** $56 + n = 104$ **7.** $n \div 25 = -12$ **9.** $9n = -171$ **11.** $n - 17 = 15$ **13.** $6d = 91$ **15.** $n + 9 = 72$ **17.** $34n = 272$ **19.** $c - 6000 = 59{,}820$ **21.** $n + 19 = 56$ **23.** A number divided by −4 is 9. **25.** 16 decreased by a number is 7. **27.** $n + (n + 1) + (n + 2) = 828$; $n = 275$ **29.** 31 **31.** −7 **33.** −13

Chapter 3 Review page 98
1. 6 **2.** 3 **3.** 17 **4.** $-8 < -2 < 2$ **5.** $-7 < -1 < 0$ **6.** $-8 < -5 < 0$ **7.** −6 **8.** −3 **9.** 3 **10.** −24 **11.** −8 **12.** 6 **13.** −16 **14.** −8 **15.** −13 **16.** −3 **17.** −17 **18.** 11 **19.** −7 **20.** −3 **21.** −12 **22.** −49 **23.** −17 **24.** 81 **25.** −93 **26.** −105 **27.** 71 **28.** $224 **29.** 9 **30.** 56 **31.** 25 **32.** −48 **33.** −8 **34.** −9 **35.** 9 **36.** −7 **37.** −4 **38.** 3 **39.** −24 **40.** −27 **41.** −3 **42.** −49 **43.** −24 **44.** −91 **45.** $10n = 110$ **46.** $n + (-15) = 60$

Cumulative Review page 100
1. $g + 9$ **3.** $v + 10$ **5.** $7y$ **7.** $16 - r$ **9.** 4 **11.** 47 **13.** 2 **15.** 64 **17.** 18 **19.** 15 **21.** 25 **23.** −10 **25.** qp **27.** $(20 \cdot 8)p$ **29.** $y + (2 + 9)$ **31.** $8a + 9a$ **33.** $10t$ **35.** $30d$ **37.** $6v$ **39.** −4 **41.** −2

Chapter 4 Decimals

4-1 pages 102–104
Practice **1a.** 478.36 **b.** 0.093 **2a.** −2.74 **b.** 2.75 **3a.** > **b.** > **c.** =
Exercises **1.** 540.76 **3.** 748.07 **5.** 578.3 **7.** 0.1 **9.** 1.33 **11.** −0.34 **13.** = **15.** > **17.** < **19.** 3.069, 3.07, 3.7 **21.** 6.010, 6.0101, 6.101 **23.** −5.404, −5.044, −5.040 **33.** −221 **35.** −25 **37.** −6

4-2 pages 105–107
Practice **1a.** 7.09 **b.** 10 **c.** 0.9 **2a.** 73.5 **b.** 0.25 **c.** 4.8 **3a.** 33 **b.** 200
Exercises **1.** 147 **3.** 127 **5.** 35 **7.** 20 **9.** 23.8 **11.** 42.7 **13.** 8.3 **15.** 17.0 **17.** 4.59 **19.** 0.28 **21.** 9.90 **23.** 8.89 **25.** 320 **27.** 40 **29.** 1300 **35.** 8 for $1.05 **37.** 2.113, 3.421, 5.534 **39.** 1.438, 2.323, 3.761 **41.** −18 **43.** −126 **45.** −72 m

4-3 pages 108–110
Practice **1a.** 293.58 **b.** 43.595 **2a.** 57.9 **b.** 0.4 **3a.** −4.95 **b.** 14.04
Exercises **1.** 48.12 **3.** 70.8 **5.** 6.03 **7.** 181.25 **9.** −12.63 **11.** 31.82 **13.** 924.82 **15.** 338.407 **17.** 121.72 **19.** 40.7274 **21.** 66.03 **25.** $8.76 million **27.** 15.89, 7.98, 13.3 **29.** 11.2, 8.38, 13 **33.** 615.92 − 231.15 = 384.77 **35.** 21 **37.** −468 **39.** 2
Numbers to Algebra **1.** $7x + 6y$ **3.** $11u + 5n$

4-4 pages 111–112
Practice **1.** −17.24 **b.** 1.953 **2a.** 17.24 **b.** 3.107
Exercises **1.** 7.9 **3.** 4.73 **5.** 113.2 **7.** 27.3 **9.** 601.5 **11.** 16.29 **13.** 369.01 **15.** 150.12 **17.** 50.17 **19.** 130.32

21. −130.32 **23.** 66.9 **25.** 17.36 = 8.24 + x, x = 9.12 **29.** 51 **31.** 12
Mental Math **1.** 17 **3.** 40.45

4-5 pages 113–115
Practice **1a.** 120 **b.** 800 **c.** 1000 **d.** 20,000 **2a.** 8.652 **b.** 0.146 **3a.** −0.0111 **b.** −0.0462
Exercises **1.** 100 **3.** 4 **5.** 8,000 **7.** 0.189 **9.** 3.46 **11.** −0.3504 **13.** 258.03 **15.** 10.2453 **17.** −52.8 **19.** 25.056 **21.** 0.0219 **23.** 33.6 **25.** 8.86 **27.** 15.43 **29.** 62.6°F **31.** 134.06°F **33.** 24 **35.** 43c **37.** −63k **39.** 12 **41.** 0.14 < 1.04 < 1.4
Mental Math **1.** 27.75 **3.** 15.1 **5.** 14.4

4-6 pages 116–117
Problems **1.** 1.5 km **3.** 8 cm **5.** 1.8 cm **7.** 2 mm **9.** 1,000,000

4-7 pages 118–120
Practice **1a.** 3 **b.** 8 **2a.** 21.25 **b.** 9.3 **3a.** 114 **b.** 0.33 **c.** 7.1 **d.** 48.1 **4a.** 0.0025 **b.** 1.6 **c.** 0.045 **d.** 0.0013
Exercises **1.** 5 **3.** 3 **5.** 3 **7.** 0.46 **9.** 0.117 **11.** 4.19 **13.** 3.4 **15.** 16 **17.** 2190 **29.** 1.2 **21.** 11.3 **23.** 8.33 **25.** 1.6 **27.** 5 **31.** 1.05 **33.** −17.46 **35.** 4.83 **37.** n + 0.95

4-8 pages 121–123
Practice **1.** 19
Exercises **1.** m = 2005 − 16; 1989 **3.** j − 17 = 53; 70 cars **5.** r + 4.52 = 29.32; 24.80 seconds **7.** 0.15r = 6 ÷ 2; 20 m **9.** n + 17 = 15 × 8; 103 people **13.** 4.4 **15.** 3 **17.** 9
Calculator Activity **1.** $76.49 **3.** $133.33 **5.** $478.79

4-9 pages 125–126
Practice **1a.** 150 **b.** −920 **2a.** 0.728 **b.** −18.56
Exercises **1.** 5.3 **3.** −7 **5.** −19.09 **7.** −15 **9.** −12 **11.** 20 **13.** −5.976 **15.** −17.28 **17.** −18 **19.** 17.5 **21.** 15.91 **23.** 113.82 **25.** 1.2x = 264; x = 220 **27.** 3 **29.** −4.2 **31.** 6.6 **33.** −12

Chapter 4 Review page 130
1. 63.8 **2.** 5.072 **3.** > **4.** = **5.** < **6.** 80 **7.** 1000 **8.** 62 **9.** 50 **10.** 8.43 **11.** 85.47 **12.** 5.88 **13.** 46.83 **14.** −28.75 **15.** 86.7 **16.** 1.46 **17.** −28.19 **18.** 29.41 **19.** 45.67 **20.** 200 **21.** 300 **22.** 300 **23.** 22.944 **24.** −1.386 **25.** 34.96 **26.** 1.462 **27.** 1750 cm **28.** 4000 g **29.** 21 **30.** −180 **31.** 8.8 **32.** 0.994 **33.** −3.63 **34.** −14.03 **35.** 37.90 − 10.75 = p; p = 27.15 **36.** 88.6 + 97.4 = c; c = 186 kg

Cumulative Review page 132
1. 18 − 7 **3.** 12 + 8 **5.** c − 9 **7.** 8 **9.** 7 **11.** 7 **13.** −7 **15.** −7 **17.** 4 **19.** −11 **21.** 13 **23.** 2 **25.** 9 **27.** 48 **29.** −34 **31.** 265 **33.** 47 **35.** 6 **37.** $843

Chapter 5 Number Theory

5-1 pages 134–136
Practice **1a.** 7, 14, 21 **b.** 9, 18, 27, 36, 45 **2a.** no **b.** yes **3a.** 1, 2, 3, 6, 9, 18 **b.** 1, 2, 4, 8, 16, 32
Exercises **1.** 3, 6, 9, 12 **3.** 7, 14, 21, 28 **5.** 6, 12, 18, 24 **7.** 9, 18, 27, 36 **9.** 4, 8, 12, 16 **11.** 20, 40, 60, 80 **13.** yes **15.** no **17.** yes **19.** no **21.** yes **23.** yes **25.** yes **27.** yes **29.** 1, 2, 4, 5, 10, 20 **31.** 1, 2, 3, 4, 6, 7, 12, 14, 21, 28, 42, 84 **33.** 1, 2, 3, 4, 5, 6, 10, 12, 15, 20, 30, 60 **35.** 1, 3, 5, 7, 15, 21, 35, 105 **37.** 91; 18, 91 **39.** 4, 9, 25, 49; squares **45.** 14.504 **47.** 20.2
Calculator Activity **1.** 1, 2, 3, 6, 13, 26, 39, 78 **3.** 1, 3, 5, 7, 15, 21, 35, 105

5-2 pages 137–139
Practice **1.** a, c, d, f **2.** b, c **3.** a, b
Exercises **1.** no **3.** yes **5.** yes **7.** no **9.** no **11.** yes **13.** no **15.** yes **17.** yes **19.** no **21.** yes **23.** yes **25.** no **27.** no **29.** yes **31.** yes **33.** yes **35.** yes **37.** yes **39.** yes **41.** yes **43.** no **45.** A number is divisible by 10 if its last digit is 0. **47.** 2520 **49.** 70; 2, 10, 14, 35, 70 **51.** > **53.** = **55.** −44.793 **57.** 26.163 **59.** 15.26 **61.** 2n + 11 = 27
Mental Math **1.** yes **3.** no **5.** yes

5-3 pages 140–141
Practice **1.** $\frac{s}{6}$ = 84; $504
Exercises **b.** $\frac{c}{4}$ = 2.41; $9.64 **3.** 2$r$ = 146; 73 **5.** 3t = 453; 151 **7.** 12c = 84; $7 **11.** −2 **13.** 20 **15.** 0 **17.** −3 **19.** −2.74 **21.** 19.264 **23.** −45.75

5-4 pages 142–143
Practice **1a.** com. **b.** prime **c.** com.
Exercises **1.** com. 2, 3 **3.** com. 3 **5.** com. 2, 3, etc. **7.** com. 2, 13 **9.** com. 2, 4, etc. **11.** com. 2, 17 **13.** prime **15.** prime **17.** prime **19.** com. 7, 11 **21.** 2, 3, 5, 7, 11, 13, 17, 19, 23 **23.** 6 **25.** 5 and 7, 11 and 13, 17 and 19, etc. **29.** 0.6125 **31.** 0.3 **33.** −19.36

5-5 pages 144–147
Practice **1a.** $3 \cdot 3 \cdot 3 \cdot 3 = 81$ **b.** $(-2)(-2)(-2)(-2) = 16$ **c.** $a \cdot a \cdot a$ **2a.** 10^3 **b.** $(-2)^2$ **c.** b^4 **3a.** $(-5)^6$ **b.** 10^7 **c.** x^5 **4a.** 1100 **b.** 650
Exercises **1.** $10 \cdot 10 \cdot 10 \cdot 10 \cdot 10 = 100{,}000$ **3.** $7 \cdot 7 \cdot 7 = 343$ **5.** $9 \cdot 9 \cdot 9 = 729$ **7.** $8 \cdot 8 = 64$ **9.** $n \cdot n \cdot n \cdot n$ **11.** 5^4 **13.** 10^4 **15.** 9^4 **17.** 3^6 **19.** 10^{10} **21.** 10^{14} **23.** 7^{27} **25.** 2^{11} **27.** 3^{14} **29.** p^4 **31.** c^{15} **33.** 48 **35.** 110 **37.** 8 + 4 = 12 **39.** $5^3 = 125$ **41.** 10^2 **43.** 10^4 **45.** 65,536 **47.** 78,125 **49.** 123 **51.** −2, 4, −8, 16, −32, 64 **53.** positive **55a.** 100 **b.** A googol or 10^{100}. **57.** −0.75 **59.** 7.25 **61.** 2 **63.** 2.3 **65.** 4.7

5-6 pages 148–150
Practice **1a.** $2^3 \cdot 5$ **b.** $2 \cdot 3^3$ **2a.** $2^2 \cdot 7$ **b.** $2^3 \cdot 3^2$ **3a.** $2 \cdot 3 \cdot 7$ **b.** $3 \cdot 3 \cdot 5 \cdot 7$

Exercises **1.** $2^2 \cdot 3^2$ **3.** $2 \cdot 3 \cdot 5 \cdot 7$ **5.** $2^4 \cdot 3$ **7.** $2^2 \cdot 5 \cdot 7$ **9.** $2^2 \cdot 3$ **11.** $2^2 \cdot 3^2$ **13.** $3 \cdot 13^2$ **15.** $2 \cdot 3^2 \cdot 5$ **17.** $2^4 \cdot 3 \cdot 5$ **19.** $2 \cdot 3 \cdot 5 \cdot 11$ **21.** $3^2 \cdot 5^2$ **23.** $2 \cdot 3 \cdot 7 \cdot 11$ **25.** $3 \cdot 3 \cdot 3 \cdot 11$ **27.** $2 \cdot 2 \cdot 2 \cdot 3 \cdot 3 \cdot 3$ **29.** $2 \cdot 3 \cdot 7 \cdot 13 \cdot 17$ **31.** 5 **33.** 23 **35.** 2268 **37.** 137,200 **39.** 141,414; 232,323; 757,575; repeats the age three times. **41.** $2 \cdot 3 \cdot 5 \cdot 7 \cdot 11 \cdot 13 = 30{,}030$ **43.** $9(12 + n) = 135$ **45.** $36 + n = 5 \cdot 4$ **47.** 2.35

5-7 pages 151–153

Practice **1a.** 1, 2, 3, 6, 9, 18 GCF = 9 **b.** 1, 3, 4, 6, 12 GCF = 4 **2a.** $12 = 2 \cdot 2 \cdot 3$, $16 = 2 \cdot 2 \cdot 2 \cdot 2$ GCF = 4 **b.** $24 = 2 \cdot 2 \cdot 2 \cdot 3$, $30 = 2 \cdot 3 \cdot 5$ GCF = 6

Exercises **1.** 1, 2, 4, 8 GCF = 1 **3.** 1, 2, 4, 8, 16 GCF = 8 **5.** 1, 2, 3, 4, 6, 12 GCF = 12 **7.** 1, 2, 3, 4, 6, 8, 12, 16, 24, 48 GCF = 16 **9.** 1, 2, 3, 4, 6, 8, 12, 24 GCF = 8 **11.** 1, 2, 5, 10 GCF = 1 **13.** 1, 3, 9, 27 GCF = 9 **15.** 1, 2, 4, 8, 16, 32 GCF = 8 **17.** 15 **19.** 18 **21.** 15 **23.** 24 **25.** 21 **27.** 2 **29.** 72 **31.** 26 **33.** 6 **35.** 6 **37.** 8 **39a.** yes **b.** yes **c.** yes **41.** 63 **43.** $2t$ **45.** -1 **47.** $6x - 4$ **49.** 0 **51.** 30 **53.** 9

Numbers to Algebra **1.** xy **3.** $6xy^2$ **5.** $8x^2z^2$

5-8 pages 154–155

Problems **1.** 80 ft **3.** 65 ft **5.** 245 ft **7.** Braking Dist = 151.25 ft, Stopping Dist = 206.25 ft **9.** 146.25 ft **11.** 95 miles

5-9 pages 156–158

Practice **1a.** 9, 18, . . . LCM = 18 **b.** 12, 24, . . . LCM = 24 **2a.** $2 \cdot 2 \cdot 3 \cdot 5 = 60$ **b.** $2 \cdot 2 \cdot 2 \cdot 3 \cdot 5 = 120$

Exercises **1.** 10, 20, 30, 40, . . . LCM = 40 **3.** 10, 20, 30, . . . LCM = 30 **5.** 12, 24, . . . LCM = 24 **7.** 15, 30, 45, . . . LCM = 45 **9.** 21, 42, . . . LCM = 42 **11.** 15, 30, . . . LCM = 30 **13.** 14, 28, 42, . . . LCM = 42 **15.** 10, 20, . . . LCM = 20 **17.** 100 **19.** 210 **21.** 280 **23.** 210 **25.** 630 **27.** 240 **29.** 60 **31.** 180 **33.** 36 **35.** 1575 **37.** 280 **39.** 540 **41.** 120 cm **43.** 540 **45.** 1260 **47a.** $\frac{48}{2} = 24$, $\frac{48}{24} = 2$ **b.** $\frac{150}{5} = 30$, $\frac{150}{30} = 5$ **c.** $\frac{216}{6} = 36$, $\frac{216}{36} = 6$; yes **49.** $(-2)^3$ **51.** 18.82

Computer Activity **1.** 252

Chapter 5 Review page 162

1. 5, 10, 15, 20, 25 **2.** 10, 20, 30, 40, 50 **3.** 70, 140, 210, 280, 350 **4.** 1, 2, 4, 8, 16 **5.** 1, 2, 4, 8, 16, 32 **6.** 1, 5, 17, 85 **7.** 2 **8.** 3 **9.** 2, 3 **10.** 5 **11.** 2, 5 **12.** 2 **13.** $218 = 2x$; $x = 109$ **14.** $12c = 144$, $c = 12$ **15.** composite **16.** composite **17.** composite **18.** $8 \cdot 8 \cdot 8 = 512$ **19.** $(-6)(-6)(-6)(-6) = 1296$ **20.** $s \cdot s \cdot s \cdot s \cdot s \cdot s \cdot s$ **21.** 6^5 **22.** a^3 **23.** $(-2)^4$ **24.** 8^3 **25.** $(-3)^6$ **26.** x^5 **27.** 36 **28.** 9990 **29.** $2^2 \cdot 3^2$ **30.** $3 \cdot 5^2$ **31.** $2 \cdot 3 \cdot 5^2$ **32.** $2 \cdot 3^3 \cdot 7$ **33.** 3 **34.** 13 **35.** 12 **36.** 40 mi/h **37.** 24 **38.** 48 **39.** 288

Cumulative Review page 164

1. 25 **3.** 6 **5.** $m - 18 = 20$ **7.** 220 **9.** 750 cm² **11.** 14 **13.** -3 **15.** -18 **17.** 3 **19.** -3 **21.** -9 **23.** 12 **25.** -11 **27.** -102 **29.** -11.55 **31.** 3.2 **33.** -4.5 **35.** 7.48

Chapter 6 Rational Numbers: Addition and Subtraction

6-1 pages 166–169

Practice **1a.** 36 **b.** 35 **2a.** yes **b.** yes **3a.** $\frac{1}{2}$ **b.** $\frac{2}{3}$

Exercises **1.** 14 **3.** 3 **5.** 1 **7.** 50 **9.** 65 **11.** 7 **13.** 35 **15.** 12 **17.** no **19.** yes **21.** yes **23.** yes **25.** $\frac{10}{13}$ **27.** $\frac{4}{7}$ **29.** $\frac{17}{19}$ **31.** $\frac{2}{3}$ **33.** $\frac{13}{14}$ **35.** $\frac{11}{63}$ **37.** $\frac{3}{7}$ **39.** $\frac{3}{5}$ **41.** $\frac{7}{15}$ **43.** $\frac{7}{9}$ **53.** yes **55.** no **57.** no **59.** yes **61.** false **65.** $5m$ **67.** $14r - 10$ **69.** $3t$ **71.** a^3 **73.** 5 **75.** -5.35 **77.** 6.56

Numbers to Algebra **1.** $\frac{2}{3}$ **3.** $\frac{7a}{8b}$ **5.** $\frac{a}{2}$ **7.** $\frac{4a}{bc}$ **9.** $\frac{3}{7}$ **11.** $\frac{12}{35a}$

6-2 pages 170–172

Practice **1a.** $3\frac{2}{3}$ **b.** 6 **c.** $5\frac{1}{7}$ **2a.** $\frac{19}{4}$ **b.** $\frac{16}{3}$ **c.** $\frac{73}{10}$

Exercises **1.** $4\frac{1}{6}$ **3.** 17 **5.** $8\frac{3}{11}$ **7.** 11 **9.** $3\frac{21}{50}$ **11.** 5 **13.** $11\frac{3}{5}$ **15.** $3\frac{1}{2}$ **17.** $\frac{31}{8}$ **19.** $\frac{41}{16}$ **21.** $\frac{52}{9}$ **23.** $\frac{26}{3}$ **25.** $\frac{137}{10}$ **27.** $\frac{223}{20}$ **29.** $\frac{86}{17}$ **31.** $\frac{791}{80}$ **33.** $4\frac{3}{5}$ **35.** $4\frac{5}{17}$ **37.** $13\frac{1}{5}$ **41.** $2 \cdot 3 \cdot 5$ **43.** 12.375 **45.** prime **47.** $n \div 5 = 40$; $n = 40$ **49.** -6.023

Computer Activity **a.** $\frac{1}{11}$ **b.** $\frac{4{,}123}{3{,}998{,}149}$ **c.** $\frac{1{,}950}{17}$

6-3 pages 173–175

Practice **1a.** $\frac{-5}{6}, -\frac{5}{6}, \frac{5}{-6}$ **b.** $\frac{-7}{3}, -\frac{7}{3}, \frac{7}{-3}$ **c.** $-\frac{11}{12}, \frac{-11}{12}, \frac{11}{-12}$ **d.** $\frac{-15}{9}, -\frac{15}{9}, \frac{15}{-9}$

Exercises **1.** $\frac{-3}{8}, -\frac{3}{8}, \frac{3}{-8}$ **3.** $\frac{-11}{16}, -\frac{11}{16}, \frac{11}{-16}$ **5.** $\frac{-5}{2}, -\frac{5}{2}, \frac{5}{-2}$ **7.** $\frac{-3}{2}, -\frac{3}{2}, \frac{3}{-2}$ **9.** $\frac{-3}{7}, -\frac{3}{7}, \frac{3}{-7}$ **11.** $\frac{-3}{16}, -\frac{3}{16}, \frac{3}{-16}$ **13.** $\frac{-9}{12}, -\frac{9}{12}, \frac{9}{-12}$ **15.** $\frac{-18}{24}, -\frac{18}{24}, \frac{18}{-24}$ **27.** $-\frac{3}{x}$ **29.** $\frac{h}{2}$ **31.** $\frac{6}{n}$ **33.** $\frac{12}{m}$ **35.** $\frac{3}{5}$ **37.** $\frac{15}{2}$ **39.** $-\frac{1}{13}, \frac{1}{15}, -\frac{1}{17}$ **41.** $4m + 8n$ **43.** -3.781

Estimation **1.** 5 **3.** 0 **5.** -4

6-4 pages 176–179

Practice **1a.** > **b.** < **2a.** > **b.** < **3a.** > **b.** >

Exercises 1. < 3. > 5. < 7. > 9. > 11. > 13. < 15. > 17. > 19. > 21. < 23. < 25. > 27. > 29. > 31. < 33. $\frac{1}{5}, \frac{1}{4}, \frac{1}{3}$ 35. $\frac{4}{9}, \frac{6}{12}, \frac{2}{3}$ 37. $\frac{3}{8}, \frac{5}{6}, \frac{6}{7}$ 39. > 41. = 43. < 45. > 47. $\frac{5}{12}, \frac{5}{9}, \frac{5}{8}, \frac{5}{6}, \frac{5}{5}, \frac{5}{4}, \frac{5}{3}, \frac{5}{2}$ 49. 55 51. 3 53. 5.22

Calculator Activity 1. 0.8 3. 0.8125 5. −0.28

6-5 pages 180–182

Practice 1a. $\frac{3}{4}$ b. $\frac{2}{7}$ c. $-1\frac{1}{9}$ 2a. $\frac{1}{2}$ b. $-\frac{1}{4}$

Exercises 1. $\frac{1}{2}$ 3. $\frac{3}{11}$ 5. $\frac{1}{4}$ 7. $\frac{2}{11}$ 9. 2 11. $-\frac{4}{19}$ 13. $\frac{11}{15}$ 15. $-2\frac{1}{5}$ 17. $2\frac{8}{15}$ 19. $-1\frac{1}{4}$ 21. $\frac{15}{16}$ 23. $-\frac{2}{3}$ 25. $\frac{1}{3}$ 27. $\frac{5}{6}$ 29. $\frac{5}{9}$ 31. $\frac{2}{7}$ 33. $\frac{7}{12}$ 35. $\frac{7}{12}$ 37. 1 39. $\frac{11}{z}$ 41. $\frac{12}{x}$ 43. $\frac{42}{u}$ 45. $7\frac{1}{2}$ 47. $\frac{1}{4}$ mi or $\frac{2}{5}$ of the course 49. 1, 2, 3, 4, 6, 8, 12, 24 51. $\frac{1}{4}, \frac{1}{4}$ 53. 1.982

6-6 pages 183–185

Practice 1a. $1\frac{13}{60}$ b. $\frac{7}{10}$ 2a. $\frac{23}{24}$ b. $-\frac{9}{10}$

Exercises 1. $\frac{7}{8}$ 3. $-\frac{7}{12}$ 5. $-\frac{3}{10}$ 7. $-1\frac{1}{5}$ 9. $1\frac{7}{12}$ 11. $\frac{11}{20}$ 13. $1\frac{11}{24}$ 15. $\frac{3}{4}$ 17. $-\frac{41}{100}$ 19. $1\frac{17}{24}$ 21. $-\frac{5}{36}$ 23. $\frac{5}{28}$ 25. $-\frac{2}{9}$ 27. $\frac{11}{18}$ 29. 5 ft $1\frac{3}{4}$ in. 31. $-\frac{2}{5} + \frac{3}{4} = \frac{7}{20}$ 33. 1, 5, 25 35. 7, 7 37. est. ≈ 28, exact: 26 39. −37.31

Estimation 1. 2 3. $\frac{1}{4}$

6-7 pages 186–188

Practice 1a. $1\frac{3}{4}$ b. $9\frac{17}{40}$ c. $7\frac{1}{5}$ 2a. $2\frac{1}{4}$ b. $1\frac{1}{15}$ c. $4\frac{1}{4}$

Exercises 1. $1\frac{1}{15}$ 3. $2\frac{16}{21}$ 5. $4\frac{1}{60}$ 7. 6 9. $12\frac{1}{12}$ 11. $3\frac{9}{20}$ 13. $-6\frac{4}{7}$ 15. $-5\frac{35}{48}$ 17. $-1\frac{3}{4}$ 19. 3 21. −4 23. 7 25. 15 27. 36 29. 5 ft $2\frac{9}{10}$ in. 31. 120 33. 0

Mental Math 1. 0 3. $9\frac{5}{6}$ 5. $\frac{5}{12}$

6-8 pages 190–191

Problems 1. 31 3/4 3. 55 7/8 5. 23 1/2 7. \$1,975 9. increase 2 1/4

6-9 pages 192–194

Practice 1a. $-\frac{1}{3}$ b. $\frac{1}{12}$ c. $\frac{5}{8}$ d. $1\frac{7}{15}$ 2a. $-\frac{19}{24}$ b. $-\frac{11}{45}$

Exercises 1. $1\frac{1}{9}$ 3. $-\frac{7}{30}$ 5. $-\frac{13}{30}$ 7. $\frac{1}{8}$ 9. $-\frac{1}{4}$ 11. $-\frac{47}{50}$ 13. $\frac{1}{2}$ 15. $-\frac{14}{15}$ 17. $-\frac{13}{40}$ 19. $\frac{1}{24}$ 21. $\frac{8}{15}$ 23. $-\frac{13}{35}$ 25. $-17\frac{11}{40}$ 27. $-1\frac{29}{60}$ 29. $1\frac{11}{36}$ 31. $-\frac{7}{12}$ 33. $-\frac{1}{2}$ 37. $\frac{1}{2}, \frac{1}{4}, \frac{1}{16}$ 39. −1.85 41. 1, 19 43. 1, 2, 3, 4, 6, 12

Mental Math 1. $3\frac{1}{4}$ 3. $3\frac{1}{5}$

6-10 pages 195–196

Exercises 1. $\frac{7}{8}$ in. 3. $\frac{17}{40}$ mi 5. 25 7. $\frac{1}{12}$ in. 11. 7 · 7 13. 2 · 3 · 3 · 5 15. 15 17. $\frac{64 + n}{12}$ 19. $7m$ 21. 84

Chapter 6 Review page 200

1. 60 2. 1 3. 20 4. $\frac{3}{4}$ 5. $-\frac{6}{13}$ 6. $\frac{12}{13}$ 7. $6\frac{1}{3}$ 8. $-11\frac{2}{11}$ 9. $6\frac{7}{30}$ 10. $\frac{36}{7}$ 11. $-\frac{42}{5}$ 12. $\frac{23}{5}$ 14. = 15. > 16. > 17. > 18. $\frac{5}{6}$ 19. $-\frac{2}{9}$ 20. $-\frac{9}{25}$ 21. $\frac{2}{3}$ 22. $-\frac{1}{3}$ 23. $-\frac{5}{8}$ 24. $4\frac{1}{12}$ 25. $3\frac{2}{3}$ 26. $12\frac{7}{10}$ 27. $1\frac{3}{4}$ lbs 28. $9\frac{5}{8}$ mi 29. $\frac{5}{8}$ 30. $-\frac{7}{10}$ 31. $1\frac{1}{4}$ 32. $1\frac{5}{8}$ yds

Cumulative Review page 202

1. 47.8 3. 5.17 5. = 7. > 9. > 11. 80 13. 7,000 15. 60 17. 60 19. 200 21. 10 23. 50 25. 28 27. 7 29. 7, 14, 21, 28, 35 31. 1, 2, 4, 8, 16, 32 33. 1, 2, 3, 4, 5, 6, 10, 12, 15, 20, 30, 60 35. yes 37. no 39. yes 41. yes

Chapter 7
Rational Numbers: Multiplication and Division

7-1 pages 204–207

Practice 1a. $\frac{5}{16}$ b. $\frac{16}{27}$ 2a. $3\frac{1}{5}$ b. $-6\frac{1}{6}$

Exercises 1. $\frac{9}{20}$ 3. $\frac{5}{32}$ 5. $-\frac{5}{6}$ 7. $-\frac{7}{10}$ 9. $\frac{7}{9}$ 11. $1\frac{1}{4}$ 13. $\frac{5}{24}$ 15. $1\frac{1}{5}$ 17. $14\frac{5}{8}$ 19. $6\frac{3}{4}$ 21. $-12\frac{8}{9}$ 23. $23\frac{4}{7}$ 25. $-1\frac{2}{5}$ 27. 22 29. −16 31. $2\frac{7}{16}$ 33. $-\frac{11}{36}$ 35. $\frac{1}{2}$ 37. $-2\frac{2}{5}$ 39. $-\frac{3}{8}$ 41. 52 ft 43. 28 45. 32 47. 8 49. 12 51. 48 53. 8 55. $2c + 3t$ 57. 1 59. $-\frac{1}{5}$ 61. $-\frac{34}{5}$ 63. $\frac{87}{16}$ 65. −0.06 67. $\frac{7}{8}$ 69. $\frac{4}{15}$

Mental Math 1. 28 3. −46 5. 34 7. 101

7-2 pages 208–210

Practice 1a. −4 b. $\frac{1}{24}$ 2a. $-2\frac{2}{15}$ b. $1\frac{1}{2}$

Exercises 1. 3 3. $\frac{5}{7}$ 5. $-\frac{5}{12}$ 7. $-\frac{3}{16}$ 9. $1\frac{2}{3}$ 11. −2 13. $\frac{13}{14}$ 15. 6 17. 4 19. $3\frac{5}{21}$ 21. $-\frac{3}{10}$ 23. $\frac{1}{21}$ 25. 310 27. $6\frac{30}{43}$ 29. $-\frac{67}{128}$ 31. $4\frac{1}{12}$ 33. $\frac{1}{8}$ in. 35. $\frac{6}{5}, -\frac{1}{5}$ 37. −2.2

Estimation 1. >14 3. >3 5. <3

7-3 pages 211–213

Practice **1a.** 24 **b.** −2 **c.** $\frac{1}{16}$ **d.** $\frac{1}{10}$ **2a.** $1\frac{2}{13}$ **b.** $-1\frac{29}{55}$

Exercises **1.** $\frac{3}{16}$ **3.** $6\frac{1}{4}$ **5.** 5 **7.** −9 **9.** $-\frac{2}{9}$ **11.** 21 **13.** $\frac{6}{7}$ **15.** −8 **17.** $\frac{6}{11}$ **19.** $1\frac{17}{26}$ **21.** $-3\frac{3}{5}$ **23.** $-\frac{54}{335}$ **25.** $1\frac{5}{11}$ **27.** 15 **29.** 18 **31.** $2\frac{1}{4}$ **33.** $6\frac{3}{5}$ **35.** 4, −4 **37.** $8c$ **39.** −33.6

Computer Activity **1.** 48.3333333 **3.** 177.015873

7-4 pages 215–216

1. 80 **3.** $16\frac{1}{2}$ lb **5.** 25 **7.** $106\frac{1}{4}$ lb **11.** $1\frac{1}{24}$ **13.** $\frac{7}{16}$ **15.** −23 **17.** $1\frac{1}{4}$ **19.** $\frac{15}{16}$

7-5 pages 217–218

Problems **1.** 13″ **3.** 35″ **5.** 99 lb **7.** 4 yd³ **9.** $206\frac{5}{8}$″

7-6 pages 219–220

Practice **1a.** $0.\overline{2}$ **b.** $0.1\overline{6}$

Exercises **1.** $0.\overline{45}$ **3.** 0.35 **5.** $0.0\overline{6}$ **7.** 1.6875 **9.** $0.\overline{6}$ **11.** $0.\overline{4}$ **13.** 0.575 **15.** $0.\overline{375}$ **17.** 0.64 **19.** $2.\overline{6}$ **21.** 0.6 **23.** $3.6\overline{1}$ **25.** $0.41\overline{6}$ **27.** $0.\overline{27}$ **29.** 33 **31.** 219 **33.** 270 **37.** 60 **39.** 6.4 **41.** 2

7-7 pages 221–223

Practice **1a.** 5^3 **b.** $(-3)^3$ **c.** 10^3 **2a.** y^5 **b.** m^4 **c.** z **3a.** $\frac{1}{125}$ **b.** $\frac{1}{4}$

Exercises **1.** 3^3 **3.** $(-4)^2$ **5.** 10^4 **7.** 8^4 **9.** 6 **11.** x **13.** t^2 **15.** g **17.** x^5 **19.** n^2 **21.** $\frac{1}{16}$ **23.** $\frac{1}{16}$ **25.** $\frac{1}{10{,}000}$ **27.** $\frac{1}{25}$ **29.** 3^{-3} **31.** x **33.** 3 **35.** $(-3)^{-5}$ **37.** 5^{-1} **39.** $(-2)^2$ **41.** 3 **45.** 9 **47.** 4 **49.** 1.8 **51.** 7.5 **53.** −8.4

Numbers to Algebra **1.** xy^2 **3.** $\frac{6n^2}{5m}$ **5.** $\frac{y^6}{x^2}$

7-8 pages 224–226

Practice **1a.** 0.00018 **b.** 655.6 **c.** 0.04 **2a.** 4.567×10^3 **b.** 2.34×10^5 **c.** 5×10^7 **3a.** 2.06×10^{-2} **b.** 8×10^{-6} **c.** 2.004×10^{-1}

Exercises **1.** 35,000 **3.** 405,000 **5.** 1.35×10^2 **7.** 3.45×10^5 **9.** 1.24×10^3 **11.** 4.55×10^6 **13.** 9.9×10^4 **15.** 7.8×10^{-2} **17.** 6.77×10^{-4} **19.** 1×10^{-6} **21.** 4.05×10^{-5} **23.** 1.01×10^{-1} **25.** 8×10^7 **27.** 3×10^1 **29.** 5.5×10^6 **31.** 2×10^5 **33.** 1.34×10^{-2} **35.** $\frac{1}{5}$ **37.** $\frac{3}{35}$ **39.** $\frac{7}{15}$ **41.** $10t$

Calculator Activity **1.** 4.029×10^{18} **3.** 1.7192×10^{14} **5.** 1.53×10^{16}

Chapter 7 Review page 230

1. $\frac{1}{3}$ **2.** $-\frac{4}{7}$ **3.** $-5\frac{5}{7}$ **4.** 21 **5.** $-\frac{7}{16}$ **6.** $2\frac{1}{4}$ **7.** $2\frac{1}{2}$ **8.** $-\frac{2}{3}$ **9.** $\frac{1}{6}$ **10.** 4 **11.** $-\frac{8}{15}$ **12.** −3 **13.** 24 **14.** 15 **15.** $1\frac{1}{2}$ cups **16.** $0.6\overline{1}$ **17.** 0.45 **18.** $0.\overline{2}$ **19.** 8^3 **20.** $(-5)^7$ **21.** x^2 **22.** $\frac{1}{64}$ **23.** $\frac{1}{36}$ **24.** $\frac{1}{64}$ **25.** 4,700 **26.** 0.019 **27.** 0.000037 **28.** 4.36×10^5 **29.** 5.7×10^4 **30.** 8×10^7 **31.** 7.22×10^{-4} **32.** 1×10^{-6} **33.** 5×10^{-2}

Cumulative Review page 232

1. 67.54 **3.** 18.5 **5.** −51.4 **7.** $\frac{6}{13}$ **9.** $-\frac{3}{5}$ **11.** $-\frac{7}{15}$ **13.** $9\frac{7}{8}$ **15.** $8\frac{5}{6}$ **17.** 14.28 **19.** $-1\frac{1}{6}$ **21.** \$32.39 **23.** \$406 **25.** 3 7/8

Chapter 8
Equations and Inequalities

8-1 pages 234–236

Practice **1a.** 16 **b.** −17 **c.** 18 **2a.** 34 **b.** −9

Exercises **1.** 7 **3.** 10 **5.** 5 **7.** 80 **9.** 648 **11.** 203 **13.** 8 **15.** −17 **17.** 4.75 **19.** −62 **21.** 9 **23.** 14 **25.** $1\frac{1}{2}$ **27.** −5 **29.** 9 **31.** 16 **33a.** $\frac{c-b}{a}$ **b.** $\frac{c+b}{a}$ **35.** $\frac{8}{15}$ **37.** −3

8-2 pages 237–238

Practice **1a.** $2j + 5 = 39$ **b.** $3s - 4 = 65$

Exercises **1.** $2j + 25 = 200$ **3.** $67 = 3v + 4$ **5.** $94 = \frac{1}{2}m + 17$ **7.** $376 = \frac{3}{4}e + 56$ **13.** 4 **15.** $9\frac{3}{8}$ **17.** $10t + 800$

Calculator Activity **1.** 56 **3.** 1,275

8-3 pages 239–240

Exercises **1.** 100 **3.** 24 **5.** 42 **7.** 16°C **11.** 3.3 **13.** −1.25

8-4 pages 241–243

Practice **1a.** 74 **b.** 30 **2a.** −6.5 **b.** 9

Exercises **1.** 12 **3.** 4 **5.** 5 **7.** 4 **9.** −6 **11.** 3 **13.** 5 **15.** 5 **17.** 17 **19.** 8 **21.** 21 **23.** 16 **25.** −8 **27.** 3 **29.** 40 **31.** yes **33.** 75¢ **37.** 9 **39.** 9.6

8-5 pages 244–246

Practice **1a.** 13 **b.** −4 **2a.** 12 **b.** −7

Exercises **1.** −9 **3.** $20\frac{1}{2}$ **5.** 4 **7.** $6\frac{3}{4}$ **9.** 5 **11.** 2 **13.** $12\frac{1}{7}$ **15.** −48 **17.** 7 **19.** $8\frac{1}{2}$ **21.** −22 **23.** 14 **25.** 8 **27.** $-3\frac{1}{2}$ **29.** 45 **31.** Juana is 26; Mary is 78 **33.** 87, 88, 89 **35.** 0.75 **37.** 0.6 **39.** 3 · 5 **41.** 2 · 2 · 7

Numbers to Algebra **1.** $x - 5$ **3.** $5t - 7$ **5.** $-2b + 15$

8-6 pages 247–249

Practice **1a.** 36 **b.** 3 **2a.** $\frac{2}{3}$ **b.** 1

Exercises **1.** 2 **3.** 3 **5.** 6 **7.** 12 **9.** 10 **11.** 5 **13.** 11 **15.** 7 **17.** 2 **19.** −3 **21.** 1 **23.** $1\frac{3}{7}$ **25.** $-5\frac{1}{4}$ **27.** $-4\frac{1}{2}$ **29.** 1 **31.** 4 **33.** −72 **35.** 30 **37.** 12 **39.** $<$ **41.** $<$ **43.** 32 **45.** m^3

Mental Math **1.** 3,599 **3.** 6,399 **5.** 4,896

8-7 pages 250–251
Problems **1.** \$2,800–\$4,200 **3.** \$6,800 **5.** yes **9.** 20,000 miles

8-8 pages 253–255
Practice **1a.** $n \leq 1$ **b.** $x < 1\frac{1}{2}$ **2a.** $b > 16$ **b.** $p < -5$
Exercises **1.** $a < 6$ **3.** $c < 5$ **5.** $p > 21$ **7.** $t < -24$ **9.** $y < -5\frac{1}{2}$ **11.** $n < -4$ **13.** $s > 9$ **15.** $n > 7$ **17.** $m \leq \frac{5}{12}$ **19.** $3 < x$ **21.** $x \leq \frac{5}{2}$ **23.** 32 **25.** \$96,500 **27.** $\{-10, -9, -8, -7, -6, -5, -4, -3, 9, 10\}$ **29.** 0 **31.** 1 **33.** 1

8-9 pages 256–258
Practice **1a.** $n > 20$ **b.** $a \geq 4\frac{1}{2}$ **2a.** $r < -4$ **b.** $x > 3$ **3a.** $b < 1$ **b.** $c \leq -\frac{1}{7}$
Exercises **1.** $a > 3$ **3.** $s < -1$ **5.** $r > -6$ **7.** $c > 12$ **9.** $p < 13$ **11.** $x < 8$ **13.** $n < 8$ **15.** $a \geq 3$ **17.** $n \geq 8$ **19.** $x < -\frac{3}{4}$ **21.** $a > 3$ **23.** $x \geq \frac{1}{7}$ **25.** $x > 12\frac{1}{2}$ **27.** $n < -10$ **29.** $x < 1$ **31.** $2n - 9 < 57$ **33.** $\frac{2}{3}n + 6 < 40$ **35.** $\frac{1}{2}n - 6 > 15$; 43 **37.** $2\frac{1}{2}q + 15{,}000 \geq 90{,}000$; \$30,000 **41.** 45 **43.** m^6n^4
Estimation **1.** less **3.** less **5.** more

Chapter 8 Review page 262
1. 10 **2.** -19 **3.** -23 **4.** 4 **5.** $5s + 3 = 33$ **6.** $2a + 2 = 100$ **7.** $3g - 2 = 22$; 8 **8.** 32 oz **9.** 6 **10.** -8 **11.** 12 **12.** 5 **13.** -8 **14.** 10 **15.** 4 **16.** 6 **17.** 8 **18.** 12 **19.** 7 **20.** 3 **21.** 75 **22.** $p < 7$ **23.** $p > -5$ **24.** $a > 4$ **25.** $f < -10$

Cumulative Review page 264
1. $9 \cdot 9 \cdot 9 \cdot 9 \cdot 9 = 59{,}049$ **3.** $t \cdot t \cdot t$ **5.** c^7 **7.** 4^5 **9.** v^4 **11.** 32 **13.** $5 \cdot 5$ **15.** $2 \cdot 2 \cdot 2 \cdot 5 \cdot 5$ **17.** 6 **19.** 30 **21.** 60 **23.** 0.875 **25.** 5^5 **27.** r^{-3} or $\frac{1}{r^3}$ **29.** $\frac{1}{9}$ **31.** 4.14×10^2 **33.** 1.2×10^7 **35.** 2.25×10^{-5} **37.** 27,800 **39.** 0.00708

Chapter 9
Ratio, Proportion, and Percent

9-1 pages 266–267
Practice **1a.** $\frac{1}{3}$ **b.** $\frac{5}{4}$ **c.** $\frac{3}{2}$
Exercises **1.** $\frac{3}{2}$ **3.** $\frac{4}{9}$ **5.** $\frac{3}{8}$ **7.** $\frac{12}{7}$ **9.** $\frac{3}{2}$ **11.** $\frac{8}{5}$ **13.** $\frac{4}{1}$ **15.** $\frac{16}{9}$ **17.** $\frac{5}{18}$ **19.** $\frac{1}{2}$ **21.** $\frac{1}{5}$ **23.** $\frac{17}{6}$ **25.** $\frac{x}{y}$, $x{:}y$ **27.** $3a{:}b$, $\frac{3a}{b}$ **29.** $\frac{m+n}{z}$, $m + n{:}z$ **31.** 2:1 **33.** 3:1,000 **35.** 24:425 **37.** 4:5:2:1 **39.** 2 **41.** $c > -6$ **43.** 0.375 **45.** 0.12 **47.** $1\frac{1}{14}$

9-2 pages 268–271
Practice **1a.** $\neq$ **b.** $=$ **2a.** 15 **b.** 63 **3.** 30
Exercises **1.** $=$ **3.** $\neq$ **5.** $\neq$ **7.** $=$ **9.** $=$ **11.** $=$ **13.** 18 **15.** 9 **17.** 18 **19.** 11 **21.** 35 **23.** 7 **25.** $15\frac{3}{4}$ **27.** 50 **29.** 20 **31.** 102 **33.** $\frac{10}{18} = \frac{5}{9}$ **35.** $\frac{7}{18} = \frac{77}{198}$ **37.** $\frac{4}{25} = \frac{32}{200}$ **39.** $\frac{3}{4} = \frac{18}{24}$ **41.** $\frac{10}{12} = \frac{15}{18}$ **43.** 15 **45.** 21 **49.** 20 min **51.** $\frac{3}{16}$ **53.** $\frac{5}{8}$ **55.** x^2 **57.** $\frac{3}{4}$ **59.** $-\frac{2}{3}$ **61.** 48 **63.** 9 **65.** 11
Numbers to Algebra **1.** 7 **3.** 25 **5.** 11

9-3 pages 272–273
Practice **1a.** 8.7 km/l **b.** 375 words/min **2.** \$12.75
Exercises **1.** \$8/h **3.** 250 words/min **5.** 937.5 km/h **7.** 3 people/car **9.** 66.5 rev/min **11.** 55 min/class **13.** 18.75 **15.** \$40 **17.** 100 beats/min **19.** 44 **23.** 1.5 **25.** -0.928 **27.** -0.08
Estimation **1.** ≈30 km/l **3.** ≈80¢/h **5.** ≈150 mi/h

9-4 pages 274–275
Practice **1a.** d **b.** $3d$ **2.** $n + 2n = 24$
Exercises **1.** k, $k + 7$ **3.** g, $\frac{1}{2}g$ **5.** $g + (g + 8) = 63$ **7.** $x + \frac{x}{2} = 110$ **9.** $p + (p + 25) = 297$ **13.** $a - 18$ **15.** -2 **17.** 6 **19.** -1

9-5 pages 276–277
Practice **1.** 12
Exercises **1.** $x + (x + 65) = 211$; 138 **3.** $f + (f - 64) = 354$; 145 male, 209 female **5.** $4r + r = 40$; large 32, regular 8 **7.** $f + 2f + (f + 12) = 48$; Fred 9, Jerry 18, Tom 21 **11.** 120 **13.** $\frac{19}{30}$ **15.** $\frac{7}{30}$

9-6 pages 279–281
Practice **1.** $L = 1.2$ m, $W = 0.8$ m **2.** 18 cm
Exercises **1.** 600 km **3.** 900 km **5.** 720 km **7.** 555 km **9.** 10 mm × 12.5 mm **11.** 2.5 mm × 7.5 mm **13.** 3.5 mm × 1.65 mm **15.** 5.375 m **17.** 3.75 m **19.** 11.6 cm × 6.4 cm **21.** c or d **23.** $21m$ **25.** $4t + 8$ **27.** $-\frac{2}{15}$ **29.** $\frac{3}{20}$ **31.** 25 **33.** 2,401 **35.** $-\frac{33}{5}$

9-7 pages 282–283
Problems **1.** 0.84, 0.81; Bob's **3.** 1.50, 1.20; A & B **5.** 2.50, 2.75; A & B **7.** Jones' **9.** Bob's **11.** about 1¢ more **13.** \$1.70

9-8 pages 284–286
Practice **1a.** $\frac{11}{20}$ **b.** $\frac{1}{25}$ **c.** $\frac{21}{100}$ **2a.** $\frac{11}{200}$ **b.** $\frac{11}{400}$ **c.** $\frac{1}{15}$ **3a.** 96% **b.** $83\frac{1}{3}$%
Exercises **1.** $\frac{9}{20}$ **3.** $\frac{1}{20}$ **5.** $\frac{1}{5}$ **7.** $\frac{1}{10}$ **9.** $\frac{37}{50}$ **11.** $\frac{3}{200}$ **13.** $\frac{2}{25}$

15. $\frac{23}{400}$ **17.** $\frac{63}{100}$ **19.** $\frac{1}{30}$ **21.** $\frac{39}{400}$ **23.** $\frac{149}{1,000}$ **25.** 75%

27. $16\frac{2}{3}$% **29.** $33\frac{1}{3}$% **31.** 80% **33.** 12% **35.** $62\frac{1}{2}$%

37. $83\frac{1}{3}$% **39.** $18\frac{3}{4}$% **41.** 34 **43.** $23\frac{9}{17}$% **45.** math

47. English **49.** 9 **51.** 1.6

Estimation **1.** ≈50% **3.** ≈$33\frac{1}{3}$% **5.** ≈$66\frac{2}{3}$%

9-9 pages 287–290

Practice **1a.** 125% **b.** 115% **2a.** $\frac{3}{4}$% **b.** $\frac{4}{5}$% **3a.** $\frac{9}{4}$ **b.** $\frac{41}{25}$

4a. $\frac{1}{200}$ **b.** $\frac{1}{800}$

Exercises **1.** 175% **3.** 225% **5.** 200% **7.** 400%

9. $133\frac{1}{3}$% **11.** $137\frac{1}{2}$% **13.** $\frac{1}{5}$% **15.** $\frac{3}{10}$% **17.** $\frac{4}{5}$% **19.** $\frac{3}{5}$%

21. 220% **23.** $\frac{3}{4}$% **25.** $1\frac{1}{10}$ **27.** 3 **29.** $1\frac{3}{4}$ **31.** 2 **33.** $\frac{1}{500}$

35. $\frac{3}{800}$ **37.** $2\frac{1}{4}$ **39.** $\frac{1}{40}$ **41.** 165% **43.** $33\frac{1}{3}$% **45.** no

47. $22\frac{2}{9}$%; $44\frac{4}{9}$% **49.** 3 **51.** $0.8\overline{3}$ **53.** 0.3 **55.** $8\frac{2}{3}$ **57.** $8\frac{3}{8}$

Computer Activity **1.** 83.3333333% **3.** 81.25% **5.** 25%

9-10 pages 291–293

Practice **1a.** 0.05 **b.** 0.0825 **c.** 1.25 **2a.** 60% **b.** $8\frac{1}{2}$% **c.** 214%

Exercises **1.** 0.4 **3.** 0.05 **5.** 0.02 **7.** 1.5 **9.** 0.9 **11.** 1 **13.** 0.045 **15.** 2 **17.** 0.12 **19.** 0.34 **21.** 0.0075

23. 0.05625 **25.** 62% **27.** 5% **29.** 80% **31.** $\frac{1}{10}$% **33.** $1\frac{1}{2}$%

35. $12\frac{1}{2}$% **37.** 150% **39.** $\frac{1}{2}$% **41.** $46\frac{1}{2}$% **43.** $7\frac{1}{2}$%

45. 438% **47.** $\frac{3}{5}$% **49.** 0.406 **51.** 0.353 **53.** $x(0.01)$

55. 12 **57.** 31 **59.** 1 **61.** −13 **63.** $c < 8$ **65.** 68 **67.** −3 **69.** 72

Calculator Activity **1.** 75% **3.** $16.\overline{6}$% **5.** $133.\overline{3}$% **7.** 15%

Chapter 9 Review page 298

1. $\frac{3}{7}$ **2.** $\frac{8}{5}$ **3.** $\frac{14}{3}$ **4.** 25 **5.** 20 **6.** 30 **7.** 38 km/h **8.** $20/day

9. 13 kg/day **10.** 5 km/h **11.** $s + 3s = 44$

12. $\frac{1}{2}g + g = 24$; 8 boys, 16 girls **13.** 4 cm × 1 cm

14. 3 cm × 1 cm **15.** 5 ft^2 for $1.30 **16.** $\frac{7}{50}$ **17.** $\frac{7}{100}$

18. $\frac{3}{40}$ **19.** 75% **20.** 36% **21.** 12.5% **22.** 225% **23.** 160%

24. $\frac{3}{4}$% **25.** $2\frac{3}{4}$ **26.** $\frac{1}{250}$ **27.** $\frac{11}{400}$ **28.** 0.04 **29.** 0.085

30. 8100% **31.** $7\frac{1}{2}$%

Cumulative Review page 300

1. $\frac{84}{96}$ **3.** $-\frac{75}{110}$ **5.** $-\frac{2}{11}$ **7.** $6\frac{5}{6}$ **9.** $1\frac{49}{100}$ **11.** $-\frac{21}{4}$ **13.** >

15. < **17.** < **19.** $\frac{2}{5}$ **21.** −8 **23.** $\frac{5}{6}$ **25.** 3 **27.** 6

29. $72 = 6t + 6$

Chapter 10 Using Percent

10-1 pages 302–304

Practice **1a.** 6 **b.** 90 **c.** $\frac{18}{5}$ **2a.** 78 **b.** 3.375 **c.** 102

Exercises **1.** 12 **3.** 24 **5.** 45 **7.** 5.4 **9.** 23.52 **11.** 3 **13.** 8 **15.** 2.5 **17.** 0.378 **19.** 12 **21.** 15 **23.** 2.205 **25.** 0.37 **27.** 0.06 **29.** 8.25 **31.** $100 **33.** $240 **35.** $14,787.50 **37.** $6.30 **39.** $5.25 **41.** 50% **43.** 75% **45.** −2 **47.** −5

Mental Math **1.** 45 **3.** 70 **5.** 15

10-2 pages 305–307

Practice **1a.** 20% **b.** $33\frac{1}{3}$% **2a.** $50\frac{5}{6}$% **b.** $13\frac{1}{3}$%

Exercises **1.** 15% **3.** 60% **5.** 80% **7.** $7\frac{1}{2}$% **9.** 40%

11. 20% **13.** $33\frac{1}{3}$% **15.** $33\frac{1}{3}$% **17.** $22\frac{2}{9}$% **19.** 60%

21. 80% **23.** $2\frac{1}{2}$% **25.** $12\frac{1}{2}$% **27.** 20% **29.** 25%

31. 44.4% **33.** 5% **35.** 52% **37.** no **39.** $x = 25$, $y = 50$

41. 0.25 **43.** 1.24 **45.** −3

Estimation **1.** 33% **3.** 67%

10-3 pages 308–310

Practice **1a.** 40 **b.** 200 **2a.** 62.9 **b.** 200

Exercises **1.** 32 **3.** 160 **5.** 500 **7.** 1,300 **9.** 300 **11.** 283.3 **13.** 29.4 **15.** 1,400 **17.** 266.7 **19.** 400 **21.** 18 **23.** 8 **25.** 62.5 **27.** 411.76 **29.** 764 **31.** 152.94 **33.** 800

35. 80 **37.** 180 yd^3 **39.** 400 mL **41.** $\frac{3}{4}$, 75% **43.** $\frac{5}{1}$, 500%

45. $\frac{9}{2}$, 450% **47.** $\frac{25}{8}$

Calculator Activity **1.** 19.2 **3.** 200 **5.** 120

10-4 pages 311–312

Practice **1.** $35 = \frac{1}{2}x + 1$; 68 customers

Exercises **1.** $g + 3g = 76$; 19 **3.** $2x + 5 = 45$; 20 **5.** $20w + 64.50 = 146.50$; $4.10 **7.** $24.30 + 0.1s = s$;

$27 **11.** 36 **13.** 4 **15.** 34 **17.** $\frac{1}{64}$

10-5 pages 313–315

Practice **1.** $12\frac{1}{2}$% **2.** 48%

Exercises **1.** 50% **3.** 25% **5.** 20% **7.** 16% **9.** 75% **11.** 43.8% **13.** 57.9% **15.** 33.3% **17.** 33.3% **19.** 117%

21. $6\frac{2}{3}$% **23.** $650 **25.** $74.25 **27.** 0.8 **29.** $2.\overline{6}$

31. 0.3125 **33.** $\frac{5}{16}$ **35.** $\frac{3}{38}$ **37.** −2 **39.** −1

10-6 pages 316–318

Practice **1a.** discount = $450, sale price = $1,800 **b.** discount = $105, sale price = $770 **2a.** $12 **b.** $31.25

Exercises **1.** $2.50, $7.50 **3.** $0.33, $11.67 **5.** $32.50, $227.50 **7.** $103.49, $586.46 **9.** $571.25, $3,998.75

11. \$1.35 **13.** \$0.71 **15.** \$165 **17.** \$23.39 **19.** 23.5% **21.** \$356, \$3,204, \$192.24 **23.** It doesn't matter. **25.** $\frac{2}{5}$ **27.** 0.25 **29.** 0.11 **31.** 6 **33.** 12 **35.** $r > -3$

10-7 pages 320–321

Problems 1. \$49.50 **3.** \$375 **5.** \$7,987.50 **7.** \$100 **9.** \$8.97 **11.** \$257.82

10-8 pages 322–325

Practice 1a. \$75, \$325 **b.** \$22.50, \$97.50 **2a.** \$15, \$140 **b.** \$180, \$2,180
Exercises 1. \$3.60, \$123.60 **3.** \$24, \$424 **5.** \$100, \$600 **7.** \$101.25, \$476.25 **9.** \$114.75, \$539.75 **11.** \$121.63, \$816.63 **13.** \$144, \$544 **15.** \$76.80, \$396.80 **17.** \$336, \$1,036 **19.** \$1,500, \$11,500 **21.** \$33.75, \$333.75 **23.** \$12.60, \$102.60 **25.** \$7.50, \$2,007.50 **27.** \$936.30, \$14.05, \$950.35 **29.** \$570.04, \$370.04, \$5.56, \$375.60 **31.** \$178.24 **33.** $1\frac{1}{2}\%$ **35.** 4 months **37.** \$38.33 **39.** 12 **41.** c **43.** t
Numbers to Algebra 1. $t = \frac{D}{r}$ **3.** $C = \frac{F - 32}{1.8}$

10-9 pages 326–328

Practice 1. 4-year college 180°, work 99°, 2-year college 54°, armed services 18°, undecided 9°
Exercises 1. adventure 180°, science fiction 72°, children's 54°, comedy 36°, other 18° **3.** walk 162°, bus 108°, bicycle 61°, car 29° **5.** popular 189°, soundtrack 76°, comedy 68°, classical 27° **7.** payments 228°, gas 66°, insurance 41°, repairs 19°, reg. 7° **9a.** 162° **b.** 126° **c.** 72° **11.** $\frac{7}{20}$ **13.** 3

Chapter 10 Review page 332

1. 54 **2.** 12 **3.** 2.25 **4.** 20% **5.** 40% **6.** 75% **7.** 25% **8.** 175 **9.** 102 **10.** 50 **11.** 700 **12.** sweater \$25, skirt \$20 **13.** 20% increase **14.** 40% increase **15.** 30% decrease **16.** \$1.80 **17.** \$5, \$20 **18.** \$70, \$1,680 **19.** \$2.85 **20.** \$10.58 **21.** \$48, \$348 **22.** \$16.80, \$176.80 **23.** mystery 36°, fiction 78°, nonfiction 126°, children's 72°, other 48°

Cumulative Review page 334

1. $-3\frac{3}{10}$ **3.** $\frac{1}{8}$ **5.** $-\frac{3}{16}$ **7.** 3.4 km **9.** 5 **11.** −13 **13.** 29 **15.** $3\frac{3}{4}$ **17.** 5 **19.** 4 **21.** 80 m **23.** 3 cm × 4 cm **25.** 16 oz

Chapter 11 Equations in Geometry

11-1 pages 336–337

Practice 1. points: W, X, Y, Z; lines: $\overleftrightarrow{WY}, \overleftrightarrow{ZX}, \overleftrightarrow{WZ}$; segments: $\overline{YW}, \overline{ZW}, \overline{XY}, \overline{XZ}, \overline{YZ}$; rays: $\overrightarrow{YW}, \overrightarrow{WX}, \overrightarrow{ZW}$, etc.
Exercises 1. any 3 of: A, B, C, D, E **3.** ACD, AED, etc. **5.** $\overline{AE}, \overline{AD}, \overline{AB}, \overline{AC}$ **7.** $\overrightarrow{DC}, \overrightarrow{DA}$ **9.** $\overline{AB}, \overline{AE}, \overline{AD}$ **11.** GCF, CGH **13.** $AEF, FBC, CGH, HDA, FGH, ABC$ **15.** 4 **17.** $x < 2.5$ **19.** $x > 2$

11-2 pages 338–341

Practice 1a. 3 cm **b.** 2 cm **2.** $31.5 + x = 47.3$ $BC = 15.8$ m **3.** 15 cm **4.** $x + 3.9 + 3.7 + 5.1 = 17$; $DC = 4.3$ cm
Exercises 1. 3.2 cm **3.** 6.1 **5.** 7.2 cm **7.** 6.4 mm **9.** 4 m **11.** 35.8 cm **13.** 35 cm **15.** 16.3 m **17.** 4 cm, 4 cm, 6 cm **19.** 0.5 km **21.** $y = 11, x = 2$; 94 **23.** $y = 4, x = 10$; 104 **25.** 1.2 **27.** 2.625 **29.** $2\frac{4}{5}$ **31.** 1.3 **33.** $1\frac{2}{5}$ **35.** $1\frac{2}{25}$ **37.** $\frac{37}{100}$ **39.** 0.3 **41.** 150%

11-3 pages 342–345

Practice 1a. $\angle CBA, \angle DAB, \angle DAC, \angle DCA$ **b.** $\angle ADC$ or $\angle ADB$ **2a.** 37° **b.** 16° **3a.** 61° **b.** 42°
Exercises 1. $\angle TYZ, \angle TYS$, etc. **3.** $\angle XYS, \angle SYZ, \angle RYZ, \angle RYX$ **5.** $\angle XYS, \angle SYZ$, etc. **7.** 17° **9.** 13° **11.** 20.5° **13.** 37° **15.** 27° **17.** 73° **19.** $180 - x$ **21.** 22.5° **23.** 72°, 108° **25.** 18° west of due north **27.** $\frac{2}{5}$ **29.** 1.2
Estimation 1. 15° **3.** 50°

11-4 pages 346–348

Practice 1. 61° **2.** $m\angle 5 = 38°$, $m\angle 6 = 38°$, $m\angle 7 = 38°$, $m\angle 8 = 142°$
Exercises 1. $m\angle 1 = 52°$, $m\angle 2 = 38°$ **3.** $m\angle 1 = 90°$, $m\angle 2 = 40°$ **5.** all = 100° **7.** $m\angle 1 = 95°$, $m\angle 2 = 95°$, $m\angle 3 = 85°$, $m\angle 4 = 95°$ **9.** 121° **11.** 20° **15.** 12.5% **17.** 60%

11-5 pages 349–351

Practice 1. $\triangle XYZ$ is right and scalene, $\triangle BCD$ is obtuse and scalene **2.** 51°
Exercises 1. isosceles and obtuse **3.** right and scalene **5.** $40 + 55 + a = 180$ $m\angle A = 85°$ **7.** $15 + 70 + a = 180$ $m\angle A = 95°$ **9.** 78° **11.** 130° **13.** 56° **15.** $x = \frac{180 - n}{2}$ **17.** $m < 3$ **19.** 85%
Calculator Activity 1. 109 **3.** 69

11-6 pages 353–355

Practice 1a. pentagon, not regular **b.** octagon, not regular
Exercises 1. pentagon, not regular **3.** octagon, not regular **5.** 118° **7.** 49° **9.** 60°, 60°, 120°, 120° **11.** 110°, 60°, 85°, 105° **13.** rectangle **15.** 4 **17.** 150%
Numbers to Algebra 1. 720 **3.** 26,640

11-7 pages 356–357

Problems 1. 27 mi **3.** 39 mi **5.** yes **7.** $4\frac{1}{2}$ h **9.** \$960 **11.** 1,310 mi

11-8 pages 358–360

Practice 1a. 10.048 cm **b.** 51.496 cm **2a.** 1.91 m **b.** 5.73 cm

Exercises **1.** 15.7 cm **3.** 62.8 cm **5.** 38.308 m **7.** 1.59 cm **9.** 3.822 m **11.** 1.465 m **13.** 1.433 cm **15.** 2.389 cm **17.** 2.357 m **19.** 87.92 in. **21.** 30.84 **23.** 26.84 **25.** A cat could walk under. **27.** 4 **29.** $\frac{1}{5}$
Computer Activity **1.** 52 **3.** 1,000

11-9 pages 361–364
Practice **1.** $A \cong G, B \cong H, C \cong I, D \cong J, E \cong K, F \cong L; \overline{AB} \cong \overline{GH}, \overline{BC} \cong \overline{HI}, \overline{CD} \cong \overline{IJ}, \overline{DE} \cong \overline{JK}, \overline{EF} \cong \overline{KL}, \overline{FA} \cong \overline{LG}$ **2.** $\overline{AC} \cong \overline{UW}$, $\angle C \cong \angle W$, $\angle A \cong \angle U$, $\triangle ABC \cong \triangle UVW$ by ASA
Exercises **1.** $\angle U$ **3.** $\angle T$ **5.** $\angle R$ **7.** $\overline{VW}$ **9.** $\angle B$ **11.** $\overline{TU}$ **13.** $\overline{AB}$ **15.** SSS **17.** ASA **19.** $\triangle AFE$, by SSS or SAS **21.** $\triangle BCE$, $\triangle CDA$, $\triangle DEB$, $\triangle EAC$ **23.** 0.1875 **25.** $0.41\overline{6}$ **27.** $0.\overline{18}$ **29.** 12 **31.** −357 **33.** $\frac{1}{40}$ **35.** 450% **37.** 140%
Estimation **1.** no **3.** no

11-10 page 365
Problems **1.** 36 **3.** 8 m, 8 m, 20 m, 20 m **5.** \$4.75 **7.** \$6 **11.** 0.5 **13.** −3 **15.** 4

11-11 pages 366–368
Exercises **21.** 5 **23.** 4 **25.** 19

Chapter 11 Review page 372
1. X, Y, or Z **2.** $\overleftrightarrow{XZ}$, $\overleftrightarrow{XY}$, or $\overleftrightarrow{YZ}$ **3.** $\overrightarrow{XZ}$ or $\overrightarrow{YZ}$ **4.** 2 cm **5.** 8 cm **6.** $\angle MNO$ **7.** $\angle NOP$ **8.** 120° **9.** acute and equilateral **10.** right and isosceles **11.** pentagon **12.** parallelogram **13.** 4.3 h or 4 h 18 min **14.** 10.99 m **15.** 37.68 cm **16.** ASA **17.** 85

Cumulative Review page 374
1. 9 **3.** −25 **5.** $p < 13$ **7.** $n > 5$ **9.** $x > -3$ **11.** 7:17 **13.** $\frac{4}{1}$ **15.** 49 **17.** 54 in. **19.** 53 km/h **21.** 64 beats/min **23.** 34 mi/gal **25.** 60 **27.** 45% **29.** 25% **31.** 140 **33.** 76

Chapter 12 Area and Volume Formulas

12-1 pages 376–379
Practice **1.** 132.86 m² **2a.** 216 m² **b.** 2,487.45 cm²
Exercises **1.** 115 cm² **3.** 150 cm² **5.** 13.23 cm² **7.** 28.12 cm² **9.** 2,214 mm² **11.** 17.2939 m² **13.** 1,029.3 cm² **15.** 66 cm² **17.** 231 cm **19.** 1.2 m **21.** 75 in² **23.** 2.5 gal **25.** 250 cm² **27.** $-\frac{1}{6}$ **29.** 2 **31.** $66\frac{2}{3}$% **33.** $62\frac{1}{2}$%

12-2 pages 380–383
Practice **1a.** 20 cm² **b.** 33 cm² **2a.** 464 m² **b.** 231 m²
Exercises **1.** 31.5 cm² **3.** 63 cm² **5.** 30 cm² **7.** 45 m² **9.** 18 m² **11.** 127.5 cm² **13.** 1,752 cm² **15.** 81 m² **17.** 57.5 cm² **19.** 117 m² **21.** 0.598 m² **23.** 12 cm **25.** 8 cm **29.** −1
Numbers to Algebra **1.** $h = \frac{A}{b}$

12-3 pages 384–386
Practice **1a.** 28.26 ft² **b.** 50.24 m²
Exercises **1.** 78.5 cm² **3.** 78.5 cm² **5.** 18.0864 cm² **7.** 196,250 m² **9.** 7,850 cm² **11.** 7.065 m² **13a.** 50.24 in² **b.** 19.625 in² **c.** 9.61625 in² **15.** 12π **17.** $144 + \frac{25\pi}{2}$ **19.** 21,892.865 m² **21.** 498.5064 cm² **23.** 277.4504 cm² **25.** \$1.80 **27.** $\frac{6}{25}$ **29.** $\frac{11}{100}$ **31.** 12 **33.** −66 **35.** 1.12 **37.** 0
Estimation **1.** $\approx\frac{1}{4}$ **3.** $\approx\frac{1}{2}$

12-4 pages 387–388
Practice **1a.** 239 m² **b.** 222.13 m²
Exercises **1.** 108 m² **3.** 48 m² **5.** 119.28 m² **7.** 72 ft² **9.** 188 ft² **11.** 320.11 m² **13.** 0.125 **15** 0.07 **17.** 5

12-5 page 389
Problems **1.** 6 ft $3\frac{3}{4}$ in. **3.** juice \$0.70, popcorn \$0.95 **5.** \$12.50 **7.** \$140 **11.** 18 **13.** −2

12-6 pages 390–393
Practice **1.** 1,528.8 cm³ **2a.** 2,512 cm³ **b.** 141.3 cm³
Exercises **1.** 352 cm³ **3.** 2,009.6 ft³ **5.** 300 cm³ **7.** 504 ft³ **9.** 72,000 cm³ **11.** 29.98 m³ **13.** 7,218.86 ft³ **15.** 602.88 dm³ **17.** 1,969,408 cm³ **19.** 565.2 cm³ **21.** 25 m **23.** 20 cubic units **25.** 6 **27.** 3.8 **29.** 1.25 **31.** 320% **33.** −75% **35.** 8 **37.** 0.25 **39.** 5
Estimation **1.** 1,200 cubic units **3.** 210 cubic units

12-7 pages 394–395
Problems **1.** 604.4 yd³; \$785.78 **3.** 15.43 yd³; \$694.44 **5.** \$3,318.75 **7.** \$3,360

12-8 pages 396–398
Practice **1a.** 198 cm³ **b.** 188.4 m³
Exercises **1.** $209\frac{1}{3}$ cm³ **3.** 339.12 cm³ **5.** 150.72 in³ **7.** 1,013.2 cm³ **9.** 235.5 dm³ **11.** 314 cm³ **13.** 401.9 mm³ **15.** $158.\overline{3}$ cm³ **17.** 188 m³ **19.** 690 cm³ **21.** 4,230 m³ **23.** 24π **25.** 72 **27.** 144 **29.** 6.9 **31.** twice **33.** 288π cm³ **35.** 176.868π m³ **37.** 20, 35, 56 **39.** 1.35 **41.** 0.194 **43.** 1.6×10^{-4} **45.** −2 **47.** −8.5

12-9 pages 399–402
Practice **1a.** 533.8 cm² **b.** 1,155.52 m² **2.** 788 cm²
Exercises **1.** 527.52 cm² **3.** 427.04 cm² **5.** 1,004.8 cm² **7.** 678.24 m² **9.** 439.6 dm² **11.** 3,165.12 m² **13.** 138 cm² **15.** 136 cm² **17.** 2,612.48 cm² **19.** 12.56 m² **21.** 300 ft² **23.** $\frac{9}{25}$ **25.** $\frac{13}{50}$ **27.** 44 **29.** 2 **31.** 2
Computer Activity **1a.** $V = 1.4587002\ E + 10$ $SA = 28866095.4$ **b.** $V = 3.9217527\ E + 10$ $SA = 55812419.8$ **c.** $V = 2.6057913\ E + 11$ $SA = 197259435$

Chapter 12 Review page 406
1. 200 mm² **2.** 128 cm² **3.** 97.92 m² **4.** 98 cm² **5.** 254.34 m² **6.** 9.0746 km² **7.** 65 m² **8.** \$4.50

9. 216 m^3 **10.** 6,908 ft^3 **11.** 21 yd^3 **12.** 506.5867 ft^3 **13.** $170.\overline{6}$ dm^3 **14.** 1,909.12 cm^2 **15.** 416 ft^2

Cumulative Review page 408

1. $\frac{17}{50}$ **3.** $\frac{17}{200}$ **5.** 65% **7.** 625% **9.** 10% **11.** $\frac{3}{400}$ **13.** 0.07 **15.** 4.25 **17.** 8.5% **19.** 50% **21.** 20% **23.** $253.20 **25.** *A, B, C,* or *D* **27.** *ABC, ABD, ACD,* or *BCD* **29.** $\overrightarrow{AB}$ or $\overrightarrow{AD}$

Chapter 13
Probability, Statistics, and Graphs

13-1 pages 410–412
Practice 1. 12
Exercises 1. 9 **3.** 20 **5.** 9 **7.** 6 **9.** 100 **11.** 16 **13.** 24 **15.** 3 **17.** 2 **19.** 150%

13-2 pages 413–415
Practice 1a. 6 **b.** 120 **2.** 12
Exercises 1. 2 **3.** 6 **5.** 6 **7.** 6 **9.** 24 **11.** 6 **13.** 3,628,800 **15.** 24 **17.** 60 **19.** 676 **21.** 720 **23.** 720 **25.** 3,276,000 **27.** 6,390,000 **29.** $3m$ **31.** $9n$ **33.** $6x - 6y$ **35.** 15.7 **37.** 20 **39.** −2
Numbers to Algebra 1. $(n + 1)$, $(n + 2)$, $(n + 3)$, $(n + 4)$ **3.** $(y - 2)$, $(y - 4)$

13-3 pages 416–418
Practice 1a. 21 **b.** 28
Exercises 1. 3 **3.** 1 **5.** 4 **7.** 15 **9.** 10 **11.** 8 **13.** 36 **15.** 28 **17.** 210 **19.** 220 **21.** 495 **23.** 28 **25.** 175 **27.** 4 **29.** 32 **31.** −40 **33.** 3 **35.** 25% **37.** 16 **39.** −4 **41.** −30 **43.** 18 cm

13-4 pages 419–421
Practice 1a. $\frac{3}{6} = \frac{1}{2}$ **b.** 1 **c.** $\frac{3}{6} = \frac{1}{2}$ **2a.** $\frac{5}{12}$ **b.** $\frac{9}{12} = \frac{3}{4}$
Exercises 1. $\frac{1}{2}$ **3.** $\frac{1}{13}$ **5.** $\frac{1}{13}$ **7.** $\frac{1}{52}$ **9.** $\frac{1}{2}$ **11.** $\frac{3}{4}$ **13.** $\frac{4}{15}$ **15.** $\frac{1}{3}$ **17.** $\frac{3}{5}$ **19.** $\frac{11}{16}$ **21.** $\frac{3}{8}$ **23.** $\frac{9}{16}$ **25.** $\frac{3}{8}$ **27.** $\frac{1}{8}$ **29.** $\frac{5}{36}$ **31.** $\frac{1}{6}$ **33.** 36 **35.** 6 **37.** 3 **39.** −8

13-5 pages 422–424
Practice 1a. $\frac{9}{20}$ **b.** $\frac{1}{5}$ **2a.** $\frac{8}{33}$ **b.** $\frac{14}{33}$
Exercises 1. $\frac{1}{48}$ **3.** $\frac{1}{4}$ **5.** $\frac{1}{2}$ **7.** $\frac{1}{48}$ **9.** $\frac{1}{2}$ **11.** 0 **13.** $\frac{1}{2{,}652}$ **15.** $\frac{25}{102}$ **17.** $\frac{13}{204}$ **19.** $\frac{4}{663}$ **21.** $\frac{4}{663}$ **23.** $\frac{1}{17}$ **25.** $\frac{1}{56}$ **27.** $\frac{1}{42}$ **29.** $\frac{15}{1{,}024}$ **31.** $\frac{5}{256}$ **33.** $\frac{1}{72}$ **35.** $\frac{5}{24}$ **37.** 60% **39.** 60% **41.** 3
Calculator Activity 1. 58%

13-6 page 425
Exercises 1. $5.25 **3.** $10.38 **5.** $525 **7.** $w = 3$ ft, $l = 12$ ft **11.** < **13.** 4

13-7 pages 426–428
Practice 1. range 3, mode $16\frac{1}{2}$
Exercises 1. range 9, mode 2 **3.** range 28, mode 73 **5.** range 20, mode 20 **7.** range 80, mode 76 **9.** range 52, mode 82% **11.** range 34, mode 28 and 34 **13.** range $5, mode $1–$2.99 **15.** 24 **17.** $c > 4$ **19.** −0.5 **21.** −3

13-8 pages 429–431
Practice 1. mean 15, median 14
Exercises 1. mean 4.1, median 4 **3.** mean 23.1, median 23 **5.** mean 49.6, median 45 **7.** mean 10.9, median 9.5 **9.** mean 6.3, median 7 **11.** mean 171.2, median 175 **13.** mean 5.45, median 5.1 **15.** mean 0.21, median 0.08 **17.** mean 3.34, median 3.5 **19.** $3.33 **21.** 105 **23.** $4.38 **25.** ≈300 **27.** $66\frac{2}{3}$% **29.** 50% **31.** $\frac{3}{4}$ **33.** 3 **35.** −1 **37.** < **39.** > **41.** =

13-9 pages 432–433
Problems 1. 20% **3.** 60% **5.** 77.5% **7.** 20 **9.** 1983: 32.67; 1984: 33.67 **11.** 25% **13.** $150

13-10 pages 434–437
Exercises 7. $9n - 9$ **9.** 4 **11.** −7 **13.** 7 **15.** −4 **17.** 10 **19.** 24 m **21.** 37.5 cm

13-11 pages 438–440
Exercises 9. < **11.** = **13.** = **15.** 4.2 **17.** 31.25% **19.** 6.25%

Chapter 13 Review page 444
1. 6 **2.** 720 **3.** 120 **4.** 42 **5.** 15 **6.** $\frac{4}{7}$ **7.** $\frac{3}{7}$ **8.** 1 **9.** $\frac{1}{36}$ **10.** $\frac{1}{12}$ **11.** $15.99 **12.** 9 **13.** 22 **14.** 22 **15.** 21 **17.** 92 **18.** 7th **19.** 9th

Cumulative Review page 446
1. $18, $42 **3.** $2.64 **5.** $337.50, $1,087.50 **7.** $\angle IHK$ or $\angle IKH$ **9.** $\angle MJI$ or $\angle JIK$ or $\angle HIK$ **11.** right and isosceles **13.** square **15.** 198 ft^2 **17.** 8,480 mm^2 **19.** 113.04 m^2 **21.** 69 cm^2

Chapter 14
Square Roots and Special Triangles

14-1 pages 448–450
Practice 1a. −5 **b.** 8 **2a.** $5 < \sqrt{28} < 6$ **b.** $7 < \sqrt{53} < 8$ **3a.** 18 **b.** 9
Exercises 1. 5 **3.** 2 **5.** 12 **7.** −4 **9.** 4 **11.** 2, 3 **13.** 4, 5 **15.** 6, 7 **17.** −6, −7 **19.** 5, 6 **21.** 4, 5 **23.** 9, 10 **25.** 10, 11 **27.** 6 **29.** 10 **31.** 11 **33.** −1 **35.** 12 **37.** 0 **39.** < **41.** < **43.** > **45.** 9 **47.** $\sqrt{5^6} = 125$; $\sqrt{6^6} = 216$; $\sqrt{n^6} = n^3$ **49.** $\angle CBD$ and $\angle DBE$ **51.** 40° **53.** 66 cm^2
Numbers to Algebra 1. 8 **3.** 12 **5.** 10 **7.** 9

14-2 pages 451–453
Practice **1a.** 3.873 **b.** 3.317 **2a.** 7.2801098 **b.** 6.6105975
Exercises **1.** 1.414 **3.** 3.742 **5.** 4.359 **7.** 3.162 **9.** 9.644 **11.** 5.657 **13.** 5.292 **15.** 9.327 **17.** 9.644 **19.** 7.550 **21.** 9.788 **23.** 91.608 **25.** 6.552 **27.** 7.565 **29.** $<$ **31.** $<$ **33.** $>$ **35.** $<$ **37.** 15 seconds **39.** 11 **41.** 0, 1 **43.** 4 cm **45.** 64 cm^2 **47.** $\frac{1}{52}$ **49.** 9 **51.** 0.5 **53.** 3
Calculator Activity **1.** 2.45 **3.** 5.57 **5.** 6.48

14-3 pages 454–455
Practice **1a.** ± 7 **b.** ± 10 **2a.** ± 11 **b.** $\pm\sqrt{39}$ **c.** $\pm\sqrt{73}$
Exercises **1.** ± 4 **3.** ± 9 **5.** ± 11 **7.** $\pm\sqrt{56}$ **9.** $\pm\sqrt{132}$ **11.** $\pm\sqrt{53}$ **13.** $\pm\sqrt{113}$ **15.** $\pm\sqrt{55}$ **17.** ± 5 **19.** ± 10 **21.** ± 7 **23.** ± 7 **25.** 0, 1 **27.** -1, 0 **29.** 55% **31.** 20% **33.** 2
Estimation **1.** ≈ 6 **3.** ≈ 10 **5.** ≈ 4

14-4 pages 456–459
Practice **1a.** $\sqrt{89}$ **b.** $\sqrt{274}$ **2a.** $\sqrt{161}$ **b.** $\sqrt{160}$
Exercises **1.** 15 **3.** $\sqrt{130}$ **5.** $\sqrt{208}$ **7.** 13 **9.** $\sqrt{356}$ **11.** $\sqrt{544}$ **13.** $\sqrt{119}$ **15.** 8 **17.** $\sqrt{133}$ **19.** $\sqrt{56}$ **21.** $\sqrt{205}$ **23.** $\sqrt{171}$ **25.** $\sqrt{924}$ or 30.4 ft **27.** 20.19 ft **29.** no **31.** no **33.** no **35.** yes **37.** yes **39.** yes **41.** $2t + 8$ **43.** $6n + 12$ **45.** 0.3
Mental Math **1.** 3,025 **3.** 5,625 **5.** 9,025

14-5 pages 460–461
Problems **1.** yes **3.** no **5.** 136.01 yd. **7.** ≈ 14.39 yd

14-6 pages 462–464
Practice **1a.** 10 **b.** 19.5
Exercises **1.** 14 **3.** 15 **5.** $a = 5$, $e = 32$ **7.** $p = 9\frac{1}{3}$, $u = 40\frac{1}{2}$ **9.** 90 m **11.** 66 m **13.** 4 **15.** $\frac{4}{5}$ **17.** 9 **19.** 5

14-7 pages 465–467
Practice **1.** $5\sqrt{2}$ **2.** 2.5, $2.5\sqrt{3}$
Exercises **1.** $3\sqrt{2}$ **3.** $3\sqrt{3}$, 3 **5.** $5\sqrt{2}$ **7.** $12.5\sqrt{3}$, 12.5 **9.** 3.464 ft **11.** 127.26 ft **13.** $BD = 8$, $AC = 8\sqrt{3}$ **15.** $\frac{\sqrt{3}}{2}$ **17.** 1 **19.** -6

14-8 pages 468–471
Practice **1.** $\sin A = \frac{12}{13}$, $\cos A = \frac{5}{13}$, $\tan A = \frac{12}{5}$ **2.** ≈ 193.75
Exercises **1.** $\cos A = \frac{15}{17}$, $\sin A = \frac{6}{17}$, $\tan A = \frac{6}{15} = \frac{2}{5}$ **3.** $\cos A = \frac{29}{36}$, $\sin A = \frac{9}{36} = \frac{1}{4}$, $\tan A = \frac{9}{29}$ **5.** $\sin A = \frac{7}{21} = \frac{1}{3}$, $\cos A = \frac{15}{21} = \frac{5}{7}$, $\tan A = \frac{7}{15}$ **7.** 1354.2 ft **9.** 260.42 ft **11.** $\frac{1}{2}$ **13.** $\frac{1}{2}$ **15.** $\frac{1}{\sqrt{2}}$ or $\frac{\sqrt{2}}{2}$ **17.** $\frac{1}{\sqrt{2}}$ or $\frac{\sqrt{2}}{2}$ **19.** $\sin A = \frac{7}{25}$, $\cos A = \frac{24}{25}$, $\tan A = \frac{7}{24}$, 25 **21.** $\sin A = \frac{4}{7}$, $\cos A = \frac{5.74}{7}$, $\tan A = \frac{A}{5.74}$, 5.74 **23.** 4 **25.** 30 **27.** 30° **29.** 30° **31.** 20° **33.** 16 cm^2 **35.** 28 in^2 **37.** 4.14 **39.** 24 **41.** 4 **43.** 3

14-9 page 472
Problems **1.** 86, 149, 172 **3.** 44 **5.** 1.83 m and 4.17 m **7.** 16 ft, 17 ft, 18 ft **11.** 4 **13.** 2 **15.** $3^2 \cdot 5 \cdot 11$

Chapter 14 Review page 476
1. 5, 6 **2.** 8, 9 **3.** 2 **4.** 11 **5.** 2.65 **6.** 10.82 **7.** 13, -13 **8.** 3.46, -3.46 **9.** 10.63 **10.** 12 **11.** 21.21 in **12.** 19 **13.** 24 **14.** 7 **15.** $9\sqrt{3}$ **16.** $\sin A = \frac{30}{42} = \frac{5}{7}$ **17.** $\cos A = \frac{14}{42} = \frac{1}{3}$ **18.** $\tan A = \frac{30}{14} = \frac{15}{7} = 2\frac{1}{7}$ **19.** 410 ft^2, 460 ft^2

Cumulative Review page 478
1. 2,115 mi **3.** 7.536 m **5.** SSS **7.** 448 m^3 **9.** 12 yd^3 **11.** $\frac{8}{12} = \frac{2}{3}$ **13.** $\frac{1}{36}$ **15.** $\frac{5}{18}$

Chapter 15 Graphs of Equations and Inequalities

15-1 pages 480–481
Practice **1a.** $x > -\frac{8}{3}$ **b.** $x < 1$ **2a.** $x \geq -2$ **b.** $x \leq 1$
Exercises **5.** $x > \frac{1}{2}$ **7.** $x < 5$ **9.** $x \leq -5$ **11.** $x > 3$ **13.** $x \leq 1$ **15.** $x \leq -\frac{9}{5}$ **17.** $x \geq -64$ **19.** $x < 9$ **29.** $1 \leq x \leq 3$ **31.** 8 **33.** 3 **35.** 1.2

15-2 pages 482–485
Practice **1.** $D(-3, -5)$; $E(5, 2)$; $F(5, -2)$; $G(-4, 2)$
Exercises **1.** (3, 2) **3.** $(-2, -4)$ **5.** $(3, -4)$ **7.** $(-6, -3)$ **9.** $(-6, 4)$ **11.** (4, 0) **25.** $(-2, 4)$ **27.** $(-1, -3)$ **39.** (2, 3) **41.** 9 **43.** mean: 13.625; mode: 12
Numbers to Algebra **1.** 13 **3.** 10

15-3 pages 486–488
Practice **1.** $(2, -3)$
Exercises **1.** (2, 3) **3.** $(-3, 4)$ **21.** $y = -4x + 4$ **23.** $y = -2x + 8$ **25.** $y = \frac{3}{2}x - 2$ **27.** $y = \frac{1}{2}x$ **29.** (1, 1) **31.** $\frac{3}{5}$ **33.** $\frac{3}{4}$ **35.** 12

15-4 page 489
Problems **1.** \$4,580 **3.** 9 gal **5.** 13 weeks **7.** 38 hours **11.** 6 **13.** 2

15-5 pages 490–493
Practice **1a.** yes, $k = 5$ **b.** no, $k = -2$ **2.** no **3a.** no **b.** yes, $k = 1$
Exercises **1.** yes, $k = 1$ **3.** no **5.** no **7.** yes, $k = 120$ **9.** yes, $k = 2$ **11.** directly **13.** directly **17.** 30 **19.** 90 **21.** 243 **23.** 0.25 or $\frac{1}{4}$ **25.** 2.4

15-6 pages 494–497

Practice **1a.** 2 **b.** $\frac{2}{8} = \frac{1}{4}$ **2a.** -2 **b.** $\frac{2}{3}$ **3a.** x-int: -3; y-int: 6 **b.** x-int: $\frac{10}{3}$; y-int: -5

Exercises **1.** $\frac{2}{3}$ **3.** $\frac{3}{2}$ **5.** -1 **7.** -2 **9.** $\frac{1}{7}$ **11.** 3 **13.** 2 **15.** 2 **17.** $-\frac{1}{3}$ **19.** 2 **21.** (5, 0), (0, 5) **23.** (6, 0), (0, -2) **25.** (5, 0), (0, 4) **27.** (2.5, 0) (0, -5) **33.** 12 ft **35.** 28 **37.** 3 **39.** 24 **41.** 7

Estimation **1.** 13 **3.** 7

15-7 pages 498–499

Problems **1.** \$8.40 **3.** \$4.80 **5.** \$3.60 **7.** \$22.80 **9.** \$0.20 **11.** ≈1.4¢

15-8 pages 500–501

Practice **1.** (2, 1)

Exercises **1.** (1, 0) **3.** (2, 2) **5.** (-1, -1) **7.** (2, 1) **9.** (3, 1) **11.** none **13.** $k = 0$ **15.** More-For-Your-Money, 100 mi **17.** 251.2 cm^3 **19.** 235.5 m^3 **21.** 75% **23.** 150% **25.** 15 **27.** 2.95

15-9 pages 502–503

Exercises **11.** $y \geq -\frac{1}{2}x + 1$ **15.** $y < \frac{3}{4}x + 3$ **17.** $5x + 7y \leq 500$ **21.** $d = 12$ in, $a = 113.04$ in^2 **23.** 2

Chapter 15 Review page 506

3. (1, 2) **4.** (-2, 0) **7.** (4, 9) **9.** \$160 **10.** yes, $k = 4$ **11.** no **12.** yes, $k = 20$ **13.** yes, $k = 15$ **14.** 1 **15.** 5 **16.** 2 **17.** 4 **18.** \$325 **19.** (2, 1) **20.** no

Cumulative Review page 508

1. 715.92 in^3 **3.** 376.80 ft^2 **5.** 20 **7.** 24 **9.** 84 **11.** 14 **13.** 14 **15.** 5, 6 **17.** 8.94 **19.** 9.4 **21.** $\frac{12}{13}$

Index